Societies and Political Orders in Transition

This book series presents scientific and scholarly studies focusing on societies and political orders in transition, for example in Central and Eastern Europe but also elsewhere in the world. By comparing established societies, characterized by well-established market economies and well-functioning democracies, with post-socialist societies, often characterized by emerging markets and fragile political systems, the series identifies and analyzes factors influencing change and continuity in societies and political orders. These factors include state capacity to establish formal and informal rules, democratic institutions, forms of social structuration, political regimes, levels of corruption, specificity of political cultures, as well as types and orientation of political and economic elites.

Societies and Political Orders in Transition welcomes monographs and edited volumes from a variety of disciplines and approaches, such as political and social sciences and economics, which are accessible to both academics and interested general readers.

Topics may include, but are not limited to, democratization, regime change, changing social norms, migration, etc.

All titles in this series are peer-reviewed.

This book series is indexed in Scopus.

For further information on the series and to submit a proposal for consideration, please contact Johannes Glaeser (Senior Editor Economics and Political Science) Johannes.glaeser@springer.com.

Juri Plusnin

Russian Provincial Society

An Empirical Analysis

Springer

Juri Plusnin
Faculty of Social Sciences
National Research University Higher
School of Economics
Moscow, Russia

ISSN 2511-2201 ISSN 2511-221X (electronic)
Societies and Political Orders in Transition
ISBN 978-3-030-97828-0 ISBN 978-3-030-97829-7 (eBook)
https://doi.org/10.1007/978-3-030-97829-7

This Springer imprint is published by the registered company Springer Nature Switzerland AG
The registered company address is: Gewerbestrasse 11, 6330 Cham, Switzerland

Acknowledgments

The initiative of field research explicitly focusing on the structure of provincial local societies came from Prof. Simon Kordonsky. Over the last few years of collecting empirical data, I have discussed this work in detail with him. He is also the author of several important ideas and concepts that I develop in this book. We jointly published several articles that preceded this monograph and the materials of which are used herein. He also inspired the very idea of writing this monograph. I am deeply grateful to my senior colleague and friend.

The text is based on data collected during field research under the project *The Social Structure of the Russian Provincial Society* sponsored by the Khamovniki Foundation for Social Research. The initial fieldwork took place in 2011–2012 (Project No. 2011-002) and was later extended to 2013–2014 (Project No. 2013-007).

Subsequent fieldwork was carried out as part of research under the Academic Fund Program at the National Research University Higher School of Economics (NRU HSE) in 2017–2018 and in 2019–2020 and under the Russian Academic Excellence Project 5-100 (Grant No. 17-01-0027 *Archaic Elements in the Structure of Modern Russian Society* and Grant No. 19-01-067 *Provincial Crafts: Informal Economic Practices of the Population*).

Many of my earlier studies undertaken in the period between 1995 and 2010, which also continued thereafter, were sponsored by field research grants from the Russian Foundation for Humanities (1996, No. 96-03-18019e; 1997, No. 97-06-18005e; 1997–1998, No. 97-06-08278; 1998, No. 98-06-18011e; 1999, No. 99-06-18013e; 2001, No. 01-06-18010e; 2006, No. 06-06-18001; 2010, No. 1-03-18022e), grants from the Moscow Public Science Foundation and the Ford Foundation (1999, No. SP-99-1-14 *Dynamics of Nonadaptive Transformations of Economic Behavior and Social Values of the Population of Provincial Russia*), grant from the Regional Scholar Exchange Program 2001–2002, USA (*Social Stability and Instability on the Local Level: the Analysis of Internal Factors in Overcoming a Crisis*), and a grant from the President of the Russian Federation (through the Institute of Public Design) (No. 36/k *The Structure of Municipal Power and its Impact on the Development of Social Solidarity and Local Entrepreneurship*, 2008-2009). My colleagues from the Institute of Philosophy and Law of the Siberian Branch of the Russian Academy of Sciences, Novosibirsk, supported me in most of these projects.

Many assistants helped me in collecting empirical data. I would like to acknowledge with gratitude the contribution made by Artemy Pozanenko, Natalia Zhidkevich, Irina Popova, Sergey Pyzhuk, Olga Molyarenko, Vyacheslav Plusnin, Anatoly Ablazhey, Yana Zausaeva, Anna Baidakova, Larisa Romanova, Artur Grishechkin, Anastasia Ivashchenko, Mikhail Olyanchuk, Alexander Pavlov, Sergey Seleev, Oleg Pisarev, Elizaveta Stepanova, Anastasia Pyanova, Alina Kulchu, Evgeny Nikolaev, Jaroslav Slobodskoy-Plusnin, and Georgy Stalinov. They participated in several expeditions and engaged in joint research. In addition, at different times, 139 young researchers from the Higher School of Economics, Moscow, took part in our study of the provincial society. Unfortunately, I cannot list them all here, but I am happy to thank them for the scrupulous and responsible collection of diverse field data in many regions of our country.

Julia Kazantseva translated the text of this monograph from Russian into English and rendered valuable technical assistance.

Contents

Chapter 1
Introduction

My long-term empirical study, the generalized findings of which are presented in this monograph, applies exclusively to the provincial society in Russia. It is not the society of large- or even medium-sized cities. It is the society of small towns and rural districts—since rural districts surround the small towns, "*localities*," forming together an organic continuity, both spatial and social. Even the small towns (as well as considerable areas of many medium-sized cities) are no or little different from our villages. In this sense, the rural district imposes its way of life, the material and spiritual practices of the population, on the small town, thus "absorbing" (devouring) it. The very system of household livelihoods in small towns is similar, and in some places identical, to that in rural areas. This was so throughout all the decades of my research—especially pronounced in the late 1980s and during the crisis of the 1990s; and still the case at the beginning of the 2020s. Therefore, I believe it reasonable to extrapolate the records of my observations covering 300 of the total 1700 local communities to a significant part of Russia's population. This part ranges from two-fifths to half of the entire population of the country. In fact, this is provincial Russia.

Initially, the purpose of the research was to describe the social structure of local communities, which was then understood quite narrowly, operationally. In fact, the empirically described local grassroots social structure failed to fit class or estate stratification patterns. Neither stratification by household income nor distribution of people by rank in the estate-based state system enables to understand the essence of relations existing between people, families, and social groups within the local community. In addition, these relations and the entire life of the community are associated with the local territorial structure. One does not exist without the other; they mutually determine each other. The physical projection of the community is an organic part of its social structure. Three components of social behavior are inseparable: habitation (in physical space), existence (relationships), and activity (subsistence). Each one has a particular and special structure but is dependent on the other two. In addition to describing relationships between people, it proved necessary to also depict their subsistence patterns—household management and economic

J. Plusnin, *Russian Provincial Society*, Societies and Political Orders in Transition,
https://doi.org/10.1007/978-3-030-97829-7_1

practices—which strongly affect the structure of relations. However, household management and economic practices turned out to be associated with the territorial structure, since for subsistence our provincial population relies primarily on the informal and shadow segment of the economy. Livelihoods depend most closely on the resources provided by nature and created by the people themselves on their own homesteads (territories). Therefore, I describe the provincial social structure herein as a three-component system: the territorial structure, subsistence patterns (economy), and the structure of relations in the system of basic oppositions describing these relations (the "us/them," "active/passive population," and "upper/lower strata" oppositions).

The diversity of essentially ethnographic records required generalization. The four methods I used to typologize local communities proved to be quite heuristic, especially when classifying communities by the degree of their spatial isolation and by the extent of external, government, impact on their development. These tools allowed me to describe the structural features of all the above-mentioned three components by grouping them into just several typical forms. I identified only six types of local communities, which are reducible to four basic types.

These two approaches—decomposition into three structural components, on the one hand, and typology of communities based on external principles, on the other hand—made it possible to distinguish several quite clear patterns in the patchwork of provincial life. Besides descriptive exhaustiveness and concision, they also have predictive value. Knowing what type a local community can be classified into—by age, spatial isolation, and impact of public resources on its development (even by the layout of its administrative center)—we can reasonably estimate various aspects of its existence: the structure of the controlled territory; the nature and even types of widespread economic practices of the inhabitants; the structure of the formal segment of the local economy; the composition of the population, including the "us/them" structure; and even the system of power relations and the determinants of individual status positions. Of course, I do not claim that the predictive value of my typologies is absolute. Provincial communities over the vast expanse of Russia are too diverse to fit readily into the Procrustean bed of sociological concepts. Nevertheless, to a certain extent this is achievable, and that is one of my most significant findings.

I believe the predictive nature of a model based on the analysis of the territorial, economic, and social components of the structure has another important merit. It allows us to assess the self-organization and sustainability of a local community, its ability to withstand various external destructive influences, whether of natural, economic, or political origin.

This book is divided into nine chapters. The first three chapters constitute a methodological and conceptual framework, which is then "draped" by the empirical structure of the local community. The research concept outlined in Chap. 2 is based on three hypotheses. The first one claims the existence at the local level of two additional structures different in nature: a formal estate structure imposed from above by the state and a local structure developing from below. The second hypothesis is based on the well-known statement about the complementarity of physical and social space; it suggests that the territorial structure of the local community quite distinctly "correlates" with the social one. The third hypothesis assumes that the above-mentioned three-axial binary framework underlies the local social structure.

Chapter 3 is devoted to qualitative methodology and describes observation and interviewing methods that form the basis of all my empirical research. The second part contains empirical data relating to nearly 300 local communities.

Chapter 4 contemplates on several typologies that can be developed to generalize empirical sociological descriptions. It proposes and substantiates four typologies based on different independent principles: age of the community; its spatial location; dependence on external sources of existence; and distinctive features of the residential structure reflecting the administrative status.

Chapter 5 addresses the territorial component of the local community structure. Up to a dozen criteria necessary and sufficient to describe the territorial structure are identified and defined. A comprehensive description of the territories under the four mentioned typologies made it possible to differentiate the territories of different types of communities according to all the selected criteria.

Chapters 6, 7, and 8 focus on the various household and economic practices of the provincial population. Besides the "thin lawn" of formal economy, I am also considering the "wild field" of informal economy. Invisible to the state, uncontrolled, unregulated, and therefore unperceived by economists, it is this part of the economy that forms the basis of provincial livelihood. I describe both archaic economic practices represented by *otkhodnichestvo* (internal circular labor migration) and "*scattered manufactories*" in small towns, as well as many modern ones represented by the "*garage economy*" and various household crafts, which are everywhere the basis of well-being for provincial households.

Chapter 9 deals with the structure of kin and neighborly relations under the "us/them" dichotomy. Kinship and neighborhood are the basis of the provincial social structure. Any relations—from professional to power—are "strung" on kin and neighborly ties. This is the radical distinction between the provincial and urban societies. The structure of kin and neighborly relations in the province can be considered as invariant, independent of the type of community. The composition of "us" depends on how a community emerged and subsequently developed—as an "agglomeration" assembled from different parts or as a "layered structure" formed by successive layers over a long period of time. The composition of "them" has only quantitative differences.

Chapter 10 focuses on the nature and individual components of the personal status of a provincial inhabitant, and on the nature of local authority. In a provincial society, status determination dominants differ from those in urban societies. Here, the most important factors that determine an individual's social status are personal influence, clan/family affiliation, formal power position, and only last of all, disposable capital (income). However, the decisive factors differ depending on the type of community. This also proved to affect the style of local (municipal) government. The characteristic styles (or strategies) of governance identified in previous studies correlate with factors of spatial isolation and dependence on public resources.

Chapter 2
Provincial Societies: Definitions and Conceptual Framework

This chapter focuses on the definitions of provincial local society and our working concepts of local social structure. "Provincial society" is an abstract sociological construct, defined in terms of the periphery and the center. The "provincial local society" is defined as a territorially organized group of communities whose members are related by kinship, neighborhood, and mutual support; live in a common self-controlled territory; and engage in predominantly informal economic activities (crafts). Individual communities rely on self-organization mechanisms, and their core institutions largely retain archaic elements. The strength of ties between communities is ensured by a shared history and state administrative mechanisms.

The conceptual framework includes three interrelated hypotheses. The main hypothesis is the idea that each modern local society in Russia has two social structures, which are complementary. The estate/class-based structure imposed by the state "from above" associates as an additional one with the "grassroots" archaic communal structure, which itself is the result of social self-organization. The second hypothesis regards territorial entities as the physical basis for the functioning of local social institutions. The territorial structure is a spatial projection of the social structure. Under the third hypothesis about the triaxial binary oppositional structure of social ties, I analyze the social structure at the local level using a set of basic oppositions: "us/them," "upper/lower strata," and "active/rent-seeking population." The consistent application of such approaches to the analysis of empirical data allows us to create a typology of the territorial and social structure of local societies, which is done in the following chapters.

2.1 Provincial Society

Objects defined by the term "provincial" do not cause any difficulties in people's everyday consciousness, although the concept has ambiguous connotations in its scientific description. In the first case, "provincial" means non-metropolitan, not

J. Plusnin, *Russian Provincial Society*, Societies and Political Orders in Transition,
https://doi.org/10.1007/978-3-030-97829-7_2

from a megalopolis or a big city, in general "not an urban dweller." Thus, in everyday consciousness, the concept is determined primarily by negative terms and is meaningfully unambiguous. In the second case, there is a lot of ambiguity: see, for example, a special issue of the journal *Otechestvennye Zapiski*, entirely dedicated to the province *Anatomy of the Province* (2006). Meanwhile, I believe that the first position—an undifferentiated definition in negative terms—is a more complete and integral perception. The province is the periphery, all that is outside the center and located around it, but inextricably linked to the center and necessarily needs a center; see also: Shils (1961, pp. 117–130). There is no periphery without a center, there is no province without a capital. That's it. The boundaries of the concept are vague, the demarcation is uncertain. Therefore, I will confine myself *to a marginal* (extreme) definition: the province is the periphery. Scale and contrast are important here. The Russian province is everything beyond the boundaries of Moscow. On a smaller scale, at the regional level, for example, the province is the environment of the City (in any region, the capitalized "City" is the regional capital for all other residents of the administrative territory, i.e., for provincials). The same is true down to the local level: for any small town, its rural district is the "province," although everyone in the town understands that he/she is a provincial for an inhabitant of the City, who, in turn, is a provincial for a resident of the capital. Clearly, the concept of "provincial" is relative. Therefore, it makes little sense to delve into the details of the definitions, especially since there are already comprehensive historical, sociological, political, anthropological, and philological descriptions of them; see, for example: Shils (1975, pp. 3–16, 34–47),[1] Zayonts (2000), Kupriyanov (2007), Donskikh (2011, pp. 25–44[2]).

For the purposes of our research, it is sufficient to confine ourselves to the definition and designation of the Russian provincial society as a society of small towns and their rural district. On the one hand, I exclude from the analysis metropolitan and major cities, as well as large- and medium-sized ones. In the Russian administrative and academic tradition, a small town is an urban settlement with a population of up to 50,000 people. Vyacheslav Glazychev attempted to capture the essence of the differences between a large- and medium-sized city and a small town. In his recent monograph, he made an overview of Russia's thousand-year history of "*exploring, appropriating, and assimilating territories*," where a large, metropolitan city emerges little by little breaking through the thick crust of provincialism under which the city is still hardly distinguishable from a village (Glazychev, 2011, pp. 144–209). Economic geographer Andrey Treyvish uses a different, formally statistical approach to distinguish cities and towns by their size (Treivish, 2009, pp. 248–267, 282–287). I intentionally do not consider the geographers' view on the

[1] In his well-known essays on the relationship between the center and the periphery, on society and societies, Edward Shils pays special attention to the moral, value, and political aspects of the mutual influence and interaction of the center and its periphery.

[2] Oleg A. Donskikh performed a detailed historical and sociological study of provinciality, where he showed the development of such a concept in relation to the establishment of an absolutist state, the system of services, and the formation of the noble status and the administrative status of the city.

subject. Apparently, by the seventeenth to eighteenth centuries, only the specific estate-based occupations of urban residents distinguished them radically from the surrounding villages, and later from the immediate suburbs (*posad*). By that time, the estates of the petty bourgeois, merchants, military nobles, and clergy constituted the majority of urban residents (Kamensky, 2007, pp. 55–90; Ivanova & Zheltova, 2009, pp. 325–404). Thus, I support the hypothesis of total opposition between the urban anomic and rural communal lifestyles ("*The city and the village oppose each other primarily not as two types of populated places, but as two principles of organizing social life* . . ." (Vishnevsky, 2010, p. 78). On the other hand, such a definition emphasizes the administrative-territorial feature of "provinciality as the periphery": what matters are not spatial (geographical) or residential aspects, but social ones, since every society is a system, both territorial and political.

Distinguishing "the province" based on the negative "non-center" = "non-urban life" criterion is a clearly inadequate and extremely simplified approach. But it is not devoid of meaning. By limiting the "provincial society" to small towns and rural areas, I am narrowing it down even more, but I am also adding substance. A decrease in scale enhances integrity and reveals signs of social self-organization, which gives us reason to treat the local community as an integral social object. At the same time, such an object becomes more *visible*. Provincial society, as such, is neither an observable nor an integral object. It is not a real object, only a designation. Such a society consists of many *local societies*, or communities. Each local society (community) is substantially, little, or hardly (negligibly) connected with its neighbors. The higher the degree of spatial isolation, the more integral and self-sufficient the community appears, and the more it approaches a single community. When various ties are very strong, the community virtually dissolves into its neighbors, and it is practically impossible to distinguish it as a special entity and to determine where the territorial and social boundaries (except the administrative ones) pass. Such almost "*dissolved*" communities cannot be singled out as a special entity, as a special social object, unless we refer to the social self-identification of their members; see especially: Tajfel and Turner (1979), Tajfel (2010), Jenkins (2008, pp. 118–131), Gowland and Thompson (2013). That is why it is always more convenient to study spatially isolated communities that have fairly clear territorial (not administrative) boundaries and limited and observable neighborly and family relations (see Chap. 4). Thus, the central concept of my research is the concept of "local society," rather than "provincial society" in general.

2.2 Local Society

The concept of "local society" is even less definite and unambiguous than (the concept) of "provincial society," although we can refer to each of them. "Provincial society" is an ideal construct, and "local society" requires a reference. Hence, it is not easy to capture common features. A local society is often identified with a community. But not every local society is a community, although it is the community that is the "*basic focus of social life*" (Murdock, 1949, p. 82), since, according to the tradition established by Ferdinand Tönnies (1887), a community is generally defined as a group of people connected by kinship and affinity, who live in the same place and directly interact and communicate with each other; see also: Murdock et al. (1945, p. 29). A local society is always a constellation of several communities. Only in the extreme case is this a single community. Anticipating the definition of "local society," I will outline its key features. As an entirety, as a relatively autonomous "social system," it has the following characteristics:

(a) *Objectiveness,* which consists in physical and/or symbolic separation from its neighbors and from the host environment by a territory and its boundaries within which a limited human population lives
(b) *Composition*—a certain composition that forms a social structure, and
(c) A system *of relations*, due to which the population of interacting individuals can sustain the social structure and turns into a self-organizing and self-sufficient social system.

To a large extent, this definition is close to the metaphorical formula "*a system is a set of interrelated elements*," which was introduced by Alexander A. Bogdanov (Malinovsky) at the beginning of the twentieth century and further developed by Pitirim A. Sorokin in the 1920s and Ludwig von Bertalanffy in the 1930s–1940s (Bogdanov, 1989, Chap. 2; (Sorokin, 1920, Vol. 1, pp. 1–22; von Bertalanffy, 1968, pp. 194–197). However, I believe that the definitions of "local society" provided in the next three sections contain an operationally more adequate explanation. Here the term "set" corresponds to "separation," "interrelated"—to "relations," and "elements"—to "composition," represented not only by elements, but also by structural components. I will consider them separately.

2.2.1 Objectiveness: Community Sizes and Boundaries

The key problem any field researcher faces when identifying and describing a local community is the ability to refer to an existing physical object, which is also a social object (Bourdieu, 1987). At the same time, this is also a classification problem, which is far from solved in sociology; see Kordonsky (2008b). One of the solutions is to answer two questions: what is the size and where are the boundaries of a local society and according to what criteria should one society be distinguished from the neighboring one? In other words, how (a) *to identify* an object called "local society" and (b) how to *distinguish it from similar* other objects? Indeed, where are the physical (in space) boundaries, and where are the population-environmental (in behavior) ones? What is the minimum and maximum population of a local society? How has the physical habitat [Lebensraum] been transformed? And how are both types of boundaries related? Certainly, not just by the density of the distribution of individuals in space.

2.2.1.1 Population Size

The size of the population is a debatable issue. The minimum size is at least determinable based on intuition—it is neither one nor even a dozen people, nor is it one or a dozen families—but how many then? Much greater difficulties arise with determining the maximum size of the population that can still constitute a local society. It is known that self-organization and self-government are possible at the level of an individual household, but even a dozen households assembled lead only physical existence and can only engage in an economy of material reproduction (production exclusively for in-house consumption). Such a community is incapable of any long-term social reproduction, neither can it exist as a biological population. A self-reproducing human population requires a minimum of 500 or even 1000 people; see MacArthur and Wilson (1967) and Kimura and Crow (1963). Anthropologists' known estimates of the size of an archaic community range from 50 to 1000 people (Peregrine & Ember, 2001), averaging 250–450 people (Murdock, 1949, p. 81). According to my observations, Russian self-sufficient and spatially isolated societies represented by a single community consist of 100–200, maximum 1000 people. (However, they are by no means self-reproducing populations, but need constant interaction with neighboring communities, as ethnographers well know.)

Here it makes sense to add a consideration about "Dunbar's number," an assessment of close, psychologically significant relationships between individuals, proposed by Robin Dunbar in the 1990s (Dunbar, 1992), as well as the respective estimates proposed at the same time by Russell Bernard and Peter Killworth (Bernard et al., 1991; McCarty et al., 2001). Both quantitative invariants—150 people in the first case and 290 in the second—as a certain constant of the number of permanent, close, and stable social connections of the average individual, perfectly coincide with the average size of rural settlements (i.e., the minimum community) in almost any local society in Russia: they have about 100–300 adult members, and that's where the most intense human interaction takes place and stable social connections are built. It is "clusters" (territorial group of villages, settlements, and townships) of such rural settlements that usually make up real communities in Russia: households are connected by kinship, neighborhood (living on a common territory), cooperation of household activities, and mutual assistance.

The upper bound of local society remains less definite. In any case, assumptions about the upper limit of local society are purely hypothetical. Nevertheless, we have some assumptions and estimates that can be used to evaluate the maximum size of a local society. Since modern, non-isolated local societies are represented by many communities, the size of such communities, in contrast to isolated ones, is substantially greater than 1000 people, usually exceeding 3000. But exceeding by how many people? We can attempt to determine the maximum size of the population using the socio-psychological approach. A well-known scientific fact introduced in 1974 by anthropologist Ray Birdwhistell asserts that each person, maintaining at least occasional contacts, can know on average 2000 other people (Birdwhistell,

1974). Based on that, we can assume that in most Russian provincial towns, not to mention the rural area, all inhabitants know each other. Indeed, if we proceed from the estimate that considering common acquaintances, an average family of three or four members can know 5000–6000 and more people, then with an average of 3000–10,000 urban families in a local society, every family will be acquainted with almost all other families. Thus, an individual can interact indirectly, through friends and relatives, with an average of 20,000–40,000 people. The average size of the provincial local society I am studying is just that—about 30,000 people. Of course, it is not one, but several—up to a dozen or more—communities. But on this basis, we can assume that this size of the local society is optimal in terms of stable and permanent social connections between people. If we also assume that Dunbar's number can be considered as an invariant multiplier of the number of vertices forming a complete graph K_{150}, or the Bernard–Killworth estimate of K_{290} (each adult person is physically able to maintain stable relations with an average of only 150–290 other people, most of whom are relatives and neighbors), then the maximum number of vertices of the complete graph will be from 20,000 to 80,000 people.

Based on the above assumptions, we can suppose that the minimum size of a local society is no less than 100–500 persons. The maximum size is harder to specify; it could be about 20,000–30,000 people. It is likely that from 40,000 people onwards, local cohesion and the ability to self-organize begin rapidly diminishing. With a population of more than 50,000 people, members of the society themselves hardly feel any local unity and mutual support, and at the level of 80,000–100,000 people, the society loses locality along with integrity—i.e., it is no longer capable of spontaneous self-organization and self-government. External bonds are required, and it is the state that provides them; see Johnson and Earle (1987), Carneiro (1981), Cohen and Toland (1988), and Kradin and Linsha (1995). A comparison of these estimates with our empirical data gives us realistic limits: the lower one is 100–500 adults, and the upper one is 40,000 people (including children). Most of our local societies have approximately 20,000–30,000 members. According to these figures, the number of communities that make up a society ranges from one to between ten and twenty. The upper estimate of the number of interconnected communities is uncertain (vague) for two reasons: different size of the communities—from 50–100 to 1000–3000 people—and a variable number of individual settlements in one community—between one and several dozen.

2.2.1.2 Territorial Boundaries and Density

The second issue—territorial boundaries—is contingent on the size of the local society. Along what frontiers, rivers and seas, mountains and forests, swamps and tundra do the community boundaries pass, enclosing an area necessary and sufficient for current sustenance and long-term existence of a population of a certain size? The answer is evident only in two cases: when the community is completely spatially isolated and when there is an insurmountable physical barrier separating a particular community from its neighbors. But both cases usually coincide. Any local society establishes and maintains boundaries insofar as it exists in a physical environment, in space, and because the boundary enclosing part of the space transforms this space into territory. The territory is a precondition for the existence of the community and the life of its members, since its size depends on the minimum necessary amount of resources gathered or produced to provide for and reproduce members of the community. The boundary also determines the territorial structure of the community. And this latter, in turn, constitutes the community as an integral entity. Therefore, the territory and its boundary are a mandatory *starting point* for both the composition and structure of any community. In fact, the territory creates the community (cf.: Murdock, 2003, pp. 106–108).

By defining physical boundaries, we also largely determine the social ones. The main reason lies in certain (limit) values of population density. Average density can vary greatly: from a meager 0.01 people per km^2 (which corresponds to one person per 100 km^2) to 100–200 people per km^2 (which corresponds to 1–2 persons per 1 ha). But these are the average population density values in terms of the entire territory of the community. It is not they that matter, but the density of the population in the administrative center. The space can be largely underpopulated, but the center must be inhabited, and with a certain density. According to my observations, in the Russian provincial society this density ranges from 300 to 1000 people per km^2, averaging about 400–500 people per km^2. Considering only the residential area, i.e., the one intended for housing (excluding industrial zones and land alienated for social infrastructure), in the administrative center each household with an average number of three people occupies between 300 and 1500 m^2. The density of households in rural villages is from three to ten times lower. Even according to officially approved standards, at least 4000 m^2 of land was allocated per household in the village. This area is just adequate for self-sufficiency in Russia's temperate climate. Thus, the historical density of habitation (not husbandry!) in the administrative center of the provincial community is 500 people per km^2 (lim: 300–1000); in the villages of the rural district the density decreases by an order of magnitude 30–100 people per km^2, dropping even further toward the outskirts of the controlled territory. A planetary system can serve as a model for such a density structure.

Thus, the decisive factor is the distribution of population density across the territory, i.e., the territorial structure of the community, which is the basis for the development of social structure and boundaries. Social boundaries capture the components that form the local community. Their choice can be quite arbitrary, since they form a multicolored variety of ethnographic forms. But despite all this diversity, there is always a certain invariant set of components that characterize any local society without exceptions. Besides gender and age, such components include ethnic and national identity, the nature of kinship and family ties, the people's main occupation, their material reproduction (informal economy), mutual support, the system of sanctions and preferences, and finally, local culture. It is the special constellation of these invariant components that generates the diversity of local communities, and this is what will distinguish, for example, the communities of Evenks and Dolgans in Siberian Anabar from the communities of Permian Komi-Zyryans, or the communities of Kostroma meadow Cheremis from mountain

Cheremis. This diversity has nothing to do with belonging to different socio-political systems, which, on the contrary, erode and dissolve to the utmost both the specific social composition constellations and the constructs that make up their invariant framework.

2.2.2 *Composition: Local Society and Communities, Provincial Town, and Its Rural District*

A local society consists of elements and components, which are often treated as synonyms but should be clearly distinguished. Elements include individual people, not as mere physical individuals but as members of the community. Outsiders, as non-members of the community, are its "alien elements." They also exist in society, just as viruses, bacteria, or other parasites are necessarily present in any organism without being—or being to a limited extent—its own elements. Strange as it may sound, elements can also include other living organisms, on which the community relies in its everyday life, such as cows and horses, cats and dogs, as well as mystical objects of local ideology that exist only in the minds of society members but have a real impact on them and their existence, for example, deceased ancestors, brownies, goblins, or devils; see Plusnin (1991). Animals, necessarily present in any human community, as well as outsiders, who are as common in our time, constitute special types of elements, along with the autochthons themselves (members of the community as elements). All three types of elements—insiders, outsiders, and others—are in special relations with each other, which already implies at least the existence of appropriate institutions; see, for example, a special study on the issue (Shipilov, 2008). Although it is often considered that elements are an essential part of the composition of society, it seems to me that they are important only as representatives of institutions, and physically they matter only as "fillers" of the community, as "elementary components" of the population (demographic accounting units).

As for the components of local society, I believe they exist in two forms: socio-territorial and spatial-organizational. The first one consists of territorial communities that compose any local society. The second form is the "center-periphery" invariant (Shils, 1975, pp. 3–16), always represented by two structural units: the administrative center (usually a small town) and its rural district. These two forms are not different but mutually complementary components of the community.

Socio-Territorial Component

This component is logically obvious, but hardly distinguishable in-situ. It is rarely possible to capture where one community ends and the other begins—both geographically and personally. Today, these boundaries are vanishingly transparent, by the way, Emile Durkheim wrote about this already a hundred years ago (Durkheim, 1893, p. 34). Although in Russian, the concepts relating to three levels of social integration—provincial society, local society, and community (Gemeinschaft)[3]—are easily differentiated. Russian provincial local societies consist of one or two to several dozen communities. When a local society is represented by just one or two communities, it is always a special, extreme situation involving pure physical isolation or social self-isolation. The latter arises due to ethnic, religious, ideological, and, less often, political reasons. An ethnic group settling on the lands of another ethnicity; adherents of another faith occupying an area among communities professing a common religion; a community of like-minded people sharing an ideology alien to their environment; a group of people forcibly displaced to a new territory. I have records of all such cases, but they constitute a small share of local societies. In Russia, spatial isolation is much more common. Up to three-fifths of the entire territory of Russia create physical obstacles to inter-communal communication. Such is the Arctic, the Far North of Siberia, and many areas in the North of European Russia. Remote areas also exist in the mountainous regions of the south, in the vast forests of central Russia, and in the Siberian taiga. The communities living here are usually isolated, have no developed road network, and often have no roads at all. In this environment, local societies are small and form one community, or are represented by several remote communities that nevertheless maintain stable family and economic ties with each other.

Most modern local societies do not comprise one community, but one or two dozen communities. Rather than consisting of one village, *aul*, or *stanitsa*, a community generally embraces a cluster of such small settlements. Communities are represented by one settlement in the central part and in the south of European Russia, in the Urals, and in the south of Siberia. Such individual community settlements are quite large, with their population often ranging from several thousand to fifteen thousand people. They can control an area between several square kilometers (in the south) to several dozen square kilometers (in the center). The situation in the Russian North and in the west of the country is different. Here the community consists of a cluster of villages ("*coost*"), which is called a "district," or "rural district" (formerly simply "*district*" or "*cluster*"); these are several hamlets and villages (up to several dozen), closely related geographically, historically, and economically. Usually, the "cluster" or "district" is inhabited by people who are somehow related, since most of them come from families whose uninterrupted presence in the area dates back for several, sometimes ten to fifteen, generations. Such "clusters" occupy areas from twenty to a hundred square kilometers. The differences between communities consisting of only one settlement and "clustered" communities consisting of several hamlets are due to the larger size and smaller

[3]Hereinafter, throughout the text, I use the terms "community," "commune," or "Gemeinschaft," "Gemeinde," and "communauté" as synonyms for community, without highlighting any special semantic shades, unless specifically indicated. I consider "local society" exaggeratedly as an aggregate of "communities" (or individual commune) interconnected as units of local social integrity and linked by relations of territoriality and neighborhood, whose members consider themselves as part of one whole. "Provincial society" as an aggregate of local societies is only a terminological, but never an ontological, unity.

controlled territory of the central, southern, and Siberian villages as compared to the northern and western ones, and to the more developed transport infrastructure of the former (for details see Chap. 5).

The modern provincial Russian community retains the most important features of the traditional community, identified by Ferdinand Tönnies: neighborhood, kinship, and reciprocal ties ("*Gemeinschaft ist des Blutes, des Ortes, des Geistes. Verwandtschaft—Nachbarschaft—Freundschaft*") (Tönnies, 1887, p. 17). The communities of one local society are linked historically and administratively. Administrative unity in most cases simply inherits historical ties. In addition, the connection is also strengthened by the church structure. In the old days, Orthodox pogosts, Catholic parishes, Muslim *mahalla*, etc., usually united inhabitants of one or, less often, several communities. However, in the Soviet period and currently, there is one church parish per entire local society in rural areas, one or two parishes in towns with 3000–10,000 inhabitants, and from three to five parishes in towns with a population exceeding 20,000 inhabitants. So, as before, the local society is bound together by kin and neighborly (clan and ancestral) ties, and in addition to them by the state and the church.

Many local societies within their communities have a long record of existence and long-established, historically determined boundaries. Young communities are usually united by administrative boundaries within a district (former uyezds or their parts, volosts). But very often current administrative borders were drawn along the historically established boundaries between long-existing local societies (in the European part of Russia), or local societies themselves emerged and developed within the administrative bounds set by the state for economic or geographical reasons (as in the Urals and Siberia, and especially in the Russian Far East). So, often, both types of borders, historical and administrative, coincide.

A community is a social entity, a unity based on "*blood and soil*." It exists as a part of local society, or, under certain circumstances, it can be a self-sufficient, self-organizing, and self-governing system. A local society is an aggregate—a composition—of communities, but not necessarily an integral social entity. The reason is the two different ways a local society emerges. In one case, the society emerges from a single community (one "cluster"); then, over generations, it differentiates and splits into several communities, which are separated territorially, but connected by kinship, local culture, and often by household practices. Such are most traditional societies of the Russian North, the west, and the center of European Russia, as well as local communities of the Ugric, Tatar, and Bashkir peoples of the Volga region, and of Caucasian and Siberian peoples. These societies are autonomous self-organizing social systems; below, I define them as a type of naturally developing societies. In the second case, the local society is "planted"—often with the help of the state, but sometimes forced by its own initiative—on the territory and initially consists of either several randomly united communities or of randomly assembled individuals, settlers. In all cases, these are migrants, new inhabitants of the area. Only over time do individuals or individual communities establish neighborly and kin relations with each other and compose a local society. This situation is typical for relatively recently populated territories of the Far East of Siberia, some territories of the North Caucasus, and the western outskirts of the country. I call such societies coercively established. Often, however, both paths are intertwined, so that some groups of people or communities emerge along the first way, while others, in the same society, along the second one (for details see Sect. 4.6 of Chap. 4).

Spatial-Organizational Component

Any society consists of the center and the periphery. In our case, a provincial local society is composed of the administrative center and the rural district. Every local society is represented by two types of settlements: the town and villages of the rural district. The center is a "*locality*," a small town, less often a village or an urban-type settlement, entrusted with a complex of necessary administrative and religious functions. These functions are what distinguishes the locality among others and gives it the status of a center. Settlements of the periphery can be comparable with the center in size and historical glory, they can be located in a more convenient or even central place, but if they are not assigned administrative functions, the inhabitants themselves do not consider them a center.[4] The rural district is a set of individual settlements (hamlets, farms, villages, and urban-type settlements) surrounding the "*locality*" and separated from the rural district of other local societies by a historically defined and administratively established territory (for a detailed description of the territorial and residential structure see Chap. 5).

Small towns usually form only one community (and there is always only one community in other types of settlements—villages or townships—if they serve as an administrative center). If the population of the town is large enough—usually more than 5000 inhabitants, neighborhoods ("*ends*") with closer neighborly ties, often segregated along ethnic and even occupational lines, begin to emerge. Such neighborhoods are a prerequisite for future intra-town communities. In young towns, neighborhoods originally emerged for economic reasons: every large enterprise was surrounded by residential "dormitory areas" inhabited mainly by workers of that particular enterprise; thus, occupation-based communities developed coercively both since the times of Peter the Great and since the early Soviet period (this is especially typical for settlements established next to mining manufactories and plants in the Urals in Imperial times, and next to factories, mining complexes, and metallurgical plants in Siberia in the Soviet period). Only later did such communities acquire the features of a real community with a predominance of not only neighborly, but also family ties. In towns with a population exceeding 20,000 people, communities are usually "blurred" and "dissolved"; they cannot be clearly identified, and the residents themselves do not distinguish them. Since relatives do not live compactly, but are dispersed throughout the town and, even more often, across the rural district, family ties permeate neighborly ones; both types of relations can be equally close for the purpose of cooperating in life. In this case, we can speak of one

[4]The administrative center is not always the most populated part of the local society. This is the situation today, but in the recent past (until the beginning of the twentieth century) the administrative and religious centers, which were not always in the same settlement, were far less populous than the villages of their rural district.

large territorial community. Nowadays, this is even more relevant, since social networks and online forums, which are available everywhere, in every town, unite the townspeople by allowing them to "communicate" continuously.

The rural district is much better differentiated into communities: here they are always territorially separated. As mentioned above, communities are represented either by one large village or several nearby settlements or by "clusters" that can occupy quite a considerable area. Meanwhile, due to exogamy, absolutely all communities in the local society are interrelated through family and affinity relations of their inhabitants. Often, such relations are very distant (see Chap. 9).

The above descriptions demonstrate that both components of local society are closely linked: territorially, communities are differentiated into the center and periphery, interpenetrating each other with the connections of their elements. The special case of a single community and a single settlement does not violate this rule: in this case, the periphery consists of farms and temporary settlements (seasonal camps, cabins) scattered throughout the territory.

2.2.3 *Social Relations: Basic Institutions*

The interaction and dependence of the components of local society—communities with each other, on the one hand, the urban center and the rural district, on the other hand—are ensured by a set of relations, which I consider necessary and sufficient for any local human population to be a self-organized community. That is, there are mechanisms of social self-organization in it. In this sense, such a set of relations is invariant, and therefore archaic, i.e., present everywhere and existing eternally. My own analysis suggests that there are eight pairwise linked types of relations. Since all these relations are well known, and only their compositional structure is not obvious, I will limit myself to a brief general description. Each pair of relations belongs to a certain sphere of life, absolutely necessary for the existence of any community.

The actual existence of a community—"here and now"—is a physical reality, actuality ("*ectio*"); it is upheld by relations of communality and synchrony (contemporaneity) of the existence of a group of people maintaining local integrity. Relations of *communality* (lat. *communality* = life within common walls) characterize joint permanent residence of community members on a common territory they consider their own (and their neighbors recognize it as such), control it and protect it from outsiders and any encroachments. These relations underlie the institutions, in whatever form they may exist, that are responsible for ensuring the physical safety of members of the community and for protecting its territory. It is quite obvious that communal relations are definitely associated with relations aimed at synchronizing people's life. Relations of *synchrony* (lat. = *synchronicity*, *modernus*) manifest themselves first and foremost locally: synchronizing the everyday life of individuals and households by regulating their behavior on a daily and minute-by-minute basis (e.g., statutory working hours); synchronizing the functioning of social institutions in line with the natural and social calendar cycle (local planting and harvesting time, the dates of general and professional holidays, etc.); the need to synchronize local traditional rites and rituals that contribute to the unity of the community and the entire local society.

Cooperation and coordination are the basic relations that determine any activity ("*actio*") of community members. Relations *of cooperation* (lat. = *cooperante*) emerge as individuals and households interact in economic and social activities, initially intended for life support and social reproduction purposes. They determine the differentiation of functions of individuals and groups, the nature of the division of labor in the family, in the household, and in the community. The first and most important form of cooperation is the complementarity of biological, social, and economic functions of husband and wife, and father and mother in the family; see Durkheim (1893, pp. 130–131) and Murdock (2003, pp. 25–30). When we talk about cooperation, we are thus talking about division of labor. Obviously, cooperation implies and requires coordination. Cooperation as such is impossible without coordination even at the level of the simplest work if that work cannot be performed by a single person. Therefore, relations of *coordination* (lat. = *coordinationem*) are paired with relations of cooperation. They are responsible for creating a system of subordination necessary for the sustainable existence and development of local society. Relations of coordination establish not only the functional (labor) and status hierarchy, but also community networking (*heterarchy*). Thus, they determine the basic components of the social structure, the status positions of functionally diverse members of the community.

We should also mention reactive activity ("*re-actio*"), which reflects productive activity. It also ensures the actual productive activity necessary for life support, for biological and social reproduction; for details see, for example Durkheim (1893, pp. 130–136). Such re-active relations are again represented by a complementary pair—communication and compassion. *Communicative* relations (lat. = *communicationis*) are in fact an accord (in particular, a consensus) on the creation and maintenance of a local communication system—a daily mutually intelligible information exchange based on local dialects and dialects of a language common to all members of the community. Relations of compassion (lat. = *compatientus*) result from reciprocal altruism. The ability to put (imagine) oneself in the position of any other member of the community and sympathize with him or her means creating and maintaining a special psycho-emotional field that gives members of the local society a sense of belonging. Mutually intelligible communication is possible only on a common psycho-emotional field. And information exchange consists largely of non-verbal messages, which constitute the basis and an essential semantic part of the content of messages. Like the aforementioned pairs of relations, there is no everyday communication without compassion, and compassion implies communication.

Finally, the fourth pair of relations results from the community members' projective activity ("*pro-ectio*"). They occur in the form of people's perceptions of their own existence and daily activities, and reflect the life ideology (world perception), mythology, and life philosophy (worldview). Such relations can be called relations of *consensus* (lat. = *consensus*) and *consciousness* (lat. = *consciousness*).

Consensus is aimed at establishing and maintaining a common opinion among members of the community. Often the result of such activity to maintain local mental unity is denoted by the term *mentality*. This is not only a perception of oneself and the world (projection of oneself onto the world and the external environment onto oneself), but also relations with other members of the community that ensure the local mentality and certify its stability, thus also confirming an ordinary person's consistent picture of the world and its full compliance with that of his fellow citizens (more precisely, fellow tribesmen). The complementary type of relation here is consciousness, i.e., relations regarding traditional empirical knowledge, regarding establishing and maintaining a system of knowledge based on long-standing local experience specific to each particular local society. Such a system of knowledge is often described as folk experience, folk knowledge, and local tradition. But it is also perceived as superstition, as knowledge based on faith and tradition rather than on science. Perception of local consciousness as superstition is the view of an *outsider*, a representative of another culture, an alien. Local consciousness does not imply and does not allow critical attitude to the world, to society, and to kinsfolk. Unity of opinion (totality of opinions) and community consciousness is therefore inherent only in members of the community and of the local society. But, on a larger scale, such unity begins "to break up" and malfunction; mental pluralism emerges, which is unacceptable, for example, in an archaic society or an old rural community, where the mere fact of dissent makes a person an outcast. Therefore, relations of local consensus and consciousness are important bonds of communal unity, the basis of local self-organization to the same extent as communality and synchrony of everyday life.

Thus, four pairs form a round of interconnected types of relations (*...—ectio—action—re-actio—pro-ectio—ectio—...*); the mandatory availability of each and all of them determines the existence of local society as an integral social object. A community exists only *there, so, then, always and forever*, if its members are "*here and now*"—engage in joint simultaneous activities; they cooperate (practice a division of labor) and coordinate (functionally subordinate) their activity "*so and in such a way*"; they speak a common language and can understand each other, communicate and have compassion to show altruism and willingness to self-sacrifice for the sake of loved ones; they have shared everyday experience, adhere to the same practices and traditions, have common ideas about themselves, about the surrounding world, about their history, their past and future. I assert that only such relations make social life consistent.

2.2.4 Local Society: Definition

Summarizing the descriptions provided in Sects. 2.2.1–2.2.3, I define "*provincial local society*" as follows. It is a territorially delimited set of several communities (a single community in the extreme case), usually linked by a common history and origin, and permeated by kinship of most families. (In particular cases, a local society is aggregated from several heterogeneous, originally alien communities; such societies are established coercively.) This is a physically existing population, represented by individual households (families) organized into settlements-demes, which are themselves organized in space into a three-level territorial structure consisting of the administrative center (town-*locality*) and its two-level rural district (*volost* = network of hamlets, villages, and townships with their centers). Community members united into households are interconnected through kin and neighborly relations due to their long-term co-existence; they are also linked by relations of reciprocity (reciprocal exchange), since they are in cooperative and coordinated interactions—they engage in joint vital activities and form a certain structure of industrial and social subordination. The most important features of local society are also people's perceptions of their unity within their social locality. On the one hand, they enable maintaining stereotypes of behavior, local traditions, and established practices, and expressing the local mentality and system of local experience. On the other hand, they protect every member of the community, not only in terms of physical security, but also in terms of locally recognized privileges and preferences, mutual concessions and benefits, social responsibilities and rights according to occupational, gender, age, neighborly, clan, and kinship principles.

Of course, such a definition is not satisfactory, if only because it is not concise. But it captures all the features, which I believe are essential for a local society:

1. Territorial delimitation, the existence of its own territory and boundaries that define it and establish that all or a certain part of natural resources and produced material assets belong to the community
2. Generations of continuous existence in one territory, which determines historical continuity
3. Composition of the local society of communities united by kin and neighborly ties, which are overlapped by relations of reciprocity resulting from reciprocal altruism and nepotism
4. An organizational structure represented by individual households, not evenly distributed in space, but organized into settlements, which themselves always have a two-tier (rarely three-tier) structure—the urban center and its periphery, the rural district
5. Functional diversity and status heterogeneity of members of society, which determine the relations of cooperation and coordination of each and everyone
6. Communicative, sensory, and mental unity of society members, ensuring social reproduction, which underlies local self-government and makes it possible

So, below I describe the social structure of "local society," which I understand [define] as a territorially delimited set of several communities (in the sense of Ferdinand Tönnies), historically and administratively interconnected and precisely due to this constituting the phenomenon of an integral social locality.

2.3 Conceptual Framework: Basic Hypotheses of Empirical Research

The description of the social structure should be based on a conceptual framework. In our case, these are three interrelated concepts. The principal one is the hypothesis that two social structures that developed on the "body" of the local society are complementary. It is the basis for two associated concepts. One asserts that the social and territorial structures of a local society are interrelated: one does not exist without the other. The other one states a triaxial binary oppositional structure of social relations at the local level.

2.3.1 Complementarity of Social Structures

The author's hypothesis that social structures are complementary is the basic concept of my empirical study of provincial local society. The essence of the concept is as follows. The social structure of each local society is not integral since it is not "one-dimensional." It is built on two complementary foundations. There is an "external" social structure, which is determined and "imposed from above" by the state. It is this social structure that is almost the exclusive subject of sociological research; see, e.g.: Goldthorpe (1987), Vidich (1995), Scott (1996), Radaev and Shkaratan (1996), Bergman and Joye (2005), Radaev (2008), Gorshkov et al. (2012), Manning et al. (2017), Anikin and Lezhnina (2018), Tikhonova et al. (2018), and Tikhonova (2019). This structure can be both class-based and estate-based. In the first case, stratification is the result of income stratification or is determined by the size of available capital, and thereby the amount of controlled resources. In the second case, it is determined by a legislatively established system of public service and is supported by tradition. Most often—and in the current environment always—a class or estate-based structure does not exist in pure form (exclusively); to a greater or lesser extent they complement each other. In the case of modern Russian society, the social structure is predominantly estate-based (Kordonsky, 2008a, b, c, 2016; Shkaratan, 2012), also (Rieber, 1982, p. 416; Becker, 1985, pp. 16–20). Although income stratification exists, it gives no definite clue to the position of classes (Tikhonova et al., 2018); the bounds of the "middle class" are especially blurred (Radaev, 2008; Tikhonova, 2020). I adhere to the principles of Simon Kordonsky's theory of the estate-based structure of modern Russian society, which he proposed and developed in the early 2000s and outlined in several monographs; see Kordonsky (2016). According to his theory, the social structure of Russian society only appears to be a class structure and is officially designated as such; however, by nature it is not a class one. All features of an estate-based structure are present (Kordonsky, 2008a, p. 52): (a) statutory rights of each estate; (b) inheritance of estate rights; (c) estate organizations with the most extensive rights, including judicial ones ("*courts of honor*," for example); (d) estate self-government; (d) external attributes of estate affiliation (uniform, insignia, award systems, appropriate lifestyle, etc.); and (e) estate consciousness.

Under his theory of the estate-based social structure, Kordonsky identifies the following four principal groups of estates (Kordonsky, 2016, pp. 80–84, 91–95):

1. "*Government*" (officials, individuals directly in the service of the state—titular service states)
2. "*The people*" (non-titular not serving estates—heterogeneous groups of pensioners, industrial, agricultural, and public sector workers, and employees)
3. "*Entrepreneurs*" (heterogeneous groups of independent professionals—privately practicing doctors and healers, lawyers, artists and private detectives, political strategists, journalists, clergymen, etc.)
4. "*Marginalized individuals*" (people with limited rights, convicted persons, individuals with a criminal record).

In each of the four estate groups, one can distinguish over a dozen separate estates, which are defined mainly either by a statutory status or by self-determination and certain rights and preferences, but not necessarily by law. The former case includes estates stipulated by special laws, namely, titular estates (first group), and "marginalized individuals"—persons convicted and limited in rights and non-estate persons (fourth group). The latter case includes "the people" and "entrepreneurs," attributed to the second and third groups, respectively.

Under the theory of the estate-based social structure, we distinguish the following features at the level of local society. First, not all estates are represented in the province, and second, they are represented differently in each group of estates. In this, provincial local societies differ significantly from societies in medium-sized and large cities. The most complete representation is among bureaucrats—titular service estates—but representatives of each estate are solitary, and their total number is often under 5%–10% of the adult population. The reason is that only local branches of government agencies operate "on site," moreover, not all of them and not everywhere (for details see Sect. 6.2 of Chap. 6). The composition of estates in the most numerous group "the people" varies greatly from society to society. Usually, a particular society does not demonstrate much diversity in the types of estates represented. Of course, pensioners and public sector employees are to be found everywhere. The categories of agricultural workers are uniform, but there are usually few or no industrial wage workers. There are very few manufacturing experts. In the estate group "entrepreneurs"—independent entrepreneurs and self-employed professionals living on income and fees—the latter are hardly represented, with petty merchants and small businesspeople from the service sector accounting for almost the entire composition. The size of this group is about 10%–15%, considering shadow entrepreneurship (when a person formally belongs to one estate group, but in fact is part of this one). The fourth estate group, "marginalized individuals," is the least represented in local societies (generally, no more than 1%–2%, which is precisely the reason for the extremely low crime rate in provincial societies). A rare society has prisoners, and then only if there are "zones"—penal colonies—on its territory (about 1%–2% of all the societies I recorded). Former convicts, even if they exist in a local society, are "flow-through people," migrants, whose presence is just temporary. In addition, they generally settle on the periphery of society, often in monasteries, which are themselves "outsiders." There are just as few people with limited status due to limited legal capacity. Almost all of them have been transferred to the status of dependents and placed in "care homes for the disabled and the elderly"; thus, they are formally included in the group of pensioners. There are hardly any permanent residents limited in rights (ex-convicts), or thieves and bandits in such societies,[5] since due to the related and neighborly environment, where the residents themselves rather than the state control a significant part of vital resources, they cannot get access to resources for "feeding." Therefore, most local marginalized individuals move to large cities, which provide more opportunities for their "area of expertise." Only solitary dropouts remain. Ex-convicts from among local residents generally have their rights reinstated upon release from prison, and upon return join the estate of "the people" or "entrepreneurs." In general, the state-defined social structure is clearly visible, clearly designed, hierarchically built, and universal for any locality, with only minor variations.

Along with this, a local society has its own local "grassroots" structure, which originates and grows from below, from its own body. In the Russian provincial environment, it generally meets the well-known criteria of a communal [Gemeinschaft] structure, i.e., it is an archaic structure. Based on the totality of all the local societies I surveyed, I can assert with certain allowances that the social structure is determined by the following criteria (for details see Chap. 9). The most important criterion is the social influence of a person, determined by his professional experience, competencies, expertise, and practical skills that are essential for the life support of the local population. Respect, which generates influence, depends not only on the intelligence, knowledge, experience, and skills of the person; it depends as much on his or her moral and ethical qualities—socially correct behavior and exemplary mental attitudes. The second most important criterion is clan affiliation. In the provinces, kinship, clan, and ethnic affiliation still play an important role and are decisive for social stratification, i.e., an individual's social position depends on different degrees of genetic kinship and affinity [clan and ethnic affiliation]. A specific feature under present circumstances is that all these types of relations intermix, and people often perceive "kin" and "kin group" as synonyms to both "clan" and "ethnic group." An individual's formal status in the system of state hierarchy (system of service) is only the third criterion of his/her social position in the province. Finally, money income, disposable capital, and the amount of controlled resources close the list in fourth place. Of course, there are instances when one person or a kin group (a group of families related by kinship and ethnicity) have absolute control over local resources; in such cases, this criterion is decisive for local

[5] The infamous period of violence of the "New Russians" in the 1990s practically did not affect the Russian province. Local bandits, even if they operated at home, targeted either "outsiders" or (less often) representatives of neighboring communities within the local society, when the society was large enough and consisted of a dozen or several dozen communities.

social stratification. But more often the situation is different, and capital is neither of first nor second priority in determining a person's local status.

Thus, the "grassroots" local social structure, which can be called "communal," results from the interaction of a constellation of criteria: influence, kinship, power, and capital. They determine to varying degrees (largely depending on the type of local society) the scope of informally established rights and responsibilities, preferences, and access to local resources and institutional positions. There is no straightforward correlation between both structures—the formal estate-based one and the grassroots "communal." There is no direct relationship between affiliation with a titular service estate and significant influence, top power positions, considerable disposable capital, or control over resources vital for the local society. Similarly, formal affiliation with the estate of marginalized individuals does not imply lack of capital or influence. Probably, but not necessarily, such a person will not occupy high positions in the formal power hierarchy—but only because he is limited in rights. Among other things, we should bear in mind that the four criteria can be continuous (influence and capital) or establish binary oppositions (clan and power). Consequently, their composition acquires additional complexity in capturing numerous options that determine the social position of each particular person in each particular local society. Consequently, the complex constellation of four estate positions and four elements of the "communal" structure creates a social stratification, which to a certain extent is unique for each local society. At least, it is unique for each of the six types of social structures outlined in Chaps. 4, 9, and 10.

2.3.2 Territorial Structure

The hypothesis that the territorial structure is the physical basis of the social structure relies on the well-known statement about the congruence of social and physical space (Christaller, 1980; Altman & Chemers, 1980; Bourdieu, 1989). To paraphrase Pierre Bourdieu, social space tends to become reified in physical space by appropriating and marking it, primarily by indicating physical and symbolic boundaries—that is, by reconstructing itself in physical space (Bourdieu, 1989, pp. 14–25). Any methods of social differentiation are represented in physical space and are physically objectified. Physical space of any size—from a few square meters to millions of square kilometers—is somehow transformed everywhere into social space, and this is done mainly by means of three universal mechanisms.

First, the social and psychological mechanism of appropriation—division into "ours" ("mine") and "someone else's." "Ours" is established with the help of borders and is formalized as a territory. It can be the individual territory of "my room" or "my estate," as well as the territory of "my town" and "my country."

The second universal mechanism is the split of space into the center and periphery ("*... the capital city can be conceptualized only in relation to the provinces ...*" (Bourdieu, 2007, p. 55). The center and the periphery form binary oppositions, which are countless: from differentiating the space of a house ("icon corner"—"*kut*" (storeroom), female and male living quarters), the space of any public building (church—altar and porch, theater—stage and gallery, etc.), any urban or rural space—into the main square where the most important institutions are located, and the outskirts (*posad*, "*shanghai*"). Any local society consists of the administrative center ("*locality*") and the rural district, any state—of the capital and the *ukraine*, outlying areas. This is the mechanism of institutional structural and functional differentiation of space.

In addition to these two established mechanisms, there is also a well-known but extreme political mechanism, specified by Pierre Bourdieu (1987, pp. 150–160): transforming "*social space . . . into physical space by uprooting or deporting some people*," as well as large groups, including entire cities, ethnic groups, and peoples. In the old days, all polities regularly resorted to this mechanism but now its use is restricted to wartime and the redrawing of state borders.

Mechanisms for transforming physical space into social space are mechanisms for transforming space into territory. They are thus also responsible for establishing the territorial structure. I think it is important to emphasize especially a structural correspondence between physical space transformed into a territory and social differentiation established in the territory and supported by institutions. The territorial structure is reflected in the social structure on various levels. Both class and estate (and especially caste) differentiation of society at the local level are manifested in the smallest signs of territorial segregation. I will mention well-known facts. Representatives of different estates or different classes prefer or are forced to settle in certain areas of cities and villages, which are respectively called either elite neighborhoods or "ghettos." Urban districts and individual residential complexes are segregated in physical space according to the emerging new estate structure. Similar segregation takes place for public spaces; a large part of the buildings and areas turn out to be either "exclusive elite clubs" or "foul places inhabited by vile people with criminal behavior." Territorial segregation representing social differentiation is most vividly illustrated by numerous "fences" that prevent representatives of other strata or occupational groups from entering enclosed areas, "public" buildings, and residential premises. That is why in the post-Soviet period, when the previously dominant ideology of the "homogenous, classless society" was "relegated to the dustbin of history," enclosures and fences, barriers and automatic locks began to appear in our urban environment everywhere—first in the metropolitan cities, then even in small towns and townships, and the number of security guards throughout the country rose to several million. A new social structure began emerging in the country, and its first and most obvious sign were changes in the organization of the territory and ways of controlling it.

The same phenomenon of spatial segregation, corresponding to (and following) social differentiation, is also observed—paradoxically—regarding the transport, energy, and utilities infrastructure. Its quality, and even its existence or lack, is to some (quite distinct) extent associated with the territories of everyday habitation of representatives of different social strata, including those differentiated by occupational characteristics or place of residence (especially urban or rural). The quality of the road surface, the marking and arrangement of streets and driveways vary significantly from area to area, which, at close examination, turn out to be inhabited by people from different classes and estates. Even the energy infrastructure varies territorially. Electricity grids differ less, whereas the heat and gas supply systems—distinctly (which can be easily captured by walking the streets of regional capitals, small towns, and small villages). The same applies to the utilities infrastructure. In different residential areas, water supply and sewerage systems are built and operated differently. The service sector and social reproduction demonstrate an even more vivid picture. Universities and schools, hospitals and clinics, health resorts and stadiums, and even public baths and brothels selectively target certain classes and estates, and the effective mechanism for this is not their restricted admission, but the cost of services. In some cases, they are accessible only for the upper-income class, in other cases low prices stop representatives of the middle-class from using them for reasons of prestige ("*but this is a hospital for the poor*!"). But all these public—according to the initial definition—places are distributed in a completely definite way in space and are elements of the territorial structure of society. It is noteworthy that this kind of "infrastructural segregation" is more characteristic of an estate-based rather than class structure of society.

I believe these reasons are sufficient to consider the phenomenon of complementarity of the territorial and social structures trivial, and to accept the hypothesis of the territorial structure as the physical basis of social structure. However, this had to be recorded. Besides, the territory is a convenient classification indicator, since in this case there is a clear procedure for checking the conformity between the phenomenon observed by the researcher and the self-identification of the people living in the territory; there is a clear correspondence between both for the researcher and for the local residents, which is a necessary requirement for any "natural" classification (Kordonsky, 2008a, p. 40). Therefore, the classification of the territorial structure can be a prerequisite for the classification of the social structure. This is the task I propose to address in Chap. 5.

2.3.3 Triaxial Binary Opposition Structure

Simon Kordonsky proposed the second working concept in the course of our joint empirical study of local societies (Kordonsky, 2008c; Kordonskiy et al., 2009). Its essence is as follows. The structure of a local society can be classified not on one, but on several grounds simultaneously. It is assumed that this allows one to give a description relevant to social reality—the concept created by the researcher will be more in line with what "actually exists" (Kordonsky, 2008a, pp. 37–40). The structure of a particular local society was meant to be described in a system of three coordinates: each coordinate represents an axis of binary opposition features. The three coordinates are: (1) the degree of an individual's inclusion in the community; (2) his/her social status; and (3) the extent of economic dependence on/independence from the state.

The "inclusion" axis is represented by the universal "us/them" ("insiders/outsiders") binary opposition. By degree of inclusion, each person in a local society can be classified as either an "insider" or an "outsider." But he can also be somewhere in-between—not completely "us" or not quite "them," that is, he can be on the way from one pole to the other. More often, this is the state of transition from the status of "outsider" to the status of "insider." The reverse situation is much less common. Obviously, a large part of the locals are "insiders." But "outsiders" are also always present in any society; in some societies they are numerous, in others—few (there is even an exceptionally rare case nowadays, where there are none). By the correlation between "us" and "them" local societies can be classified into societies with different levels of migration and size of the diaspora or diasporas. All modern communities have a larger or smaller proportion of migrants in their composition. Notably, migrants are not exclusively "outsiders"; in each local society they are on different stretches of the long way to becoming "insiders" (Collier, 2013, pp. 57–110). "Us" and "them" can be differentiated on several grounds (criteria). The most obvious criteria are: (a) residential status of the inhabitants of the settlement, recorded, in particular, in the registration documents at the place of residence; (b) permanence and duration of residence; (c) legal status of the resident based on the status of the dwelling (local residents in their own houses or apartments and summer residents in country houses temporarily residing in the territory); (d) historical circumstances (the order in which different groups of inhabitants settled the territory and appropriated its resources); and (e) ethnic factor (affiliation with an autochthonous ethnic or kin group). The "us/them" dichotomy matters for social cohesion and self-organization since the presence of outsiders consolidates local society. They are always needed, but they must be few. Outsiders must not claim the basic resources on which the local society relies for its existence. If they do claim or impinge on the resource allocation system, society stubbornly resists. But with the increasing pressure of outsiders (especially if the diaspora grows and the amount of resources it disposes of increases), the community begins to crumble from within. At the same time, outsiders are able to integrate and assimilate, and quite quickly become insiders. Therefore, the composition of "us" and "them" can be used to identify and describe the "affinity" structure for each empirical case; for such a description see, e.g., Plusnin (2013). Chapter 9 depicts the local social structure along the "inclusion" axis.

The "social status" axis is represented by the equally universal "upper/lower strata" binary opposition.[6] Obviously, by contrast to "us/them," this opposition is continuous: statuses are not accumulated at the poles but spread along the entire length of the hierarchical scale. However, one should bear in mind that hierarchy at the local level is not a primitive linear one, like in the army. There are at least several parallel hierarchies along with heterarchical (network) structures. Moreover, it is these latter ones that are often more important at the local level than hierarchies. Hierarchies are usually associated with the formal sphere, with the system of public

[6] It is still common in Russia to define status by terms inherited from Mongolian times—"white bone/black bone" (nobles/commoners).

service; therefore, they are attached to estate statuses and to the official "table of ranks." And heterarchies are associated with informal relations, with interpersonal, neighborly, and family ties. Due to multiple and ambiguous relations between the upper and lower strata, the status axis is nonlinear. Mismatches are most common between the formal status of a society member, which is established by the official table of ranks in the system of public service, and the informal status, which depends on several other factors rather than the official position. This also makes it difficult to determine operationally the status of local community members. The same person may be at the very "bottom" of the formal hierarchy (be a stoker or cleaner, for example) but at the same time be very influential in the system of informal relations and, therefore, have the highest status in the society (e.g., he may be a respected and influential "*elder*" or a reputable "*problem solver*"[7]). Conversely, a formally high status does not necessarily give a person any influence in the local society. One status rarely converts into another one. However, isolated cases do exist.[8] In fact, in a provincial society, a formally high status is most often converted into a low informal one (which is hard to imagine in an anomic urbanized society). Chapter 10 depicts the local social structure along the "upper/lower strata" axis.

On the backdrop of the first two axes, the "degree of economic dependence on the state" axis seems to be out of place. But in the Russian context, this is a very important distinction, since people are largely economically active in the informal, shadow, and criminal sectors. Moreover, in the province, a significant part of the working-age population—over a half—is not engaged in the local economy by virtue of being self-employed. It is this self-employment status that we consider as a criterion for distinguishing the "dependent/independent" opposition. Since we are talking about people's livelihoods, about the nature of their economic activity, we use the terms "active/rent-seeking population." The active population includes those who provide for themselves through their own initiative, becoming entrepreneurs or self-employed workers, since "*...they generate their own income*" (Kordonskiy et al., 2012, p. 81). The rent-seeking population includes those who largely depend on the state for their livelihood: these are the so-called "*budgetniki*"—public sector employees receiving salary from the government budget, as well as people living on pensions or welfare (non-working pensioners and various categories of people in need of social support). State-guaranteed income serves as a criterion for classifying this group as "*rent-seeking population*" (Kordonskiy et al., 2012, p. 81). At first glance, this differentiation enables to easily divide all members of a local society into active ones and "rentier" but in reality, there are many transitional states, and often one person should be attributed to both categories at once. As secondary

[7] At the provincial local level, the criminal subculture does not oppose the community at all but peacefully coexists and penetrates it. It is criminal only in relation to the state.

[8] A most recent example that shocked the Russian federal media but was not perceived by the locals themselves as something extraordinary was demonstrated during municipal elections in the fall of 2020. In one of the regions, a cleaning lady formally occupying the lowest position in the official table of ranks was elected head of municipality (which is formally the highest position in the local community).

employment is widespread in our provinces, one and the same person can be both a "*budgetnik*" and a self-employed "*garazhnik*" or even an "*otkhodnik.*" This applies even more to households where some members represent the active category, whereas others—the rent-seeking one. Nevertheless, such a division enables to classify large groups of people, splitting them fairly accurately into two polar types. The criteria for differentiation are: (a) the nature of dependence in economic activity—self-employment or service; (b) income generation method—self-sufficiency or government guarantees of security; and (c) type of income (business income, fees and salary or wages, ration, allowance, pension, or benefit). Using these differentiating criteria, we are dealing with a "motley" variance, more blurred than that defined by the "us/them" and "upper/lower strata" axes.

Three axes define a set (a three-dimensional matrix) of eight possible types, each of which quite adequately determines an individual's position in the community depending on affiliation with "us" or "them," being at the top or bottom of the social ladder, and on the main relationship with the state, financially dependent or independent. These are the following types, defined by selecting one of the eight compositions:

1. Us—upper strata—active
2. Us—upper strata—rent-seeking
3. Us—lower strata—active
4. Us—lower strata—rent-seeking
5. Them—upper strata—active
6. Them—upper strata—rent-seeking
7. Them—lower strata—active
8. Them—lower strata—rent-seeking.

Obviously, an individual or a household can be located in two, three, or more cells of the matrix at the same time. But it seems more important to capture these basic types of relations, which may be the parameters of the social structure.

Let us briefly consider which categories of the population in the local society can be attributed to each of the types. Type 1 may include local entrepreneurs with a high status in the community, both formal and informal. It may also include highly skilled otkhodniks who are respected by their neighbors. Type 2 may consist of municipal leaders and government officials or highly qualified public sector employees with a high formal status who have lived their entire life in the community and are generally accepted as "us." Type 3 may be composed of simple unskilled otkhodniks or informally engaged local unemployed. In the case of Type 4, these may be low-skilled or semi-skilled public sector employees from among local residents. This type also certainly includes most local pensioners and all those who represent the "social bottom" in need of state support and assistance, socially disadvantaged categories of the population, who are sometimes called "poor." Type 5 may include major visiting entrepreneurs who operate in the area but whom the other residents do not accept as "one of us." Type 6 may consist of officials and formally high-ranking employees, as well as skilled specialists (doctors, teachers, cultural workers, etc.), who are in the community temporarily for the period of their service. Type 7 may be composed of such different categories as former prisoners, representatives of other faiths, random and temporary people, even tourists as a category of "eternally flowing strangers." In the case of Type 8, these could be, for example, retired urban second homers who have taken up permanent residence in the community or who come only for the summer. In each particular community, the categories of people attributed to one of the eight types will be different, but the types themselves remain. Chapters 6–10 contain examples of the above. Empirical data show that with a very large variety of Russian local societies, they are quite similar in the representation of different categories in each of the eight types. Societies with any unique categories are few.[9] Communities where one or two cells of the eight types are "empty," unpopulated, are extremely rare. If this is the case, it is predominantly in spatially isolated societies. The main differences are observed not in the composition of these eight types, but in the correlation between the shares of different categories of population attributed to each type. Chapter 5 contains examples of such differences.

2.4 Summary

I am considering the Russian provincial society not by itself, in its entirety, but only as a totality—by no means an integrity—of a multitude of local communities, separated from their neighbors by historical and administrative territorial boundaries.

Besides a dual spatial organization, local societies have their own dual social structure. In the first case (spatial organization of the community), the socio-territorial component is combined with the spatial-organizational one: territorially divided communities are two-level, consist of several (dozens) "clusters" linked by an administrative center, a town.

In the second case (social structure), relations between people, mainly communal, combined with a state-defined estate structure, noticeably distinguish local provincial societies from the populations of large- and even medium-sized cities. Their social structure, in contrast to that of big cities, retains archaic—hence, invariant—features.

The social structure is closely linked with the territorial structure, since for the inhabitants of provincial societies, the local territory ("native land") is incomparably more important than for the city dweller. Based on these considerations alone, it makes no sense to compare the social structure of provincial societies with that of large cities. They are markedly different. They are neither additive nor isomorphic. The "world of the city" and the "world of the province" are disparate. It is based on this approach of contrasting the nature of social ties in the province and in the big city that I am considering the social structure of the provincial society from a "one-

[9]For example, missionaries of unconventional religious movements or sects, groups of former prisoners, monks, pagan-ecological groups—even they are widespread and can be found in every second or third local society.

sided" perspective. But this "one-sidedness"—the archaic structure of relations, attachment to the territory and the self-value of living, self-sufficiency (natural economy), independent existence, and natural [spontaneous] self-organization—is the source of strength and viability of our local societies, each one individually and all together.

References

Altman, I., & Chemers, M. (1980). *Culture and environment*. Brooks/Cole Publishing Company.

Anatomy of a Province. (2006). *Otechestvennye zapiski, 5*(36). Анатомия провинции (2006). *Отечественные записки*, 5(36).

Anikin V., & Lezhnina Y. (2018). Economic stratification: on the definition of the boundaries of income groups. *Sociological Review, 17*(1), 237–273. Аникин В., & Лежнина Ю. (2018). Экономическая стратификация: об определении границ доходных групп. *Социологическое обозрение*, 17(1), 237–273.

Becker, S. (1985). *Nobility and privilege in late imperial Russia. NIU series in Slavic, East European, and Eurasian studies*. Northern Illinois University Press.

Bergman, M. M., & Joye, D. (2005). Comparing social stratification schematas: CAMSIS, CSP-CH, Goldthorpe, ISCO-88, Treiman and Wright. In *Cambridge studies in social research, no 10*. SSRG.

Bernard, H. R., Johnsen, E. C., Killworth, P., & Robinson, S. (1991). Estimating the size of an average personal network and on an event subpopulation: Some empirical results. *Social Science Research, 20*, 109–121.

Birdwhistell, R. L. (1974). The language of body: The natural environment of word. In A. Silverstein (Ed.), *Human communication* (pp. 203–220). Lawrence Erlbaum.

Bogdanov A.A. (1989). *Tectology: A general organizational science*. "Economics". Богданов А.А. (1989). *Тектология: всеобщая организационная наука*. М.: «Экономика».

Bourdieu, P. (1987). Espace social et pouvoir symbolique, mars 1986. In P. Bourdieu (Ed.), *Choses dites* (pp. 147–166). Minuit. Russian edition: Бурдьё П. (2007). *Социология социального пространства*. М., СПб.: Алетейя.

Bourdieu, P. (1989). Social space and symbolic power. *Sociological Theory, 7*(1), 14–25.

Bourdieu P. (2007). *Sociology of social space*. Aleteia. Бурдьё П. (2007). *Социология социального пространства*. М., СПб.: Алетейя.

Carneiro, R. (1981). The chiefdom as precursor of the state. In G. Jones & R. Kautz (Eds.), *The transition to statehood in the New World* (pp. 37–79). Cambridge University Press.

Christaller, W. (1980). *Die zentralen Orte in Süddeutschland. Eine ökonomisch-geographische Untersuchung über die Gesetzmäßigkeit der Verbreitung und Entwicklung der Siedlungen mit städtischer Funktion*. Wissenschaftliche Buchgesellschaft.

Cohen, R., & Toland, J. D. (Eds.). (1988). *State formation and political legitimacy*. Transaction Books.

Collier, P. (2013). *Exodus. How migration is changing our world*. Oxford University Press.

Donskikh, O. A. (2011). Province and provinciality: The beginning. In E. I. Dergacheva-Skop & V. N. Alekseev (Eds.), *Book and literature in the cultural space of epochs (XI - XX centuries)* (pp. 25–44). Nauka. Донских О.А. (2011). Провинция и провинциальность: начало. В кн: Е.И. Дергачева-Скоп, & В.Н. Алексеев (Ред.) *Книга и литература в культурном пространстве эпох (XI – XX века)* (с. 25–44). Новосибирск. Наука.

Dunbar, R. L. M. (1992). Neocortex size as a constraint on group size in primates. *Journal of Human Evolution, 22*(6), 469–493.

Durkheim, E. (1893). De la division du travail social. In *Etude sur l'organization des societes superieures*. Felix Alcan, Editeur.

Glazychev, V. L. (2011). *A city without borders*. Publishing House "Territory of the Future". Глазычев В.Л. (2011). *Город без границ*. М.: Издательский дом «Территория будущего».

Goldthorpe, J. H. (1987). *Social mobility and class structure in modern Britain*. Clarendon Press.

Gorshkov, M., Palin, L., & Golenkova, Z. T. (2012). *Russia and China: Changes in the social structure of society*. New Chronograph. Горшков М., Пэйлинь Л., & Голенкова З.Т. (2012). *Россия и Китай: изменения в социальной структуре общества*. М.: Новый Хронограф.

Gowland, R., & Thompson, T. (2013). *Human identity and identification*. Cambridge University Press.

Ivanova, N. A., & Zheltova, V. P. (2009). *Estates society of the Russian Empire (XVIII - early XX century)*. New chronograph. Иванова Н.А., & Желтова В.П. (2009). *Сословное общество Российской империи (XVIII – начало XX века)*. М.: Новый хронограф.

Jenkins, R. (2008). *Social identity*. Routledge.

Johnson, A. W., & Earle, T. (1987). *The evolution of human society: From foraging group to agrarians state*. Stanford University Press.

Kamensky, A. B. (2007). *Everyday life of Russian urban inhabitants: Historical anecdotes from the provincial life of the 18th century*. Russian State University for the Humanities. Каменский А.Б. (2007). *Повседневность русских городских обывателей: Исторические анекдоты из провинциальной жизни XVIII века*. М.: Российский государственный гуманитарный университет.

Kimura, M., & Crow, J. F. (1963). The measurement of effective population number. *Evolution. The International Journal of Organic Evolution, 17*(3), 279–288.

Kordonskiy, S. G., Skalon, V. A., & Plusnin, J. M. (2009). *Municipal Russia: Way of life and way of thinking. Experience of phenomenological research*. TsPI MSU. Кордонский С.Г., Скалон В.А., & Плюснин Ю.М. (2009). *Муниципальная Россия: образ жизни и образ мыслей. Опыт феноменологического исследования*. М.: ЦПИ МСУ.

Kordonskiy, S., Dekhant, D., & Molyarenko, O. (2012). Estate components in the social structure of modern Russia. *Otechestvennye zapiski, 46*(1), 74–91. Кордонский С., Дехант Д., & Моляренко О. (2012). Сословные компоненты в социальной структуре современной России. *Отечественые записки*, 46(1), 74–91.

Kordonsky, S. G. (2008a). The estate structure of post-Soviet Russia (part I). *World of Russia, 17*(3), 37–66. Кордонский С.Г. (2008a). Сословная структура постсоветской России (часть I). *Мир России*, 17(3), 37–66.

Kordonsky, S. G. (2008b). The estate structure of post-Soviet Russia (part II). *World of Russia, 17*(4), 3–36. Кордонский С.Г. (2008b). Сословная структура постсоветской России (часть II). *Мир России*, 17(4), 3–36.

Kordonsky, S. G. (2008c). *The estate structure of post-Soviet Russia*. FOM. Кордонский С.Г. (2008c). *Сословная структура постсоветской России*. М.: ФОМ.

Kordonsky, S. G. (2016). *Socio-economic foundations of the Russian post-soviet regime. The resource-based economy and estate-based social structure of contemporary Russia*. Ibidem.

Kradin N.N., & Linsha V.A. (Eds.) (1995). *Alternative paths to early statehood*. Vladivostok: Dalnauka. Крадин Н.Н., & Лынша В.А. (Ред.), (1995). *Альтернативные пути к ранней государственности*. Владивосток: Дальнаука.

Kupriyanov, A. I. (2007). *Urban culture of the Russian province. Late 18th - first half of the 19th century*. New Chronograph. Куприянов А.И. (2007). *Городская культура русской провинции. Конец XVIII – первая половина XIX века*. М.: Новый Хронограф.

MacArthur, R. H., & Wilson, E. O. (1967). *The theory of island biogeography*. Princeton University Press.

Manning, N., Veit-Wilson, J., Abrahamson, P., Davidova, N., Zdravomislov, A., Zuziev, A., & Tikhonova, N. E. (2017). *Poverty and social exclusion in the new Russia*. Routledge.

McCarty, C., Killworth, P. D., Bernard, H. R., Johnsen, E. C., & Shelley, G. A. (2001). Comparing two methods for estimating network size. *Human Organization, 60*(1), 28–39.

Murdock, G. P. (2003). Sotsial'naya struktura. M.: OGI [Murdock, G. P. (2003). Social Structure. M.: OGI]. (This is the Russian edition of the Murdock's book "Social Structure (1949), The Free Press, New York; Collier-Macmillan Limited, London).

Murdock, G. P., Ford, S. C., Hudson, A. E., Kennedy, R., Simmons, L. W., & Whiting, J. W. M. (1945). *Online of cultural materials. Yale anthropologicals studies, II* (pp. 1–56). Yale University Press.

Peregrine, P. N., & Ember, M. (Eds.). (2001). *Encyclopedia of prehistory. Volume 2. Arctic and subarctic. Volume 4. Europe*. Springer.

Plusnin, J. M. (1991). *The concept of "social archetype" (why don't we understand the motives of the devil's behavior?)*. IPP SB RAS. Плюснин Ю.М. (1991). *Концепция «социального архетипа» (почему мы не понимаем мотивов поведения чёрта?)*. Новосибирск: ИФП СО РАН.

Plusnin, J. M. (2013). Friends and strangers in a Russian provincial town. *World of Russia, 22*(3) 60–93. Плюснин Ю.М. (2013). Свои и чужие в русском провинциальном городе. *Мир России*, 22(3) 60–93.

Radaev, V. V. (2008). The middle class as a normative model. *The standard of living of the population of the regions of Russia, 11–12*, 107–110. Радаев В. В. (2008). Средний класс как нормативная модель. *Уровень жизни населения регионов России*, 11–12, 107–110.

Radaev, V. V., & Shkaratan, O. I. (1996). *Social stratification*. Aspect Press. Радаев В.В., & Шкаратан О.И. (1996). *Социальная стратификация*. М.: Аспект Пресс.

Rieber, A. J. (1982). *Merchants and entrepreneurs in imperial Russia*. University of North Carolina Press.

Scott, J. (1996). *Stratification and power: Structure of class, status and command*. Polity Press.

Shils, E. (1961). Centre and periphery. In Polanyi Festschritft Committee (Eds.), *The logic of personal knowledge: Essays presented to Michael Polanyi on his seventieth birthday, 11th March 1961* (pp. 117–130). Routledge & Kegan Paul.

Shils, E. (1975). *Center and periphery: Essays in macrosociology (selected papers of Edward Shils, 2)*. University of Chicago Press.

Shipilov, A. V. (2008). "Ours", "strangers" and others. "Progress tradition". Шипилов А.В. (2008). *«Свои», «чужие» и другие*. М.: «Прогресс Традиция».

Shkaratan, O. I. (2012). *Sociology of inequality. Theory and reality*. HSE Publishing House. Шкаратан О.И. (2012). *Социология неравенства. Теория и реальность*. М.: Издательский дом НИУ ВШЭ.

Sorokin, P. A. (1920). *The system of sociology. T. 1. Social analytics. Part 1. The doctrine of the structure of the simplest (generic) social phenomenon*. Kolos. Сорокин П.А. (1920). *Система социологии. Т. 1. Социальная аналитика. Ч. 1. Учение о строении простейшего (родового) социального явления*. Пг.: Колос.

Tajfel, H. (Ed.). (2010). *Social identity and intergroup relations*. Cambridge University Press.

Tajfel, H., & Turner, J. C. (1979). An integrative theory of intergroup conflict. In W. G. Austin & S. Worchel (Eds.), *The social psychology of intergroup relations* (pp. 33–47). Brooks/Cole Publishing Company.

Tikhonova, N. E. (2019). The precariat and the prospects for changing the social structure of Russian society. *Sociological Research, 2*, 167–173. Тихонова Н. Е. (2019). Прекариат и перспективы изменения социальной структуры российского общества. *Социологические исследования*, 2, 167–173.

Tikhonova, N. E. (2020). The middle class in the focus of economic and sociological approaches: borders and internal structure (on the example of Russia). *World of Russia, 29*(4), 34–56. Тихонова Н. Е. (2020). Средний класс в фокусе экономического и социологического подходов: границы и внутренняя структура (на примере России). *Мир России*, 29(4), 34–56.

Tikhonova, N. E., Lezhnina Yu, P., Mareeva, S. V., Anikin, V.A., Karavai, A. V., & Slobodenyuk, E. D. (2018). *Model of income stratification of Russian society: Dynamics, factors, cross-country comparisons*. Publishing House Nestor-History. Тихонова Н.Е., Лежнина Ю. П., Мареева С. В., Аникин В. А., Каравай А. В., & Слободенюк Е. Д. *Модель доходной стратификации российского общества: динамика, факторы, межстрановые сравнения*. М.: Издательство Нестор-История.

Tönnies, F. (1887). *Gemeinschaft und Gesellschaft*. Fues's Verlag (R. Reisland).
Treivish, A. I. (2009). *City, region, country and world. Development of Russia through the eyes of a country expert*. New Chronograph. Трейвиш А.И. (2009). *Город, район, страна и мир. Развитие России глазами страноведа*. М.: Новый Хронограф.
Vidich, A. (Ed.). (1995). *The new middle classes. Life-styles, status claims, and political orientations*. Palgrave Macmillan.
Vishnevsky, A. G. (2010). *Sickle and ruble. Conservative modernization in the USSR*. Publishing House of the State University of Economics. Вишневский А.Г. (2010). *Серп и рубль. Консервативная модернизация в СССР*. М.: Издательство ГУ-ВШЭ.
von Bertalanffy, L. (1968). *General system theory: Foundations, development, applications*. George Braziller.
Zayonts, L. O. (2000). "Province" as a term. In V. N. Sazhin (Ed.), *Russian province: Myth - text - reality* (pp. 12–20). Theme. Зайонц Л.О. (2000). «Провинция» как термин. В кн.: В.Н. Сажин (Ред.) *Русская провинция: миф – текст – реальность* (pp. 12-20). М.; СПб.: Тема.

Chapter 3
Methodology

Qualitative research is our key methodology in studying the Russian provincial society. Every local society in its entirety is treated as a case study. Throughout, we apply two methods: direct observation in situ and various forms of interviewing, with in-depth interviews a must. Quantitative methods are auxiliary, and we use them in combination and along with qualitative ones. The empirical basis includes direct observations of about 500 local communities throughout Russia and findings of field research in 285 local communities scattered across 54 of the 81 provincial regions of Russia. I selected 142 communities—half of the total number—with a greater focus on the social and territorial structure, the daily lives of people, their sources of livelihood, the economic behavior of households, and social self-organization.

3.1 Methodology and Methods

3.1.1 Qualitative Methodology

The target of our research—the provincial local society—has unclear outlines (image) and indefinite boundaries. We can rarely see it as an integral and detached entity, clearly separated from its neighbors. Local society is always—to a greater or lesser extent—"dissolved" in a large society, and it is always "lost" against the background of big cities. One must resort to idealizations to "evaporate" and "crystallize" its social structure. At the same time, a specific description of each local society is required. But to describe in detail a provincial society in its many forms and states, observing the introduced theoretical limitations, on the one hand, and ensuring empirical reliability, on the other hand, one should apply a non-reductionist approach to research. I believe that ascent from the abstract to the concrete (the method of "*ascent*") provides such an approach. Historically, this methodology is associated with the names of Johann Wolfgang von Goethe (Steiner,

J. Plusnin, *Russian Provincial Society*, Societies and Political Orders in Transition,
https://doi.org/10.1007/978-3-030-97829-7_3

1897, pp. 87–146, 2018) and Georg Hegel (1975, 1, pp. 147–164). And the famous Russian philosopher and logician, sociologist, and writer Alexander Zinoviev made the most consistent critical presentation of Hegel's "ascent" methodology (Zinoviev, 2002, pp. 38–49, 62–66). The variety of many-sided empirical descriptions first turns into one-sided abstractions; then, in a series of subsequent steps, permeated by a theoretically limited construct, it "ascends" (*Aufstieg*) to a concrete presentation of the subject. This is the spirit of phenomenological description. Therefore, the framework of this methodology includes as constituent parts of different levels (although often perceived as alternatives) both the methodology of "*naive observation*" (Schütz, 1932, 2003)—as the level of empirically concrete—and structuralist analysis—as the level of the abstract at each new stage of "ascent." Accordingly, the specificity of such a social object requires a qualitative research methodology.

I am not introducing anything original to the qualitative analysis of this social phenomenon. I apply the methodology of this approach according to the well-established and long-standing traditional sociological spirit (see, e.g., Garfinkle, 1984; King et al., 1994; Weisberg et al., 1996; Becker, 1998; Kovalev & Steinberg, 1999; Shanin, 1998; George & Bennett, 2005). The group of scholars, of which I am part, conducts most of the research in line with this tradition, and we invariably outline qualitative methodology in our works (Plusnin, 2000; Plusnin et al., 2009; Kordonksy et al., 2010, 2011).

Meanwhile, it is important to specifically note that structural and functional analysis is an indispensable complement to phenomenological analysis. These are two sides of the "same coin" of qualitative methodology. An integral impression (picture) of a local society implies both a particular empirical outline of a specific case (case study) and a formalized depiction of the case as a typical one, which fits into structural patterns (Abbott, 1992, pp. 53–82). For this purpose, it is necessary to typologize and classify it—to identify and describe the structural elements and to determine their purpose for people's daily life. Here is a metaphorical example. Fireflies in the dark hurt the eye with their brightness and flickering but remain elusive. One could be content with describing the luminescent sparkling of bright dots and the mysterious blackness of the night, but it is necessary to catch and dissect the luminous creature in order to classify it and determine its place in the zoological system. The same applies to describing a local society: its individual present state must also be entered into the classification "register." In this approach, I adhere to the tradition of structuralism established by Roman Jakobson and Nikolay Trubetskoy, continued and developed by Claude Lévi-Strauss. The combination of phenomenology and the structuralist approach—however devoid of the logic of scientific uniformity it may seem—allows us to arrange the diversity of local social life variations and allocate these variations to structural patterns that are so necessary for *a limited understanding* of complexity. The logic of the "ascent" method implies exactly this path of multiple iterations from the "*cell*," from the simple, i.e. "one-sided abstract" to the specific abstract and then to the particular concrete (the first step of "ascent"); then from this concrete once again to the specific abstract at the next stage and then to the logically concrete (the second step of "ascent")—and so on "step-by-step," through numerous iterations that allow to reveal the internal connections of an organic entity, i.e. an entity that has its origin, history, its special path of evolution and its individual present state, but at the same time, is also a typical representative of countless other entities, which we call "social systems"; see Zinoviev (2002, pp. 52–53, 62–63, 93–94, 97–103, 167–170, 315). At the same time, the need to apply qualitative methods of research makes it necessary to present a series of case studies to obtain that generalized result, which like a picture can be "captured" at a glance. Using the methodology of "ascent" and "instant impression" I set the task of describing each individual local society in the system of kinship, neighborhood, and reciprocity relations, in the structure of social ties, thereby presenting this society as a typical object, i.e., classifying it in the idealizations I introduced.

Adherence to a qualitative approach and structural patterns certainly limits the use of quantitative analysis. Often, "accounting" and statistics of a social object are impossible or simply distort reality. Therefore, I resort to social analysis based on quantitative data (especially official statistics, which have not "descended" to the municipal level for 30 years) only where necessary, primarily to compare individual local societies or their types by such indicators as the size of the population and its density, the controlled area, and similar indicators, the social significance of which is secondary.

Direct observation on site and extended dialogues with the inhabitants are certainly the main methods of collecting field data. They are components of the case study method. But—and this is important!—its first component is the method of intellectual impression, *blink*, exhaustively described by Malcolm Gladwell (2005). Indeed, it is precisely the "thin slice of the first impression" that is the first and indispensable prerequisite for any subsequent meaningful description of a social phenomenon, and a formalized one as well. This *blink* is akin to the superficial impression of a journalist who spent an hour in the market square of a provincial town. But this *blink* can be more accurate than a hundred questionnaires collected in the same town and declared a "representative sample of the townspeople's opinions."

Thus, when studying the provincial local society, I rely mainly on the methodology of qualitative research, and as part of it I apply methods at three different levels. At the first level, which is not formalized at all, and does not even require any academic terminology, I use the method of intuitive intellectual impression, *insight* in a sense. At the beginning of the twentieth century, philosophers and scholars, including Karl Robert Eduard von Hartmann, Henri Bergson, and especially Wolfgang Köhler, focused on this particular method inherent not only in human beings (Köhler, 1921, pp. 160–175; reprint 1976). But it was mentioned by Malcolm Gladwell, who recently widely popularized this method.

At the second level, I resort to the basic methods of any qualitative research: direct observation of provincial urban life and informal interviews, complemented by in-depth interviews and group conversations, or "*ethnographical interview*" (Rogozin et al., 2020). Below, I outline their specifics as applied to the local community. These methods form the framework of the next methodological level—case study.

At the third level, I do a case study—a monographic study of the local community in its entirety. Here, I generally adhere to the principles of dramaturgical approach to qualitative field research elaborated by Vladimir Ilyin (2006, pp. 48–55), where the local society is a theater, the provincial town is a stage, and the inhabitants are actors performing the play of everyday life (residents) in front of a single spectator, the researcher, who at times jumps up from his seat and asks the actors questions, and sometimes even runs on stage (this is what makes *participant* observation). Actually, this approach is a development of the ideology and design of the classic case study in the existing variety of forms; compare, for example Glaser and Strauss (1967), Goffman (1956, 1986), Denzin and Lincoln (1998), Patton (2001), Yin (2002), George and Bennett (2005), Ilyin (2006), and Creswell (2009).

3.1.2 Methods

The main methods of obtaining results under the qualitative research methodology are direct observation of the life of local societies and informal focused interviews with residents on issues of social life. Additional methods included the comparative historical method used to describe the history of a particular local society in a comparative manner, as well as collection and analysis of local information resources available only on site—private and rare local history sources, private documents, accounts and reports, and local media publications. All this allowed applying the case study methodology to provincial local communities. In this manner my colleagues and I identified and depicted the basic components of the life of individuals and households, and the particular way in which the life of the entire society was arranged. We focused on studying the economic behavior of households, especially informal economic practices (which we call crafts). We revealed direct—neighborly and family—relations between people. We identified and described the interactions underlying reciprocal ties (mutual partnerships and friendships), as well as the system of local relations that determine the social structure (social statuses of hierarchical and heterarchical types).

A specific feature of empirical research based on direct observation was that in each surveyed community we were able to identify and describe all common and most rare economic practices of the population, formal activities, and a lot of informal crafts and trades. I consider this point essential, since the people's direct livelihood underlies the development of other types of relations and provides a better understanding of various ties. Further, in addition to exchange or formalized relations between people, we were able to record relationships inherent in the communal type of social organization (community—Gemeinschaft). Direct observation also revealed the invisible territorial structure of society. A study of archives and work in local museums and libraries made it possible to obtain published and unpublished materials describing the modern and ancient history of the local society. This gave us the tools for a local comparative historical analysis. And by comparing the social histories of several societies we were able to identify some of their important typical features.

3.1.2.1 Direct Observation

Any qualitative research is based primarily on observation which is then supplemented by other methods (see, e.g., Ilyin, 2006; Abbott, 2004). We have always paid appropriate attention to it (Kordonsky et al., 2011). Observations can be either of a stochastic or systematic (driven by a pre-set pattern) nature. We applied both approaches. My colleagues and I relied on direct observation, which is quite simple in terms of methodology, although it requires special technical skills. Observation was split into several stages and types.

The first stage was a completely informal excursion. The initial visit to a local community began with observing its administrative center, a small town. Before anything else, the researcher contacted the local administrations of the municipal district and urban settlement (or urban district) and informed of the purpose of the visit. Without exception, local leaders have always been understanding and helpful. At the same time, this first formal contact often developed into an interview with the head of administration. During the excursion, we had to make a spontaneous survey of the whole town and identify critical targets for more detailed observation and for future interviews. The researchers identified, examined, and registered such targets as best as they could; where possible, they established acquaintances with their managers and employees, and arranged future interviews.

Initially, the most important "targets" in the administrative center are (listed in order of their informational significance based on my own experience):

1. Local market (daily and weekly)
2. Library
3. Museum
4. Church
5. Community culture center (club)
6. Editorial office of a local newspaper or TV channel
7. Small grocery stores
8. Private small manufacturing enterprises
9. Municipal administration
10. Various government agencies (employment service, statistics department, archive, polyclinic, hospital, post office, bank, pension fund, social security center, nursing home, police, paramilitary units, etc.)
11. Schools and kindergartens
12. Convents and monasteries
13. Bars and pubs, restaurants, and cafes
14. Public organizations
15. Representative offices of political parties
16. Medium and large enterprises

17. Shopping centers
18. Sports facilities (sports and recreation centers, stadiums, swimming pools, football fields and hockey grounds, etc.)
19. Municipal amusement parks
20. Leisure and entertainment establishments

The second stage of observations included a purposeful round of the identified targets. The researchers examined the targets, observed the personnel in action, revealed the hidden features of their functioning, and interviewed managers and staff. Mostly, they audio recorded the pre-arranged interviews. But frequently the respondents did not allow recording, because they believed to be conveying important information. The researchers registered such interviews, as well as spontaneous conversations, immediately after they were conducted. The task was to make the most complete round of the town's institutions and enterprises. That was not always practicable. Often, government agencies, as well as medium and large enterprises, denied information to researchers.

At the third stage, observations covered villages of the rural district. Researchers aimed to visit the most important settlements of the district, surveyed the localities, and examined the surrounding landscape, especially agricultural land. Along the way, they held casual conversations in the streets and on the farmsteads of the villagers. Lengthy interviews were conducted in several types of institutions. The most important observation targets in the rural district are (in order of importance):

1. Rural library
2. Village club
3. Church (monastery, mosque, Buddhist temple, synagogue)
4. Rural health post
5. Administration of the rural settlement
6. Peasant farms
7. Small businesses, garages
8. Grocery stores

Rural settlements rarely have any government agencies; there are few enterprises and only one or two shops per village. The library often combined with the village club consolidates most of the local social life. Social activity relies on a person—usually a woman of retirement age—who is the focus of the villagers' attention, more important than the rural administration.

The last, fourth stage of observations is the final generalized look at the administrative center of the society: exploring the town and its most important sites once again, researchers clarify their first and subsequent impressions. This final tour usually takes place in the late evening hours. Due to the obtained knowledge about the town and the rural district, the researcher can note the minor details that have escaped attention earlier. In addition, armed with diverse facts about local society, the researcher more easily engages in casual street conversations, which often render very important information.

During the expeditions, we conducted various types of observations. In many cases, they were focused, with an emphasis on a certain type of the people's activity. Most often, we observed the economic activity of households and small- and medium-sized enterprises. In other cases, we focused on municipal issues or the inhabitants' social activity. Some observations pertained to self-organization and self-government mechanisms. But in all cases, acquaintance with the local society was carried out in the form of observation of the first stage, an unbiased impression. This pattern allowed the researchers, especially young ones, to get rid of any prejudice associated with the town and the district, of any stereotypes about the province, common for metropolitan residents.

In the course of observations, researchers keep field notes. The style of the field notes is free, although sometimes it takes the form of classical ethological registration (Eibl-Eibesfeldt, 1989, pp. 107–112) or recording techniques adopted in field ethnological practices (Sunstein & Chiseri-Strater, 2002, pp. 217–292). The notes constitute an informal non-judgmental description of what we see and hear. Abstaining from any assessments in the process of observation is a crucial principle that we adhere to Kordonksy et al. (2010) and Kordonsky and Plusnin (2015). This prevents hasty generalizations and often incorrect conclusions resulting from an initially biased and pre-determined notion based on previous observations or everyday life experience. Such a non-judgmental approach allowed us to steer clear of numerous "social myths" about the Russian provincial society that are widespread among journalists and armchair scholars; about these myths see Kordonsky et al. (2011). The researcher formulates analytical judgments about the local society at the very last moment—after visiting a particular place—and records them in an analytical report, not in the field notes.

3.1.2.2 Interviews

While engaged in observation, we simultaneously conduct interviews in a variety of forms: from a casual situational street conversation or focused "questioning" to an in-depth hour-long interview or a three- to four-hour narrative about the respondent's personal life. The duration always depends on the quality of the expected information. (Although it is noteworthy that the researcher never interrupts an interview for such a pragmatic reason; it either ends naturally or, much less commonly, the respondent terminates it.) Often, a casual conversation with a prevalence of non-verbal communication brings much more meaningful information than a lengthy interview. Let me refer to an already published example (Plusnin, 2018a, p. 144): ". . . from a casual conversation with a man selling mushrooms on the road in the village of Lazarevo (the Amur basin, Jewish Autonomous Region):*—Hunting must be fabulous here! The forest on the hills looks terrific.—There are lots of wild boars.—Do you hunt them?—We do. Soon the tigers from the [river] Ussuri will come to feed on the boars.—Will they [the tigers] go back?—Hm, they sure will!*" This grunt followed by a short exclamation "*They sure will!*" is alone worth several hours of "interrogating" locals about prohibited types of crafts—they never admit anything.

This example of a very brief but also very informative interview—a spontaneous conversation—is important in yet another respect. My long-term practice shows that sudden meetings and casual unplanned conversations prove to be much more informative than pre-arranged interviews, however long they may be. They often disclose unexpected, completely new information and give a much better understanding of the essence of local social life hidden from the observer.

In contrast to long conversations about "nothing" or narratives about "miserable lives," focused interviews are practical: they allow getting the expected information in a shorter time and from more people. But they also "narrow down" the impression of local life, especially if we want to get a holistic description of it. Such were our interviews about public administration—the interaction of municipal authorities with regional government officials and the interaction of NGOs (non-governmental organizations) with local authorities and the public. Such were also interviews focusing on issues of labor migration (*otkhodnichestvo*) or household economic practices (crafts). The information obtained with their help is complete but limited—it is one-sided. Conversations and spontaneous interviews provide a brighter, more colorful, and diverse picture of local life. But they are chaotic, often incoherent, and require considerable analytical work to decipher and understand the situation. In addition, such situational conversations imply that the researcher is already immersed in local life and knows a lot about it. *Sapienti sat.* Without this prior knowledge, such a conversation can go in one ear and out the other; one can fail to grasp the sense even of meaningful statements, let alone *grunts*.

All interviews, both informal and focused, were structured along two lines: conceptually defined structural components and subject matters. The conceptually defined components comprised three "binary oppositions" (see Chap. 2). During all interviews it was necessary to classify (differentiate) representatives of the local society into three categories: (1) insiders/outsiders, (2) economically active/passive (receiving income from the budget) people, and (3) nobles/commoners. In each case, we tried to identify and describe the local uniqueness of oppositional pairs. Who specifically are "insiders" and who are "outsiders" in the local society, and what is their composition? What occupational groups and in what percentage represent the economically active inhabitants, and who is included in public sector employees? What is the structure of crafts and the formal local economy? What is the actual hierarchical structure; who forms its "top" and who is at the "bottom"? Simultaneously, we attempted to identify and describe the local territorial structure—people's perceptions of the controlled territory they need for subsistence.

As for the subject matters, the interview structure contained six topics, with mandatory questions for discussion on each topic. Of course, we did not discuss all topics with every respondent. And in any case, we did not hand out any questionnaire to them. The six topics cover the following aspects of local life organization: historical, economic, psychological, social, political, and municipal.

The historical aspect involved discovering local knowledge about the history of the area, the history of its settlement in different periods, the composition of ethnic and related groups, and their distribution across the territory. This is very important for understanding the current relations between groups, especially regarding economic activities and control of natural resources, as well as the different influence of ethno-social groups in the community. We determined how well this knowledge had been preserved. The historical aspect was always supplemented with records obtained in local libraries, museums, and often from local historians, who, fortunately, can be found in every society. The knowledge of local social history allows for a better understanding of the current social and territorial structure of the society.

The economic aspect of the interview is obviously important because it is the basis for forming an idea about the entire livelihood system of both individual households and society as a whole. Among other things, often the standard *"question about the weather"—Well, and how's life here?* (or a similar "prompting," introductory question to start a conversation)—triggered a detailed story about economic needs and problems and, thus, was an invitation to a lengthy interview, which began and ended with economic issues.

Under the psychological aspect of the interview, we tried to find out the respondents' attitude to their and their family's way of life, and obtain their assessment of challenges, opportunities, prospects, and hopelessness. This is largely a component of the local mentality. It is very important for the success of any interview for the simple reason that a feature of our national psychology is the need and desire *to complain* about one's life, be it difficult or carefree. I have repeatedly written about this as a sociologist, but many writers noted this much earlier, and the first among them were Alexander Herzen and Fyodor Dostoevsky. Even foreign writers noted this feature of our national character; for example Gautier (1912, pp. 349–396). Olga Bessonova exposed some of the reasons for this in her depiction of the thousand-year economic history of Russian complaints and petitions (Bessonova, 2006, pp. 2–19). It is thanks to complaints about "miserable life and hardships," as an important component of our mentality, that we can reveal and understand a lot about the organization of our entire social life. (From an interview in the village of North Ossetia in April 2019: *"—We have a hard life. The salary is only 5,000 rubles [about $70 per month]—Really? But there's a truck in your yard, and two tractors, and a car . . . and you have a two-story brick house, . . . and a gate for seven million . . .—Well, yeah . . . But we live poorly."*) Of course, to a large extent this aspect was revealed by the interviewer's observations rather than by answers to direct questions.

The social aspect is most important for exposing and describing the local social structure; it implies focusing on the local hierarchy, is aimed at revealing neighborly and family ties, at disclosing mutual relations between socio-occupational groups, ethnic groups, and clans. It is also important to find out the interaction of status groups with the external environment: what relations do certain individuals and clans have with influential people and groups in neighboring societies. Non-economic interactions between families of ordinary people also matter.

The political aspect of the interview is relevant in terms of interaction of different categories of population with the authorities, both municipal and regional. How are certain socio-occupational groups, for example such polar ones as public sector employees and labor migrants-*otkhodniks*, exposed to administrative actions of the authorities? The former depends entirely on the arbitrariness of their bureaucratic boss, and their activities are definitely regulated. The latter, by contrast, are not engaged in the local economy and often establish their own work routine. The relations of various ethnic groups with the authorities are also essential; some of them are close to power, occupy the best and most important positions in government and municipal bodies, have greater access to resources, and are criminalized to a greater or lesser extent. These "arrangements" determine their "weight" in society and their political status in the external social environment. Finally, an important factor is the socio-political activity of individual groups that can consolidate on ethnic, occupational, party, or ideological grounds and influence local social life.

The municipal or local administration aspect consists in focusing on issues of self-government as an essential element of social self-organization. There are societies where social life is "barely ticking along," families are separated, settlements are escheated, and the administrative center is in complete decline. People are apathetic, have lost the will to live, and are not prepared to make any social effort. All this is evidence that self-organization mechanisms are disrupted. Self-government in such settlements and in such societies is non-existent. Communities or individual settlements fall into decay, and "*grass and forest reclaim the area*." I have observed quite a few settlements and communities of the sort; many of them had been established coercively through government effort and were incapable of existing autonomously without state support. By contrast, there are numerous examples to the opposite: autonomous, self-reliant, thriving local communities, with all the features of self-government. In most cases, they depend little, if at all, on the state, and they are often spatially isolated. Contrasting societies that differ in their potential of self-organization and self-government prove to be one of the most important tools (see Chap. 4).

An interview could last from a quarter of an hour (in case of external or internal hindrances, such as unexpectedly emerging circumstances, distraction by other people, the respondent's lack of time, or his/her unexpected refusal to talk, etc.) to 2 or 3 h in favorable circumstances. The average duration was from half an hour to an hour. Obviously, interviews with ordinary people differed from those with local experts.

Generally, three groups of people acted as local experts: (1) the so-called *intelligentsia*—people competent by virtue of education and occupation (librarians, teachers, doctors, engineers, artists, etc.); (2) successful entrepreneurs, as people competent in the local economy; and (3) managers, heads of institutions, and government and municipal employees, competent in organizing and managing local life. I also include certain ordinary people that we often encountered into the same category of local experts. Though they possessed no formal competencies, their knowledge and wisdom made their answers extremely informative.

Interviews with ordinary people, those who had none of the above competencies, were short and most often took the form of conversations or casual chats about no particular matter. Although even in this category there were always respondents who went on talking for 2 or 3 h, disclosing their personal life stories along with many details from the life of the entire community. Since in research we have always preferred interviews to questionnaires, the ratio of expert and non-expert interviews is shifted toward a much higher proportion of the former. Summarizing the data on several dozen separate studies, I can roughly estimate this ratio as one-third of expert interviews versus two-thirds of interviews with ordinary inhabitants.

3.2 Empirical Data

From the full list of 285 communities in which I conducted observations at different times, I selected only 142 for a detailed analysis of the territorial, economical, and social structure. Table 3.1 (Appendix) lists all the communities by the name of their administrative center. The first column contains the regions where the surveyed communities are located. They are listed according to the adopted administrative-territorial division of the Russian Federation. According to the "rank" of the region, the republics come first, followed by territories (*krais*), then by regions (*oblasts*), and finally by autonomous regions and autonomous districts (*okrugs*). The second column contains the main list of 142 communities surveyed mostly between 2000 and 2020. The third column lists 143 communities where I conducted observations also at different times between 1985 and 2020. I did not include them in the main list due to insufficient information for a comprehensive understanding of the social structure. Meanwhile, a study of these communities complements the overall picture, so I decided to indicate them, thereby believing that an increase in the size of the empirical sample somehow enhances the reliability of my generalizations.

Table 3.1 in Appendix clearly shows that the empirical data is represented irregularly across the country and by regions (see also the distribution of communities across the country on the maps in Figs. 4.1, 4.2, and 4.3 of Chap. 4). I did not seek either full coverage or balanced distribution. Full coverage is virtually impossible since I have observed almost all the communities directly. So far, I have not visited only 8 of the main 142 communities, and it were my colleagues and staff who collected data on them according to a specially developed program. By contrast, I have repeatedly visited each of the 143 communities on the additional list and conducted observations everywhere.

In view of Russia's vast territory, an equal representation of the regions is impossible. Besides, I do not consider it necessary, it is not evidence of "representativeness." In some regions, communities from either only the main or the additional list are represented. There are only 14 such regions, 8 and 6, respectively. I conducted observations altogether in 54 regions (out of the 81 constituent entities of the Russian Federation, which actually are the provincial regions). In nine regions, observations covered only one local community, whereas in 27 regions (half of the cases)—five and more at the same time (between 5 and 16). The irregular representation is due, first, to the different transport accessibility of both regions and individual communities. Second, I collected information under various research projects with clearly defined geographical borders; therefore, I could conduct detailed research in several societies, but only in predetermined regions. Third, I had the opportunity to visit some regions repeatedly on a private basis, so I used these opportunities to observe several neighboring societies at once (such are the regions of Karelia, Arkhangelsk, Vologda, Kostroma, Yaroslavl, Tver, Ivanovo, Nizhny Novgorod, Krasnodar, Novosibirsk, Irkutsk, and the Altai Republic).

The total empirical data includes records from the following local societies (communities): 57 communities (of which 32 are from the main list) in 14 out of 22 republics; 52 societies (23 from the main list) in 8 out of 9 territories; 168 societies (83 from the main list) in 30 out of 46 regions; and 8 communities (4 from the main list) in 2 out of 4 autonomous territories. Naturally, I did not conduct research in three constituent entities of the Russian Federation, which are federal cities: they have no provincial society.

Communities vary greatly in the size of population and the territory this population controls. Most local societies are geographically limited by the administrative boundaries of the districts since modern borders retain historical continuity with those existing since ancient times. The area controlled by the community is generally within the administrative boundary but does not always coincide with it. Some communities may have substantially smaller areas. Usually, two factors are responsible for this: the spatial and the ethno-religious one. There are areas, especially in the North and in Siberia, where the population is spatially dispersed within one administrative territory. In such cases, each individual part of the municipal territory forms its own local society. Such are, for example, communities in the Lovozero district of the Murmansk region (Lovozero and Krasnoshchelye), in the Loukhi district of Karelia (Chupa, Gridino, Kalgalaksha, and Pongoma), in the Primorsky district (Pushlakhta, Lyamtsy, Kyanda, and Solovki) and Leshukonsky district of the Arkhangelsk region (Leshukonskoye, Vozhgora, and Koinas), and in the Komi Republic (Udora and Usogorsk).

A special case results from the enlargement of administrative territories when they consolidate several previously existing districts with their distinct local societies. Such is Tura in the Evenk National District in the Krasnoyarsk Territory. The district unites three former districts and has only 23 settlements on a huge area of 763,167 km^2. Meanwhile, in fact, almost every settlement is isolated and represents a separate local society. Some societies consist of two, maximum three settlements. Among those I observed are not only Tura itself with the nearest villages of Nidym and Uchami, but also the remote Kislokan and Tutonchany, Vanavara and Chemdalsk, Strelka-Chunya, Mutoray, and Baykit. They are all located so that the nearest settlement is 100–200 km away and communication with it is possible only by air or by rivers (along the Lower Tunguska or Podkamennaya Tunguska). Therefore, although each of these isolated societies controls an incredibly large territory (between 50 and 200 km^2, or about 20 km^2 per person), this territory is still considerably smaller than the area of the entire administrative unit.

In areas where the population is mixed in terms of ethnic or religious affiliation, certain communities can geographically self-isolate within the administrative unit. Such are the Russian Old Believers of Sizim and Erzhey in the Kaa-Khem Kuzhuun (municipal district) of Tuva, who live surrounded by Tuvinians practicing another faith. In general, isolated communities within larger administrative units are few; they are always historically determined and the reasons for their separation from the geographically larger communities are known. My main list contains only eight such communities: Varnek (Vaygach), Gorbatov (Nizhny Novgorod), Krasnoshchelye (Murman), Kurmach-Baigol (Turochak, Altai Republic), Tompo (Tomponsky Nasleg [rural district] in Yakutia), Tura in the Evenki District in the Krasnoyarsk Territory, Erzhey-Sizim in Tuva, and Solovki (Primorsky district in the Arkhangelsk region). Except for Gorbatov, all other communities are extremely isolated.

The size of the area the communities control varies greatly. Usually, it is slightly smaller than the administrative territory. But since it is most often impossible to determine precisely the controlled boundaries of a community during a short-term observation, I roughly assume that the territory of the community coincides in area with the administrative territory.[1] An average community of 31,000 people has an average territory of about 10,000 km^2. The population density averages 18.5 people per km^2, which is 2.5 times higher than the respective figure for Russia (8.6 people per km^2) and roughly that for the European part of the country (23 people per km^2). Uninhabited areas are excluded from the estimate. Besides, almost two-thirds of the societies (90 out of 142) are located in the European part of Russia. The size of the territory and population density vary greatly and depend on geographical factors and spatial isolation. In certain areas, the population density of the whole community can be almost the same as in a small town—between 100 and 300 people per km^2 (Bolshoy Kamen in Primorye, Anapa District in Krasnodar, Kizilyurt in Dagestan, and Kachkanar in the Sverdlovsk Region). In vast isolated areas in the north of Siberia, the population density can be 0.01–0.02 people per km^2 or even less (Tompo in Yakutia, Tura in Krasnoyarsk, and Varnek on Vaygach Island). However, only 57 communities have a population density exceeding the average Russian figure; consequently, the population density in the remaining 95 communities (60%) is under 8 people per km^2.

The size of the population is equally variable. Some local societies comprise only between 100 and 1000 people (about 30–300 households); the main sample contains only six of them, and of course they are all spatially isolated (Varnek-Vaygach, Krasnoshchelye, Kurmach-Baigol, Tompo, Erzhey-Sizim, and Solovki). By contrast, there are local societies with a population of more than 100,000 people (at least 30,000 households). These are also few, only five, and all of them are located on transport thoroughfares (Anapa—rural district, Iskitim, Kineshma, Temryuk, and Ust-Labinsk). Two-fifths of all surveyed societies have a population ranging from 1000 to 20,000 people (54 communities). A third (44 communities) have from 20,000 to 40,000 people. Only 30 communities have a population of 40,000 to 100,000 people. Most communities—about 100—have a population between 10,000 and 50,000, averaging slightly over 30,000, i.e., about 10,000

[1] Chapter 5 provides a more detailed description of the territories and their variations, as well as diagrams indicating administrative borders and boundaries of the controlled area.

households. The picture is quite similar for communities of the additional (non-main) list.

On average, half of all the residents live in the administrative center, with its population averaging about 17,000 people. Most administrative centers are small towns with the number of inhabitants ranging from 3000 to 50,000. Only seven of them are formally considered medium-sized cities with a population between 55,000 and 88,000 (Birobidzhan, Gus-Khrustalny, Iskitim, Kineshma, Labinsk, Rzhev, and Chistopol). However, in terms of lifestyle and economic behavior of the population, they differ little from all other towns on both lists. The same applies to 36 administrative centers that have the status of a village or settlement: all of them differ little from centers with the status of a town. As district centers and even as centers of rural settlements, they have almost all municipal and some government organizations on their territory (see Chap. 6, Table 6.1).

The rural district, on average, is home to half of all residents of the society, but the spread of values for individual societies is between 10 and 80%. In industrial areas and in the south of the country, the share of rural residents is small (10–30%), in the north and in isolated societies it can reach 60–80%. On average, a local society comprises about 120 rural settlements. Their number varies from 1 to 2 in northern societies to 400–500 villages in societies of the temperate zone of European Russia. In the south, in the Urals, and in Siberia, there are always significantly fewer settlements—between 10 and 30, rarely more, but they are all populous. These are only officially registered settlements. The share of so-called *"escheated"* localities—those that have been either completely abandoned or where no more than four residents, usually lonely elderly people, remain—is quite high. Most of them are located in the center of the European part of Russia. Here their share ranges from one-third to half of all the recorded settlements, i.e., from 100 to 200 villages. "Escheated" localities are few in the Urals and in Siberia, averaging 4–5 per 30 settlements. There are almost none in the south of the country, and usually none at all in the Far North and the Arctic, where there are extremely few settlements in general.

I must note that I focused much more on isolated societies than on those located on transport thoroughfares. The reason is that studying their social structure is much easier descriptively and provides more insight into the nature of social organization than researching societies that permanently experience strong migratory pressure and ongoing turbulence of the social structure. Another reason is that such communities are difficult to reach, and once you get there, it makes sense to take a closer look.

The following chapters in part contain a more detailed description of the empirical data. This is done for substantive reasons of greater convenience, and also because we studied certain aspects of social organization more comprehensively in selected areas rather than everywhere. This pertains primarily to the research of the territorial (Chap. 5) and social structure of local societies (Chaps. 9 and 10) and the various forms of economic behavior of the population (Chaps. 6, 7, and 8).

Thus, between 2010 and 2020, under a program specially developed by prof. Simon Kordonsky and myself, I organized 71 expeditions to study the social structure of local societies. The expeditions lasted from 34 days (there were ten of them) with many students participating, to 2 weeks and longer. Observations covered all local societies from the main list.

Among other things, special research focused on various informal economic practices of the provincial population—household crafts, "scattered manufactories," and labor migration. Together with my colleagues and students, we conducted targeted surveys in 15 regions of Russia to depict the economic behavior of households in more detail. Special research focusing on informal economic behavior of people allowed us to record all types of household crafts and trades in 144 localities in 39 local societies (including 37 small towns and large settlements, and 107 villages). The studies took place between 2011 and 2020 in the course of 16 field expeditions. We performed a continuous survey of households: relying on direct observation and situational interviews, we tried to record the entire variety of the people's economic practices in each particular settlement. The methodology is described in the article (Plusnin, 2018b).

When focusing on a relatively rare, but locally widespread economic practice, such as the "scattered manufactory," we studied in depth local societies only in six towns, where we were able to identify this kind of economy (Rostov Veliky, Kimry, Uglich, Labinsk, Novokhopyorsk, and Uryupinsk). Between 2014 and 2020, from two to five expeditions worked in each of the towns (14 altogether) identifying and describing the organization of "manufactories," the manufacturing technology, and production chains, in which many households (generally, over a half) are involved. The methodology is described in the article (Kordonskiy & Plusnin, 2018).

My colleagues and I engaged in even more extensive research of circular labor migration (otkhodnichestvo) of residents of the Russian province. We specifically studied this type of economic behavior of the provincial population between 2009 and 2015. Seventeen expeditions surveyed the population of 157 settlements in 40 regions of Russia (Plusnin et al., 2015, pp. 67–75).

Furthermore, earlier, in the period between the late 1980s and 2009, I conducted numerous field studies of local societies under initiative projects supported by grants from various foundations. The methodology is described in the works Plusnin (2000) and Kordonksy et al. (2010, 2011). It is no longer possible, nor is it necessary to give an exact number of interviews conducted during these many years of field research.

Appendix

Table 3.1 The main and additional lists of local communities where we observed and studied the territorial and social structure

Constituent entities of the Russian Federation	Main list of local communities	Additional list of local communities
Republics		
Altai	Kurmach-Baigol Maima Ulagan Ust-Kan	Gorno-Altaisk Kosh-Agach Turochak Ust-Koksa
Bashkortostan	Karaidel	
Buryatia	Gusinoozersk Kyakhta	Ivolginsk
Dagestan	Gergebil Gunib Kizilyurt	Derbent Izberbash
Karelia	Belomorsk Chupa Kem Medvezhyegorsk Olonets Pudozh	Gridino Kondopoga Pongoma Sumsky Posad Velikaya Guba Vidlitsa
Komi	Sysola (Vizinga) Udora	Usogorsk Ust-Tsilma
Mari El	Kozmodemyansk	
Mordovia	Ardatov Temnikov Zubova Polyana	
Sakha-Yakutia	Aldan Anabar Tompo	Khgandyga Namtsy Pokrovsk
North Ossetia-Alania	Alagir Ardon Chikola (Iraf) Digora	Beslan
Tatarstan	Bolgar Chistopol	Aktanysh
Tuva	Erzhey-Sizim	
Khakassia		Abaza Askiz Tashtyp
Chuvashia		Alatyr Chivilsk
Territories (Krais)		
Altai	Charysh Kamen-na-Obi Zmeinogorsk Shipunovo	Kolyvan Pospelikha Maralikha Rubtsovsk Soloneshnoye

(continued)

Table 3.1 (continued)

Constituent entities of the Russian Federation	Main list of local communities	Additional list of local communities
Kamchatka	Esso	Kamenskoye Tigil Tilichiki
Krasnodar	Anapa rural district Labinsk Taman Temryuk Ust-Labinsk	Ladozhskaya Kavkazskaya
Krasnoyarsk	Yeniseysk Tura	Baikit Chemdalsk Kislokan Minusinsk Shushenskoye Strelka-Chunya Tutonchany Vanavara Verkh-Usinskoye
Primorie	Bolshoy Kamen Khanka (Kamen-Rybolov) Khasan Kavalerovo Olga Preobrazhenie	Anuchino Arseniev Artyom Lazo Partizansk Pogranichniy Russky Island Shkotovo Ussuriysk
Khabarovsk	Bikin	
Perm	Cherdyn Ochyor Osa	Solikamsk
Trans-Baikal	Nerchinsk	
Regions (Oblasts)		
Arkhangelsk	Kargopol Leshukonskoye Mezen Onega Solovki Varnek	Koinas Kuloi Kyanda Lyamtsy Pushlakhta Tamitsa Velsk Vozhgora
Amur		Erofey Pavlovich
Bryansk	Novozybkov Surazh Zlynka	Klintsy
Vladimir	Gus-Khrustalny Kirzhach Suzdal Yuriev-Polsky	Urshel

(continued)

Table 3.1 (continued)

Constituent entities of the Russian Federation	Main list of local communities	Additional list of local communities
Volgograd	Uryupinsk	
Vologda	Belozersk Kirillov Nikolsk Totma Veliky Ustyug	Lipin Bor Vytegra
Voronezh	Novokhopyorsk	Elan-Koleno
Ivanovo	Gavrilov Posad Kineshma	Lezhnevo Plyos Privolzhsk Puchezh Yuryevets Zavolzhsk
Irkutsk	Chuna Kachug Nizhneudinsk	Mama Taishet Ust-Orda Vikhorevka Zhigalovo
Kaluga	Kozelsk Yukhnov	Peremyshl
Kemerovo	Guryevsk	Mariinsk Taiga Tashtagol Yurga
Kirov	Slobodskoy Zuyevka	Kiknur Kotelnich Luza Sanchursk Yaransk
Kostroma	Buy Chukhloma Galich Nerekhta Soligalich Kologriv Makaryev Manturovo Neya Sharya Voznesenye-Vokhma	Bogovarovo Kadyy Parfenyevo Pyshchug Sudislavl
Leningrad	Podporozhye	Lodeynoye Pole Voznesenye Volkhov

(continued)

Table 3.1 (continued)

Constituent entities of the Russian Federation	Main list of local communities	Additional list of local communities
Moscow	Taldom	Dubna Egoryevsk Ilyinsky Pogost Mozhaisk Ruza Yakhroma
Murmansk	Kandalaksha Krasnoshchelye Umba	Polyarnye Zori
Nizhny Novgorod	Gorbatov Semenov Sokolskoye Varnavino Vetluga	Krasnye Baki Uren Vasilsursk Vorsma
Novgorod	Borovichi Demyansk Staraya Russa	Valday
Novosibirsk	Iskitim Maslyanino Suzun	Berdsk Bolotnoye Cherepanovo Kreshchenskoye Legostaevo Ordynskoe Ubinka Zavyalovo
Omsk	Tara	
Oryol	Dmitrovsk	
Pskov	Gdov Sebezh	Bezhanichy Ostrov Nevel
Ryazan	Kasimov	Spassk-Ryazansky
Sverdlovsk	Kachkanar Krasnoufimsk Verkhoturye	
Smolensk	Dorogobuzh Porechye (Demidov) Velizh	Roslavl Vyazma
Tver	Bezhetsk Kashin Kimry Rzhev Staritsa Toropets Vyshny Volochyok Zubtsov	Bologoye Kalyazin Nelidovo Ostashkov Selizharovo Torzhok Vesyegonsk

(continued)

Table 3.1 (continued)

Constituent entities of the Russian Federation	Main list of local communities	Additional list of local communities
Tomsk		Melnikovo Molchanovo Severtsk
Tula		Belev Chekalin Suvorov
Chelyabinsk		Verkhny Ufaley
Yaroslavl	Gavrilov-Yam Lyubim Poshekhonye Romanov (Tutaev) Rostov Veliky Uglich	Pereslavl-Zalessky Vyatskoe
Jewish Autonomous Oblast	Amurzet Birobidzhan Leninskoye Obluchye	Smidovich Teploozyorsk
Nenets Autonomous Okrug		Naryan-Mar Ustye
Total	142	143

References

Abbott, A. (1992). What do cases do? In C. Ragin & H. Becker (Eds.), *What is a case? Exploring the foundations of social inquiry* (pp. 53–82). Cambridge University Press.

Abbott, A. (2004). *Methods of discovery: Heuristics for the social sciences*. W.W. Norton & Company.

Becker, H. (1998). *Tricks of the trade: How to think about your research while you're doing it*. University of Chicago Press.

Bessonova, O. E. (2006). *Distribution economy of Russia: Evolution through transformation*. ROSSPEN.

Creswell, J. W. (2009). *Research design: Qualitative, quantitative, and mixed methods approaches*. Sage.

Denzin, N. K., & Lincoln, Y. S. (Eds.). (1998). *The landscape of qualitative research. Theories and issues*. Sage.

Eibl-Eibesfeldt, I. (1989). *Human ethology (Die Biologie des menschlichen Verhaltens)*. Aldine de Gruyter.

Garfinkle, H. (1984). *Studies in ethnomethodology*. Polity Press.

Gautier, T. (1912). *The travels of theophile Gautier. Volume one. Travels in Russia*. Little, Brown, and Company. Russian edition: Готье Т. (1988). *Путешествие в Россию*. М.: Мысль.

George, A., & Bennett, A. (2005). *Case studies and theory development in the social sciences*. MIT Press.

Gladwell, M. (2005). *Blink: The power of thinking without thinking*. Little, Brown and Company.

Glaser, B. G., & Strauss, A. L. (1967). *The discovery of grounded theory: Strategies for qualitative research*. Aldine.

Goffman, E. (1956). *The presentation of self in everyday life*. University of Edinburgh Social Sciences Research Centre. Russian edition: Гофман И. (2000). *Представление себя другим в повседневной жизни*. М.: Канон-пресс-Ц, Кучково Поле.

Goffman, E. (1986). *Frame analysis. An essay on the organization of experience*. Northeastern University Press.

Hegel, G. W. F. (1975). *Encyclopedia of philosophical sciences. T. 1. Science of logic*. "Mysl". Гегель Г.В.Ф. (1975). *Энциклопедия философских наук. Т. 1. Наука логики*. М.: «Мысль».

Ilyin, V. I. (2006). *Qualitative field research dramaturgy*. Intersocis. Ильин В.И. Драматургия качественного полевого исследования. - СПб: Интерсоцис.

King, G., Keohane, R., & Verba, S. (1994). *Designing social inquiry: Scientific inference in qualitative research*. Princeton University Press.

Köhler, W. (1921). *Intelligenzprüfungen an Menschenaffen*. Springer. Russian edition: Кёлер В. (1930). *Исследование интеллекта человекоподобных обезьян*. М.: Издательство Коммунистической академии.

Kordonksy, S. G., Plusnin, J. M., & Morgunova, O. M. (2010). Education through observation: Students in the research process. *Voprosy obrazovaniya, 4,* 54–69. Кордонский С.Г., Плюснин Ю.М., & Моргунова О.М. (2010). Обучение наблюдением: студенты в исследовательском процессе. *Вопросы образования*, 4, 54–69.

Kordonskiy, S. G., & Plusnin, J. M. (2018). Archaic economic institutions: Dispersed manufactures in small towns of Russia. *World of Russia, 27*(4), 6–30. Кордонский С.Г., Плюснин Ю.М. (2018). Архаические экономические институты: распределенные мануфактуры в малых городах России. *Мир России*, 27(4), 6–30.

Kordonsky, S., & Plusnin, J. (2015). Field research training in the department of local administration, National Research University – Higher School of Economics. *Laboratorium, 7*(2), 71–91.

Kordonsky, S. G., Plusnin, J. M., Krasheninnikova, J. A., Tukaeva, A. R., Morgunova, O. M., Akhunov, D. E., & Boikov, D. V. (2011). The Russian province and its inhabitants (research practices and attempted description). *Mir Rossii, 1*, 3–33. Кордонский С.Г., Плюснин Ю.М., Крашенинникова Ю.А., Тукаева А.Р., Моргунова О.М., Ахунов Д.Э., & Бойков Д.В. (2011). Российская провинция и её обитатели (опыт изучения и способ описания). *Мир России*, 1, 3–33.

Kovalev, E. M., & Steinberg, I. E. (1999). *Qualitative methods in field sociological research*. Logos. Ковалев Е.М., Штейнберг И.Е. (1999). *Качественные методы в полевых социологических исследованиях. М.: Логос.*

Patton, M. (2001). *Designing qualitative studies*. Sage.

Plusnin, J. M. (2000). *Russian towns*. Moscow Public Science Foundation. Плюснин Ю.М. (2000). Малые города России. М.: Московский общественный научный фонд.

Plusnin, J. (2018a). Territory of social wellbeing. Interaction of ethno-social groups in the Jewish Autonomous Region. *Ideas and Ideals, 4*(1), 136–159. Плюснин Ю.М. (2018a). Территория социального благополучия. Взаимодействия этно-социальных групп в Еврейской автономной области. *Идеи и идеалы, 4*(1), 136–159.

Plusnin, J. (2018b). The crafts of a province: archaic and modern economic practices of the provincial households. *The Journal of Sociology and Social Anthropology, 21*(1), 73–106. Плюснин Ю.М. (2018b). Промыслы провинции: архаические и современные экономические практики населения. *Журнал социологии и социальной антропологии, 21*(1), 73–106.

Plusnin, J. M., Kordonsky, S. G., & Skalon, V. A. (2009). *Municipal Russia: Modus vivendi and modus operandi. A phenomenological study*. CPI MSU. Плюснин Ю.М., Кордонский С.Г., Скалон В.А. (2009). *Муниципальная Россия: образ жизни и образ мыслей. Опыт феноменологического исследования*. М.: ЦПИ МСУ.

Plusnin, J. M., Zausaeva, Y. D., Zhidkevich, N. N., & Pozanenko, A. A. (2015). *Wandering workers. Mores, behavior, way of life, and political status of domestic Russian labor migrants*. ibidem.

Rogozin, D. M., Ipator, A. A., & Galieva, N. I. (2020). *Ethnographic interview*. "Delo" Publishing House, RANEPA. Рогозин Д.М., Ипатора А.А., Галиева Н.И. (2020). *Этнографическое интервью*. М.: Издательский дом «Дело» РАНХиГС.
Schütz, A. (1932). *Der sinnhafte Aufbau der sozialen Welt. Eine Einleitung in die verstehende Soziologie*. Springer.
Schütz, A. (2003). *The semantic structure of the everyday world: Essays on phenomenological sociology*. Institute of the Public Opinion Foundation. Шютц А. (2003). *Смысловая структура повседневного мира: очерки по феноменологической социологии*. М.: Институт Фонда «Общественное мнение.
Shanin, T. (1998). Methodology of double reflexivity in the research of modern rural Russia. *Sociological Journal, 3–4*, 101–116. Шанин Т. (1998). Методология двойной рефлексивности в исследованиях современной российской деревни. *Социологический журнал*, 3–4, 101–116.
Steiner, R. (1897). *Goethes Weltanschauung von Rudolf Steiner*. Verlag von Emil Felber.
Steiner, R. (2018). *Goethes Weltanschauung*. Wentworth Press. Accessed from https://web.archive.org/web/20121012031336/http://www.anthroweb.info/einleitungen.html
Sunstein, B. S., & Chiseri-Strater, E. (2002). *FieldWorking. Reading and writing research*. Bedford/St. Martin's.
Weisberg, H. F., Krosnick, J., & Bowen, B. D. (1996). *An introduction to survey research, polling, and data analysis*. Sage.
Yin, R. (2002). *Case study research: Design and methods*. Sage.
Zinoviev, A. A. (2002). *Ascent from the abstract to the concrete (based on the material of "capital" by K. Marx*). Publishing House of the Institute of Philosophy, Russian Academy of Sciences. Зиновьев, А.А. (2002). *Восхождение от абстрактного к конкретному (на материале «Капитала» К. Маркса)*. М.: ИФ РАН.

Chapter 4
Typology

I propose four principle approaches for the typology of local communities. The first criterion is the age of the local community, meaning the duration of its continuous existence, based on the date of emergence/foundation of the central settlement. I classify the communities into three types: ancient, old, and young. The second criterion is the degree of spatial isolation, according to which communities fall into one of the following categories: isolated, ordinary (common), or located on transport thoroughfares (turbulent). The third criterion is based on the manner of the community's emergence and development. The community either emerged and developed spontaneously or was established de-novo for economic and political reasons, and its existence is sustained by external forces. Accordingly, two types of communities are distinguished: those of natural or coercive development. The fourth criterion is the spatial organization of the administrative center. Four types of layouts are identified: street (rural), radio-centric (fortress), regular (Hippodamus system), and zonal (cluster). The layouts indicate the history of emergence and current development of the community. The developed typologies proved useful for the systematization of various empirical data concerning the territorial structure, local economy and informal economic practices of the population, and the structure of neighborly relations in different provincial communities of Russia. At the same time, I demonstrate the limitations of the typological approach to empirical sociological data.

4.1 Geographical and Environmental Differences

It is important to bear in mind one crucial precondition. In Russia, the latitude and longitude of the local society's location is one of the most significant indicators of social and economic dissimilarities. This geographical factor often overrides cultural, historical, and ethnic differences between communities, significantly increasing the cost of life (Kosmachev, 1979; Parshev, 1999, pp. 37–64; Treyvish, 2009,

J. Plusnin, *Russian Provincial Society*, Societies and Political Orders in Transition,
https://doi.org/10.1007/978-3-030-97829-7_4

pp. 126–145). Environmental and geographical conditions are particularly important for provincial societies, where most members are self-supporting. Due to climate and seasonality, life in the Russian North or Siberia significantly differs from that in the North Caucasus or Primorye in the Far East: it requires other types and quantities of resources, another space, and a different organization of settlements.[1] Similarly, household activities in terms of economic behavior of people in Siberia have important differences from those in the European part of Russia (for these differences, see, e.g. Plusnin 1997). So, environmental and geographical factors must be taken into account when describing both the territorial structure of communities and the economic practices of the population. Therefore, as a kind of "prototype," I distinguish three groups of local societies based on their latitude, and also, where necessary, distinguish Western communities located in the European part of Russia and eastern communities in the Urals and Siberia.

Based on the latitude criterion, the first group ("type") includes northern and Arctic communities located in the Russian North above the 60th parallel (between 60 °N and 72 °N) and in Siberia above the 56th parallel (between 56 °N and 73 °N) because of the severe continental climate. Further on, they are referred to as "northern communities." I have records on 26 of them. The second group ("type") includes communities located in the mid-latitudes between 50 °N and 60 °N (between 48 °N and 56 °N in Siberia); they are referred to as "temperate communities." In my records they form the majority of 99. The third group ("type") includes communities located in the south of Russia between 43 °N and 48 °N–50 °N—in the European part and in Primorye Territory in the Far East. They are referred to as "southern communities." I have records of 17 of them.

The majority of the surveyed communities (100) are located in European Russia. Only 42 communities are located in the east of Russia: in the Urals (6), in Western and Eastern Siberia (25), and in the Far East (11). Like the latitudinal communities, western and eastern communities mainly differ in their territorial structure and the economic behavior of the population. In all cases, the reason is the harsh continental climate, which significantly increases the cost of living and related expenses, both private and public (cf., e.g. Hill and Gaddy (2003), on additional budget expenses of the Russian Federation due to the Siberian climate). Thus, wherever necessary, I will further differentiate the societies not only by the three types of social structure stipulated below, but also with regard to factors of climate and geography. For this purpose, I will classify them by latitude into northern (Arctic), temperate, and southern societies; and by longitude into western (European) and eastern (Ural and Siberian) ones.

[1] Here is an example of how this directly affects various livelihood resources, and not just the productivity of the environment and the volume of food resources. Many settlements in Russia have stove heating, and households need firewood and/or coal to heat their homes. For an average house of about 50 m^2, the minimum annual supply of firewood for household needs is 1–2 m^3 in the North Caucasus, 20–30 m^3 in the temperate zone, and at least 40–50 m^3 in the North and Siberia—an order-of-magnitude difference.

4.2 Typology Principles

For any typology there are a variety of applicable principles. Usually the sociologist proposes a single typology of the observed objects. However, nothing prevents using several different bases and creating multiple typologies for the totality of the same objects. Especially when the objects are complex, as local communities definitely are. First of all, they differ in size—from a hundred or several hundred to hundreds of thousands of people. And these one hundred people can live on a territory ten or even a hundred times exceeding that of the one hundred thousand-strong community. But the ones and the others are equally capable of controlling their territories, and the nature and strength of their family ties may be very similar. Moreover, informal economic practices will differ only in scale, but not in diversity. Besides, one can never conduct an equally thorough survey of a large number of local communities. The collected information will always contain deficiencies and gaps, especially if the number of such complex objects reaches several hundred. However, the lack of clear classification boundaries is the inevitable problem of all empirical typologies of sociological data, which can never be made to fit inflexible and dry theoretical patterns (Kordonsky, 2008, pp. 39–40). Nevertheless, despite all typology deficiencies, the general trend is quite distinct, and the differences are especially pronounced in the people's behavior, although it is difficult or impossible to identify indicators that would record such differences.

In my case, of all the surveyed communities, I selected less than a hundred and fifty for a detailed review. But even this number can be completely confusing. Obviously, extensive empirical data, seemingly diverse, must be generalized. The obvious way to proceed is to develop a typology based on empirically substantiated criteria, moving within the methodological frame previously proposed by M. Weber (1904), or G. Murdock (1949). Criteria can be different, and social life is multifaceted. So, I decided not to limit myself to one or two arguments when selecting the criteria, but to rely on four empirically interpreted principles, the combination of which produces types of social structures that more or less reflect the social reality. All four proposed typological criteria are empirically valid and are intrinsic features of the social system as such. They produce four different typologies that I further apply to analyze the available data.

The first underlying typology principle is the age of the community: the number of years/centuries of a particular community's uninterrupted existence presuming continuity of generations. The factor of continuity—a continuous (uninterrupted, unceasing) period of social life—is significant for the social structure due to the following consideration. Initially, it is assumed—and archival data and empirical observations as a whole confirm this—that, under otherwise equal conditions, the period of a local community's continuous existence determines the stability of its internal structure. Over centuries, the structure has time to take shape and "solidify" (become *rigid*). Where there is no significant external impact, the community can for long maintain the existing structure of relations both between individual kin and neighboring groups, and informal local institutions, i.e., such institutions that emerge in the community spontaneously and relatively independently of those that the state introduces from outside.

The second empirical typology principle is the degree of the community's spatial isolation with regard to other communities, its nearest neighbors. Spatially isolated communities do not experience the same distorting and disruptive impacts as communities that are in close contact and continuous interaction with their neighbors. External social pressure on the community has many manifestations: deformation of its territorial structure (in extreme cases, the territory can be seized by neighbors and the community deprived of all the resources necessary for life); erosion of the structure of kin and neighborly relations; and forced distortion of the attitudes and values of its members (political as well as biological assimilation). If, due to spatial isolation, members of a local community have more or less limited contacts with external actors, its social structure is less exposed to change; so, it is likely that the system of social relations will be reproduced with minimal alterations. Spatially isolated local communities are easy to distinguish due to the existence of objective criteria of isolation (in particular, geographical remoteness, low space permeability, and poor transport communications). By contrast, the polar type of communities is identified based on fuzzier criteria. We have to introduce an intermediate type, which I designated as "ordinary," since it includes all communities that cannot be clearly differentiated in terms of spatial isolation. It is natural to expect that such communities are in the majority. The polar type in my classification is designated as "turbulent" community, where the term *turbulent* is used in its literal original meaning. Besides the familiar meaning of "*commotion, confusion, bustle, turmoil, fuss, disturbance, noise, quarrel, and riot*," the Latin word *turba* also meant "*crowd, gathering, flock, and mass*." A *turbula* is both a "*small crowd*" and "*bustle*." So, *turbulentus* is agitated, bustling, disorderly, etc. Hence, the term "turbulent" community. Indeed, the degree of spatial isolation is an essential factor precisely in the Russian environment, with virtually no significance in modern Western Europe. I believe this factor is much more important for maintaining a stable social structure than the age of the community.

The third typology principle is the natural or coercive manner of the emergence and further development of local communities. Historically, there are two ways for a local community to take shape and exist. The first one is spontaneous and natural emergence and further development. This is the "founder effect" and the availability of conditions for an autonomous, isolated existence, at least in the early stages of social life. The second way is when the community is established coercively, through the efforts of the state, either native or foreign. Here I share the views of theoretical anthropologists who advocate coercive theories of state formation, primarily Robert Carneiro's well-known old *Circumscription theory* (Carneiro, 1970). The three factors of political genesis and formation of modern societies (environmental circumscription, resource concentration, and social circumscription) he identified seem to be effective both at the local level and in present-day conditions.

Obviously, coercively established communities will initially consist of heterogeneous groups. Besides, their structure will be determined by certain external factors; it will be imposed on the community. Naturally developing communities draw upon internal resources, and their structure is shaped in accordance with nature, sui generis. These are, of course, ideal, polar options. In reality, most local communities go through stages of both natural and coercive development, which often alternate with each other. Many communities are known to have emerged in a coercive manner, but if over the following centuries they experienced no dramatic upheavals and did not disappear without a trace, they switched, as far as possible under the current conditions, to a natural path of development. So, the coercive manner of emergence and development pertains primarily to recent societies, the composition and structure of which have changed and are changing before our eyes—over the past three to six generations (about 200 years). Therefore, the natural/coercive manner of emergence may be considered a second-level criterion with regard to the age of the community. However, we cannot say that the criterion of natural/coercive formation eliminates that of the community's age: everything depends on the extent to which the composition and structure of a coercively formed society managed to "calm down" after "agitation." The observations of historians show that "turbulence" can last for decades and centuries. So, both criteria can be used independently to typologize the social structure.

The fourth empirical principle should be considered separately, since it forms the second level of typologization, based on the first three. This is the town-planning structure of the administrative center of the local community (town). For any local territory, its center, along with the border, is an essential element of the territorial and social structure (Rodoman, 1999). Empirical observations show that the town-planning residential structure depends on the age of the community, on the natural/coercive manner of its formation, and on spatial isolation. In this regard, the residential structure of the locality can be a diagnostic indicator of when, how, and under what circumstances the local community was created; whether it experienced, and for long, a distorting coercive impact from the state.

4.3 Age of the Community

The date of foundation (or first mention) of the settlement, which is currently the "district (*uyezd*) town"—the administrative center of the local society where state and municipal authorities are present—can serve as the simplest indicator of the community's age. It was Kirill Kosmachov who in the past came up with the idea of using this criterion to determine the age of old-developed areas and new developments (Kosmachev, 1979). Obviously, the local society usually existed even before the founding of the district town or locality ("*mestechko*"),[2] that later became the

[2]The West Russian term "*mestechko*" (locality) may be used as a general designation, since local grassroot administrative centers in Russia can be of different categories: they can have the status of a town (previously uyezd town—uyezd center, and during the Soviet period and now—district center); the status of a village (church parish center, and at the same time center of the rural

administrative center of the rural district. Of course, these future administrative centers already existed earlier as part of a *cluster of settlements* consisting of many villages and *hamlets* (see especially: Shishkov (2009, pp. 13–20)). However, in most cases, the establishment of a religious and/or (subsequently) administrative center consolidates the local society; as a result, the town or village becomes the center of attraction for the entire rural district. Generally, this very town already was the administrative center earlier, but over time its "*administrative weight*," or status, changed—from a *volost* (rural municipality) center or parish center it was "*upgraded*" to the administrative and government center of the *uyezd* (district). Although there are also reverse cases of the loss of a higher status: of the 142 local communities listed in Table 4.1, only in two cases have their centers lost their former status of an *uyezd* town—Taman and Gorbatov.

To evaluate the importance of the age factor, I split all the communities into three groups: ancient, old, and young:

1. Ancient communities—existing for more than 500 years and established in the period from the middle of the ninth century to 1500–1540, i.e., before the Tsardom of Russia was formed (according to the first mention of the town/locality in the chronicles); I chose the year 1500 as the conventional upper limit.
2. Old communities—existing 160–500 years, with the main settlement founded in the period between 1500–1540 and the second half of the nineteenth century; I chose the year 1860 as the conventional upper limit.
3. Young communities—existing no longer than 160 years, with the main settlement founded in the period between the 1860s and 1960s; I chose the year 1960 as the conventional upper limit.

I do not consider local communities younger than 50 years, since their existence is for so short term that they can still be regarded as "artificial" entities—such communities did not evolve naturally but were formed by administrative coercion. Besides, they are very few.

The division into three types of local communities is based on the historical irregularity with which towns emerged in Rus/Russia. The distribution of towns by the time of their emergence (foundation date or first mention in the chronicles) is at times condensed, at other times scattered: in some historical periods, significantly more towns were founded than in others. According to historian Mikhail Tikhomirov, chronicles mention 271 towns that existed within the borders of Novgorod and Kievan Rus already by the beginning of the thirteenth century, prior to the invasion of Batu Khan. Of these 271 towns "*240 are reliably identified with specific archaeological sites*" (Kuza, 1989, p. 30). In an insert, the same author provides a schematic map listing 262 reliably localized chronicled ancient Russian towns of the tenth to thirteenth centuries, as well as a list of 1397 archaeologically

municipality or village council, the lowest administrative-territorial unit); or the intermediate status of an "industrial community," i.e., an urban-type settlement with at least one industrial enterprise.

Table 4.1 Typology of 142 local communities by age (date of foundation or first mention of the future central settlement)

Ancient > 500 years old (800–1500) $N = 48$	Old 500–160 years old (1500–1860) $N = 59$	Young 60–160 years old (1860–1960) $N = 35$
Belomorsk	Alagir	Aldan
Belozersk	Anapa (rural)	Amurzet
Bezhetsk	Ardatov	Anabar
Borovichi	Ardon	Bikin
Demyansk	Buy	Birobidzhan
Dorogobuzh	Charyshskoye	Bolgar
Galich	Chikola-Iraf	Bolshoy Kamen
Gavrilov Posad	Chistopol	Chuna
Gdov	Chupa	Erzhey-Sizim
Kandalaksha	Digora	Esso
Kargopol	Demidov	Gusinoozersk
Kashin	Dmitrovsk	Kachkanar
Kasimov	Gavrilov-Yam	Karaidel
Kem	Gergebil	Kavalerovo
Kineshma	Gorbatov	Khanka
Kirillov	Gunib	Khasan (Slavyanka)
Kirzhach	Guryevsk	Kizilyurt
Kozelsk	Gus-Khrustalny	Krasnoshchelye
Makaryev	Iskitim	Kurmach-Baigol
Mezen	Kachug	Leninskoye
Nerekhta	Kamen-na-Obi	Manturovo
Nikolsk	Khvalynsk	Medvezhyegorsk
Onega	Kimry	Neya
Olonets	Kologriv	Obluchye
Pudozh	Kozmodemyansk	Preobrazhenie
Rostov Veliky	Krasnoufimsk	Sharya
Rzhev	Kyakhta	Shipunovo
Sebezh	Labinsk	Sokolskoye
Soligalich	Leshukonskoye	Solovki
Staraya Russa	Lyubim	Tompo
Staritsa	Maslyanino	Tura
Suzdal	Mayma	Ulagan
Temnikov	Nerchinsk	Ust-Kan
Toropets	Nizhneudinsk	Varnek (Vaygach)
Totma	Novokhopyorsk	Zuyevka
Tutayev	Novozybkov	
Udora	Ochyor	
Uglich	Olga	
Umba	Osa	
Varnavino	Podporozhye	
Veliky Ustyug	Poshekhonye	
Velizh	Semyonov	
Vyshny Volochyok	Slobodskoy	
Yukhnov	Surazh	
Yuriev-Polsky	Suzun	
Zubtsov	Sysola (Viziga)	
	Taldom	

(continued)

Table 4.1 (continued)

Ancient > 500 years old (800–1500) $N = 48$	Old 500–160 years old (1500–1860) $N = 59$	Young 60–160 years old (1860–1960) $N = 35$
	Taman	
	Tara	
	Temryuk	
	Uryupinsk	
	Ust-Labinsk	
	Verkhoturye	
	Vetluga	
	Voznesenye-Vokhma	
	Yeniseysk	
	Zlynka	
	Zmeinogorsk	
	Zubova Polyana	

surveyed ancient Russian fortified settlements (towns, forts, fortresses, etc.), "*of which only 414 are mentioned in written sources*" (Kuza, 1989, p. 12).

We can see periods with widespread emergence of towns, and periods when few towns were founded. The first illustration of the former case is the middle of the twelfth century, the time of economic prosperity of the Russian lands. This period was followed by almost four centuries of civil strife and Mongol rule, when very few towns were formed in Eastern Russia. Town founding resumed since the middle of the sixteenth century, especially since the first half of the seventeenth century. In the second half of the eighteenth century, numerous new *uyezd* towns were formed under the administrative and territorial reforms of the time. A new town-founding boom accompanied industrial development from the second half of the nineteenth century to the middle of the twentieth century.

Based on this fairly clear picture of the dynamics of town founding in Northeast Russia, in the Urals and Siberia, I distinguished three types of local communities by their age. All towns in Northeast and Northwest Russia identified as ancient were formed during the pre-Mongol political heyday and in the Mongol period until the establishment of the Tsardom of Russia in 1547. All currently existing ancient towns and cities of modern Russia were initially established as fortifications (fenced and fortified town, fortress), and from the earliest times were administrative centers (Kuza, 1989). Most of them still are. I chose 1500 rather than 1547 as the conventional upper limit only for reasons of convenience. Meanwhile, just 11 new towns appeared in the Tsardom of Russia during this half-century period; my sample includes only three of them (due to changed state borders).

The second type—old towns—were formed in tsarist and imperial times: in the period from the end of Northeast Russia's political dependence from the Golden Horde and the expansion of the Moscow Principality in 1480–1547 to the industrial crisis of the 1860s–1880s. This was the period of absolutism, and many of the then newly formed settlements were either military fortifications (forts and towns along "*abatis lines*"), or the product of administrative and territorial reforms starting with

Peter I and ending mainly during the reign of Catherine the Great. By the end of the period, in 1800–1830, relatively few new towns were founded; a boom was registered only starting from the second half of the nineteenth century. The year 1860 was chosen as the conventional upper limit also for reasons of convenience—that was the beginning of economic recession accompanied by political reforms (primarily the liberation of serfs in 1861), and also turmoil (growth of revolutionary activity in urban areas, largely caused by the restructuring of rural social life; see, e.g. Mironov (2003, Vol. 1, pp. 423–466), Ivanova and Zheltova (2010, pp. 549–600).

The third type—young towns—emerged at the end of the 1860–1880 industrial crisis, on the threshold of Russia's industrial development, and in the very period of rapid industrial development of 1890–1917, which continued into the Soviet time. This last period is characterized by a sharp, explosive growth in the number of new towns (many of which were transformed from large villages due to the establishment of manufacturing facilities). As of today, all these towns founded less than 160 years ago are a direct product of industrial development. On the contrary, very few new towns and cities emerged in Russia in the last quarter of the twentieth century and especially in the 30 post-Soviet years, i.e., over an entire half-century.[3]

Young communities have existed for 23, maximum six generations, and a living social memory prevails there. In ancient communities, the historical "chronicled" memory gains importance and can often largely determine the people's present lives and economic practices; the living memory of the society can be subordinated to the historical one. Differences between ancient, old, and young communities are also manifested in the attitude of their representatives to their past, to the natural and urban habitats, in a sharpened or suppressed sense of traditionalism. Undoubtedly, this determines the closeness of family ties, territorial relations, and the nature of land use; it also affects the people's attitude to strangers and migrants, and largely determines the absorption of migrants by the community.

Obviously, all ancient communities are located in the European part of Russia; the further east, the younger the provincial communities. In the Urals and Western Siberia, the communities are mainly old, existing since the first century of Siberia's accession to the Tsardom of Russia (from the mid-sixteenth–early seventeenth century); in addition to state forts and fortresses, they often emerged as settlements of mining and factory workers with their families, who were brought in from western parts of the country to work at numerous plants and factories. In the Far East of Siberia there are no ancient and nearly no old communities for the evident reason that the lands settled here immediately before and after signing the Convention of Peking in 1860 were empty, almost uninhabited—not only in the north, but also in the south, along the Amur River and in Primorye (Kropotkin, 1865).

[3]In the Soviet period, 15 new towns and cities were formed in the Russian Federation (RSFSR) from c 1969 to 1979, and only eight from 1979 to 1989—all of them in industrial development centers in the Urals and Siberia. In the 30 post-Soviet years, only two new cities were established—Magas and Innopolis—both for purely political reasons.

In Table 4.1 I classified all the surveyed local communities into three types by the date of foundation of their central settlement. It is noteworthy that the date of foundation or emergence of the future central settlement is not an absolute indication of how long the actual local community has been existing. Its development can be interrupted once or repeatedly. For example, local communities Anapa, Temryuk, Taman, and Labinsk in the south of European Russia in Krasnodar Territory already existed in ancient times (Taman is the ancient Russian Principality of Tmutarakan), but their current population started forming only in the eighteenth to nineteenth centuries. Similarly, large groups of migrants may settle in the area and eventually constitute a substantial part of the society. This happened, for example, in Esso (Kamchatka); Anabar (Yakutia); Amurzet, Leninskoye, and Birobidzhan (Jewish Autonomous Region); Krasnoshchelye (Murman); Kasimov (Ryazan), and Kyakhta (Buryatia). In the extreme case, the entire previous population has been replaced by new and ethnically different groups (this is typical of the Soviet North Caucasus, where during the twentieth century the initial Russian Cossack settlements were replaced by indigenous rural inhabitants—according to my sources, such communities are Digora, Ardon, and Chikola-Iraf in North Ossetia; and Kizilyurt and Gergebil in Dagestan).

4.4 Spatial Isolation

I believe, the second basic indicator—the degree of the local community's spatial isolation—is more decisive for the configuration of the social structure than the age of the community. The ability to maintain an unchanged internal structure for an extended period of time directly depends on external social impacts; they, in turn, are largely determined by spatial isolation, which is especially relevant for Russia, where over two-fifths of the territory are not easily accessible; and it is well-known that two-thirds of the total territory are not "*favorable for life*," according to the climatic and geographical criteria developed by Jacques Élisée Reclus (1878, p. 9). It is for these reasons that spatially isolated communities are located on these two-thirds of the territory.

If the community is spatially isolated, newcomers can have little or no influence on it. On the other hand, their influence can be disastrous, continuously changing, or destroying the barely established social structure. Generally, this situation is observed in communities that continuously accept large groups of migrants, and where diasporas of migrants of another ethnicity constitute a significant part of the population. This happened quite recently and in our time—in the nineteenth and twentieth centuries. Thus, a large group of Komi migrants settled on Sami territory in the community of Krasnoshchelye, Murman. Approximately at the same time, Lamuts (Evens) and later Koryaks from the north and west of Kamchatka, respectively, migrated to areas inhabited by Itelmens and Russian Kamchadals in Esso, Kamchatka. Such migrants of other ethnicities are often local rural inhabitants, who during the Soviet period were purposefully resettled to towns originally organized as

Russian Cossack settlements. Over two to three centuries, local rural migrants replaced from a third to a half of the initial Russian population in Ardatov (Erzya) and Zubova Polyana (Moksha) in Mordovia; Kyakhta in Buryatia (Buryats); and Krasnoufimsk in the Southern Urals in the present Sverdlovsk Region (Tatars). Even more radically one ethnic group, usually Russians, was replaced by others in the North Caucasus in the 1860s–1960s, where local communities of Russian Cossack migrants that settled in the foothills in mid-nineteenth century started accepting large groups of Caucasian highlanders coming down from the mountains; by now they have almost completely replaced the original Russian population (Tsutsiev, 2006, pp. 33–39, 100–104; Bezorov, 2013). Currently, many such societies are mono-ethnic; for example, according to our observations, such are the societies of Ardon, Digora and Chikola-Iraf in North Ossetia (Digor Ossetians), and Gunib and Kizilyurt in Dagestan (Dagestani Avars).

We note even more disastrous consequences for the local social structure where the community is exposed to active circulation of people, but migrants are not absorbed. This happens when a thoroughfare—highway or railway—passes through the local community.[4] (Previously, waterways were also crucial, but in the twentieth century, and especially in the past 30 years, their significance plunged, and in most cases was reduced to nothing.) Local communities exposed to the influence of thoroughfares continuously experience significant flow-through migratory pressure: both from the daily flow of passers-by and from migrants who settle here for a short period of time without the intention to integrate, become part of the community, or form a diaspora.

Based on empirical observations of the impact that a thoroughfare has on provincial local societies I formulated a "*flow-through model*." This model is methodologically based on Paul Collier's conceptual constructs explicated in his book *Exodus*, where he proposed a model of migration dynamics and the role of the migrant diaspora in accelerating immigration (Collier, 2013). Under the "flow-through model" I distinguish two types of communities—"*laminar*" (isolated) and "*turbulent*." A "laminar" community is located away from major transport routes, and often away from any railways, not just main ones. Generally, its administrative center is linked with other centers by only one regional road; often, it is the terminal point of a dead-end road. Reaching the settlements of such a local community requires a lot of time and money. Therefore, there are few or none "*passers-by*," random people, or migrants. The structure of such a community does not alter for a long time, family and neighborly relations remain unchanged, and informal social and economic institutions are stable. *Time has stopped here*, as they say. The researcher has the opportunity to "unearth" the structure of a "laminar," isolated from neighbors community layer by layer, observing them without disturbance, just

---

[4]These are, for example, 119 federal highways (see http://roads.ru/forum/index.php?showtopic=22464). There are 19 major railways in Russia, including the two longest ones—the Trans-Siberian Railway (Transsib) and the Baikal-Amur Railway (BAM) (see http://www.rupoezd.ru/spisok-zheleznyx-dorog-rossii/)

like a geologist engages in the stratigraphy of sedimentary layers on a plain that has not experienced geological disasters for millions of years.

The social structure of a "turbulent" community is completely different. Significant industrial changes (establishment of a new factory, manufacturing works, or mining enterprise) that also promote the development of transport infrastructure occur here regularly, unexpectedly for the society, and during the life of only one or two generations. Both together cause a massive inflow of new people into the area. But if, over time, the local community is able to "process," "digest," and incorporate (absorb) a large group of newcomers who have arrived once to settle for good, a continuous flow-through of numerous passers-by becomes a serious factor for the community's structural instability, because many of them become temporary migrants, who after a while move on without even trying to settle down. The community is in a state of permanent "boiling," that constantly disrupts the social order.

Having identified such a feature as the community's spatial isolation, which contributes to the stability of the social structure, I can now differentiate communities into at least two polar types—"isolated" and "turbulent." By definition, "isolated" communities must be in considerable isolation, experience little pressure from their neighbors, and not much "civilizing" intervention from the state. "Turbulent" communities are characterized by opposite features. Since such types are ideal constructions, and real social systems have no "pure forms," it is always necessary to supplement them by a third, intermediate type. Thus, I distinguish the following three types of local communities based on the extent of their spatial isolation from neighboring communities:

1. "*Laminar*," or isolated communities—spatially isolated communities, located away from any main routes, often connected with the "outside world" of major cities by a single road and/or dead-end or secondary railway; sometimes communication is possible only by air and along temporary winter roads "*zimnik*"[5] or occasionally by boat.
2. "*Turbulent*" communities, where the administrative center and a significant part of the territory are located on a federal highway and at the same time on a trunk railroad.
3. The intermediate position between these types is occupied by non-isolated communities linked with the outside world by a secondary railroad and a developed road network, where usually only one road is a regional route but not a major federal highway. Failing to find a more expressive term, I called such communities "*ordinary*" type, since they are really common being the most widespread type of local communities.

The division into three types by the degree of spatial isolation is based purely on formal grounds of the proximity or availability or thoroughfares. In quite a few

[5] A "*zimnik*" is a snow or ice road built only in winter over frozen rivers and swamps, and in the tundra in the Arctic zone and in the north of Siberia.

"ordinary" communities trunk railroads and highways pass through part of the territory, whereas many villages, often including the administrative center, are not covered by major transport routes.

To facilitate the description of the social structure, I combined the typology by the age of the community with the typology by the degree of spatial isolation. Table 4.2 presents a 3×3 distribution matrix by "isolation—age" indicators for the totality of my observations of local communities. A total of nine subtypes are possible, although in reality, due to variability, not all local community options can be diagnosed. Of the 142 surveyed local communities, 48 are ancient, 59 are old, and 35 are young. By type of spatial isolation: 35 are "turbulent" communities, 41 are isolated communities, and 66 are intermediate "ordinary" communities. This distribution over the cells of the matrix is in line with the initially adopted methodological principle of depicting the social structure of mostly ancient and old isolated or partially isolated communities, as well as young isolated ones. Their number totals 97. The remaining 45 communities are young non-isolated "ordinary" or "turbulent" ones.

Naturally, real differences between all nine subtypes of communities have blurred boundaries both by degree of spatial isolation and the age of their centers. Such fuzziness is especially specific for "ordinary" non-isolated and non-turbulent communities. This also manifests itself in the description of their structural features. Therefore, not all nine identified groups of local communities constitute a meaningful foundation for depicting specific features of the social structure. I focus on the most distinctive communities of the isolated and turbulent types. As for "ordinary" communities, I consider them only in specific cases, since this type is intermediate and therefore blurred and not always sufficiently clear-cut. In addition, the scope of my field research, undoubtedly, varies considerably from community to community.

The three sketch maps in Figs. 4.1, 4.2, and 4.3 illustrate the location of the three types of communities distinguished by the degree of their spatial isolation. The community is named after its administrative center (town). Sometimes it bears the historical name of the area. Geographical differences between the types are obvious and expected, especially between polar types. Isolated communities are more common in the North and in Siberia, although some can also be found near megacities. In the European part of Russia, isolated communities are located in the north (the Russian North), usually in the taiga zone with sandy, permafrost soils (permafrost zone). Such climatic conditions were the most important factor determining the low density and isolation of many communities. The size and density of the population here are substantially—by an order of magnitude—lower than the average figures for Russia in general and the part of the country (region, territory, republic) where these communities are located. Respectively, the lands occupied by isolated communities are vast, especially in the North. The territories here are by one and two orders of magnitude larger than in the temperate zone and south, respectively.

Table 4.2 Distribution of local communities by nine subtypes depending on their age (the foundation date of the main settlement) and spatial isolation (distance from major transport routes)

Age of the community Type of spatial isolation	Ancient >500 years old (800–1500) $N = 48$	Old 500–160 years old (1500–1860) $N = 59$	Young <160 years old (1860–1960) $N = 35$
Turbulent type $N = 35$	Kandalaksha Kem Olonets Rostov Veliky Rzhev Sebezh Vyshny Volochyok Yukhnov Zubtsov	Alagir Anapa (rural) Chupa Gavrilov-Yam Iskitim Mayma Nerchinsk Nizhneudinsk Novozybkov Ochyor Semyonov Taman Temryuk Ust-Labinsk Zlynka Zubova Polyana	Bikin Birobidzhan Bolshoy Kamen Kizilyurt Manturovo Medvezhyegorsk Obluchye Sharya Shipunovo Zuyevka
"Ordinary" Type $N = 66$	Belomorsk Belozersk Bezhetsk Borovichi Dorogobuzh Galich Gavrilov Posad Kashin Kasimov Kineshma Kirillov Kirzhach Kozelsk Makaryev Nerekhta Nikolsk Staraya Russa Staritsa Suzdal Toropets Totma Tutayev-Romanov Uglich Veliky Ustyug Velizh Yuriev-Polsky	Ardatov Ardon Buy Chikola (Iraf) Chistopol Demidov Digora Dmitrovsk Yeniseysk Guryevsk Gus-Khrustalny Kamen-na-Obi Khvalynsk Kimry Kozmodemyansk Krasnoufimsk Kyakhta Labinsk Lyubim Maslyanino Novokhopyorsk Osa Podporozhye Poshekhonye Slobodskoy Surazh Sysola (Viziga) Taldom Uryupinsk Zmeinogorsk	Aldan Bolgar Chuna Gusinoozersk Khanka Khasan (Slavyanka) Kachkanar Kavalerovo Neya Ust-Kan

(continued)

Table 4.2 (continued)

Age of the community / Type of spatial isolation	Ancient >500 years old (800–1500) $N = 48$	Old 500–160 years old (1500–1860) $N = 59$	Young <160 years old (1860–1960) $N = 35$
Isolated Type $N = 41$	Cherdyn Chukhloma Demyansk Gdov Kargopol Mezen Onega Pudozh Soligalich Temnikov Udora Umba Varnavino	Charysh Gergebil Gorbatov Gunib Kachug Kologriv Leshukonskoye Olga Suzun Tara Verkhoturye Vetluga Voznesenye-Vokhma	Amurzet Anabar Erzhey-Sizim Esso Karaidel Krasnoshchelye Kurmach-Baigol Leninskoye Preobrazhenie Sokolskoye Solovki Tompo Tura Ulagan Varnek (Vaygach)

4.5 Natural or Coercive Manner of the Emergence and Development of the Community

It is also possible to typologize and distinguish types of local communities by the nature of their development and the respective emerging family, neighborly, and status relations. Three options are possible. The first type are (1) newly emerging communities that shape their composition and structure directly before our eyes. The opposite type are (2) historically long-standing communities, which at the moment of observation appear to be developing due to natural factors (as far as possible for social entities). Finally, the third type by nature of emergence and current development are (3) communities formed coercively, by a government action to resettle people voluntarily or forcibly and found a settlement (town) for economic or political purposes; the rural district is then formed on the territory surrounding the newly established town. It is well known that the coercive factor of social development is a constant and probably leading factor of political genesis (Carneiro, 1970), acting primarily on a local level, on a community scale.

It is quite obvious that the logic of this typology is to distinguish and describe communities established coercively and subsequently developing according to some other "laws" than communities emerging and developing without any purposeful single or multiple coercive impact on them, i.e., communities that with some certainty could be considered "naturally developing."

Since the typology of natural/coercive development of communities is based, like the two other typologies, on empirical observations (and respectively, has an empirical interpretation), of the three possible types mentioned, in reality we observe only two. No actual observations of particular local communities revealed any

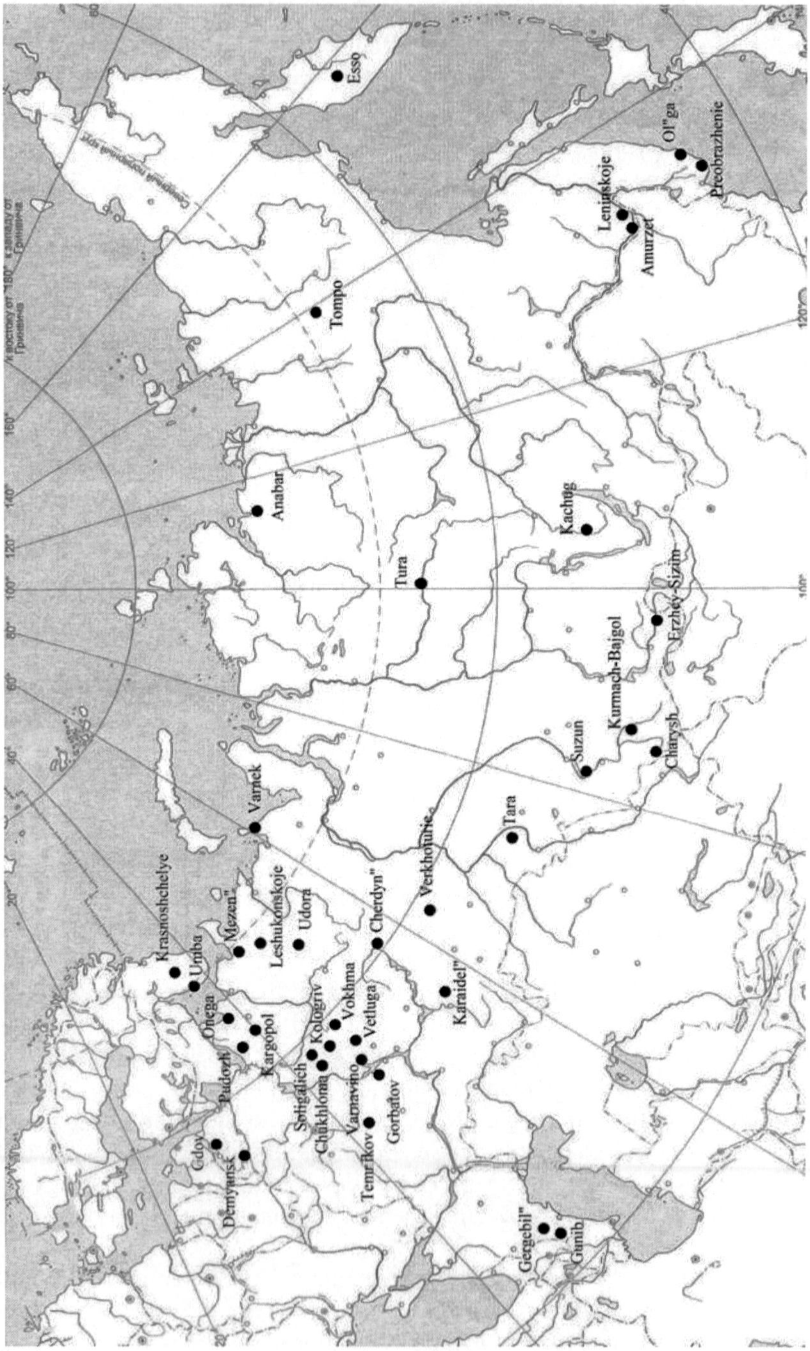

Fig. 4.1 Distribution of isolated local communities surveyed by the author across modern Russia

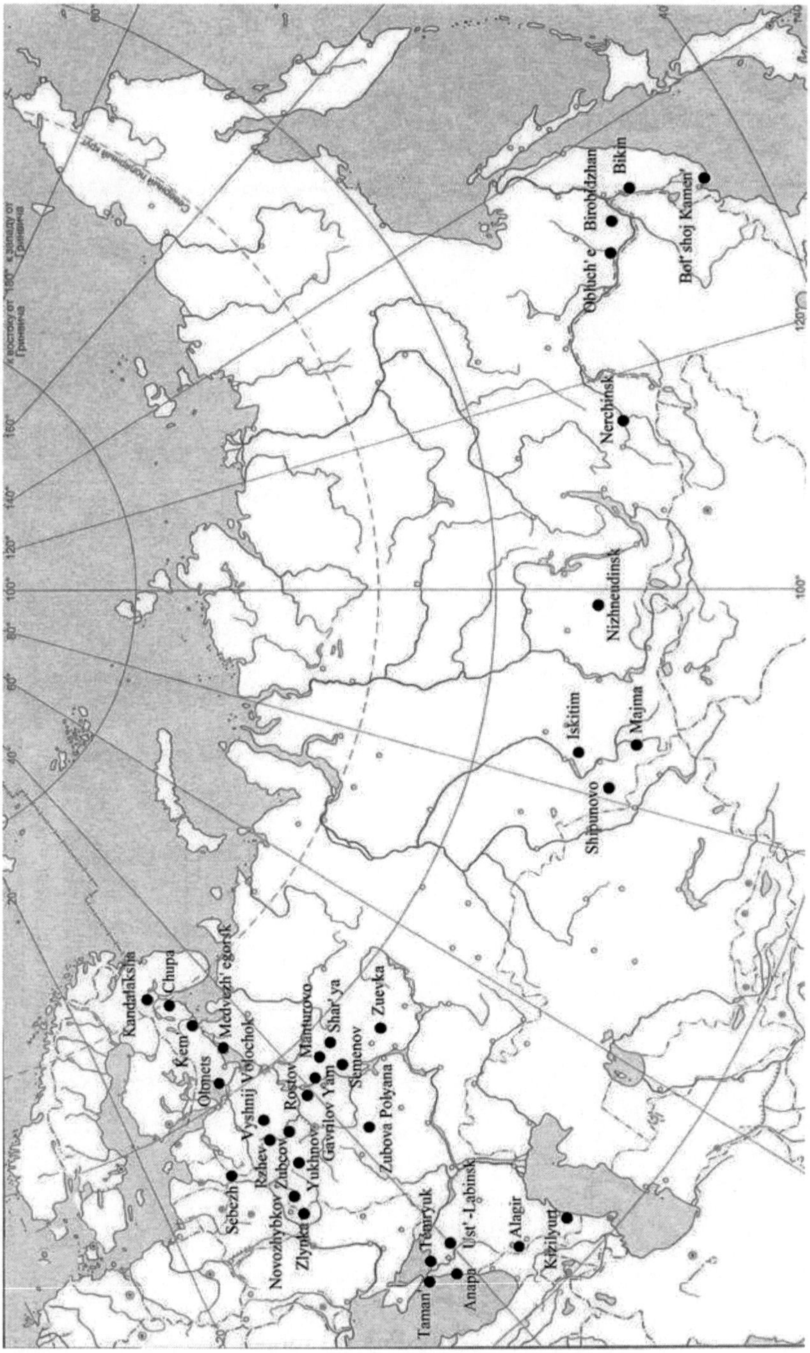

Fig. 4.2 Distribution of "turbulent" local communities surveyed by the author across modern Russia

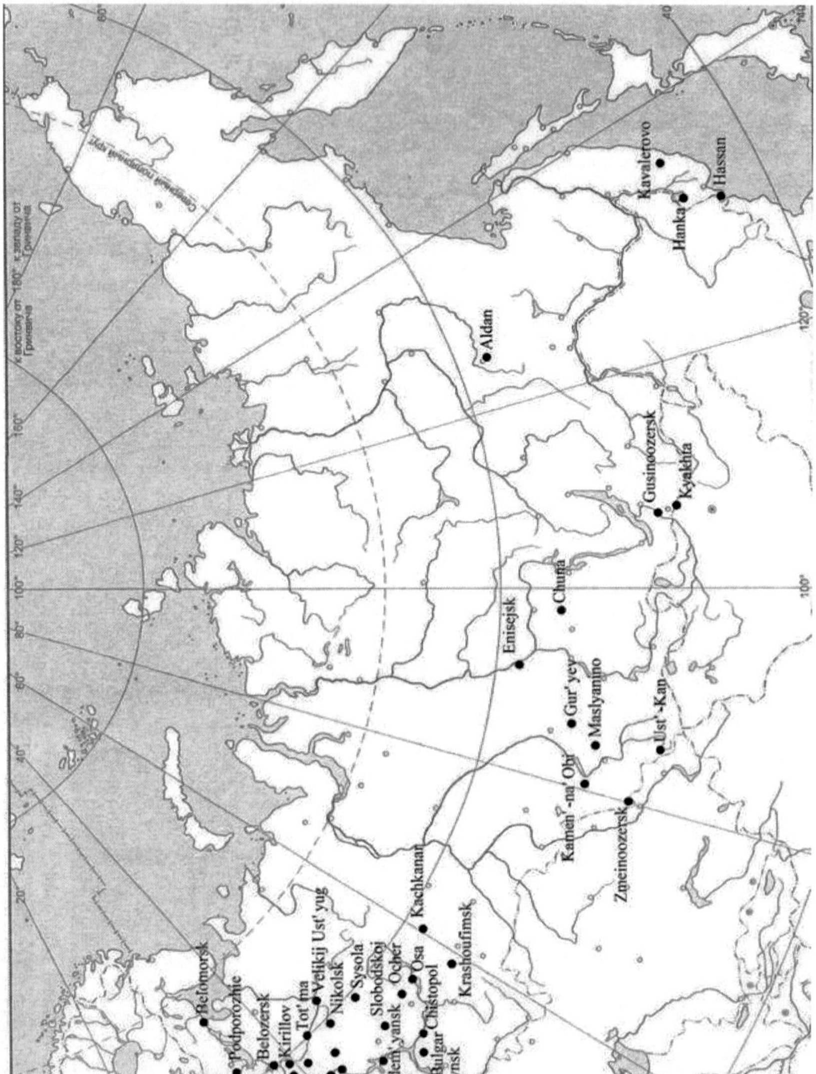

Fig. 4.3 Distribution of "ordinary" (intermediate type) local communities across modern Russia

communities of the first type. Probably, only a long-term participant observation, were it possible, would serve the purpose. Thus, we have information on local communities, developing either (1) in natural socio-historical conditions, without significant or visible external influence or coercion, or (2) under conditions of forced initiation and continuing coercive shaping of their development. I assume there are differences between these types of communities that we can distinguish in addition to those that are determined by their age and spatial isolation.

Obviously, there is a link between the factors of the communities' age and the natural/coercive manner of their emergence (development). Most communities of the first type—"natural development"—are ancient and old communities. Many coercively established communities are young. However, there is no direct or significant correlation. The more so that many communities we now classify as "naturally developed," in the early stages of their existence formed around fortress towns and forts, evolved from the adjoining settlements (*posads*). The rural district of such communities, especially in the south of European Russia, in the Urals and Siberia formed later, in the second place. Only due to the long existence of such communities, their development over centuries became "*sort-of-natural.*"

Communities of the second type (coercive emergence and subsequent controlled development) differ from the first, "natural," type primarily by the fact that the central settlement of the future community developed from scratch, anew, by government effort—initially as a plant or factory; industrial or transport hub; or as a military settlement, fort or fortress. And its entire future rural district was formed after establishing the center, in the second place; it was often moved out and developed from the suburbs. If indigenous settlements already existed in the area at the time, they were quickly assimilated, and their inhabitants were hired or moved to the factory town as workers, just as people brought in from outside. That was the way local communities formed in the Urals in the seventeenth and eighteenth centuries around mining enterprises (Lyubomirov, 1937; Kafengauz, 1949; Preobrazhensky, 1972). Communities in Siberia evolved similarly around the forts along "*abatis lines*" (Siberia, 2007), and especially in the nineteenth century with the establishment of mining enterprises in Rudny Altai (currently the territory of Kazakhstan) and in Transbaikalia (the current Buryatia, Tuva, and the Trans-Baikal Territory). The same pattern is true for most, if not all, Cossack and peasant migrant communities in the Far East in the nineteenth century (Kabuzan, 1976; Mishchuk, 2013). Migrant communities in the North Caucasus, North Ossetia, for example, formed similarly and at the same time (Bezorov, 2013).

Therefore, the most important distinguishing feature of these two types of communities is probably the primary/secondary formation of the principal structural elements of the territory: the administrative center and the rural district. In naturally developing communities the rural district is primary, and the centers are secondary, evolving from villages or settlements and pogosts (a *pogost* is originally a place arranged for periodic or permanent stay of a government official); usually it was set up for purposes of "*poliudie*" *(collection of tribute)* in the tenth to thirteenth centuries (Kobishanov, 1995) set up by government or religious authorities in rural "clusters."[6] Even if such communities were originally established as forts, and their future territorial structure and initial composition of the population were determined by state coercion, subsequently, for an extended period of time, the rural district *prevailed over* the town ("*the countryside surrounds the city*"—*Mao Zedong*) and for long dominated many components of the community's structure (e.g., the differences between the settlement as administrative center and the rural district in population, family and neighborly relations, economic behavior, and territorial organization; all these components have historically been more developed in villages).

By contrast, in coercively created communities the urban centers are primary and the rural district is secondary. There are three ways of forming it. In one case, the rural district is established de-novo, when an empty or nearly empty territory is populated, which is quite common for Russia. Usually, empty territories are populated by migrants *forcibly* resettled by the state to new lands. This situation is well known and lasted throughout the last five to six centuries of territorial expansion of the Russian state. This was the case in the steppe south of European Russia in the fifteenth to seventeenth centuries, in the Urals and Siberia in the sixteenth to – eighteenth centuries, in the Far East in the eighteenth–nineteenth centuries, and most recently in the twentieth century in the Kaliningrad and Murmansk Regions.

In the second case, the rural district is formed so that the new towns (forts and fortresses) are embedded in the existing rural communities of indigenous populations, usually small in number and weak, unable to resist waves of new migrants, therefore quickly assimilated by them; rare small villages of the former indigenous population remain only on the periphery, in places less suitable for life. Often the state helps new settlers in this by dislodging rural migrants, building new fortress towns in new places and pursuing a policy aimed at removing the indigenous population from the area of new development. Here we know quite striking examples of resettling the peoples of Crimea (Kizilov, 2016), Eastern Turkestan (Lurie, 1996), and the North Caucasus (Tsutsiev, 2006).

The third way of forming the rural district is the opposite of the second: here, on the contrary, the indigenous rural population from the outskirts of the administrative district moves closer to its center primarily for reasons of security—the newly built Russian fortress is meant to protect the surrounding population. So, the locals resettle closer to the fortress. Gradually, the rural district is populated and overpopulated, and its inhabitants head for the center itself—the fortress town. Eventually, the indigenous ethnically non-Russian population outnumbers the original residents. In a way, the indigenous ethnic population, once, in historical times evicted from their ancestral lands, returns, and moves back into an administratively developed and safe territory. Eventually, it replaces those inhabitants who had either

[6] A settlement (*selo*) is the center of a rural parish for a "*cluster*" of villages. Initially, until the middle and even the end of the nineteenth century, the settlement consisted only of a church and several buildings for the priest, clergy, an orphanage, and shelters for the poor and needy. Settlements had no more than a dozen inhabitants, whereas in the surrounding villages hundreds and even thousands of residents. The *pogosts* and *selos* were often territorially united.

earlier seized their lands or provided protection by building fortifications. This situation is typical throughout the North Caucasus—Kabardino-Balkaria, North Ossetia, Ingushetia, and Chechnya.

There are also rare variations, when a new, ethnically different population, with the support of the state, relocates to an already inhabited area and is forced to settle on infertile lands; gradually, this results in a conflict with the locals. The consequences can be harmful for both parties. Since the local community is formed coercively by government decree, everything depends on the position the state takes in such a conflict. I will illustrate this by an example obtained on site. In the 1920s–1930s, North Koreans were resettled to various districts of the Primorye Territory, namely to Khanka, Nikolsk-Ussuriysk, and others. These lands were by then occupied by Cossack communities that had arrived 50 years earlier, in the second half of the nineteenth century. Very soon, the resulting inter-ethnic conflicts, primarily because of the land, required the government to take immediate preventive measures. As a result, the entire Korean diaspora of Primorye was in a centralized way relocated to Kazakhstan.[7] A somewhat similar situation, although not comparable in scale, is observed in the Arctic communities, formed from the nomadic population by "*rooting*" it on the land. This is the way such communities as Anabar and Tompo in Eastern Siberia (Yakutia) and Esso in Kamchatka were formed. Supported by the state, larger groups of ethnic migrants settled in areas inhabited by the indigenous population, thus provoking inter-ethnic conflicts over land, which are still unresolved (demarcation and loss of ancestral lands).

Table 4.3 provides a list of communities differentiated into two types—"natural" and "coercive." Based on these types, Chap. 5 further models their territorial structures, the differences between which in many respects correlate with the nature of the community's development.

4.6 Layout of the Administrative Center

The fourth typology is more formal than meaningful, but it has proved useful for diagnostic purposes. It is the typology of administrative centers of communities based on the layout of the town's central (historical) part. Its source is a typology of the town planning pattern of ancient Russian towns, developed by architect L.M. Tverskoy in the 1920s (Tverskoy, 1953) with variations proposed by G. Ya. Mokeyev (Mokeev & Shchenkov, 2006). Empirically, I have identified four types of

[7] It is important to note that this was no deportation resulting from political repression. It was a resettlement preventing a looming conflict between Russian Cossacks and peasants on the one side and North Korean peasants on the other. The Korean settlers were not only allowed to bring along all personal property; they even took with them public school assets. At their destination, they received full compensation for the abandoned homes and were able to buy or build new housing immediately. For this reason, Korean collective farms in Northern Kazakhstan already in the first years of their existence became richer than the local ones.

Table 4.3 Distribution of communities by natural/coercive development

Naturally historically formed $N = 89$	Coercively established $N = 53$
Anapa (rural)	Alagir
Ardatov	Aldan
Belomorsk	Amurzet
Belozersk	Anabar
Bezhetsk	Ardon
Borovichi	Bikin
Buy	Birobidzhan
Cherdyn	Bolgar
Chistopol	Bolshoy Kamen
Chukhloma	Charyshskoye
Demidov	Chikola (Iraf)
Demyansk	Chuna
Dmitrovsk	Chupa
Dorogobuzh	Digora
Erzhey-Sizim	Esso
Galich	Gunib
Gavrilov Posad	Guryevsk
Gavrilov-Yam	Gusinoozersk
Gdov	Gus-Khrustalny
Gergebil	Iskitim
Gorbatov	Kachkanar
Kachug	Kavalerovo
Kamen-na-Obi	Khanka
Kandalaksha	Khasan (Slavyanka)
Karaidel	Kizilyurt
Kargopol	Krasnoufimsk
Kashin	Kurmach-Baigol
Kasimov	Kyakhta
Kem	Labinsk
Khvalynsk	Leninskoye
Kimry	Manturovo
Kineshma	Maslyanino
Kirillov	Medvezhyegorsk
Kirzhach	Nerchinsk
Kologriv	Neya
Kozelsk	Nizhneudinsk
Kozmodemyansk	Novokhopyorsk
Krasnoshchelye	Obluchye
Leshukonskoye	Ochyor
Lyubim	Olga
Makaryev	Podporozhye
Mayma	Preobrazhenie
Mezen	Sharya
Nerekhta	Shipunovo
Nikolsk	Solovki
Novozybkov	Suzun
Olonets	Tompo
Onega	Tura
Osa	Ust-Labinsk

(continued)

Table 4.3 (continued)

Naturally historically formed $N = 89$	Coercively established $N = 53$
Poshekhonye	Varnek (Vaygach)
Pudozh	Verkhoturye
Rostov Veliky	Zmeinogorsk
Rzhev	Zuyevka
Sebezh	
Semyonov	
Slobodskoy	
Sokolskoye	
Soligalich	
Staraya Russa	
Staritsa	
Surazh	
Suzdal	
Sysola (Viziga)	
Taldom	
Taman	
Tara	
Temnikov	
Temryuk	
Toropets	
Totma	
Tutayev-Romanov	
Udora (Koslan)	
Uglich	
Ulagan	
Umba	
Uryupinsk	
Ust-Kan	
Varnavino	
Veliky Ustyug	
Velizh	
Vetluga	
Voznesenye-Vokhma	
Vyshny Volochyok	
Yeniseysk	
Zlynka	
Zubova Polyana	
Zubtsov	
Yukhnov	
Yuriev-Polsky	

layouts of a small town that is the administrative center of a community. The layout can be the product of either a spontaneous chaotic expansion of the village or settlement due to population growth, or the result of implementing an urban development plan designed for defense, administrative or economic purposes. In the first case, only one type of layout is distinguished: the village (linear or street) layout, with a *stanitsa* or tract subtype (A.S. Krivov brought this option to my attention). In the second case, there are three types of layouts: radio-centric, or fortress (mainly for defense purposes); regular or grid plan (administrative purposes, Hippodamus system); and zonal or cluster (economic purposes). Following is a brief description of the above layout types.

4.6.1 Layout Types

A Street, Linear, or Village Layout
It is a chaotic arrangement of the locality, initially devoid of any town-planning design, and resulting from the expansion and merger of several neighboring villages. Historically, there is no town center as such, and the layout serves the subsistence needs of households united in one settlement. Such towns may still have meadows, pastures, and uncultivated land. As most villages in Russia, such settlements are built on river banks. They become administrative centers as a result of random choice, sometimes due to economic reasons. Many of such future centers emerged as a result of railway construction in the nineteenth to twentieth centuries, developing from railway junctions set up for purely organizational and transport purposes. The junctions were built "in the open" or in small villages that happened to be in the railway zone. Later this became the site of industrial development, so gradually many neighboring villages merged into one settlement. The best known example is Novosibirsk, which over a century has turned from a village at the construction site of a railway bridge across the Ob River into the third largest Russian megalopolis in terms of population and industrial potential. Our examples include Manturovo (Novosibirsk) and Sharya (Kostroma), which developed from half a dozen neighboring villages as Transsib stations near railway bridges across big rivers—the former across Unzha and the latter across Vetluga. Later, due to convenient communication, such transport hubs start serving other economic purposes: plants and factories are constructed in their immediate vicinity, resulting in the further merger of the neighboring rural settlements into a chaotic urban conglomerate. Such is the picture of modern Sharya, where a zonal layout supplemented the street one.

A tract (or *stanitsa*) layout means that the future town grew as a settlement along a major road—tract—contributing to the development of roadside trade, serving as a location for fairs and large markets, as well as post coach stations. Generally, such settlements were established in the south, along major tracts that were used to deliver food and industrial resources northwards, to the center of the country, whereas troops and military supplies moved in the opposite direction. Due to the fair, post coach station and military Cossack outpost, such *stanitsa* (Cossack village) gradually grew and became a district center for the neighboring *stanitsas* located further away from the tract. Since this type of settlements developed mainly in the southern steppe regions of Russia and in the south of Western Siberia, in Eastern Turkestan, where I performed few observations, this layout option is rare for my records (only five cases), so I do not distinguish it as a separate type.

The street type layout is mostly common for former villages and settlements that were assigned administrative functions. Besides, in the majority of isolated sparsely populated communities, central settlements, which are usually villages, have street layouts. Such are, for example, Varnavino (Nizhny Novgorod) and Charyshskoye (Altai), Umba (Murman), Gunib (Dagestan), and Esso (Kamchatka). Drawing in Fig. 4.4 provides example of street type layouts in Taman—a *stanitsa* in Krasnodar Territory.

Radio-Centric, or Fortress, Layout

This is probably the most historically ancient layout (Tverskoy, 1953)—the town develops historically from the adjoining settlements (*posads*), which concentrate around the fortress and marketplace. The town center is the fortress-kremlin or fort built on a *spit* at the confluence of two rivers or on a steep riverbank (*yar*) crossed by stream-filled ravines. Initially, the layout served medieval defense purposes and also its main economic function of marketplace (*torzhishche*). Such town center has two types of streets—radially diverging from the fortress and concentrically surrounding it. In a modern city, this layout of the center occupies a small part of it and may therefore not be identified on the map (Mokeev & Shchenkov, 2006). In other cases, the radio-centric layout is maintained on a large part of the city area. Notable examples are major cities Moscow and Kostroma. In my records, there are about two dozen towns with such a layout, although many of them have been reshaped by urban development changes in subsequent centuries. It is noteworthy that in all 19 cases without exception, towns with a radial layout are centers of "naturally" developing communities; none of the "coercively" formed communities has a center with the ancient radio-centric layout.

Figure 4.5 provides example of radial layouts of ancient town Soligalich (Kostroma). Soligalich is the center of an isolated community; it is linked with the outer world by a single road, and its layout is not deformed even by the Kostroma river and numerous streams flowing through the town. I have no records of young towns with radial layouts, and I believe there are none at all.

Regular Layout (Hippodamus Grid Plan)

Many large Russian cities built in the eighteenth to nineteenth centuries, as well as modern ones, can serve as examples of such military-state urban planning—from St. Petersburg and Krasnodar to Stavropol and Verny, Grozny and Makhachkala. Many of the settlements in my records were built according to the model of an antique military camp. Nearly all such originally military settlements built according to the regular plan were also intended for administrative functions. The city center is reduced; there is no such pronounced landmark as a fortress on Cathedral Square like in towns with a radial layout. But it is marked by a parade square and several administrative buildings. The original functions of such towns and cities are public administration and defense. They were often built in the open. Layouts of this type are almost equally represented in communities of both natural and coercive development. Cherdyn's layout of administrative center is presented in Fig. 4.6.

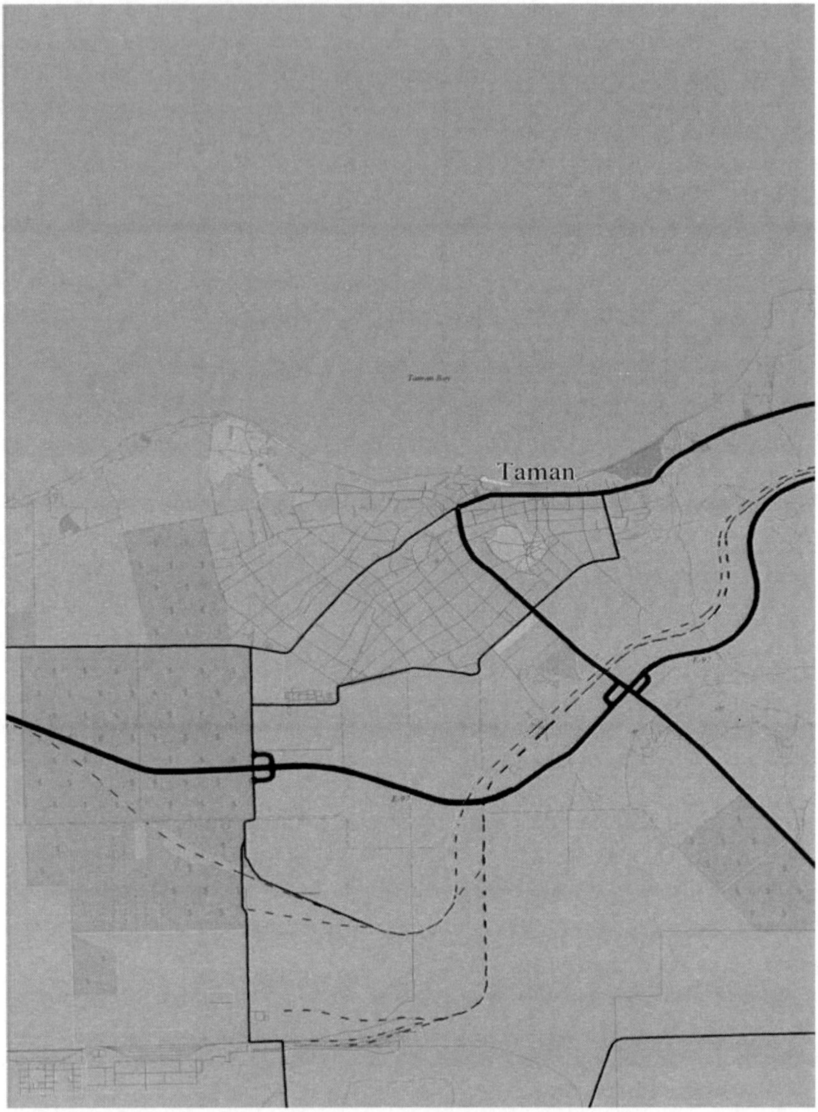

Fig. 4.4 Example of administrative centers of communities with street layouts: Taman (Krasnodar)—*stanitsa*, center of an old naturally formed turbulent community. The streets of the *stanitsa* run directly along the main road, the main tract, and the seacoast. The E97 motorway to the south is the newly built highway to Crimea

Zonal, or Cluster, Layout

When economic expedience prevails over the objectives of creating a comfortable living environment, the resulting urban layout is a bunch of isolated clusters—residential areas adjacent to industrial enterprises separated by mosaic forest and

Fig. 4.5 Example of administrative centers of communities with radio-centric layouts: Soligalich (Kostroma)—town, center of an ancient naturally developed isolated community

wasteland patches. The construction of such cluster-based towns is initially driven by economic and industrial purposes. Towns are built in areas where natural resources are concentrated and zoned depending on the profile of the enterprise. Glass works, weaving factories, food processing plants, agricultural enterprises, and creameries are embedded in villages, and here the layout is close to a street one, incorporating several neighboring settlements. Mining complexes, metallurgical

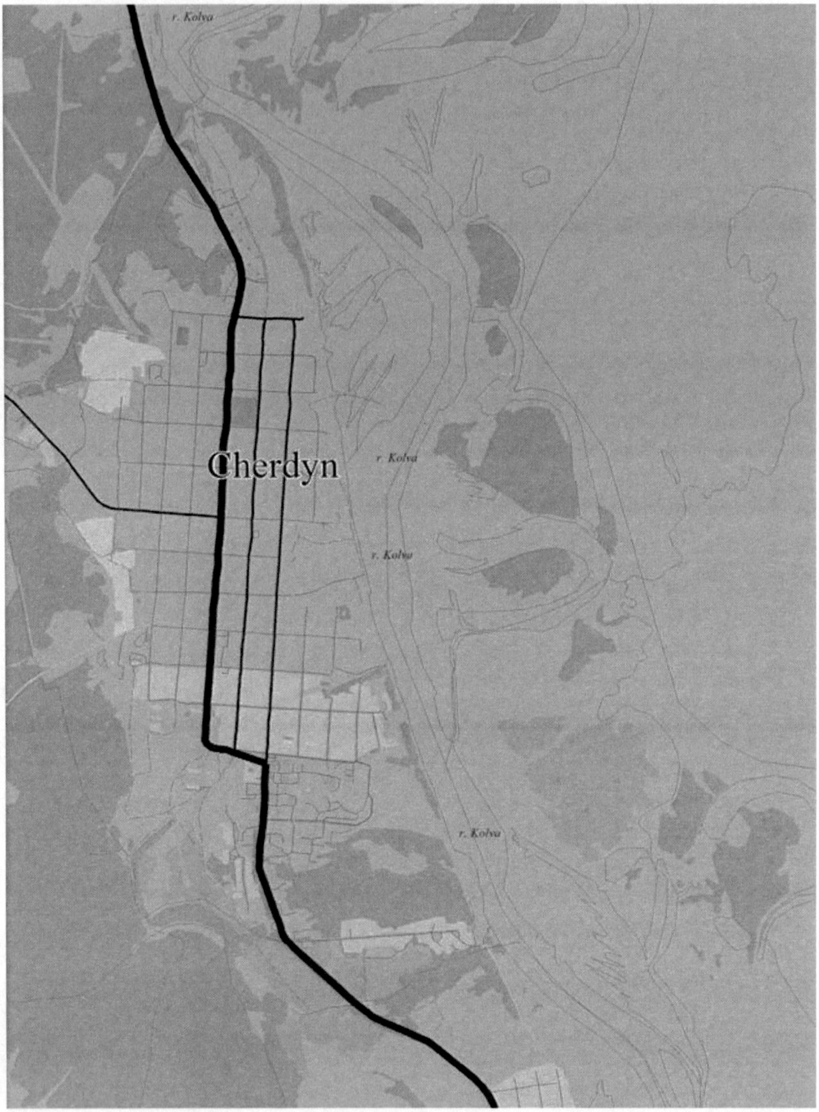

Fig. 4.6 Example of administrative centers of communities with a grid plan: Cherdyn (Perm)—town, center of an ancient naturally developed isolated community

plants, blast furnaces, coal mines, and oil derricks are built near respective deposits, and the residential areas are located next to them, so that the lives of the people are adjusted to production. As a result, a growing town, where new enterprises are commissioned, is made up of "*zones*," relatively isolated residential clusters. Many young single-industry towns have a typical zonal layout. Quite a few Ural, Siberian, and Far Eastern cities have such a layout due to their early manufacturing history. In

Fig. 4.7 Example of administrative centers of communities with zonal (cluster) layouts: Zmeinogorsk (Rudny Altai)—fortress town and polymetallic ore mine, center of an old coercively formed "ordinary" community

general, such are the centers of coercively formed communities. Less than half of the towns in my records have a clearly zonal layout; it is mostly overlapped by a grid plan, which either preceded zonal planning at the stage prior to the locality's industrial development (generally, already in the twentieth century) or emerged afterwards in the urban settlements adjoining the plants, thus overlapping the zonal layout (this is typical of industrial towns in the Urals). Figure 4.7 provides example of layouts approaching the zonal type.

4.6.2 Association Between the Center's Layout and the Types of Communities Identified According to the Three Other Criteria

To diagnose the social structure of local communities, I believe it is useful to distinguish the layouts of their administrative centers. This is illustrated by Table 4.4, which shows the frequency (in absolute figures) of the representation of

Table 4.4 Distribution of types of administrative center layouts depending on the age of the community, the degree of spatial isolation, and the natural/coercive manner of its emergence and development

Local community types		Center layout types			
		Street	Radial	Regular	Zonal
By age	Young (35)	13	**0**	9	**20**
	Old (59)	20	10	**30**	14
	Ancient (48)	15	10	**28**	16
By degree of spatial isolation	Isolated (41)	**22**	**3**	13	12
	Common type (66)	15	12	**39**	**28**
	Turbulent (35)	11	**5**	15	11
By manner of emergence	Coercive (53)	17	**0**	19	**26**
	Natural (89)	31	**20**	48	**24**

different types of layouts in various communities differentiated by type based on the above typologies: by age, isolation, and natural/coercive development.

Differentiation of communities by the age of the administrative center shows that the radial layout is most frequent in ancient towns and is not recorded in any of the young ones. This is absolutely understandable because such town-planning was conventional for ancient fortress towns. Similarly, a grid layout is not typical for young towns (25%) but is most frequently represented in ancient (60%) and old (49%) ones. Young towns have a predominantly zonal layout (56%), whereas in old and ancient towns the zonal layout is mixed with the regular and street one. The tract (*stanitsa*) layout is not represented at all in ancient towns (and it could not have developed there). Only the street layout is equally common in all three types of towns; it often completely overlaps the previous radial structure of the center, which is associated with natural disasters that befell the town (fires) or the loss of its administrative status.

Differentiation of communities by the degree of spatial isolation shows a less striking, but also notable picture of the differences in the layouts of their centers. Isolated communities are characterized by street layout, with the radial one just half of it (8% vs. 16%–17%). Both features of such town-planning of isolated communities are easily explained: there are many non-urban centers and very few early fortresses or forts. The centers of "ordinary" communities have an increased number of regular and zonal layouts, and frequently mixed ones. Turbulent communities have no distinguishing features at all. By the frequency of some layout types they are similar to "ordinary" communities (low proportion of street layouts, and an increased share of radial and regular ones); by others—to isolated communities (low share of zonal layouts).

Differentiation of communities by the natural/coercive manner of their initial development demonstrates a striking difference in the layout of their centers. Only the street layout is equally common for both types. For the three other layouts the differences are indicative. No administrative center of a coercively formed community has a radial layout—none of them was established as ancient fortresses. For them, the most typical is the zonal layout (49%) and to a lesser extent the regular one (35%). Consequently, the towns were established by a coercive effort as administrative centers or settlements to serve the needs of various industrial enterprises and mines. The centers of naturally developed communities have predominantly regular layouts (48%), less frequently street (31%) and radial (20%) ones. This reflects the fact that their town planning structure developed after the village or settlement acquired the status of a district town, and the towns were later reconstructed according to regular plans. Another option is that the locality historically had this status. This is true for all the towns where I recorded radio-centric layouts—they are all located in ancient historical areas, their coercive foundation, if any, took place ages ago, and these communities have long since switched to a state of natural development. A large proportion of street layouts is due to the fact that the administrative centers of many naturally developing isolated communities are villages.

The number of local communities of each type is shown in brackets; the most frequent and rare layout types for each type of community are highlighted in bold. Since there are 21 mixed types of layouts, they were taken into account separately when calculating and their number is greater than the number of centers.

Thus, the heuristic nature of such a parameter as the layout of the local community's administrative center is evident. It can indeed reveal how the community was formed (e.g., towns with a radial layout are never centers of coercively established communities), and also indicate the character and sequence of the development of its rural district (primary in case of a street layout and secondary if it is a zonal one). The type of layout can also imply how well the transport network is developed in the area (Tarkhov, 2018). Communities with well-developed networks most often have centers with a regular layout, followed by a zonal and less frequently by a radial one. The worst transport accessibility is typical of communities with a street layout of their centers. Local communities with a predominantly zonal layout of their centers correspond to areas of new development (Kosmachev, 1979), especially in the eastern regions of Russia.

4.7 The Ambiguity of Typology Based on Several Principles

When the typology of the social structure is based on several principles rather than one, new unexpected "analytical phenomena" arise, which are difficult to explain, but nevertheless require interpretation. One should either "turn a blind eye" to them (withhold them) or seek clarifications and make assumptions, as responsible authors like George Murdock do (Murdock, 1949, pp. 220–338). In my case the defect of "multiple typologies" is quite expected but inconvenient for analysis—"gaps" in the cells of the resulting table, when typology is based on three principles at once: the community's age, spatial isolation, and natural/coercive manner of emergence and development (Table 4.5). We find out that of the potential 18 types of local community structures, five are not represented by any community from my sample. Moreover, I cannot obtain such data even from the twice as large sample of

Table 4.5 Distribution of 142 local communities by type based on three parameters: age of the community, spatial isolation, and the natural/coercive manner of its emergence and development

Type of spatial isolation	Naturally or coercively developed community	Age of the community		
		Ancient $N = 48$	Old $N = 59$	Young $N = 35$
Turbulent type $N = 35$	Coercively developed communities $N = 17$		Alagir Chupa Iskitim Nerchinsk Nizhneudinsk Ochyor Ust-Labinsk	Bikin Birobidzhan Bolshoy Kamen Kizilyurt Manturovo Medvezhyegorsk Obluchye Sharya Shipunovo Zuyevka
	Naturally developed communities $N = 18$	Kandalaksha Kem Olonets Rostov Veliky Rzhev Sebezh Vyshny Volochyok Yukhnov Zubtsov	Anapa (rural) Gavrilov-Yam Mayma Novozybkov Semyonov Taman Temryuk Zlynka Zubova Polyana	
Ordinary type $N = 66$	Coercively developed communities $N = 21$		Ardon Chikola (Iraf) Digora Guryevsk Gus-Khrustalny Krasnoufimsk Kyakhta Labinsk Maslyanino Novokhopyorsk Osa Podporozhye Zmeinogorsk	Aldan Bolgar Chuna Gusinoozersk Khanka Khasan (Slavyanka) Kachkanar Kavalerovo Neya
	Naturally developed communities $N = 45$	Belomorsk Belozersk Bezhetsk Borovichi Dorogobuzh Galich Gavrilov Posad Kashin Kasimov Kineshma Kirillov	Ardatov Buy Chistopol Demidov Dmitrovsk Yeniseysk Kamen-na-Obi Khvalynsk Kimry Kozmodemyansk Lyubim Poshekhonye	Ust-Kan

(continued)

Table 4.5 (continued)

Type of spatial isolation	Naturally or coercively developed community	Age of the community Ancient $N = 48$	Old $N = 59$	Young $N = 35$
		Kirzhach Kozelsk Makaryev Nerekhta Nikolsk Staraya Russa Staritsa Suzdal Toropets Totma Tutayev- Romanov Uglich Veliky Ustyug Velizh Yuriev- Polsky	Slobodskoy Surazh Sysola (Viziga) Taldom Uryupinsk	
Isolated type $N = 41$	Coercively developed communities $N = 15$		Charysh Gunib Olga Suzun Verkhoturye	Amurzet Anabar Esso Kurmach-Baigol Leninskoye Preobrazhenie Solovki Tompo Tura Varnek (Vaygach)
	Naturally developed communities $N = 26$	Cherdyn Chukhloma Demyansk Gdov Kargopol Mezen Onega Pudozh Soligalich Temnikov Udora Umba Varnavino	Gergebil Gorbatov Kachug Kologriv Leshukonskoye Tara Vetluga Voznesenye- Vokhma	Erzhey-Sizim Karaidel Krasnoshchelye Sokolskoye Ulagan

300 communities that I have surveyed over the years. This is probably a pattern, and not a consequence of a small-sample error.

This suggests that the typology principles have limited explanatory value. Although we can easily justify (and I wrote about it above), for example, the complete absence of coercively developed communities in the cohort of ancient communities. Despite the fact that at least half of them can be considered to have an initially coercively established central settlement. However, subsequently, such communities developed without significant long-term invasions by the state (although in some cases they had been exposed to disastrous upheavals, for example, during wars). It is equally understandable that all young non-isolated and turbulent communities had been formed coercively. This is a direct result of industrial development, supplemented by Soviet nation building (urbanization of non-Russian rural population and the settlement of nomadic peoples).

Thus, we see that when the typology is based on one or even two principles, all possible social structure options are represented. But when there are already three underlying principles, the typological matrix loses a third of the possible structure types. The maximum number of represented options is only two-thirds of the potential total. Therefore, an integrated typology (based on three rather than one or two principles) is at best a controversial approach that does not guarantee reliable conclusions.

This limitation explains, in particular, the spread in the frequencies of urban layout types in communities classified separately under each principle (Table 4.4), since the zonal, and, to a lesser extent, the regular layout is more common for young coercively formed communities; the radial layout—for ancient and old communities, among which there are no coercively formed ones; and the street layout is typical of naturally developing isolated communities.

Nevertheless, in the following chapters I will use all typological principles to outline in general the various aspects of the local communities' social structure, particularly the territorial one.

References

Bezorov, B. P. (2013). *Resettlement of Ossetians from the mountains to the plane (XVIII-XX centuries).* Vladikavkaz: Ir. Безоров Б.П. (2013). *Переселение осетин с гор на плоскость (XVIII-XX вв.).* Владикавказ: Ир.

Carneiro, R. (1970). A theory of the origin of the state. *Science, 169*(3947), 733–738.

Collier, P. (2013). *Exodus: How migration is changing our world.* Oxford University Press. Russian edition: Коллиер П. (2016). *Исход: как миграция изменяет наш мир* (trans.: N. Edelman). M.: Изд-во Института Гайдара.

Hill, F., & Gaddy, C. (2003). *The Siberian curse. How communist planners left Russia out in the cold.* The Brookings Institution.

Ivanova, N. A., & Zheltova, V. P. (2010). *Estates society of the Russian Empire (XVIII - early XX century).* Novy Hronograph. (Иванова Н.А., Желтова В.П. Сословное общество Российской империи *(XVIII – начало XX века).* М.: Новый хронограф).

Kabuzan, V. M. (1976). *How the far east was settled (second half of the 17th - early 20th centuries)*. Khabarovsk Book Publishing House. (Кабузан В.М. (1976). *Как заселялся Дальний Восток (вторая половина XVII – начало XX века)*. Хабаровск: Хабаровское книжное издательство).

Kafengauz, B. B. (1949). *The history of the Demidov household in the 18th-19th centuries research experience in the Ural metallurgy*. Publishing House of the USSR Academy of Sciences. (Кафенгауз Б. Б. (1949). *История хозяйства Демидовых в XVIII-XIX вв. Опыт исследования по уральской металлургии*. М.-Л.: Издательство Академии наук СССР).

Kizilov, M. (2016). *Crimean Judea. Notes on the History of the Jews, Khazars, Karaites and Krymchaks in the Crimea since Ancient Times*. "Heritage of Millenia". (Кизилов М.Б. (2016). *Крымская Иудея: Очерки истории евреев, хазар, караимов и крымчаков в Крыму с античных времён до наших дней*. Симферополь: БФ «Наследие тысячелетий»).

Kobishanov, Y. M. (1995). *Polyudye: A phenomenon of national and world history*. ROSSPEN. (Кобищанов Ю.М. (1995). *Полюдье: явление отечественной и всемирной истории*. М.: РОССПЭН).

Kordonsky, S. G. (2008). The estate structure of post-Soviet Russia (part 1). *World of Russia, 17*(3), 37–66. (Кордонский С.Г. (2008). Сословная структура постсоветской России (часть I). *Мир России*).

Kosmachev, K. P. (1979). *The theory of economic development of the territory*. Institute of Geography of Siberia and the Far East of the Siberian Branch of the USSR Academy of Sciences. (Космачёв К.П. (1979). (ред.), *Теория хозяйственного освоения территории*. Иркутск: Институт географии Сибири и Дальнего Востока СО АН СССР).

Kropotkin, P. A. (1865). A trip from Transbaikalia to the Amur through Manchuria. *Russian Bulletin, 57*, 585–681. (Кропоткин П.А. (1865). Поездка из Забайкалья на Амур через Маньчжурию. *Русский вестник*).

Kuza, A. V. (1989). *Small towns of Ancient Rus*. Nauka. (Куза А.В. (1989). *Малые города Древней Руси*. М.: Наука).

Lurie, S. V. (1996). Geopolitical forms of organizing the space of expansion and their influence on the nature of popular colonization. *Civilizations and Cultures, 3*, 179–185. (Лурье С.В. (1996). Геополитические формы организации пространства экспансии и их влияние на характер народной колонизации. *Цивилизации и культуры*).

Lyubomirov, P. G. (1937). *Geographical location of the metallurgical and metalworking industry in Russia in the 17th, 18th and early 19th centuries*. Publishing House of the USSR Academy of Sciences. (Любомиров П. Г. (1937). *Очерки по истории металлургической и металлообрабатывающей промышленности в России (XVII, XVIII и начало XIX в.): Географическое размещение металлопромышленности*. М.-Л.: Издательство Академии наук СССР).

Mironov, B. N. (2003). *Social history of Russia during the period of the empire (XVIII - early XX century)*. "Dmitry Bulanin". (Миронов Б. Н. (2003). *Социальная история России периода империи (XVIII—начало XX в.)*. СПб.: «Дмитрий Буланин»).

Mishchuk, S. N. (2013). Internal and international migration in the Russian Far East in the middle of the 19th century. - The beginning of the XXI century: factors, dynamics, results. *Izvestiya RAN. Geographical Series, 6*, 33–42. (Мищук С.Н. (2013). Внутренняя и международная миграция на российском Дальнем Востоке середины XIX в. – начала XXI в.: факторы, динамика, результаты. *Известия РАН. Серия географическая*).

Mokeev, G. Y., & Shchenkov, A. S. (2006). *Planning structure of cities*. (Мокеев Г.Я., Щенков А.С. (2006). *Планировочная структура городов*). Accessed July 3, 2021, from http://rusarch.ru/mokeev1.htm

Murdock, G. P. (1949). *Social structure*. The Free Press. Russian edition: Мердок Дж. П. (2003). *Социальная структура* (trans.: Korotayev A.V.). М.: ОГИ.

Parshev A. (1999). *Why Russia is not America*. Krymsky Most-9D, Forum. (Паршев А. (1999). Почему Россия не Америка. М.: Крымский мост-9Д, Форум).

Plusnin, J. M. (1997). Socio-psychological mechanisms of life support of the population in the conditions of the economic crisis (comparative analysis of rural communities in the Russian North and in Gorny Altai). In Y. V. Popkov (Ed.), *Ethnosocial processes in Siberia* (pp. 47–56). IP&L SB RAS. (Плюснин Ю.М. (1997). Социально-психологические механизмы жизнеобеспечения населения в условиях экономического кризиса (сравнительный анализ сельских сообществ на Русском Севере и в Горном Алтае). В кн.: Ю.В. Попков (ред.), *Этносоциальные процессы в Сибири*).

Preobrazhensky, A. L. (1972). *Urals and Western Siberia in the late 16th - early 18th centuries*. Nauka. (Преображенский А.Л. (1972). *Урал и Западная Сибирь в конце XVI - начале XVIII вв.* М.: Наука).

Reclus, E. (1878). *The earth and its inhabitants. The universal geography*. J.S. Virtue & Co.

Rodoman, B. B. (1999). *Territorial areas and networks. Essays of theoretical geography*. Oecumene (Родоман Б.Б. (1999). *Территориальные ареалы и сети. Эссе теоретической географии*. Смоленск: Ойкумена).

Shishkov, M. K. (2009). *Territorial structure of Russia: Problems and prospects*. PH “Samara”. (Шишков М.К. (2009). *Территориальное устройство России: проблемы и перспективы*. Самара: Самара).

Siberia. Atlas of Asian Russia. (2007). A.P. Derevianko (ed.). *Top-book, Theoria. Design. Information*. Cartography. (Сибирь. Атлас Азиатской России. (2007). Ф.П. Деревянко (ред). Новосибирс-Москва: ООО «Топ-книга», Феория. Дизайн. Информация. Картография).

Tarkhov, S. A. (2018). Transport development of the territory. *Moscow University Bulletin. Series 5. Geography, 2*, 3–9. (Тархов С.А. (2018). Транспортная освоенность территории. *Вестник Московского университета. Серия 5. География*).

Treyvish, A. I. (2009). *City, region, country and world*. Novy chronograph. (Трейвиш А.И. (2009). *Город, район, страна и мир*. М.: Новый хронограф).

Tsutsiev, A. A. (2006). *Atlas of the ethnopolitical history of the Caucasus (1774–2004)*. Publishing House “Europe”. (Цуциев А.А. (2006.) *Атлас этнополитической истории Кавказа (1774-2004)*. М.: Издательство «Европа»).

Tverskoy, L. M. (1953). *Russian urban planning until the end of the 17th century*. State edition literature on construction and architecture. (Тверской Л.М. (1953). *Русское градостроительство до конца XVII века*. М., Л.: Гос. изд. литературы по строительству и архитектуре.).

Weber, M. (1904). Die “Objektivität” sozialwissenschaftlicher und sozialpolitischer Erkenntnis. *Archiv für Sozialwissenschaft und Sozialpolitik, 19*(1), 22–87.

Chapter 5
Local Territorial Organization

The territory is the most obvious physical embodiment of social relations. Territorial interactions determine neighborhood relations. And these latter are the primary basis of material production, of the economy *outside of and prior to* the market. Due to the universal, biologically determined, nature of territorial behavior, we must also consider human territorial relations as having grassroots, extra-social basis. Therefore, we almost involuntarily perceive the territorial structure of human societies as an invariant with roots too deep for social analysis. Or we consider it an archaic social institution. As such it has two components: invariable—archaic, and variable—determined by social and political factors. Herein I focus on analyzing the second, variable, part; however, I also constantly keep in mind the invariable component of the territorial structure. These two components create numerous territorial structures, which are based on only several permanent elements. The variance of territorial forms necessitates their typology. The typology of territories is based on the type of local communities distinguished by the degree of spatial isolation and the manner of their emergence and development. I am considering six territorial structures of provincial societies. Ultimately, they are reduced to four types of territories, which differ in all basic characteristics. These four territorial types are: (1) territories of communities existing in spatial isolation and not affected by government impact; (2) territories of communities, which are not isolated, but are developing without significant coercive government impact; (3) territories of communities formed coercively but with an inadequately developed transport infrastructure; (4) territories of communities formed coercively with a well-developed infrastructure due to their location on transport thoroughfares.

J. Plusnin, *Russian Provincial Society*, Societies and Political Orders in Transition,
https://doi.org/10.1007/978-3-030-97829-7_5

5.1 Territorial Structure

Neighborhood is the first of four basic social relations that determine the social structure. This is not an indirect connection of the local community with the surrounding physical environment; as a result of transformation, the environment becomes a landscape (often tautologically called "cultural landscape"). Neighborhood manifests itself through the territory, and its particular forms—through the territorial structure. A territory is developed and appropriated space (more precisely, resources located in physical space).

The territory of a local community has three principal components: (1) the center (town, locality); (2) its rural district, which includes from one to several hundred rural settlements; (3) and the boundaries of the territory, physical and symbolic, which uniquely represent that the area belongs to this specific community. All three components are complementary: one does not exist without the others.[1] When a community develops naturally, spontaneously, then over time, the rural district "nominates" a center that performs economic, social, and administrative functions, including public administration (in line with the well-known theory of Carnejro, 1970, 2003). If a community is formed coercively, by government effort, when the central settlement is formed first, then over time its rural district "squeezes out" (spreads out) from it. Consequently, any settlement structure, both "degenerate" and "normal" (developed), automatically creates boundaries—limits the physical space in accordance with the existing potential to control the resources available there. In fact, solely these three components constitute the basic framework underlying the entire variety of territorial structures.

The territorial structure consists of the following individual elements (see also Golts, 1995; Rodoman, 1999; Nefedova & Treivish, 2005; Tarkhov, 2005):

1. Space itself as a livelihood resource, more precisely, the totality of the host landscapes, or habitats
2. The permeability of space as a precondition for its development and transformation into a territory
3. Routes, or networks ensuring the permeability of space, i.e., transport communications that make resources accessible and facilitate their transfer inside and outside the territory
4. Boundaries, or barriers, necessary to determine the conditions for controlling and using resources
5. Territory as a limited and developed space, its size, and configuration

[1] The situation when the local community is represented by a single settlement corresponds to the "degenerate" type of community, which is an exceptional case caused by various reasons. In my records, it is Varnek on the Arctic Vaygach Island, where the entire community is concentrated in a single village for administrative, political, and economic reasons (elimination of depressed settlements and nomad camps); and Severny on the neighboring Yuznhy Island of the Novaya Zemlya Archipelago, which was established for military purposes and functions accordingly.

6. Settlements necessary for the comfortable existence of the people and the entire community, including their hierarchy—the center/district subdivision
7. Residential infrastructure and facilities of the settlements that determine the comfort of the living environment and life of the population
8. Economic (industrial) infrastructure that determines the nature and specifics of the economic activity of the population

This study focuses not on the territory as such, but on the territorial structure of the local society presented in its diversity and specific forms. To get a general picture, we should first identify and describe the types of local territories in relation to specific communities. It is impracticable to depict various territorial forms without such a typology as the simplest generalization of empirical data. Accordingly, the presentation herein requires the following sequence. First, I set forth the principles of the spatial organization of a local community, specific to the Russian provincial society. Second, I depict the nature and mechanisms of neighborhood and connectivity of members of the local community that underlie the typology of local territories. Third, I outline the typology of local territories, based on the typology of local communities discussed in the previous chapter. This allows us to differentiate the variations of local territorial structures in different regions of Russia. It also allows, fourth, to identify and present—as far as possible—the "typical" territory and residential organization of the provincial local community.

5.2 Principles of a Local Community's Spatial Organization

I identify three diverse principles that underlie the spatial organization of a provincial local community in Russia. The first principle—actually, applicable to any local community—is the structural hierarchy of the territory. The second principle—probably, specifically Russian—is the temporal "wavelike" organization of the local space. Finally, the third principle is the territorial stability of the population.

5.2.1 *The Principle of the Structural Hierarchy of the Local Territory*

It is, of course, the universal principle of organizing the space of any settled agricultural society. It is a direct consequence of the territory being organized according to the "center—periphery" principle, outlined in such theories as, for example, the central place theory (*System der zentralen Orte*) developed by Walter Christaller (1966, 1980) and Boris Rodoman's theory of "nodal regions" and "*cartoids*" (Rodoman, 1999, 2007). The territorial basis of any society with at least some forms of political organization, always and without exception, consists of two interrelated elements: the "*locality*" (town or village) and its rural district. The "locality" is the economic, business and craft, religious, and administrative center of the rural district. We observe this also in historical retrospective, irrespective of the society in question or its stage of social evolution; see Kuza (1983), Peregrine and Ember (2001–2002). However, according to the information collected by P. Perigrine in the *Atlas of Cultural Evolution* (Peregrine, 2003), the existence of a town does not always automatically assume political organization; J. Jennings and T. Earle present similar arguments (Jennings & Earle, 2016). However, there is also other point of view: see Carneiro (1970). At the same time, such organization of space is intrinsic not only to agricultural societies, but also to nomads, at least at the stage of political organization of chiefdoms and nomadic empires (Kradin, 2007).

If the issue is considered on the scale of a provincial local society, the hierarchy of places in Russia has only two, much less often three levels. The lowest first level consists of settlements—villages and hamlets,[2] that make up the economic base of the territorial structure. Under W. Christaller's theory, this is the level of the *"cultural clearing"* or the *"deme,"* village. The second level, the locality (*mestechko*, Bezirk), which together with the rural district constitute the full population-demographic and social community; at this level, local self-government, i.e., pre- and extra-public administration functions, first manifests itself and is implemented. Hence, at this level we record the most obvious signs of social self-organization, without which self-government is impossible.

Actually, this is the level of the primary local community, which is the focus of my research. It is at this level that the local community manifests itself in all its necessary components—as a population and demographic unit (community), as a social unit, as a business and craft (material livelihood for households) and economic unit, and, finally, as a self-governing political unit.

The third level of territorial organization is not encountered everywhere in provincial Russia due to the generally low population density in many of the regions. The third level consists of several localities with their rural districts, drawn toward a larger district town. This is the level of the "canton," and in Russian reality—the level of the imperial "uyezd" or the modern district. At this level, the totality of settlements united by the locality and the district town forms a socio-economic community. At the same time, it acquires the status of a grassroots political unit: public administration functions and government authorities appear, and political self-organization and local self-government become subordinate to them.

[2] In Russia, a hamlet (*khutor*) can be a small village, and in the south even a large settlement, though initially the word meant a one-homestead village, when the entire settlement consisted of only one household and one house with outbuildings.

5.2.2 *Principle of the Temporal "Wavelike" Organization of the Local Territory*

A specific Russian feature is the unique temporal organization of local space as it transforms into the territory of a local community. The temporal organization influences and possibly determines the distribution of individual settlements across the territory of the community. In particular, this feature determines a large share of *"escheat"*[3] settlements in many communities, as well as a particular dynamism of the intra-settlement structure. I believe, the distinct temporal organization of the territory is specific for the Russian society and may be a unique phenomenon, so it requires a more detailed presentation. At the same time, arguments in favor of the cyclical nature of social history have long been well known (Sorokin, 1927, 1998; Losch, 1937; Maier, 1964; Goldstein, 1988; Fischer, 1996; Nefedov, 2004, 2005). But I am discussing local cyclical dynamics. Usually, this topic is not of interest to researchers.

Throughout our history we have observed everywhere peculiar flood and ebb "tides" of the population in space, both globally, in vast expanses of the Russian Plain, and locally. I believe this movement is due to two different processes. Superimposing on each other, these processes produce a very complex pattern, which we occasionally observe and depict, but rarely decipher. This complex pattern of millennium-long *"population currents/ripples"* in the vast expanse of European Russia emerges as follows. It consists of two interfering "layers." The first, underlying layer is the repeated dispersal of the population from the center of the country to its periphery, to the outskirts. This process has been going on for the past thousand years. From time to time, the dispersal either picks up or slows down, creating centrifugal waves of population density, extended over time for decades and centuries. Although such waves are long-term and large-scale, their impact can be traced even at the local community level. The second, more local, wave process is represented by equally regular tidal demographic phenomena. Virtually everywhere, within the territorial limits of several adjacent local communities, repeated depopulation and land abandonment are followed by further resettlement two to three generations later.

The first of these "wave layers," the periodic centrifugal demographic dispersal of the population, clearly observable during certain periods already at the time of the Tsardom of Russia, has long attracted the attention of historians; they recognize this process as a phenomenon caused by military political and religious political reasons (see, e.g. Soloviev, 1990, Book V. Vol. 10, Chap. 1. pp. 357–440; Book VII. Vol. 13. Chap. 1. pp. 40–48; Chap. 2. pp. 173–175; Pascal, 2011, pp. 34–49 and 51–58; Panarin, 1999). Presumably, this periodic centrifugal process is caused

[3] An "escheat" (*vymorochnoye*) settlement is a locality abandoned by the inhabitants but meanwhile retaining all elements of the infrastructure and the administrative and territorial status of a residential unit. In Russian reality, such abandoned localities can be repopulated; there are frequent cases of repeated resettlement cycles of such "escheat" localities.

by the "generic" features of the Russian state (Lurie, 1996), its "resource" character (Kordonsky, 2016), and external factors, primarily the so-called *"nomadic brake,"* which was regular and periodic throughout the entire Eastern European and especially Russian history (Kradin, 2007). Although this latter factor is usually considered decisive (Anderson, 2000, II. 2, pp. 209–221), we cannot ignore long-term external aggression against Russia from two directions. First and foremost, from the very Dark Ages until the first third of the seventeenth century nomads regularly raided Russia from the east and southeast (Gumilev, 2006). Then, from the twelfth century and up to our days there were equally regular "German" invasions from the west and northwest (Lieven, 2002; Teschke, 2003). The interaction of the Russian population with the Russian state has its own specific consequences. The state is concerned about the availability of and control over taxable population. But, due to other underlying reasons, the tax collection process and population control mechanisms differ from those in Europe. Many consider the Mongol conquest to be the starting point of this specifically Russian behavior. The Mongol expansion brought *Space* to the Russian world. The Moscow Principality not only inherited from the descendants of Batu Khan and Uzbek Khan the judicial, political, diplomatic, fiscal, financial, and governance systems (Vernadsky, 1966, Sect. 5.3; Prokhorov, 2002, pp. 84–106, 144–160, 218–227; Yurchenko, 2012); it also received from the Golden Horde a particular inheritance: a specific development of the space and its arrangement as a *nomadic territory*. It was expressed in a new attitude of the state toward its subjects (Anderson, 2000, pp. 212–214; Kradin, 2007, Chap. 6, pp. 95–110).

New traditions emerged against the backdrop of old, pre-Mongol—and definitely democratic—ones, which had been preserved by the people; as a result, the population fled from the state. Our expanses are vast and empty. But large parts of European Russia and Siberia are covered by forests rather than steppes. Here, the expansion nomadic in spirit (*"carried-around"* space, or *"the right to migrate"*) requires other development mechanisms than those used by nomads. Such mechanisms already existed in the arsenal of our population. Rare *smoke* of villages among vast forest expanses. Roads are rivers that are uniquely numerous and abundant in Russia as compared to all other countries. We see the same picture everywhere—from Pskov and Novgorod to Tobolsk, Tomsk, and Khabarovsk. People settle in clusters amidst endless forests, clinging to numerous full-flowing rivers. Over time, the state follows its population to the new lands. And there, where the people have already settled down, the state builds fortifications, fortresses, shrines, temples, customs houses—everything that constitutes and forms the state administrative and territorial structure. The state shapes the administrative structure and imposes on the population tributes, taxes, and service in its most developed form of *serfdom*. But with a special attitude to land as a universal good, which belongs to God only and not to humans,[4] and surrounded by vast expanses, the population flees the state again and again. Since the thirteenth century onwards and up to the present time, our people have been scattering away from the center to the outskirts (borderlands). Starting from the Mongol invasion, the population fled constantly: under the yoke and the Moscow Principality, at the time of the Tsardom of Russia and up to the rule of the Soviet state. However, this widespread opinion is disputed, at least for the 250-year period of the existence of serfdom (Mironov, 2003, p. 25). People scattered in all directions from the center, geographically associated with Moscow as the successor of the Horde. They fled to Western Russia and the North, then to the south, to the Don and Dnieper, to Zaporozhye, and finally to the east to Siberia. They also fled en masse to Central Asia. The people were always searching either for *Kitezh-Grad*, the fortunate land of *Belovodye*, or the blessed *Shambhala*. This eternal escape from the state is still going on.[5] And the state yet again follows the population, and erects fortifications and *abatis lines,* and re-imposes taxes.

Owing to this, waves of dispersal arise: the centrifugal movement of the population intensifies during periods of raids, troubles, and revolutions, then ceases altogether during periods of prosperity and political calm. We tend to believe that such periods correspond to the *"collection"–"distribution"* cycles of the *"resource-based"* state according to the theory of Olga Bessonova (2006), based, in turn, on Simon Kordonsky's "resource-based state" theory (Kordonsky, 2007, 2010). This seems all the more likely, since such cycles of replacing economic resource redistribution and goods production mechanisms by non-economic (political) ones are associated with socio-political perturbations. Dominic Lieven, describing the stages of Russia's imperial expansion in the Caucasus and Turkestan, also points out that despite the seeming prevalence of economic reasons, the leading motive was political—primarily the struggle with the British Empire (Lieven, 2002, pp. 337–347). Although many historians have written about the periodic dispersal of the population or mentioned it, it is Svetlana Lourie, as far as I know, who focuses her research on this specific issue (Lurie, 1996, 1998, 2015). Incidentally, one of the visible results of this periodic dispersal of the population is the system of concentric rings of towns and cities around Moscow. It is almost regular, slightly deformed, "crumpled" in the west for military and political reasons and in the north and northeast—for geographical, environmental, and climatic reasons. There are up to seven concentric rings of towns and cities (actually—lines of defense, *"abatis lines"*) at a distance of about a hundred kilometers from each other; the clearest and most distinct picture is visible in the southern, steppe direction.

---

[4] There is an ancient Russian saying that clearly characterizes the relationship of the people with the state and their views on land rights: *"We may belong to the masters, but the land is ours."* It appeared not earlier than the fifteenth century as a reaction to the enslavement of the rural population.

[5] By the way, we have been witnessing the same process since the early 1990s in the movement of "Anastasians," pagans, and various kinds of "New Age," which in essence is not just an escape into the forests and mountains for the sake of "living in harmony with Nature," but is also an escape from the watchful "sovereign's eye" that controls every step of the inhabitant in a metropolis.

These centrifugal population waves spreading over the vast expanse of Russia, followed by "administrative waves" of establishing state territories, embodied in fortresses and towns, are overlapped by a different but anyhow associated process, namely, by smaller waves of periodic depopulation and desertification of territories, often quite large ones. Waves of this second type do not have the same scale as waves of the first type. They are local. Everywhere in European Russia, each region has the same common age-old feature: periods of population inflow and overflow in a local area are replaced by its outflow, by periods of desertification, depopulation, and *abandoning* of villages. Such tidal waves have an approximately century-long cycle. However, they usually do not coincide with the dispersal waves (unless caused by radical political perturbations). Moreover, since tidal waves are local, they do not cover the country's entire territory at the same time, and often move in opposite directions. One local area may see an outflow of population, whereas the neighboring one an inflow at the same time. Each local area of European Russia has experience five, six, or more cycles of this sort.

Tidal waves are also our unique Russian feature. It is likely that such population ebbs and flows occurred already in the fourteenth to –fifteenth centuries. Obviously, in different areas these processes happen at different times, but in general the cycles are distinguishable. Their causes can be political (civil unrest, revolutions, and wars), economic (inability for the population to achieve self-sufficiency locally leading to seasonal and temporary internal migration), or natural (crop failure and famine, and epidemics) (see, e.g. Anuchin, 1982; Dulov, 1983; Kulisher, 2004; Golts, 2002; Radkau, 2012). Of course, partly they were caused by epidemics, and crop failures, and certain climate changes. If the abundance of population in an area can be due to demographic, climatic, economic, and political factors, desertification periods are caused almost exclusively by political and economic reasons. Thus, because of the Time of Troubles and the Polish and Swedish intervention, the vast territories of Pomorye (the White Sea region in the Russian North) by the first third of the seventeenth century lost three quarters of their population, *"no more than a quarter of the former number of inhabited homesteads and cultivated lands remained"* (Pascal, 2011, p. 54). Similar examples are not so obvious, but they exist everywhere. According to Leonid Kazarinov, by the second half of the nineteenth century (from the beginning of the nineteenth century to 1874), the Chukhloma District of the Kostroma Province had almost no adult male population left. All men had left in search of work to the capitals; as a result, over three quarters of the district's arable lands were overgrown with forests and many villages were abandoned (Kazarinov, 1926, p. 20). But by 1926, only two generations later, this same district was already overpopulated and there was a shortage of land to feed over 54,000 inhabitants. Later, in the Soviet years, despite very poor farmland, the entire Chukhloma District was cultivated. Yet another three generations later the cycle repeated itself: after the 1990s people started leaving for the towns, and the local population within the same territorial borders is currently under ten thousand people. And yet again, up to half of Chukhloma's total male population has left home to seeking earnings in metropolitan cities (Plusnin et al., 2013). This time, however, "only" half of the entire agricultural land has been abandoned in the area instead of three quarters earlier. All this land is overgrown with a 30-year-old forest. But it is obvious that shortly this area will again be repopulated and the land cultivated. Absolutely similar and simultaneous demographic tides were also observed in the neighboring districts of the Kostroma Province—Kologriv, Parfenyevo, and Makaryev (Vladimirsky, 1927, p. 13 onwards).

Regular depopulation of territories required the state to take respective counter actions—to populate various important areas by new inhabitants, what it has been repeatedly doing up to our days. In the Moscow Province, its northwestern districts can serve as an example. After the Time of Troubles, in the 1630s they were populated by Finno-Ugric people (Karelians and Vepsians) from the western outskirts of the country, with the number of new inhabitants comparable to that of the former ones (Kislovsky, 2006, pp. 122, 205–211). We know similar resettlement campaigns in the Far East and the Caucasus in the middle of the nineteenth century, and in many regions of Siberia and the Russian North (Murmansk Region)—in the twentieth century. The departure of the population from a local area was subsequently followed either by its return or by coercive settlement of new inhabitants.

Thus, throughout our entire Russian history, we see two parallel socio-demographic processes: the centrifugal dispersal of the population, from time to time intensifying, then weakening, and on its background local ebbs and flows. This is a very interesting phenomenon that probably no one has ever studied in such a complex. I would describe it in the following metaphorical way: in windy weather a large rock falls into the agitated water of a large pond causing a centrifugal wave from the splash point; the interference of multidirectional wind waves with concentric dispersal waves will give us a specific picture of the superposition of a regular ring wave on the chaos of wind-generated waves. This is the model of the age-long spatial movement of the subjects of the Russian state. The length of each wave is one or two centuries, and there must have been six or seven of them over the past thousand years.

5.2.3 Territorial Stability of the Population

This is the third principle I have identified. Within a local area, the Russian provincial population is very stable—not mobile. At first glance this seems to contradict the previous principle. Meanwhile, the principles of the population's wavelike movements and its territorial stability constitute a complementary pair—they supplement each other: tidal currents across the territory and periodic flight to the outskirts of the country occur on the backdrop of stable and age-long consistent life of a certain part of the population in the same local area. Presumably, this is the uniqueness and originality of the Russian society, at least its provincial part. National population censuses, starting from the first one of 1621–1623, as well as even earlier church registers, invariably record the same families, kins, and clans in the same villages, auls, settlements, posads, and small towns. Despite constant migration, the main most numerous families—or parts of them—retain their presence in a local area for centuries. Documentary evidence—church registers and national censuses—available for the past five to six centuries everywhere records the stable presence of families and clans in local areas over a long period of 10–15 generations (see Chap. 9 for more on this).

Such territorial stability of the population is ensured by the stability of boundaries established between local communities and maintained by them unchanged for a long time, usually throughout their entire existence.

Thus, any provincial local society in Russia is characterized in its historical development by distinctive spatial patterns and territorial structure. The spatial patterns of the Russian population are distinguished by secular cycles of local ebbs and flows, and secular cycles of global centrifugal movements. Typical for the territorial structure are its two-tier organization (administrative center, "locality"—rural district) and the age-old stability of both boundaries and population (family and clan conservatism). These principles determine the universal and specifically Russian features of the local territorial structure. However, to describe the territorial structure, we must identify the categorical structure of the local territory necessary for the typology of diverse territories.

5.3 Neighborhood and Connectedness: Grounds for the Typology of Territorial Structures

Coexistence and the need for people to arrange their lives and economic activities (i.e., the daily need to physically maintain their livelihood) transform space into territory. The territory as developed and appropriated space is characterized by a certain set of features, which constitute the categorical basis for typology. The basic categories will be the foundation for developing the typology of the territorial structure. I see the following logic and ontology in identifying and depicting the totality of categories that exhaustively define the concept of territory as a specially organized physical space.

Two conditions must be met for space to become a public territory. First, the space must potentially have relevant resources, i.e., vitally important to the community in a specific period of its existence. But potential resources become actual material means of livelihood only when space becomes a territory. Even someone else's territory, according to the members of a given community. In other words, the transformation of physical space into territory and the availability of resources are interdependent.

Second, the territory emerges there, where the space is *permeable*, i.e., accessible for development everywhere within its boundaries. Thus, habitable space is characterized by the categories of landscape ("land" and its "abundance"), its permeability, and the availability of relevant resources. The space permeability precondition means that the territory of the community is always smaller than the physical space within which this territory is arranged, i.e., within the physical and geographical boundaries, where space permeability sharply decreases (Rodoman, 1999). Enhancing space permeability needed for the life of the community requires various communication routes that allow people to connect with each other and with the neighboring communities, and enable movement of resources, products, people, and information.

The existence/absence of vital resources precondition means that relevant resources must be controlled and protected from external encroachment, whether it be neighboring communities or natural agents—animals, climatic and seasonal factors, changing weather conditions, etc. Therefore, each local territory is of the size that can be controlled by community members, either due to the physical properties of the space (accessibility and the possibility of constant and regular monitoring), or because the neighbors permit (which is not always in conformity with the size of the required *Lebensraum*). Apart from the size, the second indispensable attribute of the territory are its actual borders—physical or symbolic—which allow the community to effectively control resources and protect them from destruction or plundering.

The physical habitat is transformed into a territory through establishing a system of external and internal borders that divide (and link) the grassroot (elementary) structural units—settlements. The totality of grassroot (first) level settlements—villages, farms, and hamlets—connected by territorial, historical, family, and economic ties always adjoins a hierarchically larger settlement—locality (township, town, posad, or urban-type settlement). In Russian, this totality of settlements that make up the rural district of a "locality" has long had a special name—"*koost*" (cluster).[6] The grassroot settlements vary by scale and population—from one to two households and one to ten people to dozens and hundreds of households and up to several hundred inhabitants. Despite their different size, all these settlements have only the status of *"refuge"* (Asyl) and *"village"* (Siedlung)—they are territories of direct physical and material reproduction, i.e., elementary economic units. Unlike most other countries, quite a few "villages" in provincial Russia exist in spatial isolation: numerous remote settlements, whose residents are cut off from their closest geographical neighbors for a significant part of the annual cycle, can be found on two-fifths of the country's territory. Often the "closest neighbors" are several dozens or hundreds of kilometers away. However, such an isolated settlement forms an isolated but full-fledged local community only in exceptional cases.

The two-tier (or three-tier) nature of the residential structure of the local community's territory implies the existence of two or more settlements and their hierarchy (subordination) (Christaller, 1980; Semyonov-Tyan-Shansky, 1928; Rodoman, 1999). Only one of the settlements is the *"locality"*—the administrative-territorial and economic center of the local community. The remaining settlements constitute the *rural district of* the local community. These

[6] This is where the Russian term for "handicraft production"—*koostarnoye proizvodstvo*—comes from, similar to the German or English "Heimarbeit," "handwerklich," "craft," and "artisanal."

are villages and farms where only domestic and economic activities of households are carried out.

Along with the center and borders, the rural district is one of the three major components of the territorial structure. It determines the actual (not administrative) territorial boundaries. It also mutually complements the center: without the district, the center neither emerges nor exists. In the extreme case in Russian reality, the entire rural district may consist of just several hamlets or seasonal camps, or even one single village. Such a reduced rural district is found only in spatially isolated and very remote communities. The single village becomes the community's "degenerate" center. The number of settlements in a rural district usually correlates with the population density in the area: the more of them, the higher the density and vice versa. However, in Russian reality, when the periodic outflow of the population occurs, some (sometimes many) villages of the rural district become depopulated and *fall into decay*—the population abandons them. With the reverse inflow current, inhabitants return to the abandoned villages, and the population density of the rural district grows significantly. I define as "decaying" or "escheat" those settlements where there are no permanent residents (but there are seasonal inhabitants—summer residents), or where the population is declining and at the time of registration is reduced to less than five people.

In contrast to the villages of the rural district, the residential structure of the administrative center (*"locality"*) is determined not by direct livelihood factors, but by the economic, social, political, and religious objectives this center is meant to address. Among others, these objectives are reflected in the urban layout (Kudryavtsev, 1978). The administrative status of the "locality" reflects its socio-economic, cultural, and political position (cf.: Glazychev 2003, pp. 115–122, 261–307); i.e., this status determines the local, regional, and national significance of the community. Consequently, this indicates the amount of additional resources redistributed by the state to the grassroots level, which determine the well-being of the inhabitants. Therefore, I believe the spatial organization of the administrative center, including its layout and institutions, has a certain diagnostic value for depicting the entire social structure; cf.: Nefedova and Treivish (2005).

The categories identified and described above can be considered as essential features (attributes) of the territorial structure. I will list them:

1. *"Land"*—the actual inhabited territory as an exclusive livelihood resource; what matters most is the quality of the territory, its resource intensity ("land fertility"), or, in other words, the degree to which physical space has been transformed into a landscape[7]
2. *Size of the territory* as an indication of the ability of the local community to control the resources necessary and sufficient for daily livelihoods
3. *Borders* as an essential mechanism for monitoring resources through territorial control, as a mechanism for protecting the resources from external

[7] A landscape is "cultivated" space, a reservoir of resources available for use (i.e., locally relevant).

encroachments, as well as a requirement for ensuring the safety of the inhabitants themselves

4. *Permeability of* space as a requirement for controlling and protecting the territory, as well as a precondition enabling/preventing the development of the territorial infrastructure
5. *Routes*—transport communications as a mechanism for distributing resources, ensuring the connectedness of the local population and its communication with the external environment
6. *Settlements*—the actual settlements as various forms of human habitation, everyday life and activities; at the local level, there are two, less frequently three types of settlements: the first grassroot type of the rural district includes villages, hamlets, seasonal camps, and urban-type settlements; the second type is the administrative center
7. *Infrastructure* of the settlements as a means of providing people with daily necessities
8. The administrative *status of the center*, which is captured in its urban layout

The above attributes of the territorial structure allow us to identify the indicators, which can be used to describe the territorial structure of a particular local community. But we have to reduce all the empirical diversity of nearly one hundred and fifty separate territorial configurations to several manageable types of territories common for provincial communities in Russia. For this purpose I will rely on the typologies of local communities proposed in Chap. 4. Typologies based on three different principles—(1) the time of emergence and age, (2) the degree of spatial isolation, and (3) the reasons for the emergence and development of local communities—give grounds for a typology of the second, subordinate level—typology of the territorial structures. I believe, for this purpose we can use only two of the three specified principles, namely, the degree of isolation and the reasons for the emergence of the community. The selection of these two principles is due to the negative association between the community's age and the coercive manner of its emergence. The origins of the community's emergence—natural or coercive—are more important for the structure of the local territory. Besides, this is also related to the argument that by various estimates the people's continuous memory of local and family events goes back for no more than a century. Accordingly, the local community's vital institutions are only slightly older than four to six generations. Although I have information about the stability of territories and their borders over periods of five centuries and longer, the territorial structure itself is changing faster.

5.4 Features of the Territorial Structure of Communities with Different Levels of Spatial Isolation

A high degree of spatial isolation or its absence determines the variation in the parameters of most of the above attributes of the territorial structure. Let us characterize each of the eight attributes separately for isolated, "turbulent," and "ordinary" communities. For the reasons already mentioned above, I depict the third type of communities together with the "turbulent" ones, or provide a substantially shorter additional description.

5.4.1 Isolated Communities

Nowadays in Russia, the quality of a territory as "fertile" or "barren land" is directly related to the isolation of the community. Spatially isolated communities everywhere live in areas that provide very limited resources for day-to-day autonomous livelihoods. Therefore, such communities have large and very large territories and low population density. Often both indicators differ from the average Russian ones by one or two orders of magnitude (ten-fold and hundred-fold). Naturally, such communities have almost no neighboring communities and often need no symbolic border markers, since such are physical barriers—sea coasts, mountain ranges, swampy tundra, and taiga. However, we cannot say that space permeability around isolated communities is very low. This is so mainly for modern types of vehicles, including even aviation. But for local inhabitants, the permeability of their space can be even better than that of non-isolated communities, since they have appropriate traditional means of transport and are not surrounded by a hostile or too densely populated environment; isolation is caused not by serious physical obstacles for moving around but by huge territories, and few and bad roads. There are few transport routes in isolated communities, respectively, the density of the transport infrastructure (kilometers of various standard roads per area unit) is very low, and in extreme cases it is close to zero (Varnek, Krasnoshchelye, and Anabar).

The settlement structure is reduced, especially in the rural district. Often, there are very few villages, and a large part of the population (in extreme cases, everyone) is concentrated in the administrative center. Sometimes, there is only one single settlement, and where nomadic economies prevail—just a few camps. Of all the isolated communities I surveyed, one-third has a reduced rural district.

The public utilities infrastructure of the settlements is also reduced: almost all its components are autonomous, including heating, water supply, and sewerage. That is, each household has its own separate heating system (wood stoves), water sources (wells, springs, or streams), and waste dumps for the disposal of domestic, human, and animal waste (cesspits and latrines). Only power grids and gas supply systems, if any, are centralized (many isolated communities have no centralized gas supply systems, and in some of them electricity is still generated by autonomous diesel power plants).

The administrative status of the center corresponds to the development of the municipal and transport infrastructure. Usually—in one-third of the cases (27 from 41)—the center is not a town but a village or urban-type settlement with a limited scope of public administration functions (and respective institutions); with an undeveloped local economy and extremely weak labor market; with reduced cultural and religious functions. Its layout corresponds to this state of affairs and reflects it. Most often it is either a street (village) or regular layout, since many current administrative centers of isolated communities used to be district (*uyezd*) centers, which were built in strict compliance with imperial urban planning standards. There, where the centers of isolated communities are young towns established during the industrial development of new economic regions, their layout is zonal. Radial layouts are not encountered, since this type is characteristic of centers in historical long-developed areas, where there are almost no isolated communities.

5.4.2 "Ordinary" and "Turbulent" Communities

For turbulent and many "ordinary" communities, the indicators of the territorial structure have different properties. Here, the quality of the "land"—soil fertility, the balneological properties of the area, its climate and weather conditions, the variety and attractiveness of the landscapes—is usually good or high. Due to this, the size of the territory is small, the population density is high, and agricultural landscapes, residential areas, and industrial zones prevail among the land categories. The share of other land categories is reduced; forests are especially few. There is not much *idle* or *alienated* land.

Population size and density are high, therefore, the specific load on the territory is substantial or even exorbitant (i.e., in case of autonomous existence, the territory is not able to provide for its population). Consequently, the territorial borders are clearly determined and marked with both symbolic and physical symbols to ensure constant and vigilant monitoring of resources and their protection from encroachment by neighbors. Border conflicts with neighboring communities are frequent. Space permeability is higher than that of isolated communities. There are a variety of transport routes, and usually one to two or more thoroughfares linking the local community with the most distant regions of the country. The road density is high, which drives the development of the local economy and the operation of various industries.

The settlement structure includes numerous villages of the rural district (where *escheat*—abandoned—villages are not uncommon, their share reaching from one-fifth to two-fifths of all settlements). The administrative center is sometimes represented by two levels: the rural municipality (*volost*) and the district (*uyezd*). In this case, the first municipal (*volost*) level consists of settlements that are centers of separate rural districts—"*clusters*," i.e., groups of villages autonomous in their business activities and sometimes socially (but not administratively, politically, or economically) self-contained. Such centers of the first (volost) level have limited administrative functions. This is especially typical of the Russian North and eastern regions of European Russia, where the "cluster" structure has existed since ages: Karelia (Pudozh), Archangelsk Region (Kargopol), Vologda Region (Nikolsk), Kostroma Region (Soligalich), and Kirov Region (Slobodskoy). The second settlement level of the residential hierarchy is formed by *uyezd* (currently district) towns, which unite the local community within the boundaries of current municipal districts or urban districts (in turbulent communities the administrative borders are usually broader and do not always coincide with the territory actually controlled by the community). Local communities with a three-tier territorial residential structure are of the "turbulent" type only (e.g., Anapa rural district, Temryuk, and Ust-Labinsk in Krasnodar Region, Medvezhyegorsk and Olonets in Karelia, Iskitim in Novosibirsk Region, Novozybkov in Bryansk Region, Semyonov in Nizhny Novgorod Region). There is often a very high concentration of the population in the administrative center (up to three quarters of the total population).

The physical infrastructure of settlements varies widely. Administrative centers have a full set of public utilities. Some settlements of the rural district may have an equally developed municipal infrastructure, whereas others may have nothing (apart from power grids and local roads).

The center has a full-scope administrative and territorial status. It is always a town that had received the status of a district center back in the imperial or even earlier times (of the thirty-one centers, only five have the status of an urban-type settlement, i.e., a semi-town). It has a full scope of public administration functions (and relevant institutions). Usually, the local economy is well developed; social, cultural, and religious functions are represented in full scope. This is reflected in the center's layout. In ancient and old turbulent towns radio-centric (historical) and regular (determined by urban planning standards) layouts prevail (e.g., Kem, Rzhev, Sebezh, Vyshny Volochyok, Yukhnov, Zubtsov). Young towns predominantly have zonal (industrial) layouts (e.g., Birobidzhan, Bolshoy Kamen, Medvezhyegorsk, Obluchye, Zuyevka). Only in rare cases does the center have a street (village) layout (e.g., Chupa, Kem, Manturovo, Sharya, Temryuk, Zubova Polyana).

By territorial attributes, numerous "ordinary" communities are much closer to the "turbulent" than to the isolated type. This concerns the population size of the community in general and of its center. The same applies to the size of the territory and the population density; obviously, in turbulent communities the territories are smaller and the density is higher. But the percentage of the population living in the center—over half of all residents—is absolutely similar. The same is the proportion of the rural district—up to 40%–45% of the population. A large number of escheat villages is typical of such local communities.

5.4.3 *Dissimilarities in the Territorial Structure of Communities with Different Levels of Spatial Isolation*

I will present the main dissimilarities in the territorial structure of two types of communities in a concise tabular form (Table 5.1).

5.5 Features of the Territorial Structure of Coercively and Naturally Developed Communities

Local communities developing around settlements established coercively for economic or political reasons shape their territorial structure differently than communities formed naturally and usually existing historically a long time. The age of the community seems to be of great (although unknown) relevance to the territorial structure. We must take this into account because of the big difference in the territorial structure of coercively and naturally developed communities; as can be seen from Table 4.5 in Chap. 4, among ancient communities there were none with a coercive way of development. (Although this is not so, of course, since such communities were also established in ancient times, but their initial coercive emergence has long been superseded by subsequent natural development.[8]) And among the surveyed young communities there are almost none with a natural way of development—only six out of thirty-three. These three facts are interlinked and they determine the essential differences in the territorial structure of communities with a coercive and natural manner of development, which should be taken into account.

5.5.1 *"Coercively" Developed Communities*

Surveys show that the territorial structure of such communities has the following distinctive features. At the time of establishment, the resource intensity of the territory ("land fertility," when it comes to natural resources the community needs for autonomous existence, for subsistence farming) is not essential. On the contrary,

[8]One must keep in mind the political actions of the Soviet period, which affected the residential structure of many ancient and old communities. I am referring to Nikita Khrushchev's policy of "eliminating depressed villages" in the 1960s. That is the reason why the proportion of "escheat" settlements in ancient and old communities of European Russia is so high. However, the movement to "consolidate" settlements had devastating consequences also in some parts of Siberia: thus, by the 1980s, 88% of all villages had disappeared in the immediate vicinity of Novosibirsk within a radius of just over 100 km.

Table 5.1 The components of territorial structure of communities with different levels of spatial isolation

Attribute	Isolated communities	"Ordinary" communities	"Turbulent" communities
Resources	Areas with limited resources for autonomous livelihoods	Intermediate position	High-quality "land." Agricultural landscapes prevail among the land categories
Size of the territory	Large territories	Intermediate position	Small territories
	Low population size and density	Intermediate position	Average population size and density
	Specific load on the territory varies: high in residential areas and low elsewhere	Intermediate position	Specific load on the territory is substantial or even exorbitant
Borders	Have no neighboring communities and no need to determine borders	Closer to the "turbulent" type	Frequent border conflicts with the inhabitants of neighboring communities; the need for constant monitoring and protection
	Borders are predominantly physical barriers	Closer to the "turbulent" type	Territorial borders are clearly determined and marked with both symbolic and physical signs
Space permeability	Moderate	Closer to the "turbulent" type	High
Transport infrastructure	Few transport routes of inferior quality	Closer to the "turbulent" type	Many various transport routes, including thoroughfares
	Very low road density	Closer to the "turbulent" type	High road density
Residential structure	Reduced settlement structure, especially in the rural district; number of settlements from one-two to a dozen	Closer to the "turbulent" type	Settlement structure includes numerous villages of the rural district—from several dozen to several hundred
	No escheat villages	Closer to the "turbulent" type	Many escheat villages: from 1/5 to 2/5 of all settlements
	One- to two-tier residential structure	Closer to the isolated type	Two- to three-tier residential structure
Public utilities infrastructure	Reduced: almost all components are autonomous, including heating, water supply, and sewerage	Closer to the isolated type	The physical infrastructure varies widely. Administrative centers have a full set of public utilities; settlements of the rural district may have an equally developed infrastructure, whereas others may have nothing

(continued)

Table 5.1 (continued)

Attribute	Isolated communities	"Ordinary" communities	"Turbulent" communities
	Status of the administrative center: it is not a town but a village or urban-type settlement with a limited scope of public administration functions; with an undeveloped local economy and weak labor market; with reduced cultural and religious functions	Closer to the "turbulent" type	Administrative and territorial status of the center: always a town with a full scope of public administration functions. The local economy is well developed
Layout of the administrative center	Street (village), regular or zonal layout	Predominantly regular or zonal layout	In ancient and old towns radio-centric and regular layouts prevail. Young towns predominantly have zonal layouts

the determining factor is the availability of such natural resources, for the sake of which the base settlement is established nearby. Such resources include: coal, oil, gas, polymetallic ores, gravel, granite, rare earth minerals, gold and diamonds, large rivers with dams for hydropower plants, rivers and sea coasts with large fish stocks, forest areas for logging or trapping fur-bearing animals, and finally, naturally fortified terrain allowing the construction of impregnable fortresses, forts, and military outposts. All these resources are unsuitable for livelihood. Therefore, settlements established for the sake of extracting or procuring such natural resources are highly specialized and hardly self-sufficient. Their everyday life depends on a constant replenishment of external resources, for which the state takes responsibility. In critical situations "coercive" communities face the threat of physical death.[9] This is what we have seen and are now witnessing in a number of local communities in the Russian North, in the Urals and Siberia, where some of these communities have degraded—the population has shrunk, houses and the municipal infrastructure have been destroyed. Such are twenty seven out of fifty-three "coercive" local communities from my list. This distortion—abundance of industrial, energy, and other resources, on the one hand, and a severe shortage of resources for daily existence, on the other hand—forces the population to resort extensively to specific economic practices, mainly informal, shadow, and criminal (see Chap. 6 on this).

Similarly, the territory of such communities is established arbitrarily and does not correlate with the availability and volume of resources for daily subsistence. Often, the actual area of the territory used (very relatively controlled by the community) is significantly smaller than that within the administrative boundaries. For a

[9]That is why most towns—centers of such coercively established communities—have currently received the status of *single-industry towns* characterized by narrow specialization of the local economy resulting in a tense and conflict-prone social situation.

community, where most or all members have highly specialized occupations, there is no need to control any large territory. The majority of households have no homesteads or gardens; they keep no livestock and do not engage in subsidiary farming; there are no hunting areas and no large private agricultural lands. The uninhabited territory is not controlled, since there are no or very few trades and crafts based on natural resources. Almost all households are completely dependent on wage income from employment with logging, fishing, hunting, energy, transport, or agricultural enterprises. Since for such communities the territory as a repository of resources used to have no vital importance, its boundaries were poorly controlled or even ignored by the inhabitants.

This situation with resources, size of the territory, and its boundaries existed in provincial local communities of the "coercive" type throughout the last decades of the Soviet period and in the first post-Soviet years. But from the mid-1990s it began changing quickly, because the people were forced to switch to autonomous livelihood economic practices. Now, many of the almost two dozen local communities with an initial resource "skew" in favor of government support were forced to start controlling both the natural resources and the borders of their territories (this is well illustrated by the communities Kavalerovo, Obluchye, Ochyor, Anabar, Vaygach, and Tura). However, they do not succeed as well as the "naturally developing" communities, which have traditionally and for ages controlled the natural resources on their territories. In particular, this triggers conflicts among the residents themselves, and between the residents and the authorities.

Space permeability in the territories of "coercive" communities can be very low because the initial settlements are established close to the developed natural resources, often located in hard-to-reach places (Anabar diamonds, Kavalerovo tin, Kachkanar vanadium, Tura feldspars, and Yeniseysk furs and timber). At the same time, in many other cases, space permeability can be quite high. Accordingly, the transport infrastructure is similarly skewed: the local road network is often undeveloped, with the main links being one or two roads of regional or republican significance (sometimes these are *ice roads*, i.e., routes that operate only in winter, for example, in Anabar or Krasnoshchelye).

The residential structure of a "coercive" community is generally represented by the administrative center—a settlement adjacent to the plant/factory and a few nearby villages of the rural district. However, their inhabitants, along with the residents of the central settlement, are employed at the same enterprise or its subdivisions (branches). Due to this, the rural district is represented by industrial townships rather than villages or farms—the population is engaged in industry and not in agriculture. Almost the entire population of the community is concentrated around the central settlement. Most of the territory remains uninhabited. In case of an outflow of population, it is the central settlement that becomes "escheat" and not the villages of the rural district. That is, the "decay" of the settlements starts from the "head" rather than the "tail" as in the case of naturally developing communities. Nowadays, communities of the Northern Urals, many of which were established as settlements at mining enterprises, show a striking contrast in the direction of this "decay"—from the "head" or from the "tail." Since the "decay" starts in the central settlement and its surroundings, in the immediate vicinity of the mine, mining enterprise or complex, the number and share of small "escheat" settlements-villages on the outskirts of such communities are substantially lower than in naturally developing ones.

Generally, all such settlements—not only the administrative center but also the rural district in the form of several industrial townships—initially have a well-developed utilities infrastructure. By this attribute, the "coercive" communities also differ from the "naturally developing" ones: there, the utilities infrastructure of the rural district is not developed, not centralized, and autonomous. However, in the course of the crisis, which many "coercive" settlements are currently experiencing, the infrastructure has been drastically, somewhere fatally, destroyed.

The administrative center (as well as its satellites, the industrial townships) mostly have a zonal (industrial) layout followed by a regular one. As I already mentioned, this is due to the fact that the settlement was built in the immediate vicinity of the industrial facilities. Since individual production units were initially distributed over a vast territory, the residential areas were linked to industrial zones and as a result ended up separated by large vacant lots, natural landmarks, or woodlands (e.g., Slavyanka and Zarubino in Khassan district, Primorye). When an industrial enterprise was built "in the open" and its neighboring villages grew and merged, thus creating a chaotic conglomerate of village streets, this also determined the street or zonal type of layout (e.g., Manturovo in Kostroma Region). When the central settlement was established simultaneously to extract resources, protect the territory, and perform administrative functions, its layout is regular, since such a central settlement was initially built according to an urban development plan (e.g., Zmeinogorsk, Rudny Altai). In some centers, different types of layouts emerged over time and were combined on the same territory.

5.5.2 *Naturally Developed Communities*

Such communities are of course much more numerous than the coercively developed ones, but in my records they constitute only two-thirds of the total, or 89 communities. In many respects, their territorial structures are characterized by different indicators. Generally, their territories have sufficient (though not always) resources for autonomous existence, for subsistence farming and informal economic activities (economic practices of the population) based on forest, river, and sea resources. In addition, many communities have vital resources other than natural, which are usually of two types: infrastructural (economic activities on roads, railways, pipelines, and other routes passing through the territory) and/or human resources (summer residents, vacationers, tourists, and labor migrants, for whose needs the local residents provide, thus earning an income).

Even if in ancient times the local communities classified as "naturally developed" were established coercively for the sole purpose of state defense (Buy, Verkhoturye, or Kasimov) or resource extraction (Maslyanino, Mezen, Osa, or Soligalich) or both

(Zmeinogorsk), over an extended period of natural historical development they also formed their livelihood resource base. In such communities, the size of the territory depends on the availability and volume of natural resources and the size of the agricultural landscapes, since their rural districts have long been self-sufficient. Most households, even in the central settlements, have homesteads and land for subsidiary farming. However, quite a few naturally developing communities have territories too small for autonomous existence due to the rapid growth of the local population; this is especially the case in the south of European Russia. Among the communities in my list, such is the situation in Anapa, Taman, and Temryuk (Krasnodar Territory), Gergebil (Dagestan), Khvalynsk (Saratov Region), and Uryupinsk (Volgograd Region).

Due to widespread economic activities based on natural resources, the local community controls the entire unpopulated area, which is often very small because of the intensive use of agricultural landscapes and an extremely high proportion of agricultural land (Uryupinsk). Sometimes, only such terrain is unpopulated, which is completely unsuitable for life (steep mountain slopes, mountain tundra, impassable swamps, and surrounding lakes).

Accordingly, the territorial borders are effectively controlled along their whole length. Moreover, the borders remain unchanged for a very long time, apparently, throughout the entire known existence of the local community. Isolated communities, independent of their "natural/coercive" development, have the most stable boundaries (see above). This is the information I have for most of the nearly forty isolated communities. In young communities, informal (i.e., non-administrative) borders with neighbors were established in the first decades of their existence. In ancient and old communities, as evidenced by chronicles and archive documents, the stability of borders has been maintained over the past five hundred years, which was facilitated by the administrative status attributed to them. The best picture is obtained by comparing pairs of neighboring communities, for example, Udora and Mezen, Kargopol and Pudozh, Kandalaksha and Umba, Staraya Russa and Demyansk, Voznesenye-Vokhma and Sharya, Uryupinsk and Novokhopyorsk, etc.

Space permeability is quite high, since transport routes have been developing for a long time, forming a rather dense network of local roads, including a large number of unregistered and "formally non-existent" ones. Almost any stretch of even hard-to-reach places (forests, swamps, mountains) has a network of tracks and pathways. In many cases—in Russian reality, of course—local communities are connected with their neighbors by no more than one or two roads or only by water or air; in some cases, the only link is an *ice road*, as, for example, in Kachug, Krasnoshchelye, or Udora.

The residential structure of "naturally developed" communities is well structured. The rural district is extensive with a large (dozens) or even very large (several hundred) number of settlements. However, among rural settlements, there is a considerable proportion of *"escheat"* ones, which are almost always old small villages on the outskirts of the territory (not in the center, as in the case of "coercively" developed communities). In ancient and old communities, sometimes half of all villages are "escheat," with the average figure reaching 40%. In young communities, their share is obviously lower, because the rural district had no time to "grow old." Unlike "coercive" communities, the "decay" of settlements in "naturally developed" communities starts from the "tail" rather than the "head." The administrative center is always surrounded by several—from one to two to a dozen—villages, quite thriving due to their proximity to the central settlement. In terms of homogeneous distribution of settlements across the territory, in "naturally developed" communities, the density gradient from the center to the outskirts is not as high as in "coercive" ones: in contrast to the latter, the former type has many villages on the outskirts. The territory is relatively evenly populated (as far as possible in the Russian province).

The central settlement almost always has the status of a town; rarely—the status of an "urban-type settlement" (there are only 10 villages among 89 administrative centers). The utilities infrastructure with centralized heating, water supply, and sewerage is usually developed only in the central settlement; most villages of the rural district have autonomous supply systems, especially since many of the old villages have already experienced one to two or several periods of "decay."

Since most administrative centers are towns, their layout is primarily either regular or radio-centric; less often it is zonal. Layouts of the street (village) type are rare; such urban planning is generally observed in young isolated communities formed in the late Imperial or Soviet time. I classified nine administrative centers as such, and they all developed from villages: Shipunovo, Maslyanino, Ust-Kan, Ulagan, Karaidel, Krasnoshchelye, Charyshskoye, Erzhey-Sizim, and Esso.

5.5.3 *Dissimilarities in the Territorial Structure of Coercively and Naturally Developed Communities*

I will present the main dissimilarities in the territorial structure of two types of communities in a concise tabular form (Table 5.2).

5.6 Types of Local Territories

We see that typological dissimilarities between communities stemming from the degree of their isolation and the coercive or natural manner of development produce a patchwork of territorial structures, especially given the large number of attributes. We shall try to develop a typology of local territories based on combinational logic.

For this purpose, I use a combination of two community typologies outlined in Chap. 4. The combination of community types by degree of spatial isolation and the manner of their emergence and development produces six (3 × 2) possible types of territorial structures. These are structures of (1) isolated natural, (2) isolated coercive, (3) "ordinary" natural, (4) "ordinary" coercive, (5) turbulent natural, and (6) turbulent

Table 5.2 The components of territorial structure of coercively and naturally developed communities

Attribute	Coercively developed communities	Naturally developed communities
Resources	The resource intensity of the territory is not essential for the existence of the population	The territory has sufficient resources for autonomous existence
	The principal resources of the territory are raw materials, energy, and industrial resources, which are originally not intended for everyday life	Sufficient quantity of natural resources, and also vital resources of other types: infrastructural and human
	Communities depend on replenishment of external resources for everyday life	Communities can exist autonomously
Size of the territory	The size of the territory is established arbitrarily and does not correlate with the availability and volume of resources for daily subsistence	The size of the territory correlates with volume of natural resources and the size of agricultural landscapes; rural districts are self-sufficient
	The actual used area is smaller than the territory within the administrative boundaries. Most of the territory is uninhabited	The used area corresponds to or exceeds the administrative territory
	The uninhabited territory is not controlled	Due to widespread economic activities based on natural resources, the entire unpopulated area is controlled
Borders	Inadequate border control	The territorial borders are effectively controlled along their entire length
Space permeability	The average space permeability is low, but in many cases can be high	High space permeability
Transport infrastructure	Skewed: the local road network is often undeveloped, with the main links being one or two roads of regional or republican significance	Well-developed: several roads of regional or republican significance pass through the territory
Residential structure	Represented by the center—a settlement adjacent to the plant/factory and a few nearby villages of the rural district	Rural district with a large (dozens) or even very large (several hundred) number of settlements
	Almost the entire population of the community is concentrated around the central settlement. The density gradient of the settlements from the center to the outskirts is high	The territory is relatively evenly populated. Many villages are located on the outskirts. The density gradient of the settlements from the center to the outskirts is low
	The rural district was formed later than the central settlement. It consists of industrial townships; the population is engaged in industry	The rural district was formed earlier than the central settlement. It consists of old villages; the population is engaged in agriculture
	"Decay" of the settlements starts from the "head" rather than the "tail." The central settlement becomes "escheat," not the villages of the rural district	"Decay" of the settlements starts from the periphery of the community. Almost always old small villages are affected

(continued)

Table 5.2 (continued)

Attribute	Coercively developed communities	Naturally developed communities
	Few "escheat" villages on the outskirts	The share of "escheat" villages reaches half of the entire rural district
Public utilities infrastructure	All settlements initially have a well-developed utilities infrastructure	The utilities infrastructure is developed only in the center; most villages of the rural district have autonomous supply systems
Layout of the administrative center	Zonal or regular	Regular and radial

coercive communities. By matching the descriptions of territorial structure elements provided in Sects. 5.3 and 5.4, we can differentiate each of the six types by a dozen categorical attributes. Many of the eight categories identified in Sect. 5.2 are similar or identical for particular types, but still every type has its distinctive features. Table 5.3 presents a reference list of communities differentiated by types of territorial structure.

I would like to stipulate once again that the territorial structure of "ordinary" communities is fairly similar or sometimes even identical to that of both isolated and "turbulent" communities, since in many cases the distance from their administrative centers to regional or other community centers is only several tens of kilometers rather than hundreds and thousands of kilometers as in isolated communities, but some of them exist in a natural environment that contributes to isolation due to climatic, environmental (agricultural), or infrastructural reasons. Besides, "ordinary" communities can have regional and local motor roads and railroads crossing their territory; what they don't have are highways and trunk railways. Therefore, being an intermediate type, "ordinary" communities have blurred boundaries. Accordingly, their territorial structure is often very similar to that of "turbulent" communities, whereas in quite a few cases it does not differ much from that of isolated communities. Substantially, based on the totality of specific features, we could regard many of these communities as subtypes of naturally developed "turbulent" communities or coercively developed isolated ones; however, formally, we should distinguish them as separate types (although Sect. 5.6 provides conditions for reducing "ordinary" communities to other types). Table 5.4 in Sect. 5.6 compares all six types of territorial structure by one and a half dozen indicators; I will refer to this table in the following description of the territory of each of the six types.

5.6.1 *The Territorial Structure of "Isolated Natural" Communities*

In many respects, such communities are the most convenient for analysis, since their center and borders are determined, the internal connections are relatively simple and

Table 5.3 Distribution of local communities into six types of territorial structure depending on their natural/coercive development and degree of isolation

	Nature of the community's development	
Type of isolation	Naturally historically formed $N = 89$	Coercively established $N = 53$
Isolated type $N = 41$	Cherdyn	Amurzet
	Chukhloma	Anabar
	Demyansk	Charyshskoye
	Erzhey-Sizim	Esso
	Gdov	Gunib
	Gergebil	Kurmach-Baigol
	Gorbatov	Leninskoye
	Kachug	Olga
	Karaidel	Preobrazhenie
	Kargopol	Sokolskoye
	Kologriv	Solovki
	Krasnoshchelye	Suzun
	Leshukonskoye	Tompo
	Mezen	Tura
	Onega	Ulagan
	Pudozh	Varnek (Vaygach)
	Soligalich	Verkhoturye
	Tara	
	Temnikov	
	Udora	
	Umba	
	Varnavino	
	Vetluga	
	Voznesenye-Vokhma	
"Ordinary" type $N = 66$	Ardatov	Aldan
	Belomorsk	Ardon
	Belozersk	Bolgar
	Bezhetsk	Chuna
	Borovichi	Digora
	Buy	Guryevsk
	Chistopol	Gus-Khrustalny
	Dmitrovsk-Orlovsky	Gusinoozersk
	Dorogobuzh	Iraf (Chikola)
	Galich	Kachkanar
	Gavrilov Posad	Kavalerovo
	Kamen-na-Obi	Khanka (Kamen-Rybolov)
	Kashin	Khasan (Slavyanka)
	Kasimov	Krasnoufimsk
	Khvalynsk	Kyakhta
	Kimry	Labinsk
	Kineshma	Neya
	Kirillov	Novokhopyorsk
	Kirzhach	Podporozhye
	Kozelsk	Zmeinogorsk
	Kozmodemyansk	
	Lyubim	
	Makaryev	

(continued)

Table 5.3 (continued)

	Nature of the community's development	
Type of isolation	Naturally historically formed $N = 89$	Coercively established $N = 53$
	Maslyanino Nerekhta Nikolsk Osa Porechye (Demidov) Poshekhonye Slobodskoy Staraya Russa Staritsa Surazh Suzdal Sysola (Viziga) Taldom Toropets Totma Tutayev-Romanov Uglich Uryupinsk Ust-Kan Veliky Ustyug Velizh Yeniseysk Yuriev-Polsky	
"Turbulent" type $N = 35$	Anapa Gavrilov-Yam Kandalaksha Kem Mayma Novozybkov Olonets Rostov Veliky Rzhev Sebezh Semyonov Taman Temryuk Vyshny Volochyok Yukhnov Zlynka Zubova Polyana Zubtsov	Alagir Bikin Birobidzan Bolshoy Kamen Chupa Iskitim Kizilyurt Manturovo Medvezhyegorsk Nerchinsk Nizhneudinsk Obluchye Ochyor Sharya Shipunovo Ust-Labinsk Zuyevka

visible, and the isolation from the outside world is considerable. Their territorial structure is no exception. It develops over a long period of time under the influence of mainly natural factors and without any significant impact from neighboring communities or the state.

Table 5.4 Demographic, territorial, and residential differences between six types of territorial structure of local communities, differentiated by criteria of spatial isolation and the natural/coercive manner of development

Indicator type Average figure	1 I/N $N = 24$	2 I/C $N = 14$	3 O/N $N = 44$	4 O/C $N = 21$	5 T/N $N = 17$	6 T/C $N = 16$
Population, ’000 people	13.9	10.9	34.1	36.7	44.5	45.8
Population of the administrative center, ’000 people	6.5	4.4	20.7	20.5	25.1	25.8
Size of the territory, km^2	12,060	19,005	5632	11,059	3009	7241
Population density, people/km^2	1.1	0.6	6.1	3.6	14.8	6.2
Population density of the rural district, people/km^2	0.5	0.3	2.4	1.4	6.4	2.7
Share of the population of the administrative center in total population, %	47	41	61	56	56	56
Proportion in the sample of administrative centers with the status of village, %	25	64	5	18	6	7
Share of rural population in the community, %	60	78	39	44	45	37
Number of officially existing settlements	105	20	220	46	154	61
Number of “live” settlements with >4 inhabitants	62	18	134	38	111	48
Number of “escheated” settlements with <5 inhabitants	43	2	86	8	43	13
Share of escheated settlements in relation to those recorded, %	41	9	39	17	28	24
Average number of inhabitants in one “live” rural settlement, people	122	306	101	406	165	431
Specific area of one settlement, km^2 per settlement	225	1284	50	317	27	159
Prevailing layout of the center, %	Street 54 Regular 33	Street 57 Zonal 43	Regular 68 Zonal 32	Zonal 50 Regular 36	Regular 47 Radial 29	Zonal 47 Regular 40

Average indicators are provided with the spread (range) shown below in the format of a ratio of the lower to the upper limit. Since the groups are small, and the spread of specific values is very large, it makes no sense to provide other statistics

I/N isolated communities of natural development; *I/C* isolated communities of coercive development; *O/N* “ordinary” communities of natural development; *O/C* “ordinary” communities of coercive development; *T/N* turbulent communities of natural development; *T/C* turbulent communities of coercive development

In total, I have described twenty-six communities with this type of territorial structure, of which thirteen are ancient, eight are old, and only five are young (cf.: Table 4.5). All isolated communities are strongly influenced by environmental and climatic factors, so in this and the following sections I will differentiate the description of territorial structures, distinguishing northern, temperate, and southern (where possible, due to scarce records) isolated communities according to Chap. 4, Sect. 4.1.

The "land" provides isolated communities with resources sufficient for autonomous existence. The rural district can exist autonomously for an indefinitely long period; moreover, the inhabitants of the administrative center also have the means to be self-sufficient. Almost all or absolutely all resources are natural. Households subsist primarily by using the resources of the forest and tundra, rivers, and the sea. Most households, even in the central settlements, have homesteads (private house with land) for subsidiary farming. However, the homestead is usually a secondary source of livelihood as compared to the use of natural resources.

The territories are large or very large. However, the size of the territory depends on (correlates with) the availability and volume of the required natural resources. Therefore, in northern communities areas reach tens of thousands of square kilometers (data on eleven northern communities: the average area is over 23,000 km^2). In the temperate zone of European Russia, in the Urals, and in southern Siberia, the territories of isolated communities are already by an order of magnitude smaller (data on twelve temperate communities: the average area is 2700 km^2). In the south of European Russia, territories are an order of magnitude smaller than in the temperate zone—less than 350 km^2 (data is available on only one isolated community—Gergebil in Dagestan; however, all of the remaining 16 surveyed southern communities have similarly tiny territories). Thus, between communities in Russia's Far North (Arctic) and extreme south, there is a thousand-fold difference in the size of the territory!

The population density in these communities is very low, often an order of magnitude lower than the average population density in Russia (which is about 8.6 people per km^2). Regardless of the latitude, the average size of the community is from ten to twenty thousand people (such are two-thirds of the communities of this type); in the North, the population density does not even reach one person per sq. km (0.9 people per km^2), whereas in the central part of the country it is half an order of magnitude higher (4.8 people per km^2) but still about half the average figure for Russia. In the south, the density is already tens (62.4) of people per km^2. However, the population density of the rural district (without the administrative center) is two to three times lower. In the rural district in the North it is 0.3 people per km^2, in the central part of the country 2.3 people per km^2, and in the south 46.2 people per km^2. The average population density in the rural district is 0.5 people per km^2.

In a rural district, the average number of inhabitants per village (excluding "escheat" settlements) is 122 people. And the average specific territory per "live" (inhabited, not escheated) settlement is 225 km^2. In the North, however, the average number of inhabitants per settlement (village) is higher, 146, and the controlled specific area is twice as large, 450 km^2, i.e., 3 km^2 of land per person. In the temperate zone, the number of inhabitants per settlement (village) is twice lower averaging 80 people,[10] and the specific area per rural settlement is by an order of magnitude smaller—only 35 km^2, or 0.44 km^2 of land per person. Data on the single isolated southern community show the reduction of the specific territory to 0.10 km^2 per person. Thus, every rural resident of an isolated naturally developed community has on average 2 km^2 (from 0.10 to 3 km^2) of land for subsistence purposes. Such average specific areas—large in the North and by an order of magnitude smaller in the mid-latitudes—allow each household to fully supply itself with natural resources, since the maximum required areas for this are from 1.5 km^2 in the North to 1.5 hectares in the south; see Plusnin (1997a, b).

Territorial borders are controlled by the male population of the community. The unpopulated territory, despite its huge size, is also controlled. Like in the past, the whole territory is nowadays divided into ancestral lands of indigenous local clans (small peoples of the North and indigenous Russians) or into lands rented by cooperatives and individual farmers. The institutional framework of territorial control is a wide network of various-purpose hunting lodges (*winter shelters, huts, cabins*), which are often "border posts." In these communities, the territorial borders in the most important areas remain unchanged for a very long time. My observations (Plusnin, 2006) show that some borders have been maintained for centuries by symbolic means. Thus, according to archival written sources (Cadastre, 1622), the present borders between the Udora and Mezen communities have existed for over four centuries (which the local residents also confirm, "*The stream behind Savva's house has been the boundary between Rodoma and Latyuga residents for ages*"). Similarly, hunting grounds on the borders between communities have been demarcated from time immemorial. For example, according to my field observations of different years, this is how boundaries were established between the residents of Lovozero and Krasnoshchelye in the Lovozero district of Murmansk Region (1990 observations) and between the inhabitants of Khangalassky and Namsky Districts in Yakutia (2011 observations).

In the North, and especially in the Arctic, communities have virtually no immediate neighbors in the form of settlements of other communities and often do not have and never had any hostile environment. (Clashes and confrontations sometimes happen on the borders of ancestral lands, but they are limited to conflicts of individual families and have no serious consequences.) Almost the same is true for most isolated communities in the temperate zone of European Russia and Siberia. At that, considerable parts of the territory do not adjoin the territories of neighboring communities and are separated from them by cold seas, the Arctic tundra, impassable

[10]The fact that settlements in isolated communities are more populated in high latitudes than in the mid-latitudes has environmental, historical, and political reasons: autonomous existence in the North requires communal efforts and constant mutual support of the households; here the migration of residents—most of whom are relatives—is very low, despite their very high spatial mobility. In isolated mid-latitude rural settlements, there has been an outflow of population over the past half century (mainly intraregional migration). In addition, it was here that the policy of "*eliminating depressed villages*" was carried out in the 1960s, which seriously harmed the entire non-black soil region.

swamps, forest tracts, and mountain ranges. Every single one of the twenty-four communities with this type of territorial structure has natural barriers along most of their borders. In spite of everything, the space permeability for local residents is high due to the fact that they have adapted traditional means of transport, use the entire territory for hunting and extraction of other resources, and local routes (transport communications) have for a long time formed and developed to meet special local needs. And although the density of transport infrastructure is low and the settlements are linked with the neighboring communities by only one or two roads or by ice roads, there are a lot of trails, paths, and unregistered and formally non-existent roads.

These routes help maintain close family and neighborly ties between people living at a distance of 1000–3000 km from each other in villages that have no direct transport communications. My 1991 observations in the Ust-Tsilma isolated community show that the residents of the central settlement Ust-Tsilma on the Pechora River (Komi Republic) maintain strong ties not only with relatives and friends in the city of Naryan-Mar (Nenets Autonomous District in the Arkhangelsk Region) 300 km away, but also with the inhabitants of Vananara and Chemdalsk villages in the Evenk Autonomous District of Krasnoyarsk Territory at a straight-line distance of 3000 km. For comparison I will provide absolutely similar observations that two Englishmen, William Gurdron of Hull and William Pursglov, recorded in 1611–1615 in the town of Pustozersk[11] (*Travelers trading. London, 1625, III and V*) and Alexander von Schrenck reproduced (von Schrenck, 1854). Trade contacts, friendly and family relations extended from Pustozersk to Ust-Tsilma on the Pechora River and Mangazeya (at the mouth of the Taz River near the Ob River), to Mezen, Kholmogory (now Arkhangelsk), and Kola (now Murmask).

The residential structure of northern isolated natural communities differs in several respects from that of the temperate and southern ones. What is common for all communities is that everywhere more people live in the rural district than in the administrative center. Historically, villages are numerous both in the north (on average 77 per community; spread from 3 to 244) and in the temperate zone (138; spread from 4 to 328). But they are traditionally few in the south. Although the number of villages in the north is half that of the temperate zone, the population of certain northern rural settlements is almost twice as high as in mid-latitude communities (147 and 80 people, respectively). However, both in the north and in the central part of Russia, the share of escheat settlements is high (32% and 46%, respectively). Numerous escheated villages in all provincial local communities, except the southern ones, result from several factors, the main one being the 1960's policy of "eliminating depressed villages." Besides that, in the pre-crisis 1970s–1980s and the crisis 1990s–2000s decades, the rural population was steadily drawn to the center of their community. This trend is still valid, but in the north it is

[11] An Arctic town that was located on the Pechora River just 40 km upstream from the present Naryan-Mar. By the twentieth century it had disappeared, but in the seventeenth and eighteenth centuries its administrative and economic significance was great.

more pronounced; therefore, the administrative center in the north has twice as many inhabitants as towns in the temperate zone (8800 and 4500 people, respectively). But these latter are also affected by migration to the regional center. The number of "live" villages in the north averages 52 (from 3 to 118), and in the temperate zone 75 (from 4 to 186). In considerable isolation in the Far North and in the Arctic, the average number of settlements is just two (usually, from one to four); all isolated Arctic local communities are like that.

The utilities infrastructure, not only in the villages, but also often in the administrative center is generally undeveloped. Water supply, sewerage, and heating are predominantly autonomous. The administrative center itself most often has the status of a village or settlement rather than a town (54% are villages—13 out of 24; the remaining 11 are urban-type settlements that differ little from industrial townships). Accordingly, farmstead development prevails everywhere in the "localities." As a result, more than half of the administrative centers have a street (village) layout. In one-third of the cases, but only in towns, the layout is regular. Therefore, many public functions in such centers, especially those with the status of village or settlement, are partially reduced (most government institutions are inter-district—one institution per several neighboring districts—and therefore are not represented in every administrative center). The cultural and religious functions of these centers are reduced even more.

The territorial structure of three out of twenty-four local communities of this type—Cherdyn, Pudozh, and Varnavino—most closely matches the totality of average group parameters. Therefore, as a sample territorial structure of an isolated community of natural development I present the schematic map of Cherdyn, since it is closest to the "average picture." At the same time this community qualifies as northern and Ural, thus occupying an intermediate position between the European and Siberian communities (Fig. 5.1).

We can see that the territorial structure of the Cherdyn local community is closely linked and determined by the river network. Almost all 99 settlements are located on the banks of four rivers—Kama, Vishera, Kolva, and Berezovaya. It is on these rivers that the main food resources are concentrated, and from time immemorial they have also been the main transport routes. Most of the currently "escheated" settlements (29 of them) are either located along small rivers in the taiga, where food resources are insufficient to meet the needs of all inhabitants, or were assimilated by nearby larger settlements. The population exceeds 100 people in only 29 settlements. Of these, five have over 500 residents, and another six over 1000 residents. These 11 largest settlements attract all the remaining ones, but their local territories are much smaller than those of the remote little villages. Here, as elsewhere, works the pattern of "the larger the settlement, the relatively smaller the territory," since the large settlements have additional resources for livelihood. All roads run along major rivers on river terraces; the neighboring communities (Krasnovishersk, Solikamsk, Berezniki, and Perm) are accessible by a single road (westwards, there is also a rarely used route along the Kama River and ice roads; northwards and eastwards, there are no roads at all). Many settlements, including most of the large ones, and three-quarters of the entire population—over 16,000 of the 20,000 inhabitants—are

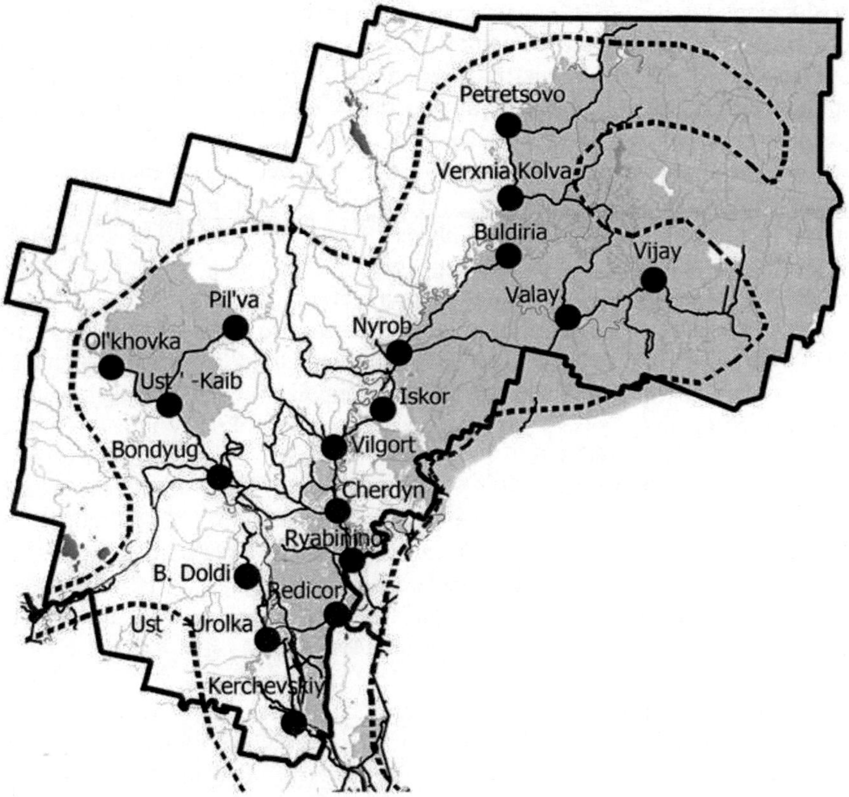

Fig. 5.1 The territorial structure of the Cherdyn local community. Hereinafter, the solid thin line shows the administrative borders of the district and the dashed line marks the approximate boundaries of the territory controlled by the local community, which are not identical to the administrative borders

concentrated along this motor road, the only link the local community has with "the big wide world."

5.6.2 *The Territorial Structure of "Isolated Coercive" Communities*

There are 15 such communities in my sample. Among them there are no ancient ones, as in the case of isolated communities of natural development, where they are in the majority. Here, on the contrary, most communities are young, formed only 150 or less years ago. Therefore, the history of their coercive emergence is well known, recorded in writing and in some places still remembered by the inhabitants. Latitudinal differences in the territorial structure of these communities are also considerable; they are even greater than in the previous case. The sample contains six northern (including Arctic) communities, eight temperate ones, and only one southern community. There are no longitudinal distinctions, since almost all communities are located in the Urals and Siberia. Therefore, many primary territorial dissimilarities these communities have with the previous type stem precisely from their location in the west or east of the country: in particular, larger territory and low population density; few settlements and a small proportion of "escheated" ones among them; number of inhabitants in one settlement; and the specific area per settlement. More important structural differences pertaining to transport, utilities, and residential infrastructure are not determined by regional factors.

The average size of the territory is the largest compared to all other types (19,000 km^2—a 100 × 190 km rectangle), and variability is considerable (1:200). At the same time, the size of the same local population is the smallest and, as a consequence, the density is very low—one or two orders of magnitude lower than in other types of communities (0.6 people per km^2). Most of the territory remains uninhabited. The resource intensity of the territory did not matter at the establishment of the communities, so they have very limited means for everyday autonomous existence and in most cases depend on external supplies ("northern deliveries" or in the mid-latitudes widespread social welfare, almost identical to "deliveries"). In all cases, the initial settlements, which later became administrative centers, were established at the development sites of natural resources, often located in hard-to-reach places. Therefore, the permeability of the space is low.

The transport infrastructure is skewed: the local road network is often undeveloped, with the main links being one or two roads of regional or republican significance. The territory has few transport routes of poor quality, and the infrastructure density is low. Many communities have virtually no neighbors; there is no borders control or protection. Hunting and ancestral lands exist, but unlike naturally developed communities, there are constant conflicts at the boundaries of these lands between inhabitants of neighboring communities. Thus, I have recorded conflicts over ancestral lands along the Popigai River between residents of Yuryung-Khaya village in the Anabar Ulus (District) of Yakutia and inhabitants of the Khatanga rural municipality in the Taimyr Autonomous District of the Krasnoyarsk Territory (2011 observations). In Kamchatka, residents of the Bystrinsky and Tigilsky Districts are also constantly disputing over their ancestral lands (1984 and 2010–2011 observations). Even within one community persistent conflicts over land are quite common.

The boundaries of all communities without exception, both northern and temperate, are determined either by natural obstacles unsuitable for habitation (sea, major river, vast tundra, taiga, or swamps), or by the boundaries of wildlife sanctuaries, closed areas, or state borders, and in half of all cases by both. Therefore, the borders are either physically impassable or the territory adjacent to them may not be used. This is an additional reason why in many cases the residents do not use their entire territory. But the main reason for not using the territory is the specific livelihood of such communities—they initially depended and still depend on the state.

The residential structure is represented by the administrative center—a settlement adjacent to the plant/factory (the main enterprise itself is now often closed down) and a few nearby villages of the rural district. Compared with other types of communities, the rural district here has the smallest number of settlements (on average 20) and almost no "escheat" villages (on average two). This is understandable, since such communities were affected neither by the elimination of "depressed villages" nor by migration of villagers to the administrative center: the settlements were initially factory townships. The settlements of the district are concentrated around the center, and like the center are highly specialized. Due to this, the population is hardly self-sufficient, and almost the entire rural district, along with the center, depends on replenishment of external resources for everyday life. In critical situations such communities face the threat of physical death. Currently some of these communities have degraded—the population has shrunk, houses and the municipal infrastructure have been destroyed. The administrative center has either a street or zonal layout, since usually (in two-thirds of the cases) it is not a town but a village or urban-type settlement with a limited scope of public administration functions. An important feature of most coercive communities is the initial establishment of the central settlement and the secondary nature of the rural district, which determines the specified changes in the territorial structure.

The northern communities (six were surveyed in detail) are all very scarcely populated; the average number of inhabitants is under 1500, of which about a thousand (from 100 to 2000 people) in the administrative center. Almost everyone lives in one or two (maximum three) closely located settlements; there are no "escheat" villages. The population is concentrated in the administrative center (over three quarters of all residents). All communities depend on external support: about 80–90% of adults receive various social benefits. The territory is very large with an average area of 42,000 km^2; the population density does not even reach 0.15 people per km^2. The specific area per one inhabited settlement exceeds 20,000 km^2—a vast partially uncontrolled expanse. The specific area per person is about 30 km^2; however, not all the territory is monitored on a regular basis, as is the case in northern communities of the first type. Meanwhile, due to resource abundance, these communities can be fully autonomous; in every community there are people—somewhere more, somewhere less—who implement the strategy of self-sufficiency through economic activities based on natural resources. But against their backdrop, there are always a lot more households entirely dependent on government support; without it, such households are doomed.

Compared to northern communities, the temperate ones (ten of them) are by an order of magnitude larger in terms of population (15,000 inhabitants on average), but much smaller in territory—slightly over 5000 km^2. Respectively, the population density averages 3.3 people per km^2, which is 20-fold higher than in the northern communities. Accordingly, there are more settlements in the rural district here, although they are still very few compared to other types of territorial structure; "escheat" villages are very rare (due to the above-mentioned geographical factor—all the communities are located in the Urals and Siberia). The overwhelming majority of settlements are concentrated around the administrative center (an average of 25 settlements and 3 escheat ones, which is three-fold and 20-fold less than the respective indicators for similar temperate isolated naturally developed

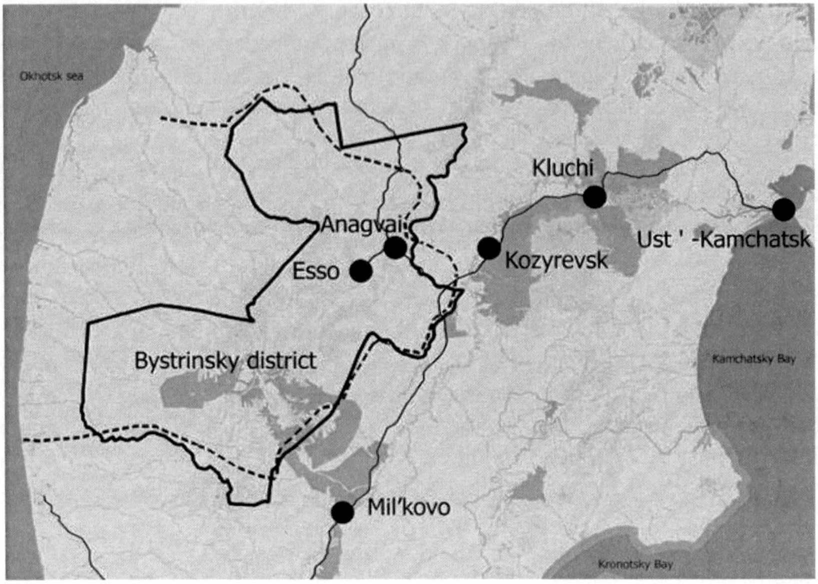

Fig. 5.2 The territorial structure of Esso northern coercive isolated local community (Bystrinsky district, Kamchatka)

communities). The transport network is fairly well developed within the territory, but the neighboring communities and the regional center can be reached only by a single road or by air, rarely by sea. The utilities infrastructure and the layout of the centers do not differ from the northern communities.

Of the southern isolated communities, there is only one (Gunib in Dagestan, once established as a military fortification), but its territorial structure is no different from that of the neighboring Gergebil community or from other communities of the North Caucasus, in North Ossetia.

Since the territorial structures of northern and temperate communities differ considerably, I have chosen two opposite examples: Esso in Kamchatka and two neighboring communities—Amurzet and Leninskoye—on the Middle Amur. The territorial structure of Esso community is extremely simple (Fig. 5.2). An only road connects the two settlements with the neighboring districts and the regional center. However, there are trails and ice roads linking the community with the eastern coast of the Sea of Okhotsk and Tigil and Sobolevo villages located there. The entire population lives on the banks of the Bystraya River, a tributary of the Kamchatka River. The inhabited territory is very small; the developed one is much larger and extends beyond the boundaries of the Bystrinsky district. Essential parts of the territory, if they are not protected areas (like the Bystrinsky Nature Park, which is located in the district), are divided between families and clans. There are seasonal camps and hunting cabins on those lands. The entire livelihood system is geographically linked to rivers. The mountains and tundra are used for roaming with reindeer and horses.

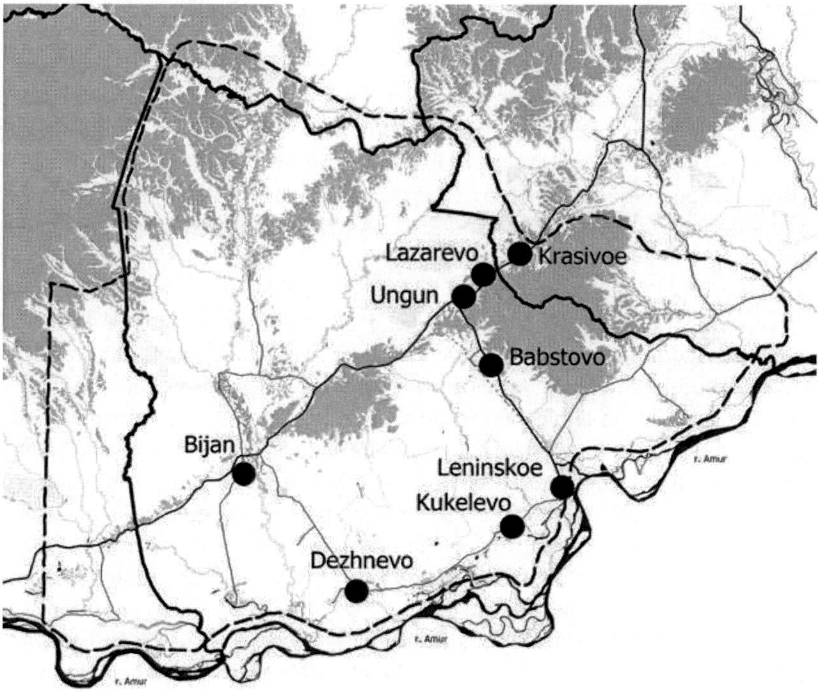

Fig. 5.3 The territorial structure of Leninskoye temperate coercive isolated local communities (Jewish Autonomous Region, Middle Amur)

The territorial structure of two neighboring local communities in the Leninsky and Sovetsky districts of the Jewish Autonomous Region is almost identical (Fig. 5.3 presented Leninsky district only). They were established according to one scenario and under the same conditions. They are also linked with the center by a single road, and their borders are formed by the swamps of the Middle Amur lowlands, the taiga-covered highlands of Lesser Khingan, and the Amur River bordering China. The few existing settlements have a different and recent history of establishment; all stand on two ring roads that connect most of the settlements; some are situated in dead ends in the taiga or along the Amur. A large part of the population is concentrated in the administrative centers (with the exception of settlements with military units), where border crossings to China are located. The inhabited space is small, along the roads; the permeability of space is also low due to numerous swamps, mountain taiga areas, and the state border. The Amur River has been withdrawn from economic use by the population. Only a small part of the population lives off natural resources; the majority depend on agricultural production and government support (public sector employees and military personnel).

5.6.3 The Territorial Structure of "Turbulent Natural" Communities

By all principal parameters, the territorial structure of turbulent communities differs significantly—manifold and by an order of magnitude—from that of isolated communities, irrespective of their type of development—natural or coercive. This is the main typological difference between local communities, differentiated by the degree of their spatial isolation. Eighteen such communities are described, of them only three are northern, three southern, and 12 temperate. The vast majority of them, with one exception, are located in the European part of Russia (see Table 5.3). This distinguishes them both from the totality of coercive isolated communities depicted above and from the following type of coercive turbulent communities, half of which are located in the Urals and Siberia, and the remaining half in European Russia.

In this type of community, agricultural landscapes, residential areas, and industrial zones prevail among the land categories. The share of other land categories is small; forests of federal significance are especially few. There is little land, which is in reserve, idle, or withdrawn from economic use. All of these features are characteristic of the old-developed areas of the country, where all the communities of this type are located. At the same time, the population engages in extensive economic practices based on natural resources. True, these resources are generally available, and people are engaged not in commercial hunting for wild animals and game, but in fishing, gathering wild plants, herbs, and so forth. Often, the products of such activities are intended for sale rather than consumption. There are plenty resources other than natural. These are usually infrastructural and/or human resources, which are also used to generate additional income.

The territory is the smallest compared to all other types of communities averaging about 3000 km^2 (a 100 × 30 km rectangle); the spread of values is relatively narrow (100-fold)—from 147 km^2 in the south (Taman) to 14,410 km^2 in the north (Kandalaksha). The territory is quite densely populated. The number of inhabitants ranges from 11,700 to 116,400 people averaging 44,500 people. The population density is moderately high. The average figure is 15 people/km^2, with the minimum of 2.4 people/km^2 in the north, the maximum of 72.8 people/km^2 in the south, and 18.5 people/km^2 in the temperate zone. At the same time, the population density of the rural district is two to three times lower—about 6 people/km^2, since more than half of the population (56%) lives in the administrative center. Meanwhile, the density gradient from the center to the outskirts is not as high as in "coercive turbulent" communities, let alone isolated ones. Quite a few villages are located on the outskirts. Thus, the territory is relatively evenly populated.

The specific load on the territory is substantial; in the south it is even exorbitant for self-sufficiency. The average area per one "live" rural settlement is 27 km^2; given the average population—165 residents per settlement—the specific area per person in the rural district is 16 ha (substantially less in the south—less than 3 ha). At first glance, this is a large specific area, but we should bear in mind that in the south substantial areas of agricultural landscapes belong to major holdings, and in the temperate zone of European Russia they have been withdrawn from farming and have not been cultivated for three decades. The inhabitants of the rural districts have been self-sufficient for a long time. Most households, even in the central settlements, have homesteads and land for subsidiary farming.

Territorial borders are determined, documented, and controlled. Space permeability is quite high. There are a variety of transport routes; one to two or more thoroughfares cross the territory. The transport infrastructure is well developed; there is a dense network of local roads, including many unregistered and formally non-existent ones. Transport communications have been forming and developing for a long time.

The settlement structure is developed and includes numerous villages of the rural district—from several dozen to several hundred—averaging 154 registered rural settlements per local community. However, the share of "escheat" villages among them is quite high (on average 43 settlements, or 28%), and they are almost always old small villages. The administrative center is always surrounded by several—from one to two to a dozen—villages, quite thriving due to their proximity to the central settlement. The share of the rural district is small—45%.

The utilities infrastructure is usually developed only in the central settlement. Most villages of the rural district have autonomous supply systems.

The central settlement almost always has the status of a town, which it received back in the Imperial or even earlier times. The administrative center is sometimes represented by two levels: the rural municipality and the district. Only "turbulent" communities can have a three-tier territorial structure. The main social, cultural, and religious functions are represented in the center in full scope. The local economy is usually well developed; every center has several medium-sized or even large enterprises. The layout of the administrative centers is predominantly Hippodamus grid (47%) or ancient radio-centric (29%).

The local community of Rostov Veliky, one of the most ancient Russian cities, provides the most common example of this type of territorial structure (Fig. 5.4). Two major thoroughfares cross the territory: the M8 Kholmogory Highway and the Trans-Siberian Railway. Accordingly, the entire territorial structure is determined by these means of communication. Especially since there are no large rivers in the area and river traffic was never an issue, and lake Nero, which used to play an important role in the economy of the region, has now lost all commercial significance and remains but a source of fish for the locals. The residential structure is fully associated with the thoroughfares. A significant part of the population is concentrated in those settlements that are in close proximity to the highway and railway. There are a very large number of villages (308) with an average of 168 inhabitants. The numerous (114) escheat settlements are all located on the outskirts. There are a lot of local small and unaccounted roads, many of which are unpaved.

Fig. 5.4 The territorial structure of temperate turbulent communities of natural development on the example of Rostov Veliky

5.6.4 The Territorial Structure of "Turbulent Coercive" Communities

The territory of coercive turbulent communities—there are 17 of them—differs from that of any isolated community in the same way as the territory of naturally developed turbulent communities. Nearly all the specified features of the structure are different.

Within the turbulent type, communities of natural and coercive development have the following territorial dissimilarities. The areas of the latter are double or triple those of the former, with a five-fold greater variation in size. At the same time, the average population density is higher, but the variation in density is also higher. The differences are most pronounced in the territorial structure of the rural district. The rural district accounts for one-third rather than half of the population. The number of registered settlements (villages) is relatively small—an average of 60 (ranging from 3 to 181). The number of escheated settlements is also small—as, indeed, in all coercive communities—and averages 13 villages. However, almost half of the communities have only one to three escheated villages or even none at all. Accordingly, the population density of the rural district is half that of the previous case (less than 3 people/km^2), whereas the specific area per one rural settlement is five-fold larger (an average of 160 km^2/settlement). The average population of the villages is identical (159 people per settlement).

The reasons for such differences in the territorial structure of the rural district (but not the central settlements) are obvious. Of all the surveyed turbulent communities, half of the coercive ones (eight out of 17) are located in Siberia and the Far East, whereas only one of the 18 naturally developed ones is situated in the east of the country. In Siberia, the rural district has always been less populated than in European Russia, and due to the vast expanses, the population density has been lower. At the same time, it is obvious that a lot more communities were formed coercively by the state in the east of the country than in its central part. In this sense, it seems incorrect to compare these two types of territorial structures in terms of homogeneous data array. But considering the situation from an all-Russian perspective, we must recognize that territorial differences are typological in nature, regardless of their external causes (primarily geographic). This applies not only to turbulent communities, but also to isolated and "ordinary" ones.

The territory has fewer resources for autonomous existence than in the case of coercive isolated communities. Since basic natural resources are those near which and for the sake of which the initial settlement was established as the current community center, and because the transport infrastructure is well developed here (in contrast to isolated settlements), most households have no homesteads, do not engage in subsidiary farming or have just small kitchen gardens, live in urban-type apartments, and largely depend on wages from employment at enterprises. In a crisis and recession, many households start using infrastructural resources as an informal primary source of livelihood. It is in such communities, mainly in their central towns, that post-archaic forms of economic behavior—"scattered manufactories" and "garage economy" (see Chap. 7)—have developed. In fact, this informal economic activity of the population is a constant source of external resources for everyday life.

Since the territory is initially established arbitrarily and does not correlate with the availability and volume of resources for daily subsistence, its size substantially exceeds that of naturally developed turbulent communities. Although compared to other coercive communities, the territory of turbulent ones is only half or one-third in area.

Another feature is that communities have no need to control their territory or borders. There are least two reasons for this: the availability of several types of resources other than natural and a critically large number of "outsiders," flow-through migrants that pass through the territory (see Chap. 9 on this). In this respect, among the six types of territorial structures, communities of this type are least capable of controlling and protecting their borders. Therefore, unlike other types, borders here are administrative, i.e., a purely formal.

Space permeability is generally high, but since many of the communities are located in Siberia, a considerable part of the territory remains uninhabited. The very uneven distribution of the population distinguishes coercive turbulent communities from the naturally developed ones. The transport as well as residential and municipal infrastructure are developed better than in any other type of community. In this respect, the distinction from the naturally developed turbulent communities is due to the difference in age: the described communities are young, and their infrastructure was shaped in the Soviet period. However, over the past 30 years, it is precisely in such communities that the utilities infrastructure of many central settlements has been completely destroyed, since many of these settlements are single-industry towns, and the local backbone enterprises were the first to take the strongest hit during the crisis. And the entire utilities infrastructure depended on them.

The administrative center performs a full scope of functions and concentrates on almost the entire local official and social activity. Therefore, the rural district is reduced, and its population is drawn to the center. Predictably, half of the administrative centers have a zonal (industrial) layout, and the other half a regular one. Both layouts are common precisely for coercively established communities.

To illustrate this type of territorial structure, I chose the community of Iskitim in Siberia, which is the southern suburb of Novosibirsk and forms a single urban agglomeration with it (Fig. 5.5). Two major thoroughfares pass through the district: the R256 *Chuysky Tract* highway leading to Mongolia and further to China and the trunk railway to Barnaul and further to the post-Soviet Central Asian states. Thus, Iskitim is located on international routes, which facilitate not only trade relations, but also a substantial flow of cross-border migrants (migrant workers) from Central Asia to Siberia, and, in addition, a very intense criminal traffic of drugs and weapons, as well as smuggled exotic and everyday goods. Quarries and mines of such important raw materials as anthracite coals, gold, marble, and limestone for the production of high-quality cement are situated in the immediate vicinity of the thoroughfares. Respective processing plants are also nearby. There are considerable reserves of commercial timber and agricultural production is well developed (there are agricultural holdings for the production of grain, meat, and eggs). The district has road links with the neighboring districts and agricultural holdings, as well as access to the Ob Reservoir, the banks of which, covered with *ribbon-like* pine forests, are a recreational (tourist) area that provides considerable additional resources for the local economy and population. The population is, therefore, large—117,000 inhabitants, with over half living in the rural area. However, up to 80% of the entire population is

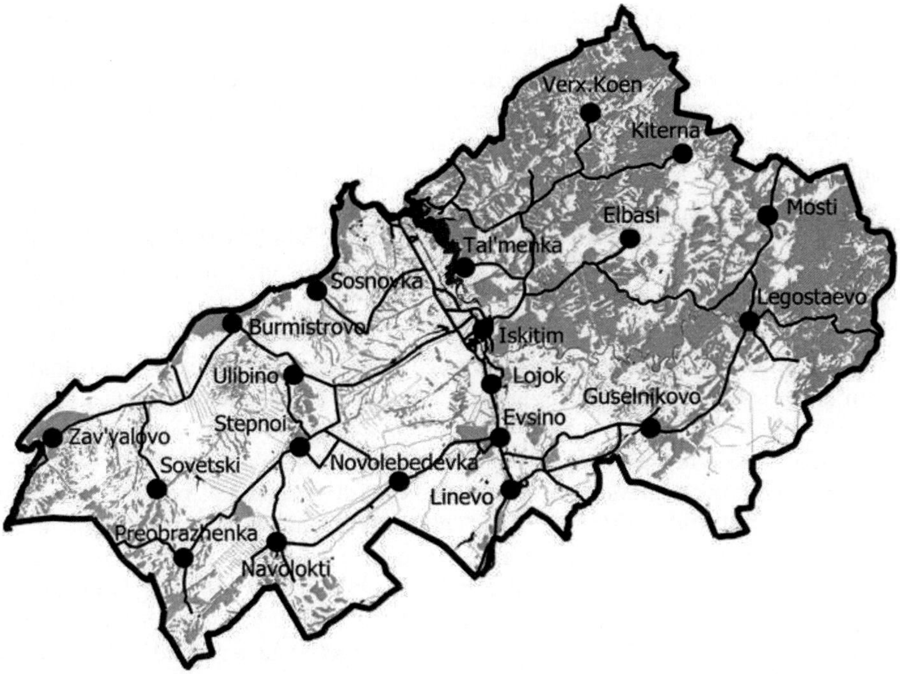

Fig. 5.5 The territorial structure of temperate turbulent communities of coercive development on the example of Iskitim

concentrated along the thoroughfares and is engaged in industrial production, in factories, mines, pits, and quarries. The territorial impact of the local community (in terms of informal economic activity of the population) extends beyond the administrative borders to Kamen-na-Obi and Suzun (to the pine and ribbon-like forests) in the south-west and south and to the Novosibirsk–Leninsk-Kuznetsky highway and the forests of the Salair Ridge on the borders of the Kemerovo Region in the east.

5.6.5 The Territorial Structure of "Ordinary Natural" Communities

The communities, which I classify as "ordinary," are the most numerous—twice the number of turbulent or isolated ones (66 altogether). However, the variability of their territorial structure is lower. And within the common type, dissimilarities between the natural and coercive communities are similar to those between isolated and turbulent communities. Actually, the "ordinary natural" communities are territorially closer to "turbulent natural" communities, and "ordinary coercive" ones—to "turbulent coercive" ones (see Table 5.4). Since in all the selected attributes of the territorial structure "ordinary" communities occupy an intermediate position between two extreme types, I will review them briefly.

I have described a total of 45 "ordinary natural" communities. Most of them are temperate communities of the European part of Russia (32). Only four are located in the Urals and Siberia, seven are northern, and two are southern. For this reason, their territorial structure is relatively homogeneous, although, of course, there are certain latitudinal differences. The average size of the territory is about 5600 km^2 (a 100 × 56 km rectangle) with a population of about 34,000 people and population density of less than 15 people per km^2. In the northern communities, the territory is about 50% larger (7600 km^2), the population is smaller (about 22,000 people), and the density is significantly lower (3 people/km^2). In the south, as elsewhere, the size of the territory is one-third of the average (2700 km^2), coinciding with that of naturally developed turbulent communities, but the population is small (about 44,000 people), and accordingly, the density is on the average level (15 people/ km^2). The spread between the minimum and maximum values is insignificant.

Since these communities are ancient and old, their territorial borders in general coincide with the administrative ones. The resources are diverse and sufficient for self-reliance—household incomes are generated not only by natural, but also by infrastructural resources. Everywhere the population is actively engaged in subsidiary farming. Transport communications are developed to the extent that is the usual "norm" for Russia in its European part. Generally, from one to several regional roads and one local railroad cross the territory of such communities in one direction only. Several low-quality intra-district (municipal) roads (unpaved or poorly paved) link the numerous rural settlements with each other and with the administrative center. Communities have on average 220 villages of various sizes with a very high proportion of "escheat" ones (39%, an average of 90 uninhabited villages per community). Among the six territorial types, communities of this type have the greatest number of villages in general, and "escheat" ones in particular. Thus, the rural district is most evenly populated; the density gradient from the center to the outskirts is the lowest; the density is less than 2.5 people per km^2, which is close to the density of the rural population on the European plain of Russia. The specific area per rural settlement averages 50 km^2; given the low average population per village (about 100 person), this produces a 0.5 km^2 specific area per person, which is more than enough for self-sufficiency in the temperate zone of European Russia.

The structure of the rural district in the north and the south differs; temperate communities occupy an intermediate position. Northern communities have four times as many villages as the southern ones (260 against less than 70), but they also have a lot more "escheat" villages (a 16-fold difference—80 against 5, respectively). These dissimilarities have a historical explanation. In the north there are many old villages with a *"clustered"* structure (rural communities, *"mirs"*), which in the Soviet years fell under the program of "eliminating depressed villages." In the south, relatively large villages and stanitsas on widely cultivated fertile lands always have more inhabitants concentrated in a few settlements.

The administrative center of such communities is almost always a town, with only one exception (Ust-Kan in the Altai Mountains). All centers are towns, and in

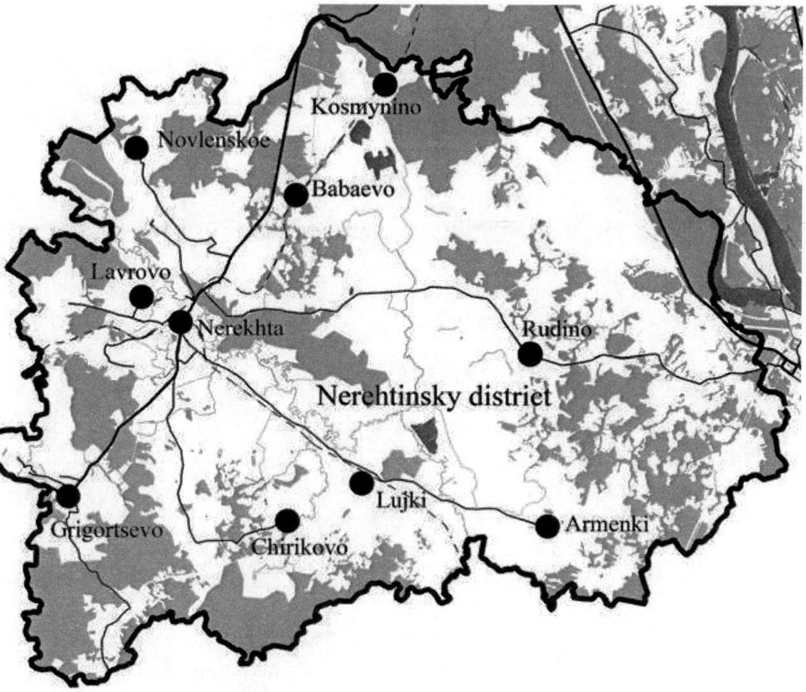

Fig. 5.6 The territorial structure of temperate "ordinary" communities of natural development on the example of Nerekhta

Imperial times they were all district towns. In the Soviet years they also became local industrial centers. This history is reflected in their layout: in two-thirds of the cases it is of the original regular type, and in the remaining cases the initial layout was subsequently replaced by a zonal industrial one. Therefore, in half of the cases (57%), these towns have a mixed layout, where the regular and zonal types are both present.

I will describe two common cases of this type of territorial structure on the examples of the Nerekhta temperate ancient community (Fig. 5.6) and the Uryupinsk southern old community (Fig. 5.7). The Nerekhta community is located between three regional centers—Yaroslavl, Kostroma, and Ivanovo; respectively, between the M8 Kholmogory Highway and three regional motor ways that do not actually cross its territory. One major road passes through the district connecting Nerekhta with Kostroma and exiting on the M8 on the other side. Another road links Nerekhta with the industrial town of Volgorechensk on the Volga River. All other roads are local and mostly unpaved. A regional railroad from Moscow to Kostroma crosses the district from south to north running just three long-distance passenger and three suburban trains a day. There are no major water bodies, and, respectively, no water-borne traffic. The territory is mostly an agricultural landscape, with small swampy woodlands left only because they are unsuitable for farming. The rural district is

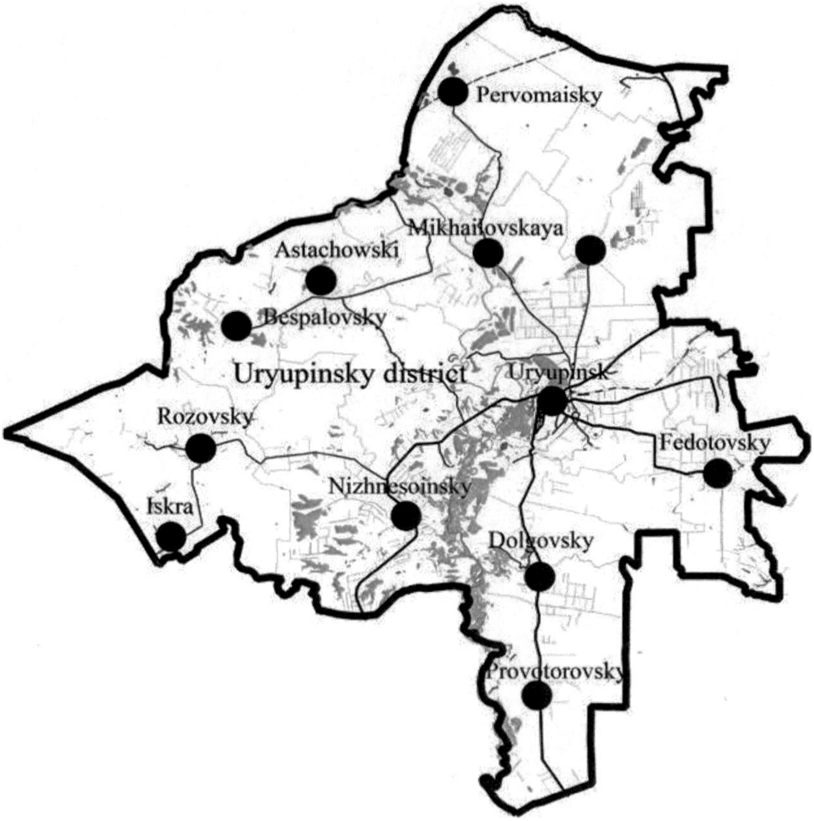

Fig. 5.7 The territorial structure of temperate "ordinary" communities of natural development on the example of southern communities Uryupinsk

represented by 161 settlements, but 59 of them (over a third) are "escheat" villages. There are seven large settlements with over five hundred residents each, but only two of them have a population exceeding one thousand people. As the district is surrounded by large cities, its territory is fairly evenly populated. This is a typical agricultural area, with a relatively high density of the rural population (10.3 people/km^2), a small territory (1140 km^2), and no large industry.

The Uryupinsk local community is located in the south of European Russia (Volgograd Region) in forest-steppe zone. Almost all the territory is agricultural land, black soil, so the local economy is based on agriculture. The Khopyor River crosses the territory from north to south. It used to be navigable and very important for the economy, but now it has lost all its functions except the recreational one. The M6 Caspian Highway (E119) runs along the eastern border of the district. But only one intraregional road branching off in Uryupinsk crosses the territory of the district. All other roads are local and connect the centers of municipal rural settlements. The railway is a dead end and has not been used for passenger carriage for a long time.

The rural district is quite evenly distributed across the area; the average density is 7.7 people per km^2. The number of rural settlements is relatively low (97), with very few "escheat" ones (5), but most of these settlements are sparsely populated farms. The main population lives in 20 stanitsas with over five hundred residents each; of them, only eight have a population from one to three thousand people. Since up to 90% of the entire territory is occupied by large agricultural enterprises and holdings, the population's self-sufficiency is based not on economic practices related to natural resources, but on income from personal subsidiary farms and on a special kind of informal economic activity—"scattered manufactory" for the artisanal production of knitwear from goat underwool (see Chap. 7).

5.6.6 The Territorial Structure of "Ordinary Coercive" Communities

The structure of "ordinary coercive" communities is closer to "isolate coercive" type (see Table 5.4). As with all coercive communities, the number of surveyed eastern communities exceeds that of European ones: the sample contains ten Siberian, two Ural, and only nine European communities. This determines the above-mentioned features of the territory's primary structure—its size, population density, number of settlements, and specific areas. In addition, this group contains quite a few both northern and southern communities (four and eight, respectively), which determined significant variability in area and population density. A combination of latitudinal and longitudinal differences predetermined the diversity of territorial structures of these types of communities. Therefore, I present several diagrams of the territorial structure in Figs. 5.8, 5.9, and 5.10.

The average population is 38,000 people, of which about 21,000 reside in the administrative center. In this respect, there is no difference between northern, temperate, and southern communities, as well as between European, Ural, and Siberian ones. The dissimilarities are in the size of the territory, the population density, and the composition and structure of the rural district. With an average area of 11,600 km^2 (a 100 × 116 km rectangle), the territory of northern communities, as well as Siberian and Ural ones, is by an order of magnitude larger than that of temperate and southern ones (48,000 km^2 and 17,000 km^2 against 2600 km^2, respectively). Population density varies accordingly: with the average figure amounting 3 people per km^2, in the north it is on the level of 0.8; in Siberia and the Urals 2.0; whereas in the mid-latitudes, the south and in European Russia in general, the population density varies from 11 to 15 people per km^2.

Since the administrative centers have approximately the same number of residents everywhere, the population density of the rural district (1.4 people/km^2) varies more. In northern communities it is 0.3 people per km^2, and in the temperate and southern ones 20 times higher (5–6 people/km^2). There are similar differences between Ural and Siberian and European communities (0.8 people/km^2 in the former

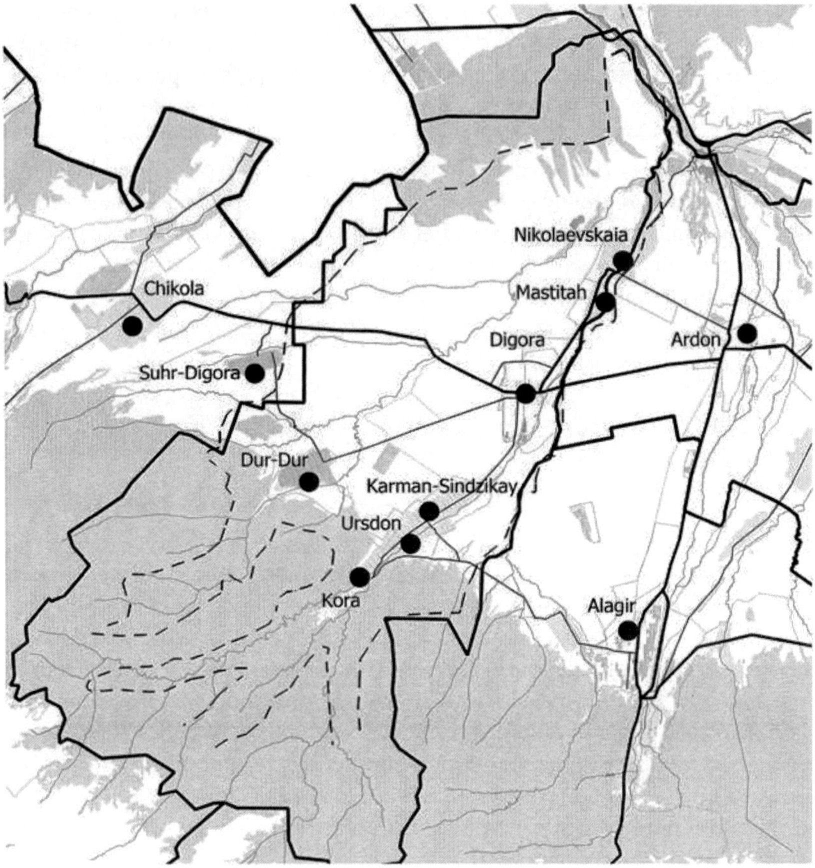

Fig. 5.8 The territorial structure of "ordinary" local communities of coercive development: southern European on the example of Digora, North Ossetia

and 7.0 people/km^2 in the latter case). The structure of the rural district is also different. The number of rural settlements in the north and in the temperate zone averages, respectively, 33 and 66, of which 4 and 14 are "escheated" villages. The average population per village is 444 residents in the north and 353 in the temperate zone. The number of settlements in the south is lower,26 (with almost no "escheat" villages—0.9 per community), and the average population of one settlement is twice higher—607 residents. Longitudinal differences are similar: in the European part of Russia, there are on average 63 rural settlements per community, of which about 13 are "escheated," and 50 are inhabited with the same 354 residents per settlement on average (three times more than in naturally developed communities in the same area). At the same time, Ural and Siberian communities have an average of 31 villages with one or two "escheated" ones; i.e., the 30 inhabited villages have about 515 residents on average.

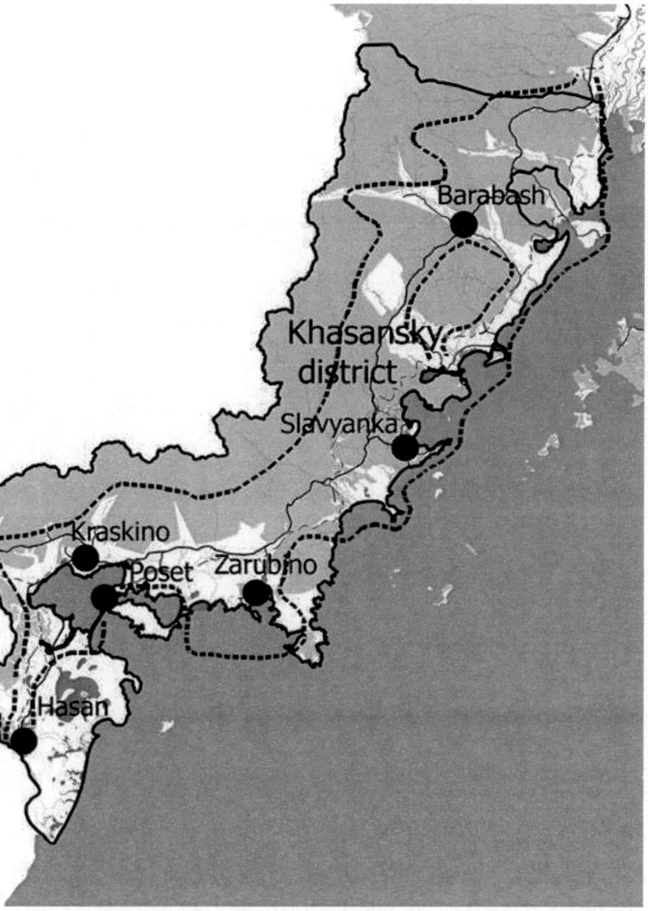

Fig. 5.9 The territorial structure of "ordinary" local communities of coercive development: southern Siberian on the example of Khasan (Slavyanka), Primorye Territory

Thus, in northern and Siberian territories, the settlements are much scarcer, and the population is concentrated in them. Therefore, the specific area per rural settlement is large—almost the same as in isolated societies, and manifold (six-fold) larger than that of naturally developed "ordinary" communities (339 km^2/village against 50 km^2/village, see Table 5.4). And the few rural settlements (most of which are industrial townships rather than villages) are concentrated around the administrative center. Hence, the territorial structure of such communities is polarized—the outskirts are unpopulated. Rural settlements in such communities almost never form "clusters" (a "clustered" structure is well illustrated by northern communities in the European part of the country—Kargopol, Totma, Veliky Ustyug, Nikolsk, Soligalich, Chukhloma, Voznesenye-Vokhma, Slobodskoy, Zuyevka, etc.). They are "drawn" to the central town. If several large rivers, forests, or major transport

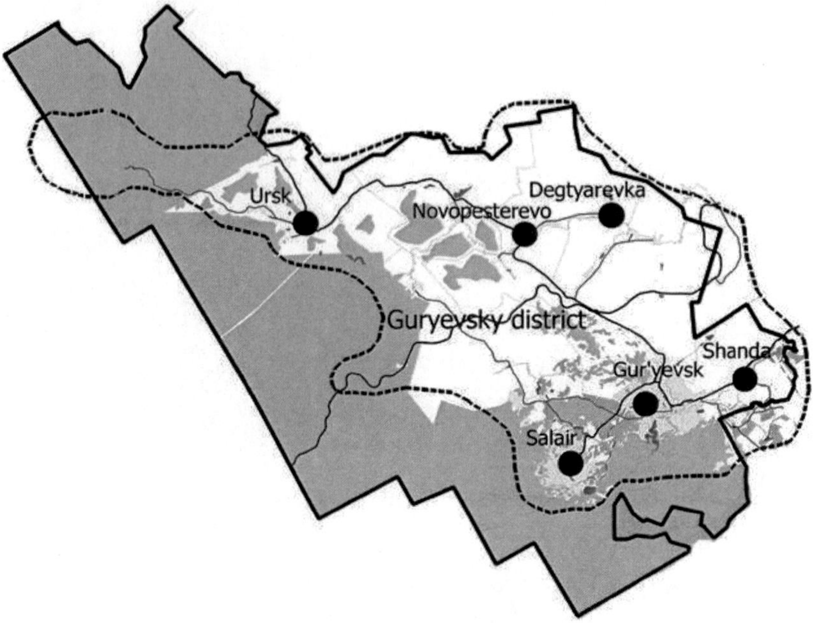

Fig. 5.10 The territorial structure of "ordinary" local communities of coercive development: temperate Siberian on the example of Guryevsk, Kemerovo

routes cut through the territory of the community, the "drawn" settlements cling to the rivers and roads. Such is the structure of virtually all nine European communities of this type.

The transport infrastructure is approximately the same as in turbulent communities, with the only difference that major federal highways and trunk railways do not actually cross the territory of "ordinary coercive" communities, although they do pass near their borders. There are many local municipal and service roads, as well as a lot of unowned (formally non-existent) ones.

The residential structure of the administrative center is similar to that of turbulent communities. Similarly, the layout of the centers in both cases is identical. Towns and industrial townships have predominantly zonal and regular layouts. Over two-thirds of the centers were established recently, in the nineteenth and twentieth centuries, and all underwent industrial development in the second half of the past century.

The territorial structure of the Digora local community in North Ossetia is extremely simple (Fig. 5.8). All settlements—six altogether with Digora—stretch in a line along the Ursdon River from the unpopulated foothills of the Caucasus Mountains in the south to the Terek River on the plain. Only the village of Dur-Dur on the river of the same name stands aside from the general line connected by three dead-end local roads. These roads lead to the intra-regional route connecting Digora with the Ossetian Chikola and further with Kabardino-Balkaria in the west, and with

Ardon in the east, where the route joins the A164 Transcaucasian Highway. There is no railway connection—the track was dismantled 15–20 years ago. All six settlements are large; there are no separate standing farms or small villages. The foothills are not populated. The population is concentrated on the plain, which has been turned into an agricultural landscape. The territory is very small (585 km^2), and the population density is 31.3 people per km^2. This would have been quite enough for self-sufficiency of the households, if only half the territory were not unsuitable for farming (mountains), and the other half were not almost completely occupied by corn, the dominant monoculture, from which numerous local and neighboring Georgian distilleries produce alcohol. Thus, the entire local community is drawn together in a single line and lives on a narrow strip of land 3x30 km, where the homesteads of about 3.5 thousand households are located.

The territorial structure of Khasan—a similar southern community, only located at the other end of the country in Primorye Territory with Slavyanka as the central town—is also linearly extended (Fig. 5.9). But here the limitations are determined not by competing neighboring communities, as in the previous case, but by four factors. The first two are of natural origin: the coastline of the Sea of Japan (also known as the East Sea) is a natural border on the southeast, and the currently completely uninhabited Black Mountains and Borisov Plateau—on the north. The two other limitations are the state border with North Korea and China and two nature reserves—a marine and a mountainous forest one (Kedrovaya Pad). These factors together severely limit the ability of the local population to control the territory and use its natural resources. Controlled territory is substantially smaller than the administrative one (although, of course, there is poaching of natural resources in closed and forbidden areas). All 37 settlements are located in a single line along the local railway track with limited passenger traffic and a regional road leading from A370 Ussuri Highway to the borders. Twelve of them have over 500 residents and almost all cling to the road. The only exception is Primorsky, which administratively belongs to the Khasan District, but is actually a suburb of Vladivostok, same as the farthermost Zanadvorka. The Khasan community, as the Digora one, does not use the entire territory for its own needs.

The third local community of this territorial type—Guryevsk in the mountains of the Salair Ridge in the Kemerovo Region of Western Siberia—is located just in the middle between the two described above (Fig. 5.10). Its transport communications are also adjacent to two highways—the north-south route from Kemerovo to Novokuznetsk and the west-east route from Novosibirsk to Leninsk–Kuznetsky. Currently, a regional road crosses the district from Belovo to Talmenka, where it connects with the Chuysky Tract. All other roads in the district are dead-end ones. The entire population is concentrated on agricultural lands in the foothills. Mountain-taiga areas are virtually unpopulated. Seven separate rural areas unite twenty-seven settlements, with most of the population concentrated in seven of them. Large areas in the west of the district serve only as a source of natural forest resources for the inhabitants. Almost the entire population, with the exception of the sparsely populated (2000 inhabitants) Ursk rural municipality in the northern part of the district, is concentrated in a limited area around Guryevsk on a local road that crosses the district from southeast to northwest along the Salair Ridge.

5.7 Significant Dissimilarities in the Structure of Different Types of Territories

An analysis of the types of territorial structures indicates that there is a combined impact of the determining factors. Spatial isolation is important not only as such, but also in combination with socio-political and economic factors. Quite a few isolated communities exist in the European part of Russia, both in the south and in the center, but still there are more of them in the north and east. The coercive manner of a community's emergence and development is much more pronounced in the east and in the north of the country. Therefore, factors that depend on the state can be deemed as latitudinal and longitudinal, and vice versa. Is it possible to take into account their different significance? Probably, yes, but this requires reviewing enormous data arrays. Modern means formally enable this, but in practice it is difficult, if only because the actual and administrative borders of local communities rarely coincide, and the population is dynamic. And it seems meaningless to use statistical approaches when there is such a considerable variability in the elements of the territorial structure. As illustration, I will present the main differentiating features of the six types of territorial structure described above (Table 5.4).

The table gives a much clearer picture of the significant differences in the territorial structure than the detailed descriptions provided above in Sect. 5.5. As I already mentioned, the most significant differences in the territorial structure are observed between two polar types—"isolated natural" communities (Type 1) on the one hand and "turbulent coercive" communities on the other hand (Type 6). At first glance it seems that in the former case, the leading factor is physical isolation in space, with the coercive impact of the state playing but a minor role, supplemented to a certain extent by the factor of the community's age. In the latter case, it seems that the influence of these factors has reversed. The factor of isolation has lost its significance, and with it the factor of the community's age. The most important factor now is the regulatory impact of the state. In any case, there are significant structural differences that determine the characteristics of the three basic elements of the local territory: the center, the rural district, and the borders.

In Type 1 the center is secondary; it is formed from the rural district, emerging initially from one of the "clusters" as either a religious (*pogost*) or economic (*torg*), or both, center of gravity for several "clusters" (rural communities, "*Mirs*"). "Appointment" as a center is determined by the availability of ancient water or, less frequently, land transport routes. Subsequently, such a center is also vested with state military and administrative functions and receives the status of a town (fort or fortress). Accordingly, the rural district is primary; it develops spontaneously, and is not limited by its neighbors' compressive impact. Generally (in the European part of

Russia), the rural district develops in the form of "clusters" consisting of several settlements on the banks of large- and medium-sized navigable rivers, which gradually spread further over forest and steppe wild lands to the watersheds. The settlements—villages—are small in terms of population, but quite numerous and located all over the territory. The density gradient from the center to the outskirts is usually low, unless the entire population is concentrated in two to three settlements, which is rare. The territory is large; its size is determined by the need to control natural resources for daily existence. The population is able to live autonomously using the procured natural resources. Borders are controlled by local inhabitants; they have been stable for long, and do not always coincide with administrative boundaries. They are determined by natural barriers and tradition: a system of long-established agreements.

In case of the polar Type 6 the center is primary and the rural district is secondary; it evolves in the form of settlements spreading from the center to the periphery. Due to this, the rural district is "drawn" to the center, and the outskirts of the territory remain unpopulated. The rural district settlement is quite large in terms of population, but few in number; by status they are usually industrial townships rather than villages. The entire community concentrates around the center. In certain periods of life, the center attracts the population of the rural district, and the district falls into neglect. At other times, the center is abandoned ("escheated"), and a large part of the population leaves the local community (this has been happening over the past 20 years). The density gradient from the center to the outskirts is high. The central settlement itself does not emerge naturally, but is established close to resources that have no immediate vital importance for the community. The residential structure of both the central and rural settlements did not develop in a slow and natural manner, but was formed "as if in a flash." The inhabited and developed territory is almost always much smaller than the administrative borders, and is not in line with the area of vitally important natural resources. Generally, the population does not develop these resources. Borders are neither protected, nor maintained; people seem to be unaware of their territorial borders, since their subsistence depends on external sources, primarily on the state.

The four other types of territorial structures demonstrate a certain cross-similarity. "Isolated coercive" communities (Type 2) are similar to "ordinary coercive" ones (Type 4), and "ordinary natural" communities (Type 3) to "turbulent natural" ones (Type 5). It turns out that the intermediate type of communities, distinguished by the criterion of spatial isolation ("ordinary" communities), splits in two, differentiated by the factor of coercive/natural manner of emergence and development. "Ordinary" communities of natural development are closer to turbulent natural ones, and those formed coercively are closer also to coercive but spatially isolated ones. The intermediate status of "ordinary" communities in terms of spatial isolation is overruled by the factor of coerciveness/naturalness, which thus appears to be most important for territorial typology (if we do not assume the combined effect of this factor with the geographical one, since coercive communities are more often located in the east of the country). Due to this, the latter four types of territorial structure can

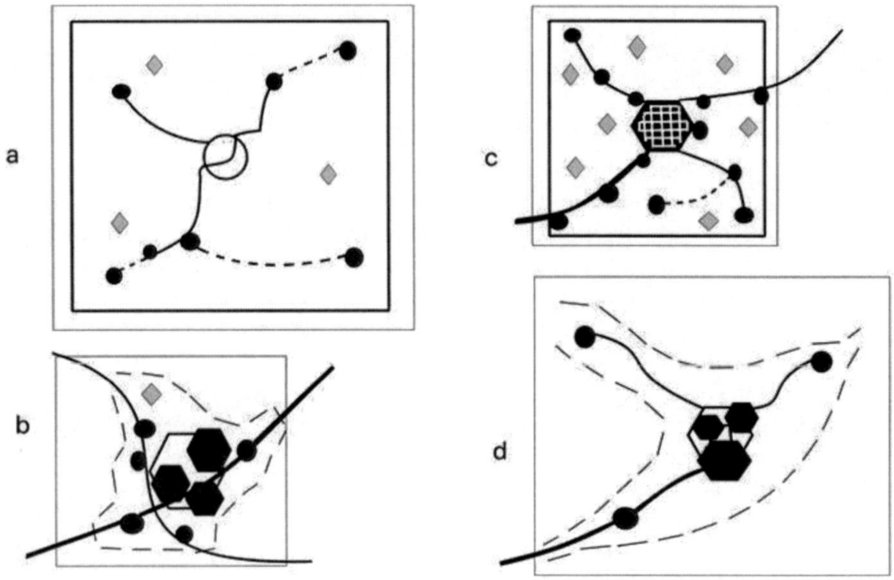

Fig. 5.11 Schematic representation of the six types of territorial structure. The two left diagrams show the first (**a** isolated natural) and sixth (**b** turbulent coercive) polar territorial types. Each of the two right diagrams unites two types of territories: (**c**) third ("ordinary natural") and fifth ("turbulent natural"); (**d**) second ("isolated coercive") and fourth ("ordinary coercive"). The relative area of the squares demonstrates the size of the territory. The boundary lines of the squares are administrative borders; the dashed lines are inhabited space. The configuration of the dashed lines reflects the degree to which the population controls its territory: rectangular—controlled; dotted curved—inadequately controlled. The size of the center shows its relative population; the hatching reflects the layout (upper circuits street and regular, or zonal at the bottom). The size, quantity, and distribution of small dots illustrate the structure of the rural district: distribution of population (black dots), number of settlements (1 dot = 10 villages), uniformity/unevenness of distribution across the territory, and availability and share of "escheated" settlements (gray crossed out dots)

be reduced to two types, which are based on "turbulent natural" communities in one case, and on "isolated coercive" ones in the other.

One of these "combined" types includes non-isolated naturally developing communities with an adequate or extensive transport infrastructure. Their territory is small; the size and density of the population are moderately high. Numerous relatively small villages spread throughout the territory. The centers of the communities are naturally established ancient and old towns. The transport infrastructure is well developed. Territorial borders are controlled. By the size of the territory, transport routes, and structure of the administrative center, these communities are closer to Type 6 "turbulent coercive" ones, and by the structure of the rural district and controlled borders to Type 1 "isolated natural" ones.

The other "combined" type includes coercively established communities with an inadequate or only moderately developed transport infrastructure. Generally, their territory is very large but uncontrolled. There are few settlements in the rural district, but they are large and populous. The settlements concentrate around the administrative center; the density gradient from the center to the outskirts is high, but most often a substantial part of the local population settles along major transport routes. Here the similarity with the two polar types of territorial structure is reversed. By the size of the territory, transport routes, and structure of the administrative center, these communities are closer to Type 1 "isolated natural" ones, and by the structure of the rural district and the borders to Type 6 "turbulent coercive" ones.

The diagrams in Fig. 5.11 are intended to help visualize the identified typological differences in the territorial structure of provincial communities. The four diagrams reflect the features of the three basic elements of the territory: the administrative center, the rural district, and the borders (I have also added transport routes). The following territorial structures are presented:

1. Isolated communities that do not experience any significant government impact (Type 1)
2. Coercively established communities located on transport thoroughfares (Type 6)
3. Non-isolated naturally developing communities with an adequate or extensive transport infrastructure (Type 3 and Type 5)
4. Coercively established communities with an inadequate or moderately developed transport infrastructure (Type 2 and Type 4)

References

Anderson, P. (2000). *Passages from Antiquity to Feudalism*. Verso. Russian edition: Андерсон П. (2007). *Переходы от античности к феодализму*. М.: Издательский дом «Территория будущего».

Anuchin, V. A. (1982). *Geographic factor in the development of society*. Mysl. Анучин В.А. (1982). *Географический фактор в развитии общества*. М.: Мысль.

Bessonova, O. E. (2006). *Distribution economy of Russia: Evolution through transformation*. "Russian political encyclopedia" (ROSSPEN). Бессонова О.Э. (2006). *Раздаточная экономика России: Эволюция через трансформации*. М.: «Российская политическая энциклопедия» (РОССПЭН).

Carneiro, R. L. (1970). A theory of the origin of the state. *Science, 169*(3947), 733–738.

Carneiro, R. L. (2003). *Evolutionism in cultural anthropology: A critical history*. Westview Press.

Christaller, W. (1966). *Central places in Southern Germany*. Prentice Hall.

Christaller, W. (1980). *Die zentralen Orte in Süddeutschland. Eine ökonomisch-geographische Untersuchung über die Gesetzmäßigkeit der Verbreitung und Entwicklung der Siedlungen mit städtischer Funktion*. Wissenschaftliche Buchgesellschaft.

Dulov, A. V. (1983). *Geographical environment and history of Russia (late 15th - mid 19th centuries)*. Nauka. Дулов А.В. (1983). *Географическая среда и история России (конец XV – середина XIX века)*. Новосибирск: Наука.

Fischer, D. H. (1996). *The Great Wave. Price revolutions and the rhythm of history*. Oxford University Press.

Glazychev, V. L. (2003). *Deep Russia: 2000-2002*. New Publishing House. Глазычев В.Л. (2003). *Глубинная Россия: 2000-2002*. М.: Новое издательство.

Goldstein, J. S. (1988). *Long cycles: Prosperity and war in the modern age*. Yale University Press.

Golts, G. A. (1995). The city and its cultural level indicators in the definition and measurement of urbanization. In E.V. Saiko (Ed.), *City as a socio-cultural phenomenon of the historical process* (pp. 47–60). Nauka. Гольц Г.А. (1995). Город и его культурно-уровневые показатели в определении и измерении урбанизации. В кн.: *Город как социокультурное явление исторического процесса*/Отв.ред. Э.В. Сайко. М.: Наука.

Golts, G. A. (2002). *Culture and economy of Russia for three centuries, XVIII-XX centuries*. Siberian Chronograph. Гольц Г.А. (2002). *Культура и экономика России за три века, XVIII – XX вв*. Новосибирск: Сибирский хронограф.

Gumilev, L. N. (2006). *Ancient Russia and the Great Steppe*. EKSMO. Гумилёв Л.Н. (2006). *Древняя Русь и Великая Степь*. М.: ЭКСМО.

Jennings, J., & Earle, T. (2016). Urbanization, state formation, and cooperation: A reappraisal. *Current Anthropology, 57*(4), 474–493.

Kazarinov, L. (1926). *Out-of-pocket trades in the Chukhloma district*. Chukhloma. Казаринов Л. (1926). *Отхожие промыслы Чухломского уезда*. Чухлома.

Kislovsky, S. V. (2006). Kashin Territory. In S. V. Kustov (Ed.), *Forgotten pages of history book*. II (pp. 122, 205–211). (Кисловский С.В. (2006). Кашинский край. В кн.: С.В. Кустов (сост.). *Забытые станицы истории*, Кн. II. Калязин, Б.и.).

Kordonsky, S. G. (2007). *Resource state – From repression to depression*. FOM. (Кордонский С.Г. (2007). *Ресурсное государство – от репрессий к депрессиям*. М.: ФОМ.

Kordonsky, S. G. (2010). *Russia. The Estate Federation*. Publishing House "Europe". (Кордонский С.Г. (2010). *Россия. Поместная Федерация*. М.: Издательство «Европа».

Kordonsky, S. G. (2016). *Socio-Economic foundations of the Russian Post-Soviet Regime. The resource-based economy and estate-based social structure of contemporary Russia. (The Cyclical Nature of Russian History)*. Ibidem.

Kradin, N. N. (2007). *Nomads of Eurasia*. "Daik-Press". (Крадин Н.Н. (2007). *Кочевники Евразии*. Алматы: "Daik-Press").

Kudryavtsev, O. K. (1978). *Settlement and planning structure of large agglomeration cities*. Stroyizdat. (Кудрявцев О.К. (1978). *Расселение и планировочная структура крупных городов-агломераций*. М.: Стройиздат.).

Kulisher, I. M. (2004). *History of the Russian national economy*. Socium. (Кулишер И.М. (2004). *История русского народного хозяйства*. Челябинск: Социум).

Kuza, A. V. (1983). Socio-historical typology of ancient Russian cities of the X-XIII centuries. *Russian City, 6*, 4–36. (Куза А.В. (1983). Социально-историческая типология древнерусских городов X–XIII вв. *Русский город*).

Lieven, D. C. B. (2002). *Empire: The Russian empire and its rivals*. Yale University Press. Russian edition: Ливен Д. (2007). *Российская империя и её враги с 16 столетия до наших дней*. М.: Издательство «Европа»).

Losch, A. (1937). Population cycles as a cause of business cycles. *Quarterly Journal of Economics, 51*, 649–662.

Lurie, S. V. (1996). Geopolitical forms of organizing the space of expansion and their influence on the nature of popular colonization. *Civilizations and Cultures, 3*, 179–185. (Лурье С.В. (1996). Геополитические формы организации пространства экспансии и их влияние на характер народной колонизации. *Цивилизации и культуры*).

Lurie, S. V. (1998). The people's perception of the territory being developed. *Social Sciences and Modernity, 5*, 61–84. (Лурье С.В. (1998). Восприятие народом осваиваемой территории. Общественные науки и современность).

Lurie, S. V. (2015). The game of cat and mouse: models of Russian peasant colonization in the XIX - early XX centuries. *International Research Journal, 42*(11), 129–131. (Лурье С.В. (2015). Игра в кошки-мышки: модели русской крестьянской колонизации в XIX – начале XX веков. *Международный научно-исследовательский журнал*).

Maier, J. (1964). Cyclical theories. In W. J. Cahnman & A. Boskoff (Eds.), *Sociology and history: Theory and research* (pp. 42–61). Free Press.

Mironov, B. N. (2003). *Social history of Russia during the period of the empire (XVIII - early XX century).* "Dmitry Bulanin". (Миронов Б. Н. (2003). *Социальная история России периода империи (XVIII—начало XX в.).* СПб.: «Дмитрий Буланин»).

Nefedov, S. (2004). A model of demographic cycles in a traditional society: The case of Ancient China. *Social Evolution & History, 3*(1), 69–80.

Nefedov, S. A. (2005). *Demographic and structural analysis of the socio-economic history of Russia. Late 15th - early 20th century.* Yekaterinburg: UGGU Publishing House. (Нефёдов С.А. (2005). *Демографически-структурный анализ социально-экономической истории России. Конец XV – начало XX века.* Екатеринбург: Изд-во УГГУ).

Nefedova, T. G., & Treivish, A. I. (2005). Town and country: Convergence or divergence? In: Y. G. Lipets (Ed.), *Interaction of urban and rural areas in regional development* (pp. 4–22). IGRAN, MARS. (Нефёдова Т.Г., Трейвиш А.И. Город и деревня: конвергенция или дивергенция?. В кн.: *Взаимодействие городских и сельских местностей в региональном развитии.* М.: ИГРАН, МАРС).

Panarin, A. S. (1999). *Russia in the cycles of world history.* Publishing House of Moscow State University. (Панарин А.С. (1999). *Россия в циклах мировой истории.* М.: Изд-во МГУ).

Pascal, P. (2011). *Archpriest Havakkum and the beginning Schism.* Znak. (Паскаль П. (2011). Протопоп Аввакум и начало Раскола. М.: Знак).

Peregrine, P. (2003). Atlas of cultural evolution. *World Cultures, 14*(1), 2–88.

Peregrine, P., & Ember, M. (Eds). (2001–2002). *Encyclopedia of prehistory* (Vols. 1–9). Springer.

Plusnin, J. M. (1997a). Models of life support of the Pomor population of the Russian North in modern conditions. *Bulletin of the Russian Humanitarian Scientific Foundation, 3*,180–192. (Плюснин Ю.М. (1997a). Модели жизнеобеспечения поморского населения Русского Севера в современных условиях. *Вестник Российского гуманитарного научного фонда*).

Plusnin, J. M. (1997b). Psychology of material life (paradoxes of rural economy of survival). *ECO: economics and organization of industrial production, 7*, 169–176. (Плюснин Ю.М. (1997b). Психология материальной жизни (парадоксы сельской экономики выживания). *ЭКО: экономика и организация промышленного производства*).

Plusnin, J. M. (2006). Mezen: The realities of natural life. *Otechestvennye zapiski, 32*(5), 147–156. (Плюснин Ю.М. (2006). Мезень: реальности натуральной жизни. *Отечественные записки*).

Plusnin, J. M., Zausaeva, Y. D., Zhidkevich, N. N., & Pozanenko, A. A. (2013). *Othodniki.* New chronograph. (Плюснин Ю.М., Заусаева Я.Д., Жидкевич Н.Н., Позаненко А.А. (2013). *Отходники.* М.: Новый хронограф).

Prokhorov, A. P. (2002). *Russian control system.* Journal "Expert". (Прохоров А.П. (2002). *Русская система управления.* М.: Журнал «Эксперт").

Radkau, J. (2012). *Natur und Macht. Eine Weltgeschichte der Umwelt.* Verlag C. H. Beck.

Rodoman, B. B. (1999). *Territorial areas and networks. Essays of theoretical geography.* Smolensk: Oecumene (Родоман Б.Б. (1999). *Территориальные ареалы и сети. Эссе теоретической географии.* Смоленск: Ойкумена).

Rodoman, B. B. (2007). *Geography, regionalization, cartoids: Collected works.* Smolensk: Oecumene. (Родоман Б.Б. (2007). *География. Регионализация. Картоиды: Сборник работ.* Смоленск: Ойкумена).

Scribal book of black-sowed volosts of Kevrola and Mezen with districts of letters and measures of Osip Yakovlevich Pronchishchev and clerks Semyon Retkin and Peter Sharapov 131 year. (1622). Book. 185. (Писцовая книга черносошных волостей Кевролы и Мезени с уездами письма и меры Осипа Яковлевича Прончищева и подьячих Семена Реткина и Петра Шарапова 131г. (1622г.). Кн. 185, Л. 1–471 Подлинник за скрепами О.П. Прончищева, С. Реткина и П. Шарапова).

Semyonov-Tyan-Shansky, V. P. (1928). *Region and country.* GIZ. (Семёнов-Тян-Шанский В.П. *Район и страна.* М.-Л.: ГИЗ).

Soloviev S.M. (1990). *History of Russia since ancient times* (Vol. 10). Mysl. (Соловьёв С. М. (1990). *История России с древнейших времён.* Кн. V. Т. 10, М.: Мысль).

Sorokin, P. A. (1927). A survey of the cyclical conceptions of social and historical process. *Social Forces, Baltimore, 6*(1), 28–40.

Sorokin, P. A. (1998). Review of cyclical concepts of the socio-historical process. *Sociological Research, 12*, 3–14. (Сорокин П.А. (1998). Обзор циклических концепций социальн-о-исторического процесса. *Социологические исследования*).

Tarkhov, S. A. (2005). *Evolutionary morphology of transport networks*. Oikumena. (Тархов С.А. (2005). *Эволюционная морфология транспортных сетей*. Смоленск: Ойкумена).

Teschke, B. (2003). *The Myth of 1648: Cass, geopolitics, and the making of modern international relations*. Verso. Russian edition: Тешке Б. (2011). *Миф о 1648 года: класс, геополитика и создание современных международных отношений*. М.: Издательский дом ВШЭ.

Vernadsky, G. (1966). *The Mongols and Russia*. Yale University Press. Russian edition: Вернадский Г. (2018). *Монголы и Русь*. М.: Ломоносовъ, 2018.

Vladimirsky, N. N. (1927). *The withdrawal of the peasantry of the Kostroma province for work*. Edition of the Kostroma provincial department. Владимирский Н.Н. (1927). *Отход крестьянства Костромской губернии на заработки*. Кострома: Издание Костромского губстатотдела.

von Schrenck, A. (1854). *Reise nach dem Nordosten des europaisehen Russlands, durch die Tundren der Samojeden zum arktischen Uralgebirge*. Dorpat.

Yurchenko, A. G. (2012). *Khan Uzbek: Between empire and Islam (structures of everyday life). Book-synopsis*. Eurasia. (Юрченко А.Г. (2012). Хан Узбек: Между империей и исламом (структуры повседневности). Книга-конспект. СПб.: Евразия).

Chapter 6
Local Economy

The phrase "The depleted lawn of formal local economy and the wild field of informal economy" can serve as the subtitle of this chapter, since the Russian provincial economy exists in two forms—different by nature and origin but deeply interpenetrating. The first one is the formal economy, where individual business depends more on government control or support than on private initiative. The second one is the wild field of informal economy, legitimate in its scope but far from legal. It largely consists of shadow and criminal economic activity. I consider the balance between formal and informal provincial economies, focusing here on the first component. The Russian province has distinctive features not only in informal economy but also in the structure of its formal part. The public sector of the formal economy is of particular significance to provincial society. Against its background, the other components of the local economy—material production and services—appear substantially less developed. Small business, particularly sole proprietorship, plays an important role in the province. Its position is specific and its dynamics are peculiar, as it constantly and continuously switches between formal and informal economy. Sole proprietors are the most vibrant, essential segment of the local economy, a significant part of which is constantly in the economic "shadow."

6.1 The Local Economy and Crafts: Two Types of Provincial Economy

The moment we cross the boundary of any provincial local community, we bump into a statistical paradox confusing for any young researcher or economist dealing purely with official statistics. The local economy employs no more than two-thirds, often only a half, of the working-age population. What do the remaining employable people do? State statistics has no answer to this. Neither have the local authorities. Moreover, many of those unaccounted for in the economy are mostly absent from

J. Plusnin, *Russian Provincial Society*, Societies and Political Orders in Transition,
https://doi.org/10.1007/978-3-030-97829-7_6

their town or village. Where are they? Neither government bodies nor municipal authorities have any idea.

The reason for this is quite simple. In contrast to the Soviet era, where every employee was clearly associated with the workplace, the past 30 post-Soviet years have witnessed widespread development of informal economic practices. Of course, such practices also existed in the Soviet Union, but they were nowhere near the current scale and consisted predominantly in subsistence farming for personal needs (the so-called pervasive "household economy") (Barsukova, 2003a, b, 2009, pp. 183–204; Kulisher, 2004; Schumacher, 1973; Gimpelson & Kapelyushnikov, 2014; Vorontsov, 2015) and in shadow and criminal activities (Grossman, 1977, 1979; Sampson, 1987; Shokhin, 1987; Rutgeizer, 1992). Nowadays, household crafts are mostly developed in the province, in small towns and rural areas, rather than in large cities (Shanin, 1999; Kalugina & Fadeeva, 2009; Nikulin 2012). The reason is that in the 1990s, the state-regulated labor market in the province virtually "*collapsed*;" the population lost official sources of income and was forced to seek independently new sources of livelihood in addition to and along with expanding the "household economy." This resulted in the emergence of numerous informal economic practices. By then, government recording and statistics of such practices had long been discontinued and have still not been re-established.

So, rather than considering the local economy in general, we have to deal with two of its types. They differ radically, but intersect and deeply interpenetrate everywhere, up to the point of becoming completely unrecognizable; cf.: Guha-Khasnobis et al. (2006) and Barsukova (2015). On the one hand, there is the local economy recorded by government statistics agencies. On the other hand, there is the informal economy predominantly represented by household economic practices or crafts. (I do not consider such types of informal economy as reciprocal and criminal, focusing on the most widespread types of household and shadow economy, which form the basis of household livelihoods (Scott, 1976; Alexeev et al., 1995; Guha-Khasnobis et al., 2006; Ledeneva, 2018).

The first type of economy is "visible," the second—"invisible." In the first case, the structure is quite simple. It is captured in the statistical records of territorial government statistics agencies. It is also recorded in municipal reports and reflected in documents published by municipal authorities on their official websites. In the second case, the structure of the provincial informal economy needs to be identified, deciphered, and reconstructed. It has its own specifics and species diversity in every community and in every region. This is not typical of a "statistically visible" economy. Let us consider the difference between the two types of economy in terms of the social income structure.

Economists usually distinguish six types of sources in the structure of social income, see, e.g. Standing (2011, pp. 26–30), Tikhonova et al. (2018, pp. 10–48). Some of them originate in the formal, and others—in the informal economy: (1) wages and salaries; (2) various public allowances and welfare payments; (3) corporate benefits and allowances; (4) rental income; (5) informal mutual family support (reciprocal non-monetary exchange); and (6) self-sufficiency (homesteading, household economy). The two latter types are generally associated with informal economy. In Russia, however, rental income is more often informal than officially registered, and corporate benefits/allowances are often unrecorded, as it is common practice for private companies to pay their employees "under the table." Obviously, this list must be supplemented by a new source of income not included in the above structure. It involves income from crafts and trades, which can be generated either by formally registered individual (family) businesses or—most often—by informal activities, both shadow and criminal. Thus, of the seven types of social income, only the first three are formal and taxable. It is quite challenging to reveal the proportion of various types of income in the budget of a household. Indirect appraisal methods (for example, the income/expenditure ratio) constantly confirm that the actual expenses of Russian provincial households are at least the double of their official monetary incomes. In the Soviet era, the share of informal economy in household spending was also significant (see, e.g. Grossman (1979, pp. 834–855), Sampson (1987, pp. 122–130), Shokhin (1987), Rutgeizer (1992, pp. 39–72). But nowadays, its scale has substantially increased; see Shabanova (1992), Alexeev et al. (1995), Nikulin (1998), Plusnin (1997, 2000, 2016), Shanin (1999), Pilikhovsky and Stolbov (2000), Steinberg (2002), Gimpelson and Kapelyushnikov (2006, 2014), Barsukova and Radaev (2012), Plusnin et al. (2015), Seleev and Pavlov (2016), and Kordonskiy and Plusnin (2018).

For the specific task of describing the local provincial social structure, I deem it possible and sufficient to distinguish only three segments of formal economy (previously the so-called "first economy," see Grossman (1987, 1988), Shokhin (1987). These three segments are (1) public sector employees, (2) local material production and services, and (3) local small business. Obviously, small business covers both material production and services, so, proceeding from the traditional approach, we are violating the principle of a uniform basis for classification. However, I distinguish these three segments of the local economy on other grounds. They differ in sources of funding for the employees, the nature of their labor efforts, and the type of income they receive. The last distinction is important. Public sector employees receive a fixed *salary* from the government budget (therefore, such employees have traditionally been called *budgetniki*). In material production and services, hired personnel earn *wages* based on the results of their labor efforts and labor productivity. Sole proprietors or owners of small companies gain *income* and profit generated by their own economic initiative, where they bear all possible risks.

The most clearly defined segment is the first one—public sector employees who receive remuneration for their work in the form of salary paid from the government or municipal budget. This category includes employees of all government and municipal institutions (education and science, health care and social welfare, culture and sports), including the local administration and numerous territorial government bodies. Their salary is fixed (determined by the rate scale); its size is small; incentives and deductions depend little on the employee's labor effort. Therefore, *budgetniki* are often not motivated to increase labor productivity and be efficient performers. In the regions where I conducted research, public sector employees accounted for thirty to sixty percent of all the working-age population engaged in the local economy (as, indeed, throughout provincial Russia). The reason for such seemingly exorbitant figures is the fact that the local economy officially employs only from half to two-thirds of the working-age population. Therefore, *budgetniki* actually constitute from one-fifth to a third of the economically active population of a provincial local community. This is still too much, and the trend has been developing since 2004, triggered by the decision to *"establish a top-down vertical of power."* As a result, grassroots territorial government bodies mushroomed in the district centers, increasing the number of employees.

The second segment includes all economic activities performed in an organized manner by large and medium-sized state-owned and municipal enterprises and private companies that operate in the district, employ local residents or migrants, and pay taxes here. The share of state-owned enterprises is now significantly lower than 15–20 years ago (except for single-industry towns and closed administrative-territorial entities where large state-owned enterprises are located). There are also few municipal enterprises and institutions. The main share goes to private enterprises and retail outlets (small- and medium-sized businesses). Almost everywhere, one or two large producers are also present—agricultural holdings in the rural area and major retail chains in district centers. The goods they produce and ship and services they provide are included in local statistics. Enterprises and companies usually pay taxes to the local budget. Their personnel receive income in the form of wages. Besides, they always receive additional, *"shadow,"* payments.[1] Such enterprises and companies employ from ten to twenty percent of the district's working-age residents (which constitutes from twenty to forty percent of the population engaged in the local economy). This segment is covered by statistics and records of employment, wages, output, volume of services, paid taxes, raised investment, etc. Here, it makes sense to distinguish between material production and services, as local statistics makes a point to treat them separately.

The third segment of the *"visible"* local economy consists of local small businesses—from farms to timber processing enterprises (sawmills), and from bakeries to local shopping centers. Formally, this category also includes sole proprietors, who are an absolute majority in provincial societies. The usual proportion between the number of SMEs or companies incorporated as legal entities and the number of officially registered sole proprietors is 1:5. I distinguish this segment from the second one, represented by medium-sized businesses, because small business intersects and even merges with informal economy. In the province, most of these entrepreneurs operate in the *"gray"* zone of the economy, as they do not report a significant part of output and revenue.[2] According to data obtained from insiders,

---

[1] For example, sales clerks everywhere earn officially 7000–15,000 rubles per month (USD 100–200); however, some of them receive additionally as much or even more "under the table." The official monthly wages of workers at small enterprises range from 20,000 to 40,000 rubles and more (USD 300–600), but there are always some unregistered workers, and "visible" earnings are split among them.

[2] In the past 30 years, it has been common practice for the timber industry to report officially only 20%–25% of the output. The remaining 75%–80% of the produced timber and lumber is usually sold "on the side" unrecorded and, obviously, untaxed.

unregistered self-employed people always largely outnumber the registered ones, but any quantitative assessment is impossible.

Thus, of the three segments attributed to the local formal economy, two are also part of the *"shadow"* economy. Due to firm family ties and extensive neighborly relations, this is not as carefully concealed in the province as in large cities; moreover, the local authorities are not inclined to persecute the *"informals"* for such violations.

Informal household economic practices, or crafts, form a substantial part of the local economy. I define crafts as independent household economic activities based on in-house means and technologies and aimed at supporting the life (survival) of the family and achieving other, usually social, goals. Such activities are usually outside the scope of capitalist business patterns; they do not rely on modern or innovative technologies (which is actually disputable), but widely use cooperation and artel or communal organization of labor. Craft practices imply neither entrepreneurship nor business in their original meaning (Kordonsky, 2010, pp. 45–58). Thus, in many cases, crafts are archaic economic institutions draped in modern legal and organizational forms.

This definition basically corresponds to the definitions of other authors, who focus on the predominantly informal nature of crafts, including non-market exchange: Scott (1976), Ilyin (2001a, b), Barsukova (2003a, b, 2004, 2015), Barsukova and Radaev (2012), on homesteading rather than business activities: Vodarsky and Istomina (2004), Pavlov and Seleev (2015), and their relation with the estate-based structure of the Russian society: Kordonsky (2010), Vakhitov (2017). But I agree with the phenomenological definition of crafts presented and extensively considered in a recent publication by our colleagues: Pavlov and Seleev (2015, p. 26). Obviously, such a definition of crafts is narrower than the definition of informal economy in general. It is in many respects synonymous with "household economy" but not limited to it; it is broader. Crafts do not aim solely at achieving self-sufficiency of the household; they often result in marketable goods. Therefore, "*household crafts*" are "*household economy*" plus shadow economy, or what we used to call "*second economy*" 40–50 years ago.

However, one should keep in mind that in contrast to large cities, informal economy in the province develops mainly for the sake of daily subsistence, and not for commercial production in its pure form, not for capital growth. Even commercial production resulting from the population's household crafts is intended primarily to achieve self-sufficiency. Where formally registered sources of income are insufficient, it forms the basis of the family's livelihood and well-being. All the above researchers are well aware of this circumstance and specifically point it out. According to my on-site estimates, informal economic activity accounts for up to half of the total volume of the local economy in those frequent cases, where there are no major industrial enterprises or agricultural holdings in the area. For this reason, when speaking about informal economy in the province, we may imply the people's crafts and trades.

They can be classified into several basic areas, with each one further subdivided into many types. I distinguish only four areas (or craft types) based on such principles as the workplace and specific operation arrangements. They include: (1) "*garazhniki*," (2) "*scattered manufactories*," (3) "*otkhodniks*," and (4) household crafts (a broader concept than '*household economy*'). The crafts and trades are practiced at home or away from home ("*otkhod*" is a special form of seasonal recurrent labor migration; it does not fall into the category of "*household crafts*"). The craft types are also differentiated by the type of locality where the participants reside and by the cooperation of their activities.

"*Garazhniki*" form a distinctive group, widely represented in large and medium-sized cities of Russia but not numerous in small provincial towns. This is a special category of self-employed, quite recently identified and described by Alexander Pavlov and Sergey Seleev (2015), Seleev and Pavlov (2016).[3] According to them, "garazhniki" are those self-employed businessmen and their teams (crews and artels) who produce goods and provide services in individual garage "boxes" on the premises of garage-building cooperatives. Most of these cooperatives are located in large cities, where residents live in apartment houses and have neither land plots nor private outbuildings where they could work. In provincial societies "garazhniki" are few—they are a marginalized group of informally employed entrepreneurs. In small towns, many residents have private housing with their own garages on the estate. However, even there some people live in apartment buildings and are forced to establish garage cooperatives. So, the few "garazhniki" in the provinces are concentrated in the administrative centers; there are virtually none in the rural district. Local experts generally treat them as "shadow" sole proprietors. But here "garazhniki" are the most vague group, merging with registered small businesses and at the same time forming the backbone of unregistered self-employed entrepreneurs. The above authors managed to record 110 various occupations in the garages of 14 large cities and nine small and medium-sized towns (Seleev & Pavlov, 2016, pp. 36–37). Entrepreneurs carry out the various "garage-based" trades using personal competencies obtained through occupational training or know-how or investing their vital resource (personal time and physical effort). Due to scarce data, my description of "garazhniki" is no more than a sketch.

"Scattered Manufactories" This type of informal economic activity of the provincial population was identified and depicted by Simon Kordonsky and myself (Kordonskiy & Plusnin, 2018). Unlike household crafts, widespread everywhere and especially significant in rural areas, "scattered manufactories" are a special form of economic activity of the population. This economic practice is represented only in small towns and the adjacent rural district and is inherent in communities that have unique resources and/or unique industries. "Scattered manufactories" are less common than other forms of economy, but where revealed, they engage a lot, if not the majority, of households.

[3] The same authors proposed the term "*garage economy*," which was quickly accepted and is now commonly used in Russia.

"Otkhodnichestvo" By contrast, the most widespread phenomenon is unregistered circular (cyclical) labor migration of small town and rural residents to large cities and industrial centers of Russia. We first described this in the early 2010s (Plusnin et al., 2013, 2015). In the past 15–20 years, cyclical labor migration has spread throughout the country, affecting all provincial societies without exception; residents of all types of villages and hamlets (*auls*), of the smallest towns and major cities are engaged in otkhodnichestvo. Originally a purely male activity, it currently also involves many women. This labor practice is largely informal and unrecorded.

Domestic, or household, crafts are formally unrecorded types of household economic activities within the local community using various resources. I distinguish five principal types of resources used:

1. In situ resources (obtained as a result of backyard production or personal farming)
2. Natural resources (mainly forest and water)
3. Infrastructural resources (transport, utilities, and residential)
4. Human resources, which are a direct source of livelihood for the household; and
5. The state as a resource, i.e. crafts based on public resources provided to certain categories of people

Obviously, different types of resources mingle with each other. For example, people as a resource almost always assume the availability of infrastructural, and often certain natural, resources. Vacationers drawn by a specific landscape usually also require a developed transport and municipal infrastructure on the spot; thus, the locals can profit from all three types of resources at once.

Household crafts presume that resources are extracted and utilized on the spot, within the local community itself, specifically, in one's backyard or on the farmstead. Resources are often consumed directly and with minimal processing. Indeed, they frequently serve as a source of livelihood rather than commodity, although it is hardly possible to distinguish clearly, whether the purpose of the craft is personal or commercial. I recorded about a hundred and fifty different household crafts, which rely on one or several types of resources. Within one community household crafts vary greatly, and in different parts of Russia, this variability is even higher. By type and diversity, crafts in the south radically differ from those in the north; there are also many distinctions between the European part of the country and Siberia. At the same time, where basic resources are similar in type and volume, I revealed the effect of *"homologous"* crafts and trades in regions distant from each other. In the provincial local society, the variability of household crafts results mostly from the activity of unregistered self-employed entrepreneurs, classified as "garazhniki" in large cities. However, there are no reliable criteria for assigning them to one or another category, since the "garages," where resources are processed and finished products manufactured, are located on the household's property.

Specific household crafts can be attributed to any informal economy type identified by researchers (Barsukova, 2009, pp. 112–123). They can be in the form of a household economy as such—economic activity of a household for daily subsistence, which is based on individual family ties and has no commercial purpose. The overwhelming majority of households are included in this type of informal economy, and every single one—in the communities, which I classify as isolated natural ones. Household crafts also form the basis of "reciprocal economy," which establishes non-market and non-monetary networks of mutual (reciprocal) exchange between related households (often between neighbors as well). In many of our provincial societies, everyday life is impossible without the support of neighbors and relatives. In many cases, one cannot do without cooperation, teamwork, and mutual aid. This is equally true for communities in the north of Siberia and the Arctic, where people simply cannot survive in isolation, for temperate ones in the non-black soil regions, and even for southern communities of the North Caucasus or Primorye. We find such mutual support of households in any local community, somewhere to a lesser extent, and somewhere in full scope (however, this is typical not only of the Russian provincial society, see Ledeneva (2018, pp. 125–212).

Many households are also engaged in the shadow and criminal economy. This particularly concerns procuring prohibited resources (such as salmon, sturgeon, and Red Book species: animals—tigers and leopards; birds—swans and snowcocks; and plants—ginseng, golden, maral or red roots) and producing and marketing prohibited goods and services (for example, cultivating cannabis and poppy; manufacturing and selling synthetic drugs; private pig farming, banned in some regions; soliciting prostitution; selling moonshine and base wine). Despite all the prohibitions, many households all over the country are engaged in such criminal activities, operating on the basis of personal and clan ties and using closed criminal markets, which due to their local nature and "mutual cover-up" (mutual support of acquaintances) are still accessible for outsiders.

The next two chapters are dedicated mostly to informal economic practices—"*scattered manufactories*" and *otkhodnichestvo*, then extensive household crafts,—mainly because such economic activities are hardly known or completely unknown, whereas "visible" people and organizations are well known and described. Besides, communities do not differ much in the specific features of their local provincial economy. "Garazhniki" are also informally self-employed people; however, I do not deal in detail with this category, because in the province, it is a small and marginalized group.

Figure 6.1 illustrates how crafts and trades depend on the residential structure. Household crafts and otkhodnichestvo are widespread in rural areas and small towns and shrink in medium-sized and large cities. Otkhodnichestvo is the destiny of people living in small towns and villages; however, in the past decade, this type of activity has started spreading to larger cities. "Scattered manufactories" can be found only in small towns and their adjacent rural area; I have seen none either in medium-sized or in large cities and I suspect they cannot exist there (more on this below). By contrast, the "garage economy" is widespread only in large and medium-sized cities; in small towns, it is rare, and in the countryside—non-existent. We must however bear in mind that in small towns and villages, the volume and variety of informal economic practices is much greater than in medium-sized and large cities. Therefore, the figure shows only relative shares for each type of settlement separately. One should not compare the volumes of household crafts and the "garage economy"

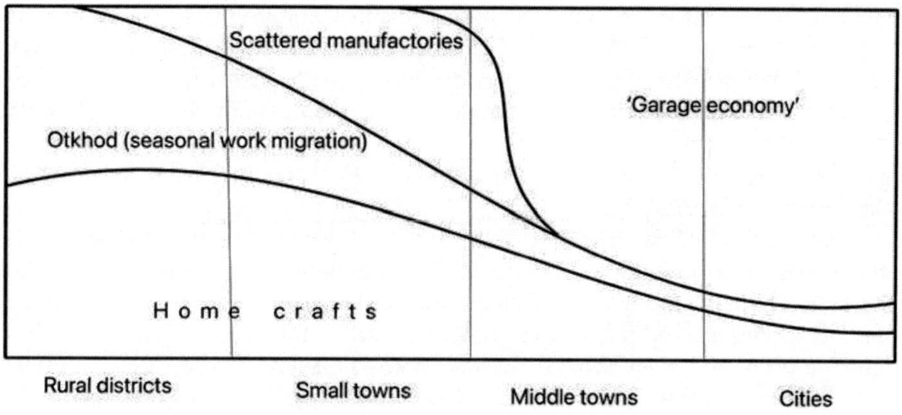

Fig. 6.1 The structure of informal economic practices (crafts and trades) depending on the settlement type. For details, see the text

based on their respective areas in the figure—the former is significantly higher than the latter. Similarly, *otkhodniks* are much more numerous than *"garazhniki."* Besides, the figure indicates the approximate correlation between the shares of crafts and trades in different settlement types. Obviously, these correlations are tentative, because the same families can be engaged simultaneously in various household crafts, as well as other types of activity, such as otkhodnichestvo, "scattered manufactories" and the "garage economy."

What can such a dissociation of *"residential and economic niches"* indicate? Please note that the greatest variety of crafts can be encountered only in small towns. This can be seen in the figure. There, all the four main types of informal economic practices are represented, including even the "garage economy." The rural district relies primarily and exclusively on household crafts and otkhodnichestvo. Only those rural residents who live in the immediate proximity of towns may participate in "scattered manufactories." In medium-sized and large cities, the "garage economy" is prevalent. Household crafts and otkhodnichestvo are of little significance; they are mostly the lot of residents living on the outskirts and in the suburbs. Large homesteads[4] in the village imply developed household production. Low population density and abundance of natural resources imply highly profitable crafts based on these natural resources. A lack of "cash" and no local sources of income because of the non-existent labor market forces rural residents to engage in otkhodnichestvo. The reverse is true for large and medium-sized cities. They have fairly developed

[4]The average area of the rural farmstead is formally 4000 m^2 (0.4 ha or 1 acre), but often it is larger. Many households have also remote field plots for growing potatoes and other vegetables; in addition, they can rent over 100 hectares of farmland for hayfields and grazing grounds. A tenth of the farmstead's area would be sufficient to provide an ordinary family of three–four people in the temperate zone of European Russia with potatoes; from a third to a half of this area (1500–2000 m^2) can yield a full supply of various vegetables, berries, and fruits. The rented hayfields and grazing grounds are sufficient to keep from ten to twenty cows plus several horses.

labor markets, and scarce sources of cash income always exist. But there is no chance to earn one's living by natural resources. Here, household crafts are limited to farming small (usually 300–600 m^2) garden plots, which can hardly serve as sources of income, though most urban families have them (Averkieva et al., 2016, pp. 300–335). Therefore, all additional income is obtained through *"odd jobs"* in garages, unless a person is engaged in criminal activities or seeks higher earnings in Siberia or *"the North."*

Small towns—those administrative centers of local communities—are in the worst position, both in terms of self-sufficiency opportunities and in terms of labor markets. This particularly affected small-town residents in the 1990s; the collapse of the local economy and the lack of sources for self-sufficiency resulted in poverty, extreme need, and even hunger; see my 1992–2000 field studies: Plusnin (1997, 2000). As a result, over the past three decades, the population of small towns was forced to develop various adaptation mechanisms, and in fact, by now it has become *"eurytopic"* in terms of subsistence patterns in a volatile environment. Therefore, the analysis of a local community's informal economy demonstrates significant differences between its two components—the administrative center and the rural district. In the rural district, crafts and trades are diverse, but homogeneous. In the administrative center, they are also diverse, but heterogeneous. Besides, the bulk of the local formal economy is concentrated there—four to eight dozen publicly funded institutions (that can hardly be found in the rural district), most manufacturing and service enterprises, and the majority of local businesspeople. Thus, a small town concentrates all local formal and informal economic practices. I perceive this as an essential achievement resulting from the population's successful adaptation to the economic collapse of the early 1990s.

6.2 The "Visible" Local Economy

In this subsection, I provide a very brief overview of the part of the local economy that is registered and recorded by the state statistics authorities, where enterprises and companies pay tax to the local budget; the local government reports to higher level public authorities based on the performance of all entities—large, medium, small and micro-enterprises and publicly funded institutions; and the aggregate economic performance is reflected in the relevant documents.[5] As mentioned above, I am considering the local economy in its simplest perspective by dividing it into three conditional segments: (1) the public sector, (2) material production and

[5] Such documents include the *Strategy for the Economic and Social and Development of the Municipality*, the *Forecast of Economic and Social Development…*, *Program…* or *Plan…*, as well as *Passport of the Municipality* and annual *Reports of the Heads of Municipalities on the Achieved Indicators for Evaluating the Performance of Local Self-Government Bodies…*

services, and (3) medium-sized and small businesses (which are also largely services).

6.2.1 The Public Sector

Every district has a significant number of publicly funded entities of regional government or local municipal subordination. As an illustration, I provide a fairly complete list of such entities in Table 6.1 below. Not every municipality has all of them, which is due to two reasons: historical and organizational. First, since the early Soviet days, many districts were established either as industrial or agricultural ones when transformed from the previous administrative-territorial units—*uyezds* of the Russian Empire. Accordingly, they received a different set of public entities. This distinction still exists. Secondly, some time ago (in the early 2000s) organizational changes significantly affecting provincial communities were undertaken to optimize the management of the public sector. In particular, same-type institutions in several neighboring districts were abolished with their functions transferred to an inter-district organization established in one location and serving several (24 or more) neighboring districts. Such are now many military commissariats, specialized hospitals, social security services, employment centers, etc. Therefore, Table 6.1 contains two columns, with the first one listing institutions available in any municipal district, and the second one—those located in districts with a special administrative status or there where inter-district territorial organizations have been set up.

The public sector can be classified by level of subordination (state or municipal) and by the scope of activity of the institutions and enterprises. The main group consists of "social reproduction" institutions. They engage the largest number of employees, and the local authorities focus on them in their annual reports and programs (*Plans* and *Strategies*) of the district's economic and social development. These are educational establishments: schools and childcare centers (kindergartens), educational facilities for children (art schools, music schools, etc.), additional education and secondary vocational education (colleges, apprenticeship training schools, and technical schools) institutions, and branches of higher education establishments. Education costs with regard to all of the above positions are the main expense item in the budget of the municipal, and often the urban, district. It accounts for 40 to 60 percent of all budget expenditures and, accordingly, the bulk of inter-budget transfers. In terms of staff, the second most numerous component unites municipal cultural institutions. These include community culture centers, libraries, museums, and cinemas. Financing these institutions is very costly; nevertheless, almost all municipalities still provide library services and maintain community culture centers in rural areas, as this is one of the most important factors of self-organization and self-government in rural settlements. Another component is physical culture and sports facilities (stadiums, football fields, ice hockey rinks, swimming pools, gyms, skiing centers, etc.), which are financed from the municipal budget with some financial support from the government. In any local community,

Table 6.1 List of public entities of government and municipal subordination in the status of territorial directorates, departments, services, etc., available in an urban/municipal district and located within the local community

Everywhere (in any local community)	In certain cases (see note)
District court	Arbitration court
Justice of the peace	Military Prosecutor's office
Bailiff service	Garrison
Prosecutor's office	Criminal investigation department
Military commissariat	Customs administration
District Department of the Interior (ROVD)	Fiscal supervision
Federal Security Service (FSB)	Geological supervision
Civil defense and Ministry of Emergency Situations District Department	Hydrometeorological and environmental monitoring administration
Pension fund department (PF)	Mining and industrial supervision
Social security fund division	Antimonopoly service
Social insurance	Subsoil use agency
Tax office	Natural resource use supervision
Federal Migration Service Directorate	Aviation rescue bases
Compulsory health insurance (fund)	Radiation control service
Forestry (forestry department)	Road supervision
Fisheries inspection (fisheries directorate)	Technology and environment supervision
Public health and social development supervision (Roszdravnadzor)	Drug control
Consumer rights protection (Rospotrebnadzor)	Territorial Administration of the Ministry of natural resources
Cadastral office	Penitentiary service (UFSIN)
Property management	Communications supervision
Labor inspection	Veterinary and phytosanitary service
Registration service (civil registry office—ZAGS)	Supervision of communications, information technology and mass media
Local mass media (district newspaper, local TV)	State registration, cadastre and cartography service
Road maintenance and construction department (DRSU)	Protected area (reserve/National Park/Nature Park/wildlife sanctuary)
Employment office	Additional vocational education
Sanitary and Epidemiological Station	Branches of higher educational institutions
Office of the Federal Treasury	Boarding schools
Branches of state-owned banks (Sberbank, VTB)	Care homes for the disabled and the elderly
Kindergartens	Correctional schools for juvenile delinquents
Secondary schools	Secondary vocational schools
Cultural institutions (community culture centers, libraries, museums, cinemas)	Health resorts, preventative clinics, health centers, infectious disease wards, etc.
Additional education facilities for children (culture and art studios, youth centers, art schools, music schools)	State District Power Station (GRES), Combined Heat and Power Plant (CHPP),

(continued)

Table 6.1 (continued)

Everywhere (in any local community)	In certain cases (see note)
	Hydroelectric Power Plant (HPP), Nuclear Power Plant (NPP), Gas Generator Plant (GGP)
Physical culture and sports facilities (stadiums, gyms, sports and recreation centers, swimming pools, junior sports schools)	
Health care facilities (district hospital, polyclinic, FAP = rural health post)	
Post office	
Telegraph, telephone, internet	
Local power distribution Authority of Electric Grid Companies	
Urban District or Municipal District Administration	
Administration of Urban and Rural Settlements	
Water supply and sewerage	
Housing and utilities management company	
Municipal cemetery	
Gas service	
Solid waste landfill ("garbage dump")	

The second column provides an expanded list of government and municipal entities when the administrative center of the local community is a significant regional town, an important industrial or transport hub housing inter-district territorial directorates of government entities; the district is a border area, or has a special administrative and territorial status (e.g., ZATO—closed administrative-territorial entity)

all people engaged in social reproduction institutions of the public sector (education, culture, and sports) account for over half of all public sector employees.

A significant proportion of public sector employees are health care workers. In the administrative centers, they work in district hospitals and clinics, in the rural district—in numerous rural health posts. Some communities (generally, this concerns industrial towns) have specialized health care facilities, which provide high-tech medical care. Unlike other "social reproduction" organizations mentioned, which are of municipal affiliation, health care was reinstalled under government management about 8–10 years ago due to the apparent inability of municipalities to manage this sphere at their own level (at a certain point, we focused on this process devoting several sociological field studies to it in 2009–2012; see Krasheninnikova (2017). Now, all health care institutions are public (obviously, with the exception of private health care, which is quite rare in the provinces, as opposed to large cities).

Municipal institutions and enterprises are a specific category of public employers. Primarily, they include the municipal administration of four types of municipalities: urban district, municipal district, and two types of settlements: urban and rural. All in all, they employ a small number of people—from 20–50, or 30 on average. Municipal institutions other than those involved in childcare, education, culture, and sports are quite few. Municipal unitary enterprises (MUPs) are more numerous, but most of their employees are hired workers who are paid based on operating results; only some of the employees are "*budgetniki*."

Government entities represented in local communities include various funds; financial institutions; courts; numerous monitoring and supervisory agencies, including public prosecutors, the police, Federal Security Service, financial and economic monitoring and industry supervision services, and communications and information technology supervision services; military and paramilitary organizations; and public utilities services. They are also listed in the second column in Table 6.1. From half to two-thirds of all public sector employees work in such entities. The largest number serves in law enforcement bodies: district departments of the Interior (ROVD) have a staff of 200–300 people. Therefore, in small municipalities, these organizations are often the principal employers.

Thus, any small municipality has at least 40–50 public entities; in frequent cases (where the population ranges from 50,000 to 100,000 people), their number can even exceed 80. That is why the public sector constitutes such a significant part of the local economy in terms of people employed. The smaller the local community, the higher the proportion of "*budgetniki*." On average, they range from 20 to 40 percent of the total working-age population. In some cases, where only half of the residents are engaged in the local economy, their share reaches even 60–70 percent.

6.2.2 Material Production

Material production generally accounts for about 40 percent of all engaged in the local economy; in certain cases, this share ranges from 20 to 60–70 percent depending on the degree of industrial development. If the area is industrial and has several medium and large enterprises (mines, mining and processing plants, high-tech production plants, woodworking plants, food processing plants, agro-industrial complexes, farms, etc.), a significant part of those engaged in the local economy work there. At most, this amounts to about 40 percent of the total working-age population (or the total economically active population, which exceeds the working-age one by about 10 percent). However, such communities are few, with the share of those engaged in material production averaging 15–25 percent. For the provincial society, this is a considerable skew, since only 20–30 years ago, this figure reached 50–70 percent. It is also one of the main reasons why senior age workers are eliminated from the local economy. They no longer have the individual ability and technical capacity to undergo vocational retraining in a new occupation, especially in the service sector, which is unusual and psychologically unacceptable for them; so, they are left with only two options—engage in the "shadow" economy or undertake low-wage unskilled jobs. Since in the provinces, wages in this latter sphere are 25–30 percent lower than average pensions, people see no reason to seek such earnings and spend their time, which they can successfully devote to significantly more lucrative shadow crafts.

The backbone of material production in provincial Russia is formed by private companies and enterprises engaged in the light industry, agriculture, construction, and transport. Large enterprises are few here, usually, from one to three, and in three-fifths of the communities—none at all. In my main sample, only 60 communities have large enterprises (42%). Generally, local statistics record large enterprises together with medium-sized ones, listing the former separately. The number of the latter ones (medium-sized enterprises) directly depends on the size of the local population. The relative number of large and medium-sized enterprises per 10,000 residents is about a dozen and a half. This would mean from 40 to 50 enterprises of such scale per average provincial community with just over 30,000 residents; from 10 to 30—per 20,000 inhabitants; and about a hundred—when the population exceeds 40,000 people. In reality, of course, the spread is much larger: from several units to a few hundred enterprises. At first glance, it seems easy to count such enterprises in each local community. In practice, however, reporting statistics are very vague with figures varying in different documents; therefore, it is unclear, what information to rely on.

In industrial areas, large and medium-sized enterprises form the basis of the local economy, accounting for over two-thirds of the value of all produced and shipped goods. The output of small and micro-enterprises, which are considerably more numerous (dozens of times), is significantly lower.[6] In rural areas, of which there are more in the country, the economy is based on agro-industrial complexes (if any—they operate mainly in the south of European Russia and in south Siberia), meat and dairy complexes, butter and cheese factories, and peasant farms. Livestock herding is practiced in Arctic communities (reindeer herding) and in the south of Siberia and European Russia (cattle, sheep, and horse breeding). In recent decades, private domestic animal husbandry and livestock herding have been "*squeezed out*" by agro-industrial complexes, which focus on indoor livestock breeding (especially pig farming).

In many northern communities and throughout Siberia, the economy is based on the timber industry: logging, transportation of timber, and to a lesser extent its on-site processing (production of sawn timber, which usually accounts for only a quarter of all the timber harvested). Small businesses (logging camps and sawmills), which were widely engaged in harvesting and primary processing of commercial timber in the 1990s and 2000s—at that time, every timber-oriented local community had from 10 to 50 of them—since the 2010s have been replaced by large enterprises. Most of them are "alien" not only to the local community, but also to the entire region. Since they pay no taxes to the local budget, while displacing local timber merchants, such enterprises are perceived as *"thieves"* robbing both local resources and the population. There are plenty examples of such predatory behavior of outsiders—almost every community in the forest regions (Kargopol in the Arkhangelsk

[6]This is typical of the entire Russian economy: according to Rosstat, only 0.1% of the largest enterprises in the real sector of the economy (6000) generate two-thirds of all output (https://www.gks.ru/folder/10705)

Region, Kologriv in Kostroma Region, Yeniseysk in Krasnoyarsk Territory, Chuna in the Irkutsk Region, Kavalerovo in Primorye Territory, etc.) has a story to tell.

Many local communities specialize in a very narrow range of activities. My sample also contains single-industry towns—a total of 21 out of 142 communities (15%), which roughly corresponds to the share of single-industry settlements in all urban settlements in Russia (out of 321 such settlements, see (http://моногорода.рф/ and https://regnum.ru/news/1886332.html)). In single-industry towns, over a quarter of working-age residents are employed at a large and usually only enterprise; in small towns, this figure can exceed half of the population.

6.2.3 Services

In provincial societies, the service sector is represented mainly by trade and to a lesser extent, by transport services (taxi, freight carriage, and car repair and maintenance). Consumer services (repair of household appliances, private construction and minor renovation of premises, beauty parlors, and utilities) bring up the rear. In contrast to the Soviet era, consumer service providers have seriously deteriorated. Except perhaps for funeral services and hairdressers. In any provincial town, a visitor is certain to find up to two dozen hairdressers and half a dozen funeral parlors. Such practices flourish in the west and south of the European part of Russia (here, towns with only 20,000–30,000 residents can have several—up to a dozen—cemeteries; often, they are not municipal but private, and many of them are unregistered, i.e., formally non-existent). In general, consumer services in the formal segment of the economy are completely undeveloped. This is due to the fact that back in the early 1990s, such services quickly and easily migrated to the informal segment; many services are home-based, provided privately and untaxed.

In the provinces, the basis of the service sector is trade, where over 90 percent of all private businesses are engaged. There are three basic types of trade entities here: (1) local retail outlets, (2) supermarkets, and (3) weekly markets. The first type is represented by private shops operating from a variety of locations—former apartments in residential premises; basements of multi-storey buildings; specially built separate booths; or solid shopping centers. There are still quite a few vendor kiosks that were the most widespread type of "*retail outlets*" in the 1990s. An important characteristic of provincial retail outlets is a certain invariance in the correlation between their number and the number of households in each particular settlement. My long-term diverse observations show that a retail outlet in the province can break even and survive only if it serves at least 30 households (approximately 100–120 people). By now, this correlation has stabilized in most local centers—they are all saturated with sales outlets.

However, in the past 5–7 years, this balance has been broken by the mass emergence of grocery retail chains in the province (especially *Magnit, Pyaterochka, Dixy, Perekrestok, Maria-Ra*, etc.). They draw customers away from small shops forcing those to close. Local residents and local experts alike, rightly regard these trends as detrimental to the local economy. Goods in supermarkets are cheaper than in the local shops, but their quality is much lower. More importantly, besides ruining the local trade, such policies of retail chains also destroy local production of foodstuffs, which are generally of much higher quality but more expensive. Thus, retailers deal a double or even triple blow to the local economy. Firstly, they squeeze out local trade; secondly, they destroy the real sector of the local economy; and thirdly, reduce thereby the local labor market.

The third basic type of trade in the province is the market. Insignificant and inconspicuous at first glance, in reality it is a very important institution. Market trade takes place every week on a specified day in all, without exception, district centers of the country, and in some large villages. It goes on only from morning to noon, but it is one of the most significant social institutions, because it performs several important functions. Besides being an actual marketplace (which can well be replaced by chain stores and retail outlets), the market acts as a classic *forum*. On a certain day of the week, people gather from all over the area to meet with their acquaintances at the market and to chat. Women demonstrate their outfits. Men arrange fishing, hunting, and get-togethers. This is an archaic institution, which has remained unchanged in the province since Imperial and earlier times, just as it has been in Europe since ages (Pirenne, 1937, pp. 9–10). It continues to perform these functions throughout provincial towns. There is no single district center without a weekly market. On such days—usually workdays rather than weekends—public entities stand empty; shops and clinics are overcrowded; banks and offices issuing various certificates and permits display long queues. People come to the market to buy food for a week, and to settle other issues at the same time. In these few market hours, the town transforms: people and cars fill all the nearby streets and space. In the afternoon, the center with the market square empties, and merchant vehicles head out of town to meet the following day in another district center where the next market is scheduled. The tradition is important and its significance is more social than commercial.

Transport services are a relatively recent segment, which has emerged along with and following the motorization of the population and simultaneous deterioration of public transport in the province. Similar to large cities, in the past 30 years the province has gone the way from rare private cars to sweeping motorization: almost every family owns one or two vehicles. In addition, many provincial households also have tractors, trucks, snowmobiles, quad bikes, motorcycles (somewhere even private helicopters, as in some Far Eastern and Arctic settlements). All this equipment requires repairs and maintenance, so respective services, above all for cars, have surged. According to my rough estimates, administrative centers have one auto repair shop per 300–500 families. But there are even more private unregistered workshops in garages. In addition, many people continue repairing their cars themselves. Private taxi services have grown significantly. Every town now has three to five taxi operators with 5–10 hired taxi drivers. "*...Only students and pensioners take cabs nowadays*"—those who have no cars of their own yet. Trucking services have expanded. Meanwhile, a significant part of all transport services remains in the "*shadow*;" according to local experts, the ratio of registered and "shadow" enterprises is 1:2.

Besides the above three types of services, there are also two new ones, which emerged only in the post-Soviet years and are developing as rapidly as in the large cities. These are information services and private home building. Internet is available in all towns and large villages, with many of them enjoying high-speed fiber optic communication; besides satellite television with dozens or even hundreds of channels, most families have personal computers, laptops, and smartphones. It will not be an exaggeration to say that the entire population of the province is provided with information services. Television and telephone connections already lag behind Internet communications. Adults and teenagers, small children and senior citizens alike are all immersed in the information field. Accordingly, the volume of services provided via the Internet has grown immeasurably, both within the local community and with the outside world. Purchasing various goods online from China has become common practice for many families. Local e-commerce is also developing. The Internet is now a marketplace for self-made foodstuffs (cakes, pastry, gingerbread, jam, etc.), wine and moonshine, books and antiques, and also criminal deals (drug trafficking). Construction and renovation services have evolved similarly due to a boom in private home building, which the province has been experiencing since the 2000s, a while after the major cities. Yet, these service sector segments, other than trade, have only one foot in the formal economy, with most of the business conducted informally.

6.2.4 Small Business

Small and micro-business is the most complicated and least-known segment of the local economy. Only a minor part of it is registered, with the bulk staying in "shadow." Rough estimates, based on indirect data, local expert opinions and direct observations, suggest that the ratio of registered to unregistered businesses is between 1:2 and 1:5, perhaps even more. The ratio is very volatile and depends on repressive policies of the government. For example, the recent campaign of "bringing the self-employed out of the shadows" has reduced the number of both informal and formally registered entrepreneurs everywhere. In the 1990s and the 2000s, few sole proprietors believed in conducting *"visible"* business. This affected, in particular, the attitude of researchers when depicting small business in different periods; e.g. Radaev (1999), Alimova et al. (2011), Chepurenko et al. (2017), Chepurenko (2019a, b). According to my observations, in the 1990s, the ratio of formally registered and *"shadow"* businesses in some small towns reached 1:10. This is no longer the case. Therefore, I am able to provide only a fragmentary description of small business in the formal economy relying exclusively on municipal reports and statistics compiled by territorial registration authorities. However, all reports are inaccurate with data varying considerably from year to year. Thus, in the interval over the past 5–8 years, discrepancies in municipal reports regarding the number of registered legal entities, sole proprietors, service enterprises, and people employed in small business reach 20%–25% and more.

The number of small and medium-sized enterprises registered in a municipality with a population of approximately 30,000 people averages 400. Figures vary from two dozen to two-three thousand enterprises. In terms of 10,000 population, the relative number of such enterprises ranges from 10–15 to 200. Such differences stem from the type of community. Isolated communities have relatively few enterprises (in the range of 20–80), whereas turbulent ones—a lot more (in the range of 100–200). In coercively established communities, they are about a third fewer in number than in naturally developing ones, since the former almost always have large backbone enterprises employing a lot of people.

Small businesses employ from one-fifth to a third of the total working-age population, or from a quarter to two-thirds of those engaged in the local economy. In isolated communities, their share is high (40–60 percent of the employed in the local economy), whereas in turbulent communities, it does not exceed 25–30 percent. Such businesses employ an average of ten people, although in different communities, figures vary from five to fifty plus personnel.

The number of formally registered sole proprietors ranges from under a hundred to five-six thousand; the average figure per community is 800–900. Per every thousand residents, there are about twenty-six sole proprietors (approximately every fifteenth family). However, with regard to the working-age population, the number of sole proprietors ranges from thirty to sixty per thousand inhabitants. Given the average family size in Russia (2.7 people), this means every tenth family (spread from 1:15 to 1:7). In other words, a very large proportion of families are engaged in business: with two able-bodied adults, from every seventh to every third family is somehow involved in business activities. We should, however, bear in mind that this concerns primarily commerce, small trade: over three quarters of all sole proprietors are in the service sector (trade, public catering, consumer services, tourism and hospitality).

Differences in the number of sole proprietors are associated with the type of community: in isolated and "ordinary" communities, they are about half as many as in turbulent ones (30–35 versus 55–60 per 1000 inhabitants). This is most likely due to the fact that compared to the inhabitants of turbulent communities, people living in isolation have more opportunities to conduct business *"in the shadow,"* and that is indeed what they do. Generally, such businesses employ from one to four workers.

Meanwhile, all these ratios can vary greatly not only from decade to decade, but even from year to year; they depend on the state's legislative and fiscal policy, which is highly inconsistent and unpredictable when viewed from a grassroots perspective. Therefore, any change almost always rapidly reduces the number of formally registered sole proprietors by several, sometimes by a dozen, percent. Therefore, the administration of a municipality may within a year "lose" from fifty to a hundred sole proprietors who liquidated their business and slipped into the "*shadow*."

Sole proprietors in the province are most closely linked (and often merge) with "*garazhniki*." Here, it is difficult, and often impossible, to distinguish them. What are the features of the *"garage economy*" in provincial communities?

6.3 "Garage Economy" and Shadow Self-Employment

As I already mentioned, the "garage economy" in the province is very sporadic and can be encountered almost only in the administrative centers of turbulent communities, where there are many multi-storey buildings and, respectively, garage-building cooperatives, which host the "garage economy." Therefore, in most provincial communities, such business does not concentrate in garages, and rather than being specialized it is fuzzy and indistinguishable from shadow self-employment in production and services. Moreover, the "garage economy" in the province is almost indistinguishable from many other "home-based" crafts, as I will outline further in Chap. 8.

Obviously, when considering small business in the formal economy, we clearly distinguish business owners from others occupied in the real sector—both hired workers engaged in production and services, and public sector employees. It is quite another case with informal economy, where the differences are far from obvious. A significant part of "garazhniki," many artel workers in "scattered manufactories," as well as otkhodniks are in fact—though not in form—entrepreneurs. Each of them engages in some business (is a *"businessperson"*). Otkhodniks independently and proactively offer their own products and services on external (for the local community) markets. "Garazhniki" and "manufactureres" do the same, only from home. Of course, some of these people are not entrepreneurs, but only informally hired artel workers, where there is a need to form production teams, artels (of course, this is not always necessary). A team operating locally (within the community) usually consists of a foreman-entrepreneur and two to four hired workers. Otkhodniks earning their living far from home generally form larger teams—from four to ten people. We should, however, bear in mind that the participation of team members in an artel is radically different from that in an ordinary production or office team. In an artel, each participant is an entrepreneur, even though subordinate to the will of the superior and the objectives of the artel.

Given these considerations, a lot more people are actually engaged in real, though "unexposed," business activities than those recorded in state registers as small (and individual) entrepreneurs. According to insider estimates obtained in small towns only (without the rural district), the ratio of registered and unregistered entrepreneurs ranges from 1:3 to 1:5. My estimates from various areas of Russia indicate that in the period from 2000 to 2020, in each municipal district "shadow" enterprise accounted for up to eighty percent of all small business, both in terms of output and number of people engaged (especially where it concerned economic practices based on natural resources).

It is, however, difficult to make such estimates, because the majority of even formally registered small (and individual) businesses disclose only a minor part of their products/services in the financial statements, and it is unclear whether a certain entrepreneur operates openly (with statutory reporting) or mostly in the "shadow." At the same time, it is much easier in the provinces than in large cities to operate completely in the "shadow," without registering one's business at all, due to reciprocal family and neighborly ties and available facilities (many households have large private grounds or "scattered" outbuildings, even unregistered in the cadastre).

I will attempt to demonstrate the features of the provincial "garage economy" by comparing it with similar "*garage-based*" trades recorded by my colleagues in large cities (Seleev & Pavlov, 2016, pp. 36–37). I used their Table 3 listing more than 110 types of garage-based crafts and trades that they identified in 21 Russian cities to compile the following Table 6.2, which includes only those trades and crafts that I recorded in provincial towns. Once again, most of them are practiced only in the administrative centers of turbulent communities. Their scale is extremely small compared to the "garage economy" in large cities. However, these practices exist in the province, and they should not be ignored. Provincial towns feature at least half of the crafts that S. Seleev and A. Pavlov identified in large cities. Certain crafts do not exist, because the lack of specialized works or hi-tech production facilities in the province means that there are also no craftsmen capable of performing similar work in private garages. On the other hand, some trades cannot be practiced in large cities. This primarily concerns the procurement and processing of specific natural resources unavailable in a major city. All these types of "*garage-based*" crafts and trades are largely informal shadow or criminal economic activities of the population. Almost everywhere, they are "*invisible*," and hence unrecorded in municipal reports.

A look at the table shows that the use of garages not in line with their main purpose (car storage) is associated with activities that are dangerous or cannot be performed at home, such as repairing tools and mechanisms and processing natural or technical products. In the province, garages are used either for their intended purpose or as sheds, storehouses, and workshops. They rarely serve as production facilities. In general, the "garage economy" in the province is not diversified and has not gone beyond addressing transport and repair problems. Garages serve to store vehicles, repair them and perform activities directly associated with transport, carriage, and transportation services. And in this respect, such activities should be attributed, by and large, to household crafts.

6.4 Conclusion: Uniformity of the Formal Economy

The most notable and most important feature of the formal, "first," economy in the Russian province is its uniformity. It is the same everywhere, primarily because its backbone is the public sector, which has a standard arrangement throughout the country. The service sector is similar and similarly underdeveloped everywhere. Even the format of market trade (weekly visiting bazaars) is the same throughout Russia. It would seem that at least material production should demonstrate diverse types and variable forms. But in the province, this sector has withered away 30 years ago, and only here and there local plants and companies deliver to the federal market. Individual enterprise, everywhere under a quarter of local production, is extremely unimpressive. The formal economy of the province creates a uniform gray background, with shades barely discernible from area to area and region to region.

Table 6.2 Crafts practiced in private garages and garage-building cooperatives in small towns (Seleev & Pavlov, 2016)

Type of economic activity					
Type of craft		Procurement	Processing	Manufacturing	Sales
Crafts and trades based on natural resources	Forestry, hunting		Producing hunting supplies. Woodworking workshops. Processing hides and antlers	Lumber workshops	
	Fishing	Fishing bases. Boat stations, boathouses	Fish and seafood processing (drying, smoking, and canning)	Growing fish bait (bloodworms)	Sale of fresh fish and seafood; sale of processed products
	Procuring local minerals		Ferrous and non-ferrous metal scrap yards	Production of ornamental materials (stones for bathhouses)	Sales of building stone, gravel, and sand
	Household production and processing	Dovecotes, poultry yards, pigsties, stables	Processing of medicinal and narcotic raw materials (cannabis, gold and red roots, ginseng, mushrooms)	Making wood and metal handicrafts (toys, home decorations, household appliance parts)	Sales of homemade alcoholic beverages (moonshine, chacha, arrack, wine, home brew, alcohol).
Infrastructural crafts and trades	Manufacturing	Purchase of used spare parts and cars	Tool workshops	Dressmakers, shoemakers, down and fur workshops	
	Construction		Machines for processing wooden and metal structural elements	Production of furniture, doors, windows, and floors	Sales of construction materials (wood, stone, crushed stone, sand)
	Transport		Auto repair shops, car service, motorcycle service, bicycle service, tire shops	Manufacturing and reconditioning spare parts for cars and tractors	
	Real estate transactions, leases			Construction of garages for sale	Residential garages; hobby clubs
Services	Trade	Garage-warehouses	Retail packaging of goods		Shops. Vendor kiosks
	Utilities			Argon welding, sharpening and repair of household tools	Specific relaxation services

And against this bleak background, a vibrant diversity of informal economic practices are flourishing. Latently, in the "shadow" rather than the light, the people's economic activity is bubbling. Every household and every person, young and old, is engaged in it. This is not a metaphor: the informal economy embraces the elderly, adults, and children. Each household practices up to a dozen types of crafts, each village—several dozen, and each local community—up to a hundred diverse crafts and trades. Therefore, considering the provincial economy, we must first and foremost focus on informal economic activities of households.

In the two following chapters, I deal with distinctive informal economic practices: firstly, represented by two archaic institutions with opposing fundamental principles—"scattered manufactories" (workshop-based production process) and otkhodnichestvo (circular labor migration), and secondly, by numerous crafts based on households.

References

Alexeev, M., Gaddy, C., & Leitzel, J. (1995). Economic crime and Russian reform. *Journal of Institutional and Theoretical Economics/Zeitschrift für die gesamte Staatswissenschaft, 151*(4), 677–692.

Alimova, T. A., Chenina, A. V., & Chepurenko, A. Y. (2011). Economic crisis and entrepreneurial activity of the population of Russia: starting a business or leaving a business? *The World of Russia, 20*(2), 142–160. Алимова Т.А., Ченина А.В., Чепуренко А.Ю. (2011). Экономический кризис и предпринимательская деятельность населения России: открывать свое дело или выходить из бизнеса? *Мир России*. 20(2), 142–160.

Averkieva, K. V., Antonov, E. V., Kirillov, P. L., Makhrova, A. G., et al. (2016). *Between home and ... home. Reversible spatial mobility of the population of Russia*. New Chronograph. Аверкиева К.В., Антонов Е.В., Кириллов П.Л., Махрова А.Г., и др. (2016). *Между домом и. . .домом. Возвратная пространственная мобильность населения России*. М.: Новый Хронограф.

Barsukova, S. Y. (2003a). Informal economy: Concept, structure. *Economic Sociology, 4*(4), 15–36. Барсукова С.Ю. (2003a). Неформальная экономика: понятие, структура. *Экономическая социология*, 4(4), 15–36.

Barsukova, S. Y. (2003b). Networking mutual aid of Russian households: Theory and practice of the economy of the gift. *World of Russia, 12*(2), 81–122. Барсукова С.Ю. (2003b). Сетевая взаимопомощь российских домохозяйств: теория и практика экономики дара. *Мир России*, 12(2), 81–122.

Barsukova, S. Y. (2004). *Informal economy: Economic and sociological analysis*. Publishing House of the Higher School of Economics. Барсукова С.Ю. (2004). *Неформальная экономика: экономико-социологический анализ*. Москва: Изд-во ГУ ВШЭ.

Barsukova, S. Y. (2009). *The informal economy*. Publishing House of the Higher School of Economics. Барсукова С.Ю. (2009). *Неформальная экономика*. Москва: Издательский дом Гос. ун-т – Высшая школа экономики.

Barsukova, S. Y. (2015). *An essay on the informal economy, or 16 shades of gray*. Publishing House of the Higher School of Economics. Барсукова С.Ю. (2015). *Эссе о неформальной экономике, или 16 оттенков серого*. Москва: Издательский дом Высшая школа экономики.

Barsukova, S., & Radaev, V. V. (2012). Informal economy in Russia: A brief overview. *Economic Sociology. The European electronic newsletter, 13*(2), 4–12.

Chepurenko, A. (2019a). Different types on informal entrepreneurs in fragile 'transitional' context: Case based evidence in Russia. In B. Dallado & E. Tortia (Eds.), *Entrepreneurship and local economic development: A comparative perspective on entrepreneurs, universities and governments* (pp. 1–29). Routledge.

Chepurenko, A. Y. (2019b). Flexibility of the organizational structure and typology of informal small business in Russia. According to a longitudinal study (2013–2015). *Economic Sociology, 20*(4), 39–69. Чепуренко А. Ю. (2019). Гибкость организационной структуры и типология неформального малого предпринимательства в России. По данным лонгитюдного исследования (2013-2015). *Экономическая социология*, 20(4), 39–69.

Chepurenko, A., Popovskaya, E., & Obraztsova, O. (2017). Cross-regional variations in the motivation of early-stage entrepreneurial activity in Russia: Determining factors. In A. Sauka & A. Chepurenko (Eds.), *Entrepreneurship in transition economies. Diversity, trends, and perspectives* (pp. 315–342). Springer.

Gimpelson, V. E., & Kapelyushnikov, R. I. (Eds.). (2006). *Precarious employment in the Russian economy*. Publishing House of the Higher School of Economics. Гимпельсон В.Е., Капелюшников Р.И. (ред.) (2006). *Нестандартная занятость в российской экономике*. М.: Издательский Дом ГУ-ВШЭ.

Gimpelson, V. E. & Kapelyushnikov, R. I. (Eds.) (2014). *In the shadow of regulation: Informality in the Russian Labor Market*. Publishing House of the Higher School of Economics. В тени регулирования: неформальность на российском рынке труда (2014). / Под ред. В.Е. Гимпельсона и Р.И. Капелюшникова. М.: Изд. дом Высшей школы экономики.

Grossman, G. (1977). The second economy of the USSR. *Problems of Communism, 26*(5), 40.

Grossman, G. (1979). Notes on the illegal private economy and corruption. In G. Grossman (Ed.), *The Soviet economy in a time of change, by U.S., Congress, Joint Economic Committee* (pp. 834–855). Government Printing Office. Accessed from https://www.jec.senate.gov/public/index.cfm/1980/12/report-da446217-b7f8-42d5-896f-c7092e64b031

Grossman, G. (1987). The second economy in the USSR and Eastern Europe: A bibliography. *Berkeley-Duke occasional papers on the second economy in the USSR*, 1. University of California, Berkeley, and Duke University. Accessed from http://public.econ.duke.edu/Papers//Treml.BDOP.html

Grossman, G. (Ed.). (1988). *Studies in the second economy of communist countries*. University of California Press.

Guha-Khasnobis, B., Kanbur, R., & Ostrom, E. (2006). *Linking the formal and informal economy: Concepts and policies*. Oxford University Press.

Il'in, V. I. (2001a). Gift as a social phenomenon. *Frontier (almanac of social research)* 16/17. Accessed from http://socnet.narod.ru/Rubez/16-17/il'in.htm. Ильин В.И. (2001a). Подарок как социальный феномен. *Рубеж (альманах социальных исследований)* 16/17.

Il'in, V. I. (2001b). *Russian bazaar: Social organization and marketing*. Syktyvkar. Ильин В.И. (2001b). *Российский базар: социальная организация и маркетинг*. Сыктывкар.

Kalugina, Z. I., & Fadeeva, O. P. (2009). *Russian village in the labyrinth of reforms: Sociological sketches*. Publishing House of IEOPP SO RAN. Калугина З.И., Фадеева О.П. (2009). *Российская деревня в лабиринте реформ: социологические зарисовки*. Новосибирск: Изд-во ИЭОПП СО РАН.

Kordonskiy, S. G., & Plusnin, J. M. (2018). Archaic economic institutions: Distributed manufactories in small cities of Russia. *World of Russia, 27*(4), 6–30. Кордонский С.Г., Плюснин Ю.М. (2018). Архаические экономические институты: распределенные мануфактуры в малых городах России. *Мир России*, 27(4), 6–30.

Kordonsky, S. G. (2010). *Russia. Local federation*. Publishing House "Europe". Кордонский С.Г. (2010). *Россия. Поместная федерация*. Издательство «Европа».

Krasheninnikova, Y. (2017). *Informal healthcare in contemporary Russia. Sociographic essays on the post-soviet infrastructure for alternative healing practices*. ibidem.

Kulisher, I. M. (2004). *History of the Russian national economy*. Socium. Кулишер И.М. (2004). *История русского народного хозяйства*. Челябинск: Социум.

Ledeneva, A. (Ed.). (2018). *The global Encyclopaedia of informality. Understanding social and cultural complexity*. UCL Press.

Nikulin, A. N. (1998). Enterprises and families in Russia: Socio-cultural symbiosis. In T. I. Zaslavskaya (Ed.), *Where is Russia going? Transformation of the social sphere and social policy* (pp. 218–229). Delo. Никулин А.Н. (1998). Предприятия и семьи в России: социокультурный симбиоз. В кн.: *Куда идет Россия? Трансформация социальной сферы и социальная политика*/Под общ.ред. Т.И.Заславской. М.: Дело. С. 218–229.

Nikulin, A. M. (Ed.) (2012). *The Second Russia: Differentiation and self-organization*. Delo Publishing House, RANEPA. *Вторая Россия: дифференциация и самоорганизация* (2012). (Под общ.ред. А.М. Никулина). М.: Издательский дом «Дело» РАНХиГС.

Pavlov, A. B., & Seleev, S. S. (2015). Phenomenological description of modern crafts. *Universum: Obschestvennye nauki, 3*(13), 25–41. Павлов А.Б., Селеев С.С. (2015). *Феноменологическое описание современных промыслов*. Универсум: Общественные науки. Accessed from http://7universum.com/ru/social/archive/item/2015

Pilikhovsky, A., & Stolbov, V. (2000). Informal cooperation in rural communities. *Sociological Research, 1*, 34–36. Пилиховский А., Столбов В. (2000). Неформальная кооперация в сельских общинах. *Социологические исследования*, 1, 34–36.

Pirenne, H. (1937). *Economic and social history of medieval Europe*. Harcourt Brace.

Plusnin, J. M. (1997). Psychology of material life (paradoxes of rural economy of survival). *ECO: Economics and Organization of Industrial Production, 7*, 169–176. Плюснин Ю.М. (1997). Психология материальной жизни (парадоксы сельской экономики выживания). *ЭКО: экономика и организация промышленного производства*.

Plusnin, J. M. (2000). *Small Russian towns*. Moscow Public Science Foundation. Плюснин Ю.М. (2000). *Малые города России*. : МОНФ.

Plusnin J.M. (2016). Far from the state: Migrant workers and power in modern Russia. *Public Administration Issues, 1*, 60–80. Плюснин Ю.М. Вдали от государства: отходники и власть в современной России. *Вопросы государственного и муниципального управления*, 1, 60–80.

Plusnin, J. M., Zausaeva, Y. D., Zhidkevich, N. N., & Pozanenko, A. A. (2013). *Othodniki*. New chronograph. Плюснин Ю.М., Заусаева Я.Д., Жидкевич Н.Н., Позаненко А.А. (2013). *Отходники*. М.: Новый хронограф.

Plusnin, J., Zausaeva, Y., Zhidkevich, N., & Pozanenko, A. (2015). *Wandering workers. Mores, behavior, way of life, and political status of domestic Russian labor migrants*. Ibidem.

Radaev, V. V. (1999). Shadow economy in Russia: Changing contours. *Pro et Contra, 4*(1, 10), 5–24. Радаев В.В. (1999). Теневая экономика в России: изменение контуров. *Pro et Contra*, 4(1, 10), 5–24.

Rutgeizer, V. (1992). The shadow economy in the USSR. In G. Grossman, & V. G. Treml (Eds.), *Berkeley-Duke occasional papers on the second economy in the USSR* (pp. 1–77). Durham, NC: Duke University. Paper No 34.

Sampson, S. L. (1987). The second economy of the Soviet Union and Eastern Europe. *The Annals of the American Academy of Political and Social Sciences, 493*(1), 120–136. https://doi.org/10.1177/0002716287493001009

Schumacher, E. F. (1973). *Small is beautiful. Economics as if people matter.* Blond and Briggs. Russian edition: Шумахер Э.Ф. (2012). Малое прекрасно. Экономика, в которой люди имеют значение. М.: Издательский дом Высшей школы экономики.

Scott J. (1976). *The moral economy of the peasant: Rebellion and subsistence in Southeast Asia*. Yale University Press. Russian edition: Скотт Дж. (1999). *Моральная экономика деревни*. В кн.: *Неформальная экономика: Россия и мир*. Т. Шанин (отв. ред.). М.: Логос. Accessed from https://yalebooks.yale.edu/book/9780300021905/moral-economy-peasant

Seleev, S. S., & Pavlov, A. B. (2016). *Garages*. Strana OZ. Селеев С.С., Павлов А.Б. (2016). *Гаражники*. М.: Страна ОЗ.

Shabanova, M. A. (1992). Modern otkhodnichestvo as a sociocultural phenomenon. *Sociological Researches, 4*, 55–63. Шабанова М.А. (1992). Современное отходничество как социокультурный феномен. *Социологические исследования*, 4, 55–63.

Shanin, T. (Ed.) (1999). *The informal economy. Russia and the World*. Logos. Шанин Т. (ред.), (1999). *Неформальная экономика. Россия и мир*. М.: Логос.

Shokhin, A. (1987). Struggle with unearned income: Socio-psychological aspect. *Planned Economy, 2*, 83–89. Шохин А. (1987). Борьба с нетрудовыми доходами: социально-психологический аспект. *Плановое хозяйство*, 2, 83–89.

Standing, G. (2011). The precariat. *The new dangerous class*. Bloomsbury Publishing Plc. Russian edition: Стэндинг Г. (2014). Прекариат: новый опасный класс. М.: Ад Маргинем Пресс.

Steinberg, I. E. (2002). Real practice of rural family survival strategies – "network resources". In T. I. Zaslavskaya (Ed.), *Where is Russia going? Formal institutions and real practices* (pp. 183–189). MVShSEN. Штейнберг И.Е. (2002). Реальная практика стратегий выживания сельской семьи – «сетевые ресурсы» В кн.: *Куда идет Россия? Формальные институты и реальные практики* (с. 183–189). Под общ.ред. Т.И.Заславской. М.: МВШСЭН.

Tikhonova, N. E., Lezhnina, Y. P., Mareeva, S. V., Anikin, V. A., et al. (2018). *Model of income stratification of Russian society: Dynamics, factors, cross-country comparisons*. Publishing House Nestor-Istoriya. Тихонова Н.Е., Лежнина Ю.П., Мареева С.В., Аникин В.А., Каравай А.В., Слободенюк Е.Д. (2018). *Модель доходной стратификации российского общества: динамика, факторы, межстрановые сравнения*. М.: Изд-во Нестор-История.

Vakhitov, R. (2017). Handicraft as a phenomenon of estate society. *Economics and Management: Scientific and Practical Journal, 1*(135), 51–57. Вахитов Р. (2017). Промысел как феномен сословного общества. *Экономика и управление: научно-практический журнал*, 1(135), 51–57.

Vodarsky, Y. E., & Istomina, E. G. (2004). *Rural handicrafts of European Russia at the turn of the XIX-XX centuries*. IRI RAN. Водарский Я.Е., Истомина Э.Г. (2004). Сельские кустарные промыслы Европейской России на рубеже XIX-XX столетий. М.: ИРИ РАН.

Vorontsov, V. P. (2015). *Essays on the handicraft industry in Russia*. LENAND. Воронцов В.П. (2015). *Очерки кустарной промышленности в России*. М.: ЛЕНАНД.

Chapter 7
Archaic Economy: Wandering Workers and Scattered Manufactories

In the Russian province, people also practice special forms of economic behavior, which remain completely "invisible" to official statistics. Their status is special because these are archaic forms of economy, long-standing and long-forgotten, but spontaneously resumed in a new, transitional socio-political environment. Our research team is a pioneer in identifying and describing two such forms. The first one is mass seasonal circular labor migration—*otkhod* or *otkhodnichestvo*. The second one, opposite in scale, is a rather rare, but locally mass economic activity—"*scattered manufactories*." Both forms are identifiable and visible only through direct on-site observation. In many ways, these economic activities are polar. But in essence, they are mutually complementary forms of economic behavior of the population. "Scattered manufactories" have been revealed and described only in some small towns. They emerge only in local communities with unique production resources and/or unique professional skills. People engaged in "scattered manufactories" are linked into a single technological chain and do not leave their place of residence, often working in their own backyard (homestead) or apartment. By contrast, a wandering worker (otkhodnik) always leaves home to seek work far away, since locally, there is no labor market. Most otkhodniks are residents of rural areas, villages, settlements, and small towns. Many are low-skilled and undertake mass low-wage jobs. So "scattered manufactories" and otkhodnichestvo are common for different settlements and different communities, require different labor skills and patterns, and finally, a different *modus vivendi et modus operandi*.

7.1 Otkhodnichestvo: Internal Circular Labor Migration

Russian otkhodniks (wandering workers) are a specific group of labor migrants—internal temporary (circular) self-employed or hired workers. (Herein, I partially used my own records presented in the following publications (Plusnin et al., 2015; Plusnin, 2019)). Among them, seasonal and agricultural laborers are but a tiny

J. Plusnin, *Russian Provincial Society*, Societies and Political Orders in Transition,
https://doi.org/10.1007/978-3-030-97829-7_7

minority. These Russian labor migrants differ from both circular (circulatory) cross-border migrants and seasonal rural migrants, well known in many countries of the world. They certainly also differ from foreign migrant laborers. A self-designation for such *wandering* workers appeared in Russia about three or four centuries ago. People started calling them *otkhodniks* [from the Russian *otkhod*—temporary departure], and this is the term they themselves and some Russian scientists still use.

The main features of modern otkhodnichestvo—in fact, a special type of independent economic activity of the population—distinguishing it from other types of labor migration are similar to those of non-agricultural industrial otkhodnichestvo of the second half of the nineteenth—first third of the twentieth centuries:

1. Otkhodnichestvo originates in the province: from small towns and rural areas, people head to metropolitan cities and industrial centers, to the North and to Siberia.
2. Otkhodniks and their families have no intention of relocating; therefore, unwillingness (and much less often—inability) to leave home permanently for the sake of work is the main precondition for a person to become an otkhodnik.
3. At the stage of developed otkhodnichestvo, labor migration is most often caused by the wish to improve the well-being of the family rather than by need.
4. Independence and enterprise are critical factors in the search for work: initiative comes from the worker, who either markets products of his labor (acting as a self-employed worker-entrepreneur, similar to the handicraft industry of the past), or takes up various jobs, most of which do not require high skills.

Over the past 30 years, this form of circular labor migration has experienced rapid growth. From the early 1990s to the early 2020s, the number of otkhodniks has increased from several thousand to fifteen and more million. I even venture to suspect that about 20 million men and women from the Russian province are currently engaged in various occupations far away from their homes. The rapid development and expansion of modern otkhodnichestvo and the considerable diversification of activities concerned, raise the issue of the economic, political, and social significance of otkhodniks. I believe that the otkhodniks' specific labor behavior and motivation, as well as their socio-demographic features, make otkhodnichestvo a new important factor of Russia's economic and political life with those involved becoming the notorious "new dangerous class" (Standing, 2011)—the precariat. However, otkhodniks also played an important role in other periods of Russia's history. In particular, there are grounds to consider them an important factor of century-old socio-political transformations, since this numerous group of Russian peasantry was distinguished by mobility and a high potential for modernization. I am referring to the causes and origins of the 1905–1920 Russian revolution; see Shanin (1986).

7.1.1 Otkhodnichestvo in Imperial Russia

In the second half of the nineteenth and first third of the twentieth centuries, otkhodnichestvo was a very widespread phenomenon among the peasantry in the Russian Empire. From a half to three-quarters of the total male peasant population of the non-black soil (non-chernozem) central and northern provinces headed off for earnings (generally in winter and early spring) to neighboring and distant districts, and other provinces, reaching the very outskirts of the empire (it is noteworthy that otkhodnichestvo was virtually unknown in the Urals and Siberia). The number of otkhodniks rapidly increased, and by the middle of the nineteenth century reached no less than three to 5 million peasants. And after the 1860s, immediately after the reform to free the peasants from serfdom and with the beginning of a long period of economic recession, the number of otkhodniks at least doubled. By the late 1920s, about half of the male peasant population (in some places, up to 80%–90%) were engaged in otkhodnichestvo in the most affected provinces (Vladimirsky, 1927, pp. 76–121). But at the very peak of the mass character of this phenomenon, by the 1930s, it had disappeared from the socio-economic life of the country for five decades. As an independent economic practice, otkhodnichestvo re-emerged in the very first post-Soviet years, demonstrating extremely rapid growth over a quarter of a century (see Fig. 7.1). Meanwhile, the roots of otkhodnichestvo can be traced back through the ages for half a millennium.

Although the practice of engaging in seasonal work away from the native villages dates back to the sxiteenth to seventeenth centuries (Kulisher, 2004, pp. 353–381 and 415–424), otkhodnichestvo, presumably, received the most perceptible, strong impetus from the state itself at the beginning of the eighteenth century. That was the time when peasants were forcibly displaced on a mass scale to toil at the "*great construction sites*" (St. Petersburg and many other new cities, especially along the border) and fight in the great wars (beginning of recruitment for 25 years of military service). Researchers of the nineteenth-early twentieth centuries shared the opinion that widespread otkhodnichestvo in Russia was triggered by Peter the Great's reforms, which "shifted" the country's population to the new capital and the borders. The people bound to the land for life by the state, the commune or the landowner, could not leave their places of residence without a valid reason. Two preconditions are necessary for otkhodnichestvo to emerge as a pattern of economic behavior: the relative or complete binding of a person and his family to the land serves as a prerequisite; and the inability to feed the family from local sources forcing the person to seek external means of existence, acts as a driver. It was impossible to subsist either in the poor non-black soil areas of central Russia, already densely populated by the eighteenth century; or in the practically undeveloped and even poorer forest-covered northern regions. Peasants living in areas where the crops were poor, could not properly feed their families from the small land plots they had. Besides, they had to pay quitrent and state taxes (researchers pointed out that taxation in Imperial Russian was underdeveloped and considered this to be an important trigger for otkhodnichestvo: Kachorovsky (1900), Vladimirsky (1927), Lenin (1971), Burds

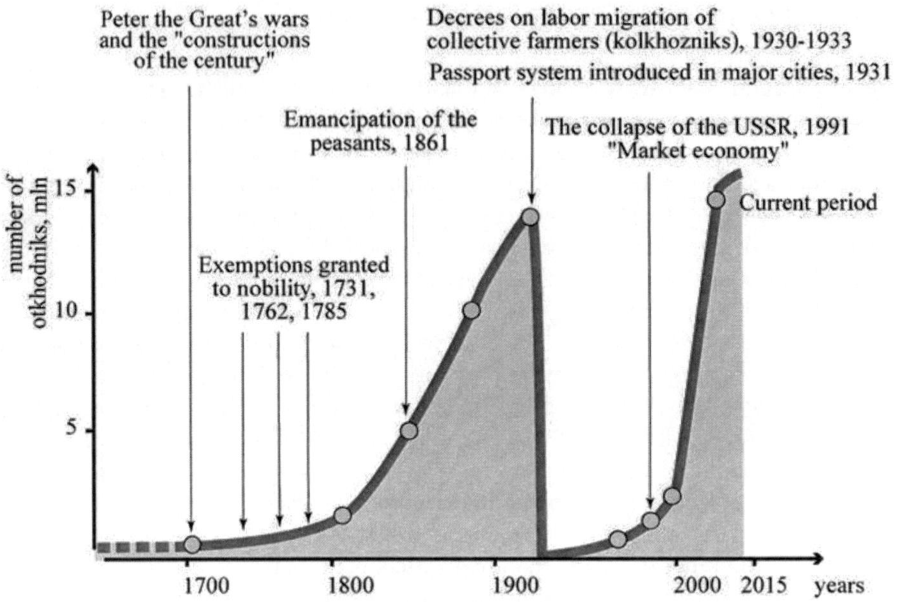

Fig. 7.1 The evolution of Russian otkhodnichestvo in the Imperial, Soviet, and current (post-Soviet) period. The changes in the number of otkhodniks since the beginning of the seventeenth century are provided according to the estimates of different authors mentioned herein (marked as dots on the curve). The timeline shows the major political and economic events, which various researchers consider to be the drivers of otkhodnichestvo. For explanations see the text below. Source: Plusnin et al. (2015, p. 51)

(1998), Vodarsky and Istomina (2004)). As a result, they were forced to send some family members, usually young men and boys, to labor in towns.

At a certain point, the state, the rural commune, or the landlord "realize" this contradiction and take respective measures.[1] The state engages the population in nationwide construction sites or "wastes" it in wars. The rural commune is less reluctant to let its skilled craftsmen seek jobs in towns; their external earnings help the commune pay state taxes, the burden of which had become excessive under Peter's rule. As for the landowner, by the beginning of the nineteenth century, he starts to realize that he can profit from quitrent (*obrok*) much more than from corvee (*barshchina*); so, he allows more and more serfs to leave the estate temporarily to labor on the side. Moreover, he now promotes their training in various crafts. Otkhodnichestvo thus gradually develops, spreading across the central and northern provinces of the Russian Empire. The landowner is mostly the driver in central areas, and poor crops—in the northern ones. In some provinces—for example, Vladimir,

[1] We also know counterexamples of the ruling class addressing this contradiction: Count Sergei Witte's memoirs reveal that the imperial family most strongly opposed the release of private peasants, since the high density of the population bound by serfdom made "*land expensive and labor cheap*".

Kostroma, Yaroslavl, and Nizhny Novgorod—both factors were equally important, so these areas always served as the main source of mass otkhodnichestvo.

The population of otkhodniks by the beginning of the eighteenth century was estimated at about 1 million people (Karyshev, 1896). According to my estimates,[2] that was over a half (!) of all adult male peasants aged from 20 to 59 years,[3] living in rural areas of European Russia at the beginning of the eighteenth century.

The period from the early eighteenth century to the mid-nineteenth century is characterized by an implicit development of otkhodnichestvo, which implied its subsequent rapid growth. Initially, this growth was driven by the right granted to the landlords in 1731 to collect poll tax from their serfs. Accordingly, they quickly realized the benefit of allowing their serfs to seek work outside the commune. Thirty years later otkhodnichestvo was bolstered by the Manifesto on exempting landlords from compulsory civil and military service (*Manifesto on Granting Freedom and Liberty to the Russian Nobility,* 1762); subsequently, by an additional confirmation of the "*liberties*" (*Charter of the Nobility*, 1785); and finally, by the permission for landlords to mortgage their estates (together with the serfs). Only 99 years later did the process finally culminate in "emancipation reforms"—the *Emancipation Manifesto* of 1861, although the very first "nobility liberties" were taken by the peasantry as a sign of imminent automatic liberation of peasants from serfdom, see Herzen (1859), Mironov (2003, pp. 377–387). Therefore, the subsequent emancipation of peasants (the foundation for which was laid down a century earlier by the change in the status of landlords) triggered their rapid transition to otkhodnichestvo (especially tenant farmers, whose allotments were too small, and peasants who had redeemed their land parcels—up to 1881).

This practice, initially caused by dire need, already three to four decades later, by the 1890s, becomes the main factor of peasant well-being. To a large extent, such changes were prompted by rapid industrial growth in Russia following the extended economic crisis of the 1860s–1880s (Sukhanov, 1913; Lenin, 1971; Fedorov, 2010). Another important factor was rural overpopulation in the European part of Russia caused more by inadequate farming rather than land capacity. The peasant commune resisted any innovations, and the peasants themselves were not motivated to raise the fertility due to continuous land repartition (Mironov, 2003, pp. 401–412; Davydov, 2018, pp. 35–42). Otkhodnichestvo peaked in the first decade of the twentieth century, bolstered by both Stolypin's reforms (Danilov, 1974), and the cooperative movement in the province, based on the principle of positive feedback. Largely driven by otkhodnichestvo and the home crafts triggered by it, cooperation

[2] Based on a fairly rough assumption about the invariability of the age and gender composition of the peasant population (men comprising 49%, of them 44% aged 20–59 years) and the share of peasants (about 84%–87%) in the population of European Russia, which was home to 73% of the Empire's entire population of about 14 million or less by the 1720s. So the estimated total number of male peasants aged 20–59 years was about 1.87–1.90 million people.

[3] Both in the past and now, men over 60 do not participate in otkhodnichestvo. And although before the revolution, quite a few adolescents and young men temporarily worked away from home, their share among the otkhodniks was small (though unknown).

developed in giant strides and in the 1920s outpaced similar processes in Europe (Nikulin, 2008). The fairly accurate statistics on passports and permits issued to peasants in those years allows estimating the number of otkhodniks at approximately 10 to 12 million people (Vladimirsky, 1927; Mints, 1926). Applying the same approach but using more accurate data of the 1897 All Russian Census and additional figures on the structure of the population in 1910, I assess the share of otkhodniks to be the same half of all male peasants of European Russia (47%–56% of 21,542,000 men aged 20–59 years—i.e. 10–12 million people). It is noteworthy that otkhodnichestvo was mostly widespread in the non-black soil provinces of the central and northern part of European Russia. In the southern black-soil provinces, it was less common and was triggered mostly by the scarcity of arable land. In those areas otkhodnichestvo was generally seasonal and agricultural. In spring and autumn, peasants could get hired as day laborers. Authors of the early twentieth century claimed that almost the entire male population of the non-black soil provinces engaged in otkhodnichestvo, which in view of the above does not seem unrealistic.

7.1.2 A Brief History of Otkhodnichestvo in the Soviet Period

It is noteworthy that throughout history, the attitude of the state toward otkhodniks changed significantly. During the Imperial period, the otkhodniks were first "*at the mercy*" of the rural commune and the landlord; later—only the commune; and finally they were left on their own. In the Soviet period, the state took over control. Before the abolition of serfdom, otkhodniks were sometimes very advantageous for landowners in the non-black soil regions—they often generated more income than the "*poor plough.*" In many provinces, peasants considered land to be an evil necessity, since it rendered practically no income, and taxes on it had to be paid from external earnings. Due to this, a "profit-generating" otkhodnik serf had to pay much more than a simple farmer or local craftsman to buy out his freedom: for him, the cost of obtaining a "manumission" was several-fold higher.[4]

Already by the end of the nineteenth century (in the 1920s especially), otkhodnichestvo was at the same considered to be a result of agrarian overpopulation (i.e., the imbalance between the number of workers in a peasant household and the actual possibility to engage them productively) and a way to overcome it (Mints, 1929; Suvorov, 1968; Shanin, 1972). On the one hand, otkhodnichestvo was perceived as a progressive phenomenon, since "socially and professionally, peasant otkhodniks were a direct and immediate reserve of Russia's working class" (Andryushin, 2012, p. 232). On the other hand, mass otkhodnichestvo was a serious

[4]The rural commune (*mir*) also quickly realized the benefits that such craftspeople provided; therefore, the redemption fees for a skillful craftsman, who earned money to pay public taxes and levies, were fivefold and tenfold higher than those for a simple unskilled peasant.

concern for the People's Commissariat of Labor, being a source of urban unemployment, which it was supposed to control (Danilov, 1974). Rural dwellers migrated to the cities on such a large-scale, that in less than 15 years (already by 1930), the urban population more than doubled. The "*influx was so enormous that one of the official goals of the passport system introduced in 1932 was to lessen the burden on the cities*" (Andryushin, 2012, p. 205). Therefore, passports were introduced temporarily and initially only in four metropolitan cities—Moscow, Leningrad, Kharkov, and Kiev, as they were experiencing the greatest difficulties due to a two to threefold increase in the number of residents. It is well known that shortly prior to that Moscow and St. Petersburg were the main recipients of rural otkhodniks. Therefore, the growth of metropolitan population in the 1920s was driven exclusively by otkhodnichestvo.

Attempts made by the Soviet State to regulate otkhodnichestvo treating it as part of the cooperative movement came in conflict with the goals of industrializing the country. By the early 1930s, concern that the scale of otkhodnichestvo was inadequate to achieve the industrial development of the country emerged. Consequently, this phenomenon was inventoried and institutionalized, thus changing its essence (including by changing the designation *otkhodnik* to *sezonnik* (seasonal worker) and turning spontaneous otkhodnichestvo into organized government recruitment of workforce from the villages (vivid examples of that time are the construction sites of Donbass, Kuzbass, Komsomolsk-on-Amur and many others, which were reflected both in official propaganda, including Soviet films and songs, and in folklore). For this purpose, in the period from 1930 to 1934, the Government (the Central Executive Committee and the Council of People's Commissars) passed several special decrees regulating otkhodnik activities of the population.[5] Consequently, otkhodnichestvo dropped out of public discourse as a contemporary phenomenon and remained only as a historical one. The war which broke out shortly finalized the process.

Later, in the period from 1946 to 1991, otkhodnichestvo in the Soviet Union existed as an extremely marginalized phenomenon and took distorted forms. The only form that was more or less approved by the authorities was the seasonal *recruitment* of workers from some southern and western Soviet Republics, where labor was excessive (Moldavia, Ukraine, Armenia, Uzbekistan, and Kirghizia), to work at logging enterprises in the northern forest-covered areas (Arkhangelsk, Karelia, Komi, Vologda, Kostroma, and Perm) and in Siberia, where there was always a shortage of labor.[6] *Recruitment* of laborers for the logging camps started in the late 1940s and peaked in the 1950s. Such *recruitment* involved primarily rural inhabitants, who worked at collective and state farms. Since timber is harvested

[5]Decrees of the Central Executive Committee and the Council of People's Commissars of the USSR dated 16 March 1930 and 30 June 1931 *On Otkhodnichestvo* and, subsequently, the Decree of the Council of People's Commissars of the USSR dated 17 March 1933 *On the Procedure of Otkhodnichestvo from Collective Farms*.

[6]The *recruited* laborers were referred to simply as *recruits*; that is how they were nicknamed in all the locations where they worked.

mostly in winter, this form of employment became seasonal. The collective farmers regularly returned home in time for summer work in the fields.

However, it did not take long for the arrangements to change. Collective and state farms in southern republics experienced constant acute shortage of lumber for construction, so they quickly seized the initiative from the state and started sending their own teams to the logging camps. In winter, such farmers earned money for their families and also harvested timber (extremely scarce in the south) for their collective farms and fellow villagers. At the same time, besides logging, the former *recruits*, now sent by their collective farms, participated in the construction of various facilities in the forest settlements and villages. By the late 1970s, when the need for timber harvesters started to decline, this process "went out of control" and lost its organized nature. The *recruits* started forming their own logging teams and went to work in familiar places independently of the collective farms. Accordingly, new labor relations required new designations: people nicknamed such independent workers *shabashniks*—a derivative from the slang word *shabashka* meaning an independently found side job, which generates relatively quick and high earnings.

In the 1980s, "Moldavian," "Armenian," and "Uzbek" building teams were already rather numerous, working not only in the northern parts of European Russia but practically all over Siberia. Finally, this working pattern attracted the attention of researchers, economists and sociologists (Shabanova, 1992).[7] In fact, these seasonal loggers in winter (*recruits*) and, at a later time, builders in summer (*shabashniks*) were not quite genuine otkhodniks, as they did not possess all attributes of this type of labor migration. The *recruits* were sent by their principal employer to work for the benefit of the employer and not the worker. In this respect, they were neither independent, not enterprising, although they did depart from home for seasonal work. The *shabashniks* left home for the sake of additional, temporary, and occasional earnings and not because of need or necessity; such work for them was not regular (although some of them, especially team leaders, were already real otkhodniks). Neither the society nor scientists (with a few exceptions, see Shabanova (1986), Shabanova (1992)) treated these two phenomena as a particular type of labor migration, as otkhodnichestvo.

Repeatedly, otkhodnichestvo re-emerged as a new mass phenomenon of Russian social and economic life in the early 1990s (Shabanova, 1992). Following the shock experienced at the beginning of the 1990s, which forced the population to return to the archaic pattern of subsistence farming (at that time, both urban and rural families spent 90% of their budget on food), otkhodnichestvo gradually re-emerged as one of the most effective, and currently the most widespread economic practice of the population. In the early 1990s, abandoned subsistence patterns started rapidly

[7] The 1980s were the only decade of the Soviet era when the village was thriving: not only farms and complexes were being built everywhere, but also roads and houses for collective farmers. In addition, collective and state farms had more flexibility in using the funds allocated for construction purposes, than was granted to urban enterprises. Due to this, at that time almost all collective and state farms every summer hosted *recruits* and *shabashniks* from western and southern Soviet republics.

developing in Russia as a response to the domestic economic chaos, as people were left on their own to seek and find means of existence (and survival). Long-forgotten archaic folk crafts were "remembered" and rekindled, the first among them being the return to subsistence farming and the revival of otkhodnichestvo.

Rather than reappearing in its historic center—the non-black soil regions—the new otkhodnichestvo emerged as temporary labor migration from the outskirts, the former Soviet republics, to the center. That was where the Soviet otkhodniks—the *recruits* and *shabashniks* lived, who had been the first to master this subsistence pattern. It took some time for this centripetal movement to spread to the central regions of Russia, which used to be the major starting point of otkhodnichestvo. Therefore, by its principal features, otkhodnichestvo as domestic Russian labor migration, is indistinguishable from seasonal labor migration to Russia from such new post-Soviet states as Ukraine, Moldavia, Uzbekistan, Kirghizia, and Tajikistan. By nature, these currently cross-border, but essentially domestic (within the borders of Big Russia) labor migrations are closely related. Probably that is the reason why otkhodnik activities currently affect not only residents of the traditional "old otkhodnichestvo" regions, but also the population of virtually all post-Soviet republics, as well as the eastern, Siberian areas of Russia, which had never been involved before.

7.1.3 Two Stages in the Evolution of Contemporary Otkhodnichestvo

Although contemporary otkhodnichestvo is a relatively recent phenomenon—only about 30 years old, – I would distinguish two stages in its development. The first one—Growth—was characterized by the emergence (actually, re-emergence) of otkhodnichestvo and its large-scale growth in the small towns of European Russia. The second one—Expansion—consists in shifting the sources of otkhodnichestvo "deeper down" and "out."

The rapid re-emergence of otkhodnichestvo in small towns, mainly in the same areas as during the Imperial period, was the main feature of the first stage. In the mid-1990s, two factors initiated this process. First, the absence of any labor market specifically in the small towns due to the collapse of all production. In the early 1990s, major and small state-owned enterprises, which existed in every small town and district and served as principal employers for the local residents keeping them in place, went bankrupt and came to a standstill. During the Soviet period, employment at such enterprises greatly reduced labor mobility. Therefore, in the early and mid-1990s, it was considered that intra-regional labor markets were virtually non-existent, and labor migration as such was completely undeveloped.

Many families in small towns and industrial townships suddenly lost work and, respectively, the means of existence. Most of them had no or inadequate land plots for gardening, and this aggravated the situation. Rural families were in a better position, as subsidiary farming made it easier for them to overcome the collapse of collective and state farms. In the mid-1990s, over half of all schoolchildren in the provinces took meals mainly at schools, as there was nothing to eat at home. The situation was so widespread that no one even considered it a social disaster—it was everyday life (Plusnin, 1997). Many urban families were left without work and they had neither farms nor gardens to feed. People must seek urgently new sources of subsistence. Otkhodnichestvo was one of them. As time went by and the labor market in the regional centers and metropolitan cities developed, it became increasingly widespread.

The first factor—the absence of a local labor market—triggered the need to leave home in search for work. The second one—the well-known specifics of our residential system, where families were bound to state-owned housing and could neither sell nor exchange their apartments—shaped labor migration in the form of otkhodnichestvo, because families could not relocate with their breadwinners. The mass revival of otkhodnichestvo was preconditioned by a new form of "serfdom"—"*apartment serfdom,*" the absence of widely available rental housing and affordable mortgage, which hindered easy and quick relocation of the families. This form of "serfdom" still strongly affects contemporary otkhodnichestvo, which would never have reached its current magnitude, if the people had not been "bound" to their housing. The Soviet people were sufficiently prepared to change their place of residence due to necessity. However, for most families, the negative implications of moving residence far outweighed the consequences of a temporary, even though lengthy, absence of a family member.

Thus, the first stage of contemporary otkhodnichestvo was shaped. It was spontaneous and driven by need, and it involved primarily the dwellers of small towns, who were "trapped" between the big city, where job opportunities were always available, and the village, where there were always opportunities to produce food. In the 1990s, the small town had none of these opportunities.

At the first stage, otkhodnichestvo was dominated by professional builders, carpenters, joiners, drivers, mechanics, and engineers—all those, who could independently market their skills and products. In those difficult years (in the 1990s), the industrial centers and even the capitals still required significantly more labor for the manufacturing industries than for the service sector (according to my data, by the mid-1990s, manufacturing in the province accounted for no less than 54% of all employed, whereas by the end of the 2000s, this figure dropped under 20%; labor was now more in demand in the service sector, which by then accounted for 60%–70% of all employed). By the end of the described first stage, the number of otkhodniks in just a decade had increased to 7–10 million people, or 18%–26% of working-age men.

The second stage consists in otkhodnichestvo expanding "deeper down"—from the small town to its rural district, and "out"—eastwards, beyond the Urals and into Siberia. Besides, it is no longer a purely male occupation: over the past decade, the proportion of female otkhodniks has been rising rapidly. This new stage has been developing since the early 2000s and is unfolding before our eyes. It was characterized primarily by the rapid shift of the source of otkhodnichestvo from the district center to the rural area. Apparently, this was triggered by the economic stabilization and growth of the 2000s, when in many small towns old enterprises were re-opened and new ones were commissioned. Besides new job openings, which brought some otkhodniks back home, other interesting changes occurred in the occupational structure, in particular due to "the power vertical finally reaching the local level," meaning the implementation and strengthening of the top-down command structure effected during the first two terms of Vladimir Putin's presidency, especially starting from March 2004. As a result, the district centers experienced a significant growth of public sector employees, including those engaged by regional and federal government bodies.

These two reasons—growing local production and the development of the public sector—somehow contributed to downscaling otkhodnichestvo in small towns, the administrative centers of local communities. Some otkhodniks residing in the district centers simply engaged in the local economy. However, the path was already well-trodden, and "*nature abhors a vacuum*": jobs in the capitals vacated by small-town otkhodniks were quickly filled by their village counterparts. Where previously jobless villagers looked for work in their district centers, now, directed by their colleagues from these district centers, they increasingly depart to make a living in the City (meaning the regional center) or in Moscow and the Moscow Region. Otkhodnichestvo filters down deeper and deeper into provincial life.

The eastward shift of otkhodnichestvo stands somewhat apart. Timewise, it follows the shift to the rural areas in the western parts of the country, however, the underlying factors are different. In Imperial times, otkhodnichestvo (except for long-distance horse-drawn carriage) was completely alien for the rich and resource-abundant Siberian towns and villages. (Although there is a different point of view: e.g., Remnev and Suvorova (2010)), still, the Chinese accounted for the majority of otkhodniks in Siberia (Dyatlov & Grigorichev, 2013). Until the 1930s, the population of Siberia did not need to seek any additional earnings. Siberia was sparsely populated, arable lands were abundant, and the people had enough money from hunting, fishing, cattle-breeding, logging, precious metal mining, and many other occupations. And after the 1930s, no one heard anything about otkhodnichestvo in Siberia, although Siberia was the destination for many teams of *recruited* loggers and *shabashnik* builders from the southern and western republics of the USSR. Nowadays, facts of apparent otkhodnichestvo are revealed all over Siberia. However, as far as I can judge based on my observations, the structure of Siberian otkhodnichestvo differs from that in the European part of Russia by the following significant details. First, we have not noticed any large-scale involvement of town-dwellers; otkhodnichestvo is mainly practiced by villagers and people from industrial townships. True, in recent years, residents of single-industry settlements have started engaging en masse in external jobs. Second, otkhodnichestvo here is "*aligned*" with the rotation form of labor migration. People take up jobs at construction sites, factories, mining enterprises, or join fishing vessel crews in response to formal vacancy ads. However, unlike organized recruitment, they do it independently, form their own teams, and often negotiate with the employer on a team, rather than individual, level.

The third important feature of the second stage of otkhodnichestvo is the growing proportion of women. If in the 1990s, women practically did not engage in this type of activity, by the mid-2010s, their numbers began to increase sharply. Female otkhodniks are mainly older women (40–50 years of age and older) with grown-up children, who they can afford to leave the family for a couple of weeks or a month (or even for a year) to take up a job in a metropolitan city. A significant part of women are employed in the service sector (sales clerks, stallkeepers, cleaners, domestic help, and concierges) or in social reproduction (nurses, nannies, and teachers). However, more and more of them are employed at plants and factories; the number of women signing up for rotation shifts in the North is also increasing.

7.1.4 The Composition of Contemporary Otkhodniks

Unlike earlier, when a significant part of the otkhodniks were artisans offering self-made articles for sale, contemporary otkhodniks quite often sell only their labor. The share of artisans among otkhodniks used to be very high. Many, if not all, peasant craftsmen were at the same time otkhodniks. For the overwhelming majority of peasant farms, income from crafts and trades accounted for over half of their budget. In general, according to some estimates (Delarov, 1928), proceeds from crafts and trades constituted more than a quarter of the notional net income of a peasant household in the non-black soil areas of European Russia.

Nowadays, few otkhodniks are marketing their own products. Among them are carpenters who build log homes and other wooden facilities and offer them for sale in the Moscow Region and in the regional capitals, where demand is high. As for daily household articles domestically manufactured by otkhodniks, part of this cottage industry has shifted to another format—the so-called "*ethno-format.*" The majority of contemporary otkhodniks take up employment in industry, construction, transportation, and also in security, trade, services, and domestic services. In this respect, compared to Imperial times, the substance of otkhodnik activities has changed: from a sole proprietor (artisan), the otkhodnik has turned more into a wage-worker.

Contemporary otkhodniks engage in very few principal activities as compared to their predecessors; based on a survey of over 500 people, we identified no more than 15 types of activity, whereas a century ago, otkhodniks from every big settlement practiced up to 50 various occupations (Vladimirsky, 1927). Currently, the otkhodniks are mainly occupied in construction, transportation, long haul trucking, community services (various communal services related to construction and maintenance of grounds around buildings), trade (both at market stands, and in supermarkets). The security "business" is rather popular among otkhodniks: in the major cities, the numerous army of office and factory security guards consists almost exclusively of otkhodniks. Various jobs at big enterprises are taken up by organized groups and teams consisting of friends and relatives (the team principle). Generally, such teams are engaged in non-core, unskilled operations. For the most part, employment is informal.

The second stage in the evolution of otkhodnichestvo is characterized by its diversification. People with low skills or employed in unskilled jobs now engage in otkhodnichestvo along with builders, carpenters and other skilled workers. In major cities, the demand for labor in the service and social reproduction sectors had grown significantly. As a result, residents from the province stepped in to fill in the positions of cleaners, nannies, governesses, sales personnel, and even heath workers and teachers. In the service sector, there are fewer otkhodniks engaged in skilled labor. Over 5 million people may be occupied in different segments of the service sector. However, it is currently absolutely impossible to determine the actual size of this motley cohort. According to our very rough estimates based on data on the size of the working-age male population of the Russian province (about 20–23 million people) and selected data on the share of the population not employed in the local economy (which varies from 15 to 47 percent and more), from 10 to 15 million people in Russia were engaged in otkhodnichestvo as of 2015. (Plusnin et al., 2015, pp. 85–98). This figure is now most likely higher (since Siberia has joined in). Of the roughly 44 million men of working age, otkhodniks account for over one-third, i.e., just like two-three centuries ago, out-of-town occupations are currently the most widespread form of employment.

Contemporary otkhodniks can be classified into four major categories depending on their principal occupation:

1. Skilled carpenter builders and industrial workers and engineers (rotation workers and former Soviet *recruits* and *shabashniks*).
2. Generally unskilled personnel in the service sector.
3. Security guards composed mostly of unskilled persons.
4. Long-haul truckers. In addition to these, there are several other categories.

Figure 7.2 presents the approximate changes in the otkhodnik population, by category as of 2015; in recent years, the overall situation has not changed, but the numbers have increased.

Among all otkhodniks, the share of skilled workers is relatively small, since such people can find employment in line with their proficiencies back home. They engage in otkhodnichestvo for several major reasons. First of all, in their region, there may be no or insufficient demand for the goods or services they offer. Such is the situation, for example, with entrepreneurs building wooden houses. The frame is manufactured at the home site and assembled on the customer's premises, usually in the suburbs of a large city. Another common reason currently is the shut down of specialized production facilities in the home area (factories, mines, mining and processing plants, etc.). These enterprises always employ highly skilled but narrowly focused personnel. In order not to lose their proficiency, such people are forced to seek similar enterprises and jobs elsewhere and leave their homes and families for lengthy periods, generally for a year. Such is the situation in the Alagir local community—the town itself and the villages of Mizur and Buron. After the lead-zinc ore mining and processing complex shut down, many specialists signed up for

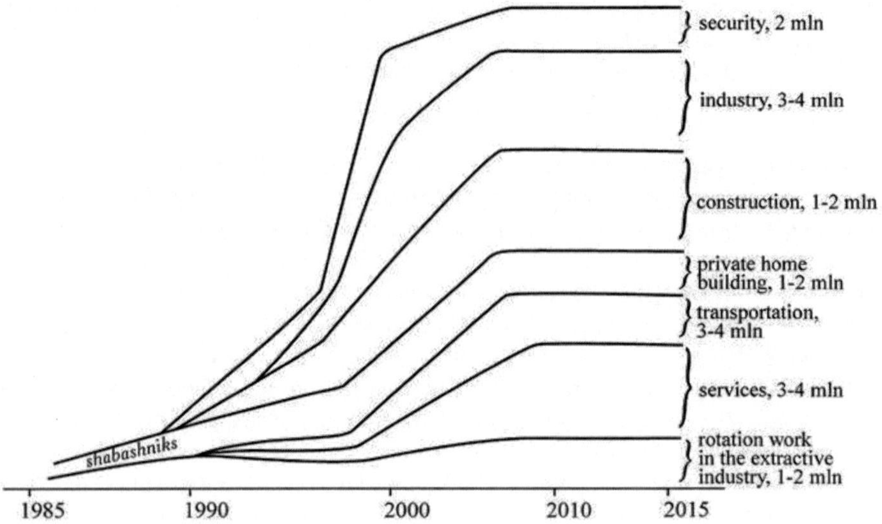

Fig. 7.2 The composition of otkhodniks and its current dynamics. For explanations see the text above/below. Source: Plusnin et al. (2015, p. 51)

rotation jobs in Norilsk, Krasnoyarsk Territory, 7000 km away from their home in North Ossetia. The main reason for a skilled specialist, technician or engineer, specialty vehicle driver, etc. to engage in otkhodnichestvo is significantly higher wages that can be earned on a rotation basis as compared to local opportunities.

The category of otkhodniks employed in the service sector is very numerous and diverse—from trade, taxi services, carriage and domestic help to socially significant occupations of nanny, educator, teacher, nurse, and doctor. In this sector, the number of female otkhodniks is quite high; most of the women come from remote villages or are former Soviet citizens from currently independent Kyrgyzstan, Uzbekistan, Tajikistan, Moldova, and Ukraine. Many people in this category take up relatively long-term jobs—from several months to a year—since they come from far away and have no farmsteads.

Two occupationally compact groups of otkhodniks are especially numerous—security guards and long-haul truckers. Myriads of companies, trade centers, establishments, and even hi-rise residential houses hire security guards. The number of these people exceeds the number of fences erected in any major Russian city. According to a very rough estimate, there are over 3 million security guards in the country. Almost all of them are provincial residents from the regions surrounding the capitals. They work on a 2 weeks on, 2 weeks off rotation basis, and hold jobs about 500–700 km from home.

Long-haul trucker is a category of workers that has become another important element of the second stage of evolution of contemporary Russian otkhodnichestvo. Similar to the Imperial times, Russia is once again experiencing a rapid development of long-distance carriage—only now it is "long-haul trucking" [in Russian—

"*dal'noboy*"], or simply "trucking." Russian "trucking" emerged in the 1990s, and in the early 2000s, it experienced rapid development, the scope of which has still not been assessed. The "regulatory clamp-down," increasing failures experienced by the Russian railway monopolist OJSC Russian Railways and the excessive growth of its tariffs could have been the principal reason for such a boost in long-haul trucking. Today, "trucking" unites a multi-million, well-staffed, well-equipped and well-connected organized army of carriers. According to the most approximate estimates, professional truckers currently number from 3 to 5 million people. Only 5–10 years ago, at least half of them were sole proprietors, working independently, at their own risk, driving their own trucks (which they often repair and maintain themselves), and negotiating business directly with the freight consignors. The other half were those who hired themselves out as drivers to currently numerous freight forwarding companies. Their only responsibility was to deliver goods by corporate trucks. Specialized teams of mechanics were in charge of repairs and maintenance, and dedicated professionals took care of all business arrangements. However, both trucker categories rely on the already existing and well-developed system of dispatcher services, which seems to become unified. The development of private dispatcher services has contributed even more to consolidating the truckers and making them professionally more self-contained. Freight hauling orders are no longer incidental. In the past decade, trucking in Russia has followed general development trends, which are well-known from U.S. experience—anything but voluntary organization of independent drivers into small and large trucking companies (Wyckoff, 1979). Private individual carriers have become increasingly rare in recent years.

7.1.5 Typical Features of the Contemporary Otkhodnik

The people from traditional areas of otkhodnichestvo are very conservative in their selection of otkhodnik occupations, and this is a matter of special emphasis. Not only have contemporary otkhodniks "recollected" the lifestyle of their grandfathers, they have also "remembered" and reproduced the principal occupations that were common in those areas over a hundred years ago. Thus, log home building (manufacturing and transportation of log cabins to be installed as summer homes and bathhouses for urban residents) is the principal occupation of otkhodniks from Makaryev, Kologriv, Chukhloma, and Soligalich (Kostroma Region); whereas residents of Kasimov, Temnikov, Ardatov, and Alatyr, who previously used to hire themselves out as unskilled laborers, day workers, or barge haulers, now mostly seek employment as security guards and sales personnel. Residents of Lyubim (Yaroslavl Region) who used to work as *waiters* in all pubs and restaurants of St. Petersburg are even now employed in the same city and the same service sector.

The destinations are now somewhat different than a century ago, but considering the changes in the administrative-territorial division of the country, we have to state that in this respect otkhodniks are also very conservative. If one or two centuries ago people from the Trans-Volga region were "drawn" to St. Petersburg, now they switched to Moscow. In both cases, however, they aimed for the capital city. The same is true for regional centers: otkhodniks from district towns head for regional centers, wherever those may be. If previously, Mordovian workers from Temnikov and Ardatov traveled to Nizhny Novgorod, Moscow, and Penza, now they aim for Nizhny, Moscow and Syzran, since Syzran is currently their regional capital instead of Penza.

Otkhodnichestvo has expanded its geography, but no radical changes have occurred. In the nineteenth century, residents of Kargopol and Veliky Ustyug also used to work as servants and janitors in Kronstadt and Tiflis, Georgia. Nowadays, people are still going from Kasimov to mine diamonds in Yakutia, and from Toropets and Kashin—to harvest beetroot and grapes in Krasnodar. Since during the past century, travel speeds have increased by an order of magnitude, otkhodniks now travel more frequently and cover greater distances. Where previously a workplace located from 100 km to 600–700 km from home meant that an otkhodnik would be absent from 6 months to a year, now a 1- to 2-week rotation shift would not be uncommon. However, structurally, the geography of otkhodnichestvo seems to have remained unchanged. As previously, up to half of all otkhodniks do not go far from home and look for jobs in a radius of 200–300 km. At least three quarters of all otkhodniks depart to destinations no further than 500–800 km from home (nowadays, this distance can be covered by train or car in about half a day); and only about a quarter travels to distant locations, which take a long time to be reached (over one-tenth of the working time). The people carefully and precisely assess the economic aspects of their hard work—not only the time outlays, but also the net earnings.

How much money does an otkhodnik actually bring home? I will provide data as of the mid-2010s (Plusnin et al., 2015, pp. 151–163). In 5 years, they have hardly changed. Contrary to popular belief, on average, an otkhodnik does not bring home "big money." Earnings on the side are greatly dependent on the skill and activity. Per season, carpenter builders can earn up to half a million rubles (EUR 6000—EUR 8000). Those, engaged in industry, transportation or construction earn less—from 20,000 to 50,000 rubles per month, but they work almost all year round, so their annual income is from EUR 3000 to EUR 8000. Less skilled otkhodniks earn 20,000–25,000 rubles per month, and security guards—up to 15,000 rubles. Thus, on average, skilled otkhodniks earn from 300,000 to 500,000 rubles per year (EUR 5000–EUR 8000), and unskilled—from 150,000 to 200,000 rubles (EUR 2500–EUR 3000). Such earnings are generally higher than those a person would have received if he were to work in his hometown, where the salaries of public sector employees do not exceed 100,000–150,000 rubles per year, and the wages of a sales clerk—100,000 rubles.

So, currently it is worthwhile to be an otkhodnik, but only a high-skilled otkhodnik, and that compared to neighbors engaged in the public sector. Because if you deduct the expenses that the otkhodnik incurs while working, the resulting amount will be far from impressive. According to our sources, despite generally miserable living conditions (except for the "*North*") and regardless of the otkhodnik's desire to save on everything and bring home as much money as possible, life in the city costs him from 5000 to 15,000 rubles monthly, which he covers from his average wages of 25,000 to 40,000 rubles. Therefore, usually he brings home about 20,000–25,000 rubles monthly, rather than the 50,000–70,000 rubles he mentions.

What awaits the otkhodnik at home? Here he has his family, homestead, and neighbors. And he intends to spend his earnings on the children, house, farming needs, and leisure. These are the four main items of essential and conspicuous expenses that the otkhodnik spends all his earnings on. The expense structure in otkhodnik families can differ significantly from that in the families of neighboring public sector employees or pensioners. Since by this criterion, the otkhodniks stand apart from their neighbors, this in a way triggers envy and hostility toward them. In general, however, the otkhodniks have normal good relations with their neighbors; the neighbors have long since understood how hard the work of an otkhodnik is, and their envy is wrapped in compassion. Besides, the neighbors do not observe any conspicuous consumption in otkhodnik families, so there is less reason for them to be jealous.

As for the otkhodnik's actual social status, it is not an object of envy for the neighbors. Often, in the local community, an otkhodnik has no access to resources that are available to a public sector employee, especially a civil servant (bureaucrat). We believe the underlying reason is the "distance" of such people from the state (Plusnin, 2016). Municipal and local government authorities do not "notice" these people either as labor resources, or as part of the population entitled to social security and public benefits. A significant part of the otkhodniks work informally and provide services bypassing the state. The state does not partake of the fruits of their labor. Their travels between cities and regions can not be tracked. They are uncontrolled, "unregistered," and "unenserfed."

Assuming (Plusnin et al., 2015, pp. 92–94) that all but two-fifths of all Russian families are engaged in otkhodnichestvo, the scope of their productive activity, "invisible" for the state (and therefore "shadow"), must be enormous; this has been established by many sociological and economic studies (Radaev, 1999; Barsukova, 2003, 2015; Barsukova & Radaev, 2012; Gimpelson & Kapelyushnikov, 2006, 2014).

But does the state actually need this "invisible giant"? Practically left out of all public social security programs, and beyond the control of the government, it is also excluded from political activity. Although otkhodniks take part in the "electoral process," they are ultimately of no interest to the federal authorities, who treat them as unimportant political subjects. The otkhodnik remains largely aloof from the local authorities also. His only value for them translates into the share of grants and subsidies the local administration receives to perform their functions, as such, receivables are determined based on the number of residents. Therefore, the otkhodnik is useful for the authorities only as a demographic unit due to the "per capita share." Apparently, he brings home lots of money, thus raising the purchasing power of the population and stimulating the local economy. Usually, this is the only argument in favor of the otkhodnik. But is this really important for the local administration?

7.1.6 The Importance of Contemporary Otkhodnichestvo as a New Economic and Political Factor

The seasonal non-agricultural departure of provincial residents in search of work to major Russian cities is a very old practice, which has existed for the past 400–500 years. The prevalence, mass character and diversity of such economic behavior gives reason to consider it the main economic self-organization practice of the population and the basic subsistence pattern, along with private subsidiary farming. However, in contrast to the latter, otkhodnichestvo creates socio-political risks, because it fuels social tension. This happened in the Russian Empire at the turn of the nineteenth—twentieth centuries. It took great sacrifices and efforts to overcome the risks; total industrialization and collectivization served the purpose.

Currently, at the beginning of the twenty-first century, otkhodnichestvo has acquired the same mass character as a century ago. But if previously otkhodniks could partly rely on subsistence farming, now otkhodnichestvo has become the principal, if not the only source of family income. At the same time, the predominantly hired and informal nature of otkhodnik occupations and lack of any social guarantees from the state for most of the otkhodniks, transfers these people to the category of «*precariat*». And this "new class" again has something to fight for.

I believe the following features determine the importance of otkhodnichestvo as a new economic factor:

1. Predominantly shadow informal employment
2. Diversification of activities
3. Large number of people involved
4. Significant production volumes
5. Latent small business.

    1. Over half of the otkhodniks we interviewed are engaged in the informal economy. Informal employment is more pronounced in the northern towns of the European part of Russia, where many otkhodniks are self-employed entrepreneurs. Hired workers at metropolitan enterprises and in northern and Siberian rotation camps are formally employed, although even here, informal employment is widespread in the service sector. This circumstance creates well-known problems. The first one is tax evasion, which has reached an alarming scale in Russia, with otkhodniks probably being the main "contributors." The second issue is faltering social security due to poor or often lacking social protection of the workers. Third, otkhodniks are often not entitled to any benefits under the government social policy.

2. Since the first third of the 1990s, otkhodnik activities are embracing an increasing number of economic sectors. By the mid-2010s, otkhodniks are present in almost all spheres of economic activity, especially in transportation (long-distance carriage and intracity services); all types of services (primarily trade, security and private services); construction (industrial and residential, especially private housing); industrial and agricultural production; and social reproduction (education, health care, municipal service, banking and finance). The diversification and mass presence of otkhodniks in all sectors of the economy changes economic motivation, non-economic behavior (structure of recreation and leisure) and interaction between people representing different cultural and ethno-territorial traditions.
3. Over the past 30 years the number of otkhodniks increased rapidly—from several (unknown) thousands of *shabashniks* and less than 1 million circular labor migrants in the largest Russian cities to 15 and even 20 million such workers in metropolitan and regional agglomerations, in all regional centers, and everywhere "in the North," i.e. in Siberia and the Arctic. Otkhodnichestvo affected not only all small towns (as in the 1990s), but also small rural settlements; it spread throughout the south, north, west and east of Russia. Any additional increase in the number of wandering workers is limited by the demographic potential of rural areas: almost half—and often more—of all able-bodied men in the province are engaged in otkhodnichestvo. Nevertheless, we predict that the "army" of such labor migrants will continue growing due to the rising participation of female villagers.
4. I assume that the volume of goods and services produced by the otkhodniks in the shadow sector of the economy—in the so-called "garage economy" and "scattered manufactories"—is extremely high and exceeds by far the existing official estimates. The Ministry of Labor assesses this level at over a quarter of the gross national product, whereas it is likely to exceed half of the GDP. Besides various finished products (from shawls and fur coats to cars). the "garage economy" also manufactures components (not only the simplest elements and parts but, as it turned out, even components for the nuclear and space industries are handcrafted). This suggests that the actual output generated by the otkhodniks, including in the shadow segment, is substantially higher than the official records.
5. In small towns and villages, many active residents were forced to turn to otkhodnichestvo, although they would have preferred to engage in small business locally. Many otkhodniks are actually small entrepreneurs, but they do not register their business. According to our estimates, in all rural areas and small towns, every formally registered sole proprietor or small business is matched by five to ten unregistered but actually operating ones. Excessive inspections and reporting requirements, unreasonable government regulation of business, coupled with the authorities' failure to fulfill their obligations, become an insurmountable obstacle for small businesses; consequently, people either slip "into the shadow" or give up and leave home to continue their trade as otkhodniks in other areas, evading control and regulation. The recent

sharp decline in the share of "new enterprise" may be explained by the surge of otkhodnik practices. Otkhodnichestvo becomes an alternative to doing business at home; it generates more income and allows avoiding interaction with government and municipal authorities.

The following features determine the importance of otkhodnichestvo as a new political factor:

6. High skills
7. Education and political "awareness"
8. Organization of many otkhodnik occupational groups
9. Mass character
10. Destructive social and cultural activity

6. Many otkhodniks (among men this share exceeds two-thirds) are skilled workers with secondary vocational and less frequently higher education, often engaged in jobs requiring no skills whatsoever. This means unjustified spending of public funds on vocational education and loss of social capital due to ineffective use of labor.
7. Many of the otkhodniks are not only skilled, but also well-educated, with critical thinking abilities and established political views. Meanwhile, according to the findings of my 1990s research of latent social tensions, it is educated skilled middle-aged men who represent the most active and organized category of the politically active population. It is this category that public authorities must focus on to prevent and reduce social tension.
8. Many otkhodnik groups are well organized and independent. Professional truckers are the best example. Across the country, they are already forming a linked network (and not a virtual one!) of mobile organized teams that can act quickly and efficiently. Carpenters and log home builders are organized into artels. The high level of organization of some mass otkhodnik groups implies that they can be used to facilitate certain public tasks (e.g., similar to the "*Labor Army*" or "self-defense squads"), or they can be a potential threat to internal security.
9. Becoming a mass phenomenon, otkhodnichestvo introduces new features to the local social structure, which on the one hand, lead to its degradation, and on the other, make it more complicated. The social structure degrades because the youngest and most active part of the population most of the time lives and works far away from their small towns. In the municipalities, the active working-age population is eroded; consequently, pensioners and people in need of social support or prone to social pathologies gradually prevail. At the same time, there is a tendency everywhere to replace local workers with outsiders, often similar labor migrants from the former Soviet republics. Both processes require changes in local social policies, which the municipal authorities are not ready to introduce. They also demand changes in the national policy, which is not launched nor yet conceptualized.

10. We should not underestimate the role that otkhodniks play in eroding the joint integrity of many local communities. In a certain sense, the otkhodniks involuntarily disintegrate the community's natural self-organization processes. Due to their lifestyle and activities, which proceed outside the local community, as the community gradually "crowds them out," the otkhodniks and their families increasingly become inhabitants of a large city, rather than their native town or village. As a result, the provincial local society of today perceptibly differs even from that of the late Soviet period: rooted large new groups of "outsiders" and groups of "insiders" currently pushed to the outskirts of local life are increasingly imposing their differing perceptions of what is "right" and "appropriate" on the local community. Both the native otkhodniks, and the foreigners that replace them introduce something new: the former—metropolitan cultural patterns; the latter—alternate domestic and ethnic cultural habits, and a different lifestyle, which affects the local community, even if it rejects it.

Thus, the otkhodniks are emerging as a new factor of public life that exists everywhere but on a local level. However, the existence of otkhodnichestvo as a fact of social life requires considering not only the economic, but also the social and political implications it can have or already has. One of the most important consequences of the development of economic activity in a form unusual until very recently, but also traditional, is the emergence of a new socio-occupational group, which, following some social scientists and economists, can be diagnosed as a new class—the precariat, see Standing (2011), Tikhonova (2019), Manning et al. (2017), Toshchenko (2018), and my own earlier publication (Plusnin, 2016). An important Russian feature is that the precariat's (otkhodniks') economic enterprise is constrained by state and local authorities, and the socio-political initiative is completely suppressed by the way of life. In the meantime, otkhodniks possess quite a high potential for political activity (especially the businesspeople). However, their low socio-political status is an obstacle to realizing this high potential. And as high potential must always be discharged, a certain "discharge" is only to be expected from such people. How and in what areas and how can these people manifest themselves? Can contemporary otkhodniks once again become a destructive factor of social life, should that life need to be changed, as was the case just a century ago?

7.2 "Scattered Manufactories"

In 2014, we identified a new phenomenon of economic behavior of the population in small towns of provincial Russia—"scattered or dispersed manufactories." After several years of study, we depicted it in a recent article (Kordonskiy & Plusnin,

2018).[8] The empirical "clue" for this was our field research in two neighboring towns in the south of European Russia: Novokhopyorsk and Uryupinsk. Here the population has long been engaged en masse in manufacturing and selling items from goat down yarn (downy shawls and other wearables). This business also embraces many rural inhabitants of these two adjacent districts in the Voronezh and Volgograd regions. In subsequent years, we identified and depicted "dispersed manufactories" in several other small towns: a "fur manufactory" in Labinsk, Krasnodar Territory, a "shoe manufactory" in Kimry, Tver Region, a "Rostov enamel manufactory" in Rostov Veliky, Yaroslavl Region, and several other similar "folk crafts"– all concentrated in small towns. Typologically, they resemble the "down manufactory" of Uryupinsk and Novokhopyorsk. Still pending a detailed description are presumably a "clock manufactory" in Uglich (Yaroslavl), a fishing net manufactory in Kasimov (Ryazan), and a "cucumber manufactory" in Demidov-Porechye (Smolensk). There is also an assumption requiring empirical confirmation that such "manufactories" emerged and exist in certain single-industry towns with specialized (highly specialized) production of unique products.

The term "*dispersed manufactory*" for such activity stems from the fact that the entire production chain from procuring or producing and processing the resource to manufacturing and selling goods is accomplished within the local community, including the townspeople and the villagers, while it is scattered across many households, with the households specializing in separate components of the technological process, being different links of a single processor chain.

7.2.1 History of the "Scattered Manufactory"

My further observations in the abovementioned towns and their rural districts confirmed that the described phenomenon had all features of scattered manufacturing, a long-forgotten phenomenon of early capitalism.

As is well known from economic history (Mokyr, 1976; Mathias & Postan, 1978; Kahan & Hellie, 1985; Ogilvie, 1993), scattered manufactories that originally emerged in Italian cities in the fourteenth century and later in the Netherlands and other European countries, as well as in Russia, were an early capitalist response to the guild organization of craft activities. They were not encumbered by professional guild restrictions of the time and enabled mass output of consumer goods, which contributed to the subsequent success of such production management. Scattered manufactories quickly became widespread and engaged a lot of small village artisans, as well as poor and needy urban residents, thus providing them with a labor market and additional sources of income. They were generally established in industries with labor-intensive production chains that needed a large workforce but did not require high skills. They were therefore most common in the textile industry

[8] This section is based mainly on the text of the abovementioned article.

(weaving, cloth, fur, and down manufacturing), in logging and timber processing, in specialized construction (shipbuilding and housebuilding), in the mining industry (in iron, copper, silver mines and ore-smelting and metallurgical plants).

In Russia, manufactories have been well known since the seventeenth century (Blum, 1992, p. 293; Kahan & Hellie, 1985, pp. 121–136), therefore, the beginnings of manufacturing could have existed by the end or even by the middle of the sixteenth century (Kulisher, 2004, pp. 353–378, 399–412, 569–570), and from the first quarter of the eighteenth century, the manufacturing system in Russia experienced rapid growth. For example, in 1725, there were 233 manufactories, and in 1796—already 3360, both very large and small, mainly around Moscow (in addition to mining and metallurgical plants) (Blum, 1992, pp. 293–294). And by the beginning of the nineteenth century (1803), the village of Ivanovo alone (now a regional center), for example, had 49 manufactories for producing linen and printed cotton fabrics (Blum, 1992, pp. 300–301). It is noteworthy that besides Ivanovo, the neighboring districts adjacent to Moscow had many other large settlements with surrounding villages hosting numerous manufactories established mainly by Old Believer communities (e.g., in the Guslitsa area and in Meshchyora (Commercial and Industrial Russia, 1899). In Russia, the term manufactory was usually attributed to weaving enterprises—perhaps, for historical reasons and due to the mass nature of this phenomenon. Besides, mines, metal works, and specialized metallurgical and machine-building plants were controlled by the state or owned by the treasury (Blum, 1992). The government actively encouraged the development of manufactories in Russia (including in the form of lease or assignment). According to Fernand Braudel, the sudden loss of substantial government revenues from sales of Siberian furs in European markets (due to competition from North America since the 1730s) could have been a possible relatively unknown reason for developing mining and other manufactories in Russia "at the behest of the State" from the mid-eighteenth century (this industrial "pre-revolution") (Braudel, 1979, pp. 473, 478; Kulisher, 2004, p. 567). According to Gerald Blum, the Russian pre-industrial industrial development of the eighteenth century equaled and sometimes even surpassed that of the rest of Europe (Blum, 1992, p. 294); this is also evidenced by comparative data, for example, for Germany of the same period (Mathias & Postan, 1978, pp. 498–511).

Scattered manufactories characterized only the initial period of capitalist development in both Europe and Russia (the pre- or proto-industrial stage of capitalism, see Mendels (1972), Rudolph (1980), Houston and Snell (1984)), Ogilvie (1993)) and relatively quickly abated as a result of two interrelated processes: due to the development of monopoly and financial capitalism, which requires an appropriate dispersion of commodity chains to exclude the transparency of capital, and also due to diversification of production, preconditioned, by the way, by industrial specialization, akin to manufactory. This process was certainly accompanied by state protectionism against the background of growing sovereignty (Teschke, 2003, pp. 285–308). However, on the economic periphery, such (now archaic) institutions continued to exist for a long time, apparently in a greatly reduced form, as evidenced by the impressive development of handicrafts and artisanal production in Russia right until the 1930s (Gindin, 1925; Vladimirsky, 1927; Mints, 1929; Vodarsky & Istomina, 2004; Pavlov & Seleev, 2015); this was also always a precondition and prerequisite for scattered manufacturing. However, I found no explicit indications that manufactories in such archaic forms still existed at the end of the nineteenth century and even less so throughout the entire twentieth century. Therefore, I believe it likely that this phenomenon is a "new formation" of the turn of the twentieth–twenty-first centuries, a forced return of Russian provincial society to economic archaism.

The systemic economic crisis of the 1990s, underdeveloped and collapsing local labor markets, and widespread informal and shadow economy (Buev, 2010; Alimova et al., 2011; Gimpelson & Kapelyushnikov, 2014) forced the active population in small towns and adjacent rural areas to develop (or more precisely, to "remember") special economic behaviors, once characteristic of the early stages of capitalism in Europe and Russia (we traditionally call them "crafts"), in the form of so-called scattered manufactories. By the totality of features, such modern scattered manufactories in small towns represent an archaic economic institution, since they reproduce all the attributes of the classical scattered manufactory of the fourteenth to eighteenth centuries. Dispersed manufacturing involves a large part of the working-age population, both in the small towns themselves and in the surrounding rural areas. Households are included in dispersed production processes when obtaining (procuring) resources, making traditional local goods from them and selling those goods (retail and wholesale trade).

Meanwhile, modern *distributed manufacturing* is also well known. It widely relies on information technologies; it is not localized in one place, but constitutes a "*network of loosely connected and interacting intelligent entities for the production of individual components*" (Kühnle, 2009, p. 1); and it is generally located in third countries and distributed over a large area (Kühnle, 2007; Kühnle & Bitsch, 2015). This new form of distributed manufacturing is now seen as a promising, complementary, and alternative option to traditional industrial, conveyor production (Coughlan et al., 2010; Kühnle, 2009; Kostakis & Bauwens, 2014; Dekkers & Bennett, 2009). However, the key feature of the dispersed production processes that we identified and depicted is precisely their archaic nature and full compliance with classical scattered manufactories rather than modern distributed manufacturing based on innovative and IT technologies.

7.2.2 Features of Classical and Modern "Scattered" Manufactories

All the modern "scattered" manufactories that we identified and described turned out to be typologically similar. They are all concentrated (which is important) in small towns and the surrounding rural districts. The basic features of these economic institutions and the origins of their emergence in a particular area in one or another form are the same everywhere. Both the classical scattered manufactory of the early modern period and the current Russian provincial dispersed manufactory have certain distinctive features. I have identified eight of them.

1. Numerous separate independent components in the production chain. Manufacturing implies that the production process consists of many separate, relatively independent elements, which do not necessarily have to be located on the same premises (in some cases, that is even impossible). In fact, it is actually the need for several separate and relatively independent processing lines for the production of the finished goods that makes it possible to establish a scattered manufactory.
2. Combination of simple labor-intensive activities (the majority) with complex operations. This is the second precondition for the organization of a scattered manufactory. Time-consuming but simple operations do not require highly skilled workers. However, in the overall production chain, they are generally combined with complex operations, which imply high proficiency. This combination of simple and complex components in the finished product, which requires diverse working skills, is specific of manufacturing.
3. Specialization in certain types of operations. The third prerequisite is that workers (not individuals, but households or artels and teams) specialize in certain types or groups of production activities. Often, such specialization led to the emergence of working dynasties, where knowledge, skills and trade secrets were passed on within the family, thus giving its members a competitive advantage over neighbors. It is noteworthy that "dynasties" are characteristic mainly of highly skilled workers. This important element of the historically very early guild organization has been preserved to this day, and it is equally typical of the classical scattered manufactory. At the same time, since scattered manufacturing is often based on the use of unique or hard-to-get local raw materials, specialization also depends on external constraints: rather than high skills, certain operations require access or lack of access to resources or individual components of production.
4. Local concentration of production. Scattered manufacturing requires that the entire production process be concentrated within a single controlled area of one or more neighboring local communities on the backdrop of dispersed fabrication of its individual components. This is the key difference between the classical scattered manufactory and modern distributed manufacturing, since the production process implies direct physical interaction between workers engaged in different links of the chain.
5. Self-organization and artel cooperation. It is absolutely necessary to cooperate production activities and all elements of the scattered manufacturing process. This means that the participants have to organize themselves into specialized artels and groups of artels. Artel cooperation is one of the most important features of archaic economic institutions. It implies predominantly neighborly rather than family relations; communal rather than personal responsibility; and distributive remuneration for work.

6. Self-government institutions. Consequently, artel self-organization triggers the spontaneous emergence of self-government in its simplest (archaic) forms of *skhodki* (conventions), *razborki* (fights), *tyorki* (negotiations), and *avtoritetniy reshatel'* (reputable problem solver) (see the recent study of crafts (Seleev & Pavlov, 2016)). Generally, this results in the establishment of a single local source of control over all components of the manufacturing and sale of finished products (the organizational center can be in the form of a kulak peasant, merchant, industrialist, entrepreneur, bandit, "protector," government entity, or corporation). It is such artel cooperation and self-organization of the population, along with enterprise and economic self-sufficiency, that allow to record such economic practices of the population as crafts.
7. Unique raw materials. An important but not necessarily existing feature is the availability of a unique local raw material (or the ability to produce mass quantities of such raw material) for manufacturing mass market goods. Presumably, the development (re-emergence) of certain scattered manufactories in the 1990s was primarily due to the availability of such raw materials, which the local economy did not use. This situation gave members of the local community a natural competitive advantage over both the local economy and the neighboring communities. A vivid example of a unique resource is a special breed of Khopyor goats, which give an extremely fine long and durable downy yarn.
8. Unique technology. Another important, but also not always existing feature, is availability of a production resource in the form of a unique technology used for manufacturing a specific product. The local community has maintained the traditions of a unique craft that once ensured the welfare of most households. This unique craft (economic practices) determines the sustainability and "preservation" of scattered manufacturing based on such practices due to no or weak competition. Rostov enamel miniatures are a notable example of a unique technology. It is noteworthy that scattered manufacturing is not possible without either a unique craft, or unique raw materials, or both.

Observing and describing modern scattered manufacturing in small towns, in all the cases outlined below we recorded the entire set of traditionally distinguishable attributes of the early capitalist (currently already archaic) scattered manufactory.

7.2.3 *Specific Operation Arrangements of Four "Scattered Manufactories" of Uryupinsk/Novokhopyosk, Labinsk, Kimry, and Rostov Veliky*

All four scattered manufactories (producing down in Novokhopyorsk and Uryupinsk, fur in Labinsk, shoes in Kimry, and Rostov enamel miniatures in Rostov Veliky) are similar in their operation, employment, logistic, and marketing arrangements. Therefore, I provide a generalized description of the individual components of the production process.

7.2.3.1 Raw Materials and Primary Processing

Only the down manufactory produces goods from specific raw materials. It uses high-quality goat down, either hand combed or shorn from goats reared along the middle reaches of the Khopyor river; it is this down that adds special value to the shawls and other downy items woven in Uryupinsk and Novokhopyorsk. For this reason, down goats have long been raised here not only in villages but also on urban homesteads. The unique qualities of the down obtained from Khopyor goats, like the Orenburg ones, give the local population a competitive advantage over their neighbors and have long been the main source of well-being for local households. There are two ways to harvest down fiber—comb out or shear. This affects the quality of the finished product. Combing out is a more time-consuming process, and high-quality items are made from such a down. Sheared down is used to manufacture mass cheaper knitted products of lower quality.

The other three manufactory types do not use unique raw materials. Although the Labinsk fur manufactory works mostly on fur supplied by local private fur farms from almost half the rural area of Krasnodar and Stavropol Territories, it also uses a lot of raw materials brought in from Siberia. Prior to sewing, secondary processing—fur dressing—is often carried out on the spot, in the workhouses of Labinsk and neighboring villages. Kimry shoemakers, apparently, use only purchased leather, already tanned, which is delivered not only from different parts of the country, but also from abroad. In Rostov Veliky, all the main components for manufacturing the local enamels (copper plates, silver, enamel, and paints) are also imported, often from Europe (primarily paints). Thus, only the manufactories in Uryupinsk/Novokhopyorsk (exclusively or mainly) and Labinsk (partly) work on local raw materials, whereas the ones in Kimry and Rostov use only materials brought in from afar. However, in all cases, it is the retailers and wholesalers of the finished goods that mostly arrange the supply of raw materials to those involved in the initial stages of the production chain. At the same time, there are also specialized suppliers, including individual carriers (taxi drivers and truckers). As far as we can judge, some of those who control significant output and sales volumes are at the same time major suppliers of raw materials to the workers involved, thus representing a group of people controlling a significant share of the manufactory market. Eventually, these groups become key players in arranging and controlling the production of goods at all stages. Probably this has already happened, as is noticeable in Rostov and evident in clock manufacturing in Uglich. (Please note that these people, "concentrators of scattered manufacturing," are a factor in transforming the scattered manufactory into its classical form, exhaustively described by Karl Marx).

7.2.3.2 Production of Workpieces: The Simplest and Most Labor-Intensive Stages of Manufacturing

The production cycle in all scattered manufactories consists of both specialized and simple, labor-intensive and time-consuming operations. They employ a large number of people, not necessarily skilled, who can work together, *in artels*, at workhouses—premises specially allocated for such hazardous stages of production.

At the down manufactory, this involves primarily cleaning and washing the down, spinning (winding the down fiber on a cotton or silk thread using a hand or electric spinning wheel), and fluffing the finished product (fluffing downy shawls in a centrifuge to make them look marketable) at the final stage. All these operations can be (and used to be) performed within one family, at home, but are increasingly moved to specially allocated premises. Down along with the thread is often distributed to neighbors for spinning yarn; all family members are engaged in this.[9] Not many families have "*fluffers*" and self-made electric centrifuges, so people pay the owners of these specific devices to fluff their finished products.

In fur manufacturing, workhouses are mostly used for labor-intensive fur dressing prior to sewing. For these purposes, either existing facilities on the homestead of one of the families are adapted or new ones are specifically built. There, up to ten workers—neighbors and relatives—collectively engage in dressing and cutting the skins. Separate premises are necessary, since these operations are the "dirtiest" ones in fur manufacturing. Cutting skins is a more complex stage of production and is usually performed by those who sew the finished items. So fur clothes are often but not always sewn at the same premises where the fur is dressed. The least-skilled workers, unable to cut and sew, labor in the workhouses.

In shoe manufacturing, labor-intensive and simple procedures are probably minimized, since Kimry currently boasts of four shoe factories, which at different times had spun off from a single one. For private manufacturers, they are the most likely major suppliers of leather and materials for shoe soles and inner lining. For certain stages of production, shoe uppers are also delivered to various workshops and facilities in the surrounding towns and cities, including Moscow. Since semi-finished products require no processing, rough work is reduced to cutting out outer, middle, and inner soles, yuft and other fabrics according to patterns, which is done at private premises in Kimry and the neighboring towns.

In the production of enamel, labor-intensive operations are also minimized and limited to cutting and bending small copper plates, which are then enameled and burned in a muffle furnace. The enameler often works with metal himself. This requires appropriate skills, since not only the condition and color of the surface, but also the durability of the product depend on the quality of enamel burning (as well as on the bend of the copper plate). Furnaces are mostly rented since few people have them. Burning is a power-consuming process triggering widespread arrears on

[9] Earlier, in the 1990s, when this activity was the basic source of livelihood, men also spun yarn.

electricity bills and significant power losses in Rostov. The municipal administration held several special meetings regarding this issue.

Thus, where simple labor-intensive procedures are few (as in Kimry and Rostov), the technological chain has a larger share of operations requiring high skills and several areas of expertise. This determines the exclusive combination of proficiencies required to manufacture the product, which compensates for the uniqueness of the raw materials used (Uryupinsk and Novokhopyorsk).[10]

7.2.3.3 Manufacturing Stages that Require High Proficiency and Unique Professionals

It is characteristic that all the identified scattered manufactories contain links in their production chains that require special knowledge, skills, and abilities, which often run in the family. Apparently, it is precisely these specific features in the production of goods that make the development of such archaic economic institutions possible.

In down, fur, and shoe manufacturing, special knowledge is not as required as in the production of Rostov enamel miniatures, however, such skills are deeply rooted in tradition, which is maintained, among other things, by a significant local concentration of workers highly skilled in one or another area. Many women knit shawls, but the best knitters are greatly appreciated and learn this art. Moreover, a lot of down products are made on knitting machines, but their price is several-fold or even by an order of magnitude lower than the cost of a shawl handmade by a good knitter. The situation is quite similar in fur production, where almost all the work is manual and there are stringent requirements for cutters, fashion designers and workers who make hats and other products from the highest quality fur: here, too, the role of tradition is great and there is home-based (in workhouses) training in the art of sewing hats. At the same time, a large segment of production is routine, and most fur products, according to the manufacturers themselves, are of medium and low quality and are designed for mass buyers; meanwhile, there are always orders entrusted to the most skilled craftspeople. Handicraft production of footwear in Kimry is based on the work of fashion designers, who undergo special training, not only locally, but also allegedly in Italy, and shoemaking itself (tailoring of boots and shoes for particular purposes, for example, for pilots of polar aviation) is an art, so good shoemakers are extremely appreciated.

The production of Rostov enamel miniatures requires the participation of high-class specialists of two or three specialties: the lowest requirements apply to enamelers who cover copper plates with enamel and burn them, although it is believed that the final quality of the product depends on the experience and skill of the enameler; often the artists themselves do this work, but not for mass production. The artist's work is labor-intensive and time-consuming (it takes from several hours to weeks

[10]The Labinsk fur manufactory is the only one where we cannot specify any uniqueness, though it may consist in the special skills of the seamstresses.

and months to complete one miniature or painting), but the work of a filigree jeweler creating a silver frame for the miniature is three to five-fold more labor-intensive. The artists themselves buy and prepare paints; they trace pictures mainly from samples, but, of course, there are original works, and a number of works are recognized as of very high artistic value. Recognized craftsmen often work independently and no longer associate themselves with the few enamel miniature enterprises still remaining in Rostov. The filigree artist also usually makes all the components for the frame on his own: rolls and twists the wire; cuts and winds the individual parts of the frame; welds them; and makes the frame according to a previously prepared drawing (the frames are often original). The work of a jeweler is the third and final stage of product manufacturing, which requires high skills. All these craftsmen get vocational training at the enterprise and in specialized educational establishments. Some are trained by parents and relatives. There are still many working dynasties of artists and jewelers in Rostov who pass on their art and professional secrets from father to son.

7.2.3.4 Sales, Retail and Wholesale Trade of Scattered Manufactories

This component of modern scattered manufactories remains minimally accessible, and therefore least described for obvious reasons: it involves large shipments of goods and big amounts of money; interaction takes place between few well-acquainted people, and information is unavailable to outsiders. Obviously, there is considerable internal competition at this stage, but as all participants are closely connected, they jointly protect their common business from outsiders, if only because it is totally in the "shadow." However, along with several large entrepreneurs (up to a dozen, according to our observations), each manufactory has many small vendors, including both artisans (artists and jewelers, shoemakers and furriers, knitters and farmers) who sell their own products in local markets, and small merchants who buy items from several craftspeople, rent a booth, stall, or table in the town's municipal market, and engage exclusively in sales. They rarely register as sole proprietors, but they ensure interaction between individual participants of the production process: purchase raw materials and distribute them among workers engaged in primary processing; pick up the workpieces and hand them over to the next stage for further processing; sell finished products on the market; pay at all stages of production; and often lend money to the workers. The same people associate with both external wholesale suppliers of raw materials (down from Kalmykia and Dagestan, yarn thread from Ivanovo, fur skins from Novosibirsk and Krasnoyarsk, leather from Kirov and Italy, copper from Moscow, silver from Kostroma, etc.) and with wholesale buyers of final products. Therefore, the milieu of these numerous small vendors (many of whom used to be mediocre artisans themselves) gradually coins major local merchants who specialize exclusively in commerce and fiercely compete to monopolize the local market. This process remains invisible not only for outside observers but also for locals. It seems that large local merchants not only control entire rows of stalls in municipal markets, but also set up (or buy) forwarding companies to transport raw materials and goods, and open workhouses where they employ unskilled workers. In general, the process follows a well-established pattern, although production relations are currently at the stage of pre-classical manufacturing.[11]

In all manufactories, besides the two interlocking categories of merchants (artisans peddling or selling their products in the market, and specialized vendors engaged in retail and wholesale trade and enabling interaction between all links of the production chain), there is a third group of traders and resellers—the local Roma communities. According to respondents, gypsies are part of the shadow business everywhere; trading in downy shawls, fur items, leather footwear, and enamel jewelry is also a screen for their criminal business (usually drug and precious metal trafficking).

Merchant buyers are the cementing component of the manufactory that forms and ensures its integrity; this milieu promotes participants of the enterprise who gradually begin to control and manage the whole business. At the present stage of manufactory development, these new small companies are still just emerging, crystallizing; by appearance and nature of business, they resemble the remnants of formerly state-owned enterprises, factories, which used to and still produce the same goods that modern scattered manufactories specialize in. However, already here, in small towns with scattered production of unique or rare goods, accumulation of capital is approaching.

7.2.3.5 Participation of the Population

It proved difficult to assess the extent of engagement of the population of small towns and nearby villages in scattered manufactories. The reasons are obvious: absence of municipal and regional records on residents unemployed in the local economy and on the structure of the self-employed population (Plusnin et al., 2015; Kordonsky et al., 2009). Therefore, we are forced to rely exclusively on the opinions of respondents and local experts, on our own comparisons, and on calculations based on statistical and municipal reports. As a result, we have come up with the following estimates. In the 1990s and the 2000s, the entire population was engaged in the down manufactory of Uryupinsk and Novokhopyorsk. Currently, significantly fewer people participate, but still no less than a third of the households. Earlier, not only able-bodied family members and pensioners, but also children were involved in down production. Now the number of goats has decreased considerably; many townspeople no longer keep them in their backyards, and the main herd is concentrated in the rural area. Knitting is no longer a permanent side business for households; other

[11] However, our recent observations show that in Uglich and Kimry, for example, scattered manufacturing is already developing into a classical manufactory. Homestead as place of work is giving way to workshops, and each town currently boasts of several specialized enterprises, watchmakers and shoemakers.

sources of income have emerged. Estimates based on observations made in the spring of 2017 indicate that from a third to half of the households are engaged in scattered manufacturing, which means at least a third of all working-age residents, or about 10,000 of the 25,000–30,000 households (exact figures on the number of households in both districts were unavailable). In Labinsk, approximately a fifth of the adult population, representing 4000 of the total 20,000 households, is involved in different stages of fur manufacturing. Of the 10,000 households in Rostov, a thousand is associated with manufacturing enamel miniatures. We were not able to estimate shoe manufacturing in Kimry. No matter how great the error of such estimates, it is quite obvious that a large part of the local population is engaged in scattered manufactories, and that is the basis of their livelihood and source of well-being, although neither statistics nor local authorities are aware of this.

7.2.4 Common Features of Modern "Scattered Manufactories"

What are the characteristic common features of the "scattered manufactories" depicted and those identified but not yet described? There are six of them.

7.2.4.1 Traditional Production

First, all these industries have long-standing traditions of local crafts, which in the Imperial and Soviet periods were developed and industrialized: in all the towns, factories based on traditional crafts, skills, and economic practices of the population were established long ago. Artisanal down crafts in the middle reaches of the Khopyor River (Uryupinsk, Novokhopyorsk) have been known since the eighteenth century. In Labinsk, industrial production of fur items was launched in the 1930s, whereas artisanal one—much earlier. Several fur factories operated in the Soviet years, and even now, there are seven of them. In Kimry, artisanal footwear production and tanneries have been known since the beginning of the seventeenth century (allegedly, since the sixteenth century), and shoe factories—since the beginning of the twentieth century (1903). Currently, there are five factories, which are gradually eliminating scattered manufacturing. Rostov enamel miniatures as hand painted art on enamel have existed since the 1760s, the enamel factory—since 1918. At present, there are already four or even five enamel factories, which are a threat to the survival of scattered manufacturing. It is noteworthy that the early eighteenth century is the time when manufacturing demonstrated an explosive growth in various areas of the national economy (Blum, 1992, pp. 293–294), although the beginning of the process dates back to the middle of the seventeenth century, when diverse manufactories were set up in the vicinity of Moscow, Tula, Kashira, in the Urals and Trans-Urals under the patronage and assistance of the state (with the involvement of foreigners)

(Kulisher, 2004, pp. 399–412). In other words, small-town scattered manufactories described herein have a long history of precisely this kind of local production.

7.2.4.2 Unique Resources/Practices

Second, scattered manufactories rely either on unique local resources (such as the breed of Khopyor goats with a special quality of down) or on traditional, often unique, practices of the population (such as the long-time tradition of high-quality shoemaking in Kimry,[12] and Rostov enamel manufacturing). In all cases, raw materials and supplies that require special processing skills constitute the most important competitive edge of the population involved in the dispersed manufacturing process. But along with resource-based superiority, there is also an advantage provided by professional (guild) skills, which are still carefully protected and inherited in each town.

7.2.4.3 Simplicity and Labor Intensity of Individual Production Operations

Third, the manufacturing of goods requires several simple but labor-intensive operations, which can be carried out separately and at different times with no need for an orderly one-time assembly of components, i.e. conveyor production is of no benefit. This allows distributing the operations among different workers to be performed independently. It is likely that the artisanal nature of production and the autonomy of its components ensures their sustainability. Raising goats, shearing or combing out their down, spinning yarn, knitting, fluffing the finished products (making them fluffier) and selling them—all these operations are dispersed among rural and urban households not only geographically, but also in time, embracing an annual cycle. The same is happening with manufacturing fur items from both imported fur and that supplied by private fur farms of Labinsk and its vast rural surroundings (raising fur-bearing animals on private farmsteads is widespread in the villages of the Stavropol and Krasnodar Territories). Until recently, many households in Kimry independently purchased and cut leather, made patterns, soles, and tailored boots (and other leather footwear); the emergence of several specialized factories brought this activity virtually to a standstill. Manufacturing copper and silver base plates for various Rostov enamel miniatures, enameling, painting and burning them, making filigree, and applying the final jeweler's touch are also independent technological processes, which are still dispersed among many

[12]However, since the times of Catherine the Great, Kimry shoemakers have also been notoriously known for their swindles with paper soles, when they flooded Moscow markets with footwear of inferior quality; even during the Crimean War, the soldier boots they supplied under large military orders were of extremely poor quality (see, e.g., Vladimir Gilyarovsky's essay *Sretenka* in *Moscow and Muscovites* for this).

households, despite the increasingly obvious consolidation of production by several factories. Apparently, a similar process has gone a long way in Uglich, and nowadays households are virtually not engaged in watchmaking; everything is once again concentrated at factories.

7.2.4.4 Combination of Simple and Complex Operations

Fourth, the production cycle of scattered manufactories combines two kinds of operations. Most of them are labor-intensive but very simple (like making copper base plates for the enamel miniatures, raising goats and fur-bearing animals, treating leather, fur, or down). However, there are always a couple of operations that generally require high professionalism and special skills (the work of miniaturists and filigree jewelers, pattern makers and fashion designers of leather products, fur seamstresses, and knitters of handmade fluffy shawls). Because of them, the entire production cycle focuses on the places where people with such rare or unique skills reside, while simple and work-intensive components of the process are often dispersed not only throughout the town but also the rural district. This is especially typical for Khopyor goats and Labinsk household animal farms scattered over large areas (however, in the case of the alleged Uglich manufactory, the resource base consisted of huge stocks of spare parts for watches left at the factory, which were embezzled: "... *we then made watches from those parts for another twenty years* ...").

7.2.4.5 Co-Operation of Autonomous Laborers

Fifth, some simple elements of the production cycle are concentrated in workhouses: several people (from two-three to ten) unite and perform one operation together. Generally, this takes place on the premises of one household, usually in a dedicated room (not necessarily specially built—utility rooms, outbuildings, sheds, garages, basements, etc. also serve this purpose). The cooperation effect is in force here: it is easier and faster to perform individual homogeneous operations together, so many workhouses uniting laborers according to the artel principle were set up in all the towns. The laborers are not necessarily relatives. More often, they are close acquaintances and neighbors (which is most typical for the artel organization of labor). This forms the basis for artel cooperation within scattered manufactories, which we believe is a key factor underlying the stability and sustainability of this type of economic practices.

7.2.4.6 Widespread Market and Long-Distance Trading

Sixth, retail and wholesale trade in finished goods is not limited to local markets; it is becoming regional and even international. In the towns, merchants dealing in finished goods have formed coalitions ("clans"), which closely cooperate and at the same time fiercely compete, keep outsiders out, and actively develop long-distance wholesale trade (domestic and international). This component of scattered manufacturing is associated with many other types of business activities, of which there are several categories. The first includes suppliers of raw materials (copper, silver, leather, fur, down). The second category consists of major wholesale buyers, often large organizations of different forms of ownership, including, for example, the Russian Orthodox Church and state military departments. The third comprises door-to-door vendors, like gypsies, Chinese merchants, otkhodniks engaged in rotation work, and specialized online sellers. Finally, the fourth category are those who provide additional, primarily transportation, services—truckers, private carriers, and local taxi firms.

These features can serve as diagnostic indicators when searching for, identifying, and describing similar dispersed industries in other small Russian towns. Very recently, we have started searching for such "scattered manufactories" all over Russia, focusing on numerous single-industry towns, where the socio-economic situation is known to remain unfavorable (Lipsits, 2000; Turgel, 2010) forcing inhabitants to seek en masse additional sources of income besides the almost non-existent local economy; in the meantime, most single-industry towns are distinguished by resource specialization, unique technologies and products.

7.2.5 *The Concept of Craft and Technological Uniqueness*

It is important to note the following: the identified features of the manufactories that appeared de-novo just three decades ago indicate that the development of certain economic institutions is contingent on the environment (territory) and the people's household and economic practices (crafts). I believe it is relevant to characterize territories and crafts in terms of their uniqueness, by which I mean the availability of rare, singular, or extraordinary local resources used in the production process; a craft can be unique due to long-standing historical traditions (no one does it anywhere, or nearly anywhere, else) in manufacturing those goods that give the local community a competitive advantage over others.

A typical local territory, as well as typical practices (indistinguishable from many other territories and similar crafts) determine the conditions for mass (industrial or conveyor) production. A territory unique in terms of its resources (raw materials), developed practices and distinct local historical tradition, as well as unique household and economic practices (crafts) themselves determine the conditions and create opportunities for the development of a modern scattered manufactory. Rather than calling this process *de-novo* development, I suppose we should speak of restoring the once abandoned/forgotten way of organizing local crafts of the population.

Thus, it is possible to propose a phenomenological concept of the development of household and economic practices (crafts) of the population based on local resources and historical traditions and the prevalence of a craft. I will illustrate this with the

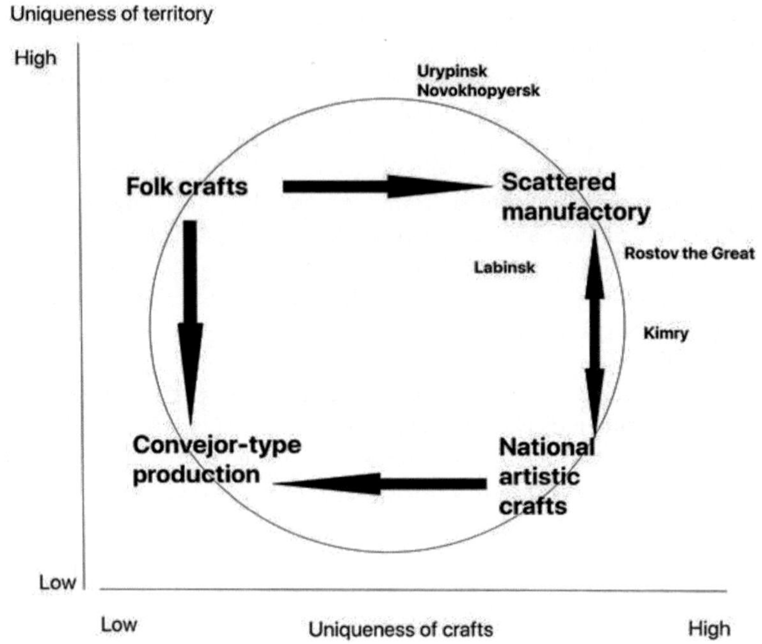

Fig. 7.3 Development of economic institutions under the concept of unique territory and/or crafts. Source: Kordonskiy and Plusnin (2018)

following chart (see Fig. 7.3): the abscissa shows the degree of uniqueness (more precisely, rarity) of a craft; the ordinate—the degree of uniqueness of the local territory in terms of resources and traditional economic practices. A unique territory and unique crafts determine the way to a scattered manufactory or, more likely, to the long-term preservation of archaic economic institutions in some localities (which is also the preservation of archaic practices in time and space). The opposite trend—toward an indistinguishable, similar territory in terms of natural and climatic conditions (resources) and ordinary, non-specific history of its economic development and homogeneous crafts—determines the way to mass production, industry, and assembly line.

Other types of household and economic practices can also be distinguished in the same "territory/crafts" coordinate space. Common (non-unique) practices implemented in a territory with unique resources (raw materials) pave the way for the development of diverse handicrafts. This provides insight into the situation when on the backdrop of extremely well-developed handicrafts in Imperial Russia and in the early Soviet years, individual provinces and neighboring uyezds (districts) differed so much in the types of crafts prevailing there: one district specialized only in earthenware; another—in wooden spoons; the third—in logging and timber rafting; whereas the fourth (in the same situation)—exclusively in otkhodnichestvo, and so forth (Ezersky, 1894; Vladimirsky, 1927). Everywhere, area-specific resources, nature and climate gave local communities at least some competitive edge over their closest neighbors.

By contrast, unique crafts of the population in a territory that has no exceptional features (for example, does not have particularly important resources) lead to the development of so-called folk arts and crafts. Such are all modern artistic folk handicrafts associated with "crafts" (Pavlov & Seleev, 2015, pp. 30–31), e.g., Fedoskino lacquer miniatures; hand paintings of Palekh, Khokhloma, Mezen, and Leshukonye; clay toys from Kargopol and Petrovskoye, Dymkovo and Guslitsy, and hand painted Gzhel ceramics.

Thus, the phenomenon of the modern scattered manufactory is determined by the uniqueness of the local territory and/or the uniqueness of household and economic practices (crafts). Thick arrows in Fig. 7.3 indicate alternative ways of development, and the thin ones—likely transitions from one type of production to another. I assume that the existing archaic scattered manufactories cannot directly transform into industrial conveyor production (the arrow is broken). I believe the reasons and conditions for the development of these types of institutions are different. The chart also shows the conditional location of scattered manufactories in the designated "territory/crafts" coordinates. The manufactories of Uryupinsk, Novokhopyorsk and Labinsk are to a certain extent less unique in household and economic practices of the population, but more unique in terms of territory (resources); Rostov Veliky and Kimry, on the contrary, are unique in practices (crafts) and less unique in terms of territory (resources and raw materials). A scattered manufactory can also cover the areas labeled "handicrafts" and "folk arts and crafts."

7.3 Summary. Likely Reasons for the Renewal of Archaic Economic Institutions

The described patterns of economic behavior common for provincial residents pertain mainly to the informal and shadow segment of the economy and are in no way officially recorded. Depending on the type of activity, from two-thirds to three-fourths of otkhodnichestvo is in the "shadow." Almost all production and trade activities of the population relating to scattered manufactories are informal and shadow, with very few exceptions. Although nowadays these exceptions are increasingly becoming the rule. When a household-based scattered manufactory concentrates, "solidifies" into a classical manufactory—a factory producing enamel miniatures, boots, fur items, knitwear or watches, such an enterprise is forced to report officially at least part of its output and turnover. But as long as production is "scattered" or "wandering," the revenue it generates is considered as income from personal subsidiary farming, which no one ever records; moreover, it cannot be recorded. Exchange relations between the performers of individual operations in a "manufactory" are very rarely formalized. Relations in an otkhodnik artel are almost never formalized, simply because only one team member is generally formally employed, whereas the remaining five to ten people are not registered as workers. Some people do register sole proprietorship or even a small business, but do it only due to necessity (for example, to set up a permanent market booth, open a private shop, get a factory job, rent resources and equipment required for production, etc.). Private enterprises are also established for international trade in manufactured goods (such enterprises exist in all towns). Volumes of raw materials and output, the cost of goods produced, trade turnover and the number of people involved in scattered manufacturing are not recorded and not reported in either municipal accounts and financial statements or, even more so, in state statistics. The same applies to the overwhelming majority of our wandering workers, about which we wrote a lot (Plusnin et al., 2015, pp. 143–150).

One should note an important feature of otkhodnichestvo and "scattered manufactories: such types of crafts emerged in the early 1990s and still exist mainly in the province (otkhodnichestvo) and only in small towns ("manufactories"). In large cities we find no otkhodniks but observe everywhere the shadow "garage economy" as a form of post-workshop organization of production; however, there is no sign of either otkhodnichestvo or "scattered manufactories." By contrast, in small towns garages are still mainly used as intended (Seleev & Pavlov, 2016, p. 44) or as workhouses in scattered manufacturing.

There are several reasons underlying the "emergence" and prevalence of otkhodnichestvo and "scattered manufactories." The trigger was the critical situation that developed in small towns in the early 1990s and put the residents in an unfavorable position compared to inhabitants of large cities and rural areas. In contrast to large cities, the few backbone enterprises that had existed in small towns since the Soviet era collapsed literally at the same time, leaving most residents jobless and with no chance of finding work locally. As opposed to the rural district, the majority of small-town households could not immediately switch to subsistence farming due to lack or inadequacy of farmland (Plusnin, 2000).[13] So in order to adapt promptly to the situation, residents of small towns resorted to such archaic forms of activities as otkhodnichestvo (it actually originated primarily in small towns and only later spread to the rural district) and artel work based on kin and neighborly relations and using unique local resources or techniques of manufacturing unique products. In some small towns (presumably only a few, but we are not yet certain), the latter subsistence pattern fairly quickly developed into "scattered manufactories"—a form of economic behavior as archaic as otkhodnichestvo. However, it is noteworthy that these two essentially additional forms of economic behavior of the population in Russia have always developed side by side in one and the same province (depressive, as currently viewed) (Mints, 1929; Vladimirsky, 1927).

The second reason for the shadow nature of both "scattered manufactories" and otkhodnichestvo appears to be the domestic policy of the state, as Simon Kordonsky

[13] In most small towns, households own land plots of 200–400 m^2 (0.05–0.1 acres); their size rarely reaches 1000–1200 m^2 (0.3 acres), and almost never equals the 4000 m^2 (1 acre) necessary for subsistence.

expressly wrote (Kordonsky, 2018). I presume that the main driver in the development of "scattered manufactories" and the widespread of otkhodnichestvo, as archaic economic institutions, is excessive government regulation of small business. We know that such pressure almost always "inhibits" new business (Chepurenko, 2008), and over time forces even the existing small business into "the shadow" or causes its collapse. This is especially so in provincial Russia, in small towns and their rural districts (Chepurenko, 2019). As a result, emerging provincial "scattered manufactories" and otkhodnichestvo are two typologically different reactions—flight to a private backyard and workhouse or flight from the home town/village—of the active, self-employed and enterprising population to increasing supervision from the "focusing state." Potential local entrepreneurs choose one of two evils, but in both cases prefer to evade rather than overcome.

I see no other significant reasons for the re-emergence of such archaic economic institutions as scattered manufactories and otkhodnichestvo in the Russian province. These two causes (inadequate local labor market and excessive regulation of local business) are interrelated as the driving force and trigger, making their combined action cumulative. Undoubtedly, there are local conditions that serve as additional factors stimulating or inhibiting the development of archaic forms, especially "scattered manufactories," otherwise we would observe similar forms everywhere, as is the case with modern otkhodnichestvo in provincial Russia. Meanwhile, unlike mass otkhodnichestvo, "scattered manufactories" are relatively rare. The reason for this is precisely the availability or lack of unique resources and unique manufacturing techniques, which give the local community a competitive advantage over its neighbors. In this case, however, unique local resources and/or techniques are a prerequisite rather than reason for development.

Obviously, mass otkhodnichestvo of rural residents and the "scattered manufactories" of small towns are a temporary, transient phenomenon. Resumed due to necessity in a crisis, they are bound to degenerate soon or, more precisely, undergo transformation first into classical manufactories and then into institutions more typical of the new time. Otkhodnichestvo will hardly fade away completely but considering the increasing prevalence of modern distributed manufacturing and remote employment, its current forms will inevitably degrade. It is, therefore, even more, challenging to identify and describe such archaic institutions, which re-emerge only in times of sweeping change but remain intact in nature, thus giving us reason to consider them archaic.

References

Alimova, T. A., Chenina, A. V., & Chepurenko, A. Y. (2011). Economic crisis and entrepreneurial activity of the population of Russia: starting a business or leaving a business? *The world of Russia, 20*(2), 142–160. Алимова Т.А., Ченина А.В., Чепуренко А.Ю. (2011). Экономический кризис и предпринимательская деятельность населения России: открывать свое дело или выходить из бизнеса? *Мир России*. 20(2), 142–160.

Andryushin, E. A. (2012). *From the history of the USSR labor law and human resource policy of the Soviet government*. Novyj Khronograf. Андрюшин Е.А. (2012). *Из истории трудового законодательства СССР и политики советского правительства в области трудовых ресурсов*. М.: Новый хронограф.

Barsukova, S. Y. (2003). Informal economy: Concept, structure. *Economic Sociology, 4*(4), 15–36. Барсукова С.Ю. (2003a). Неформальная экономика: понятие, структура. *Экономическая социология*, 4(4), 15–36.

Barsukova, S. Y. (2015). *An essay on the informal economy, or 16 shades of gray*. Publishing House of the Higher School of Economics. Барсукова С.Ю. (2015). *Эссе о неформальной экономике, или 16 оттенков серого*. Москва: Издательский дом Высшая школа экономики.

Barsukova, S., & Radaev, V. V. (2012). Informal economy in Russia: A brief overview. *Economic Sociology. The European Electronic Newsletter, 13*(2), 4–12.

Blum, J. (1992). *Lord and peasant in Russia from the 9th to the 19th century*. Princeton University Press.

Braudel, F. (1979). *Civilisation matérielle, économie et capitalisme, XV-XVIII siècle T.3. Le temps du monde*. Armand Colin. Russian edition: Бродель Ф. (1992) *Время Мира. Материальная цивилизация, экономика и капитализм, XV–XVIII вв.* М.: Прогресс.

Buev, V. V. (2010). Shadow activity of small businesses. *Public Opinion Monitoring, 4*(98), 57–74. Буев В.В. (2010). Теневая деятельность малых предприятий. *Мониторинг общественного мнения*, 4(98), 57–74.

Burds, J. (1998). *Peasant dreams and market politics: Labor migration and the Russian village, 1861–1905*. : University of Pittsburgh Press.

Chepurenko, A. Y. (2008). Early Entrepreneurship in Russia: Intermediate Results of GEM. *Mir Rossii, 17*(2), 22–40. Чепуренко А.Ю. (2008). Раннее предпринимательство в России: промежуточные результаты GEM. *Мир России*, 17(2), 22–40.

Chepurenko, A. (2019). Different types of informal entrepreneurs in fragile 'transitional' contexts: Case based evidence in Russia. In B. Dallago & E. Tortia (Eds.), *Entrepreneurship and local economic development: A comparative perspective on entrepreneurs, universities and governments* (pp. 1–29). Routledge.

Commercial and industrial Russia. (1899). Sankt-Peterburg. *Торгово-промышленная Россия* (1899). СПб.

Coughlan, D., O'Connell, J., & Murphy, I. (2010). Knowledge, innovation and creativity as the basis of economic development in the 21st century. *Vestnik mezhdunarodnykh organizatsij, 5*(3), 21–32. Коклан Д., О'Коннел Дж., & Мерфи И. (2010). Знания, инновации и творческий потенциал как основа экономического развития в XXI в. *Вестник международных организаций*, 5(3), 21–32.

Danilov, V. P. (1974). Engagement of peasants in external wage earning in the 1920s. *Istoricheskie zapiski, 94*, 46–88. Данилов В.П. (1974). Крестьянский отход на промыслы в 1920-х гг. *Исторические записки*, 94, 46–88.

Davydov, M. A. (2018). On the problems of Russian modernization. *Russian History, 3*, 33–44. Давыдов М.А. (2018). О проблемах российской модернизации. *Российская история*, 3, 33–44.

Dekkers, R., & Bennett, D. (2009). Industrial networks of the future: Review of research and practice. In R. Dekkers R. (Ed.), *Dispersed manufacturing networks. Challenges for research and practice* (pp. 13–34). Springer.

Delarov, D. I. (1928). The northern oblast and its role in the economy of the USSR. *Sever. Vologda, 7–8*, 135–160. Деларов Д.И. (1928). Северная область и её место в народном хозяйстве СССР. *Север*, 7–8, 135–160.

Dyatlov, V. I., & Grigorichev, K. V. (Eds.) (2013). *Migration society of Asian Russia: Migration, space, community*. "Ottisk". Дятлов В.И., Григоричев К.В. (ред.) (2013). *Переселенческое общество Азиатской России: миграции, пространства, сообщества*/Науч. ред. В.И. Дятлов, К.В. Григоричев. Иркутск: «Оттиск».

Ezersky, N. (1894). *Handicraft industry and its importance in the national economy*. Printing House A.I. Mamontov. Езерский Н. (1894). *Кустарная промышленность и ее значение в народном хозяйстве*. М.: Типография А.И. Мамонтова.

Fedorov, A. N. (2010). The real support of Soviet power: Socio-demographic characteristics of the urban population of Russia in 1917–1920 (based on materials from the Central Industrial Region). *Journal of Social Policy Research, 8*(1), 69–86. Фёдоров А.Н. (2010). Реальная опора советской власти: социально-демографические характеристики городского населения России в 1917-1920 годах (на материалах Центрального Промышленного района). *Журнал исследований социальной политики*, 8(1), 69–86.

Gimpelson, V. E., & Kapelyushnikov, R. I. (Eds.) (2006). *Precarious employment in the Russian economy*. Publishing House of the Higher School of Economics. Гимпельсон В.Е., Капелюшников Р.И. (ред.) (2006). *Нестандартная занятость в российской экономике*. М.: Издательский Дом ГУ-ВШЭ.

Gimpelson, V. E. & Kapelyushnikov, R. I. (Eds.) (2014). *In the shadow of regulation: Informality in the Russian labor market*. Publishing House of the Higher School of Economics. В тени регулирования: неформальность на российском рынке труда (2014). /Под ред. В.Е. Гимпельсона и Р.И. *Капелюшникова. М.: Издательский Дом ВШЭ*.

Gindin, Y. (1925). Our economic growth and new tasks facing labor market regulation. *Voprosy truda, 11*, 38–44. Гиндин Я. (1925). Наш хозяйственный подъем и новые задачи регулирования рынка труда. *Вопросы труда*, 11, 38–44.

Herzen, A. I. (1859). *Russian Germans and German Russians*. [Electronic resource]. Accessed from http://opentextnn.ru/man/?id=1299&txt=1. Герцен, А.И. (1859). *Русские немцы и немецкие русские* [Электронный ресурс]: Очерк/А.И. Герцен.

Houston, R., & Snell, K. D. M. (1984). Proto-industrialization? Cottage industry, social change, and industrial revolution. *The Historical Journal, 27*(2), 473–492.

Kachorovsky, K. R. (1900). The Russian community, Vol. 1. SPb. Качоровский К.Р. (1900). *Русская община*. Т. 1. СПб.

Kahan, A., & Hellie, R. (1985). *The plow, the hammer, and the knout: An economic history of eighteenth-century Russia*. University of Chicago Press.

Karyshev, N. A. (1896). Concerning a study of our otkhodnik occupations. *Russkoe Bogatstvo, 7*, 1–24. Карышев Н.А. (1896). К изучению наших отхожих промыслов. *Русское богатство*, 7, 1–24.

Kordonskiy, S. G., & Plusnin, J. M. (2018). Archaic economic institutions: Distributed manufactories in small cities of Russia. *World of Russia, 27*(4), 6–30. Кордонский С.Г., Плюснин Ю.М. (2018). Архаические экономические институты: распределенные мануфактуры в малых городах России. *Мир России*, 27(4), 6–30.

Kordonsky, S. (2018). The social structure of Russia. In I. Studin (Ed.), *Russia. Strategy, policy and administration* (pp. 76–85). Palgrave Macmillan.

Kordonsky, S. G., Plusnin, J. M., & Skalon, V. A. (2009). *Municipal Russia: Lifestyle and mentality. Phenomenological study*. TsPI MSU. Кордонский С.Г., Скалон В.А., Плюснин Ю.М. (2009). *Муниципальная Россия: образ жизни и образ мыслей. Опыт феноменологического исследования*. М.: ЦПИ МСУ.

Kostakis, V., & Bauwens, M. (2014). *Network society and future scenarios for a collaborative economy*. Palgrave Macmillan. https://doi.org/10.1057/9781137406897

Kühnle, H. (2007). Post mass production paradigm (PMPP) trajectories. *Journal of Manufacturing Technology Management, 18*(8), 1022–1037.

Kühnle, H. (Ed.). (2009). *Distributed manufacturing: Paradigm, concepts, solutions and examples*. Springer.

Kühnle, H., & Bitsch, G. (2015). *Foundations & principles of distributed manufacturing: elements of manufacturing networks, cyber-physical production systems and smart automation*. Springer.

Kulisher, I. M. (2004). *History of the Russian national economy*. Socium. Кулишер И.М. (2004). История русского народного хозяйства. Челябинск: Социум.

Lenin, V. I. (1971). The development of capitalism in Russia. The process of the Formation of a home market for large-scale industry. V.I. Lenin. In *Complete set of works*. Izdatel'stvo politicheskoj literatury. Ленин В.И. (1971). Развитие капитализма в России. Процесс образования внутреннего рынка для крупной промышленности. *Ленин В.И. Полн. собр. соч.* М.: Изд-во политической литературы.

Lipsits, I. V. (Ed.) (2000). *Single-industry cities and city-forming enterprises: An overview report*. Chronicler. Липсиц И.В. (Ред.) (2000). *Монопрофильные города и градообразующие предприятия: обзорный доклад*. М.: Хроникер.

Manning, N., Veit-Wilson, J., Abrahamson, P., Davidova, N., Zdravomislov, A., Zuziev, A., & Tikhonova, N. E. (2017). *Poverty and social exclusion in the new Russia*. Routledge.

Mathias, P., & Postan, M. M. (Eds.). (1978). *The Cambridge economic history of Europe. Vol. VII. The industrial economies: Capital, labour, and enterprise. Part I: Britain, France, Germany, and Scandinavia*. Cambridge Press.

Mendels, F. F. (1972). Proto-industrialization: The first phase of the industrialization process. *Journal of Economic History, 32*(1), 241–261.

Mints, L. E. (1926). *Engagement of peasants in external wage earnings in the USSR*. Voprosy truda. Минц Л.Е. (1926). *Отход крестьянского населения на заработки в СССР*. М.: Вопросы труда.

Mints, L. E. (1929). *Agrarian overpopulation and the labor market in the USSR*. GIZ. Минц Л.Е. (1929). *Аграрное перенаселение и рынок труда в СССР*. М.-Л.: ГИЗ.

Mironov, B. N. (2003). *The social history of Russia in the imperial period (18th – Early 20th centuries)*. "Dmitry Bulanin. Миронов Б. Н. (2003). *Социальная история России периода империи (XVIII—начало XX в.)*. Т. 1. СПб.: «Дмитрий Буланин».

Mokyr, J. (1976). Growing-up and the industrial revolution in Europe. *Explorations in Economic History, 13*(7), 371–396.

Nikulin, V. N. (Ed.) (2008). *North-west in the agrarian history of Russia*. Kaliningrad: Publishing House of the Russian State University. I. Kant. Никулин В.Н. (Ред.) (2008). *Северо-Запад в аграрной истории России*. Калининград: Издательство РГУ им. И. Канта.

Ogilvie, S. C. (1993). Proto-industrialization in Europe. *Continuity and Change, 8*(2), 159–179.

Pavlov, A. B., & Seleev, S. S. (2015). Phenomenological description of modern crafts. *Universum: Obschestvennye nauki, 3*(13), 25–41. Павлов А.Б., Селеев С.С. (2015). *Феноменологическое описание современных промыслов*. Универсум: Общественные науки. Accessed from http://7universum.com/ru/social/archive/item/2015

Plusnin, J. M. (1997). Psychology of material life (paradoxes of rural economy of survival). *ECO: Economics and Organization of Industrial Production, 7*, 169–176. Плюснин Ю.М. (1997). Психология материальной жизни (парадоксы сельской экономики выживания). *ЭКО: экономика и организация промышленного производства*.

Plusnin, J. M. (2000). *Small Russian towns*. Moscow Public Science Foundation. Плюснин Ю.М. (2000). *Малые города России*. Москва: МОНФ.

Plusnin, J. M. (2016). Far from the state: Migrant workers and power in modern Russia. *Public Administration Issues, 1*, 60–80. Плюснин Ю.М. Вдали от государства: отходники и власть в современной России. *Вопросы государственного и муниципального управления*, 1, 60–80.

Plusnin, J. M. (2019). Russian otkhodnichestvo: milestones of a centuries-old history. *ECO, 10*, 94–115. Плюснин Ю. М. (2019). Российское отходничество: вехи многовековой истории. *ЭКО*, 10, 94–115.

Plusnin, J., Zausaeva, Y., Zhidkevich, N., & Pozanenko, A. (2015). *Wandering workers. Mores, behavior, way of life, and political status of domestic Russian labor migrants*. Ibidem.

Radaev, V. V. (1999). Shadow economy in Russia: Changing contours. *Pro et Contra, 4*(1, 10), 5–24. Радаев В.В. (1999). Теневая экономика в России: изменение контуров. *Pro et Contra*, 4(1, 10), 5–24.

Remnev, A. V., & Suvorova, N. G. (2010). Controlled colonization and spontaneous migration processes on Asian peripheries of Russian Empire. *Politia, 3–4*(58–59), 150–191. Ремнев А.В.,

& Суворова Н.Г. (2010). Управляемая колонизация и стихийные миграционные процессы на азиатских окраинах Российской империи. *Полития*, 3–4 (58–59), 150–191.

Rudolph, R. L. (1980). Family structure and proto-industrialization in Russia. *Journal of Economic History, 40*(1), 111–118.

Seleev, S. S., & Pavlov, A. B. (2016). *Garages*. Strana OZ. Селеев С.С., Павлов А.Б. (2016). *Гаражники*. М.: Страна ОЗ.

Shabanova, M. A. (1986). Seasonal builders in Siberian villages. *Izvestiya Sibirskogo otdeleniya Akademii nauk SSSR. Ser. Ekonomiki i prikladnoj sotsiologii, 7*(2), 48–57. Шабанова М.А. (1986). Сезонные строители в сибирском селе. *Известия Сибирского отделения Академии наук СССР. Сер. Экономики и прикладной социологии*, 7(2), 48–57.

Shabanova, M. A. (1992). Modern otkhodnichestvo as a sociocultural phenomenon. *Sociological Researches, 4*, 55–63. Шабанова М.А. (1992). Современное отходничество как социокультурный феномен. *Социологические исследования*, 4, 55–63.

Shanin, T. (1972). *The awkward class: Political sociology of peasantry in a developing society, Russia 1910–1925*. The Clarendon Press.

Shanin, T. (1986). *Revolution as a moment of truth: 1905–1907→1917–1922*. Yale University Press.

Standing, G. (2011). *The precariat. The new dangerous class*. Bloomsbury Publishing Plc. Russian edition: Стэндинг Г. (2014). *Прекариат: новый опасный класс*. М.: Ад Маргинем Пресс.

Sukhanov, N. N. (1913). Concerning the description of the Russian proletariat. *Sovremennik, 4*, 320–328. Суханов Н. Н. (1913). К характеристике российского пролетариата. *Современник*, 4, 320–328.

Suvorov, K. I. (1968). *The historical experience of the CPSU on eliminating unemployment (1917 – 1930)*. Izdatel'stvo «Mysl'». Суворов К.И. (1968). *Исторический опыт КПСС по ликвидации безработицы (1917 – 1930)*. М.: Издательство «Мысль».

Teschke, B. (2003). *The myth of 1648: Class, geopolitics, and the making of modern international relations*. Verso. Russian edition: Тешке Б. (2011). *Миф 1648 года. Класс, геополитика и создание современных международных отношений*. М.: Издательский Дом ВШЭ.

Tikhonova, N. E. (2019). The precariat and the prospects for changing the social structure of Russian society. *Sociological Research, 2*, 167–173. Тихонова Н.Е. (2019). Прекариат и перспективы изменения социальной структуры российского общества. *Социологическиен исследования*, 2, 167–173.

Toshchenko, Z. T. (2018). *Precariat. From proto-class to new class*. Nauka. Тощенко Ж.Т. *Прекариат: от прото-класса к новому классу*. М.: Наука.

Turgel, I. G. (2010). *Monofunctional cities of Russia: from survival to sustainable development*. Publishing House UrAGS. Тургель И.Г. (2010). *Монофункциональные города России: от выживания к устойчивому развитию*. Екатеринбург: Издательство УрАГС.

Vladimirsky, N. N. (1927). *The withdrawal of the peasantry of the Kostroma province for work*. Edition of the Kostroma provincial department. Владимирский Н.Н. (1927). *Отход крестьянства Костромской губернии на заработки*. Кострома: Издание Костромского губстатотдела.

Vodarsky, Y. E., & Istomina, E. G. (2004). *Rural handicrafts of European Russia at the turn of the XIX-XX centuries*. IRI RAN. Водарский Я.Е., Истомина Э.Г. (2004). *Сельские кустарные промыслы Европейской России на рубеже XIX-XX столетий*. М.: ИРИ РАН.

Wyckoff, D. D. (1979). *Truck drivers in America*. Lexington.

Chapter 8
Crafts

This chapter focuses mainly on the informal household economy. This is where informal economic activity opposes the formal economy in many respects. At the same time, it is hardly or inadequately described, especially in terms of specific forms of economic behavior of households and particularly on the microlevel of individual local communities and settlements. Therefore, herein I focus on the crafts and trades practiced by individual households in one and a half hundred settlements of several dozen local communities throughout provincial Russia. Using direct observation methods, we have identified numerous crafts and classified them by the type of resources involved. We have distinguished five types of resources, which determine the procurement method, labor intensity, consistency, seasonality, prevalence, and effectiveness of specific types of crafts and trades: natural, household, infrastructural, human, and social resources. In addition, we have also classified the crafts into archaic (traditional) and modern depending on how long they have been practiced locally. An analysis of the prevailing archaic and modern crafts based on different types of resources has allowed us to formulate the concept of the commercial evolution of local societies. Households are always looking to move from available but labor-intensive archaic crafts to modern ones that are not as time-consuming. However, this makes them less resistant to unfavorable external circumstances. Therefore, in the event of force majeure, households generally switch back to archaic crafts. They are the starting and end point of self-sufficient existence of any local society. I conclude the chapter by associating the diverse crafts and trades people practice with six types of local communities distinguished by the degree of spatial isolation and the manner of their emergence and development.

J. Plusnin, *Russian Provincial Society*, Societies and Political Orders in Transition,
https://doi.org/10.1007/978-3-030-97829-7_8

8.1 Household Crafts: Types of Attracted Resources and Practices Duration

Informal economic activities of people referred to as "*household crafts*" are very diverse primarily due to the multitude of resources used and drawn upon and also because of the variety and types of manufactured products. They are known to exist everywhere, somewhere barely noticeable, somewhere overwhelming (Schneider, 2005, 2012; Williams, 2009). In order to somehow systematize the variety of such crafts, one should first of all focus on the types of resources people use when practicing them. My systematization of household crafts is based precisely on this criterion (some of the content in this section was published in my recent article (Plusnin, 2018). The other criteria are not so clear, since all types of household crafts are practiced on site, in situ. They are performed by individual households within the historically established and controlled territory of the local community. This is the only reason for uniting such diverse economic activities into one group. Most household crafts are informal with the entire household participating, which largely resolves the issue of the structure of the social group involved in such activities. An important common feature of household crafts is well-developed family and neighborly cooperation, long duration and mass engagement of the population in such practices. Most of these crafts are extremely rarely legalized, e.g. registered as an individual enterprise or peasant farm (Chepurenko, 2018). But it is important that they are always locally legitimate—people do not disapprove of criminal crafts; on the contrary, they totally support them (Gladnikova et al., 2013; Gimpelson & Kapelyushnikov, 2014). Crafts generate significant revenues, often far higher than the official ones (Ledeneva, 2018). In many cases, such income is received in a non-cash form (Scott, 1976; Barsukova, 2004; Barsukova & Radaev, 2012). Crafts are diverse and varied: depending on the nearest available resources, neighboring settlements in the same local community can differ greatly in the nature of practiced crafts. By contrast, local communities from different, often distant regions can be very similar in the composition of their crafts. Thus, there are quite typical *"homologous series,"* similar to those studied in biology.

A special study of crafts and trades practiced by the population and their complete registration is a laborious and time-consuming task. The more so that it involves a direct household survey of several or most settlements in each local community. Therefore, this chapter contains survey data for only 26 local communities from the main list, supplemented by information for another 13 from the additional list (see Chap. 3). Household crafts and trades were recorded in 144 settlements of 39 local communities in 15 regions. Registering crafts in several settlements of a community at the same time (with several exceptions when the study was conducted in only one settlement or in a small town, the administrative center of the community) makes it possible to extrapolate the obtained data to the entire local society. Obviously, some rare or exotic types of local crafts could not be recorded. Similarly, certain criminal trades escaped our attention, since people were either afraid to talk about them for various reasons, or were simply ignorant. At the same time, some widespread criminal crafts were easily recorded, as people did not avoid mentioning them. For example, collecting plants prohibited for use by the population—hemp, ginseng, golden root in Primorye and Altai—or hunting rare and protected animals. Nevertheless, I believe that in a particular settlement we managed to record all mass crafts and most of the less widespread ones.

I describe the entire variety crafts and trades (we recorded over 130 types of them) based on two principles: (1) resources used to generate income from the craft and (2) traditional nature of a specific economic activity, allowing to differentiate crafts into archaic and modern.

8.1.1 "Resource" as a Criterion for Classifying Crafts and Trades

The characteristic of a resource includes its designation (raw material for the activity), availability for the population, labor intensity, and seasonality of procurement, as well as the procurement method. This allows providing a comprehensive description of resources as sources of crafts and trades. For reasons of obviousness and convenience only (i.e., criteria absolutely alien for classification), we can propose the following subdivision of resources: (1) natural, taken from the natural environment, (2) economic, produced on the homestead (in the household), (3) infrastructural (transport network, residential structure, and utilities as a resource), (4) human (people as a resource), and (5) social (state as a resource). However, it is impossible to single out one "pure" type of resources for a particular craft or trade. Almost every practice requires several types rather than one. Nevertheless, it makes sense to differentiate crafts by the main type of resources used; the other types should be considered auxiliary, though necessary.

Obviously, the most "apparent" resources are those people traditionally use—natural and economic. The former are obtained directly "*from nature,*" the latter are derived from processing natural resources in the household, "*on the homestead.*" For example, beekeeping is a resource for honey trade in the form of roadside sale of honey. In turn, beekeeping is based on transforming a natural resource—honey gathering by bees. For roadside honey trade there is no difference where the honey comes from—from beehives in an apiary or from wild hives in the taiga. Some economic resources are produced in vegetable gardens and barnyards. Therefore, in a sense, it is difficult to distinguish between natural and economic resources, be it wild honey, or sheep, pigs, and horses grazing in "the wild" in the steppe or in the forest that the owner has to hunt with a rifle, which is not uncommon in Russia. The same applies to the medicinal plant ginseng, which many households in Primorye have cultivated for centuries in the taiga. Even more obvious is the situation with strawberries, both picked in meadows and on woodland edges and harvested in private gardens, but sold along motorways from the same basket. Even such economic resources as sea cucumbers and oysters grown on aquafarms or wild caught in the sea directly next to the farm require the availability of natural resources in the marine area. Therefore, when deciding which resource is the main one for a particular craft, emphasis is made on the availability of the raw material, on the labor intensity and nature of processing it, and on the specific features of the process. Natural resources can be used directly without processing (mushrooms and berries are sold along the motorway immediately after picking) or with minimal processing (cut birch and fir branches are on site tied into bunches for use in a steam bath and sold along the same road). In the case of economic resources, cultivation and processing on the farmstead are the main and most labor-intensive component. For example, canning wild or garden mushrooms and berries is equally more labor-intensive than just picking them, so pickling mushrooms or making raspberry jam, regardless of the purpose—to be eaten in winter or sold along the road, should be classified as a craft based on economic resources.

I believe it important to emphasize an essential point: in Russia, natural resources include mainly forest-taiga and sea-river resources. People use these resources extensively. At the same time, the state cannot adequately control this process or does not control it at all (Plusnin et al., 2015, pp. 112–115). This—the ability of the population to use natural resources for subsistence uncontrolled by the state—is one of the many important unique features of Russia distinguishing it from all European and most of the other countries.

Infrastructural resources "emerge" when crafts utilize the transport, utilities, residential, and industrial infrastructure of the territory as a basic resource. They also intersect with natural resources, since neutral properties of the landscape become natural resources only if an infrastructure is in place. For example, the natural balneological health resort properties of the Black and Azov, Caspian and Eastern seas, their estuaries, bays, and beaches become relevant for crafts and trades of the local population only when there is an available transport and utilities infrastructure that satisfies the physical needs of vacationers and tourists (roads and hotels, restaurants and clubs). Using the territorial infrastructure as a resource for crafts and trades, the locals can make money both on the tourist flow and on passing travelers. Therefore, infrastructural resources also actualize the economic ones—people begin to produce more agricultural products than they need and put them out for sale.

It is in this case that a new type of resources emerges—the human one. A large mass of tourists, vacationers, and passers-by become a source for a variety of services. Such services are possible only subject to an available infrastructure. It is not actually the people that are a resource, but their considerable stream that flows through the territory, sometimes slowing down on the way. This flow constitutes a resource for crafts and trades of the population. For example, the construction of the Crimean Bridge connecting the Taman and Crimean peninsulas triggered the development of the transport and industrial infrastructure, brought many workers to Taman and Temryuk, and resulted in new tourist flows. This created new opportunities for the informal economy of the local population, which largely switched to new types of resources (leasing apartments and engaging in prostitution, opening cafes and restaurants, growing large quantities of grapes and selling illegally wine and moonshine, etc.) abandoning many traditional crafts based on natural resources; see for details: Plusnin (2018).

The state as a resource becomes important when people use its social policies as a source of informal—and usually criminal—income. Illegal allowances and benefits, such as fictitious disability pensions or pensions for long-dead relatives; maternity capital for unborn children; or 4—even 12!—old-age pensions; manipulations with foster children in families[1]—all this I call trades on the state, which in this case acts as a source of income. Such trades are provoked by the social policy of the state, which offers certain allowances and benefits to particular categories of the population. The trade becomes criminal, when such allowances and benefits are granted to people who had fraudulently enlisted in the entitled categories. The mass nature of crafts and trades on the state makes them a significant factor of support for some local societies. Such are, for example, northern isolated communities, where large groups of the population receive both legally and fictitiously many "northern" benefits and special allowances. The situation is similar in the extreme south of Russia. Hence, there are such absurdities as "prevailing" disability in every fifth (20%) family in Russia, or the situation when a significant part (still unknown how large) of Ukrainian citizens receive a pension both in Ukraine and in Russia. Similarly common since long is the practice of "unemployment crafts" (Plusnin & Poshevnev, 1998, pp. 33–35), especially in rural areas, when people generating income from personal subsidiary farming register as unemployed to get a higher (often twice as high) old-age pension than they would receive if they were not employed anywhere. For the same purpose, people get fictitious jobs as caregivers to pensioners with limited mobility. A new type of trade on the state has emerged—obtaining a bank loan without reimbursing it. In some areas, this has become a mass phenomenon. As for combining different types of resources for a specific craft or trade, the state as a resource in some respects stands apart—often no other resources are needed to use it. Therefore, by using this type of resources in their economic practices, people turn into highly specialized "recipients," which is fraught with negative consequences for the household, and for the whole local society. Such examples are known.

The five types of resources thus identified differ in their availability, seasonality, labor intensity, and method of procurement. These differences are largely due to the type of local community, above all the degree of its spatial isolation. Isolated and "ordinary" communities are distinct from turbulent ones by all the indicated attributes characterizing resources, except for the seasonality and use of a particular kind of resource. Usually, residents of isolated and "ordinary" communities have better access to natural, economic, and social (state) resources than the inhabitants of turbulent communities for reasons stated in Chaps. 5 and 9. However, infrastructural resources are obviously much more available to people living in turbulent communities. In this respect, local communities varying in the manner of their development and degree of isolation, use for subsistence different types of resources and occupy

[1] These are really recorded illegal but fairly common practices of the population.

Table 8.1 Availability of resources used by people in their crafts and trades in different types of communities

	Kind of resource				
Type of community	Natural	Economic	Infrastructural	Human	Social
Isolated natural $N = 24$	23 0.9	23 0.9	0 0.0	5 0.2	23 0.9
Isolated coercive $N = 14$	13 0.9	8 0.6	2 0.1	5 0.4	13 0.9
"Ordinary" natural $N = 44$	21 0.5	33 0.8	18 0.4	8 0.2	25 0.6
"Ordinary" coercive $N = 21$	12 0.6	11 0.5	16 0.8	3 0.1	11 0.5
Turbulent natural $N = 17$	4 0.2	11 0.7	16 0.9	6 0.4	7 0.4
Turbulent "coercive" $N = 16$	8 0.5	9 0.6	13 0.8	5 0.3	8 0.5

Note: the degree of availability of each type of resource is indicated in the event that the population has mass access to a particular type of resource, as a share of communities from the total number in each type of community (the absolute number of communities is indicated and the fraction of a unit)

distinct and non-adjacent "economic niches," similar to ecological niches. Table 8.1 presents my detailed estimates as to the availability of various kinds of resources to the inhabitants of different types of local communities. These estimates are based on direct observations of the population's crafts and trades. Natural resources are most available to all isolated communities. The other types of communities have average or minimal access to them. The same applies to economic resources, but they are more available to naturally rather than coercively developed communities. The availability of infrastructural resources negatively correlates with spatial isolation. Human resources are generally quite rare, since they appear only in the southern resorts of Russia, which are few, and in areas with publicly accessible tourist attractions, which are just as few. Therefore, "ordinary" and isolated communities have the least access to human resources. As compensation, it is the residents of isolated communities that use the state as a resource to the utmost; in other types of communities, this practice is common but not widespread.

Seasonality is important for the first three types of resources—natural, economic, and human, and does not matter for infrastructural and social ones. For natural and economic resources, seasonality is compensated during the annual cycle (in summer and winter, people use different natural and economic resources, without loss switching from one to another). By contrast, in Russian conditions, the seasonal factor makes human resources excessive in summer and unavailable in winter, thus causing distortions in income flows from related occupations. Therefore, it is the population of turbulent communities that suffers most from the seasonal irregularity in the arrival of vacationers and tourists. Residents of "ordinary" and isolated communities usually do not have this resource.

In terms of procurement, natural and economic resources are more labor-intensive than the other three kinds. In this respect, people in isolated communities are in a less favorable position than the population of turbulent communities. So whenever possible, the crafts are reoriented to less labor-consuming ones. This triggers specific consequences for the local community, as will be shown below.

8.1.2 Diversity of Household Crafts

People largely practice informal economic occupations in all communities—in each settlement, one can identify from two to three or four dozen various kinds of crafts. And at least from 60 to 80 kinds of crafts were recorded in each local community. Although there is a significant variation in prevalence and informality of different crafts in different territories everywhere. Some trades are formally registered, especially those related to the hotel business, services for vacationers and tourists, guest houses, cafes, and dentists, i.e. those using human resources. The same trades are also widely represented in the informal sector. There are certain crafts and trades, even those using natural resources, that exist only in the formal field. They are the ones that cannot be hidden from the fiscal authorities, because they are in plain sight (for example, aquafarms, fish ponds, and sawmills). However, even in this case, the formal field is only partially represented. Businesses officially report no more than 20%–30% of their output or services; the remaining—larger—part is delivered to the local, regional, and even international market illegally.

Table 8.3 of Appendix 1 lists all the economic activities of the population that we identified in 15 regions. It is noteworthy that these are generalized data on several local communities, similar socially, environmentally, and climatically, albeit differing by the type of landscape. However, they show a general, very characteristic preference pattern for one or another craft or trade. The table contains data obtained in 39 local communities, each of them represented by several settlements—from one-two to three and six. The recorded crafts cover the entire territory of the country, although in Siberia, the studies were conducted in four regions, all of them in the south, with only two cases in the Far North, whereas in European Russia—in eight regions located in the north, south, west, center, and east. Herein below, I will review in greater detail crafts practiced by residents of only 26 local communities from the main list.

The generalized characteristic of crafts for all the surveyed communities depending on their sources is as follows. Crafts are predominantly or exclusively informal (such are 96 of the 135 identified ones, i.e. nearly three quarters). These are mainly crafts based on natural and economic resources. By contrast, crafts on the state, though illegal, are all in the formal field by definition.

Rare crafts identified only in some communities (e.g., illegal gold mining or ginseng plantations, trade in homemade gasoline or scams with bank loans) or in individual households (e.g., providing esoteric services or home-based religious practices, begging) have been recorded in just over a quarter of the communities

(28%, first quartile, the prevalence of crafts and trades in the totality of all communities ranges from 1% to 25%).

Up to half of all the identified crafts and trades (42%) are specific, but fairly common—represented in at least one-third to half of all the communities (second quartile, from 26% to 50%). In total, almost three quarters (70%) of all the identified crafts and trades practiced by the population are rare and specific and can be encountered either only in the south or the north, in Siberia, or in western Russia. In central Russia, such practices are few, with the most common practices prevailing. This is evidence of both the diversity of economic practices and significant ecological, geographical, and climatic differences throughout our country.

At the same time, up to a quarter of all kinds of crafts (24%) are widespread and represented in most communities (third quartile, 51%–75%). They exist everywhere. Most of all, they are based on infrastructural resources, least of all—on human resources. "Crafts and trades on the state" are not among them—although illegal and criminal activity is pervasive, it is not widespread.

Finally, mass occupations practiced by virtually all communities and most households account for less than 6% of various crafts and trades (fourth quartile, 76%–100%). We recorded only seven activities, which exist in almost all provincial communities and settlements, and are common for the overwhelming majority of households. Picking wild berries in forests and meadows is the only craft on natural resources. Three crafts are based on economic resources: vegetable gardening, potato gardening, and preservation of garden fruits and vegetables. Crafts on infrastructural resources include passenger carriage (taxis) and trade in shops. The only craft on human resources is otkhodnichestvo, a really mass and pervasive kind of economic practice.

Summarizing the resulting picture of mass crafts, one could say that the entire population of provincial Russia in winter takes to the road in search of external sources of income, returns home by summer, grows potatoes and vegetables, picks berries in forests and meadows, and preserves all this for the coming year. Self-sufficiency based on personal enterprise.

The identified diversity of crafts and trades practiced by the people should be considered in two aspects. First, it results from the fact that most areas have abundant resources of various nature—natural, traditional agricultural, and new ones, triggered by the development of tourism, infrastructure, and industry. Second, it indicates the sustainability of the local society—the more diverse the crafts and trades of the population based on resources of different nature, the easier the transition of households from one main occupation to another one without changing the source of resources. For example, if a local community's leading crafts are fishing, viticulture, meat and dairy production, and hospitality services to vacationers, the loss of this last resource due to a shrinking tourist flow will not force households to resort to the "lifebelt" of otkhodnichestvo. However, if the community had nothing else "up its sleeve" but hospitality services, the threat of losing this business would more likely drive people away from home in search of external earnings rather than encourage them to provide for their families by engaging in cattle-breeding or fishing.

In the meantime, we see that local societies differ significantly in the number of crafts and trades. The differences are probably due to the correlation between the number of archaic (traditional) and modern practices in a particular society.

8.1.3 Archaic and Modern Crafts

The totality of independent economic practices of the population can be differentiated according to the criterion of novelty: any local society has traditional crafts, known "since ages," and new ones, which appeared in our time. We can set a "more precise" criterion: crafts, which have been practiced for several or many generations, can be considered traditional, and crafts, the appearance of which people can recall, can be considered new for a particular local society. Such can also be ancient economic practices recently transferred to local soil as crafts new to the population. Moreover, a society can preserve rudiments or actively develop the most ancient, archaic crafts, which can reproduce archaic forms not only by the type of economic activity, but also by the technologies and techniques used. Therefore, they can be perfectly well called "archaic" without referring to the terms "pseudo-archaic" or "post-archaic." Such centuries-old archaic crafts should be regarded as highly adaptive and effective economic practices, completely independent of changeable socio-economic and political conditions.

Archaic crafts are the most ancient, they have been known since time immemorial. They are based mainly on natural and economic resources available to everybody but seasonal and labor-intensive. Human resources are used to a much lesser extent. Infrastructural and social resources are generally not utilized. Such crafts are inherent in all societies without exception, but their representation (development and prevalence) varies greatly from community to community. Generally, archaic crafts prevail in isolated communities, but in turbulent, especially turbulent coercive ones, they are few or non-existent.

Apparently, due to the long history of archaic crafts, people perceive them as natural circumstances of life and do not reflect on their nature. The may not consider such activity as a special craft. Thus, viticulture and winemaking is a widespread occupation in Taman, Temryuk, and Anapa, which is known to have continued uninterrupted for over 2000 years. Almost every family grows grapes and makes wine. A significant (no one, including us, knows how large) part of the residents have vineyards, and either sell grapes as raw material or produce wine for sale directly on the homestead; however, the remaining inhabitants do not consider this a special and separate craft, although viticulture and winemaking (but not wine trade) definitely plays an important role in the structure of the social income of the population, contributing to self-sufficiency of the homesteads and the mutual support and reciprocal exchange between families in the community. The situation is completely similar in all northern societies with hunting, fishing, and gathering wild plants (berries, mushrooms) and heating fuel (deadwood and firewood). These basic life support practices (salvation from cold and hunger) date back thousands of years; people always had to resort to them, so they view such activities not as crafts but as irreplaceable and unchanging "eternal" existence practices. Nothing can replace them here, just as nothing can replace viticulture and winemaking in the south.

Very close to archaic crafts are such occupations that can be called traditional in the sense that they have existed for over a century, or "for ages" in the memory of the currently living generations. Since everyday social memory does not go back further than one century, people perceive traditional crafts as archaic ones, even if they have been practiced in a particular society no longer than one or two centuries. Thus, *maral* breeding in the form of raising *maral* deer in corrals to obtain their antlers and subsequently sell this medicinal raw material to China, Korea, and Japan emerged in Gorny Altai a little over 120 years ago, but has already become so widespread that the locals consider it a very old, and even ancient occupation.

For some societies, traditional crafts are objectively new—they did not exist among the economic practices of a particular area, and people knew nothing about them. Such are some agricultural practices of local Ossetian communities in North Ossetia, namely, corn cultivation (since corn is no longer used to produce mixed fodder but serves as a raw material for making alcohol or *araka*, local moonshine). Such are also practices of growing ginseng and hemp or illegal gold panning for the Russian population of the forest areas in Primorye. In both cases, the current inhabitants of these areas have been engaged in such occupations for less than 150–200 years, although the practices themselves have a thousand-year history. Therefore, it is not easy to identify and distinguish crafts that are ancient in fact but new for a specific population—to determine how traditional this or that practice is for the inhabitants, one should know the history of a particular local society. In this respect, traditional crafts occupy an intermediate position between archaic and modern ones not only formally, by the duration of existence, but also logically. So, we have to put them in the same category as ancient crafts.

The situation with identifying modern crafts and trades is completely different. Generally, the researcher is well aware of whether a particular craft is modern for two reasons. First, the inhabitants themselves know this, since the new practice appeared within the recollection of only one or two, maximum three generations. Second, modern trades and crafts rarely or never use natural resources, and quite rarely—economic ones. They rely primarily on the other three types of resources, the origin of which in a particular area is well known.

Modern crafts are much less labor-intensive than the archaic ones, so when the transport, residential, and utilities infrastructure is well developed and the landscape of the territory is suitable, the population massively switches to them, abandoning the more labor-intensive archaic crafts. At the same time, new types of crafts may be unestablished, not fully formed. They can be effective for a short period and depend on external (especially non-economic) circumstances. If these circumstances and the conditions for the development of the new crafts change, people are forced to give them up. They do it quite easily, because a craft innovative for the community has not yet been sufficiently tested, has not become widespread, and has not proved effective in the opinion of local society. Therefore, such new types of crafts cannot be numerous—they are sporadic and short-lived. They cannot always be recorded, because even if they remain in the memory of the population, then only as unsuccessful experiments. For example, despite regularly combing the coastline at a considerable distance from settlements both in the Krasnodar Territory on the Black Sea coast from the Tsemes Bay to the Kerch Strait and in Primorye on the Sea of Japan coast from Zerkalnoye (Kavalerovo) to Posyet Bay (Khasan), we recorded only isolated cases of aquafarms (mussels, oysters, sea cucumbers, scallops, crabs). Meanwhile, it has long been well known that the Black Sea and Far Eastern coasts are favorable for sea farming, and only minor investments are required to set up and launch the production of highly profitable seafood (according to expert estimates, initial investments here start at RUB 50,000 = less than USD 1000, see Kholodov et al. (2010)). The reason, most likely, is not that this new type of craft is unprofitable, but that it is "in plain sight" and required formal registration of business activity; thus, one cannot "hide" or shift the production of mussels and oysters, sea cucumbers and scallops "into the shadow," as people do everywhere when raising pigs in private farmsteads, in spite of this now being universally prohibited by Ministry of *Rosselkhoznadzor*.

There is a certain paradox here. The active population is ready to commit criminal and administrative violations engaging en masse in illegal pig farming, while generating income primarily or exclusively to provide for the family (selling domestic pork in the market risks high punishment, though it is carried out everywhere—literally "from under the counter"). But this occupation is traditional and the people are not ready to give it up. Just as for the same reasons they are not prepared to abandon such prohibited crafts as fishing for shrimp in the limans of Taman (the fine for one caught shrimp is 30 rubles [$0.5], so the resulting fines may be astronomical for the locals), catching sturgeon in the Sea of Azov, shooting snow leopards in Gorny Altai, or hunting tigers in the Amur basin and the Sikhote-Alin Mountains (which is already subject to severe criminal punishment). In all these cases, the crafts of the population are traditional, informal, and "shadow" or even criminal under acting law. It seems that this, along with the traditional nature ("usual thing"), outweighs for the people their significance as compared to the unconditional benefits of new economic activities.

I have attempted to split the totality of recorded economic activities of the population into archaic and modern crafts (see Table 8.4 in Appendix 2, which is transformed from Table 8.3 in Appendix 1). This division is to a certain extent conventional, because, as mentioned above, almost any craft or trade classified as new may also be traditional. For example, "black archeology" was already known in antiquity, but there was no routine or widespread engagement of the population in tomb raiding and search for ornaments and jewelry. The same applies to handicrafts for the manufacturing and sale of ironmongery and forged products—now it is almost exclusively a souvenir business on vacationers rather than the production of consumer goods for the local population, as was the case just 150 years ago. Trade in wine and moonshine (homemade wine, beer, vodka, *chacha*, *araka*, and cognac spirits) is also an industry targeting exclusively the same tourist contingent; it is not intended for local needs, since every provincial family used to provide and still provides itself with wine and moonshine. And if we bear in mind that during the Soviet era this activity was considered criminal, we should classify current wine trade (despite the deep roots) as a new kind of economic activity of the population, which also has a new market. Similarly, home-based medical practices and "folk dentistry" have existed at all times, but now they qualify as healing and herbalism. And modern medical practices are already a professional activity. Smuggling is also an ancient occupation, but in recent times a special form of "legal smuggling" has emerged—hiring people as one-time carriers of goods across the border. In Siberia they are called "*camels,*" and in Primorye—"*helpers*" ("*pomogayka*" in Russian), with reference to "*help received from an unrespected person with the lowest social status*".[2] Renting out houses and apartments existed at all times—peasants rented out "corners" in their houses to travelers or wanderers for a night or two and urban dwellers rented out rooms in their apartment; and this was and remains a widespread practice. But when this practice involves almost exclusively the hotel business and informally established guest houses and hostels targeting the flow of vacationers, then this is already a new business. Moreover, this is actually so, since the local population has never been engaged en masse in such practices before (for example, many Far Eastern coastal villages only in the past 10–15 years began to master completely new crafts for themselves on holidaymakers and tourists).

Basically, traditional and archaic crafts require no explanation, since all such occupations are known to have existed since ancient times. Moreover, it is known, for example, that in a particular area, fishing and winemaking or hunting and gathering wild plants formed the basis of the population's economic life even in prehistoric times; for many households, these occupations are still the main sources of livelihood. In the same group of crafts, I distinguish as separate types such occupations as smoking and salting meat, fish, and seafood and preserving both garden and wild fruits, berries, mushrooms, and herbs (ferns, wild leek, and rhubarb), since besides producers, they involve numerous dealers, and the crafts themselves have always been a source of livelihood. Let me especially mention a mass folk craft still almost unknown to researchers—otkhodnichestvo (internal circular labor migration), which is indicated as a traditional craft of the local population, as opposed to commuting, a completely new phenomenon for the Russian province.

In other words, I define a craft as new if it has a new market, has acquired a completely different content than before (a new market and a new type of service), or actually did not exist previously. By contrast, traditional and archaic crafts are those that have not changed either in form or essence for a very long time and have always been a more or less important part of the livelihood system for many households in local societies. However, one must admit that despite the formal validity of such distinctions, the subjective factor remains very strong.

[2]By the way, such an ancient occupation as *meshochnichestvo* (black-market traffic in grain and scarce goods; from the Russian word *meshok*—bag, in which such goods were transported), which resumed in the early 1990s in the form of mass cross-border "shuttle traders" (*chelnoki*), virtually disappeared in the 2010s, and we have not recorded this trade in any border area.

As can be seen from Table 8.4 in Appendix 2, I classified 84 of the identified economic practices as archaic and traditional crafts, and nearly half as many—only 51 (60%)—as modern ones. I see the main reasons for such quantitative differences in the fact that household crafts are focused on households, and their economic practices are mostly informal. We did not record many types of economic activity represented solely or predominantly by economic actors (state-owned enterprises or private firms). Among them there are quite a few economic practices innovative for the territory.

8.1.4 Crafts and Trades in Different Local Societies

Let us transform the contents of Tables in Appendices 1 and 2 into a graphical form (Fig. 8.1) in order to correlate the economic practices of different local societies located in different climatic and geographical zones. For the analysis, I selected the above 26 local communities from the main list and added two neighboring communities from the full list. The indicators on the chart are the types of crafts: archaic (traditional) ones on the abscissa and modern ones on the ordinate. The *x:y* coordinates show the correlation between the number of traditional and modern crafts identified and recorded in a group of several settlements in each local community. It is expedient to adopt the following convention, which I consider important: if a particular craft is widespread in the community, i.e., practiced by most households, it is assigned a coefficient of 3; if a craft is common but not practiced by the majority of households, it gets a coefficient of 2; and isolated recorded cases of crafts rare for a particular community or settlement get a coefficient of 1 (this is accordingly marked in Table 8.3, Appendix 1; see note). Thus, summing up the types of crafts with regard for the extent of their prevalence in the totality of households, makes it possible to differentiate local societies more distinctly. Accordingly, the sum of the number of crafts with regard for their prevalence (rare*1 + common*2 + widespread*3) is bigger than the simple sum of all recorded crafts. The maximum possible values, if all crafts without exception were widespread, which is unrealistic, would be 252 for archaic and 153 for modern crafts, based on their total recorded number (84 and 51, respectively). Actual observations (including available data not presented in the chart in Fig. 8.1) produce values for crafts with their prevalence ranging from 40 to 152 for archaic crafts and from 15 to 65 for modern ones. This corresponds to 25–65 archaic and 5–30 modern crafts recorded in each community. However, since each local community is represented by several dozen localities (villages, settlements, townships, as well as a small town), the inhabitants of which differ—sometimes greatly—in the types and number of economic practices, pooling crafts for the whole community give a more generalized and, perhaps, somewhat blurred (distorted) picture compared to that obtained when describing crafts in each particular settlement, on a microscale. I try to consider and overcome this circumstance in the next section of this chapter, which examines and compares the informal

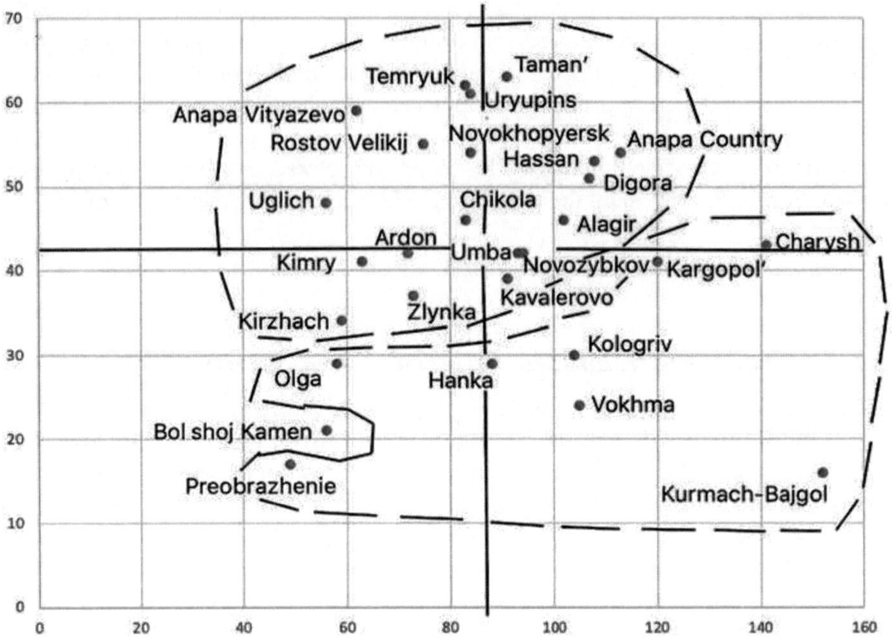

Fig. 8.1 Correlation between the number and prevalence of recorded household crafts classified as archaic (traditional) or modern, for a total of 28 local communities. The horizontal and vertical lines with values $x = 86.0$ and $y = 42.5$ indicate, respectively, the median values of the number of modern and archaic types of crafts (they practically coincide with the average values: $x = 88$ and $y = 42$)

economic practices of residents of individual settlements in several dozen local communities.

The analysis of the resulting picture is interesting but quite obvious. First of all, the set of crafts and trades practiced in isolated and turbulent communities is well differentiated—practically without intersecting—(for more details, see Sect. 8.2 below). In the case of modern crafts, all isolated communities are located below the horizontal median line and mostly to the right of the vertical median line. Archaic crafts prevail in the households of such communities, whereas modern crafts are very or relatively few. By contrast, all turbulent communities (except for Bolshoy Kamen), as well as all "ordinary" ones (also with one exception—Khanka) are located at the top of the chart around and above the horizontal median line and around the vertical median line. Modern types of crafts relatively prevail in the economic practices of their population, whereas archaic crafts are less developed.

The second common feature is, on the one hand, the similarity of informal practices of neighboring communities, and on the other, quite opposite, significant differences between neighbors. In the first case, these are such pairs of communities as Temryuk and Taman, Uryupinsk and Novokhopyorsk, Digora and Alagir, Ardon and Chikola-Iraf, Olga and Preobrazhenie, Kologriv and Vokhma, as well as the trio

Uglich, Kirzhach, and Kimry. Here we observe a similarity in both the number and prevalence of all kinds of crafts. Although, of course, they can differ in substance. For example, the population of neighboring (their centers are located at a distance of only 90–120 km from each other and connected by regional highways) mostly urban communities of Rostov Veliky, Kimry, Kirzhach, and Uglich show a 30% difference from each by type of crafts, although they are similar in their number and prevalence.

Households of neighboring communities, the territories of which, both administrative and actually controlled by the population, have a common border, but whose economies rely on different types of resources demonstrate considerable differences in the number and prevalence of crafts. Among the cases considered, such are the following pairs: Anapa-Vityazevo and Anapa rural district, Kavalerovo and Olga, Zlynka and Novozybkov. For example, distinctions between households of Anapa-Vityazevo and Anapa rural district (distances between centers are only 15–25 km) exceed 90%: of the 55 crafts described in Vityazevo, 52 are different from those of the rural district. The informal crafts of Vityazevo residents are based on people—vacationers and tourists, whereas the inhabitants of the Anapa rural district rely on household agriculture. The population of the Kavalerovo community is focused on the natural resources of the taiga, while the neighboring population of the Olga community—on marine resources and the transport infrastructure. By contrast, the households of Zlynka and Novozybkov (the distance between the administrative centers is less than 20 km) vary only by about a quarter in the crafts they practice (19 of, respectively, 71 and 79 types of crafts are different), but the dissimilarity is due to the different prevalence of the same crafts; otherwise, these two communities are very similar. So in each case, both the similarities and differences in the correlation between archaic and modern crafts in these pairs of communities are easily explained by landscape, infrastructural, and economic factors.

Among other things, as contrasting examples I added for comparison the Alagir mining community, which is adjacent to the Digora, Ardon, and Chikola-Iraf communities in North Ossetia. Here, industrial development ceased 20 years ago after a catastrophic flood, and residents are forced to master crafts that are new for them. As a result, there is a visible evolution of crafts and trades. The industrial community of Alagir should have had mainly modern infrastructural resources, since it has fewer opportunities to use economic and natural resources than Digora, Ardon and, especially, Chikola-Iraf. Meanwhile, the complete collapse of the local economy forced the population to turn to archaic crafts. As a result, over 20 years, the number of economic practices based on natural and economic resources has increased, but at the same time there has been no decrease in the number of modern practices. And the Alagir society started to resemble the Digora society, where the economic practices of the population rely mainly on the economic resources of households and where there are no or few infrastructural resources that Ardon and Chikola-Iraf have.

Finally, let us consider the three communities in extreme positions on the chart. The community of Kurmach-Baigol stands out in the bottom right corner—archaic crafts absolutely prevail here with virtually no modern ones (we have recorded 58 and 7, respectively). This is a very small and very isolated community in the taiga of northern Gorny Altai. The livelihood of the population is based almost exclusively on the use of natural resources. This is a typical and striking example of preserved archaic forms of self-sufficiency. Even the rare modern crafts here are also based on natural resources: criminal hunting, trade in hunting souvenirs, and timber poaching. In addition, people practice a "craft on the state" registering as part of a small people (the Chelkans) in order to receive allowances and benefits, to which many are not entitled (but here support from the state is very small, as compared, for example, to the equally isolated Anabar community, located 4000 km north in Eastern Siberia). Against this background, the informational self-organization of the population is quite spectacular: they have their own "village chat" and social networks, through which all residents, young and old, are connected and exchange various services and trade. However, in the past decade, this kind of craft has become widespread in many Russian rural communities.

At the opposite pole (bottom left on the chart in Fig. 8.1), there are two very vivid examples of underdeveloped (or reduced) crafts, not only modern but also archaic. These are the Bolshoy Kamen and Preobrazhenie communities in the south of Primorye Territory. They can be supplemented by a very similar Olga community, neighboring on Preobrazhenie and located to the north-east on the coast of the Sea of Japan. Here, the reduction of informal crafts and trades of the population is caused by the same reason—the availability of a large industry employing a considerable number of residents. The earnings are quite high, and people have little time for informal economic activity.

Bolshoy Kamen is an urban district with a special administrative status, until recently a closed territory, where the largest ship-repair enterprise of the Ministry of Defense "Zvezda" is located. The population of the town with an extremely small rural district basically does not need crafts and trades, and has no opportunity to engage in them.

The isolated Preobrazhenie community, represented by a town and five small settlements, adjoins the protected areas of the Sikhote-Alin in the north and west and is limited by the coastline of the Sea of Japan in the east and south, where there are also protected areas. Large-scale use of the natural resources not only of the taiga, but also of the sea is objectively impossible. But this is the location of one of the largest Far Eastern enterprises—Preobrazhenskaya Base of Trawling Fleet—a core enterprise employing up to half of the working-age population. Here, crafts are hardly possible and not needed either for subsistence (on the basis of natural and economic resources), or for generating income from serving vacationers and tourists (of which there are few, since the area is very remote).

The Olga community is located even further, 150 km northeast of Preobrazhenie. There are no restrictions related to protected areas here, and poaching the natural resources of the taiga is widespread. There are no less than a dozen quite large resident enterprises engaged in logging and timber processing, building stone, maritime transportation of cargo, marine fishing and fish farming, and agriculture. A large share of this entire complex of economic activity is in the shadow. Therefore, the residents, on the one hand, are employed at these enterprises, and on the other hand, cannot compete effectively with organizationally stronger firms in informal practices based on the same resources. Therefore, they have as few archaic crafts as their neighbors, but the availability of new production technologies contributes to the development of modern types of crafts. In this respect, Olga can be compared with the neighboring Kavalerovo community (distance between the centers is 60 km), which is located northwards in the mountains of Sikhote-Alin and has a narrow and inconvenient outlet to the sea. Informal practices in Kavalerovo are much more developed than in Olga and especially in Preobrazhenie.

Finally, let us consider the entire extreme left vertical row of communities forming the line from Preobrazhenie at the bottom of the chart to Anapa-Vityazevo at the top. These are communities with minimal development of archaic crafts, but with an increasing share of modern crafts. In addition to the three already considered, this line includes Kirzhach, Kimry, Uglich, and Anapa-Vityazevo. All these communities are located very close to major regional centers or metropolitan areas (Moscow). Everywhere the administrative center, a small town, clearly prevails over the rural district. All of them are focused on tourism, urban summer residents, and travelers and vacationers. Therefore, the population has everywhere abandoned many types of archaic crafts and switched to modern crafts based on infrastructural and human resources. Rostov Veliky could also be included in this group but it has a natural base (Lake Nero) and has not lost its ancient crafts, so Rostov's coordinates are slightly shifted to the center of the chart—here the population has considerably more archaic crafts.

The situation is similar with the Zlynka community in Bryansk Region, where many archaic crafts based on forest and agricultural resources have been developed. However, the 30-year-long practice of the population to profit en masse from the state (forgery and criminal practices on benefits granted as compensation for the consequences of the 1986 Chernobyl accident) has reduced both modern and archaic crafts in the local society. The "commercial attitude" of Zlynka residents can be compared with that of neighboring Novozybkov, which is located in the same geographical, landscape, and socio-political environment, but has preserved significantly more archaic types of crafts.

Besides Anapa-Vityazevo, the extreme top position in this group is occupied by the communities of Temryuk, Taman, and Uryupinsk. In fact, in these communities, modern crafts relatively (not absolutely) prevail over archaic ones. The reasons for this vary, but all have the same effect—they reduce the number of archaic crafts and increase the number of new, modern ones.

The Anapa-Vityazevo community in the Krasnodar Territory neighbors on the rural communities of Anapa rural district, Taman, and Temryuk, but the informal economic practices of the residents here target people, constituting a variety of services to vacationers and tourists based on the balneological resources of sandy Black Sea beaches. The seasonality is spectacular: in summer everything bubbles, in winter all activity dies down, freezes. The society specializes narrowly in certain types of trades.

Taman and Temryuk, located in the immediate vicinity, have substantial natural and economic resources, and until recently, archaic types of crafts were more common here. They have survived and are still widespread. However, several major federal infrastructure projects were launched on the territory at the same time: the Taman sea port, the Crimean Bridge, the railway and highway to Crimea, along with pipeline communications. All this greatly changed the nature of the informal economic activity of the population. It began switching en masse to modern crafts and is approaching the position occupied by the population of Anapa-Vityazevo. Presumably, already in the near future the population of Temryuk and especially Taman will abandon many archaic crafts and will increasingly specialize in modern ones.

The neighboring Uryupinsk and Novokhopyorsk communities, as well as Rostov Veliky are distinguished by the pronounced commercial specialization of their population—all of them have the so-called scattered manufactories operating on their territories (for a detailed description, see Chap. 7 above). Manufactories are traditional crafts, but their markets are modern. Therefore, in these three communities, there is a moderate decrease in the number and prevalence of archaic crafts and a significant increase in the number of modern ones (as in Kimry, but there specialization resulted in a much greater degradation of archaic crafts).

The provided examples give us a general picture of the evolution of household crafts and trades depending on the available resources, location, landscape, and infrastructure. The development of some types is accompanied by the reduction of others, by the rejection of less profitable and more labor-intensive practices in favor of more lucrative and less time-consuming ones, or vice versa. This aspect is discussed in detail below. But first, it is interesting to look at the same processes on a microscale, at the level of individual settlements. The resulting picture is similar, but evolutionary trends are more pronounced because of the greater constraints that the resources, landscape, and infrastructure impose on the economic behavior of residents of individual settlements.

8.1.5 Trades and Crafts in Selected Settlements

Figure 8.2, which formally duplicates Fig. 8.1, presents the mutual correlation of people's trades and crafts not in total for a particular local community but in 50 separate settlements constituting 27 local communities. In half of the cases, for each local community, I provide data for both the central town and one to three largest rural settlements. In other cases, data are available for only seven administrative centers and six rural settlements, one in each community. In several cases, data on settlements duplicate that on communities, for example, Bolshoy Kamen, Preobrazhenie, and Kurmach-Baigol, since almost all of their population is concentrated in the administrative center. I provide sample data on settlements of several communities in the following regions: Krasnodar, Altai and Primorye Territories; Arkhangelsk, Murmansk, Kostroma, Yaroslavl, Tver, Voronezh, Volgograd, and Bryansk Regions; the Republic of Yakutia, North Ossetia, and the Altai Republic. This includes the north, center, west, and south of European Russia, the far north and south of Siberia, and the Far East. Initially, I applied this approach only to the settlements of Anapa, Temryuk, and Taman in the Krasnodar Territory and published the results (Plusnin, 2018). Adding a significant amount of new data did not change the initial findings in this publication. Therefore, I analyze the presented results in a similar way.

At first glance, there is a connection between the number of inhabitants in a settlement and the number of crafts and trades. But it is not clear-cut. One cannot assert a positive correlation between the number of crafts and the population of a town or village (although there can always be a systematic error due to the fact that in a large settlement, not all crafts were taken into account or, conversely, in a small village, every single one was recorded). Pearson's correlation coefficient for the presented sample is only +0.20, which cannot be considered a statistically valid correlation; the relationship may be random. A possible reason is that the correlation between the number of inhabitants and the number and prevalence of archaic and modern crafts is of the opposite sign. Archaic crafts demonstrate an insignificant negative correlation ($r = -0.16$), while modern crafts show a distinct positive correlation ($r = +0.41$). Both are quite obvious and expected. The role of urbanization is important here. In towns, regardless of the larger population, archaic crafts cannot be widespread due to the lack of natural resources and the relatively small specific volume of economic ones, while modern crafts, on the contrary, are more frequent, owing to significant human and infrastructural resources.

Analyzing the craft distribution pattern in Fig. 8.2, we do not see any obvious groupings, except for two or three. There is a cluster in the bottom right corner of the diagram representing settlements with a strong predominance of archaic crafts over modern ones. The "blurred" group at the top and in the center of the diagram signifies settlements with many modern crafts against the background of a considerable number of archaic ones. Finally, there is a cluster in the bottom left corner of the diagram, grouping settlements with few archaic and modern crafts. Actually, this cluster consists of two categories of settlements. The first includes industrial towns with a reduced craft-related activity of the residents. The second comprises villages and towns-like-villages, where the lifestyle is rural, and the residents practice crafts based exclusively on natural and economic resources. This second category of settlements merges with those of the first cluster—located at the opposite end of the diagram.

If we consider only settlements with a contrasting number and prevalence of the two types of crafts—many archaic crafts and very few modern ones (for example, the values of the former exceed 100, and the latter are under 20), then such a more than fivefold predominance of archaic crafts over modern ones indicates such settlements have few or no vacationers and tourists, no industrial or transport construction, and the informal economic activity of the population is based primarily on natural resources and on homestead farming. Traditional otkhodnichestvo is also widespread here, since there is no labor market. The other subgroup of the same cluster unites settlements with few crafts of both types. This underdevelopment of crafts and trades can be due either to the availability of industrial enterprises and a labor market, as described above in the case of Bolshoy Kamen and Preobrazhenie, or the collapse of industry that used to support the existence of settlements such as

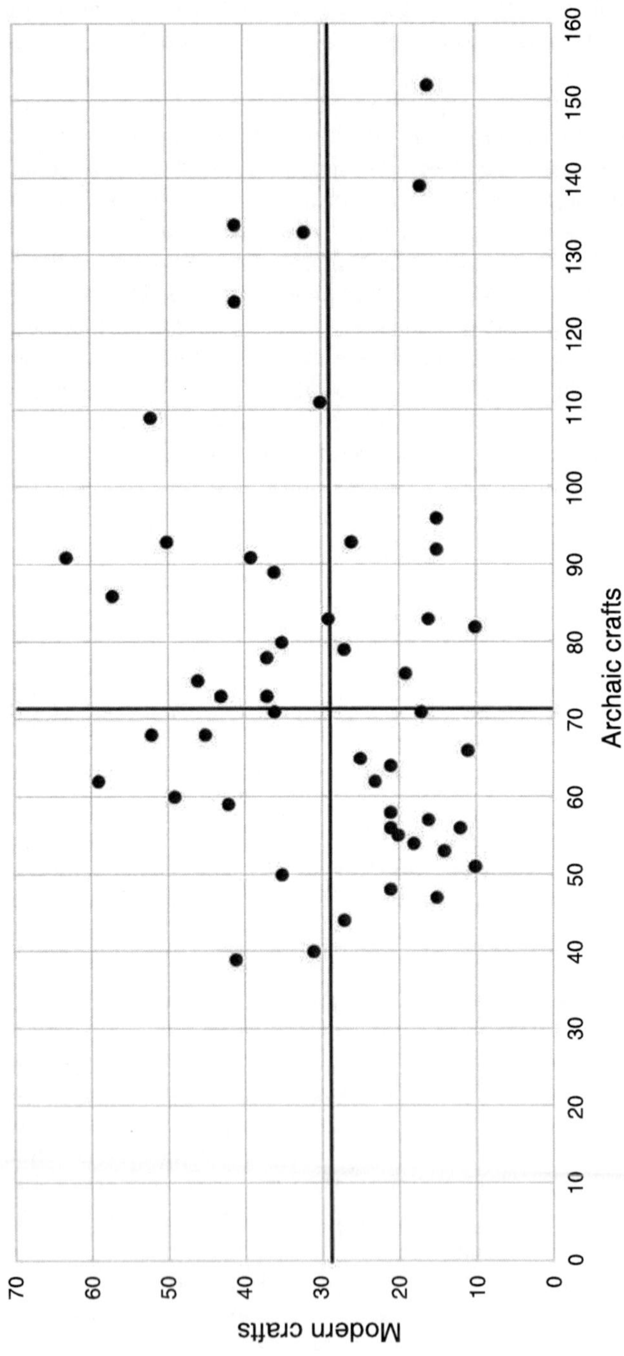

Fig. 8.2 Correlation between the number and prevalence of recorded household crafts classified as archaic (traditional) or modern, in settlements of various local communities. The horizontal and vertical lines with values x = 71 and y = 29 indicate, respectively, the median values of the number of modern and archaic types of crafts

Rudny in the Kavalerovo community of Primorye, or Mizur in North Ossetia, or Yuryung-Khaya in Anabar, Yakutia. There is also a third reason for the reduction of household crafts and trades in such settlements—specialization in few but high-income types of crafts. For example, all the surveyed villages and settlements of North Ossetia (not only those represented in the diagram) specialize in growing corn for the production of alcohol. This generates significant income (including illegal) and requires substantially less efforts and risks than crafts on prohibited natural resources.

Let us consider another, alternative group of settlements—the "blurred group at the top and in the center of the diagram." These are communities where the population equally intensively develops both archaic and modern types of crafts. The specific feature of most settlements in this group is that until recently their population relied almost exclusively on natural and economic resources; abundant infrastructural and human resources appeared in the areas only in the past decade or two. Thus, a large group of rotation workers engaged in the construction of the Crimean Bridge settled in Taman (Krasnodar Territory). Other settlements from this list, namely, Zarubino, Andreyevka, Vityaz, and Slavyanka (Primorye Territory), Chikola and Alagir (North Ossetia), Zamulta, Saratan, and Mendur-Sokkon (Altai Republic), Charyshskoye (Altai Territory), and Umba (Tersky Coast of the Murmansk Region) are annually experiencing an increasing flow of vacationers, especially tourists. All these radical changes in the resource base of the population have rapidly transformed the types of crafts in favor of many new modern ones. As is always the case in social systems, the emergence of a new type of resource in abundance, initially contributes to a substantial increase in the number of certain types of crafts and their expansion (mass nature and prevalence). Therefore, by the nature of the commercial activity of the residents, these communities are in a transitional state from predominantly traditional crafts and trades to modern ones: the former still remain in full scope but many new ones have already appeared; both types coexist in the same community and often on the same homestead. However, it is to be expected that more profitable trades on new resources may displace traditional ones, as has already happened elsewhere.

This is the picture that the communities that make up the group on the left-hand side of the chart demonstrate. This group includes settlements where modern crafts are numerous; consequently, the residents are much less focused on traditional crafts. In some cases, the prevalence of modern crafts exceeds that of archaic ones. Such are all Krasnodar settlements that specialize exclusively in resort-related crafts: Golubitskaya, Sukko, Varvarovka, Blagoveshchenskaya, and Vityazevo villages, and the town of Temryuk. The town of Slavyanka in Primorye, as well as equally specialized Uryupinsk and Novokhopyorsk are also part of this group. Notably, the neighboring settlements—Taman in the Krasnodar Territory and Zarubino, Andreyevka, and Vityaz in Primorye—have retained developed archaic crafts, although the population is increasingly switching to high-income and less labor-intensive modern types of crafts. The infrastructure or often almost exclusively vacationers and tourists serve as the resource base underlying all kinds of crafts—not only the hotel business, but also construction and repairs, wine production and sales, processing of home-grown agricultural produce, taxi services, prostitution, numerous balneological services, and all handicraft souvenirs. Actually, all traditional crafts here are also focused on making money on vacationers and tourists. An extra "ordinary" abundance of one or two types of resources diminished the resource diversity promoting a specialization in the crafts and trades of the population.

The curious phenomenon of *"homologous series"* in the economic practices of people using the same types of resources in similar climates and landscapes is also worth mentioning. There are only two territories in Russia with similar and most favorable weather conditions and resort potential. They are separated by 10,000 kilometers—these are the coastal areas of the Black Sea and the Sea of Japan. In both cases, similar conditions contributed to the development and consolidation of the same—even identical—crafts and trades of the population. In some towns and villages, people are engaged in providing services to tourists and vacationers and profit from this activity. Neighboring territories do not provide such opportunities, and people in the settlements located there profit mainly from natural resources. This homology in the economic activities of the population is clearly manifested in the southwest of the Krasnodar Territory and in the southwest of the Primorye Territory. Thus, despite somewhat different conditions, the coastal settlements of Vityazevo and Slavyanka, Blagoveshchenskaya and Vityaz, Golubitskaya and Andreyevka, and Volna and Posyet with Podnozhye are homologous. The villages of Akhtanizovskaya and Kraskino, Gostagayevskaya and Khorol, somewhat distant from the sea, are also homologous (Fig. 8.3).

I would like to specifically point out the following important consequence of the degradation of crafts and trades of the population. I observed this in Sukko and Varvarovka in the Krasnodar Territory, in Saskylakh and Yuryung-Khaya in Anabar in Yakutia, and in several settlements in Primorye: Rudny, Fabrichny, and Bogopol in the Kavalerovo community; Rakushka, Vesyoly Yar, and Nord-Ost in Olga district, and Pogranichny and Podnozhye on Russky Island. The same trends are already being felt in Taman, Volna, and Golubitskaya in the Krasnodar Territory and in Olga, Slavyanka, Andreyevka, Vityaz, and Kraskino in Primorye Territory. Degradation is accompanied by increasing social tension in various forms: crime growth, rising drug addiction, and the emergence of prostitution. One cannot help but assume that the criminalization and drug addiction of the local society is an aftermath of the loss of a highly specialized livelihood resource base.

The example of local societies polar by the structure of trades and crafts demonstrates that where people have access to natural resources only, they retain mainly or almost exclusively traditional crafts. The emergence of new types of resources leads to a dramatic increase in the diversity of activities. The abundance of any one type of resources promotes specialization, which in extreme cases leads to narrow specialization. However, communities that practice archaic crafts are resistant to external impacts, because they have natural and economic resources that external agents do not control, and their economic behavior is very flexible—households tend to have several types of crafts "up their sleeve" and can switch from one to another if necessary. Local societies that have switched to new types of resources face certain risks in developing new economic practices and expose the well-being of the

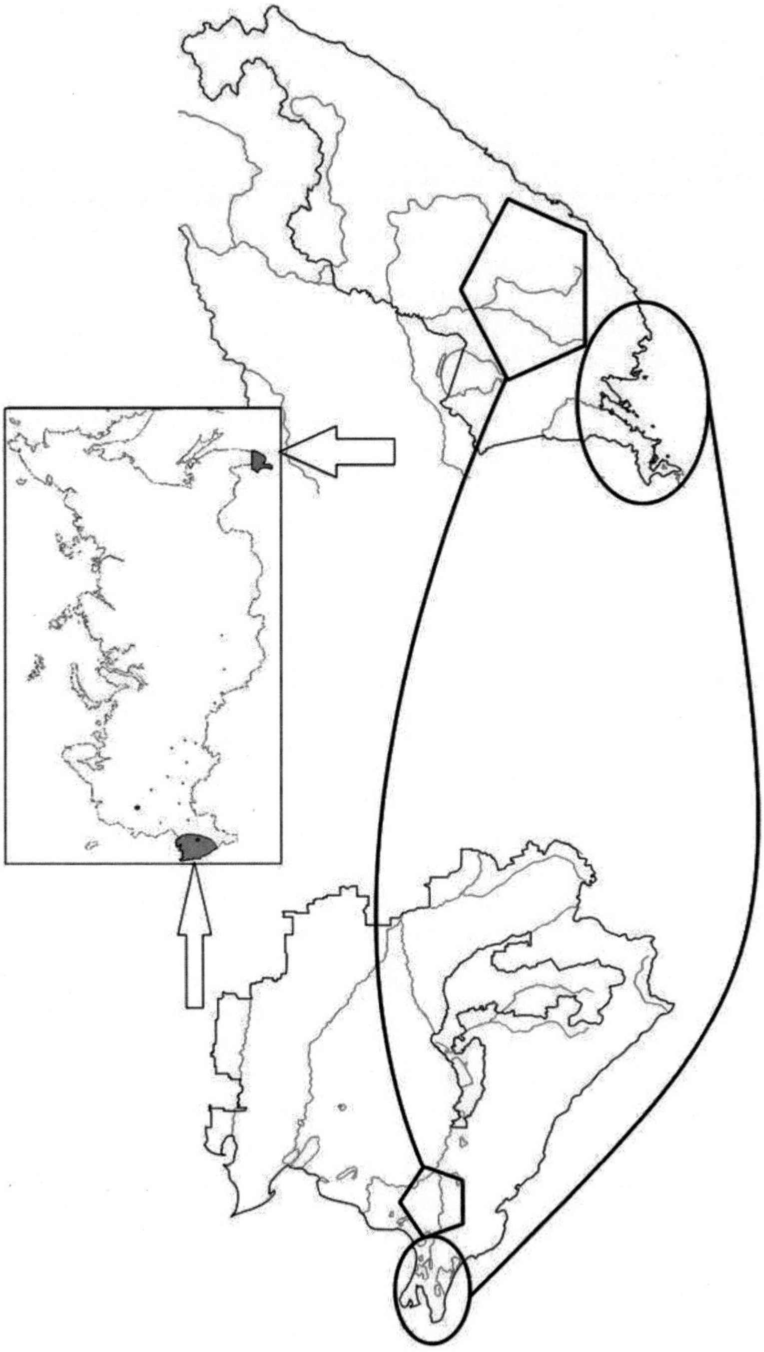

Fig. 8.3 The *"homologous series"* in the economic practices of people using the same types of resources in the coastal areas of the Black Sea and the Sea of Japan (Krasnodar Territory and Primorye Territory)

households to threats from external agents, since new resources promote narrow specialization of crafts and trades and, consequently, reduce the sustainability of the community.

The sword, as always, is double-edged: commitment to tradition does not bring stunning economic success, but provides high stability on the backdrop of moderate well-being. If one relies only on something new, success is certain but short-lived and risks are high that the entire local economy based on such crafts will collapse. This prompts the conclusion that the best position is midway, but the solution is hardly so simple, since the factor of variability must be taken into account. The resources on which people base their crafts are not eternal (except, perhaps, natural resources, but even here "eternal" should be taken literally, meaning the life span of three to four generations). Many types of resources appear and disappear suddenly and quickly, not so much for economic as for socio-political reasons. Therefore, local societies that practice crafts based mainly on new types of resources are always "walking on thin ice," as they depend on the ups and downs caused by the economic conditions, consumer preferences, leisure and cultural traditions, and political circumstances.

8.1.6 The "Commercial Evolution" Model

The prevalence of traditional and new crafts and trades depending on resource-based and non-economic factors, which was described on the example of both local communities and individual settlements, allows us to create a model of "commercial evolution." I believe, the following concept explains the diversity of crafts and the differences in the predominance of modern crafts over archaic ones and vice versa. Figure 8.4 shows its logical structure. The evolution of people's crafts and trades in local communities is considered as opposition of archaic and modern crafts, which are exposed to factors affecting both their correlation and number. It is essential that such an evolution should be cyclical. The description of the model is as follows:

Point 1 In any local community, the informal economic activity of households is based on natural resources. In the case of complete self-sufficiency and in conditions of social isolation, the livelihood system of such a community is based solely on natural resources. Historical and modern anthropological data give us reason to assume that such isolated local communities practice few crafts, specializing in one or two principal ones. Almost always, such crafts are exclusively archaic, starting from gathering wild plants, hunting, and fishing. Point 1 marks this position in the Figure above. I cannot provide examples of settlements from the list that most closely correspond to this position, because this is a marginal case and modern local communities are interconnected; there are always new crafts using some new resources.

Point 2 In the context of exchange (transfer of technologies of new crafts) and competitive interaction, not only new types of crafts are emerging, but also the

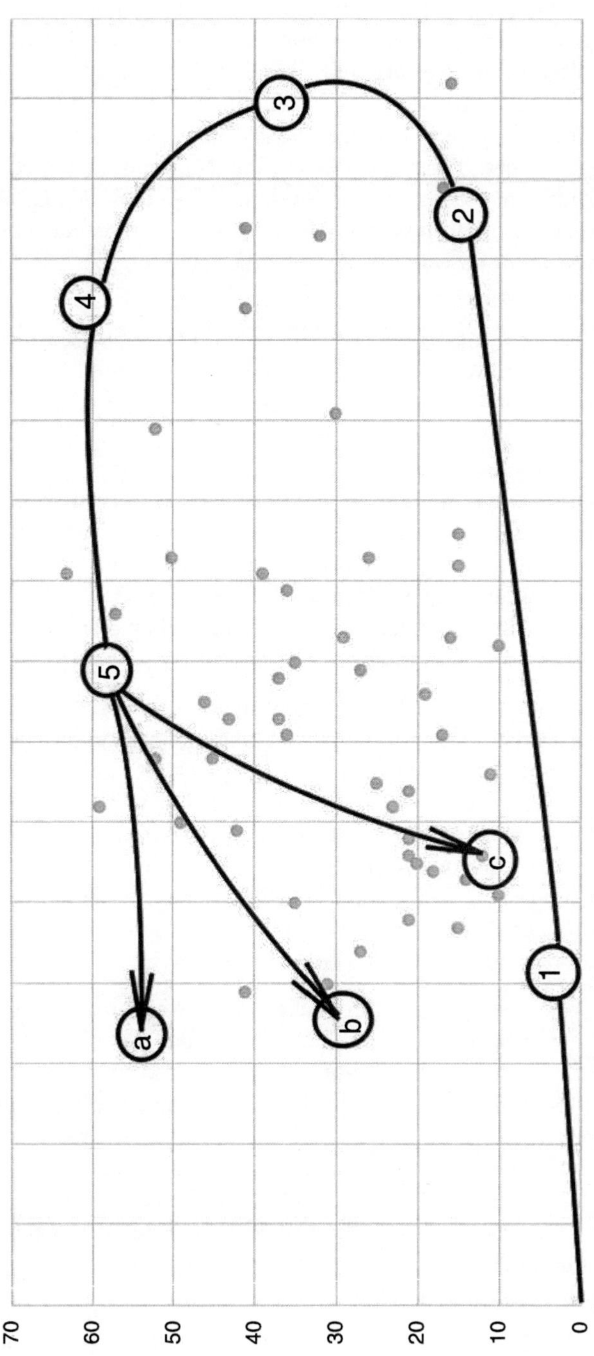

Fig. 8.4 A model of the cyclical evolution of archaic and new crafts and trades of local communities. Explanations are provided in the text

number of traditional ones based on borrowed technologies of agricultural production is increasing. Point 2 marks this position. This is a conservative, most stable state of the local community's socio-economic system: crafts that use permanent natural and agricultural resources are supplemented with new types, thus enhancing the sustainability of the entire livelihood system of the community. An example of settlements closest to this position are the already mentioned Kora-Ursdon in North Ossetia, Varzuga on the Tersky Coast in the Murmansk Region, Talitsa in Voznesenye-Vokhma in the Kostroma Region, Oshevensk in the Arkhangelsk Region, and Kurmach-Baigol in Gorny Altai. All these settlements are completely self-sufficient; they are in no way affected by other communities and have minimal support from the state.

Point 3 The emergence of new types of resources leads to rapid growth of competitive household interactions within and among local communities, but also to increased interdependence. In the evolution of crafts, the number of traditional practices "peaks to saturation" and the number of new crafts significantly increases. Point 3 marks this position. Examples of the settlements closest to this position are the village of Charyshskoye in the Altai Territory and the three surveyed villages in the Altai Republic—Saratan, Mendur-Sokkon, and Zamulta. The inhabitants of all these settlements actively use both natural resources and those produced in households. In addition, they also have infrastructural resources (located on motorways) and the opportunity to attract human resources, which is evidenced by the growing flow of tourists.

Point 4 The effect of external factors contributing to the abundance of new types of resources now causes the number of new economic practices to increase to "saturation." At the same time, the number of traditional practices begins to decline due to both a diminishing resource base and their lower efficiency compared to modern, almost always more accessible and less labor-intensive types of resources. Point 4 in the Figure marks the transition from the predominance of archaic crafts to the predominance of modern ones. Examples of settlements closest to this position are the towns of Digora and Alagir in North Ossetia, the village of Taman in Krasnodar Territory, and Zarubino and Kamen-Rybolov in Primorye.

Point 5 Finally, with the continued abundance of new resources, there is a natural shift toward the specialization of household crafts and trades: against this background, the number of traditional practices is significantly reduced, as they are substantially less profitable and usually more labor-intensive than modern ones. Modern crafts still retain their diversity, but subsequently, the development of commercial evolution diversifies. This is due to the natural and universal tendency toward narrow specialization. The already mentioned towns of Uryupinsk, Novokhopyersk, Temryuk, and the village of Vityazevo serve as examples. Diversification is possible in three directions (unless we consider the return path to point 4), which are marked with the letters A, B, C.

Option "A": a good resource base with high competition. Where there is both a sufficient resource base for new types of crafts and considerable competition between households and between neighboring communities, commercial evolution develops in the direction marked by point "A." The population concentrates its efforts almost exclusively on crafts backed by new resources, preserves their diversity, but abandons archaic practices as ineffective compared to new ones. Examples of settlements closest to this position are Slavyanka in Primorye and the villages of Golubitskaya and Blagoveshchenskaya in Krasnodar Territory.

Option "B": a good resource base with low competition. Where there is a constant abundance of new types of resources, which decreases competition in the local community, households start specializing in the few most profitable crafts. The community occupies a narrow "economic niche." The commercial income of households provides them with a higher standard of living compared to their "non-specialized" neighbors (which is also reflected in external attributes of the quality of life). However, the sustainability of such a livelihood model is low and is strongly exposed to external threats. Examples of settlements closest to this position are Sukko and Varvarovka in Krasnodar Territory and Vesyoly Yar and Podnozhye in Primorye.

Option "C": poor resource base and/or self-isolation. This option implies isolation (primarily self-isolation) of the local community and/or lack of new types of resources. Both limit the development of crafts and trades. In the event of self-isolation, modern types of crafts are deliberately rejected—though currently not uncommon, this is a specific case of development along the "sectarian" path, which we do not discuss. In the event of a shortage of new types of resources or the disappearance of their source, the local community returns to occupations based on natural resources, and often these are precisely archaic crafts. This is not always possible. Under such circumstances, the most frequent and probably typical option for the province is for many households to return to otkhodnichestvo—to seek earning opportunities away from home. I suppose that this option is still a rather short-term state for the modern local society. I have no examples of settlements for this point in the available sample.

It appears that all three endpoints of "commercial evolution" ("A," "B," and "C") are unstable states of the livelihood system. Internal risks and external threats force households to either reduce their crafts and trades to archaic ones or to adopt a cyclic pattern and eternally move "in a circle" where the correlation between traditional and modern crafts depends on external variables. All three options of the "commercial evolution" allow me to assert that the entire diversity of economic practices does not appear from scratch and does not disappear irrevocably but is preserved in social memory and "retrieved" from there whenever needed—when the right time comes and circumstances favor it.

This "circular race," which is the logic of life for local communities simultaneously using and preserving ancient and modern crafts and trades, naturally makes them highly resistant to any external impacts. When communities "drop out" of the circular race, i.e., households switch en masse to crafts based exclusively on modern resources and new markets, this is an indication of commercial specialization, which poses many threats: degradation of the community, loss of traditional crafts by the population, decline of independent economic activity, and, ultimately, collapse of the local livelihood system. We observe such outcomes in all territories with a previously high concentration of industrial production, where households were "relieved from the burden" of providing for themselves. Some vivid examples are the villages of Mizur in North Ossetia; Saskylakh and Yuryung-Khaya in Anabar, Yakutia; Rudny and Fabrichny in Kavalerovo, Primorye; and Nyrob in Cherdyn, Perm Territory.

The discussion of household crafts leads to the assumption that different correlations between archaic and modern economic practices play an important role for the local society or an individual community (settlement). First of all, it seems that the abundance of crafts and the diversity of economic practices of the population may indicate that the local society is resistant to various external impacts and threats. The more crafts there are and the more diverse they are, the more resilient the local society is to any adverse impacts. Conversely, the specialization of households in one or just a few crafts may indicate a decline in the community's ability to respond to adverse external impacts. In fact, this assumption is a well-known theoretical concept, which has long been empirically substantiated, that narrow specialization narrows the "ecological niche" reducing thereby the sustainability of any population and social system; see, e.g. Von Foerster and Zopf (1962), Prigogine et al. (1972).

Among other things, I assume that archaic crafts retain their importance and role in current economic activities of the population along with new and newly emerging crafts, insofar as society always preserves archaic elements of the social structure, primarily at the "*grassroots*" level of the family, clan, or local community. In other words, I argue that the preservation of local pseudo-archaic social institutions that support the relevant economic practices of the population is a positive phenomenon. Actually, this statement contradicts the generally accepted thesis on the destructive role of archaization of social relations and institutions; see, e.g. Akhiezer (2001), Heylighen (2008), Kordonsky (2010), Sergeev (2012), and Yadov (2014). The reason why I hold an alternative opinion was stated above: the destruction of archaic crafts and their replacement with new ones that yield higher economic returns but are not yet "mastered" can ruin the basic structural elements of local society and result in its degradation.

8.2 Types of Communities and Kinds of Crafts

I will now resume considering the economic behavior depicted in Chaps. 6 and 7 and in Sect. 8.1 herein, as related to the typology of communities. What is the correlation between the types of local communities set out in Chap. 4 above and the various kinds of economic practices represented in them? Certainly, besides the pervasive informal economy, all the main sectors of formal economy—the public sector, material production, and services—are represented in any local community. Typological differences between communities are manifested only in the correlation between the number of workers and organizations in different sectors of the economy. The differences may be critically large, but they are only quantitative. This is not the case with informal economy. Not all kinds of crafts described above can be found in every community. This is especially true for "scattered manufactories" and for "garazhniki," which we discovered in very few communities. Otkhodnichestvo, which re-emerged only 30 years ago, became widespread only in the past decade. Therefore, the significance of this practice and the relative number of otkhodniks vary greatly from place to place. By contrast, household crafts have always existed and they are developed everywhere; what differs is their scale and the resources used. But these differences can be enormous.

Therefore, when speaking about the correlation between the types of local communities and the kinds of crafts practiced, we are considering primarily informal economic practices. It is also obvious that when speaking about the representation of economic activities in local communities of certain types, we mean not the existence or lack of a particular kind of practice, but the extent to which it manifests itself in different types of communities. I would also like to specify that almost all kinds of economic activities are represented in each of the six established types of local communities. Only in some communities they manifest themselves, in others they are depressive or rudimentary, yet in others—completely absent. It is precisely this imbalance in economic activities that needs to be discussed in the context of the typology of local communities.

In Table 8.2, I present my estimates of how each kind of economic activity described in the preceding sections is expressed (represented) in each of the six types of local communities. How were these estimates obtained? I analyzed all 142 local communities and assessed the extent to which informal economic practices are expressed relative to a certain subjective average, which I have determined based on empirical data. The specifics of the local formal economy can be determined through direct observation and by analyzing municipal reports presented on the official websites of district and urban administrations. Expert estimates are made for each segment of the economy in each community and are averaged by type of community. They are represented as fractions of a unit. Average values are 0.5–0.6. The value "1.0" corresponds to the mass nature of a particular kind of economic practices in all local communities of the same type, without exception. A value of "0" means that this kind of practice is not represented in all surveyed communities of a particular type; this was recorded only for "scattered manufactories." The table also shows the percentage of the working-age population not employed in the local economy, according to municipal reports. These are either various categories of non-working people (for example, housewives or socially unprotected "dropouts"), or, for the most part, unregistered self-employed in various household crafts or otkhodniks who went to work in other regions of the country. In addition, I chose several communities in each of the six types to illustrate the typological features of the local economy.

A quick glance at the table shows that there are significant differences between all types of communities, except for the two "ordinary" types—the structure of their economies is almost identical in all the selected indicators, both according to official municipal reports and according to expert estimates resulting from direct

Table 8.2 Representation of certain economic practices in different types of communities (expressed in fractions of a unit, from 0 to 1; for details, see the text)

Type of local community, number of observations	Percentage of the population not engaged in the local economy	Public sector	Industry	Small business	Garazhniki	Household crafts	Scattered manufactories	Otkhodniks
Turbulent communities of coercive development, $N = 17$	24	0.4	0.5	0.8	0.7	0.4	0	0.2
Turbulent communities of natural development, $N = 18$	33	0.3	0.8	0.8	0.8	1.0	0.1	0.3
"Ordinary" communities of coercive development, $N = 21$	42	0.8	0.4	0.5	0.6	0.6	0.1	0.5
"Ordinary" communities of natural development, $N = 45$	34	0.9	0.4	0.5	0.3	0.5	0.1	0.5
Isolated communities of coercive development, $N = 15$	38	0.5	0.5	0.5	0.4	0.8	0	0.6
Isolated communities of natural development, $N = 26$	44	0.9	0.4	0.5	0.2	1.0	0	0.9

observations. This, however, is understandable, since the grounds for differentiating "ordinary" communities into naturally or coercively developing ones are not as clear as in the case of isolated and turbulent communities. I will describe the distinct features of the local economy and informal practices for each type of community starting with the isolated type.

8.2.1 Isolated Communities of Natural Development

The distinctive feature of these communities is the low proportion of working-age people among the residents owing to two principal interrelated reasons: the migration outflow of working-age families due to a lack of jobs and a large proportion of pensioners. This feature is complemented by an important and widespread skew in the employment structure: the local economy employs only from one-third to three-fifths of the working-age population (an average of 56%). The remaining working-age residents—from 40 to 60 percent and mostly men—are not engaged in the local economy; they make up the "army" of otkhodniks or unregistered "shadow" entrepreneurs, those who mainly constitute the so-called self-employed population. The share of otkhodniks here is lower than in other types of communities and they leave home for longer periods due to the relative isolation of their communities. "Shadow" business is widespread, since household crafts are based almost exclusively on natural resources and homesteading (subsidiary farming and peasant farms). The procured resources significantly exceed personal consumption and need to be sold on the market. Moreover, crafts on prohibited resources are common in such communities (for example, procuring or cultivating ginseng and hemp; gathering roots of medicinal plants and mushrooms; hunting specially protected species of animals, such as tigers and snow leopards; or raiding archeological sites). Since proceeds from selling such resources are hundreds and thousands of times higher than official earnings, and state control in isolated communities is problematic, many residents are tempted by the prospect of easy money. Groups of specialized *procurers* engaged in the procurement, processing and disposal of such products emerge. It is impossible to determine the extent of such activities, but estimates based on indirect evidence indicate that they are very widespread; see the recent full-scope study of hunting in the Altai Republic conducted in 2018–2019 by A. Pozanenko and V. Plusnin (2021). At the same time, along with "shadow" entrepreneurs, there are many registered sole proprietors and small and medium businesses in isolated communities.

To illustrate the structure of the economy in this type of community, I chose typical isolated communities of natural development in the north and south of European Russia (Kologriv in the Kostroma Region and Gergebil in Dagestan) and in Siberia (Kachug in the Irkutsk Region). All of them have a small population, common for this type of isolated communities—from six thousand in Kologriv to seventeen thousand in Kachug and twenty thousand in Gergebil. The share of the working-age population is everywhere less than half (43%–47%), which is due to the above reasons. And of the entire working-age population, the local economy employs only from a half (in Kachug) to two-thirds (in Kologriv and Gergebil); if we consider the economically active population, which is more numerous than the working-age one, the share of people employed in the local economy will decrease in all communities to a half. Accordingly, from a third to half of all able-bodied residents (mainly men) of isolated communities are engaged either in otkhodnichestvo in large cities and industrial centers or in crafts based on natural resources in the surrounding taiga and in the mountains.

The population formally employed in the local economy is distributed very unevenly across various segments. The public sector (education, health care, culture, sports, state and municipal administration, security) is the cornerstone of employment accounting for half of all the employed (52%–54%). Engagement in material production and services varies greatly from community to community (this is typical not only for the three communities described). The share of material production (agriculture and forestry, industry, construction, energy generation, transport and communications) in total employment is two-thirds in Gergebil due to developed agriculture, two-fifths in Kologriv (forestry), and only one-sixth in Kachug because of numerous penal colonies in the area. The service sector is underdeveloped everywhere; its share in total employment ranges from 10 percent in Gergebil to 20–25 percent elsewhere. The reason is that this sector includes primarily trade and consumer services, which in many cases are home-based. There are very few or no catering or hotel services; many consumer services are lacking. Information and financial services are scarce. Usually, there are either no large enterprises at all, or just one. In each district, no more than a dozen medium-sized enterprises are operating (Gergebil and Kachug each has only three of them). Formally registered small businesses are just as few. And the number of micro-enterprises and individual entrepreneurs varies greatly due to the different nature of the principal economic activity of the population. In Gergebil, many entrepreneurs are engaged in agriculture, in Kologriv—in forestry. In both cases, there are more than 40 of them per 1000 able-bodied residents. By contrast, in Kachug, the number of registered individual entrepreneurs is disproportionately small (only 9.3 per 1000 able-bodied residents), which almost always indicates that the majority of such entrepreneurs operate in the "shadow."

The distribution of the economically active population by type of informal economy in this category of communities is specific and close to that seen in rural areas. Without exception, all households are engaged either in crafts on natural resources (the taiga and river in the case of Kologriv and Kachug), or in subsidiary farming, which provides for autonomous existence (especially typical for southern communities, in particular, Gergebil). The third source of income in all communities is otkhodnichestvo, mass circular labor migration either to the nearest large cities of the region, or further—to "the North," to the industrial centers of the Far North and Siberia. There is no "garage economy" or "scattered manufactories" in such communities. In general, a significant share of household incomes is generated by informal household, shadow, and criminal crafts. According to my estimates, informal incomes are twice or three times as high as formal ones; for certain households in such communities, the ratio of formal to informal earnings ranges from 1:10 to 1: 100 and more.[3]

8.2.2 Isolated Communities of Coercive Development

The distinctive feature of these communities is the lack of pronounced originality of both informal economic practices and employment in the local economy. Informal economy is represented only by household crafts. Of the 15 observed communities located mostly in Siberia, the population of half rely for their livelihood on crafts on natural resources (sea, taiga, and tundra), and of the other half—on developed livestock herding (reindeer herding, horse and sheep breeding); many combine both. Part of the population—young men—are otkhodniks that migrate mainly far away and for long periods.[4] The garage economy exists in its most rudimentary forms and only in a few communities. In this respect, there is no difference with the first type of isolated communities described above. The differences lie in the structure of employment in the local economy by industry. First of all, these communities have the largest share of residents employed in the economy—over 63 percent in general and in some communities even exceeding 70 percent—owing to the large number of working pensioners, many of whom are quite young, since under "northern benefits" people retire at the age of 50–55. The share of residents employed in the local economy is the currently usual two-thirds of the working-age population. The structure of employment by sector is also typical: a quarter in the public sector, a quarter in services, and up to half in material production. The number of individual entrepreneurs and small and medium-sized enterprises is the same as in other isolated communities.

I will consider the specifics of the economy on the example of several communities. The Arctic community of Anabar (Yakutia, in the north of Eastern Siberia), where a small population of about 3400 residents, represented mainly by the indigenous peoples of the Far North, Dolgans and Evenks, is concentrated in only two settlements, is very distinct. The basis of the local economy is reindeer herding and marine fisheries, which, however, employ only under five percent of the working-age population. The entire remaining sphere of material production—another ten percent—consists of state-owned enterprises that supply electricity, gas (heat), and water to the population and provide communication and transport (aviation) services. Given that another 71 percent of the employed population is

[3]For example, crafts on forest resources in Kologriv and Kachug—timber, firewood, and wild plants—or on agricultural crops in Gergebil—orchards and sheep breeding—can annually generate from $40,000 to $100,000 and more in revenues, whereas the official monetary income of a family with two working members is only $4000–$6000 per year.

[4]Although if job opportunities arise nearby due to pipeline construction, deposit development, operating mines and pits or seaports, the surrounding communities form teams and undertake the most unskilled, menial work.

engaged in the public sector, small business accounts for only 14 percent, with nearly all 77 individual entrepreneurs providing trade services to the population and hiring a meager three percent of personnel. Indeed, the Anabar local society is largely dependent on the state; all production and a significant part of everyday supplies are contingent on "summer deliveries from the mainland." "Crafts on the state," primarily unemployment payments, child allowances, and various benefits due to small aboriginal peoples also play an important role. Of course, for all that, the population fully provides itself with wild game (there are more than a thousand hunters here—one in each household!), and half of the population—with fish and reindeer products. But everything else is delivered by winter trails from the outside, from a distance of two to four thousand kilometers. There is also a rare semi-criminal trade—the procurement of "*mammoth bone,*" or mammoth tusks, the annual yield of which in the Arctic zone of Eastern Siberia, according to old and current estimates, reaches from ten to twenty tons and more; see Zenzinov (1914, pp. 64–65), Kipriyanov (2018, pp. 1–8). All these exotic goods are smuggled to the "mainland."

The Olga community at the other end of the country in the south of Primorye has a different structure of the economy. The formal segment is represented by a significant share of employed residents—80 percent of the total working-age population (5000 people),—and over half of them are engaged in material production. The reason for that is a fairly large seaport, where many people find jobs as crew members on fishing trawlers; they spend a lot of time at sea, so there are few independent otkhodniks here. In addition, extensive logging is underway in the Olginsky district, with lumber and timber exported to China. There are also some naval mariners and border guards. The public sector accounts for up to a third of the employed population, but the service sector is underdeveloped, as in most isolated communities. Registered business activity is high: every six out of a hundred able-bodied people are formal entrepreneurs (every ninth family is entrepreneurs). Meanwhile, the population is much more active in the informal economy. All households engage in crafts on resources of the forest (hunting, gathering wild plants, harvesting timber and firewood) and sea (fish, crabs, shellfish, and algae); both crafts for personal needs (hunting and fishing, picking berries and mushrooms for food), and for commercial purposes, especially harvesting pine cones (pine nuts), ginseng, medicinal plants (lemongrass), herbs (wild leek and ferns), and medicinal mushrooms (*reishi* and *matsutake*) for further export to China and Japan. Criminal trades on the same natural resources are also very common: growing hemp and ginseng on forest plots, poaching seafood and hunting sea animals (seals), hunting in protected areas, and smuggling timber and lumber. With an abundance of two sources of natural resources at once—the taiga and the sea,—the local population makes little effort to produce something on their homesteads.

The third example is provided by the local community of Charyshskoye (Altai Territory). It is located in the foothills of the Altai Mountains. A large part of its territory is covered by hilly forests, but the main wealth is agricultural land—highland black soils. Therefore, the main activities are crop production, beekeeping, vegetable growing, hunting, maral breeding, and meat and dairy farming. Everything that is produced in the local economy, the residents themselves either produce on their homesteads or procure in the taiga. Therefore, the local economy employs slightly over a half of the total working-age population, while more than half of the economically active population (including some pensioners) are self-employed engaging in personal subsidiary farming and forest-based crafts. Both are very widespread: almost everyone has a subsidiary farm and hunts in the mountain taiga, gathers wild plants, medicinal herbs, harvests pine nuts, procures maral antlers and other medicinal animal derivatives (musk deer castoreum, bear bile and fat, etc.). Criminal crafts are also widespread. Besides developed material production, services associated with providing for the needs of numerous tourists trekking in the mountain taiga or river rafting are also expanding. The increasing significance of crafts on people (tourists) has launched the "garage economy." Since the local community directly borders on the newly formed state of Kazakhstan, although the border is not protected, smuggling flourishes. However, I have no details about this type of activity.

Thus, we see that some isolated communities of coercive development have an economy entirely dependent on the state (Anabar, as well as Tura and Esso); others generate informal incomes from rich natural resources and at the same time have developed material production (Olga, as well as Preobrazhenie and Suzun); yet others, located in natural environments favorable for the development of agriculture, base their economy on personal subsidiary farming and the use of taiga resources (Charyshskoye, Amurzet, Leninskoye, and Kurmach-Baigol). All isolated communities of the coercive type have in common extensive reliance on rich natural resources, which they have the opportunity to use both under natural law and illegally.[5] The second common component of their economy is strong state support or developed material production based on the same natural resources (agriculture, forestry, fishing, and animal husbandry). In the first case, their economy is identical to isolated communities of natural development, in the second case—not at all. It is important to note the wide variety of economic practices and the pronounced specialization of isolated communities, which is determined by environmental and geographical factors.

8.2.3 "Ordinary" Communities of Natural Development and "Ordinary" Communities of Coercive Development

Reviewing the local economy of communities, which I classified as intermediate in terms of transport communications, I found neither expressive distinctions nor

[5]Resources of the sea and large rivers—Amurzet, Anabar, Varnek, Leninskoye, Olga, and Preobrazhenie. Tundra resources—Anabar, Varnek, Tompo, and Esso. Taiga resources—Amurzet, Verkhoturye, Kurmach-Baigol, Leninskoye, Olga, Preobrazhenie, Suzun, Tompo, Tura, Charyshskoye, and Esso. Agricultural land resources—Amurzet, Verkhoturye, Gunib, Leninskoye, and Charyshskoye.

differences related to the source of the communities' development, natural or coercive. Therefore, it is not reasonable to consider these two types separately.

As in other types of communities, the share of the working-age population engaged in the local economy ranges from just over a half to two-thirds. The proportion of public sector employees is large—from one-third to half of all the employed. Due to the interaction between these two indicators—employment in the local economy and employment in the public sector,—engagement in material production and services varies greatly from community to community. It is common and understandable when a decline in the share of employment in the local economy is accompanied by a rise in the proportion of public sector employees and a decrease in employment in material production: a shortage of jobs in manufacturing "washes out" potential workers into otkhodnichestvo, shrinking the economy even further, while employment in the public sector remains unchanged. Small business is moderately developed accounting for one-third of all those employed in the local economy. Formally registered entrepreneurs are quite numerous: nine to ten small and medium-sized enterprises per 1000 population, and 30–37 sole proprietors per 1000 able-bodied people (there is one household of entrepreneurs per every nine to ten households). However, there are also quite a few "shadow" entrepreneurs in these communities: as many or even more people do not register their business. The "garage economy" is somewhat developed here, primarily in communities of the coercive type. There are also "scattered manufactories," in which almost all workers are in the "shadow." Since both otkhodnichestvo and many types of household crafts on all types of resources are widespread here, the informal economy of such communities is often better developed than the formal one. I have already repeatedly indicated the reasons for this: the economic collapse of small towns in the 1990s, which required the urgent development of informal economic practices. As a result, we still observe the same situation in most local societies.

I will consider the specifics of the economy on the example of several communities of the "ordinary" type. The first two of them—Totma and Uryupinsk—are of natural development. The Totma community (Vologda Region) is located in the northern forests of European Russia. Most of the settlements cling to the large Sukhona River. Two-thirds of the population live in two hundred small villages and forest settlements (logging camps), with under a hundred inhabitants in each. Most residents are engaged in informal economic practices primarily on forest and river resources. Homesteading is less developed, although it provides the population with basic essentials, and crafts on the roads (the only regional motorway passes through the district) are virtually non-existent. A significant part of able-bodied men work on a rotation basis in the north or engage in otkhodnichestvo in major cities. For half of the population, these types of informal practices form the basis of employment and self-employment. Only 49 percent of the able-bodied residents are employed in the local economy; of them, 40 percent are public sector employees, although the basis of the local economy is forestry and timber processing. There is a large number of both individual entrepreneurs (forest and trade) and small and medium-sized businesses. Such a high entrepreneurial activity of the population is very characteristic of the traditional northern Pomor societies. People are active in both the formal and informal segments of the economy.

The Uryupinsk community (Volgograd Region) is located on the Khopyor River in the southern forest-steppe zone of Russia. About two-thirds of its population are concentrated in the administrative center. The rural district is represented by two dozen large villages with 500–1000 residents each and seven dozen hamlets with very few inhabitants. The landscape and geographical features indicate a developed agriculture: here, all households, not only rural, but also urban ones have large farmsteads. In addition, everyone raises goats here, even the townsfolk. Goats are a source of income for most households. Uryupinsk has a "scattered manufactory" for the production of items from goat down, in which the majority of households are engaged, so other types of informal economy have not developed here: there are few otkhodniks, few registered sole proprietors, and few small and medium-sized businesses. Besides the downy "scattered manufactory," all informal economic activity of the population is concentrated on household crafts in private subsidiary farms—crop production and animal husbandry. Natural resources, which can be a source of livelihood, are very scarce here. Only half of the community's population are employed in the local economy, the backbone of which is the public sector (over 40% of those employed) and agriculture, crop production. Material production relies on enterprises engaged in processing agricultural products.

The community of Ardon (North Ossetia) is located further south, on the sloping Ossetian plain in the foothills of the North Caucasus. I have classified it as an "ordinary" community of coercive development. It was established in 1824 as a military fortification to guard the road that runs along the left bank of the Terek River and connects with the Georgian Military Road. Initially, this was a Russian Cossack settlement. But Ossetians from the mountainous Alagir Gorge also moved here. Currently, they are the predominant population, with Russians accounting for just 17 percent. Thirty-two thousand people occupy a very small territory by Russian standards, with two-thirds of the inhabitants concentrated in the town and the remaining third—in only 11 villages. Almost the entire territory is occupied by agricultural land, which is used to grow only one crop—corn for the production of alcohol. Only a small part of the population—less than a third—is employed in the local economy, which is based on industrial crop production. Of this small share, nearly half (47%) are public sector employees. The service sector is well developed—there are numerous retail outlets, freight and passenger carriers, and private taxis. However, a significant part of the population lives off subsidiary farming, animal husbandry, and vegetable gardening. This is not always sufficient, so people widely resort to "shadow" and criminal crafts, such as smuggling wine materials; producing and selling moonshine, *chacha* (grape moonshine), *araka*, and alcohol (from corn); poaching; and illegally providing services, especially in road transportation, tourism, catering, and hospitality for tourists.

A completely different local community, although also of the "ordinary" coercive type, is located in the east of Russia, on the Aldan River in the south of Eastern Siberia. This community was established in a very harsh environment in the first third of the twentieth century at the site of gold and mica mining to host workforce for the respective mining enterprises. Therefore, its current population of 40,000 consists of urban dwellers (94%), with half of them (about 16,000) employed at the gold mines and related transport enterprises in four small towns and their satellites. Over three quarters of the working-age population are engaged in the local economy, which is based on material production (gold mining and processing, logging and timber processing). There are quite a few small and medium-sized businesses (about 500, i.e. one enterprise for every 40 workers). But at the same time more than 31 percent of the residents work in publicly funded institutions (half of all families in the local towns have at least one adult employed in the public sector). The area is extremely unfavorable for agriculture, and only about 5% of the indigenous population, the Evenks, are engaged in reindeer herding. Though many townspeople have small land plots for growing vegetables and potatoes. But the informal economy is completely underdeveloped for self-sufficiency; only a small part of rural inhabitants in four villages provide for themselves. Hunting and fishing supplement household crafts based on natural resources, but they are no more than a supplement. Besides employment in the local economy, people also live off their own business activity—every tenth household is engaged in business. Rotation work (otkhodnichestvo) is not developed. On the contrary, otkhodniks come here, to Aldan, Tommot, and Nizhny Kuranakh, to work. But the "garage economy" is flourishing. Since most people live in apartment buildings, the garages are concentrated in garage-building cooperatives, where the conditions allow setting up any business, individual or cooperative. In fact, only this kind of informal crafts is the most widespread and profitable. But the main source of the community's livelihood is the formal local economy.

As can be seen from the descriptions, formal and informal local economy play an equally important role in "ordinary" communities of both natural and coercive development. In those communities, where the local industry has not come back to life, the informal economy exceeds the formal one. The share of public sector employees is high everywhere, which, considering the large number of senior citizens (from 30 to 40 percent of the total population), creates an additional burden on the manufacturing sector. Almost all such local communities (except for Aldan) have subsidized budgets, which are largely socially focused, with social spending accounting for forty to sixty percent of all expenditures. Material production is based either on natural resources (commercial timber, hunting, marine fisheries, metal mining, extraction of construction materials and energy resources) or on agricultural production. The economic specialization of such communities is quite distinctive. For example, the communities of Belozersk, Veliky Ustyug, Kirillov, Suzdal, and Uglich specialize in tourism and vacationers. Surazh, Uryupinsk, Khvalynsk, Ardon, Bolgar, Digora, Labinsk, Maslyanino, Novokhopyorsk, Khanka, and Chikola-Iraf specialize in agro-industrial production. Aldan, Guryevsk, Gusinoozersk, Kavalerovo, and Kachkanar are known for their mining and power generating industries. There is a large proportion of self-employed people everywhere. Generally, the crafts are diverse but associated with the principal specialization of the area and the main available resources (forest, river, sea, agricultural landscape, transport infrastructure, tourism, or balneological resources).

8.2.4 Turbulent Communities of Natural Development

Unlike the previous types, turbulent communities have distinctive features in the structure of their informal economy, which is determined, of course, by their location on transport routes. The share of the population not engaged in the local economy is high—about a third, sometimes more. At the same time, a significant part of the population is engaged in industry, construction, and transportation. The share of public sector employees is relatively small and does not exceed one-fifth of those employed in the local economy. Small business is well developed; besides many small and medium-sized enterprises, there are also a lot of individual entrepreneurs. Furthermore, due to quite a few garage-building cooperatives, "garazhniki" are numerous as well. The number of registered and informal individual entrepreneurs is approximately equal (comparable). Like in "ordinary" communities, we have identified several "scattered manufactories" here, in which residents of both the administrative centers and the surrounding rural areas are engaged. Otkhodnichestvo is rare or non-existent due to the development of local industry, where many potential otkhodniks are employed. Household crafts are typically widespread in such communities. However, rather than being based on natural resources, the crafts and trades rely primarily on infrastructural and domestic resources—people process products from their private subsidiary farms and sell them along major roads. Roadside trade is a typical feature of these communities. In certain places, the roadside is lined with "sales outlets"—makeshift stalls piled with homemade foodstuff: jams and pickles, salted and smoked products. Prohibited goods are often sold here too (for example, homemade wine, cognac spirits, and moonshine). Crafts on people, such as providing various services to travelers and vacationers, are also developed. Rostov Veliky and Temryuk are examples of such communities.

I will once again turn to the records on Rostov Veliky (Yaroslavl Region) to illustrate the economy of this type of communities. Industrial production is fairly well developed in both the town and district. However, the local economy employs only 46 percent of the working-age population. Therefore, although the share of those employed in industry exceeds 80 percent, this is still only 46 percent of the total working-age population of the community. Nevertheless, by present standards, this is a very high figure. There are three reasons for low employment in the local economy: the proximity of the major city of Yaroslavl—only an hour's drive away—causes large-scale commuting, and the proximity of Moscow—only a 3–4 h drive—enables short-term otkhodnichestvo (i.e., labor migration on a weekly or fortnightly basis). Low employment in the local economy is complemented by the engagement of many people in the "scattered manufactory" for the production of enamel miniatures, which underlies almost the entire informal economy here. In addition, rural residents live off trade on the M8 highway, where they offer travelers homemade farm products, smoked, salted, dried, and fresh-caught fish from Lake Nero, and mushrooms and berries from the surrounding forests. In addition, Rostov is an important tourist site with a high tourist traffic. Thus, most of the population lives off crafts on human resources.

The southern community of Temryuk (Krasnodar Territory) is located on the road linking Rostov and Krasnodar with Crimea. Now it is the main federal highway used for almost all cargo carriage and a significant part of passenger flow to the peninsula and back. Over 70 percent of the working-age population is employed in the local economy, which, besides industrial production, is also represented by a large seaport and a transport railway and road junction, fishing and fish farming enterprises, significant production of wine materials, and several large wine producers. The service sector is well developed, and the share of public sector employees is less than a quarter of those employed in the local economy. Due to the development of both material production and services, less than 30 percent of the working-age population are not included in the economy. Most of them are engaged in making wine and moonshine (cognac spirits) on their homesteads, selling them, along with selling fruits, vegetables, and canned food, and providing extensive services to vacationers (guest houses, cafes, taxis, sea activities, etc.). All this is carried out without registration, in the "shadow," or is part of criminal business (such is sturgeon poaching, "black archeology," etc.).

The two communities, which served as examples, are characterized by both a developed formal economy (high-tech industrial production, fishing and agriculture, maritime, rail and road transport) and a developed informal economy based on three types of resources at once: people (tourists and vacationers), transport infrastructure (railway and highway), unique local production (enamel miniatures), or balneological services (the sea, peloids). This situation is quite typical for at least 11 of the 17 communities of this type.

8.2.5 Turbulent Communities of Coercive Development

In this group of communities, informal economy is less common than in the other types. There is a high proportion of urban population, which often has no opportunity to be self-sufficient. Many are employed in the formal economy. Given the well-developed local industry and especially small business and the service sector—even more so than in turbulent communities of natural development described above—these communities have the smallest share of people not engaged in the economy—usually less than a quarter, and an equally small share of public sector employees—about one-fifth of those employed in the economy. For households, the main source of livelihood are formal earnings—wages and salaries. Additional informal income can be generated only in the "garage economy," but it is much less developed than in large cities. We have identified no "scattered manufactories" in such towns, and there are very few otkhodniks (enterprises once in a while organize recruitment for work on a rotation basis). Household crafts are not developed everywhere—usually natural resources are not sufficient for commodity production. Personal subsidiary farms are underdeveloped and rarely produce meat, milk, vegetables, fruit, and root crops for sale. There is roadside trade and crafts on people—provision of services to travelers, vacationers, or tourists, for example, when crossing the state border (the so-called *helpers* and *camels*). At the same time, informal activities are diverse because these communities are linked to various raw materials, which are not directly associated with vital resources. People "do business" on the illegal use of such resources (extraction, smuggling, criminal activity). Among other things, informal economic activity of the population is suppressed by the proximity of large cities, regional centers, to which many residents commute to work (such are 10 of the 17 turbulent towns of this type).

I will illustrate this on the example of two communities with a similar location respective to their regional centers, similar transport infrastructure and population, but situated far away from each other—Iskitim in the Novosibirsk Region and Ust-Labinsk in the Krasnodar Territory. The administrative centers of both communities are located only 1 h drive from the regional center; both communities have a considerable rural district with developed agriculture, and although the share of urban population is only 40 to 50 percent, industry and services are also developed. Iskitim has high employment in the local economy (85%), while the majority of those not included in it commute to the nearest cities of Berdsk and Novosibirsk, as well as to the surrounding large industrial enterprises. The share of the population engaged in the service sector is very large—more than half, which is associated with attending to the needs of the nearest regional city and the highway. Therefore, the proportion of those engaged in small and medium-sized business is high, as are the numbers of both such enterprises and individual entrepreneurs. There are many large and medium-sized enterprises, including those that produce unique products. The structure of employment in the informal economy is very different from that described for other types of communities. The "garage economy" exists, but to a limited extent. There are no otkhodniks. Certainly, there are no "manufactories." Household crafts are developed, but more for in-house consumption, although rural residents engage in roadside trade and on demand supply meat, milk, vegetables, and potatoes to residents of the town and suburbs. Shadow and criminal crafts are developed (in particular, drug trafficking—transshipment from Central Asian regions).

Due to its suburban location, Ust-Labinsk resembles the community of Iskitim (industrial suburbian of Novosibirsk city), but has specific features determined by better developed agro-industrial production, where many are engaged, and an underdeveloped service sector in the formal segment of the economy. However, in the informal segment, such services as trade, passenger carriage, and freight transportation are very widespread. As everywhere in the south, personal subsidiary farming and associated crafts—trade in own products and provision of services to travelers and vacationers—are highly developed. Criminal crafts are presumably less developed than in Iskitim, but I have no reliable information. As for the other sector of the informal economy—otkhodnichestvo, "garazhniki," and "manufactories,"—Ust-Labinsk is far behind isolated and "ordinary" communities.

8.3 Summary: Community Types and Features of the Economy

In general, the six types of communities have the following features of the local economy. Isolated communities tend to have abundant natural resources and a much more developed informal economy than turbulent communities. The population is left to its own devices to the greatest extent. Between a third and half of the working-age population are not engaged in the local economy. The informal economy of isolated communities of both natural and coercive development mostly relies on crafts on natural resources, personal subsidiary farming, and to a certain extent on labor migration (otkhodnichestvo). At the same time, such communities enjoy strong support from the state, as a result of which many people work in the public sector and a lot of families receive various government benefits and allowances. An important feature of the informal economy of such communities is a great diversity of crafts and trades, predominantly archaic ones.

The economy of "ordinary" communities partly relies on natural resources and partly on industry and agriculture. Both equally constitute the economic basis of their population. The share of unemployed people is also large. The local economy's employment structure is pairwise similar in "ordinary" and isolated communities of natural development and, respectively, in those of coercive development. The public sector is outsized and the service sector is underdeveloped. The informal economy is based primarily on personal subsidiary farming and secondly on natural resources. An important feature is the specialization of many communities in certain types of crafts, which makes them dependent on changing market conditions.

Turbulent communities have the smallest share of the population not engaged in the economy. They have a much more developed local economy, material production, and services. The public sector is relatively small. The informal economy is less common here. It is more focused on modern crafts and on human and infrastructural resources than on natural resources and archaic crafts. The population often has no opportunity to be self-sufficient.

Finally, the structure of the formal local economy also demonstrates type-related distinctions: there are fewer differences between communities of coercive development—isolated, ordinary, and turbulent—than between those of natural development. This may be due to the considerably greater participation of the state in the local economy due to its focus on raw materials and developed material production; the substantial share of the public sector is also important. By contrast, in the structure of the informal economy, there is a greater difference between isolated and turbulent communities than between those of natural and coercive development.

Appendices

Appendix 1

Table 8.3 Diverse crafts and trades of the provincial population

Craft or Trade	Anabar (2)	Tersky Coast (4)	Moscow Region (4)	Novozybkov Zlynka (12)	Uryupinsk Novokhopyorsk (11)	Taman and Anapa (13)	Kargopolye (11)	Primorye (41)	North Ossetia (20)	Altai Republic (4)	Charyshskoye (4)	Kologriv Voznesenye-Vokhma (18)
Natural Resources												
Subsistence hunting	xxx	xxx	x	xx		x	xx	xxx	x	xxx	xxx	xxx
Commercial hunting	xxx	xxx					xx	xxx		xxx	xx	xx
Tourist hunting		xxx						xx	xx	xx	x	x
Criminal hunting		x						xxx	x	xx	x	xx
Fowling	xxx	x		xx	x	x	x	xxx	xxx	xx	xx	xx
Animal derivatives (navel, castoreum, bile, fat)	xx	x					x	x		xxx	xxx	xxx
Hunting souvenirs (skins, fangs, horns, etc.)	x						x	x	x	xxx	x	x
Subsistence fishing	xxx	xxx	x	xx	xx	xxx	xx	xxx	x	xxx	xx	xxx
Illegal fishing for sale	xx	xxx			xx	xxx	x	xxx	x	x		
Criminal fishing		xxx				xx	x	xxx				
Seafood fishing (crab, shellfish)		x						xxx				
Algae harvesting (agar, ahnfeltia)		xx						x				
Wild berries	xxx	xxx	xx	xxx		x	xxx	xxx	xx	xxx	xxx	xxx
Wild mushrooms	xxx	xxx	xx	xxx			xxx	xxx	xx	xxx	xx	xxx

(continued)

Table 8.3 (continued)

Craft or Trade	Anabar (2)	Tersky Coast (4)	Moscow Region (4)	Novozybkov Zlynka (12)	Uryupinsk Novokhopyorsk (11)	Taman and Anapa (13)	Kargopolye (11)	Primorye (41)	North Ossetia (20)	Altai Republic (4)	Charyshskoye (4)	Kologriv Voznesenye-Vokhma (18)
Edible wild plants (wild leek, ferns)							xx	xxx	xx	x	xxx	
Wild plants—pine cones (pine nuts)								xxx		xxx	xxx	
Wild plants—ginseng								xxx				
Wild medicinal mushrooms								xxx		x	x	
Wild plants—hemp					xxx			xxx	x			
Wild medicinal herbs		x	x	x			xx	xxx	x	xxx		x
Wild plants for industrial use (moss, bark, branches)	xxx	xxx	x	x			xxx	xx	xx	xx	xxx	xxx
Deadwood gathering	xxx		x	x				x		xx	x	
Firewood harvesting		xxx	x	xx			xxx	xxx	x	xx	xxx	xxx
Commercial timber harvesting		xxx		xxx			xxx	xxx	xx	xxx	xxx	xxx
Commercial timber-poaching		xx		xx			xxx	xxx		xxx	x	xxx
Gold panning								xx				x

Economic resources procured/produced by individual households												
Viticulture						xxx						
Winemaking and trade					x	xxx		x	xxx	x	x	
Moonshine brewing (beer, home brew, moon-shine, araka, chacha)	xx	xx	x	x	x	x	xxx	xxx	xxx	xxx	xxx	xx
Gardening (vegetables)		x	xxx	xxx	xxx	xxx	xxx	xxx	xxx	xxx	xxx	xxx
Gardening (fruits and berries)			x	xx	xx	xxx		xxx	x	xxx	xxx	x
Greenhouses (winter vegetables)	xx	x	xx	xx			xx	x		xx	xxx	xx
Beekeeping			x	x	x	xx	xx	xxx	xx	xxx	xxx	xx
Production of milk		x		xx	x	xx	x	xxx	xx	xxx	xxx	xxx
Production of butter and cheese				x	x	xxx	x	xxx	xxx	xxx	xxx	xxx
Production of juices					x			xx	xx		x	
Maral breeding (antlers)								x		xxx	xx	
Horse breeding		x		x			xx	x	x	xxx	xxx	
Animal husbandry (cows, sheep, goats)		xx		x	xxx	xx	xx	xxx	xx	xxx	xxx	xx
Pig farming				xxx	xx		x	x	xx	x	xx	xx
Livestock herding (sheep)									xx	xxx		

(continued)

Table 8.3 (continued)

Craft or Trade	Anabar (2)	Tersky Coast (4)	Moscow Region (4)	Novozybkov Zlynka (12)	Uryupinsk Novokhopyorsk (11)	Taman and Anapa (13)	Kargopolye (11)	Primorye (41)	North Ossetia (20)	Altai Republic (4)	Charyshskoye (4)	Kologriv Voznesenye-Vokhma (18)
Reindeer herding	xxx	x										
Poultry farming			x	xxx	xxx	xx	x	xxx	xxx	xx	xxx	xx
Pond fish farming			x	x	xx	x	x	x			x	x
Algae processing (agar, ahnfeltia)		x						x				
Seafood processing (roe, fish, shellfish, crabs)	xxx	xxx				xxx		xxx				
Preservation of edible wild plants	xxx	xxx	xx	xx			xxx	xx		xxx	xxx	xxx
Preservation of medicinal wild plants								xxx		x	x	
Preservation of garden fruits and vegetables		xx	xxx	xxx	xxx	xxx	xxx	xxx	xx	x	xxx	xxx
Salting and smoking of meat and lard	xxx	xx	x	x			xxx	xx	xx	xxx	xxx	xxx
Fish preservation, salting and smoking	xxx	xxx			x	xxx	xx	xxx			x	x
Forage grasses, hay		xx		x	xxx		xxx	xxx	xx	xxx	xxx	xxx

Plants for industrial use (corn, soybeans, rice, sunflower)					xxx	xx		xxx	xxx		x	
Tobacco cultivation				x	x	x		x	x	xx	x	
Growing hemp								xxx		x	x	
Growing ginseng and golden root								xx		x		
Potatoes		xx	xx	xxx	xxx	xx	xxx	xxx	xxx	xx	xxx	xxx
Cereals				xx	xx	xxx		xx	xxx		xxx	x
Bakery production			x	x	x	xx	x	xxx	xx	xxx	xx	xx
Food (pies, dumplings, buns)	x	x		x		xx			xxx	x	xx	x
Cottage industries												
Jewelry			xx					x	x			x
Ethnographic souvenirs	xx	xx	xx	x	xx	xx	xx	x	x	xx	x	x
Folk arts and crafts		xx	xxx	xx	x	xx	xx	x	x		x	x
Ironmongery (forging)			xx	x		x	xx	x	x		x	x
Domestic services—repair of equipment	xx	x	xx	xx	xx	x	x	x	x	xx	xxx	xx
Knitting, spinning (down, wool)			x	x	xxx	x	xx	x	xx	xx	x	x
Leatherwork (tailoring and repairing shoes)	xx	x	xxx				xxx	x	x		x	x

(continued)

Table 8.3 (continued)

Craft or Trade	Anabar (2)	Tersky Coast (4)	Moscow Region (4)	Novozybkov Zlynka (12)	Uryupinsk Novokhopyorsk (11)	Taman and Anapa (13)	Kargopolye (11)	Primorye (41)	North Ossetia (20)	Altai Republic (4)	Charyshskoye (4)	Kologriv Voznesenye-Vokhma (18)
Tailoring and repairing clothes	xx		xx	xxx	xxx	x	xx	x	x		x	x
Technical processing of materials (felt, carpets, covers)	xxx		x		x				xx	xx	x	
Wood carving, bone carving, wicker furniture	x	x		xx	xx		xx			x	x	xx
Infrastructural resources												
Trade—shops	xx	xxx	xxx	xxx	xx	xxx	x	xxx	xx	x	xx	xx
Trade—kiosks		x	x	xx	xx	xx	x	xxx	xx	x		x
Trade—stalls, mobile shops, markets		xx	x	xxx	xxx		xxx	xxx	x	xxx	xxx	xx
Criminal street trade (alcohol, drugs, gasoline)	xx		x		xx	xx		xx	xxx			
Home-based trading (e-commerce)	x	x	xx	xx	xx	xxx	xx	x	x	xxx	xxx	xx
Passenger carriage (passenger taxis)		x	xx	xxx	xxx	xxx	xx	xxx	xxx	xxx	xx	xx
Freight transportation (delivery vans)		x	xx	x	xxx	xx	xx	xxx	x	xx	xx	xx

Delivery of homemade products					xx	xx		xxx	x			x
Car repair service		x	xxx	xxx	xxx	xx	xxx	xx	xx	x	xxx	xxx
Car business (driving to destination, overhaul, sale)				xxx	x			x	xx	x	x	
Car rental			x	x	xxx	x	x	xx	xx	xxx	x	
Sawmill—primary processing		xxx		xxx			xxx	xxx	x	xxx	xxx	xxx
Construction of houses, bath houses, outbuildings		xx		x		xxx	xxx	x	x	xx	xxx	xxx
Repair of houses, bath houses, outbuildings		x	x			xxx	xxx	x	x	xxx	xxx	xxx
Construction materials manufacturing						xx	xx	x	x	x	xx	xx
Carpentry		x	x			xx	xxx	x		x	xx	xxx
Joinery work		x				xx	xxx	x		xx	xx	xxx
Locksmithing		x					xxx	x	x		xx	xx
Balneological services		x			x	xxx		xx	xx		x	
Informational self-organization ("village chat," Telegram, Vkontakte, Odnoklassniki)			xxx	xx	xx	xx	xx	xx		xx	xx	xx

(continued)

Table 8.3 (continued)

Craft or Trade	Anabar (2)	Tersky Coast (4)	Moscow Region (4)	Novozybkov Zlynka (12)	Uryupinsk Novokhopyorsk (11)	Taman and Anapa (13)	Kargopolye (11)	Primorye (41)	North Ossetia (20)	Altai Republic (4)	Charyshskoye (4)	Kologriv Voznesenye-Vokhma (18)
Odd street jobs—“moonlighting”	xx	x		x	xx		xx	xx	x	x	x	x
Ferrous and non-ferrous scrap metal collection		xx	xx	x	x		xxx		x		xx	xxx
“Black archeology”				x		xx		x	xx			
Mariculture—aquafarm						x		xx				
Production and sale of clean water									xx			
Human resources												
Tutoring		x	xx	x		x			x	x		x
Writing academic papers (diplomas, essays)			xx		xx				x			
Vacationers-services		x				xxx		xxx	xxx	x	x	
Tourists-services		xxx	xx	xx		xxx	xx	xx	xx	xxx	xx	x
Summer residents-services			xxx	x	xx		x	xxx				
Healing, herbalism				x	xx	x	x	x	xx	x	x	
Esoteric services (witchcraft, shamanism)	xx			xx	xx	x	xx	x	xx	xx		

"Home-based" religious rites	xx	x		x		x	xx	x	x	x		
Medical practices (home treatment)	x	x		x		x	x		x	x	x	
Medical practices (dentistry)			xxx	xx	x	x	x	x	x		x	x
Prostitution			xx	x	x	xxx		xx	x	x		
Usury									xx			
Financial services—pawnshop, microfinance organization	xx	xx	xx	xx	xxx	xx	xxx	xxx	xxx	x	x	
Hygiene services (massage, hairdresser)		x	xxx	x	xx	x	xx	xxx	xx		x	x
Sports services (equipment, trekking)		xxx			x	xxx	xx	x	xx	xx	xx	
Outdoor entertainment services		xxx				xxx		xx	xx	xx	x	
Guest houses, hostels, holiday hotels		xx	xxx	x	x	xxx	x	xxx	xxx	xx	x	x
Canteens, cafes, restaurants		x	xxx	x	x	xxx	x	xxx	xx	x		x
Cross-border trade services—"helpers," "camels"					x			xx	x	x	x	
Help (free services)	xxx	xxx		x	x		xxx	x	xx	xx	xxx	xxx

(continued)

Table 8.3 (continued)

Craft or Trade	Anabar (2)	Tersky Coast (4)	Moscow Region (4)	Novozybkov Zlynka (12)	Uryupinsk Novokhopyorsk (11)	Taman and Anapa (13)	Kargopolye (11)	Primorye (41)	North Ossetia (20)	Altai Republic (4)	Charyshskoye (4)	Kologriv Voznesenye-Vokhma (18)
Begging (beggars)			x					x		x		
Petty theft	xx		xx	xx	xx	x	x	x	xx	x	x	x
Smuggling				xx		x		xxx	xx	xx	x	
Crime (banditry, racket, “protection”)		x	x	xx	xx	xx		x	x			
Commuting			xxx	x		xxx		xx	xx			
Otkhodnichestvo (circular labor migration)		xx	x	xxx	xxx	xx	xxx	xxx	xxx	xxx	xxx	xxx
Social resources (state as a resource)												
Professional unemployed	xx	x	x	x		x	x	x	x	x	x	x
Position for status									xx			
Natural disasters (floods, fires, radiation)	xx		x	xxx				xx	x	x	x	
“Aboriginal people”	xxx							x		xx	x	
Special categories of the population (Cossacks, liquidators)					xxx	xx					xx	
Bank loans without reimbursement									xxx			

Assistance to those in need (caregivers)									x			
Business on foster children (family orphanage)		x	x	x	x				x	x	x	x
Business on own children (maternity capital)	xx	x		x	x	x		x	xx	xx	x	x
Disabled people	x	x	x	x	x		x					
Agricultural shares (leasing)				xxx	xxx	xxx	xxx		xxx	x	xxx	
Welfare	xx		x	x			xx		xx	xx		x
Cemetery business									x			

The crafts and trades are divided into groups according to the type of the main resource used
The designations of the territories where the studies were conducted include the name of the region or district, the years of observation, in brackets the number of surveyed settlements, small towns, and villages
The prevalence (mass nature) of the crafts and trades is indicated by a gradation of three levels
xxx—the craft or trades is of a mass nature; most or all of the households are engaged in it
xx—the craft or trade is common in the community, but is not of a mass nature
x—the craft or trade is rare or sporadic, but it has been recorded

Appendix 2

Table 8.4 Subdivision of the identified crafts and trades of the provincial population into archaic and modern types

Archaic and traditional crafts $N = 84$	Modern crafts $N = 51$
Subsistence hunting	Tourist hunting
Commercial hunting	Criminal hunting
Fowling	Hunting souvenirs (horns, skins, fangs)
Animal derivatives (bile, fat, castoreum)	Criminal fishing
Subsistence fishing	Algae harvesting (agar, ahnfeltia)
Illegal fishing for sale	Commercial timber-poaching
Seafood fishing (crab, shellfish)	Algae processing (agar)
Wild berries	Plants for industrial use (corn, soybeans, rice, sunflower)
Wild mushrooms	Ethnographic souvenirs
Edible wild herbs (wild leek, ferns)	Folk arts and crafts
Wild plants—pine cones (pine nuts)	Home-based trading (e-commerce)
Wild plants—ginseng	Criminal street trade (alcohol, gasoline, drugs)
Wild medicinal mushrooms	Delivery of homemade products
Wild plants—hemp	Passenger carriage (passenger taxis)
Wild medicinal herbs	Car repair service
Wild plants for industrial use (moss, bark, branches)	Car business (driving to destination, overhaul, sale)
Deadwood gathering	Car rental
Firewood harvesting	Balneological resources—services on their basis
Commercial timber harvesting	Production and sale of clean water
Gold panning	Ferrous and non-ferrous scrap metal collection
Viticulture	"Black archeology"
Winemaking and trade	Mariculture—aquafarm (oysters, sea cucumbers, sea urchins)
Moonshine brewing (home brew, moonshine, araka, chacha)	Informational self-organization ("village chat," Telegram, Vk.com Ok.ru)
Gardening (vegetables)	Writing academic papers (diplomas, term papers)
Gardening (fruits and berries)	Vacationers-services
Greenhouses (winter vegetables)	Tourists-services
Beekeeping	Summer residents-services
Production of milk	Medical practices (home treatment)
Production of butter and cheese	Medical practices (dentistry)
Production of juices	Financial services—pawnshop, microfinance organization
Maral breeding (antlers)	Sports services (trekking)
Horse breeding	Outdoor entertainment services
Animal husbandry (cows, sheep, goats)	Hygiene services (massage, hairdresser, bath)
Pig farming	Guest houses, hostels, holiday hotels

(continued)

Table 8.4 (continued)

Archaic and traditional crafts $N = 84$	Modern crafts $N = 51$
Livestock herding (sheep)	Canteens, cafes, restaurants
Reindeer herding	Cross-border trade services—"helpers"
Poultry farming	Crime (banditry, racket, "protection")
Pond fish farming	Commuting
Seafood processing (roe, crabs, sea cucumbers)	Professional unemployed
Preservation of edible wild plants	Position for status
Preservation of medicinal wild plants	Crafts on natural disasters (floods, fires, radiation)
Preservation of garden fruits and vegetables	Benefits for "small people"
Salting and smoking of meat and lard	Special categories of the population (Cossacks, liquidators)
Fish preservation, salting and smoking	Bank loans without reimbursement
Forage grasses, hay	Assistance to those in need (caregivers)
Tobacco cultivation	Foster children (family orphanage)
Growing hemp	Business on own children (maternity capital)
Growing ginseng and golden root	Disability benefits and allowances
Potatoes	Agricultural shares (leasing)
Cereals	Welfare
Bakery production	Cemetery business
Food (pies, dumplings, buns)	
Jewelry	
Ironmongery (forging)	
Domestic services—repairs	
Knitting, spinning (down, wool)	
Leatherwork (shoes)	
Tailoring clothes	
Tailoring shoes	
Technical processing of materials (felt, carpets)	
Wood carving, furniture making	
Trading—shops, kiosks, stalls	
Trade—kiosks	
Trade—stalls, markets	
Freight transportation	
Primary timber processing (sawmill)	
Construction materials manufacturing	
Construction of houses, bath houses, outbuildings	
Repair of houses, bath houses, outbuildings	
Carpentry	

(continued)

Table 8.4 (continued)

Archaic and traditional crafts *N* = 84	Modern crafts *N* = 51
Joinery work	
Locksmithing	
Odd street jobs—“moonlighting”	
Tutoring	
Healing, herbalism	
Esoteric services (witchcraft, shamanism)	
“Home-based” religious rites	
Prostitution	
Usury	
Begging (beggars)	
Theft and fraud	
Neighborly help (free services)	
Smuggling	
Otkhodniks (circular labor migration)	

References

Akhiezer, A. S. (2001). Archaization in Russian society as a methodological problem. *Social Sciences and Modernity, 2*, 89–100. Ахиезер А.С. (2001). Архаизация в российском обществе как методологическая проблема. *Общественные науки и современность*, 2, 89–100.

Barsukova, S. Y. (2004). *Informal economy: Economical-sociological analysis*. Izdatel'stvo SU HSE. Барсукова С.Ю. *Неформальная экономика: экономико-социологический анализ*. М.: Издательство ГУ-ВШЭ.

Barsukova, S., & Radaev, V. V. (2012). Informal economy in Russia: A brief overview. *Economic Sociology. The European Electronic Newsletter, 13*(2), 4–12.

Chepurenko, A. (2018). Small family business in Russia: Formal or informal? *International Journal of Sociology and Social Policy, 38*(9/10), 809–822.

Gimpelson, V. E., & Kapelyushnikov, R. I. (Eds.) (2014). *In the shadow of regulation: Informality in the Russian labor market*. Publishing House of the Higher School of Economics. В тени регулирования: неформальность на российском рынке труда (2014). / Под ред. В.Е. Гимпельсона и Р.И. Капелюшникова. М.: Издательский Дом ВШЭ.

Gladnikova, E., Naghernyak, M., Roshchina, Y., & Sukhova, A. (2013). *The informal economy in Russian households in the first half of the 2000s: Domestic work, agricultural production, and interfamily transfers*. Publishing House of the Higher School of Economics. Гладникова Е., Нагерняк М., Рощина Я., Сухова А. (2013). *Неформальная экономика в российских домохозяйствах в первой половине 2000-х: домашний труд, агропроизводство и межсемейные трансферты*. М.: Издательский дом Высшей школы экономики.

Heylighen, F. (2008). *Complexity and self-organization. Center "Leo Apostel"*. Free University of Brussels.

Kholodov, V. I., Pirkova, A. V., & Ladygina, L. V. (2010). Холодов В.И., Пиркова А.В., Ладыгина Л.В. (2010). *Выращивание мидий и устриц в Чёрном море*. Севастополь: Институт биологии южных морей.

Kipriyanov, V. M. (2018). *Russian heart of the Arctic. Mammoth riddle*. В.I. Киприянов В.М. (2018). *Русское сердце Арктики. Загадка мамонта*. Вохма: Б.и.

Kordonsky, S. G. (2010). *Russia. Local federation*. Publishing House "Europe". Кордонский С.Г. (2010). *Россия. Поместная федерация*. М.: Издательство «Европа».

Ledeneva, A. (Ed.). (2018). *The global Encyclopaedia of informality. Understanding social and cultural complexity*. UCL Press.

Plusnin, J. M. (2018). Crafts in the province: Archaic and modern economic practices of provincial households. *The Journal of Sociology and Social Anthropology, 21*(1), 73–106. Плюснин Ю.М. (2018). Промыслы провинции. Архаические и современные экономические практики провинциальных домохозяйств. *Журнал социологии и социальной антропологии*, 21(1), 73–106.

Plusnin, J. M., & Poshevnev, G. S. (1998). *Behavioral psychology of unemployed*. CSA. Плюснин Ю.М., Пошевнёв Г.С. *Поведение и психология безработного*. Новосибирск: ЦСА.

Plusnin, J., Zausaeva, Y., Zhidkevich, N., & Pozanenko, A. (2015). *Wandering workers. Mores, behavior, way of life, and political status of domestic Russian labor migrants*. Ibidem.

Pozanenko, A. A., & Plusnin, V. M. (2021). *Hunting and hunters of Gorny Altai*. Country OZ. Позаненко А.А., Плюснин В.М. (2021). *Охота и охотники Горного Алтая*. М.: Страна ОЗ, (в печати).

Prigogine, I., Nicolis, G., & Babloyantz, A. (1972). Thermodynamics of evolution. *Physics Today, 25*(12), 38–44.

Schneider, F. (2005). Shadow economy around the world: What do we really know? *European Journal of Political Economy, 21*(2), 598–642.

Schneider, F. (2012). *Size and development of the shadow economy of 31 European and 5 other OECD countries from 2003 to 2012: A further decline* [electronic resource]. Accessed from https://www.researchgate.net/publication/268185661_Size_and_Development_of_the_Shadow_Economy_of_31_European_and_5_other_OECD_Countries_from_2003_to_2012_Some_New_Facts

Scott, J. (1976). *The moral economy of the peasant: Rebellion and subsistence in Southeast Asia* (p. 246). Yale University Press.

Sergeev, D. V. (2012). Socio-cultural situation in Russia at the beginning of the XXI century: Recurrent culture, archaization, invented archaism. *World of Russia, 21*(3), 100–118. Сергеев Д.В. (2012). Социально-культурная ситуация в России начала XXI в: рецидивная культура, архаизация, изобретенная архаика. *Мир России*, 21(3), 100–118.

Von Foerster, H., & Zopf, G. W. (Eds.). (1962). *Principles of self-organization*. Pergamon Press.

Williams, C. (2009). Formal and informal employment in Europe: Beyond dualistic representations. *European Urban and Regional Studies, 16*(2), 147–159.

Yadov, V. A. (2014). Transformation of post-Soviet societies: Which is more significant - historically traditional or recent past. *Sociological Research, 7*, 47–50. Ядов В.А. (2014). Трансформация постсоветских обществ: что более значимо – исторически традиционное или недавнее прошлое. *Социологические исследования,* 7, 47–50.

Zenzinov, V. M. (1914). *Ancient people by the cold ocean. Russian Ustye of the Yakutsk Region of the Verkhoyansk District*. Printing House P.P. Ryabushinsky. Зензинов В.М. (1914). *Старинные люди у холоднаго океана. Русское Устье Якутской области Верхоянского округа*. М.: Типография П.П. Рябушинского.

Chapter 9
Kinship and Neighborship

Since Ferdinand Tönnies we know that kinship and neighborship are closely interrelated and interdependent. Kinship implies neighborship. Neighborship implies kinship. People living together are often related. Relatives tend to be neighbors. This is the basis of the opposition "us-them," or "locals-aliens." In this chapter, I look at the attributes of both members of an opposition couple in order to make analytic assessments of kinship and neighborhood ties in the local community. I am describing the specific differences between residents and migrants ("aliens"). There are also significant structural differences between "locals" and "aliens" in the identified six types of communities.

9.1 "Us" and "Them" in the Provincial Society

It is well known that the "us-them" concept underlies the local socio-group identity. The "us" versus "them" opposition is a basic stratifying indicator, universal for any community (at least of the Indo-European origin, as clearly demonstrated by Emile Benveniste (1974, pp. 354–364, 1995, pp. 212–217 and 233–237). In the Russian language these notions are even linked terminologically: "related" and "close" are synonyms (there is also the notion of "close relative"). Later Luigi Luca Cavalli-Sforza and Walter Bodmer provided important empirical evidence of this relationship based on the reproductive behavior and demographic structure of local populations in Southern Europe (Cavalli-Sforza & Bodmer, 1999, pp. 181–189). Like elsewhere in the world, Russia also demonstrates a similar pattern of closely intertwined family and neighborly relations. In terms of sociology, how does kinship and neighborship function in the Russian provincial society? To consider the issue substantially, we must define the notions of "us" and "them." Who is considered "one of us" in a local society, and what features distinguish him or her from "one of them"? But, I will not dwell on the speculative academic aspect of the issue, as it has been sufficiently covered. The more so that culturological, anthropological, and

J. Plusnin, *Russian Provincial Society*, Societies and Political Orders in Transition,
https://doi.org/10.1007/978-3-030-97829-7_9

linguistic literature abounds in all sorts of definitions of the "us" vs "them" opposition, considering and "decomposing" the category in every possible way. Besides Edmund Husserl and Bernhard Waldenfels (Waldenfels, 1997–1999), who largely followed Husserl in studying the issue of "alien" and "alienness," I would like to mention papers by Russian authors containing numerous references on the subject issue (mainly linguistic texts). There are also ethnographic and sociological academic publications, which specifically focus on defining the "us" and "them" categories. Therefore, for the purposes of this study I am more interested in a specific question: who is "us" and who is "them" in the Russian community on the local level as seen by the members of the local community *themselves*. This chapter includes fragments previously published by the author in a 2013 article (Plusnin, 2013).

Being one of the key concepts for researchers of culture, the "us/them" dichotomy is also important in anthropology, ethnology, sociology, and social psychology. However, researchers of culture define this concept differently from population biologists or physical anthropologists. Sociologists define "us" and "being one of us" primarily through *adopted* mental constructs. Psychologists—through *socialization mechanisms;* ethnologists—through *belonging* to the community, clan, i.e. through *blood* and *social relationships*; whereas anthropologists and population geneticists—through the coefficient of relationship, the *genetic distance*. In everyday life anyone can distinguish "us" from "them" without really understanding the criteria for such a classification. A specific analytical approach is required to distinguish "us" from "them" based on certain criteria of distinction. This approach must rely on both anthropology and psychology. However, it should not be limited to the "objective" anthropological classification, where "one of us" is a "*relative and member of the community*" as opposed to "*a stranger.*" Neither should this approach be limited to the psychologically subjective "*acceptance,*" or to the time required for the process of "*acceptance*" as such. Actually, Ferdinand Tönnies had already formulated this approach back at the end of the nineteenth century. He highlighted the familiar attributes of polar types of social life—"the community" and "the society," thus formulating the principal criteria for treating any individual as either "one of us" or "one of them" (Tönnies, 1887, pp. 16–18, 1959, p. 181). These criteria are certain types of relations. Besides these criteria there are also others, which being physical attributes can be defined as "objective."

9.1.1 "One of Us" Attributes

The first, simplest, and seemingly obvious indicator of "one of us" is the length of residence in a local society. The longer a person lives in the community, the more likely he or she is to be "one of us." This is obviously a sufficient criterion for people born in a particular community. Therefore, it is precisely the fact of birth locally that young, *emerging* communities usually use as the sole criterion for recognizing an individual as "one of us." In such young societies, the institution of the state directly borrows this criterion to determine who belongs to the nation (citizenship by birth).

The length of residence in a specific location is an objective indicator that does not depend on people's views and attitudes, which makes it seem important. However, this criterion is absolutely insufficient. The length of residence as an attribute is no longer clear, definite, and unambiguous with regard to people who were born in a specific community but left it early in life. And it becomes even less definite for immigrants. How many years should an immigrant live in the host community for the residents to accept him or her as one of them? Are 10, 30, or 50 years sufficient? Will the local residents accept the immigrants' children, who have been living their whole life in the community, as "us"? This question is relevant at all levels—both locally and nationwide—and has neither specific, nor clear answer; see, e.g. Collier (2013). Thus, although "affinity" as an attribute of being "one of us" based on how long a person resides in the native or new community is an objective indicator, it is neither unique, nor sufficient when considered by all the participants. This criterion is relevant (applicable) only as a coarse sieve when the local community is regarded as something organic in a perfunctory and remote manner. Probably due to this, and not only because of its "objective properties," this criterion is determining in the state-bureaucratic system of young societies.

However, if the duration of life in a community is not a criterion for "affinity" ("kinship," including "social kinship," "proximity," or "neighborship"), what other criteria are significant? I believe what matters is recognition by members of the community. In the past, in ancient, archaic times it was much easier to make such a distinction: it was sufficient (a) to be born "legitimately" into a system of established family relations, including social kinship, to be accepted by the society (Graburn, 1971; Klimova, 2002a; Dziebel, 2007; Belkov, 2013, pp. 9–26), and (b) to know who was in front of you—a slave, i.e., not a free individual, or a foreigner; everyone else was "one of us"—"befriended" (*prijateli*—friends) and free people (who had a "*free day,*" according to Homer), community members and relatives (Benveniste, 1995, pp. 215–217; Lotman & Uspenskij, 1982). A person is treated either as an insider, or as a stranger or social outcast. But "recognition–non-recognition" is hardly an operational or interpretable criterion. It is not a measurable indicator; therefore, it is subjective for external observers and community members alike. Indeed, every member of the community—simply by virtue of membership—can clearly distinguish insiders from outsiders, but is hardly able to formulate the distinctions and will only offer a list of random adjectives (Klimova, 2002b). Besides, the situation is aggravated by the disruptive factor of immigration: modern societies, even provincial ones, are characterized by a significantly greater influx of migrants than a century or two ago. Even 50 years ago the situation was different (Collier, 2013, pp. 41–78; Goldin et al., 2011).

Therefore, to add "objectivity" to a set of vague attributes, we must adopt an additional indicator of affinity. Besides the length of residence, we must also consider the *time required for a person to settle down in the community.* Countless ethnographic (ethnological) works indicate this as a factor that determines the straight path of transition from "outsider" to "insider." Here, however, we have no objective "critical value"—the least span of time, which serves as a threshold for the community, the time after which any migrant will be regarded as settled down and local. This value can only be established formally. Generally, formal time requirements extend to decades. However, when formally determining the term of transition to "one of us," it is necessary to distinguish between the national and local levels. In the first case, everything is ultimately determined by the government migration policy, which is governed more by political expediency than the logic of public life (Hatton & Williamson, 2008). At the local level, the term required for a stranger to "settle down" in a new community is determined by local norms and traditions, but to a large extent depends on the behavior of the stranger. In a provincial society, the "settling in" period generally lasts as long as is takes to adopt local rules and regulations and assimilate local behavior and communication patterns. Therefore, everything depends on how quickly a migrant picks up local mental and behavioral stereotypes. The birth of children is an important milestone in the transition to the "insider" camp. Their arrival significantly accelerates the recognition of a migrant as "one of us." However, there is a considerably faster mechanism of integrating into the local community. It is social kinship. Entering into a relationship with the locals automatically grants "citizenship" and important local privileges, "*. . . And how can I get hunting grounds here?—No way. . . Only if you marry our girl, then her father's hunting grounds will become yours as well*" (from an interview with a man of about 40 years, resident of the Vozhgora village on the Mezen river, Arkhangelsk Region, July 2006). In this specific case, hunting and fishing form the backbone of the local community's subsistence patterns; therefore, assigning family hunting grounds to a new member of the community automatically indicates his acceptance. It is important that in this case the settling in period loses meaning. Social kinship, just as blood relationship, is an indisputable indication of belonging.

The *acceptance period* of a new member (or, in other words, *the integration period*), together with the duration of cohabitation, accompanied by joint household support in the same location determines family and neighborly relations, as well as reciprocity (altruistic behavior). Finally, acceptance is associated with adopting the "local mentality"—the system of local social perceptions and attitudes. On the contrary, in a "large society," where civil institutions are well developed, but family, neighborly, and friendly relations are pushed to the periphery of everyday life, an individual due to his/her anonymous status becomes neither insider, nor outsider, but both at the same time. The "us/them" dichotomy, extremely important for community life (in Gemeinschaft), loses its relevance in social life (in Gesellschaft). Similarly, opposing a "free person" to one who is not free, who is a slave forced to labor, is no longer relevant. However, as we are actually dealing with an intermediate situation—even provincial towns now lack purely community relations, but they also have no or very little anonymity (anomie) typical for the dwellers of big cities—we must acknowledge that "community" relations largely retain here their initial meaning as attributes of "affinity." Hence, the term "provincial society," which by intuition differs from the community in big cities and medium-sized towns (Vyacheslav Glazychev attempted to capture the essence of the differences between a big city and a small town. In his monographs, he made an overview of Russia's thousand-year history of "exploring, appropriating and assimilating territories," where a big, metropolitan, city emerges little by little breaking through the thick crust of provincialism under which a town or city is still hardly distinguishable from a village (Glazychev, 2003, 2011, pp. 144–209)). Economic geographer Andrey Treyvish (2009, pp. 248–267 and 282–287) and the well-known Russian geographer G.M. Lappo (2012, pp. 152–179) use a different, formally statistical, approach to distinguish towns by their size. However, I intentionally do not consider the geographers' view on the subject. Apparently, by the seventeenth–eighteenth centuries, only the specific estate-based occupations of urban residents—the vast majority of them were merchants, military nobles, and clergy—distinguished them radically from the surrounding villages, and later from the industrial suburbs (*posad*) (Kamensky, 2007, pp. 55–90). For my own criteria of essential differences that distinguish small towns from medium-sized towns and big cities, see Plusnin (2000, pp. 7–13). Exchange relations are quite common for the province as well, but such relations are not impersonal. They are based on preferences allowing for privilege, i.e., they are so prone to particularism and paternalism that they cease to be truly anonymous.

In other words, the attributes of an "insider" in a local community include, on the one hand, a lengthy residence, extensive family relations, and spatial proximity, or neighborship. These attributes are anthropologically significant; moreover, they are calculable. On the other hand, there are such attributes as reciprocity (understood as altruism) and privileged exchange based not on individual, but clan and social kinship interests (nepotism and corporatism). Therefore, I propose that a member of the local provincial community may be considered "an insider" if he/she meets all of the five following criteria.

Criterion (1). "*Rootedness.*" A person was born or has been living for an extended period of time in a community and considers himself either a native (hence, the notion of "small homeland"), or a local. It is unknown whether "integration and rooting" actually requires half a century, or whether a decade or two would be sufficient; however, it is absolutely clear that this period is nowhere limited to several years. When a new member is accepted—*befriended*, it means he has become and is a *friend*, if not a relative to the other members of the community.

Criterion (2). *The duration of cohabitation.* For most of the other community members this person is a neighbor, which means that he permanently lives among them (his premises border on those of his neighbors), knows many (if not all) members of the community and regularly personally interacts with them, thus establishing private relations.

The two criteria—acceptance of the individual as a member of the community and cohabitation (spatial proximity) seem interdependent and interchangeable, but I believe a distinction between them is necessary. The first criterion is necessary and sufficient, but applicable only to a limited extent, since it is difficult to objectify. The second criterion—neighborship—is necessary but not sufficient. Any migrant may be a neighbor, but remain an "outsider." On the contrary, an "insider" by birth may not reside in the local community and by this criterion will not be a member of the community at the time of observation, in spite of everyone else recognizing him as such.

Criterion (3). *Kinship*, including social kinship, is the oldest criterion of "affinity." Many provincial townspeople and rural residents descend from the same ancestor or are related through marriage; therefore, a person must be a relative or in-law at least to some of the neighbors. At the same time, an individual must be bound by social kinship with a particular—significant—part of the local society. We must also keep in mind the institution of nepotism, which still plays an important role in provincial life. This symbolic kinship is established between unrelated adults through their newborn offspring.[1]

Criterion (4). *Reciprocity*. An individual constantly interacts with other members of the local community on principles of mutual aid and self-sacrifice, demonstrating reciprocal altruism. He is ready to help his neighbor, loan or give away personal property, money, time, and efforts, being confident, in turn, that the neighbor will do the same. At the grassroots level—when it comes to providing for the family, such reciprocal exchanges form the basis of the entire local economy (Scott, 1976; Barsukova, 2003).

Criterion (5). *Privileged status*. Altruistic relations provide an "insider" with a certain local set of privileges unavailable to any random inhabitant of the area, to all those considered "outsiders." Due to this system of privileges, an insider interacts with such outsiders as a *representative* of the local community, a representative of the corporation, the kin, the clan; thus, even in exchange relations he acts not on his own, but representing and protecting the interests of his group as a part of or the entire local community, as one possessing and protecting the local privileges.

Criterion (6). *Mentality*. The local system of perceptions about the surrounding world, what can be called the "worldview" as the awareness of one's belonging to the community and the representation of this awareness expressed in attitudes, values, and mental constructs, specific more or less for the local community or group of close communities.

I explicitly do not discuss linguistic, cultural, and socio-historic differences, because in our case the us/them divide does not concern nations, but takes place within the society, separating some people from others, one local community from another one. However, even this list of attributes of "affinity" seems sufficient. It consists of indicators varying by nature: population-genetic (neighborship and kinship), socio-biological (neighborship and reciprocity), psychological and anthropological (length of residence, reciprocity, and clan system), sociological (privilege, clan system, and community mentality). However, this does not mean that indicators different by nature may not be additive as the criteria for distinguishing "us" from "them."

[1] In his short novel *Grandma's Yarns*, Andrey Melnikov-Pechersky tells a curious story of excessive passion for the ritual of nepotism, which brought about unpredictable, and even tragic, consequences in a traditional culture, where this institution is very important. A certain retired general was so fond of baptizing infants, that he soon became godfather to all the children of the local landlords. When the children grew up, they were unable to marry each other, since all the maidens and young men had the same godfather. Consequently, the men had to look for brides elsewhere, whereas the girls were forced either to commit suicide, or leave home for good.

9.1.2 "One of Them" Attributes

Since the "us/them" category is a binary opposition, we must also define its second part—"them"—at least in general terms. It is common practice to formulate the determinants for the alternative notion symmetrically by negating the characteristics obtained for the first member of the pair. In order to define "alienness" sociologically, I believe we must use the same notions that we adopted as attributes of "affinity." Let us consider whether the determinants of "alienness" are negative with regard to the determinants of "affinity." Are all determinants of "affinity" also negative determinants of "alienness"?

"Them" are those groups of people in a local community (often present out of necessity), different in origin and name, which *the community members themselves do not identify* as belonging to "us." A stranger (foreigner) is at the same time an enemy and a guest (cf., e.g., the ancient Russian saying: "*An enemy in the field, a guest in the house*"). Even the reconstruction of linguistic data and historical documents shows that "one of them" is not always an individual opposed to "one of us." In any community an "insider" can become an "outsider." The mechanism is well known. A person can be expelled from the community, outlawed, i.e. deprived of privileges and protection. (In my opinion, the most striking early historical and sociological study of the process of "an insider" turning into "an outsider," an outcast, was carried out in the famous Grettir's Saga (Grettla, 1965).) There is even a special term for this status—"outcast"—which is no longer used as initially intended (Lotman & Uspenskij, 1982). Symmetrically, an "outsider" can become an "insider." All people in all cultures have a universal ritual for welcoming a stranger as a guest, and thus accepting him as "one of us." This is the ritual of hospitality "*...the heart and sole of which is a joint meal... as means of introducing the newcomer to the house and making him 'one of us'*" (Bayburin & Toporkov, 1990, p. 121). In any traditional community this means the transition from the status of a stranger—an enemy—to the status of a guest, i.e. a person protected by the laws of hospitality or transformed into an almost full-fledged "*free individual*" entitled to "*a free day*" as the most important privilege. Incidentally, the process of early socialization, when a child adopts correct behavioral patterns and social norms, is essentially the transfer from an "outsider" to an "insider." As a result, the child also obtains the privileges of a full-fledged adult member of the community. And due to residing in the community for a certain period of time necessary to master and adopt the social norms, the child also becomes "an insider" (on the contrary, if he/she died in infancy or left the community in babyhood, such a child will not be considered an insider). To a certain extent, recognition as "us" depends also on family relations: the status of "bastard" limited a person's rights and privileges despite all the other attributes of "us" being in place.

Let us consider the determined attributes of "affinity" one by one applying them to the opposing notion of "alienness." The first attribute is the length of residence in the local community. This indicator is objective and symmetrical regarding the definition of "us": obviously, anyone who moved to the community recently will be regarded as a stranger. However, the duration of residence has no lower limit for an "outsider," just as there is no upper limit for an "insider." There are no objective time criteria for changing the status of "outsider" to that of "insider." (Certainly, there exist legal deadlines for obtaining the status of "insider." Generally, these regards granting citizenship to immigrants. However, this is the prerogative of the state, not the community.) It is known empirically that to become "us" at least several years are needed—exactly how many is best described by the proverb requiring "*to eat a pood of salt*"[2] with somebody to know him.

Criterion (1). *The time of residence*. The duration of residence is not an independent criterion. As an indicator, it is determined by the lengthy process of *accepting* a stranger and developing relations of *reciprocity* between the former "outsider" and his new neighbors, probably even his future relatives. It would be misleading to state that the process of *acceptance* has a specific duration. Recognizing a newcomer as "one of us" can be a very lengthy process in communities with predominantly traditional behavior, where etiquette forms take up to three quarters of the entire time people communicate. This process will involve numerous conditions, with mastering etiquette being a crucial one (Bayburin & Toporkov, 1990, pp. 65–93). In other circumstances, especially in communities formed by many random people, i.e., migrants of different origin (for example, as was the case in early Icelandic or early North American history), the process of "assimilation" as such goes very quickly, since the entire community is being "built" from scratch and has still neither guardian of standards and morality, nor its own "*lawspeaker*." In particular, for these very reasons the "us/them" divide is impracticable in local communities experiencing a significant migration burden, as well as in modern big cities. (In this sense, the current keen desire of "native Muscovites"—it is well known that almost all of them "took root" in Moscow only after 1931 (Andryushin, 2012, p. 230)—to distance themselves from "outsiders," the numerous "brand-new arrivals," in any case is doomed to complete failure; see the interesting text of Rustem Vakhitov (2012).)

Criterion (2). *Neighborship*. A stranger can acquire the status of neighbor only subject to occupying, securing, *appropriating* a certain land plot—albeit symbolic, of several square meters—within the local community. The community must allow him/her to obtain the plot. The acquired land plot transforms a previously complete outsider (business traveler, tourist, guest, seasonal worker, evacuee, exiled person, even forced long-term temporary settler) into the holder of a transitional "quasi us" status. I believe that the expansion of apartment housing (moreover, with no adjacent territory) in modern cities eliminates the attribute of neighborship as a criterion for classifying a person as "one of us." People living on the same landing stay for years unacquainted, thus remaining strangers to each other. The situation with

[2]"*A pood of salt*" (16 kg) is a fairly accurate criterion: based on current physiological standards and traditions, it is assumed that a human being consumes this amount of salt in 10 years; apparently, this time is enough to obtain the status of "us." However, those who have read William Faulkner's Snopes family trilogy know that the villagers of Frenchman's Bend, Yoknapatawpha County, Mississippi, believed that a newcomer should live half a century among them to be accepted as local.

neighborship is already significantly different in the case of townhouses, not to mention stand-alone houses—in both cases there is a personal controlled area. The land plot provides for the existence of a household. This is already an attribute of rootedness, albeit not sufficient. I will give an example of such insufficiency. In the past 20 years we have been witnessing a specific process in Russia—urban dwellers "taking root" in the countryside. A new type of summer residents (*dachniki*) has emerged in large numbers. Such people buy farmsteads in villages and houses in small towns, formally becoming their residents. However, they are "quasi" rather than real residents. The issue of urban dwellers turning into proprietors of houses and farmsteads and the resulting emergence of a new category of summer residents has been studied in detail by Tatiana Nefedova and Andrey Treyvish (Nefedovam & Treivish, 1999, 2010; Nefedova, 2012). However, in spite of buying solid houses and obtaining land plots, often in the form of a large farmstead, such summer residents do not become accepted community members, because the land has to be farmed and the house permanently inhabited. Regrettably, lots of houses and farmsteads in rural communities and small towns have been purchased as a second home by city-dwellers, who hardly ever live in them. According to studies of the abovementioned authors, there are over 60 million "dachas" (summer residences) in Russia (Russkaya dacha, 2015)—but officially registered 72 million,—which is more than throughout the whole world. This new social fact is disruptive: *neighborship* ceases to be an attribute of "affinity" not only in a big city, but also in the provincial society. People in such small towns and villages no longer perceive and treat their urban neighbors as "us," as members of the local community.

Thus, based on the attribute of neighborship, an "outsider" is a person who has no appropriated land and no permanent dwelling on such land. Moreover, he/she does not run the house or farm the land, which, in turn, is a sign of impermanence, also a mandatory component of (non)neighborship. The transitional status from "one of them" to "one of us" arises when the local community recognizes land within the community appropriated (purchased) by the "outsider" as belonging to this "outsider." We see that if the local community has a significant proportion of temporary residents (seasonal urban dwellers) or high net migration, "neighborship" as a criterion of "outsider" is not applicable.

Criterion (3). *Kinship*. "One of us" must necessarily be related by blood or marriage to a social group within the community. At least, "one of us" must have symbolic relatives among members of the local community. An outsider may also be a relative (in modern kin relationships, where relatives are not always united by neighborship), but genetic relatedness as such is not enough to become rooted in the local community, in contrast to the modern large society, where genetic kinship has been the primary criterion of "us" for some time. (Compare the evidence presented in article 21 of the collected works published in 1998 under the editorship of Irenäus Eibl-Eibesfeldt and Frank Kemp Salter (1998), as well as that provided by Frank K. Salter in his monograph on the long-standing issue of "ethnic genetic interest" in terms of human sociobiology (Salter, 2003a)). Of course, it is easier for a person with family ties in the local community to become an insider; the *acceptance* procedure for him/her is greatly facilitated. It is even enshrined both in customary law through assigning certain local privileges to a related outsider, and in written law, in particular, in the right of inheritance. Meanwhile, this criterion for "us" and "them" is not symmetrical, and, importantly, it is not a segregating factor. One may or may not have common genes with other members of the community, but still remain an outsider. However, observations and calculations show that the coefficient of relationship is relevant to establishing social proximity between people (Harpending, 1974; Salter, 2003b), especially see the interesting issue of the genetic evolution of Ashkenazi Jews (Cochran & Harpending, 2006): the lower its value, the less likely it is for an "outsider" to become eventually an "insider." In general, however, if in archaic and traditional communities' genetic kinship was an undisputed criterion of both "affinity" and "alienness," in modern societies, this uniqueness is largely lost. At the same time, modern communities retain the significance of the symbolic "soulmate relationship," the so-called social kinship—by profession or occupation, hobby, faith, cultural or religious preferences.

Criterion (4). Like kinship, the attribute of *reciprocity*, reciprocal altruism does not clearly determine the status of an "outsider." Any outsider may get help and support from the local community, just as the community may expect altruistic behavior from an outsider. Moreover, the community is even likely to expect such behavior from a stranger without reciprocating. Any outsider depends on the local community and is forced to demonstrate more altruism than he/she expects to receive in exchange. Thus, when it comes to strangers, we encounter unilateral self-sacrifice rather than reciprocal altruism: an "outsider" intending to become an "insider" must make efforts, demonstrate friendliness, and donate part of his personal resources to his future "people." An "outsider" may even be more altruistic in behavior than "insiders" and not expect any reaction from them. The host society, however, expects an outsider to be friendly and altruistic, controlling his behavior more strictly than that of its members for any deviations from the accepted rules, since the outsider retains atavistic features of both enemy and guest, whose statuses are always and everywhere meticulously regulated. An outsider must be very sensitive to all subtleties of etiquette behavior, because the community watches him much more closely than its own members. Thus, provincial residents consider tourists to be impudent and arrogant. The reason for this may be that most tourists come from big cities, where they have lost the ability to feel the boundaries of traditional behavior. On the other hand, migrant workers from Central Asia, brought up in a traditional cultural environment, remain inconspicuous in our towns and do not trigger open hostility (our respondents generally stated their awareness of Tajik, Uzbek, and Kyrgyz teams permanently working in town, "*but we don't see them, as if they were not there*").

Criterion (5). *Local privileges*. An "outsider" does not have the privileges a local community grants its members. Sometimes, an "outsider" may have no "insider" rights at all even in our days (in old times this was common practice). However, the disenfranchised status of an "outsider" is a rather rare occurrence in our local community and may concern, for example, illegal migrants, refugees, or people "on the run." Nowadays, we encounter this only with regard to the state registration system. But the procedure of granting privileges is still governed by archaic rules. A newcomer may already have certain privileges or legislatively determined benefits that he relies on, but he will not be able to obtain local privileges even by pulling strings ("*blat*"). This will be possible only when he eventually becomes "one of us." Meanwhile, an "outsider" in the status of a guest has the opportunity to "get a taste of the privileges"—he will be taken hunting, fishing, or mushroom-picking; offered a steam bath; introduced to particular people and shown something locally revered and secret. Consequently, an "outsider" as a "guest" has more rights and privileges than an "outsider" in the process of becoming an "insider."

Criterion (6). *Referentiality*. Of course, any stranger represents a certain society, but rarely in the current status. The stranger cannot demonstrate his reference group, but can only name (indicate) it, otherwise he will be qualified as an enemy (compare the ancient formula: "*A guest has come to visit you*," which signified mortal danger). Thus, the stranger is deprived of protection and does not find it in the local society. The community may provide him protection, but at its own discretion; only an outsider with a "guest" status is entitled to such protection. Based on this attribute, the status of "us" is determined, whereas that of "them" is blurred. Unlike "one of us," we cannot be sure whether "one of them" will receive support and protection in a given society, whether he will become "a guest." Similarly, it is not determined how a stranger interacts with members of the local community—*represents* his own community or adjusts to the new community in line with the saying "*When in Rome, do as the Romans do.*"

Thus, it is possible to cross the border between "us" and "them"; it is also possible to apply the same criteria for "alienness" as for "affinity," but with less precision. There is a gradation of forms from actually "us"—relatives and in-laws—through neighbors and members of the community to a guest, stranger, and enemy as receding images of "them." Two symmetric concepts describing the transitional forms between "us" and "them" stand apart, but they are aligned—the now almost forgotten outcast and slave. Both statuses are enforced. An outcast is banished, expelled from the community, deprived of privileges and the protection of the society. The traditional Russian rural community—"*Mir*"—to a certain limited extent classified "outcasts" into several groups, which served as transitional stages to an increasing estrangement from the *Mir*, and the *Mir's* gradual rejection of an individual. These were "*bobyl*," "*cossack*," and "*wolf*"—different degrees of waiving responsibilities toward the *Mir*, and the respective stages of the *Mir's* rejection of an individual. A "*bobyl*" still fully belongs to the *Mir*, he has all the rights, but he does not possess the basic attributes of a full-fledged community member—he has neither land, nor family. A "*cossack*" is historically a northern term that refers to a free man, a "wanderer," who takes up different jobs and embarks on various adventures; he is no longer bound to the community either by family, land, or commitments. A "*wolf*" is already a status that almost merges with that of an outcast, since the person in question had violated fundamental rules of community life and had consequently been deprived of many basic rights (see, for example, a typical description of the process of turning a person into a "*wolf*": the captive is dressed in a freshly skinned hide of a sheep or a bull and led on a rope through the villages beaten on the way. Usually, hundreds of people gather to watch this. After this execution, a person will never be a full-fledged member of the community, although the community still recognizes him as "one of us" (Melnikov-Pechersky, 1958, pp. 108–109). The gradual process of rejection indicates that the rural *Mir* did everything possible to retain a person among "us." A slave is forcibly introduced into the community—historically initially only as a prisoner of war, a stranger; the practice of selling one's own people into slavery, including by turning them into outcasts first, emerged much later. Eventually, a slave can become a member of the community, acquire the status of "freedman," former "outsider," formally possessing all the rights of an "insider." Obviously, the described types in their initial form do not exist anymore. However, by certain key indicators, there is a match in reality for every case. This is especially evident in the province, where family and neighborly ties are strong, and the mobility of the population (migration activity) is very low.

9.2 Family Ties and Neighborhood Relations

I shall consider the "us/them" issue empirically from two perspectives: analytical and phenomenological (typologically). First approach has two different aspects: family ties and neighborly relations.

9.2.1 Analytical Assessment of Family Ties: Genealogical and Surname Analysis Findings

It is problematic to study kinship in local populations using sociological methods. Either research should focus on a meticulous and long-term study of family ties (including calculating the coefficients of relationship), but this is feasible in a very little community (commune), given the time input and the likely magnitude of random error. Or it is possible to use indirect methods of assessment. The surname analysis, or isonymic method (Crow & Mange, 1965; Crow, 1989; Elchinova et al., 1991; Sorokina & Churnosov, 2008; Rossi, 2013) is well known for its reliability. It is widely used despite the recognized methodological errors (the analysis focuses predominantly on males; the error is quite significant due to a high proportion of illegitimate children genetically unrelated to the father). At the local level of provincial populations, the surname analysis always shows a prevalence of several local surnames and stability over time—the same surnames are retained in the community for centuries; see, e.g., papers on the rural population of central Russia (Sorokina et al., 2011), the Finno-Ugric people of the Volga region, *Cheremisy—Meadow Mari* (Elchinova et al., 1996), and small peoples of the south of Western Siberia (Kucher et al., 2002) and in Yakutia (Kucher et al., 2010). In addition, in rural areas, where the level of migration is low, the extent of surname elimination as well as the emergence of new surnames in a given community is insignificant. All this indicates that families of one local community retain close family ties in the long run.

I have few examples of my own of applying the surname analysis method in the study of specific communities. However, the existing scattered data from different territories provides the same picture. Extracts from *Household Registers*,[3] which I made all the years of field research in Siberia and in the northern and central regions of the European part of Russia (I have such extracts for individual communities in Karelia and Yakutia, the Murmansk, Arkhangelsk, Vologda, Kostroma, Nizhny Novgorod, and Novosibirsk Regions, the Altai and Krasnoyarsk Territories), allow us to identify three facts relevant for the issue in question. First of all, the *Household Registers* record a very high stability of families (households) in an area: the same families (households) are registered throughout the entire recording period (generally over half a century). A comparison with church registers ("*Metrix book*") shows that many families have been in the area for centuries. In addition, according to most respondents, they and their neighbors have lived together for several, even many generations. I know cases in local communities in the Russian North, when members of one clan live in the same village from 7 to 13 generations. Their ancestor founded the settlement at the very beginning of the sixteenth or seventeenth century,[4] and they go on living in this village, where almost all residents have the same surname. This is the situation in many old settlements where I conducted my research, namely, in the coastal villages on the White Sea: Umba on the Tersky Coast; Pushlakhta, Lyamtsy, and Kanda on the Letniy Coast; and Gridino on the Karelsky Coast. This is so in the local communities of Voznesenye-Vokhma, Nikolsk, Leshukonskoye (Ust-Vashka), Mezen (Vozhgora, Koinas), and Udora (Syol-Yb, Chernutyevo, Bolshaya Pyssa, and several dozens of small Komi villages). The close kinship and long-term neighborship of many families in isolated communities give reason to assert that the composition of "us" here is genetically very homogeneous. Even if there had been other ethnic groups (clans, families), that was a very long time ago and left no memories in the minds of current residents. Traces thereof can only be found among the exhibits of local history museums.

The second significant fact is the extremely low migration mobility of the population: over a period of five, ten, or more years, the share of newly registered or departed families (and their members) was less than one twentieth in all the communities. Even in the "special-purpose" settlements with an intended life span of 25–50 years, which the state set up for migrants only (like, for example the so-called *logging camps*, which mushroomed in the forest-covered areas of Russia in the

[3] *Household Registers* have been kept in rural Russia since old times. They were updated every 3 years and included records of all family members, their relationship, occupational status, and mobility (birth, death, arrival, departure), as well as a description of the farmstead (the house; other buildings, such as bathhouse, farmyard, woodshed, garage, shed, barn, etc.; farmland; livestock and poultry; and fruit trees). In many areas, such records were discontinued in the early 1990s, but in 2007 resumed.

[4] The earliest period is determined by the earliest available universal censuses of the peasant population in Russia.

1930s–1950s, or the no less numerous settlements around the mining enterprises, mines and open pits in the Urals and Siberia, as well as closed isolated military posts in border areas), households demonstrated stable existence for twenty or more years. Even today, over sixty years later, most families go on living in these long abandoned logging camps, mining towns, and military posts. Of course, life stopped and people were forced to leave the mining towns that consisted of apartment houses with central heating and plumbing, because staying there was physically no longer possible. However, even there one or two families go on living in absolutely unbearable conditions. I observe such facts in logging camps in the Murmansk, Vologda, Kostroma, Kirov, Nizhny Novgorod and Arkhangelsk Regions, and in Karelia and Komi. The same is true for mining towns and former military posts in the Primorye, Khabarovsk, Kamchatka, and Perm Territories. Families in the Russian province are very reluctant to migrate, even when conditions become not simply unsuitable for comfortable life, but physically pessimal.

The third identified fact seems to contradict the statement about the stability of family ties, but only at the first glance. Everywhere in the *Household Registers* I found records of families with children, usually the older ones, registered under surnames different than that of the father, less often of the mother. These children were born before marriage or out of wedlock and then adopted (in some cases, but not always). In different communities, especially in the 10–15 post-war years (1945–1960), such children accounted for up to one third of all children in the families. A high proportion of illegitimate and premarital children seems to indicate a significant "dilution" of family ties. However, it turns out that in many cases, the fathers of such children are from the same or neighboring communities. After family break-ups, new families are started in the same social environment.

Other sources of data on family ties are archives, primarily church registers and national population censuses, which have been conducted in Russia since olden times.[5] The most comprehensive data on the population of selected rural communities in the above European regions of Russia was obtained from the *Cadastre* (*Pistsovaya Kniga*) of 1623, the ten censuses of 1719–1869, and the All-Russian censuses from 1897 onwards. A sample analysis of population migration in the "core" Russian provinces (the central provinces where serfs were few or non-existent) also shows high stability of families and clans (Gerasimov, 2006, 2015). It is recorded that throughout the communities kin groups remain in the same localities, reproducing and subdividing in an ever greater number of individual family households. At least from the middle of the seventeenth century to our days, the same clans inhabit different villages in the local community, often remaining loyal to their original settlement. The level of migration is extremely low in the old settlements established in the area in the 1620s. In the three–four centuries, only less than a dozen new surnames—respectively, new migrant families—appeared in the

[5]For the Russian history of population censuses since ancient times, see, e.g. http://novosibstat.gks.ru/wps/wcm/connect/rosstat_ts/novosibstat/resources/0ddf82804f5a9868b734f7e1000af5d8/история+переписей.htm

villages, which initially consisted of people bearing the same surname, i.e. all close relatives. Moreover, once registered, these new surnames almost always remain on the records subsequently. The pronounced uneven distribution of surnames in the villages is indicative; it evidences the equally pronounced territorial stability of the clans and kin groups. It is known that many modern Vyatka (and Vologda) surnames on the Volga-Dvina watershed mentioned above emerged around 1620–1640, and the vast majority of them survived in the same places to our days. Other researchers record a similar picture in the traditional Russian regions (Sorokina et al., 2011; Nikonov, 2017).

The prevalence of surnames in the area always indicates that the population is stable, that individual clans have for many centuries been attached to the area where their name was initially recorded. Moreover, the surname analysis also allows to record the stability of the population at the level of pathology, for example, by the probability of accidental inbreeding due to the high concentration of relatives in the local population (Ginter et al., 1994; Kucher et al., 2002). Unfortunately, against the background of general population studies, there are few "focused" studies relating to the description of a specific local society. They are often published only in the local and regional press and are not widely available. However, where such an analysis is performed, it always gives clear-cut results: the prevalence of surnames indicates a high concentration of people related to each other. The results are always much more indicative in case of a focused study of surnames based on limited material—in one town, one county or district. A relatively recent monograph by A.M. Kamensky on the history of the provincial town of Bezhetsk in the eighteenth century, demonstrates that quite a significant number of ancient Bezhetsk surnames have survived till today. The author did not specifically study the names of the residents, but intentionally or incidentally mentioned several well-known local surnames (Kamensky, 2007). In the course of my short visit to this town in November 2011, I learned that many famous Bezhetsk surnames of the eighteenth century are still widely represented; these names are known to the townspeople, and their bearers are among the local residents.

A very recent article by a team of ten authors (Balanovskaja et al., 2011) published in the Moscow University Bulletin issue dedicated to Mikhail Lomonosov's 300th anniversary, provides information on the prevalence of 40 surnames of Lomonosov's relatives in five districts of the Arkhangelsk Region, including Kholmogory, where the bearers of these 40 surnames lived 300 years ago. It turned out that over these centuries only three surnames disappeared from the original area (the probability of loss was only one name per century, or about 0.7% per generation). All other surnames survived, with the maximum percentage of their bearers still living in the Kholmogory District (69%). The remaining bearers were recorded in the other four districts of the Arkhangelsk Region. These results confirm in greater detail the well-known fact of the age-old stability of provincial surnames. The same picture with low migration and a high level of inbreeding emerges in the works of research teams led by G.I. Elchinova in Tatarstan and Mari-El (Elchinova et al., 1996), Lavryashina et al. (2009), V.V. Nikonov (2017), and A.N. Kucher and co-authors in Eastern and Southern Siberia (Kucher et al., 2002, 2010).

I did not specifically focus on the prevalence of surnames in my sociological research of local societies; however, some sporadic observations allow me to assert that every provincial town, the population of which was not subjected to a "migration shift" at the time, has its own "list of surnames," which remains unchanged for ages. This is true for Mezen and Kologriv, Nikolsk and Cherdyn, Soligalich and Chukhloma, Bezhetsk and Kashin, and even for the relatively numerous communities of Toropets, Vyshny Volochyok, Kineshma, and Belozersk. Focused research shows that compared to southern and western areas, the central and northeastern regions of European Russia are characterized by a very low mobility of the provincial population resulting in high levels of accidental inbreeding, which can be recorded using the indirect "surname" indicator (Ginter et al., 1994, pp. 109–110; Balanovskaja et al., 2005, p. 9).

Nonetheless, I will provide indicative evidence of the local stability of surnames, which I obtained in the course of long-term observations studying the communities along the watershed of the Volga and Northern Dvina rivers (the outback bordering three regions: Vologda, Kostroma, and Vyatka-Kirov). Comparing the data of national population censuses and church registers from the second half of the seventeenth century onwards, published in the works of local historian Semyon Gerasimov (Gerasimov, 2015; *About Vokhma Lands* 2015), with the findings of local Vyatka historian Vassily Starostin, presented on the website https://rodnaya-vyatka.ru and in the *Book of Vyatka Clans* by the same author (http://herzenlib.ru/kniga/), and my own observations in these communities, I obtained results on the degree to which the surnames of the first settlers remained intact to our days. Almost all the names listed in the earliest records dating back to the beginning of the seventeenth century, when Pomors from the Dvina founded their settlements here, still existed both at the end of the nineteenth century and at the beginning of the twenty-first century. (The settlement of these lands was forced; at the end of the Time of Troubles (circa 1618–1622), the Pomors fled en masse from Polish troops led by Lisovsky and Sapieha, and from the Cossacks, whose plundering drove away three quarters of the population of the Russian North, Pomorye (Pascal, 1939, p. 52)).

What is important for us is that a significant part of the local community for an extended period of time—ten and more generations (up to thirteen generations, according to my personal data)—lives in the same area and remarries; as a result, the share of relatives among them is very high. Although many people in the local community may not suspect that they happen to be quite close relatives, the very concentration of common genes results in more than just similar appearance and expressive behavior. It has more serious consequences for the entire system of relations in a particular local society. This is what Frank Salter writes, arguing that common genes (from one common relative) drive a person to support another carrier of such genes intuitively and without hesitation, such support being unconditional and not rationally motivated (Salter, 2003b, pp. 91–108, 115–117).

9.2.2 *Analytical Assessment of Neighborly Relations: Residents and Migrants*

The assessment of neighborly relations is another fairly reliable indirect method of evaluating family ties. For this I will refer to the findings of my two sociological studies of 1999 and 2009, which involved extensive and representative field research of the provincial population (Plusnin, 2000, pp. 9–20; Plusnin et al., 2009, pp. 9–24).[6]

In order to assess the *length* of residence in one area and *neighborship* as attributes of "affinity" in the modern provincial society, I used two variables: the respondent's (1) age and (2) duration of permanent residence at the time of survey ("residency"). The difference between age and "residency" produces a new variable. By subtracting the second value from the first, we find out the age from which the respondent permanently resides in town. Both indicators characterize residency: the first—the duration of permanent residence in one location; and the second—the age at which a person became a resident of the town.

The distribution of "residency" durations for the inhabitants of small towns is presented in two curves (histograms) of the graph in Fig. 9.1.

Since individual segments of the curve are significant, I presented the distribution not in general, but at short two-year intervals. This resulted in frequency fluctuations, interferences. Peaks of the curve at "round" dates are followed by sharp drops. The peaks can be explained by quite natural psychological reasons well known to sociologists: people tend to round off far removed stages of life to five-year periods, especially when asked to give an interval estimate. Therefore, all intervals containing multiples of five have higher frequencies. Due to the objective of the research, it is impracticable to extend the interval to five-year periods. Although this would eliminate the fluctuations, distribution elements relevant for the analysis will be lost. Therefore, we shall ignore the peaks and look at the overall picture. Important features of the graph are hardly discernible, nevertheless, they exist.

First, by the form of the curve, the residency distributions are absolutely similar in 1999 and in 2009. The central high frequency part of the histogram is the same. The difference is noticeable in the "tails" of the distributions. The biggest difference between the 1999 and 2009 samples is apparent in the left "tail" of short residence periods. The share of people residing less than nine–ten years is higher than the respective percentage ten years later. In 1999, this share is slightly over ten percent,

[6] In 1999, the total sample amounted to 1718 people, of whom 1188 respondents were residents of 26 small towns and their rural districts in European Russia and Siberia (three towns are formally classified as medium-sized, since their population exceeds 50,000 inhabitants). Field work was sponsored by grants of the Moscow Public Science Foundation, the Ford Foundation, the Russian Foundation for Humanities, and the Russian Foundation for Basic Research. In 2009, the sample included 1243 respondents—residents of 15 small towns and their adjacent rural districts in the European part of Russia. Research was sponsored by a grant provided to the Center for Empirical Research of Local Self-Government by the Institute of Public Design by order of the President of the Russian Federation.

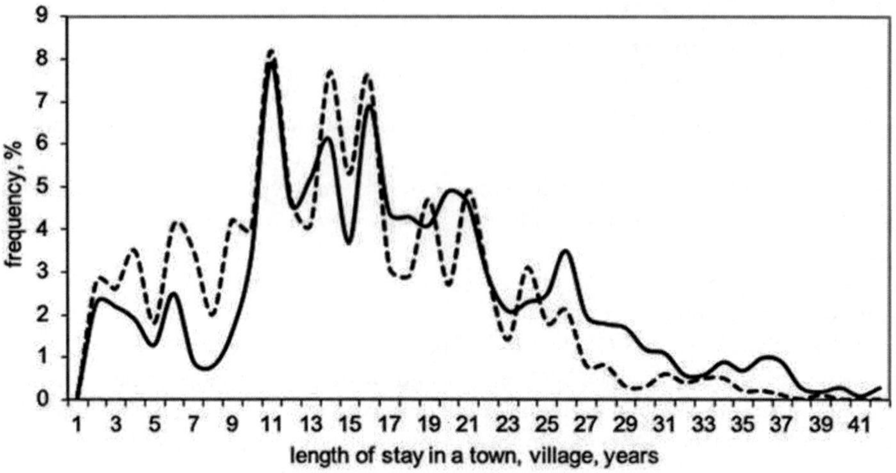

Fig. 9.1 The distribution of an individual's residence duration in the community. The dotted line indicates the frequency curve for 1999, the solid line—for 2009. Source: Plusnin (Plusnin Ju, 2013, p. 75)

whereas in 2009—below eight percent; although the difference is statistically unreliable, it is noticeable graphically. Accordingly, the percentage of people living in the community longer than 25 years decreases proportionally. This is best seen when comparing average "residency" values: in 1999, the average duration of residence was 26 years (the dispersion was ca. 14 years), whereas in 2009—almost 32 years, or six years longer (the dispersion was 16 years).

I believe that such differences between the two distributions are due primarily to the residential status of the respondents, and secondly—to the timing of the surveys. The 1999 survey covered respondents in the western, northern, central, Ural, and Siberian regions of the country, whereas the 2009 survey included only residents of provincial communities in the European part of Russia. It is known that migration in the east of the country significantly exceeded and exceeds that in the central regions (Zayonchkovskaya, 1993; Mkrtchan, 2005). In addition, in the 1990s, small and medium-sized towns experienced positive rather than negative net migration rates (except for the Far Eastern Federal District), and they were considerably higher than nowadays. In the 2000s, migration flows in small towns virtually zeroed out and even became negative (Mkrtchan, 2011). Respectively, in the 1990s, the share of migrants was high not only in the eastern regions, but also in small towns in general (positive net migration rate of 2.0–3.4 per 1000 people, and in the central and southern regions—even 5–7 per 1000). On the other hand, in 1999, less than ten years had passed since the time when almost a quarter of the population was "uprooted" from their homes and forced to seek a better life elsewhere. Thus, the Soviet economic policy and the crisis of the 1990s affected the stability of provincial life. I therefore believe that the 2009 distribution pattern is more typical for the stable

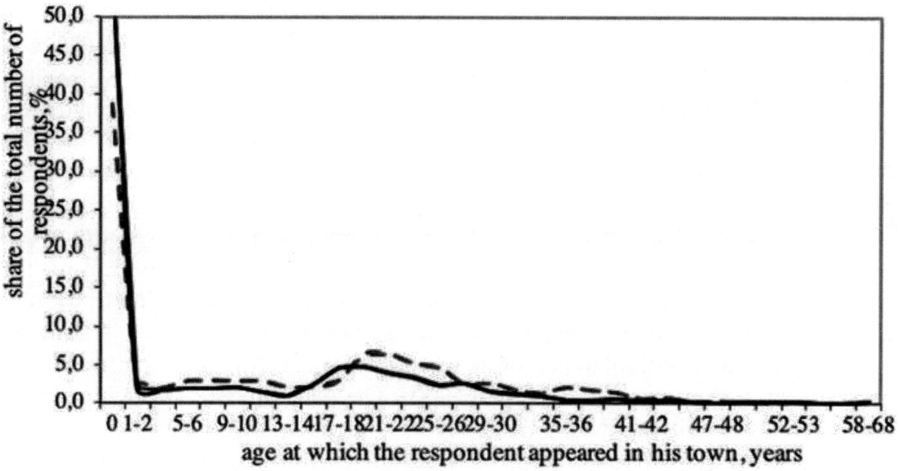

Fig. 9.2 The respondent's "settlement period." Histogram of the distribution of the respondent's time of arrival in the town or village where he was living at the time of the survey, or, in other words, from what age he has been living permanently there. Source: Plusnin (Plusnin Ju, 2013, p. 75)

existence of community and gives a better picture of the residential status of provincial residents.

What is interesting in the pattern of both distributions? A significant drop in the intervals of 6–9 years is followed by a sharp growth of frequency in the intervals of 9–14 years. This may indicate the process of "adapting" and gradually integrating into the local society. Presumably, strangers, migrants need from five to seven years to look around and adapt to a new society. Some of them (about a half) leave, whereas the others adapt, and after 10–15 years of settling down feel no more urge to "move on." They have taken root and become "us" in the local society. After the peak interval of 10–15 years, the frequency distributions gradually decline, reflecting nothing more than the impact of the natural population movement on the age structure. Therefore, the following figure is more interesting.

The graph in Fig. 9.2 presents two quite similar curves relating to the same studies of 1999 and 2009 (the frequencies are grouped into two-year intervals for a more detailed "view" of the distribution curves). However, these are already histograms of the distributions of the derived indicator obtained by subtracting the empirical residency value from the empirical age. The difference of these two values produces the age at which the respondent first appeared in the locality. This derivative indicator can be called the "settlement period" parameter, and it seems to be more important than the original "residency" indicator, because it shows how the person appeared in the local community—whether he was born there, brought over by parents, or moved himself in adulthood.

What do both distributions in Fig. 9.2 show? Four points are important. First, certainly, is a very large share of respondents in the sample that are native inhabitants. Since birth, they have been living their whole life not just in their native community, but in one and the same locality. In the 1999 records, this share is approximately 2/5 (39%), and in the 2009 records—about 3/5 (56%). The smaller share of native residents in the 1999 sample covering provincial communities throughout Russia can be easily explained by the two abovementioned reasons: the contribution of the migratory more active Siberian and northern parts of the population and the enormous migratory input of the "turbulent 1990s," when over 50 million people (more than 20% of Russia's total population) were forced to migrate from the places of their permanent residence. So, it seems typical for the provincial community when the share of exclusively native residents in one locality ranges from a half to two-thirds of the entire local population.

The remaining one-third to half of the residents born elsewhere demonstrate three scenarios of settling down in the community. The most obvious one regard those who arrived as children. They were brought by their parents to the locality where they lived at the time of the survey at a pre-school or school age. Consequently, they did not choose the place to live themselves, and stayed on forever, or at least until the moment of our survey. This category of respondents is easily cut off at the interval of 16–18 years—the age of graduation from school (although this category also includes those who started an independent life by pursuing primary and secondary vocational education). In both our samples, the share of residents from childhood approximated one-fourth to one-fifth (24% and 19%). One way or another, we will have to classify them all also as native residents. Although brought by their parents, they themselves were not disposed to migration and have not moved on since then. One should bear in mind that most respondents in this group were brought by their parents from nearby villages within the same local society, that is, they have always been members of this society. Consequently, the overall percentage of native residents, who are known to have never left their community, ranges from two-thirds to three quarters of the inhabitants of one settlement.

The second scenario of settling down is associated with vocational education. Please note the "bulge" in the distributions at the intervals from 19–22 to 24–25 years. It is more prominent in the 1999 distribution (18%) than in the 2009 one (one third less—12%). What caused the increase in the share of newcomers to the locality in this age range? The answer is obvious, as in the case of those brought in childhood. These newcomers are young specialists assigned to jobs upon graduation from colleges and universities.[7] In 1999, this category includes Soviet-time specialists, whereas in 2009, such a "postgraduate work assignment system" is no longer existent, and the "bulge," therefore, is less prominent. Nevertheless, it exists because young specialists still have to look for jobs, but all by themselves. They often return home, but to the district center (town) rather than their native village.

[7] According to the Soviet law on vocational education, all secondary and higher vocational education institutions (technical schools and colleges, institutes, and universities) provided jobs for their graduates by assignment. Such an assignment had to be held for a minimum of 3 years. This practice seems rational, since vocational education in the Soviet Union was completely free of charge, and subsequent work by assignment was meant to compensate education costs.

Therefore, these are people who had moved to the town upon graduation and, quite likely, decided to stay there forever. Given that in both our samples the provincial inhabitant's "residency" (duration of permanent residence) constitutes more than a quarter and one-third of a century, we can assume this conclusion to be correct. A respondent who first came to town as a young specialist upon graduation from college or university, by the time of the survey has been living there for two–three decades. He has become a "local" even by Frenchman's Bend standards. Thus, by recognizing the former young specialists as "rooted" and, therefore, most probably accepted by the local community as "us," we again raise the overall share of "locals" to 80%–88%.

The third scenario of settling down involves about 11%–19% of the townspeople, who for various reasons themselves in adulthood decided to settle down in the town or village, and by the time of the survey had been living there for the past 10–15 years. These respondents moved to the locality for family rather than occupational reasons. Based on the introduced "settlement period" criterion, it is these people that we can regard as no longer "them," but still not "us."

Finally, the rightmost "tail" of the distributions is formed by people who were aged over 50 when they moved to the locality. These are few—below one percent—and represent two categories: parents who came themselves or were brought over to live with grown-up children. In addition, these are summer residents from major cities who moved to the "backwater" after retirement (many of them, however, have family roots here).

So, according to purely statistical estimates, at least eight to nine out of ten residents of a provincial town, the center of the local society, are "natives." This result is consistent with the impression of visitors, with the estimates of the respondents themselves, and of course with our direct observations. Obviously, not all of these people will be full-fledged "us," i.e. recognized as such by the local community. However, based on the "neighborship" criterion, they are all neighbors in the sense that most "natives" are personally acquainted. Moreover, this acquaintance is quite close. People do not simply know about most of the other members of the local community; they have met on numerous occasions and communicate with many of them. I can just make a quite banal conclusion: almost all members of a provincial community are residents and neighbors. Residents because they have no urge to move and prefer to be born, grow up, and die in their hometown. Neighbors because they have known each other for ages—if not everyone, then every other one. This statement is even more true for rural districts. A typical Russian village has few inhabitants. The average population of all rural settlements with at least one resident is 280 people; in 62 percent of the villages the number of residents does not exceed one hundred.[8] There, all people without exception are residents and neighbors. The analytical assessment of the share of "rooted" inhabitants in towns, centers of the local society,—at over 90 percent—indicates a rigid "us/them" structure. The share

[8] According to the Federal State Statistics Service (*Socio-Demographic Portrait of Russia*, 2012: http://www.gks.ru/free_doc/new_site/perepis2010/croc/Documents/portret-russia.pdf).

of "outsiders" does not exceed ten percent; on-site observations generally produce a much lower figure. A significant part of these ten percent "outsiders" are urban dwellers that moved to the towns and villages in the past ten to thirty years and have actually become "insiders."

Unfortunately, it seems difficult to find statistical or analytical arguments for "us" and "them" with regard to other attributes mentioned above, namely, reciprocal altruism and joint behavior of members of the local society. To some extent, researchers of informal economy deal with this issue when studying household and reciprocal economies (Barsukova, 2004). However, they focus on the economic behavior and the results of exchange relations rather than on the motives underlying the actors' behavior. We can reveal such motives only through meticulous observations of local life phenomena. However, it seems possible to record the last of the proposed attributes—the "community will" as explicitly represented by the set of values and mental constructs reflecting local worldview configurations. Everyone knows that in any provincial town "*the mode of speech differs, and the thoughts of the townsfolk twist and turn like the river flowing through the town.*" Despite the current uniformity of perceptions of the world shaped by the mass media, every local community demonstrates its own subtle identity, local uniqueness. It is easily felt but hardly recordable—sociological tools are too crude and inaccurate for this. However, cultural anthropology and comparative linguistics do possess such tools. We should just refer to the research conducted by representatives of these disciplines and try to locate the relevant information.

Now, however, I will proceed to a more particular and detailed phenomenological analysis of the issue, who specifically is considered "us and them" in a provincial society. I intend to provide some typical examples of the provincial social structure, distinguished by the "us/them" divide. I linked individual descriptions to the complexity of the "us" structure. At the same time, I ignored the complexity of the "them" structure, since it changes little and largely depends on spatial (isolation), historical (age of the community), and economic factors. Due to the need to summarize a lot of empirical data on 142 local communities, I propose the simplest formalizations. I will present a two-component model of the "us/them" structure based on the concept of "laminar/turbulent" communities outlined above (Chap. 2, Sect. 2.4).

9.3 A Two-Component Model of the "Us"/"Them" Structure

Instead of describing numerous individual cases, I prefer to systematize them for a more indicative phenomenological analysis. For these purposes I use a two-component model based on the concept of "laminar"/"turbulent" communities. The first component is the age of the local community (T), the second component is the degree of spatial isolation (I). These two basic indicators correlate with the

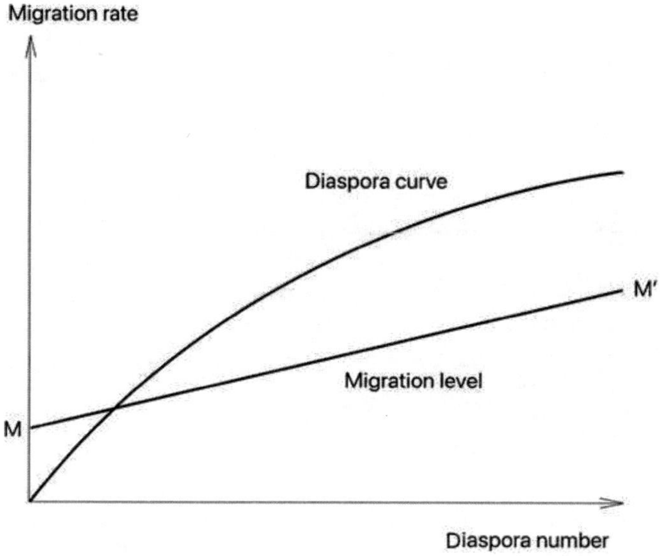

Fig. 9.3 Working model of a migrant diaspora development in the host community depending on the diaspora size, migration rate and level, and absorption rate. Source: Collier (2013), p. 65); clarifications in the text, pp. 63–72

dependent figures of the in-migration rate and the number of "outsiders" (or, similarly, the size of the local diaspora, when the "outsiders" represent one ethnic group/people distinct from the population of the host community; the diasporas in our provincial community are generally formed by ethnic groups from the former Soviet Caucasian and Central Asian republics). I rely on the immigration absorption model developed by Paul Collier (2013, pp. 63–72 and further pp. 122–152 of the Russian edition), illustrated by the graph on page 65 of his book (see Fig. 9.3).

Based on the presented correlation between the size of the diaspora and the migration rate, I propose a model describing how the number of migrants and the migration rate influence the social structure of the local society. I assume that both parameters—(1) the number of migrants (or, similarly, the size of the diaspora where all migrants represent one ethnic group) and (2) the migration rate are variables that themselves depend on the age (*T*) and isolation (*I*) of the local community. In both cases, the dependence is inversely proportional. The level of migration will increase (decrease) exponentially depending on the size of the diaspora, which, in turn, will depend, first, on the degree of spatial isolation, and, secondly, on the age of the community. The three-dimensional model is presented in Fig. 9.4. The number of migrants decreases exponentially on both coordinates—faster on *I* and significantly lower on *T*.

Converting the model in Fig. 9.4 into a table (see Table 9.1), we can determine what distinctions must be identified and described in order to consider all structural component options on the "us–them" axis. Obviously, it is necessary to review at least four out of nine potential types of "us-them" relationships: from the highest

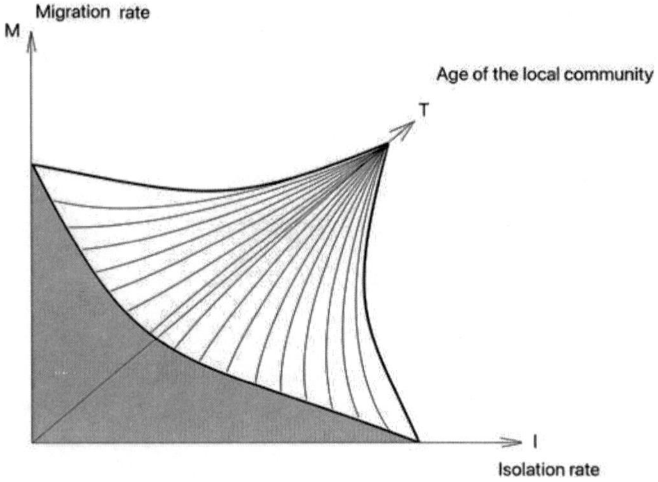

Fig. 9.4 Dependence of the level of migration (M) on spatial isolation (I) and the age (T) of the local community. In-migration decreases faster when spatial isolation increases than when a community grows older

Table 9.1 Change in the proportion of "outsiders" depending on the age and spatial isolation of the local community

	Age of the community		
Spatial isolation	Young (under 150 years)	Old (150–500 years)	Ancient (over 500 years)
Isolated	+	–	–
"Ordinary"	++	+	+
"Turbulent"	+++	++	++

share of migrants in young "turbulent" communities (marked with three crosses ++ +) to the lowest one in isolated ancient and old communities (marked with one cross +, or even left blank where there are no "outsiders" at all).

Thus, of the nine potential options for describing the social structure based on the "us–them" principle depending on the migration rate and the share of "outsiders" in the community, we should focus on four types only. Ancient and old isolated communities have the lowest proportion of "outsiders." Such isolated communities do not accept migrants readily due to the prevailing and entrenched mechanisms of self-imposed isolation. Besides, their absorption capacity is extremely low, and migrants have next to no chance to settle down there. This is especially true for isolated communities populated by ethnic non-Russians, where the share of one ethnic group is overwhelming (from over a half to 100 percent of all residents).

Young isolated communities have a low percentage of "outsiders": migration here is possible and taking place; migrants are actively absorbed; but migration itself is objectively very difficult due to spatial isolation. Old and ancient non-isolated ("ordinary") communities also have a small share of strangers, but for other reasons: even if migration is significant enough, these communities have developed strong social protective self-isolating mechanisms preventing absorption. Is the structure of "outsiders" in the first and second cases similar or different? A brief review does not reveal any differences. But a more detailed analysis shows that due to the easy absorption of migrants in young isolated communities, various occupational, social, ethnic, and religious groups of "outsiders" are able to take root in the society. Lack of spatial isolation in old "turbulated" and "ordinary" communities causes a greater influx of migrants, but self-isolation mechanisms serve as a selective factor that filters "strangers" by all the above features, especially by religion and ethnicity.

The proportion of migrants is high in ancient and old communities through which transport routes pass, and in young non-isolated ("ordinary" coercive developed) ones. Here, the existing transport routes and related industrial infrastructure contribute to a significant influx of strangers, which even powerful self-isolation mechanisms cannot curb. Due to considerable turbulation, the social structure is constantly "eroded."

The highest share of various "outsiders" is expected in young "turbulent" coercive developed communities, if only because they all consist of migrants or their descendants in the first to third generations, and the process of admitting new community members may not be over. Besides, due to underdeveloped self-isolation mechanisms, the absorption of migrants is facilitated to the utmost. Moreover, as such communities are located along transport routes, the migration flow through them is very high, this creating turbulence which continuously erodes and destroys the social structure.

This is clearly only a model approximation, and the reality in certain cases can differ significantly. Nevertheless, I use this particular model to depict structural differences.

It is also noteworthy that I analyze the "us/them" divide in the structure of the provincial community not throughout the entire local community but primarily in its principal and key point—the town (township) as center of all social life. The rural area "is drawn" to the town, but it remains "socially pure" everywhere—it has no "outsiders" at all. Moreover, the rural area does not admit "outsiders." All newcomers are gathered in the center of the local society. As for its outskirts, besides the "social xenophobia" inherent in any provincial society, the specific Russian climate is a factor to reckon with. It is extremely difficult or even impossible for a single person or family to survive long in isolation in our natural environment, in boreal and Arctic latitudes. In rural areas, "outsiders" cannot do without the help and support of their new neighbors, even if they have sufficient financial resources to buy the services of others to meet their daily needs. On their own, they are not able to provide fuel (firewood) or food supplies for themselves. In any case, an "outsider," who is not just a summer resident but lives in the village all year round, needs the help of neighbors. Without such help from the local residents, an "outsider" can survive in the village two–three years at the utmost. Usually he leaves after the first winter. However, a central town, no matter how small it is, has the necessary infrastructure and a developed system of government support, which allow an "outsider" to settle, take root, and live for an extended period of time without having to become "one of us." Local communities of the "turbulent" coercive developed' type is a special case. Here the rural area is degraded and can be so reduced that it shrinks to the outskirts of the central town. Since migratory pressure in such communities is high, the rural area also experiences its full force, and specific categories of "outsiders" appear there.

So, we will consider the provincial structure of communities along the "us"-"-them" axis with several gradients of migratory pressure: from the most homogeneous isolated ancient communities to young "turbulent" and coercive developed ones exposed to ongoing strong influence.

9.4 "Us" and "Them" in Isolated Communities

I am focusing a lot on isolated communities for the simple reason that here the "us/them" structure is represented in its purest form, without distortions caused by ongoing migration. Unlike "us," whose structure (but not composition) is quite homogeneous in all types of communities everywhere, the picture of "them" varies strongly depending on the two abovementioned factors—degree of isolation and age of the community. Structural differences based on the "us/them" divide are often determined by the ethnic composition of the population and by religious aspects. On these grounds isolated communities proved to differ considerably from the "ordinary" or "turbulent" ones. Here, the share of ethnically non-Russian residents in the community is quite high, so is the number of local communities with a predominantly non-Russian population. Although ethnic composition was not a criterion for me when selecting local communities, it turned out that isolated communities were ethnically much more heterogeneous than the "turbulent" and "ordinary" ones.

My records contain information on 41 isolated local communities (see map on Fig. 4.1). Of these, 12 communities have a considerable non-Russian population, this share being three times higher than for 101 communities of the two other types (by the spatial isolation criteria), where ethnically mixed population was recorded only in 18 cases. Two-thirds of the isolated local communities are ethnically exclusively Russian. In four communities, the share of non-Russian residents is significant ranging from 20 to 40 percent. Together with the Russians, they form an integrated local society. These are the peoples of the Volga region—the Bashkirs, Tatars, Mari, Moksha, and Komi, and the peoples of the Far North of Siberia—Evenks, Yakuts, Dolgans, Evens, Itelmens, and Koryaks.

In one-fifth of the other isolated communities (in eight), non-Russian population constitutes from 80 to 100 percent, i.e. these communities are ethnically homogeneous. These are two North Caucasus communities—Gunib and Gergebil—populated by Avars and Dargins, with virtually no other ethnic groups represented. The third local community is located in the Volga region on the Belaya River (Karaidel), where a mixed Bashkir and Tatar population lives with a small proportion of Russians and Mari. The five other communities are very small and extremely spatially isolated; they are located in the European Arctic and in the north of Siberia, in Yakutia. These are three communities in the Arctic zone of European Russia—

Krasnoshchelye on the Kola Peninsula (Murman) formed by Izhma Komi on the Sami ethnic substrate, the Nenets community of Vaygach Island (Varnek), and community in the lower reaches of the Anabar River, where the population is represented by Evenks (Tungus), Dolgans, and Yakuts, It is also a community of the Tompo River, where the population is represented by Evens (Lamuts), Evenks (Tungus), and Yakuts, and the community of the Kurmach-Baygol, where the population is represented by Chelkans.

I know that in at least five other isolated local societies, the Russian population comprises a significant—but unknown—share of the local ethnic substrate: Komi in Mezen, Leshukonskoye and Cherdyn (Lukyanchenko, 1993; Smirnov, 2012), Chulym Tatars in Tara (*The Tara Mosaic*, 1994; *On the occasion of the 400th anniversary of Tara*, 1994), and Mari in Vetluga (Ogloblin, 2010). However, most representatives of these ethnic groups have long called themselves Russians. Ethnic self-identification outweighed ethnogenetic traits.

Preservation of ethnic diversity directly depends on the share of the rural population: the larger the proportion of rural residents in a community, the slower the Russification, especially during the Soviet period (Plusnin, 2008). Isolated communities not only retain a large percentage of rural population, but also most often have villages as their centers. Such are 29 centers in 41 isolated societies, this being significantly higher than the proportion of rural centers in the other types of societies. The share of the rural area—the totality of small localities, villages, hamlets, and settlements—is relatively high and amounts to half of the local society's total population. That is why the population of most isolated communities is not monoethnic; usually, two or three ethnic groups coexist there. Generally, the town (township) has a significant part of Russian population, whereas the majority of rural residents belong to other ethnic groups. By this ethno-territorial feature such communities differ considerably from non-isolated ("ordinary") societies, where Russian population prevails almost everywhere, and the rural district itself has to a large extent degraded in terms of both population and residential areas.

What is the composition and origin of "us/them" in isolated societies? The very fact that many of them comprise different ethnic groups indicates that such communities were formed by incoming Russians that mixed with the already existing local ethnic substrate. They have long since integrated. It generally takes about five centuries for the "melting pot" to produce a single whole. All in all, the structure of "us" in isolated communities emerges along three different lines: (1) from different ethno-religious substrate; (2) from homogeneous non-Russian substrate; and (3) from homogeneous Russian substrate.

9.4.1 Different Ethno-Religious Substrate

In the first option, most distinctly represented in young isolated communities, ethnic mixing is still in full swing. The process, still painful, is perhaps the central topic of daily debates among the residents. As usual, the key issue is the struggle for natural resources, which representatives of one ethnic group believe to be theirs since olden times, whereas recent newcomers (who arrived only 100–150 years ago!) also claim their share. Such is the situation in half of the dozen young isolated communities. Here, the process of developing a “social monolith” from ethnically diverse parts is still under way. I will illustrate this on the example of two societies: Esso in Kamchatka and Anabar in Yakutia.

The local community Esso (Bystrinsky district, Kamchatka) is represented by less than 3000 people, all of them living in two settlements (Esso and Anavgay). This community developed from four sources virtually "before our eyes,” i.e., there are written records thereof. Since ancient times this area was populated by Itelmens—the indigenous population of Kamchatka. In the seventeenth century, Russian Cossacks arrived and started actively mixing with the locals (the reason is common—a shortage of women among the Russians), which soon produced the Kamchadal sub-ethnic group. The current indigenous population of Esso consists of these two long-mixed groups. However, in the nineteenth century, Evens (Lamuts) moved in from the north and occupied part of the ancestral lands of the Itelmens and Kamchadals. The process of inter-ethnic mixing is not yet over, neither are the territorial disputes between them over natural resources. Finally, new settlers appeared in the twentieth century, in Soviet times. Those were Koryaks from the western Okhotsk coast of Kamchatka. At the same time, throughout the century, Russians were resettling to the area from distant European parts of the country. The processes of ethnic mixing ended here only by the 1980s, and the past half century this extremely heterogeneous material has been “melting together.” Of course, all residents have long become “us” to each other, and even relatives, but debate about "birthright,” inspired by competition for hunting grounds, fishing areas (“*toni*”) and “ancestral territories” is not subsiding.

The Anabar local community (the official name is the Anabar National Dolgano-Evenk Ulus [District], Yakutia) is also represented by only 3500 residents in two settlements—Saskylakh and Yuryung-Khaya. The community comprises three core ethnic elements. The largest group (up to half of the population) are Dolgans—a people formed in the nineteenth–twentieth centuries by mixing local and incoming Evenks (Tungus), Yakuts, and Russian peasants. The second largest group, 900 people, are Evenks, with whom Dolgans are in friendly and family relations. The Evenks are joined by a small (100 people) group of Evens (Lamuts). Despite being relatively recent settlers in the area, the representatives of these ethnic groups are indigenous. With the Dolgans, they oppose the fourth group—the Yakuts (ca. 700 people), who are recent settlers in the area, as are the Russians of whom there are about 250 people. But if Dolgans, Evenks, and Evens are neutral and friendly with Russians (largely due to completely different occupational and resource and environmental *niches*), their relations with Yakuts are clearly aggressive, and have failed to stabilize for years and years. This is due to the fact that the Yakuts have seized all the most “lucrative” and profitable positions in the economy and displaced the aborigines from their hunting grounds and reindeer pastures. Considerable spatial isolation cannot compensate for weak social consolidation mechanisms.

In both Siberian local societies, "outsiders" comprise very small groups of people, who appear here for a short time and often not of their own free will. In the latter case, this is the personnel of military units (which, in particular, largely influenced the ethnic composition of the local population, leaving many descendants of Russian blood) and professionals—pilots, power engineers, mining engineers, etc. Besides, there are quite isolated "outsider" groups—rotation workers at mining enterprises. An example is the diamond mining and processing plant at Ebelyakh, whose workers, security guards, and specialists lived in complete isolation from the Anabar local society. The situation with "outsiders" is similar in Esso, where employees of the Bystrinsky National Park are often episodic inhabitants. All these "outsider" groups live relatively isolated from the rest of community.

Only two or three specific categories of "outsiders" appear in such local communities of their own accord (actually, they are pervasive). These are rare small teams of seasonal builders (usually one or two teams of 20–30 workers, and not every summer), and retired townspeople who buy houses and apartments as a second home for the summer. There is another tiny category of "outsiders"—missionaries of various sects, usually Jehovah's Witnesses and Evangelical Protestants, as well as various environmentalists (the so-called *Pagan Slavs* and *Anastasians*). These people are always "apart"; they demonstrate the distinctive behavior of strangers and make no attempts to integrate. In the event of frequent failure of their enterprise on local soil, they disappear forever, leaving behind an only trace in the form of a purchased and decaying house of worship.

9.4.2 Homogeneous Non-Russian Substrate

The second case of shaping "us" in isolated communities is when the local community develops from ethnically homogeneous population that had not mixed with the incoming Russian settlers. The mixing did not happen for various reasons, the main one being considerable spatial isolation due to the inaccessibility of the area. The North Caucasus mountains (Gunib and Gergebil), the tundra along the coast of the Arctic Ocean (Vaygach and Krasnoshchelye), the cold mountain tundra deserts of the Suntar-Khayat range (Tompo), or the black taiga of the Kuzbass Alatau mountain (Kurmach-Baygol)—none are attractive for Russian settlers.

Due to significant isolation and strong self-isolating mechanisms based on kinship, the population of such communities is largely homogeneous, consisting virtually of one or several clans. New residents appeared only because of political or administrative reasons. One of the major reasons was the forced relocation of people from the surrounding and distant (hundreds of kilometers away) villages to the district centers. This process started in the early 1960s. It was these new forced residents that formed minor groups of other ethnicities in the local social structure.

A good illustration thereof is the small (under a thousand residents) Tompo community (Topolinoye settlement, Tomponsky Nasleg [rural district], Yakutia). The settlement was established in the 1970s. Its first inhabitants were Even families brought from all over the Tomponsky District. They formed the majority of the local extremely isolated community (the distance to the nearest locality, the administrative center Khandyga, is about 300 km). In addition to the prevailing Even (Lamut) population, the settlement is home to a few Evenks (Tungus), Yakuts, and Russians. Many have long since become relatives, but there are marital ethnic preferences. The confrontation between Evens and Evenks with the Yakuts is expressed in the refusal to enter into mixed marriages with them, whereas there are no such marriage avoidances between Lamuts, Tungus, and Russians.

A somewhat similar reason underlies the establishment of the equally isolated Krasnoshchelye community (Murman). Originally, Sami (Laplanders) reindeer herders roamed these lands. There were numerous small Sami villages of one or several families and *sieidis* throughout the Kola Peninsula; in the eastern part the settlements were, apparently, semi-nomadic. During the Second World War and in the first two decades after it, all small Sami settlements were destroyed or eliminated. The first large settlements were established here in the beginning of the twentieth century by Izhma Komi, also reindeer herders, coming from Karelia, where they migrated in the middle of the nineteenth century from the Izhma and Pechora rivers (currently in the Komi Republic) more than a thousand kilometers away, to save their reindeer from plague. Here they formed a single community with the Lapps (Sami), since both had similar livelihood patterns (Lukyanchenko, 1993). Later, in the twentieth century, the community incorporated a small number of Russian Pomors and a mixed Russian-speaking population, specialists from outside. Currently, Krasnoshchelye and two other remote villages form a small, but autonomous and self-sufficient community (Kozlov et al., 2008; Pozanenko, 2017, 2018). There are hardly any outsiders in such communities, except for representatives of specific occupations (meteorologists, for example).

9.4.3 Homogeneous Russian Substrate

Isolated communities with native Russian population are the third option of the "us" structure. Generally, such communities have existed since ancient times, and their initial structure has remained unchanged till today (with the few exceptions when all former inhabitants were displaced or died out, and the area was populated by settlers brought in from afar). In a number of such communities, social homogeneity resulted primarily from social disasters rather than physical isolation, which was secondary.

In some cases, the reasons were political, such as the Time of Troubles in the early seventeenth century, when entire rural communities throughout regions like *Pomorye* (the Russian North) were forced to leave their homes and flee to the Volga, Urals, and Siberia, where they established small homogeneous rural communities and mixed with the local ethnic substrate. Such examples are numerous: the Pomors and Cheremis on the watershed of the Northern Dvina and Volga; the Chaldons and Tungus on the Angara; the Semeyskiye Old Believers, Buryats, and Kerims in Transbaikalia. In other cases, the reasons were related to natural elements causing epidemics, epizootics, crop failures, and famines, which forced people to flee in search of new places to live, which were always abundant in Russia.[9] Yet in other cases, the reasons were related to religious differences, primarily, the Schism (*Raskol*) of the seventeenth century: many isolated communities remained committed to the old faith (the *Old Belief*) and developed strong protective self-isolation mechanisms, which allowed them to maintain the uniqueness of their community not only in another ethnic environment, but also among ethnically homogeneous New Ritualists (Pascal, 1939). In my sample, these are the ancient communities of Varnavino (Nizhny Novgorod), Mezen (Arkhangelsk), Pudozh (Karelia), Soligalich (Kostroma), Udora (Komi), Umba (Murman), and Cherdyn (Perm), as well as the old communities of Vetluga (Nizhny Novgorod), Kachug (Irkutsk), Leshukonskoye (Ust-Vashka, Arkhangelsk), and probably Tara (Omsk). Of the young societies, these are the modern old-faith villages of Erzhey and Sizim in Tuva—a single community of Russian Old Believers among an entirely Tuvan population.

Two ancient isolated local societies with a "purely Russian" population—Soligalich and Cherdyn—can serve as examples. Located in similar ecological and climatic conditions in the north of European Russia and in the Urals, they differ significantly in the composition and process of forming "us" and "them."

Ancient Cherdyn in the north of the Perm Territory is a classic backwater town, although there have been some famous people among its residents; see (Cherdyn and the Urals, 1999). By the composition of the population, it is a typical Russian town (over 95% of the inhabitants consider themselves Russian and in the hundred years after the first census the ethnic composition of Cherdyn's population has not changed at all; see (Book of Remembrance ... for 1892, pp. 64–67; Chagin, 2004, pp. 39–41)). The town is quite small: two centuries ago, in 1814, it had 2793 inhabitants, a century later—in 1920—4578 residents (Chagin, 2004, pp. 91–92), and nowadays, its population is probably under 5000 people. In terms of households, only about 1800–2000 families live in the town and its immediate surroundings, mostly in their own homesteads. But the Cherdyn local society certainly spills over the boundaries of the town. It includes several other nearby settlements within a range of 10 km. Here, Cherdyn residents have their summer homes; from here they shuttle to work. Here, one can also see the main links of the Cherdyn society with the outside world. Nyrob, a village with almost two thousand residents lies 40 km to the north. Economically and historically, it is closely linked with Cherdyn, and is therefore included in the circle of "distant insiders." This is the only remote large settlement, the inhabitants of which Cherdyn residents consider to be "us." The equally remote Krasnovishersk is already definitely "them." The communities of Solikamsk and Berezniki are also perceived as "outsiders"; the only road southward connects Cherdyn with them.

[9] For example, it is known that the Pskov and Novgorod lands in the fifteenth century were inhabited by Muscovites, whereas the Moscow lands in the seventeenth century—by Karelians and Veps. Pomors from the Russian North went to colonize Siberia, and in the nineteenth century, Komi from the Cis-Urals moved in the opposite direction. Examples are countless.

Everyone here knows each other; everyone belongs having lived all their lives together. Over the past twenty years, the negative natural growth in Cherdyn, as elsewhere, has been exacerbated by a slightly negative balance of migration. Few leave, with an average of 20–25 people per year, which, estimated roughly, is no more than one percent of the total number of households. Among other reasons, the population of the area is decreasing because of the recent disbandment of numerous penal colonies located here. Some prisoners released from the "home" Nyrob "zones" do not leave immediately but settle for an indefinite period in the town and the surrounding villages. Until recently, the "population" of the Nyrob colonies was about 4000 people. Some of the ex-convicts—annually from twenty to thirty of them—stay behind for a couple of years (between one and three) before leaving for the "mainland." Not many of the ex-cons are able to adapt to life in Cherdyn. It is difficult to find a job, and one must engage in homesteading to feed oneself. It is impossible to buy a house, one usually has to marry, which subsequently generates new problems. Therefore, after an unsuccessful attempt to gain a foothold in the Cherdyn society, the ex-cons join the ranks of out-migrants, constituting a significant (but unknown) share of them. They definitely are outsiders. However, their status in the local society is specific because they establish stable relations with many Cherdyn residents from among the security personnel when serving a term in the Nyrob penal colony, Of course, Cherdyn residents consider them outsiders, and that is what these people effectively are.

In addition to former prisoners, the local Cherdyn society distinguishes four other small groups of outsiders. A relatively new group are monks of the re-opened St. John the Theologian Monastery. The monastery is famous for being the first Christian church and the first stone building in the Urals where liturgical service has been conducted continuously since the middle of the fifteenth century. However, the locals pay little attention to the monastery. Remarkably, just like the locals steer clear of the monks, the monks themselves do not favor the locals and interact mainly with the ex-convicts residing in town. Two groups of "outsiders" found each other in an alien homogeneous and united environment of Cherdyn residents. Another group of new "outsiders" are two-three teams of ubiquitous Uzbek or Tajik builders, between twenty and thirty people. Although the townsfolk rarely meet these people physically, they know about their existence and undoubtedly consider them "outsiders." Along with the Uzbeks-Tajiks, there is another "flow-through" group of "outsiders"—tourists. Unlike the former, these "outsiders" are noticeable; they are always in plain view of the residents. Between 100 and 150 tourists visit Cherdyn weekly. These strangers show up in town for two–three days and all look alike to the locals. On a summer day, the "dynamic density" of tourists on the streets is about 25 people. They are harmless, even useful, diversify the leisure of the townsfolk and remind them that there are "aliens" in town.

A specific group of "them" stands out among these definitely "alien" groups of the population, hardly touching or only slightly penetrating the periphery of the local society. These are inhabitants of Ryabinino village. A significant part of its population consisted of Volga Germans who were resettled here during World War II. By now, many of them have long left for Germany, but some stayed behind. These "them" are almost "us." Here we encounter a typical case of "outsiders" gradually—over 40–60 years—"growing into" the body of local society. The Cherdyn society is sufficiently isolated, and this alone unifies it and makes it resistant to penetration by alien elements. But because of long-term coexistence, some of these "outsiders," though distant in ethnicity, lifestyle, and mentality, gradually penetrate deeper and deeper into society and become almost "insiders." Ryabinino Germans almost became "us." But they left.

Thus, among the residents of Cherdyn there are in total no more than a couple of hundred "outsiders," which, considering the adjacent villages, accounts for only two–three percent of the local population. This is very little for a cohesive society, especially since we see what all these "strangers" are like: all five identified groups differ in their way of life, in the place in the social structure, and many are of another ethnicity. There are no other "them" in Cherdyn, and those who exist cannot be confused with anyone. A member of the local society has no difficulty whatsoever to determine the degree of "affinity" of any person he encounters on the way. Especially since all "us" are natives of Cherdyn, descendants of several generations of townspeople. Those "them" who do become "us" are almost all from the neighboring more distant villages. This is the great advantage of spatially remote (isolated) local societies. This is also a purely external condition for the solidarity of the local society.

The second society, Sol-Galitskaya, a settlement adjacent to the saltworks of the Resurrection Monastery founded in 1334, has a well-known written history, not only as one of the largest salt-making crafts of medieval Russia, but also as one of the oldest resorts with chalybeate mineral waters. This is also the site where the still operating largest lime plant in the Soviet Union was constructed in 1973–1975. The three specified circumstances of the history of Soligalich—the saltworks, health resort, and lime plant—were factors that determined the historical specifics of the structure of local society along the "us/them" axis. Salt production and numerous rich saltworks constantly attracted new people from many surrounding areas, not only from Galich, but also from Moscow and Veliky Novgorod. Up to the middle of the eighteenth century, when salt-making began to decline, migrants constantly replenished the population of Soligalich.

Records show that new settlers intended as workers at the saltworks were brought in in a "planned manner"—by government decrees or by transfer of monastic peasants. In old times, the Sol-Galitskaya local society was formed through "organized recruitment" and settlement of people in "dormitory areas" around the saltworks, which were located quite compactly on the bank of the Kostroma River right next to the monastery walls. Each new portion of settlers was brought in as jobs emerged at new saltworks, so it is safe to assume that there was no significant competition between the old and new inhabitants of Soligalich, and the latter in no time joined the ranks of "us."

However, the social structure did not stabilize (stagnate), because in 1835, shortly after salt-making almost completely ceased, wells drilled in town produced mineral water with healing properties, which immediately began serving medicinal purposes (Figurovsky, 2010, pp. 162–163). The opened hydropathic establishment (which, by the way, still operates successfully) attracted many new people to town, including medical doctors, and generated a constant "flow" of health resort visitors from outside, whose annual number ranges from several hundred to several thousand. The hydrotherapy clinic occupied an extensive fenced area right in the center of the town at the site of the former saltworks. Housing for the specialists was built next to the clinic. The engineers and doctors did not deprive the locals of their jobs, so most likely they seamlessly integrated into the local society. Their contribution to the qualitative composition of the residents was very positive: they brought with them education and intelligence. However, even before that Soligalich was distinguished by highly skilled engineers trained at the saltworks.

Finally, in the middle of the twentieth century, the largest limestone deposits in central Russia were discovered in the immediate vicinity of Soligalich. Consequently, a lime plant was constructed a dozen kilometers north of the town. Numerous engineers were engaged to work there, and a separate residential district was built to accommodate them. The commissioning of the lime plant and the arrival of a couple of hundred engineers and technicians to work there also did not trigger any tension in the local society. The engineers and technicians did not compete with the locals for either housing or jobs. Despite the initial isolation of the newcomers—they were allocated two streets on the outskirts of the town for living—over the past half century everyone has already integrated, especially since working dynasties have formed at the plant, and many newcomers have intermarried with the locals.

Thus, unlike Cherdyn, during the seven centuries of its existence Soligalich has always been a local society experiencing regular, every two–three generations (in fact, every 50–70 years), replenishment of its composition by new people in the form of compact occupational groups. Instead of tourists, a large group of health resort visitors lives right in the center of the town—about 1500 annually; consequently, between 100 and 150 "outsiders" of this category stay in town at the same time, and the weekly load on the local society is almost the same as from tourists in Cherdyn.

For the reasons noted above, "us" in the local society is not a compact and isolated group, as in Cherdyn, but a certain "layered" structure. Each successive group of "them" settling in the town as new permanent residents, gradually integrated into society and within 30–40 years became "us." We can assume that this process regularly occurred in ancient times, when with each new major owner of the saltworks (the principal ones belonged to the prince and the monastery), new groups of workers resettled to Sol-Galitskaya. This was the case with the (initially small) staff of the hydropathic establishment in the nineteenth century; this happened about 50 years ago with the group of specialists for the lime plant. This has been taking place in the past five–ten years, when villagers from the Soligalich district began moving en masse to Soligalich. They resettled in two mass waves. The first one took place in the early 1960s, when collective farmers finally received passports. The most active of them quickly moved to Soligalich and shortly after got themselves "recruited" to work in large cities—St. Petersburg (Leningrad at that time) and Murmansk (it is these people that upon retirement began returning to Soligalich and taking residence there as "Muscovite" pensioners). The second wave of the villagers' resettlement began in the 2000s and is still actively underway. But the local urban society already perceives these "villagers" as "outsiders," and aggressive "outsiders" who settle in the town center in the houses of "indigenous" Soligalich residents and go after the highly valued "cushy jobs" in the public sector. Due to their more developed family ties and nepotism, they help each other in obtaining the lucrative jobs. In all respects—both economic and social—the villagers, being new "outsiders," compete with the "indigenous" townspeople. And in this they differ significantly from the previous groups of "outsiders"—specialists of the hydrotherapy clinic and the lime plant—who had "grown into" the body of the local society. Therefore, the attitude to the "villagers" as to "them" is more acute than to the other few "outsiders." Despite perceiving the villagers as "outsiders," the local Soligalich society is not confined to the town only. It includes many surrounding hamlets and villages in all four directions. But it does not go even halfway along the road to Chukhloma. Like in Cherdyn, this road is the only connection with the outside world. To "enter" that world, a resident of Soligalich must move first to Chukhloma, then to Galich, then to Kostroma, and only after that settle in Moscow. The transition of villagers to townspeople is the first stage of centripetal migration through four filter cities.

In addition to health resort patients and spa guests, "distinct outsiders" include two small groups that have already become familiar over the twenty years of their existence. The first group comprises between sixty and seventy seasonal workers from Uzbekistan. Uzbeks work on a rotation basis at the sawmills and in timber processing. In the space of just a few years, some of them managed to settle down and even start new "families." They are not visible in town, although they have formed their own football team and take part in local sports events. They are out of sight, so they arouse neither compassion nor irritation among the locals. In addition to the Uzbeks, there are also permanently residing newcomers from Central Asia and the Caucasus, from the Vologda and Ivanovo Regions; almost all of them are engaged in trade.

The attitude to the second group—also common only since the early 1990s—is somewhat different. It consists of summer residents who bought houses in town. Until recently, their presence was not felt in Soligalich, since it was exclusively retired former native residents who bought the houses and settled down here. However, the past ten years have seen an influx of younger people new to the area and the local society immediately noted the presence of new outsiders. Locals consider "Muscovites" to be rich, arrogant, and cunning, living not on wages, but on capital and rent; therefore, they treat them with prejudice and rejection. However, this is the case everywhere.

Thus, the structure of the Soligalich society is distinguished by the following features: "indigenous" residents live in the town and are increasingly being edged out by assertive villagers, both groups competing with each other; there is also a new group of "us"—"the industrial folk" "*. . . who still live under socialism.*" These three groups—rather layers with different degrees of "affinity"—are joined by three groups of "outsiders": spa guests, Uzbeks, and summer residents. The groups of "outsiders" are less conspicuous and do not trigger such rejection from the local society as almost “their own” villagers. However, the summer residents are perceived with wariness and aggression because they grow into the body of local society like metastases: they have significant resources, a different mentality, and other attitudes, and the society still sees no benefit from them.

We see that by the composition and nature of “them” the Soligalich society is similar to that of Cherdyn (only instead of tourists it hosts patients and spa guests), but the structure of “us” is different and more complex. This “layered” structure results from the periodic introduction of various new groups of outsiders into local society, who gradually become an integral part of it. These groups were brought in not only for economic reasons. Economic expediency was backed up by political considerations; sometimes, the reasons were purely political. In all cases, each new layer of “us” was formed by coercively introducing (“planting”) an alien and occupationally compact group into the local society. Their tension-free integration was ensured by separating “ecological niches”: outsiders did not compete with locals for resources. Only in the latest case competition emerged in the contest for publicly funded jobs, which put “almost our” villagers in the position of “outsiders,” although this does not prevent them from successfully integrating into local society. Here, kinship and neighborhood coupled with a long common history override the economic motives for not recognizing “us.”

9.4.4 The Main Features of “Us”/“Them” Structure in Isolated Communities

Please note that the three ways of shaping “us” in isolated communities are determined by the duration of their existence. A heterogeneous composition is recorded only in young communities—here the “us” structure is still developing. A homogeneous ethno-religious composition of “us,” both Russian and non-Russian, is observed in old and ancient communities—here the structure has long been formed, and it was either initially homogeneous, or the previous ethnic substrate has long been processed and assimilated and by now completely forgotten.

Family ties are decisive for “us” in isolated communities. In ancient and old societies, the share of namesakes is high, with just a few surnames dominating (being the most frequent). This indicates high coefficients of relationship (r) between community members. However, I did not specifically study this issue, except for a few cases depicted above.

The “us” structure in isolated communities is distinguished by its agglomerated nature: individual originally heterogeneous components of the local community are united simultaneously. All the young communities I observed were recent, and the history of their establishment is well known. Such communities are composed from three types of agglomerates: (1) either from different ethnic groups previously spatially separated from each other (Anabar, Krasnoshchelye, and Esso); (2) or—in the event of ethnically homogeneous structure—from clans that used to live in different areas and gathered together only in the new locations (Vaygach, Tompo, and Tura); (3) or these are coercive developed communities composed of completely different people (not always related to each other), made or forced to settle in the area due to economic or socio-political reasons (Amurzet, Leninskoye, Olga, Preobrazhenie, Erzhey-Sizim). In all three cases, the structure of the population is initially genetically heterogeneous—at the level of individuals, at the level of kin groups, and at the level of different peoples. The structure is agglomerated, since it forms almost simultaneously.

Agglomeration is also typical for ancient and old isolated communities, but as it dates back a long time, it is less vivid and visible than in young isolated societies. In addition to it, we find the existence of different "layers." What does it mean? Throughout the life of the local society, every three–five generations or less frequently, new compact groups of residents move into the area. They differ most often by socio-occupational characteristics (principal economic activity of the migrants) or by ethnicity. In both cases, the new inhabitants are genetically distant from the local substrate. Of course, we see this process in the young isolated communities also. However, in ancient and old communities, the successive layers (in-migration) of new inhabitants appeared long ago, and current residents hardly remember their origin, unlike the population of young isolated communities, where conflicts between groups of different origin have not yet subsided. Such conflicts are relevant in the abovementioned communities of Esso and Anabar, Krasnoshchelye and Tompo, and in the equally young Amurzet and Leninskoye (Birobidzhan) communities. In ancient and old communities, information about these different layers can be found and recorded only in archives, regional studies, and museums. In addition to the described Cherdyn, Nikolsk, and Soligalich, we should also mention a similarly layered "us" structure in such communities as Vetluga (Nizhny Novgorod), Chukhloma and Voznesenye-Vokhma (Kostroma), Mezen (Arkhangelsk), Umba (Murman), and Temnikov (Mordovia).

For example, the old Vetluga community consists of four principal "us" layers, all of them ethnically different. The native Cheremis population—*Meadow Mari*—were assimilated by mass waves of Slavic and *Meryan* migration from the west, from Suzdal and Kostroma-Galich in the fifteenth to seventeenth centuries. Later, at the end of the nineteenth century, there was a wave of forced peasant migration from the east, from Vyatka. The Vyatka peasants settled in isolation in the south-west of the Vetluga area. Finally, in Soviet times in the twentieth century, there was an inflow of specialists and workers from different regions of European Russia. They settled also in relative isolation in logging camps in the north-west of the area. A layered structure of the population emerged, albeit split geographically: the three main groups of newcomers still live separately. The origins, however, have long been erased from the community's memory (although the Vetluga community clearly remembers that seventy years ago it belonged to the Kostroma and not the Nizhny Novgorod Region, as currently).

The "us" structure developed absolutely similarly in the old community of Voznesenye-Vokhma (previously Vologda, currently Kostroma Region) on the watershed of the Volga and Northern Dvina rivers (Popov & Popov, 2014). Here also Meadow Mari (Cheremis) constituted the native substrate, but the overriding population were the Pomors, who migrated from the tributaries of the Northern Dvina during the Time of Troubles and subsequent Schism (starting from about 1620, although the first monastic settlers appeared in the fifteenth century, around the 1430s). Like Vetluga and many other Vologda and Kostroma societies, this old local community also experienced a peasant migration influx at the end of the nineteenth century, this time from the east, from Vyatka. After that, there was no new in-migration, and for the past almost a century and a half the "us" structure of the Voznesenye-Vokhma community has remained stable and unchanged.

Of course, not every ancient and old community has recorded traces of the "agglomerated" or/and "layered" structure of their "locals." Apparently, in many cases it developed from a single ethnic or related substrate; individual members of community were genetically close to each other. I assume this for the almost mono-ethnic communities of Gergebil and Gunib (Dagestan), Digora and Chikola (North Ossetia), and also Udora (Komi) (Plusnin, 2006). In other cases, the native substrate is currently completely overridden by long-time immigrants, and the "layered" structure of the "locals" is not at all obvious and definitely has left no imprint in the collective memory of the people themselves. Such are, probably, the communities Varnavino (Nizhny Novgorod), Gdov (Pskov), Demyansk (Veliky Novgorod), Kargopol and Onega (Arkhangelsk), Pudozh (Karelia), Kachug (Irkutsk), Kologriv (Kostroma), Suzun (Novosibirsk), Tara (Omsk), and Charyshskoye (Altai).

I would like to emphasize once again that isolated communities, even young ones, have few or next to no "outsiders," whose composition and structure can be described as consisting of four categories.[10]

The first category consists of seasonal residents who come for economic or recreational reasons. Such groups are often the only "outsiders" in isolated communities. Their origin differs. "Economic outsiders" include the already mentioned seasonal rotation crews and construction teams made up of internal wandering workers (otkhodniks) or migrants from post-Soviet countries. They come regularly from year to year but only for a month or two in summer. Every local community in central European Russian and in Siberia hosts teams of seasonal migrant builders (*wandering workers* would be more correct)—Tajiks, Uzbeks, or Kyrgyz from post-Soviet Central Asian republics. They are pervasive, but not numerous—two–three teams of seasonal workers totaling from ten-thirty to a hundred people. Due to their extended stay in certain areas, some of them start new families, settle down, and gradually integrate into the local society. This process has acquired the most radical forms in the Jewish Autonomous Region (Leninskye, Amurzet, Obluchye, and Birobidzan), where the share of non-Russian ethnic groups from post-Soviet Central Asian states has been rapidly growing over the past 25 years (Plusnin, 2018a).

[10]These same categories of "outsiders" exist, of course, in the other types of communities, therefore I will not mention them specifically further.

"Recreational outsiders" include tourists, who come for a couple of days also mainly in summer, but as they constantly succeed each other, the locals, to whom they all "look alike," get the feeling that they are always present.

The second category of "outsiders" consists of urban second homers, residents of major cities and medium-sized towns, who buy houses and apartments in the central settlement and live there either all year round or only during the short summer. Although urban second homers are scarce in isolated societies. This category is also heterogeneous in nature. There are summer residents who have roots in the local community in the second or third generation, so they have a sense of belonging. They merge with those who returned to their native village upon retirement. Some summer residents settled by chance; they are often from afar, with their main home located 1000–5000 km away. There are urban dwellers who were driven by environmental and/or religious reasons when selecting an isolated settlement. Such are groups of "*Anastasians*," "*Pagan Slavs,*" "*Roerichians*" (followers of Nicholas Roerich), and various "New Age." This group of "outsiders" is especially numerous in turbulated-type communities. In the mono-ethnic isolated communities, "outsiders" often include Russians, Ukrainians, Byelorussians, and all other Russian speakers, since mostly they are non-indigenous, and, moreover, recent inhabitants. There is no ethnic division in mixed communities, since Russians and other non-indigenous peoples have been living together with the native population for ages. For communities with a predominant or purely Russian population, ethnically and/or religiously distant peoples, usually geographically distant also, qualify as "outsiders."

The third category consists of specific groups of "outsiders" that appear in the community for reasons other than economic or religious: Orthodox monks, missionaries of other faiths, and former prisoners. Finally, the fourth category includes random people, who are very few in isolated societies. This last category of "outsiders" is "flow-through people," who flow through the central settlement of the local community in their continuous movement across the country. Generally, "outsiders" of the last two categories stay for a couple of years, but never longer than five–seven years. Then, not finding their place in the community, they leaving. In contrast to these two and the first category—regular but seasonal inhabitants,—"outsiders" of the second category are the most persistent group in isolated societies. I would like to repeat that in isolated communities all four categories of "outsiders" are very few; certain categories, like second homers or "flow-through" people, may not be available at all. Of course, it is the few and most remote communities, such as Udora (Komi), Gunib (Dagestan), Anabar and Tompo (Yakutia), Varnek (Vaygach Island, Nenetsk Autonomous District), Krasnoshchelye (Murman), and Erzhey-Sizim (Tuva), that give the perfect example of having next to no strangers.

I have focused in detail on the "us/them" structure in isolated communities, because there it appears in its purest form, not distorted by the strong migratory pressure experienced by their antipode—the "turbulent" community, where due to a strong migration flow this structure is in a state of turbulent mixing. We shall now proceed to consider the structure of such "turbulent" communities, along with largely similar "ordinary-type" communities (an intermediate type), differing only by the degree to which "us" is diluted by "them."

9.5 "Us" and "Them" in "Turbulent" and "Ordinary" Communities

The observed 101 local societies, which I classified as "turbulent" or "ordinary" depending on the degree of their spatial isolation, differ from isolated communities both in their residential structure and in the ethnic composition of the population. The centers of these communities are mostly towns that have long been administrative centers for the rural district (in imperial times they used to be *uyezd* [district] towns). Such are 30 of the 35 "turbulent" and 59 of the 66 "ordinary" communities. This is a statistical contrast to the above isolated communities, where the community in the administrative center and its rural district is almost homogeneous.

The same is true of ethnic differences. Russian population entirely prevails in both "turbulent" and "ordinary" communities. Other ethnic groups are concentrated in the rural district. In my records, only eleven of these local communities have a predominant non-Russian population, constituting just one-tenth of the total, which is also statistically significant lower than the share of non-Russian residents in isolated communities (of whom there less than a third). In another seven societies, the share of non-Russian residents reaches 10–30 percent, almost all of them living in the rural area.

9.5.1 The Composition and Structure of "Us"

The principal feature in the structure of "us" in ancient and old "turbulent" communities is that their inhabitants have been repeatedly replaced over centuries by deported populations from other territories,[11] or new numerous groups of migrants moved into the area (as, for example, after the Time of Troubles, in the 1630s, when several thousand Karelian peasants were resettled to the Kashin district from the regions ceded to Sweden under the Treaty of Stolbovo (Kislovsky, 2006)). Since this process was repeated, large scale and frequent, people do not recall the history of

[11] For Moscow, for example, one of the earliest known replacements was when in 1478, Prince Ivan III mutually replaced Novgorodians and Muscovites following the seizure and looting of Veliky Novgorod. One generation later, in 1510, his son Vasily III replaced Pskov residents by Muscovites. The two latest large-scale inflows happened in the twentieth century. Shortly after 1931, seasonal workers from rural areas (peasant otkhodniks) of the nearest provinces moved to the city taking the place of many evicted native Muscovites. Later, in 1960–1980, the arrival of "quota workers" ("*limitchiks*") significantly increased the population of the capital. Thus, over 500 years, Moscow has renewed its population at least a dozen times—virtually every two-three generations.

even recent migrations of their neighbors, or of their own clans. Over an extended historical period of time, this creates a "layered" structure of the community. As a result, the composition of "us" becomes more homogeneous, but relationships of affinity—more fragmented. In contrast to most isolated communities, there are hardly any distinct aggregates (clearly distinguishable components) in the composition of the population. On the surface, the community appears homogeneous, but the people are not bound by close kinship or even neighborly relations, as in isolated societies. Kin groups (clans) are also much less common due to the very high percentage of residents, who came from the most remote places to settle here at different times. In this regard, "turbulent" communities are close to societies of major cities. They are not communities, but societies. Fragmented relationships and a degradation of ties between "us" are typical of most communities of the "turbulent" type. Among them, it is easier to single out those, where the "us" structure is somewhat closer to that of the isolated societies. They are: Sebezh (Pskov), Gavrilov-Yam (Yaroslavl), Zlynka (Bryansk), Nerchinsk (Trans-Baikal Territory), Semyonov (Nizhny Novgorod)—a total of seven out of twenty ancient and old "turbulent" societies.

Fragmentation of relationships and degradation of ties is already less typical of "ordinary" communities. They occupy a distinctly intermediate position between "turbulent" and isolated communities, with most of them leaning toward the latter type. Of the ancient communities such are Belozersk and Kirillov, Nikolsk and Totma (Vologda), Dorogobuzh (Smolensk), Kashin and Staritsa (Tver), Makaryev and Nerekhta (Kostroma), and Yuriev-Polsky (Vladimir). Old communities with a structure resembling that of isolated ones include Ardatov (Mordovia), Ardon, Digora and Chikola (North Ossetia), Velizh and Demidov-Porechye (Smolensk), Guryevsk (Kuzbass), Dmitrovsk Orlovsky (Oryol), Yeniseysk (Krasnoyarsk), Zmeinogorsk and Kamen-na-Obi (Altai), Lyubim and Poshekhonye (Yaroslavl), Novokhopyorsk (Voronezh), Ochyor and Osa (Perm), Uryupinsk (Volgograd), Slobodskoy (Kirov), Surazh (Bryansk), and Sysola (Komi). Of the young societies, such are Bolgar (Tatarstan), Kavalerovo (Primorye), Maslyanino (Novosibirsk), Neya (Kostroma), and Ust-Kan (Altai).

By contrast, "ordinary" communities resembling "turbulent" ones by the structure of "us" are in the minority: such are ancient Veliky Ustyug (Vologda), Galich (Kostroma), Kasimov (Ryazan), Kineshma (Ivanovo), Kozelsk (Kaluga), Suzdal (Vladimir), and Tutayev-Romanov and Uglich (Yaroslavl). Of the old communities these are Buy (Kostroma), Mayma (Altai), Gus-Khrustalny (Vladimir), Krasnoufimsk (Ekaterinburg), Labinsk (Stavropol), and Podporozhye (Prionezhye). Such are also the young communities of Aldan (Yakutia), Gusinoozersk (Buryatia), and Kachkanar (Ekaterinburg). Thus, more than half (thirty-eight) of the "ordinary" communities lean toward isolated societies, whereas only a quarter (eighteen)—toward the "turbulent" ones.

It is also noteworthy that due to the considerable degradation of the rural district and overpopulation of the administrative center, many of these communities experience weakening relationships of affinity in the villages. In contrast to isolated societies, "outsiders" are numerous in the villages of all "turbulent" and some "ordinary" communities; in some places they even prevail. In many villages, kin and neighborly relations have been destroyed. Many rural settlements here are in decay (depopulated), as their inhabitants moved to the district center, closer to the main roads. For this reason, administrative centers in some communities accumulate 70–80 percent or more of the total population. It is also natural that these two types of communities are more numerous than the isolated ones (administrative centers have an average of five times as many residents, respectively).

In these two types of spatial isolation, there are differences between ancient and old communities on the one hand, and young ones on the other. Young communities recall better the origin of individual kin and occupational groups, which founded it—quite recently, in certain cases even witnessed by the current inhabitants. Please note that almost all of such observed young communities (ten of them) are composed of two categories of residents: (1) those who came from very remote places and (2) those who resettled from the surrounding villages. The former often consist of different occupational and ethnic groups, whereas the latter themselves initially developed from groups of distant migrants, who moved to the administrative center a couple of generations later. This is one of the main reasons for the existence of many decaying (and even depopulated) villages in the immediate vicinity of the district center. As a further consequence, summer residents from regional centers and capitals settle in such villages, thus increasing the share of "outsiders," especially in "turbulent" communities.

The first of the above methods of shaping the "us/them" structure is clearly demonstrated by young "turbulent" and coercive developed local societies, for example, Birobidzhan and vicinity, Leninskoye, Amurzet, and Obluchye—the Jewish Autonomous Region. The various ethnic and socio-occupational groups, which currently live there together, have very different backgrounds. First of all, these are descendants of Old Believers from the Urals, Trans-Volga region, and Pomorye, who from the seventeenth century founded unauthorized scattered settlements in mountainous taiga valleys. The next to appear were descendants of the Cossacks, settled by state decree on the left bank of the Amur river. Three–four generations later, they were joined by two waves of Jewish settlers—in the 1920s–1930s and after 1947—who came from western areas of the Russian Federation, Belarus, Ukraine, and partly Poland. In the 1970s–1990s, these three ethno-national and religiously different groups were supplemented by numerous settlers from central Russia, the Urals, and Siberia. The newcomers were mostly Russian, but also included quite a few Ukrainians, Belarusians, Udmurts, Mari, Mordovians, Tatars, and Buryats. The fifth group consists of numerous military personnel, who stayed after demobilization, especially after the 1990s. The sixth group comprises large diasporas of Tajiks, Azerbaijanis, Armenians, and Chechens that appeared in the post-Soviet years. There are many Muslims among them. All this largely heterogeneous conglomerate constitutes a young "turbulent" and coercive developed type communities, where it is almost impossible to distinguish between "us" and "them," since all remember their roots but at the same time form a community and feel that they belong (Plusnin, 2018a).

The young "turbulent" coercive developed communities of Manturovo and Sharya (Kostroma) and Zuyevka (Kirov) provide a different example. Their administrative centers developed at the turn of the nineteenth to twentieth centuries as railway stations on the Trans-Siberian Railway under construction. Nearly all their current inhabitants are descendants of local villagers. In this regard, the population is homogeneous, since in imperial and earlier times peasants in these areas were not mobile at all. The Soviet period saw an active centripetal inflow of local inhabitants to their administrative centers. However, the population was supplemented by very diverse new groups owing to active economic migration—due to the opening of defense enterprises in the area, and because of administrative and political reasons—due to the establishment of corrective laborcamps. Former enterprise employees and ex-prisoners of several "*convoys*" remained here for permanent residence, and their numerous descendants constitute a considerable part of "us" in local societies. Thus, "us" in these three local communities consist of two principal components: (1) the local peasant one and (2) the incoming, composed of "recruited" workers and specialists, and the descendants of former "*convicts.*" Despite the difficulties of mutual adjustment, they all consider themselves to be "us." At the same time, the process of incorporating and adapting "them" is significantly facilitated in such societies.

The "us" structure in ancient and old "turbulent" and "ordinary" communities is more complex than in the young ones. Besides the same two categories of residents currently forming this structure in all three age groups of communities—descendants of migrants from distant areas and inhabitants of the local rural district—here we see a predominantly "layered" structure, which has developed over many generations (as in Soligalich). Over time, consistently appearing new large socio-occupational and ethnic or religious groups "grow" into the body of the community and take root. The earlier, respectively, more ancient, layers dissolve, and all memory of them disappears. In a significant part of such communities the initial ethnic substrate is either completely unknown, or the only traces can be found in local history museums. The memory of living people retains knowledge of social events no more than a century old. In many "turbulent" communities it is even more superficial: people often know nothing about local events that occurred ten to thirty years prior to their birth.

Typical and quite striking examples of "turbulent" natural developed communities include Kandalaksha (Murmansk) among the ancient and Taman (Krasnodar) among the old ones. In nearly all cases, the majority of the population in such communities are descendants of migrants in the first generation, and the migratory pressure is extreme, annually reaching ten percent and more immigrations and emigrations.

Kandalaksha has always been a "transit lane" to Kola and Murman, standing on almost the only water-land way, flanked by the White Sea coast in the east and impassable swamps in the west. It is well known since the twelfth century, although chronicles first mention it in the middle of the fifteenth century. By the sixteenth century, Kandalaksha was already a significant town. Initially, these were the territories of nomadic Lapps (Sami), and the coastal area was inhabited by

Novgorodians. Gradually, the Pomor sub-ethnic group—a mixture of Lapp, Karelian-Finnish, and Russian components—emerged in the White Sea area. Except for native Lapps (Sami), all the principal inhabitants of these places have always been migrants since ancient times. The Pomors lived in close contact with the Lapps. They had no conflicts because of significant differences in livelihood patterns (the Lapps were reindeer herders and hunters, whereas the Pomors were fishermen and farmers). The joint existence of two peoples produced a friendly and conflict-free local society. The community had—and still has—a very small rural district, with Kandalaksha being the dominant center. The principal life of the community was concentrated in the town and in three–four Pomor villages located on both coasts of the Kandalaksha Gulf at a distance of up to 30 km. Lapp nomads set their camps in the sub-tundra zone away from the sea. Throughout its existence, the local community experienced three–four major disturbances: Oprichnina and the Swedish aggression at the end of the sixteenth century; the Time of Troubles at the beginning of the following century; the British intervention in 1855; and the front-line position during World War II. At the end of the nineteenth century, there was a forced inflow of Komi peasants from the eastern districts and Karelians from the southern districts of the Arkhangelsk province. Some of them soon assimilated and became part of the local society. The biggest changes occurred in the twentieth century due to the construction of the Murmansk Railway and the city of Murmansk. During the Soviet period, from the 1920s to the 1970s–1980s, the population increased significantly—from 5000 to almost 60,000 people. Migrants from central—mainly non-black soil—regions of European Russia (Twer, Vologda, Kostroma) prevailed among the new inhabitants. The current residents are descendants, in the third–fourth generations, of those migrants. The indigenous inhabitants—the Pomors and Lapps (Sami)—now constitute a minor share of the population and live mainly in the rural district of Kandalaksha. Presently, there are almost no new migrants. On the contrary, since the mid-1990s, there has been a rapid outflow of population, which halved over twenty years. In this respect, ancient Kandalaksha is populated almost exclusively by the descendants of recent migrants and in fact represents a young community in terms of community standards, family and neighborly relations between people. Migratory pressure is high: over the past 20–25 years, the population has been annually declining by two–three percent, with the number of arrivals and departures exceeding 1500 people each; i.e., the annual outflow and inflow are six and five percent, respectively (*Murmansk Region in Figures*, 2019, pp. 28–30).

Old Taman is ancient Greek Hermonassa and medieval Russian Tmutorakan, Polovtsian Matarkha, and Genoese Matrega, and finally, Turkish Taman. But the history of Taman's local community begins only in the late eighteenth century, when the Black Sea Cossacks, in fact, re-founded the settlement. The ethnic polyphony, characteristic of the peninsula for two millennia, gradually faded away. Currently, Taman and two neighboring settlements Volna and Tamansky are home to just over twelve thousand people, of whom 77 percent are Russians and 15 percent—Tatars, including Crimean ones. Most inhabitants are descendants of the Cossacks. Until the mid-2000s, the local community did not experience much migratory pressure. However, since 2009, a major international cargo seaport is being built in the south of the Taman Peninsula to transship grain, coal, natural gas, oil and petroleum products iron ore and steel, mineral fertilizers, and timber. And in 2016, the construction of the Crimean Bridge with a motorway and railway was launched. All this resulted in a rapid development of transport infrastructure and the arrival of numerous rotation workers in Taman. In the late 2010s, there were nearly twenty thousand of them—twice the number of local residents. In addition, the tourist flow through Taman to Crimea increased tenfold, daily reaching ten thousand people—the entire population of Taman. The tourists, of course, make a stop in Taman and greatly contribute to the composition and movement of the local society. In fact, the total number of people—rotation workers and tourists—daily "flowing" through the local community is two per one local resident. This launched tremendous upheavals in the society, which had to adapt to such disastrous migratory pressure in just a few years. The community has undergone significant structural transformations, which, I expect, will destroy it in the coming years (Plusnin, 2018b).

Examples of "ordinary" communities include ancient Nikolsk in the Vologda Region and old Digora in North Ossetia. Both are located on major motorways, but away from railroads, although in former times a narrow-gauge track (the remains are still in place) used to cross Nikolsky district, and a local railroad (scrapped for metal by residents) used to pass through the Digorsky district. A local road passes through Digora linking it with the Transkam and Kavkaz (Georgian Military Road) motorways, which connect Ossetia with the Transcaucasian republics. Nikolsk is located at the crossroads of three routes: west to Vologda, north to Veliky Ustyug, and south to the central regions of Russia—Nizhny Novgorod, Kostroma, and Moscow.

Ancient Nikolsk is an old settlement and trading post that emerged on the watershed of an important trade route connecting the rivers Volga, Vetluga, and Vokhma with Yug and Northern Dvina. By the origin of its residents, this is a purely Russian town and also Russian rural district. The local community has Novgorod and Pomor roots—the ancestors of the present inhabitants came from the rivers Sukhona and Northern Dvina a long time ago, back in the fourteenth to fifteenth centuries, and grew into the *Komi-Cheremis* soil, now long forgotten (*Around Nikolsk*, 2011). During Catherine's provincial reform, Nikolsk became a district (uyezd) town and controlled a considerable area, now partly located in the Vologda and partly in the Kostroma regions. The lack of trunk roads, along with the fact that there have never been any large enterprises here, has contributed to long-term social stability with minimal migration movement. The population increased primarily due to internal growth. Currently it amounts to twenty-five thousand people, of whom the majority (about sixteen thousand) live—and have always lived—in the rural area. This gives reason to assume that with the remote (in the east and west) and border (in the north and south of the district) settlements, the local Nikolsk community consists of about six-eight thousand families. The rural district is closely linked with the town, with no distinction being made between nearby and remote villages. Many townspeople have numerous relatives in the villages and readily move there themselves, building new homes for their families away from the town center. Good roads and dense cluster development of the area, typical of the Russian North, allow people to spread out and live as they please. By far not all provincial towns enable such a lifestyle. It is driven by the integrity and solidarity of the local community throughout the entire district. The villagers settle in town as easily as the townsfolk in the rural area. There is no spatial segregation in this society, but its solidarity is great ("*. . . there are no tourists, there are no migrants, we live here in our own little world*"). Indeed, tourists rarely appear here; those who do pass by, are usually on their way to Totma or Veliky Ustyug. And the migration rate in the district is extremely low—it is estimated at under 0.1 percent per year. Even "outsiders" here mostly seem to belong. These are summer residents from Murmansk, "*all our own folk, coming back to their roots,*" who upon retirement settle mainly in the rural area rather than in town. Besides these "almost local" summer residents, I could locate only two tiny groups of real "outsiders" in Nikolsk: a small group of a dozen representatives of the Jehovah's Witnesses sect and an equally small group of about two dozen seasonal migrant workers from Tajikistan and Uzbekistan. They appeared relatively recently and are hardly noticeable, but the population is extremely wary of both groups. Even given chance visitors, the percentage of "outsiders" here is under half percent. Thus, the local community of Nikolsk is a clear case of a homogeneous and undifferentiated structure: there are no outsiders, everyone is an insider, descending from Pomors and Novgorodians with a history going back half a thousand years. Moreover, the "insiders" did not unite or evolve from disparate parts; they developed as a whole in a space that for centuries was not affected by any political perturbations or economic innovations.

The Digora community in North Ossetia has an "us" structure quite similar to that of Nikolsk. The history of the Digora local community is well known (Kuchiev, 1992). The population consists of two diverse parts: Russians and Ossetians. The Russian authorities bought vacant Kabardian lands in the foothill valley of the Terek river and settled Ukrainian Cossacks from the Poltava and Kiev provinces on them after suppressing the Polish uprising in 1832–34. The Cossacks founded the still existing Nikolaevskaya, Arkhonskaya, and Zmeyskaya villages. In 1852, the Volno-Khristianovskaya village was founded for Digor Ossetians, who were resettled from the gorges to the "*plain*," to fertile lands. Due to favorable living conditions, the initial population of 1300 people rapidly increased four-fold over half a century, reaching by 1900 already 5757 residents. Over the following 120 years, the Ossetian population showed another three-fold increase, whereas the number of Russians grew insignificantly. Currently, Ossetians constitute 88 percent of the 18 thousand inhabitants, and Russian Cossacks—only eight percent (about 1500 people). Meanwhile, the representatives of both peoples always maintained friendly and kin relations (based on "*kunachestvo*"—consecrated friendship). In the course of two centuries, many families intermarried and became related. Children were sent to each other's families to learn the Russian language and Ossetian traditions. Ossetians and the Cossacks still intermarry. The rapid and conflict-free development of a single community from heterogeneous parts seems to be due to the fact that the entire Caucasian environment of Russians and Ossetians is Muslim; the Kabardian and Ingush communities are largely hostile to Ossetians, thus contributing to their isolation. Therefore, the composition of "us" in the Digora local community (as well as in the neighboring Irafsky—Chikola—and in Ardon and Alagir, all populated by Digor Ossetians) formed very quickly and consists of two ethnic groups—Russians and Ossetians—the representatives of which have become interrelated, with many having mixed families. Kin and neighborly ties are widespread and strong; they underlie the whole system of private relations and local statuses. There are no other "locals" here, except for the descendants of Cossacks and Ossetians, who have maintained their ancestral homes in the mountain villages of the North Caucasus (where they are nowadays gradually resettling due to new favorable living conditions). Representatives of all other ethnic groups are definitely "them," especially Ingush, Chechens, and Kabardians (religion does not matter, since some Digor Ossetians are Muslims). There are also distant "outsiders" represented by Koreans, Vietnamese, Meskhetian Turks, Armenians, Azerbaijanis, and Georgians living here as seasonal workers.

9.5.2 The Composition and Structure of "Them"

"Outsiders" in "turbulent" and "ordinary" communities are of the same categories as in isolated societies. However, here their share in the population is substantially higher, not only in towns but also in the rural district. In the villages, the number of permanently residing "outsiders" may even exceed that of local "insiders," especially if they are urban second homers. The share of "flow-through" people—migrants staying here only a short while—is also relatively high (they are few or non-existent in isolated societies). Local "insiders" rarely classify others as "outsiders" based on ethnic grounds; even religious differences are not always a sign of segregation. Since family ties are rather weak, work relations, on which the system of mutual social support is largely built, gain importance. Even groups that differ greatly in patterns of everyday behavior, as well as in etiquette and ritual forms of behavior (such as various "environmentalists," widespread "*Anastasians,*" or missionaries of non-traditional religions and sects) can assimilate quite quickly and become "us" in a dozen or two years.

There are several modifications to a generalized socio-demographic portrait of an "outsider," a migrant intending to settle permanently, who acquired housing, became a neighbor, but is not yet accepted as "one of us." The first category includes single people, adults, not youngsters, mostly not settled in life, without a household, and with a poor or dilapidated dwelling (apartment or more often a house with a garden) purchased on occasion. These are mostly single unskilled men, long divorced, not bound by children, often after serving a prison term, who failed to start a family in the new place as well. Occasionally, these are also single 30-40-50-year-old women, almost always residents of large cities, escaping from family troubles and hoping to change their life. They are also unskilled. Almost all of them are come-and-go people. Despite the acquired housing, after another unsuccessful attempt to take root, failing to find common language at work and in everyday life, rejected by their colleagues and neighbors, they disappear from the town or village forever.

The second category are families with children, usually two–three or more children, who seek provincial life most often for ideological reasons (pure nature, simple life and interpersonal relations, ideals of "living from the land," etc.). They prefer the rural district as often as the town. In the past thirty years, starting from the 1990s, the number of such urban families has increased significantly; in some villages, such new settlers, "outsiders," are in the majority. They have replaced all the local residents having bought their houses. Some of these families live all year round and engage in farming. Besides a vegetable garden and potato field, they keep livestock and poultry. Other urban dwellers remain in the status of permanent vacationers—they live seasonally, but often the whole summer and part of the autumn and winter rather than only during the holidays. A feature of such urban families with children, including those who live seasonally, is the need for earnings, so they start looking for sources of income locally, not only in private small businesses, but also in the public sector (where competition is very high, with locals holding all publicly funded jobs due to widespread cronyism, "*blat*"). And since they have children, often three or more, they need schools, kindergartens, and clinics. These two factors—the need for sources of income and availability of social institutions—as well as the need for daily assistance from neighbors, force this category of "outsiders" to integrate actively into local life, adapt, absorb the principles and rules of behavior—to become "us" as soon as possible. Successfully integrating families quickly become "insiders"; the rest are forced to leave even after spending from seven–ten years in the local community.

The third category includes urban second homers past childbearing age; generally, these are retired couples who have decided to live in the village or township. In addition to pensions, they receive rental income from leasing their apartment (sometimes even two or three apartments) in the city. Given the quite cheap life in the village, the total income from pensions and lease significantly exceeds the cash earnings of local villagers. By choosing this life strategy, retired urban dwellers greatly enhance the quality of life, even as compared to what they had in the city. They do not have to engage in subsidiary farming; they have neither livestock, nor potato fields, at times even no vegetable garden; some do not even make any winter stocks of mushrooms, berries, nuts, and other forest products, absolutely indispensable in the rural area, as they can buy everything on the spot. Therefore, for local villagers such urban dwellers are moneybags and outsiders without limitations—"them" forever.

However, this group of retired urban dwellers includes people who are not complete strangers. These are former local residents, who returned home or came to live with grown-up children already in advanced age. Such groups of returning elderly people are pervasive. This is due to the well-known facts of our socio-economic history. Before and after World War II, till the late 1980s, there was widespread practice in the Soviet Union to recruit provincials, mainly from non-black soil regions, to work far away from home. Work destinations included "Great Construction Sites of the Century," such as the Baikal-Amur Railway; oil, gas, and mining enterprises in the "North" (Extreme North, Siberia, and the Far East); and plants and factories in Moscow that had quotas for non-resident industrial personnel (such workers were called "*limitchiks*"). As a result, over fifty years, many non-black soil regions experienced a several-fold decrease of population (in Kostroma Region, for example, the decrease was five-fold over the period from the 1960s to the 2010s). Since the 1990s, retired former residents have started slowly but steadily coming back. Most return to their homeland, especially since many still have their parents' houses there. Being former "us," these retirees, returning en masse, are accepted by the local community, and re-integrate very quickly. Bacause they come back to numerous relatives and childhood friends. But for a short while, they remain "outsiders" for the local society, at least until they recall the forgotten stereotypes of behavior and their native dialect.

9.6 Summary. "Agglomerated" and/or "Layered" Structure of the "Us-Them" in Different Types of Communities

The composition of "us" in isolated communities (both natural and coercive developed) has two typical common features: an agglomerated and "layered" structure. Actually, the same applies to the other—non-isolated—types of societies, but there these features manifest themselves differently than in isolated societies. An agglomerated structure, when the population is heterogeneous by origin, composed of different clans and ethnic groups, is typical of young communities. A layered structure, composed of earlier and later groups of people differing by origin, is identified in old and ancient societies. Agglomerates signify that heterogeneous groups of people settled in the area almost simultaneously. Therefore, agglomeration can be recorded only in modern young societies; in old and ancient societies, the process of mutual assimilation has long been completed. On the other hand, young communities have no traces of "layers," which can be registered only in old/ancient ones. In isolated societies, "affinity" is based on family and ethnic ties; the ancient ethnic substrate has been preserved there, albeit implicitly.

In the two other—non-isolated—types of local societies, the composition and structure of "us" is predominantly "layered" rather than agglomerated. The individual agglomerate components have long merged, leveled out, and dissolved in each other. Due to the destruction of family ties, the structure of "us" is fragmented and homogeneous: there are no large kin groups in the local society, just as there are few isolated ethnic groups, and if they do exist, they mutually merge (members of different ethnic groups have become interrelated). Consequently, the share of other ethnic groups is small, with Russians prevailing everywhere, especially in "turbulent" communities, where migratory pressure is high, thus over time promoting the adaptation and assimilation of non-Russian migrants. In such communities, especially in coercive-types, the rural area is underpopulated, and the administrative center is excessively overpopulated, concentrating up to eighty percent of all inhabitants. Rural settlements degrade; there are many *decaying* (depopulated) villages. In addition, kin and neighborly relations are destroyed and degraded not only in the administrative center, but also in the rural district.

The composition and structure of "them" in "turbulent" and "ordinary" communities differs from those in isolated communities by a considerably higher number and a significant share of "flow-through" people. "Outsiders" prevail not only in the administrative center of the local society, but in the villages as well, which is also different. There is not much ethnic or religious filtering, so both the town and the rural district attract many migrants of different ethnicities, various sectarians, and people with differing worldviews (mentality). A significant reverse flow of urban residents to the village, which has picked up in the past twenty-five years, sharply increased the share of urban dwellers in many provincial societies. Some of them stay on a seasonal basis, others reside permanently. Otherwise, the composition of "them" in "turbulent" and "ordinary" communities is similar to that in isolated societies. It includes individual families and groups of people that differ from the local residents in social, occupational, ethnic, and religious/ideological terms.

References

About the Vohma lands of the late 19th century. Materials of the Ethnographic Bureau of V.N. Tenisheva. (2015). Kostroma: B.I. *О Вохомских землях конца XIX века. Материалы Этнографического бюро В.Н. Тенишева*. (2015). Кострома: Б.И.

Andryushin, E. A. (2012). *From the history of the labor legislation of the USSR and the policy of the Soviet government in the field of labor resources*. New Chronograph. Андрюшин Е.А. (2012). *Из истории трудового законодательства СССР и политики советского правительства в области трудовых ресурсов*. М.: Новый Хронограф.

Balanovskaja, E. V. et al. (2005). «Family's portrets» of fife Russian provinces. *Medicinskaja genetika, 1*, 2–10. Балановская Е.В., Соловьёва Д.С., Балановский О.П., Чурносов М.И., Сорокина И.Н., Евсеева И.В., Аболмасов Н.Н., Почешхова Э.А., Серёгин Ю.А., Пшеничнов А.С. (2005). «Фамильные портреты» пяти русских регионов. *Медицинская генетика*, 1, 2–10.

Balanovskaja, E. V., et al. (2011). Gene pool of Russian North: Slavs? Finns? Indo-Iranians? *Vestnik Moskoskogo universiteta. Seria XXIII. Antropologiya, 3*, 27–58. Балановская Е.В., Пежемский Д.В., Романов А.Г., Баранова Е.Е., Ромашкина М.В., Агджоян А.Т., Балаганский А.Г., Евсеева И.В., Виллемс Р., Балановский О.П. (2011). Генофонд Русского Севера: Славяне? Финны? Палеоевропейцы? *Вестник Московского университета. Серия XXIII посвящается 300-летию М.В. Ломоносова. Антропология*, 3, 27–58.

Barsukova, S. Y. (2003). Networking mutual aid of Russian households: Theory and practice of the economy of the gift. *World of Russia, 2*, 81–122. Барсукова С.Ю. (2003). Сетевая взаимопомощь российских домохозяйств: теория и практика экономики дара. *Мир России*, 2, 81–122.

Barsukova, S. Y. (2004). *Informal economy: Economic and sociological analysis*. Publishing House of the State University - Higher School of Economics. Барсукова С.Ю. (2004). *Неформальная экономика: экономико-социологический анализ*. М.: Издательский дом ГУ-ВШЭ.

Bayburin, A. K., & Toporkov, A. L. (1990). *At the source of etiquette. Ethnographical essays*. Nauka. Байбурин А.К., Топорков А.Л. (1990). *У истоков этикета. Этнографические очерки*. Л.: Наука.

Belkov, P. L. (2013). *Australian kinship systems. Foundations of typology and elementary transformations*. Nauka. Белков П.Л. (2013). *Австралийские системы родства. Основы типологии и элементарные преобразования*. СПб.: Наука.

Benveniste, E. (1974). *Problemes de linguistique generale*. Gallimard. Russian edition: *Бенвенист* Э. (1974). Общая лингвистика, М.: Прогресс.

Benveniste, E. (1995). Le *Vocabulaire des Institutions Indo-Europeennes*. Les Éditions de Minuit. Russian edition: Бенвенист Э. (1995). *Словарь индоевропейских социальных терминов*. М.: Прогресс-Универс.

Cavalli-Sforza, L. L., & Bodmcr, W. F. (1999). *The genetics of human populations*. Dover.

Chagin, G. N. (2004). *The cities of Greath Perm. Cherdyn and Solikamsk*. "Knizhny mir". Чагин Г.Н. (2004). *Города Перми Великой. Чердынь и Соликамск*. Пермь: «Книжный мир».

Cherdyn and Ural in Russian Historical and Cultural Heritage. (1999). Perm: B.I. *Чердынь и* Урал в историческом и культурном наследии России (1999). Пермь: Б.и.

Cochran, G., & Harpending, H. C. (2006). Natural history of Ashkenazi intelligence. *Journal of Biosocial Science, 38*, 659–693.

Collier, P. (2013). *Exodus. How migration is changing our World*. Oxford University Press. Russian edition: Коллиер П. (2016). *Исход. Как миграция изменяет наш мир*. М.: Институт Гайдара.

Crow, J. F. (1989). The estimation of inbreeding from isonimy. *Human Biology, 61*(5/6), 935–948.

Crow, J. F., & Mange, A. P. (1965). Measurement of inbreeding from the frequency or marriages between person of the same surname. *Eugen Quart, 12*(4), 199–203.

Dziebel, G. V. (2007). *The genius of kinship. The phenomenon of human kinship and the global diversity of kinship terminologies*. Cambria Press.

Eibl-Eibesfeldt, I., & Salter, F. K. (Eds.). (1998). *Ethnic conflict and indoctrination. Altruism and identity in evolutionary perspective*. Oxford Berghahn Books.

Elchinova, G. I., Kadoshnikova, M. Y., Mamedova, R. A., Bukina, A. M., Petrova, N. V., & Startseva, E. A. (1991). About the frequency criteria for the family name selection in the research of population genetic structure. *Genetics, 27*(2), 358–360. Ельчинова Г.И., Кадошникова М.Ю., Мамедова Р.А., Букина А.М., Петрова Н.В., Старцева Е.А. (1991). *О частотном критерии выбора фамилий для изучения генетической структуры популяций//Генетика*, 27(2), 358–360.

Elchinova, G. I., Kravchuk, O. I., Startseva, E. A., et al. (1996). Meadow Mari: genes, surnames and migrations. *Genetics, 32*(10), 1421–1422. Ельчинова Г.И., Кравчук О.И., Старцева Е.А. и др. (1996). Луговые марийцы: гены, фамилии и миграции. *Генетика*, 32(10), 1421–1422.

Figurovsky, N. A. (2010). *Essays on the medieval history of the city of Soligalich*. Avantitul. Фигуровский Н. А. (2010). *Очерки средневековой истории города Солигалича*. Кострома: Авантитул.

Gerasimov, S. S. (2006). *From our olden times*. B.i. Герасимов С.С. (2006). *Из нашей старины*. Кострома: Б.и.

Gerasimov, S. S. (2015). *World War I and Vokhma lands. Historical and local history collection*. B.i. Герасимов С.С. (2015). *Первая мировая война и вохомские земли. Историко-краеведческий сборник*. Кострома: Б.и.

Ginter, E. K., Mamedova, R. A., Elchinova, G. I., & Brusinceva, O. V. (1994). Genetic structure of Kirov region population and the territorial distribution of autosomal-recessive diseases specific. *Genetics, 30*(1), 107–111. Гинтер Е.К., Мамедова Р.А., Ельчинова Г.И., Брусинцева О.В. (1994). Генетическая структура популяций и особенности территориального распределения аутосомно-рецессивных заболеваний в Кировской области. *Генетика*, 30(1), 107–111.

Glazychev, V. L. (2003). *Deep Russia: 2000-2002*. Novoe Izdatelstvo. Глазычев В.Л. (2003). *Глубинная Россия: 2000-2002*. М.: Новое издательство.

Glazychev, V. L. (2011). *City without limes*. Publishing House «Territoria Buduschego». Глазычев В.Л. (2011). *Город без границ*. М.: Издательский дом «Территория будущего».

Goldin, I., Cameron, G., & Balarajan, M. (2011). *Exceptional people: How migration shaped our world and will define our future*. Princeton University Press.

Graburn, N. H. H. (1971). *Readings in kinship and social structure*. Harper & Row.

Grettla. (1965). *Grettir's Saga or the Saga of Grettir the strong: The Saga of Grettir the strong*. Dent.

Harpending, H. C. (1974). Genetic structure of small populations. *Annual Review of Anthropology, 3*, 229–243. https://doi.org/10.1146/annurev.an.03.100174.001305

Hatton, T. J., & Williamson, J. G. (2008). *Global migration and the world economy: Two centuries of policy and performance*. MIT Press.

Kamensky, A. B. (2007). *Everydays life of Russian citizens Everymen. Historical jokes of XVIII centure' provincial life*. RGGU. Каменский А.Б. (2007). *Повседневность русских городских обывателей: Исторические анекдоты из провинциальной жизни XVIII века*. М.: Российский государственный гуманитарный университет.

Kislovsky, S. V. (2006). *Kashin Territory*. B.I. Кисловский С.В. (2006). *Кашинский край*. Калязин: Б.и.

Klimova, S. G. (2002a). The criteria for determining the "us" and "them" groups. *Sotsiologicheskie Issledovaniia, 6*, 83–92. Климова С. Г. (2002a). Критерии определения групп «мы» и «они». *Социологические исследования*, 6, 83–92.

Klimova, S. G. (2002b). Breaking social identities, or "we" and "they" yesterday and today. *Otechestvennye Zapiski, 3*, 106–122. Климова С. Г. (2002b). Ломка социальных идентичностей, или «Мы» и «Они» вчера и сегодня. *Отечественные записки*, 3, 106–122.

Kozlov, A. I., Lisitsyn, D. V., & Kozlova, M. A. (2008). *Kola Sami in a changing world*. Institute of Heritage, IL "ArktAn-S". Козлов А.И., Лисицын Д.В., Козлова М.А. (2008). *Кольские саамы в меняющемся мире*. М.: Институт Наследия, ИЛ «АрктАн-С».

Kucher, A. N., Tadinova, V. N., Maksimova, N. R., & Sanchat, N. O. (2002). Population structure of the indigenous and newcomer population of Siberia: An isonymous approach. In Puzyrev, V. P. (Ed.), *Human genetics and pathology*, Vol. 6. (pp. 87–94). Tomsk State University Publishing House. Кучер А.Н., Тадинова В.Н., Максимова Н.Р., & Санчат Н.О. (2002). Популяционная структура коренного и пришлого населения Сибири: изонимный подход. В кн.: В.П. Пузырев (Ред.), *Генетика человека и патология*, Вып. 6. (pp. 87–94). Томск: Издательство Томского государственного университета.

Kucher, A. N., Danilova, A. L., Koneva, L. A., & Nogovitsina, A. N. (2010). Marriage structure of Yakut population: Ethnic composition and isonimy inbreeding. *Genetika, 46*(3), 408–416. Кучер А.Н., Данилова А.Л., Конева Л.А., Ноговицина А.Н. (2010). Брачная структура якутской популяции: этнический состав и инбридинг на основе изонимии. *Генетика*, 46(3), 408–416.

Kuchiev, V. D. (ed.), (1992). *History of Digora town*. Ir. Кучиев В.Д. (ред.), (1992). *История города Дигоры*. Владикавказ: Ир.

Lappo, G. M. (2012). *Cities of Russia. Geographer's view*. New chronograph. Лаппо Г.М. (2012). *Города России. Взгляд географа*. М.: Новый хронограф.

Lavryashina, M. B., Ulyanova, M. V., & Balanovskaya, E. V. (2009). Family composition dynamics as an indicator of changes in the population structure of the indigenous peoples of southern Siberia. *Moscow University Bulletin. Series XXIII. Anthropology, 3*, 14-22. Лавряшина М.Б., Ульянова М.В., Балановская Е.В. (2009). Динамика фамильного состава как показатель изменения популяционной структуры коренных народов Южной Сибири. *Вестник Московского университета. Серия XXIII. Антропология*, 3, 14–22.

Lotman, J. M., & Uspenskij, B. A. (1982). *«Outlaws» as a social-psychological status in the Russian culture, especially before Peter the Great's period: «Ownes» and «alien» in the history of Russian culture. Works on Sign Systems*. Publishing House of Tartu University. Лотман Ю. М., Успенский Б. А. (1982). "Изгои" и "изгойничество" как социально-психологическая позиция в русской культуре преимущественно допетровского периода: ("Свое" и "чужое" в истории русской культуры). В кн.: Труды по знаковым системам. Вып. XV. Тарту. Издательство Туртусского университета.

Lukyanchenko, T. V. (1993). Sami in Russia: On the issue of the adaptive function of traditional culture. *Siberian Ethnographic Collection, 6*(1), 11–23. Лукьянченко Т.В. (1993). Саамы в России: к вопросу об адаптивной функции традиционной культуры. *Сибирский этнографический сборник*, 6(1), 11–23.

Melnikov-Pechersky, A. (1958). *Collected works in 6 volumes*. Pravda. Мельников-Печёрский А. *Собрание сочинений в 6 т.* М.: Правда.

Mkrtchan, N. V. (2005, January 10–23). Migration in Russia: The west drift. *Demoskop Weekly*, 185–186. *Мкртчян Н.В.* (2005) Миграция в России: западный дрейф. *Демоскоп Weekly,* 185-186, 10-23 января 2005 г. Accessed from http://demoscope.ru/weekly/2005/0185/tema01.php

Mkrtchan, N. V. (2011). Russian cities migration balance: To the question about grown and disposition influence in the system of central-peripheral relations. *Nauchnye Trudy Instituta Narodnokhozjajstvennogo Prognozirovanija RAN, pp.* 416–430. MAKS Press. Мкртчян Н.В. (2011). Миграционный баланс российских городов: к вопросу о влиянии размера и положения в системе центро-периферийных отношений. *Научные труды ИНП РАН,* 416-430. М.: МАКС Пресс.

Murmansk Region in Numbers. (2019). Federal State Statistics Service, Territorial Body of the Federal State Statistics Service for the Murmansk Region. Murmansk. *Мурманская область в цифрах* (2019). Федеральная служба государственной статистики, Территориальный орган Федеральной службы государственной статистики по Мурманской области. Мурманск.

Nefedova, T. (2012). City dwellers and dachas. *Otechestvennye Zapiski, 3*(48). *Нефёдова Т.* (2012). Горожане и дачи. *Отечественные записки*, 3(48).

Nefedova, T. G., & Treivish, A. I. (2010). Cities and Vesi: The polarized space of Russia. *Demoscope Weekly,* 437–438, October 4–17 2010. http://demoscope.ru/weekly/2010/0437/tema01.php. *Нефёдова Т.Г., & Трейвиш А.И.* (2010). Города и веси: поляризованное пространство России. *Демоскоп Weekly*, 437–438, 4–17 октября 2010.

Nefedovam, T. G., & Treivish, A. I. (1999). *Crisis and new trends in urbanization in Russia. Migration and urbanization in the CIS and the Baltic states in the 90s.* Adamant. *Нефёдова Т.Г., Трейвиш А.И.* (1999). *Кризис и новые тенденции урбанизации в России. Миграция и урбанизация в СНГ и Балтии в 90е годы.* М.: Адамантъ.

Nikolsky Territory in the XVIII-XXI centuries. Local history through the eyes of contemporaries and researchers. (2011). Nikolsk: B.I. *Никольский край в XVIII-XXI столетии. Местная история глазами современников и исследователей.* Никольск. Б.И.

Nikonov, V. A. (2017). *Geography of surnames*. URSS. Никонов В.А. (2017). *География фамилий.* М.: URSS.

Ogloblin, N. N. (2010). *River country roads*. "Knigi". Оглоблин Н.Н. (2010). *Речные просёлки.* Нижний Новгород: «Книги».

Pascal, P. (1939). *Avvakum et les débuts du raskol: La crise religieuse au XVIIe siècle en Russie*. Centre d'Etudes Russes Istina. Russian edition: Паскаль П. (2011). *Протопоп Аввакум и начало раскола.* М.: Знак.

Plusnin, J. M. (2000). *Russian Townes*. Moscow Public Science Foundation. Плюснин Ю.М. (2000). *Малые города России.* М.: Московский общественный научный фонд.

Plusnin, J. M. (2006). Mezen: The reality of natural life. *Otechestvennye Zapiski, 32*(5), 147–156. Плюснин Ю.М. (2006). Мезень: реальность натуральной жизни. *Отечественные записки*, 32(5), 147–156.

Plusnin, J. M. (2008). Factors in the development of local self-government. Assessing the importance of isolation and isolationism. *Issues of Public Administration, 3*, 38–50. Плюснин Ю.М. (2008). Факторы развития местного самоуправления. Оценка значения изоляции и изоляционизма. *Вопросы государственного и муниципального управления*, 3, 38–50.

Plusnin, J. M. (2013). Friends and strangers in a Russian provincial town. *World of Russia, 22*(3), 60–93. Плюснин Ю.М. (2013). Свои и чужие в русском провинциальном городе. *Мир России*, 22(3), 60–93.

Plusnin, J. M. (2018a). Territory of public welfare. Interaction of ethno-social groups in the Jewish Autonomous Region. *Ideas and Ideals, 4*(1), 136–159. Плюснин Ю.М. (2018a). Территория общественного благополучия. Взаимодействие этно- социальных групп в Еврейской автономной области. *Идеи и идеалы*, 4(1), 136–159.

Plusnin, J. M.. (2018b). Trades in the province: archaic and modern economic practices of the population. *Journal of Sociology and Social Anthropology, 21*(1), 73–106. Плюснин Ю.М. (2018b). Промыслы провинции: архаические и современные экономические практики населения. *Журнал социологии и социальной антропологии*, 21(1), 73–106.

Plusnin, J. M., Kordonsky, S. G., & Skalon, V.A. (2009). *Municipal Russia: Modus vivendi and modus sapienti. The experience of phenomenological research.* IPR OKSO. Плюснин Ю.М., Кордонский С.Г., Скалон В.А. (2009). *Муниципальная Россия: образ жизни и образ мыслей. Опыт феноменологического исследования.* М.: ИПР ОКСО.

Popov, V. I., & Popov, A. V. (2014). *History of the Vokhomsky Krai of the Vologda (since 1944, Kostroma) province from ancient times to 1917.* Nauka. Попов В.И., & Попов А.В. (2014). *История Вохомского края Вологодской (с 1944 г. Костромской) губернии с древнейших времен до 1917 г.* М.: Наука.

Pozanenko, A. A. (2017). Two types of isolated local communities as old and new Tennis communities in modern Russia. *Journal of Sociology and Social Anth*ropology, *20*(3), 161–178. Позаненко А.А. (2017). Два вида изолированных локальных сообществ как старые и новые тённисовские общности в современной России. *Журнал социологии и социальной антропологии*, 20(3), 161–178.

Pozanenko, A. (2018). "A separate type of republic": structural features of spatially isolated local rural communities. *World of Russia, 27*(4), 31–55. Позаненко, А. (2018). «Отдельная типа республичка»: структурные особенности пространственно изолированных локальных сельских сообществ. *Мир России, 27*(4), 31–55.

Rossi, P. (2013). Surname distribution in population genetics and in statistical physics. *Physics of Life Reviews, 10*(4), 395–415.

Russian dacha: sweet home without amenities, gas and access roads. (2015). *Press release №2605.* Omnibus-VTsIOM. Accessed from http://wciom.ru/index.php?id=459&uid=114861. Русская дача: милый дом без удобств, газа и подъездных путей. *Пресс-выпуск №2605.* Омнибус-ВЦИОМ.

Salter, F. K. (2003a). *On genetic interests: Family, ethnicity, and humanity in an age of mass migration.* Peter Lang.

Salter, F. K. (2003b). Ethnic genetic interests and bio-policy. *Philosophy of Science*, *4*(19), 84–122. Салтер Ф.К. (2003b). Этнические генетические интересы и биополитика. *Философия науки*, 4(19), 84–122.

Scott, J. (1976). *The moral economy of the peasant: Rebellion and subsistence in Southeast Asia.* Yale University Press.

Smirnov, I. N. (2012). *Permians. Historical and ethnographic sketch.* Book House "LIBROKOM". Смирнов И.Н. (2012). *Пермяки. Историко-этнографический очерк.* М.: Книжный дом «ЛИБРОКОМ».

Sorokina, I. N., & Churnosov, M. I. (2008). Using the "frequency" criterion for selecting surnames to analyze the structure of the population's gene pool. *Bulletin of Tomsk State University, 13*(5), 401–407. Сорокина И.Н., & Чурносов М.И. (2008). Использование «частотного» критерия отбора фамилий для анализа структуры генофонда населения. *Вестник Томского государственного университета*, 13(5), 401–407.

Sorokina, I. N., Evdokimov, V. I., & Churnosov, M. I. (2011). About genetic characteristics of population Central Russia. *Vestnik Tomskogo gosudarstvennogo universiteta, 16*(6), 1535–1538. Сорокина И.Н., Евдокимов В.И., Чурносов М.И. (2011). О генетических характеристиках населения центральной России. *Вестник Томского государственного университета*, 16(6), 1535–1538.

Tara mosaic (history of the region in essays and documents from 1594–1917) (1994). Omsk: Omsk book publishing house. *Тарская мозаика (история края в очерках и документах 1594–1917 гг.)* (1994). Омск: Омское книжное издательство.

To the 400th anniversary of the founding of Tara and the 60th anniversary of the Tara district (1994). Omsk: Omsk Department of Statistics of the State Statistics Committee of Russia. *К 400-летию основания г. Тары и 60-летию Тарского района* (1994). Омск: Омское управление статистики Госкомстата России.

Tönnies, F. (1887). *Gemeinschaft und Gesellschaft. Grundbegriffe der reinen Soziologie*. Leipzig: Fues's Verlag (R. Reisland). Russian edition: Тённис Ф. (2002). Община и общество. Основные концепции чистой социологии. СПб: Владимир Даль.

Tönnies, F. (1959). Gemeinschaft und Gesellschaft. In A. Vierkandt (Ed.), *Handworterbuch der Sociologie*. Ferdinand Enke Verlag.

Trejvish, A. I. (2009). *City, district, country, and world. Russian development through the geographers eyes*. Novyj Khronograf. Трейвиш А.И. (2009). *Город, район, страна и мир. Развитие России глазами страноведа*. М.: Новый хронограф.

Vakhitov, R. (2012). Moscow for the Moscovites. *Otechestvennye Zapiski*, *3*(48), 145–152. Вахитов Р. (2012). Москвичи как сословие. *Отечественные записки*, 3(48), 145–152.

Waldenfels, B. (1997–1999). *Studien zur Phänomenologie des Fremden* 1–4. Suhrkamp.

Zayonchkovskaya, Z. A. (1993). *Population migration and the labor market in Russia. Migration Research Program*. Issue VII. IND RAN, RAND. Зайончковская Ж.А. (1993). *Миграция населения и рынок труда в России. Программа по исследованию миграции*. Вып. VII. М.: ИНД РАН, РЭНД.

Chapter 10
Status and Authority

In the social stratification of provincial society, income stratification, education, proficiency, and even occupational prestige (professional status) are not the main criteria of personal status. The status of an individual in local society is determined by the following factors (in order of priority): social, ethnogenetic, political, and economic. Status depends first on personal influence in the local society (public respect), then on clan affiliation (belonging to a kin group and/or ethnic group), then on the position in the power hierarchy, and only last of all on monetary income. This hierarchy of factors determining status positions is due to the fact that in contrast to urban societies the determinants of status in a provincial society are not anonymous. The social structure is heterarchical (networked) rather than hierarchical. It seems that the political organization of a local society's life depends on how individual status is determined. We have identified four polar types of power relations in provincial public administration: true local self-government, "*estate*" governance, state governorship ("Soviet-type" administration), and competitive governance in politicized municipalities. The establishment of one or another type of governance correlates with the type of community in terms of spatial isolation and the natural/coercive nature of its development to draw on the prevailing stratification factors giving access to formal leadership positions in municipal administration.

10.1 Personal Status in Provincial Society and Its Criteria

It is almost useless to investigate status stratification in a local society. Questionnaires do not work in this case and interviews of the type "*and who is the most influential/rich/almighty here*" provide no clue, even if the entire adult population of the locality is interviewed, as experience shows. Everywhere, the formal local political status—be it head of the municipality, chairman of the local town council, or the town manager—hardly determines the actual status of that person in the community. One must live here a year or ten to grasp the essence of the local status

J. Plusnin, *Russian Provincial Society*, Societies and Political Orders in Transition,
https://doi.org/10.1007/978-3-030-97829-7_10

system and to understand the details of the mutual relations between people and their personal histories, which determine the current (existing now) status of everyone in the local society. Since this is not possible, the external observer in each case must limit himself to sporadic observations and create an overall picture from *multicolored* pieces of different quality. Often one stumbles upon such pieces' by pure chance. Therefore, all this usually remains a blind spot for the researcher, who ignores such facts and stories, being not immersed in the local cultural field. One can still find out something about the assigned status, but little about the actual status of a person.

I will illustrate this with the following example. Once, in one of the Ural towns, I tried unsuccessfully for several days in a row to meet with the head of the municipality or the head of the town administration (these are different positions usually held by different people). However, every time I was sent to the chairman of a local public organization, the Union of Small Business Owners, with whom we had daily conversations about the various aspects of local life. A very intelligent and informed respondent. Knows all there is to know. But he has long been retired and holds no official position. Sort of not convincing enough. Not an authority on current governance issues. Finally, on the last evening, just before departure, I also visited the abbot of the local monastery. He invited me to tea, and we talked about the monks, the laity, and the authorities. In the middle of the conversation, we touched upon the influential people of the local society, and I voiced regret that I was not able to meet with anyone from the administration. He then dropped a phrase referring to the above respondent, *"But he actually is the 'overseer' here; he is the one who got them their jobs"* (meaning that he was the most influential person, to whom everyone in the administration reported, since he had appointed them to official positions). So inadvertently and incidentally I learned that for a whole week I had been daily receiving information from the most powerful person in the district, who was "*overseeing*" order and controlling all local political and economic life. One casually dropped phrase instantly clarified the situation in the local society and brought the whole picture of the formal social hierarchy into focus, and not just the formal one.

Long-term observations in many local societies have enabled me over time to identify criteria that determine a person's status. Of course, such criteria are largely consistent with the well-known ones; see, e.g., Shkaratan (2012), Wodtke (2016). However, there are important differences in the order of relevance of individual criteria; one should bear in mind that the order (rank) of the criteria was determined not by interviewing, but by observation. Two crucial points relating to the characteristics of the social status of an individual in the local community should be noted. First, nowhere are individual social positions hierarchical; instead, we observe heterarchical (often networked) relations. Second, the "grassroots" social structure is such that it can still be called "communal," or more precisely archaic. It is thus determined by the direct interaction of its members (i.e., neighborship); the genetic and social (symbolic) kinship of most of them; by historically established (traditional) systems for managing the behavior of community members and for assessing this behavior (standards); and the existence of mechanisms for regulating the use of local resources through control over territory; cf.: Kordonsky (2010, pp. 76–80).

First, provincial status positions are not hierarchical. There is no rigid hierarchy like in the army, except for government and municipal institutions, and even there not everywhere. Hierarchy is of an individual nature; it is determined only by formal power positions in the official "table of ranks," which are not many in local society. Even if formal hierarchy, traditionally based on such simple criteria as disposable income and capital (the degree of control over various resources), is operational in a provincial society, then only on a limited scale (Tikhonova et al., 2018, pp. 3–4, 10–48). Heterarchical relations [heterarchy] are definitely more important. (According to the original definition of "heterarchy" by Warren McCulloch (1945, pp. 89 and 91), further developed by Carole Crumley (1979, p. 144) and detailed on the example of complex anthropological systems in the monograph (Ehrenreich et al., 1995); see also (Bondarenko et al., 2002, pp. 54–80), (Bondarenko, 2007, p. 142).) Relations between members of a local society are more of a coordinating, equal nature than that of super- and subordination. One can argue that all previously identified structural forms of heterarchy are present here; see Brumfield (1995, p.125)—from an array of mutually independent homogeneous elements, as observed in informal quasi-economic interactions of households, to discrete (independent) hierarchies that are in equal relations, as seen in interactions between local government and municipal employees. Moreover, since all modern local communities are under constant and strong external economic and political pressure, any spontaneous emergence and establishment of a stable hierarchy, especially a one-dimensional one, is in principle impossible here; see Small (1995, pp. 81–82), also Bondarenko (2007, pp. 164–183).

Network (heterarchical) relationships established between groups of families (clans) and between individuals linked by childhood friendship regularly evolve into situational hierarchies: into a struggle for formal power positions and for control of resources, and most often for access to local natural resources. But they do not result in any stable hierarchy of families or clans, and if they do, then only for a short while. Where the local society is made up of several different ethnic groups, there is also occasional competition between their representatives. However, in none of the cases I considered did competitive relations result in any domination of one ethnicity over the others, although representatives of different ethnic groups often have different access to resources and/or formal power positions. I suppose this is largely the legacy of the Soviet policy of "*equalizing differences*" (which has long been abandoned in other post-Soviet states) that persists in the Russian province. Thus, at the local level there is a system of "*dispersed governance*" as one of the most important features of heterarchical relations (McCulloch, 1945, p. 91).

Secondly, the community's grassroots social structure, which in itself is heterarchical, determines the status positions of individuals based on a constellation of several factors. The four main ones are ranked in the following order of importance: influence, kinship, power, and capital. These factors determine to varying degrees (largely depending on the type of local society) the scope of informally established rights and responsibilities, preferences, and access to local resources and institutional positions. It is these four factors that can be considered criteria that determine the status of an individual in a provincial local society.

Influence and kinship matter most. If the former depends mainly on the professional competence and moral qualities of a person, the latter is predetermined by his or her affiliation with a family, clan, or ethnos. Their correlation as status factors is the correlation between the dynamic and static components. Influence depends on the person himself and changes during his life, whereas clan affiliation changes very rarely, if ever (for example, through marrying into a new family or becoming a godfather or godmother, a symbolic relative).

Two other status factors—formal power position (usually in public administration and in enterprises large by local standards) and capital (access to control of resources, cash income and corresponding consumption level)—are largely determined by influence and kinship and depend on them. In this respect, they can be regarded as secondary. A person's power positions are relatively stable: even after their loss, people's memory of a person's previous status in the formal hierarchy persists for a long time, often until the end of his life. At the same time, possession of significant capital does not leave a "trail" after its loss. People remember this fact, but it ceases to exist as a factor. The same is true for the opposite: sudden (for the local society) possession of capital and a respective increase in wealth and consumption do not change much the locals' opinion about the status of the nouveau riche *("new Russian")*. These factors are important primarily for studying income stratification (Shkaratan, 2012, pp. 141–186; Grigoriev & Salmina, 2013; Wodtke, 2016; Tikhonova et al., 2018, pp. 201–224). Therefore, this pair of secondary factors also correlate with each other as a relatively stable and a dynamic component that determine an individual's status in the local society.

Thus, the four status criteria can be cross-differentiated: in one case, they are classified into static (kinship and power) and dynamic (influence and capital) components, and in the other—into determining, primary (influence and kinship) and determinable, secondary (power and capital) components. I believe that influence, being the most important status factor, is essential, among other things, for acquiring/losing formal power positions, especially when such positions result from elections rather than appointment. There is no strict correlation with kinship and capital. The factor of kinship correlates with those of power and capital, but in a specific manner: only if representatives of one clan were in power for a long time and could control local resources. Formal power and capital have at least a one-way connection: formal status gives control over local resources. However, as traditional social condemnation of conspicuous consumption persists, this connection can hardly be consolidated. In addition, the widespread presence of much richer and more powerful external players ("*Muscovites*") in the provincial local economy, does not allow representatives of the local society to assert themselves by means of power and/or capital only. These *pillars* are too unstable; it is safer to rely on kinship and personal influence.

Obviously, the importance of each of the four main status factors varies among local societies. In general, we can correlate their significance in the six basic types of local communities I have identified. The factor of influence is important everywhere, but since it is determined only by public opinion and can neither be counted as capital, ranked as a power position, nor even nominated, as kinship affiliation, the variations are inestimable. (At least, I would not undertake to determine the degree of variability of the influence factor even if we use only such well-documented indicators as the level of education and socio-occupational status; cf.: Shkaratan (2009, pp. 385–465).) By contrast, the other three factors quite distinctly depend on the type of community and are probably related to the principles on which my typology of communities is based. Kinship has a relatively greater importance in naturally developing communities, whereas formal power—in those of coercive development. This differentiation may be due to simple reasons. Naturally developing communities have long established family ties and individual clans—especially if they belong to different ethnic groups,—which are often more or less stratified in terms of access to resources and power positions because of long-term competition on local soil. We see this situation in the North Caucasus and the Siberian North. By contrast, the factor of formal power has a somewhat greater significance in coercively developing communities for an equally simple reason that I considered in Chaps. 4 and 6 above: the livelihood of local communities here is largely dependent on the state; the local community has less control over its own territory and resources; and respectively, the formal power position is more closely related to the real status of the individual, as it is relatively more important for the life of the community. We see this in relatively young communities, especially in the Far East of Siberia. The fourth factor, disposable capital, has a relatively greater importance in turbulent and ordinary communities, whereas in isolated communities it is often quite insignificant. The reasons consist in less opportunities to accumulate capital, both in monetary terms due to the lack of a market, and in the form of control over significant natural resources, since these are controlled by all members of society and so far, no one is allowed to accumulate "surplus" resources. Turbulent communities have transport links to large cities, which allows an individual to convert the factor of capital into a formal status position. This is typical of societies in the European part of Russia. Here, *"new Russians,"* who obtain informal, and often formal statuses mainly due to income stratification[1] rather than personal moral or professional qualities, have been emerging much more often. This virtually never happens in isolated communities either in the Russian North or in Siberia.

[1] One should also bear in mind that the practice of buying diplomas of vocational education became quite common in the post-Soviet period. Due to this, the factor of education level lost its real significance, especially in the provinces, where along with simply "purchasing education," one can "acquire a profession" in extremely dubious educational establishments, moreover, not through routine training but by primitively paying for exam scores. The resulting "certified specialist" has no clue even about the basics of the "acquired" profession, but applies for status positions, sometimes successfully. According to various estimates obtained from the Russian Internet, up to a quarter of all false certificates of secondary and higher vocational education are bought for the purpose of taking up leadership positions, including in public administration.

10.1.1 Influence

In every local community that I visit repeatedly, I often maintain ongoing friendly relations with several of my former respondents. They are usually the most valuable informants since they are competent and yet completely frank with me. So, in a society I have been visiting regularly for more than a quarter of a century, a few years ago I met with my long-time acquaintance, who over the years has grown from a small entrepreneur into a large businessman and has become, moreover, a "respected person." We were lunching together and discussing the changes—very significant ones—that have taken place in local society over the course of three decades. I asked how the status positions of several formerly most influential people, including those in formal positions of power, had changed. Among other things, he replied, *"Well, you know, the patriarch now comes here every year. And we host a gala dinner in his honor, to which we invite about fifty of our local people. They are the influential ones here…"*

How does one determine influence? What are the indicators of influence? Based solely on my empirical observations rather than scholastic assumptions, I record the following. Of the objective indicators, neither gender nor origin (kinship) of a person has any relevance here. What matters for the traditionally-minded people is age. In provincial society, influence correlates with age. Young men and women, even those who have reached a high professional level or formal status, are perceived as less influential and respected compared to older people. This is an archaic legacy, but it continues to shape ordinary people's perceptions of a person's status. Given this background of age discrimination (probably unconscious and therefore spontaneous), there are two most important attributes of influence: a person's moral qualities and his/her professional competence (knowledge and skills).

Although it is difficult or impossible to find criteria to rank these two most important attributes of influence, I still think that a person's moral and ethical qualities are primary. Consistently proper behavior in compliance with generally accepted standards and traditions (impeccable behavior), along with moral (exemplary) conduct, strong will, intelligence, and wisdom that comes with age, determines a person's reputation above all else. Thus, an influential person is a wise, ethical, properly behaving individual of middle or senior age who participates in establishing and maintaining a system of social control by setting local patterns and norms of behavior and forming local expectations.

The second component of influence, professional competence, develops at a younger age and is the most important requirement for respecting a person as a "competent specialist." And this is not related with education as such; a person can have one, two, or even three diplomas certifying proficiency in one or several occupations, but this has nothing to do with how other people judge his or her professional competence. Including for the reasons mentioned above. Vocational skills are also assessed similarly, and judgments do not depend on the prestige of the occupation. A skilled self-taught bricklayer or carpenter will enjoy much greater respect than a doctor or lawyer who was educated at a metropolitan university or simply bought a diploma but fails to demonstrate the competencies expected of him. In the opinion of neighbors, the status of "certified specialist" gives its bearer no advantages compared to those who are not "certified" but really skilled. That is why the level of education and even its quality (education at a prestigious university) is of little or no value in determining the status of a person in local society, especially nowadays. It matters only as a criterion for competitive selection for a formal position, and even then, it is incomparably less relevant than it could be in a major city. In a provincial society, a person cannot improve his social status through, inter alia, the level of education: this factor here is almost reduced to nothing. Moreover, with few exceptions, education here does not correlate with income levels. Usually, it also does not correlate with the ability to hold official positions, since in the province this depends more on clan ties and patronage (assume a position "by inheritance"; see Zhukov and Seltzer (2019)). Therefore, it is not the level of education as such, but the professional competencies actually achieved by a person that determine his local social status.

Consequently, an influential person in the province is a person with an excellent reputation in those occupations that are locally important, a reputation based on skills demonstrated and confirmed in practice, regardless of the level and quality of the vocational education received. At the same time, he must also be a respected person by virtue of his moral, ethical, and intellectual qualities. Since both influence factors are developed and firmly established by a fairly mature age, it is possible that in provincial public opinion they are perceived as dependent on age. It is common for sociological literature to differentiate status factors into influence and education, with priority given to the latter; e.g. Shkaratan (2009, pp. 154–169). But in provincial society, what matters most is not the level of vocational education itself, but its consequences in the form of acquired skills. Since these skills and not the level of education is a prerequisite for influence, I do not regard the latter as a significant status factor.

10.1.2 Clan

I use the word "*clan*" as a status factor somewhat conditionally, as a totality of related families that originate from a common (including mythical) ancestor and are connected by ethnic kinship. The closest ethnological definition is: "*A unilinear consanguineous corporate group whose members trace their origin to a common ancestor but cannot trace all their family ties genealogically*" (Artyomova, 1999, p. 886). And the coinciding political science definition is as follows: "*…clans, informal organizations based on kin and fictive kin ties, are political actors that have a profound impact on the nature of post-transitional regimes and the potential for regime durability*" (Collins, 2004, p. 224). The term "clan" is now quite common not only in the Russian political science dictionary (Mote & Trout, 2010; Young, 2009, pp. 256–258), but also in everyday Russian life, including—and especially—in the province, since here family ties and the mutual support of relatives are still very important. And since this also matters in the race for formal power positions, the use of this concept becomes one of the ways to explain the results of the struggle for power in local society; a study of socio-occupational developments of local elites in central Russian regions over the past three decades demonstrates this very clearly (Zhukov & Seltzer, 2019). The term "clan" thus applied often replaces the Russian concepts of "family" and "kin" more appropriate to the situation. But referring to "clan" has become a tradition. An important reason for this is the additional hidden connotation here: "persons who achieve their goals not always by legal means, who resort to kin, friendly, and neighborly ties," and therefore the term is often perceived as "mafia family." Very often, it is in this explicit meaning that the term is used when describing the activities of a family group in power in the local society, "*. . .they are the mafia over there.*" In addition, the factor of clan affiliation records the existence of real group relations: the status of an individual in a community is determined not through autonomous indicators (income level, formal power position, and individual prestige), but through relative ones, which seems more important.

In some local societies, a "clan" can include one or several related families, in other societies "clans" are formed by representatives of one or more ethnic groups (nationalities), conflicting with each other for power, whether formal (the head of the municipality) or informal (the local "*problem solver*" or "*overseer*"). Clan affiliation has little or no relevance to a person's influence. But it is an important asset contributing to the ability of a person to assume a formal position in public entities and authorities. It is undoubtedly crucial for status differentiation in private organizations and firms. This factor began to play an increasingly important role in provincial societies immediately after the collapse of the Soviet system of government, which I pointed out already in the early 1990. I noted that municipal positions could, first, be bought, which opened the door to representatives of the criminal world, and second, inherited, i.e., in local self-government bodies and local branches of government agencies, the number of people connected by family (clan) relations began to increase rapidly (Plusnin, 1999, 2000, 2002). This was also recorded by subsequent observations; see Young (2009), Mote and Trout (2010). New research shows that this situation at the municipal level in the province persists and even deteriorates (Ledyaev et al., 2014; Zhukov & Seltzer, 2019). With weakening or even completely lacking mechanisms of vertical social mobility on a competitive basis, focus has shifted to mechanisms of "hereditary" transfer of status positions in the formal hierarchy of public authorities and criminalized control over local natural resources. Clan (kin and criminal) affiliation has virtually become the decisive status factor in the formal hierarchy of power in local societies of European Russia (Zhukov & Seltzer, 2019, p. 53; Ledyaev & Chirikova, 2019a). However, according to my observations, the situation did not go that far in Siberian and northern societies, although in the south of Russia it is similar to that described by the above authors. Because the clan factor is so important in the eyes of the local community, political scientists almost always consider formal power positions as dependent, determined by it; e.g. Blyakher (2008).

10.1.3 Power

Power in local society implies holding a formal status position, generally or exclusively in the system of public service (in this case, this is also true for municipal service, since despite the formal independence of local self-government from the state, the positions of municipal leaders are not determined by the will of local voters; any significant municipal position requires coordination with the curator, a regional official).

Since power is formal, its personal source has generally little to do with an individual's wealth. It is quite common for a rich businessman or a local crime lord ("*avtoritet*") to fail repeatedly in securing a position, usually elected, of deputy of a local representative assembly or head of administration. It was easy to "buy a position" in the 1990s and in the early 2000s; now it is much more difficult, and over time the appeal of such positions has significantly decreased.[2] We see that everywhere the share of "bought positions" has dropped sharply compared to the 1990s (Plusnin, 1999, 2000; Zhukov & Seltzer, 2019). Power positions are in general taken up by representatives of clans, who get them "by inheritance." But in the past decade, their share has been somewhat declining because of party and professional "appointees." However, even these latter, upon close examination of their connections, most often turn out to be "insiders" belonging to a certain clan dominant at the moment, who got the job by virtue of being relatives or close acquaintances of the leaders; compare, for example: Ledeneva (1998, pp. 83–87, p. 175), Barsukova (2013, p. 119), Chirikova and Ledyaev (2017). It is absolutely impossible for an outsider, a migrant or a recent urban resident, to get an administrative position, either by election or appointment. This can work out only for a "*Varangian,*" i.e., an external appointee or protégé of the regional authority.

Such is the situation on the upper levels of government (usually elected municipal positions, or appointed positions in local branches of government agencies). On the lower levels—those of municipal service,—the situation is different. On the one hand, there is a drastic shortage of professionally trained specialists,[3] on the other hand, the quality of such training is inferior for the reasons mentioned above. But on the third hand, a relevant reason for refusing to assume low-level municipal and public positions is very small salaries: it is a paradox but the usual salary of such a public sector employee is lower than the pension due to him upon retirement. Only those lower power positions are attractive which give control over any important local resources—natural, financial, or human (participation in official appointments).

[2] Perhaps due to changes in the structure of inter-budget transfers, with a sharp decrease in the share of subsidies, which allowed arbitrary spending of public funds allocated to the municipality.

[3] Although Russian universities have over 430 departments of state and municipal administration with thousands of graduates annually, such specialists at best assume public office in large cities, whereas in the provinces they usually engage in commerce straight away, thus joining the service sector.

All publicly funded positions are ranked within each institution. The power status is institutional and hierarchical. Each person (usually) holds one uniquely defined position in the hierarchy of linear subordination in one or less often several institutions established and controlled by the state with a statutory (legally) specified organizational form. However, the "public hierarchy," the subordination of positions in a publicly funded institution, is not related to the perception of a person's actual status by the local community. Due to professional competence, a simple schoolteacher or a doctor in a district hospital may have an incomparably higher social status than their professionally worthless superiors—the school director or the chief physician. Thus, positions in power as such, as well as the formal level of vocational education, poorly correlate with a person's real status in the local society. The reasons lie mainly in inflation of both vocational education and official appointments. Due to the widespread purchase of education diplomas and to pseudo-training in numerous private educational institutions, along with sweeping distribution of positions to acquaintances and relatives ("by inheritance"), the social and formal statuses of one and the same person usually coincide nowhere. Social status is the status of real group relations. Formal status is just an atomic characteristic of a person in the estate-class system. In the Russian environment, both former and current—in the system of estate relations. Let me give you the most impressive example, from my point of view.

Probably our cemeteries provide the clearest and most illustrative ground (literally) projection of social differentiation based on formal atomic hierarchy. Previously—both in the Imperial and Soviet periods—cemeteries also were a visible physical projection of the estate structure of society. They still are, first and foremost, on a local scale (although each metropolitan city has its own special estate-based cemeteries, with the Kremlin wall in Moscow topping the list). It is in the cemeteries of the administrative centers of local communities that the structure of society manifests itself in its entirety, as it was a century or half a century ago and as it is now. The deceased are always located according to their rank both in the formal and local informal hierarchy. The high-status ones are buried in the center of the cemetery. The graves of wealthy but lower status people, as well as those of crime lords, "mafiosi," are located nearby on the central alley. All "*important people" are laid to rest* as close as possible to the cemetery church or chapel. The poor are buried along the outskirts, and the homeless and wretched ones who were fortunate enough to make it to the cemetery are buried next to garbage dumps and often beyond the fence, as was the case with suicides and actors in the old days (now these latter belong to the elite and are usually located in the center).

The estate-occupational differentiation reaches the point of absurdity when sites in cemeteries are allocated to individual government agencies. This is very typical for closed administrative-territorial entities, as well as for former "*sharashki*" such as Novosibirsk Akademgorodok or similar academic settlements. Usually, such cemeteries allocate plots not only for an estate or occupational group, but also for each specific institution. The graves of leaders, military personnel, builders, and scientists are located in different segments of the same cemetery, and in the best places. And the graves of ordinary residents ("all the rest") are meant to be in the worst places, often in the lowlands and swamps. Within the segments allocated for the estates (for deceased scientists, for example), each institution (university or research institute) gets a separate, clearly demarcated land parcel. And on this parcel, the deceased bosses lie at the head of their former subordinates, with minor clerks buried at the very rear. So, these sites of the institutions are arranged in straight rows with the leaders in the first row, their deputies in the second, followed by others further down the rank (however, ordinary workers, like cleaners, are buried in the segment for "common people"). The two-level hierarchy—between the estates and within the estate—is strictly observed among the dead also. All of them are forever aligned according to the hierarchy under their penultimate status (the ultimate one is engraved on the tomb). Such is the disposition in central and "prestigious" cemeteries in the administrative centers of local communities. There are usually one or two of them per community. Not so in village cemeteries, which are egalitarian in this respect. Although even here we can often see the segregation of the location *of the deceased* on grounds of kinship, ethnicity, religion, and even occupation. Our cemeteries are the best age-old—and certainly not instantaneous—cross-section of the social structure of society both at the general and local levels.

In contrast to urbanized territories (especially in contrast to metropolitan cities), distribution of power in the province has its distinctions, which contribute to the development of particular styles of local government. I consider the typology of such styles in Sect. 10.2.

10.1.4 Income

Above, I mentioned an important contradiction in the fact that researchers often shape the social structure using the model of income stratification (Shkaratan, 2009; Wodtke, 2016; Tikhonova et al., 2018), whereas at the level of local society, differences in income between people or households are not significant in determining a person's actual social status. Capital is not synonymous with status. Capital—the control and possession (appropriation) of various resources (from natural to financial and information)—only then determines a person's real status when it conjugates with a formal power status. However, this usually applies only to a few individuals; for the vast majority, there is no direct link between capital and power.

At the local level, it also seems appropriate to consider income-based stratification of households as synonymous with social stratification. This is relevant only for the very ends of the social ladder—the very top and the very bottom. The remaining "body of society" will not be stratified in any way. Households or individuals can be ranked only by formal income, but not by social status. Moreover, household incomes from informal economic activities can exceed formal (declared) ones manifold, as was demonstrated in Chaps. 6, 7, and 8. For example, how should we rank an average provincial household (of three people) with a formal monthly income corresponding to the regional median level, where each family member earns a salary of RUB 9000–15,000 [$150–250], thus totaling about $560 for the household, according to 2018 data (Tikhonova et al., 2018, pp. 182–183)? Our field observations show that the same household makes monthly from $2500 to $5500 on various informal crafts, thus placing it in the uppermost high-income stratum ≥4 of the median. However, the household will not have many durable goods; it will not use the services inherent in this stratum; and the family members themselves will unanimously rank themselves as poor; cf.: Tikhonova et al. (2018, pp. 59–65, 117–143, 157–172). This is not a hypothetical example at all, but a perfectly typical common case. Such households are widespread. Such a discrepancy between self-assessments of respondents and their level of income creates a quite understandable cognitive dissonance in the field researcher/interviewer.

The opposite situation is just as common in the province: a household belongs to a lower stratum in terms of income stratification, but its family members do not consider themselves poor, and the social status of their adult members is highest due to the respect they enjoy. Such, for example, are the vast majority of professional workers employed in social security and reproduction—precisely those whose remuneration and status is so inconsistent with their actual social role, thus raising an important issue in new crisis conditions and on the threshold of a new world ("*In the future, will society accept that a star hedge fund manager who specializes in short-selling (whose contribution to economic and social welfare is doubtful, at best) can receive an income in the millions per year while a nurse (whose contribution to social welfare is incontrovertible) earns an infinitesimal fraction of that amount? In such an optimistic scenario, as we increasingly recognize that many workers in low-paid and insecure jobs play an essential role in our collective well-being, policies would adjust to improve both their working conditions and remuneration.*" (Schwab & Malleret, 2020, p. 36)). In any case, whenever we observe the relations of people in small and relatively isolated local communities, there is no correspondence whatsoever between income and consumption levels, on the one hand, and social stratification, on the other. Turbulent and larger communities have a greater resemblance to major urbanized communities. But, in general, a person's genuine status depends on relations in the local community, and not on atomic externalities, such as income.

10.2 Provincial Authority and Its Types

Finally, we are interested in the relations between the local authorities and the local society. How do they actually interact? What are the typical forms of local authority? How and why are these standard forms determined by local society, or are they shaped by some external circumstances?

Legislatively, municipal authorities, or "local self-government," have clearly defined functions and a structure consistent with them. This is stipulated by federal laws. However, life has its own way. And the real forms of local authority do not always follow written law. More often they obey the law of life. As municipal leaders sometimes admit, "*we live by the code [of the underworld] rather than by law.*" Over the decades of existence in a new political environment, the newly established municipal authorities have learned to live "by the code" shaped by specific local conditions. Diverse forms of government have emerged: the nature of local government is different; the social groups that serve it and are served by it are different; even the objectives of local government bodies have changed and been partially replaced (Ledyaev & Chirikova, 2019a, b).

Therefore, rather than recording legislative uniformity, empirical research highlights diverse forms of municipal government. For the central government, all this diversity creates unnecessary hassle, makes the results of administration more uncertain, and reduces governance efficiency. Barring exceptional cases, such diversity is almost indistinguishable at the top, federal level. But for the regional authorities, it is becoming an increasing challenge over the years. According to observations, the main problem is the relationship between the local authorities and local society. In other words, are the authorities perceived as part of society, or are they treated as something alien, external, imposed from outside? Have the authorities developed within local society as an institution of true self-government, or do they essentially represent "external governance" appointed and controlled by the state?

We proposed the principle of "inclusion-exclusion" of the municipal authorities in/from the local community as an operational principle indicating how the authorities correlate with local society. This is synonymous with the extent to which regional government bodies control the local authorities. Here, we must distinguish two aspects: the formal one—the degree to which the municipal level of public authority is included in local society, and the substantive one—the functional focus of the local authorities.

The formal characteristic is the inverse function of dependence of local administration on superior—federal and regional—government bodies. This is expressed primarily in the dependence of the municipal head's administrative decisions on the arbitrariness of the regional official. The official's task is to control and facilitate such decisions, which is rarely limited to that. Local leaders may be highly, moderately, or hardly dependent on government officials. Accordingly, if the local authorities are largely independent of the arbitrariness of government officials and of the "guidance" of regional administrations, this generally (but not always) indicates their inclusion in local society. In other words, the local government is in fact local self-government. By contrast, complete dependence on external governance indicates exclusion of the authorities from the life of local society.

The substantive characteristic of the "inclusion-exclusion" principle consists in the objectives of governance and forms of responsibility to the population that the authorities focus on. Law defines three objectives of local government, in order of relevance: social, economic (including local development), and political. It also defines its three forms of responsibility: to the state, to the population, and to individuals and legal entities. Law requires that all forms of responsibility and the entire set of objectives be met. In life, the ideal is rarely achievable, often not at all. Local authorities may shift focus if forced to select one, two, or all three objectives as the main ones, or if they prefer one form of responsibility to the other two. It is hardly possible to be equally successful in pursuing, for example, political and local development objectives, or to combine responsibility to the population with responsibility to the state. Observations show that in practice municipal authorities always put emphasis on certain forms of responsibility as well as on certain objectives. For example, the authorities can organize local governance focusing exclusively on political objectives and "professing" responsibility only to the state. Obviously, in this case, the substance of governance will differ radically from that of authorities emphasizing responsibility exclusively to the population and focusing on social objectives. Authorities committed to the former style of governance will be excluded from local society both in substance and form, while those committed to the latter will be included in it in the substance of governance, even if dependent on superior government bodies in its form. In these latter, we will record features of true local self-government, while in the former ones we will find none at all. At best, it will be "crisis management." Such formal and substantive accents can be driven by conditions and circumstances, both objective and quite subjective. The reason often consists in the composition of the population of the local society and the nature of its everyday life, especially the prevalence of informal practices of economic behavior.

Thus, considering the formal and substantive aspects of the "inclusion-exclusion" principle, we can arrange the local authorities' governance styles along two orthogonal axes: (1) by the degree of control by regional government bodies and (2) by the extent of true local self-government. After consolidating numerous empirical observations of municipal life arrangement, we distinctly identified four main municipality types (we already depicted these standard organizational forms of municipal administration earlier: Plusnin (2009), Kordonskiy et al. (2011). The types are differentiated not only by the style of governance, by focus and priorities, but also by the way municipal leaders interact with government officials; for more details, see Plusnin and Mitroshina (2017).

The diagram in Fig. 10.1 demonstrates the correlation between the four identified municipality types in terms of the extent of local self-government and the degree of dependence on/control from government bodies (indicated on the axes). The largest gray-filled circle represents a considerable number of municipalities, which I find difficult to classify into one or another of the four types: such municipalities are numerous. The relative size of the circles indicates the share of a particular type of municipal administration. The position of the circles relative to the abscissa and ordinate axis shows the extent of local self-government and the degree of dependence on government bodies. We can see that the correlation between the types of governance is not oppositional: the type circles are not symmetrical.

The estimates are derived from expert interviews from an empirical sample of approximately 1000 municipalities that we accumulated during 297 field studies between 2005 and 2020. The typology described back in 2009 (Plusnin, 2009) remained unchanged; new observations only confirmed the revealed picture. If we assess the distribution of local authority types in the 285 local communities I

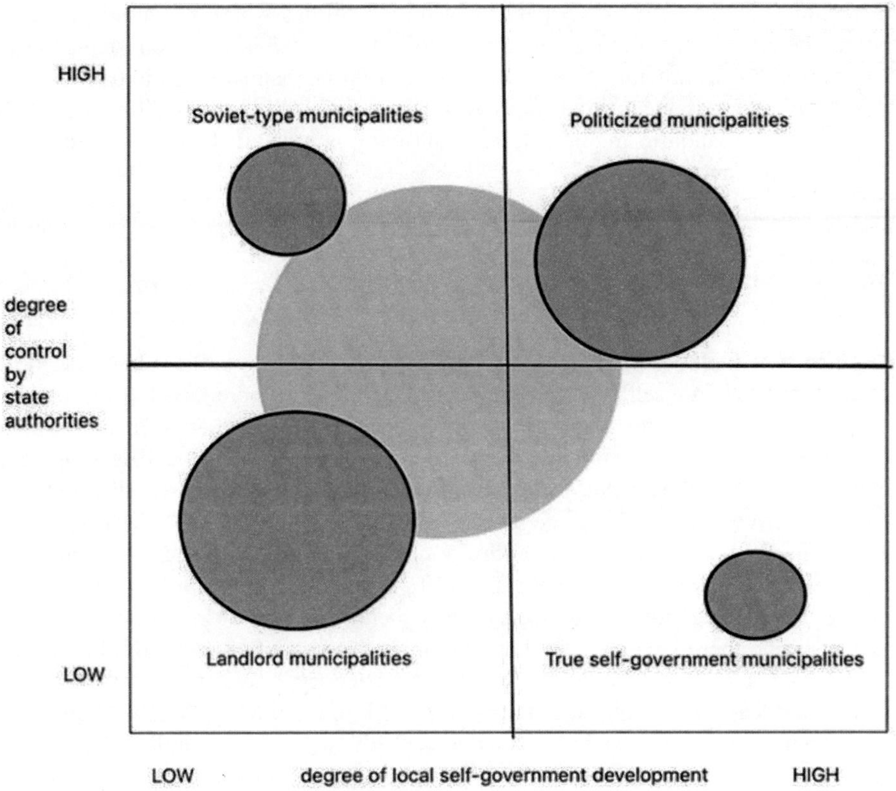

Fig. 10.1 Types of municipal administration in provincial local communities

surveyed, the picture is as follows.[4] Municipalities with true local self-government make up the smallest share—from six to seven percent. The share of municipalities retaining "Soviet-style governance" with full subordination to government bodies is slightly higher, but also small—up to ten percent. Municipalities with politicized governance account for about twenty percent. "Landlord municipalities" have the highest share—twenty-five percent. Finally, in about forty percent of the cases I could not clearly define the type of governance; the circle is not symmetrical relative to the center, which suggests that many of these uncertain types of municipal administration lean toward the "Soviet" and "landlord" styles. Politicized municipalities, where there is a struggle for power between individuals and clans, are fairly easy to diagnose. The same is more or less true for municipalities with true self-government. "Landlord" and "Soviet-style" municipalities are not so clearly

[4]In each local society, we observed between one-two and seven-ten various municipalities, but the estimate here relates to municipal authorities on the level of the entire local society. Most often these are municipalities of two categories: "municipal district" or "urban district." There are fewer municipalities of the "settlement" (rural and urban) category.

differentiated. The above sixty percent of municipalities where we could precisely define the type of governance correlate as follows: 1:1.5:3:4. For each municipality with true self-government, there are one and a half times as many municipalities with Soviet-style governance, three times as many politicized municipalities, and four times as many landlord municipalities. Following is a detailed description of each type of governance.

10.2.1 Municipalities with True Local Self-Government

The first type includes municipalities established "according to the rules": the local society here has true self-government. The local authorities are largely independent of government bodies (actually—of the arbitrariness of government officials), which is in line with law. The administration focuses on social and local development objectives, i.e., on the everyday needs of the community; therefore, strictly speaking, these objectives are not always economic (they have nothing to do with the market). The main responsibility is to the entire population and only partially—formal and legal responsibility to government officials. In this sense, responsibility to the state is only of a reporting and accounting nature (which, in fact, is how it should be).

Generally, these are quite small communities in terms of population. The municipalities are mostly of the "rural settlement" category, less often—"urban settlement," and least often—municipal district. In addition to the fact that the boundaries of the municipality successfully coincide with the natural boundaries of the local society's territory, such societies are often spatially isolated and represented by one or several communities. For the population, the main sources of livelihood are natural resources and subsidiary farming. It is these factors—isolation and self-sufficiency—that determine that power emerges from the body of local society as a full-fledged self-government, and only then is institutionalized in the form of municipal authorities; for more details, see Plusnin (2008). Here, the representative of the authority (head of the municipality and administration) is often purely nominal, chosen from among random and incompetent people who do not command respect; it is the entire society or a group of activists who perform the actual administration; for examples, see Kordonskiy et al. (2011). Self-government is generally direct rather than representative. The potential of such societies is relatively high—the authorities and society are consolidated, act in concert, and governance is always effective (largely because results have to be achieved under considerable resource constraints). Meanwhile, such municipalities are of no interest to regional authorities. There is "nothing to take" from them and "manual" external management is not applicable to them: local authorities, integrated with society, are resilient and do not give in to the simple administrative manipulations, which are the only thing regional officials are capable of. That is why little is known about such municipalities at the regional level. Only direct observation during field research can provide insight into the organizational specifics of true self-government, including the structure of the local authorities. It is impossible to record such features formally (statistically). I would like to point out that this form of governance is too close to the ideology of Russian anarchism for the central government to allow its existence. Why then do such municipalities exist? Apparently, because the local society exists "*apart from the state*"; there are quite a few such societies in Russia (Plusnin, 1999).

10.2.2 Landlord Municipalities

For specific reasons, the second type of local administration is called "landlord municipalities" (Simon Kordonsky proposed the name and used it in the title of his monograph, see Kordonsky (2010)). This organizational form is distinguished by the *estate-like* nature of authority. Such municipalities in fact serve as estates of business-people or municipal officials (usually both statuses are combined if not in the same family, then in the same clan). This form of authority is most evident in district or urban district municipalities with a vast territory but sparse population. There may be two reasons for the correlation between the type of governance and these indicators. First, such administrative units have abundant natural resources on their territory, and the local authorities participate in managing them. Second, district and urban district municipalities are subject to considerable control by the regional authorities due to relatively large amounts of financial resources allocated to the local level (inter-budgetary transfers) and to the fact that the regional administration directly interacts with the municipal authorities rather than the local population. Therefore, such administrative-territorial units (municipal districts and urban districts) are subject to the archaic but effective practice of "placing the governor," who gains access to resources and control of the local economy in exchange for faithful service to "the sovereign." This becomes relevant when the local situation "gets out of control." Accordingly, parochial tyranny, legalized racket of business, and censorship of social and political activity flourish in such municipalities. Almost all income-generating assets belong to the heads of municipalities, their family members, and agents. Or such important enterprises belong to businesspeople formally not in power, but in fact governing the municipality. Usually, such entrepreneurs are former district leaders who have accumulated administrative and financial resources, have formally retired but continue governing the district or town through their henchmen.

The local authorities here are substantially more included in the structure of state power: the focus is shifted to economic and political objectives, and the forms of responsibility—to the state and individuals on which the status of the municipal leader depends. The inhabitants here are in "serfdom" and live by the principle: "*we would dig in if we had a master.*" In such municipalities, the "population" includes municipal and government employees, pensioners, "socially unprotected categories of citizens," the wretched, sick, and public sector employees. Independent people—entrepreneurs, merchants, otkhodniks, and any other categories of active residents are not considered to be part of the "population." The concern of the authorities is the socially fair distribution of available resources; for details, see Kordonsky (2006). Such municipalities are usually seamlessly integrated into the system of regional government. They are closed for external observation, and the municipal authorities fiercely oppose any attempt by "outsiders" to understand how life is arranged there.

There is one special feature, a certain diagnostic indicator of this type of power relations, which always distinguishes landlord municipalities. Absolutely everywhere, the heads of administration have their houses in full view of everyone, in the best and highest places—entirely in line with Imperial and Soviet traditions. The two or three-story mansion is usually connected to the heating main by a branch-off from the nearby hospital, and water supply and sewage are extended from the administration building. Sometimes, the power supply is free of charge. Since the landlords are forced to replace each other, at least for the sake of decency, there are usually several such mansions. Often, they form *"lordly settlements," "kulak corners," "villages of the poor,"* and other areas designated for the elite (all the names are real). Landlord municipalities are usually established in isolated or ordinary societies; there are almost none in turbulent societies, as well as in those of coercive development. As mentioned above, this is related to the specifics of the allocation of local resources and the ability of the regional authorities to control them directly. This type of municipal administration is rare in the vicinity of major cities and regional capitals, as well as on "high roads" (in turbulent societies). Almost always, factors of clan and capital determine formal power positions.

10.2.3 "Soviet-Type" Municipalities

These are resource-oriented municipalities that still retain the Soviet-style system of administration. Such municipalities are totally reliant on the state; management is not independent; the administration pursues social and economic objectives; and focuses on responsibility exclusively to the state, i.e., to regional officials. This type is polar to the first type of municipalities with true self-government and somewhat similar to the second type, landlord municipalities.

It is distinguished by a largely intact Soviet structure of administration and focus on resources distributed by state authorities. In fact, such municipalities are like structural units of regional administrations implementing their own policy, which has little to do with the municipal specifics and independence of subordinates. Generally, such municipalities are led by former functionaries of communist party district committees or Soviet executive committees, who have been in power for 34 or more terms, or they are headed by highly dependent executives who rode the wave of early democracy of the 1990s and, therefore, often have no adequate administrative skills. There is no question of any real integration of the authorities into local society, especially of their emergence from local self-government. The authorities here are in fact the grassroots level of state authority. There is absolutely no freedom of community-oriented local governance; governance here is a simple transmitter of administrative impulses, based on the distribution and redistribution of budget resources. For this type of municipality, like for the landlord one, the "population" means exclusively people receiving income from the budget:

pensioners and public sector employees, as well as numerous groups of benefit and welfare recipients. All these categories are fully dependent on the state social policy.

Since this type of governance requires external resources and depends on their centralized distribution, it is usually implemented in local communities of coercive development, either spatially isolated or ordinary; it is not relevant for turbulent communities with diverse resource flows that the authorities do not control.

10.2.4 "Politicized" Municipalities

Municipalities with this style of governance can be heavily or moderately dependent on government bodies; their responsibility focuses on both the population and the state. This type of municipality is positioned closer to the center of the axes, as shown in Fig. 9.1. The objectives of governance are predominantly or exclusively political. Formally, this type is opposite to "landlord municipalities," and there is a high personal turnover of functionaries (heads of administration "change like gloves"). The political nature stems from the fact that the system of municipal government represents the interests of many officials, wealthy landowners from among the summer residents, and businesspeople. Their might and influence are comparable, and no one has a landslide victory in the struggle for power. The municipal authorities are caught in the crossfire of external—appointed by the regional authorities—and local—home-grown—"elites" claiming resources and therefore power; so, they govern by balancing the interests of these groups; cf.: Ledyaev and Chirikova (2017). Such municipalities are always a problem for regional administrations. But for the residents, the political life of their community is interesting and eventful. The entire population, including completely apolitical individuals, is immersed in administrative squabbles, which are in full view of the public. In some of these municipalities, the authorities seek greater autonomy from regional administrations, in others, on the contrary, they are closely linked to individual regional officials (for an example of such a municipality, see Plusnin (2000, pp. 102–142). There are a lot of such "politicized" municipalities in Russia.

"Politicized" municipalities are characteristic of both isolated and turbulent societies; this type of administration emerges primarily due to the factor of coercive development of local society. Therefore, it is not clan affiliation, but influence (professional competence of the contenders for power) and capital (because the outcome of the contenders' political struggle often depends on a massive election campaign supported by regional and local mass media) that determine formal power positions here.

The four types of municipal administration identified by direct observation are borderline cases of the organizational forms of authority. In most cases (over forty percent of all provincial municipalities), however, we observe a structure of authority, which is more or less in line with legislation, and only a closer scrutiny can reveal whether it is skewed in one of the four directions. According to our observations, regional administrations prefer municipalities that are dependent, subsidized, and therefore relatively easily controlled from the outside. Least of all do they favor "politicized" municipalities; the authorities are too troublesome there. The regional authorities often aim at depriving municipalities of any autonomy; for this purpose, they can subject the heads of politicized municipalities to various kinds of persecution, including criminal prosecution. In addition, competing "elites" here must seek the support of the population and among other things they strongly rely on the civil and environmental activity of people who are more concerned with health than employment and for whom social justice is more important than democracy. Municipalities with true self-government are of no interest whatsoever to the regional authorities; maybe that is why they leave them alone. Especially since local authorities here strive to develop socially focused practices and social entrepreneurship as their most important component; it is this form of economic activity that unites the two main objectives of local self-government: provision of services and social support of the population. Therefore, regional authorities concentrate on municipalities with the "Soviet" and "landlord" types of administration. Municipal leaders seeking one or the other style of governance are focused on handouts of financial resources "from above" in the first case and on the ability to redistribute natural resources "from below" in the second case.

10.3 Summary. The Configuration of Status and Authority in Different Types of Local Societies

Do different styles of municipal governance somehow correlate with the factors that determine a person's social status, on the one hand, and with the types of local societies identified on grounds of spatial isolation and coercive/natural manner of development, on the other hand? Although typology always focuses on extreme (marginal) forms, which are rarely represented in their pure state, one can find some correspondence between the type of community and the way of implementing local government there, as I noted above. It is more difficult to associate the typology of societies with the factors determining social status, since these latter are not only universal but also interdependent. Meanwhile, with certain reservations, a correlation is traceable in both cases. It is certainly more pronounced in the extreme types of communities—isolated communities of natural development and turbulent communities of coercive development—than in societies in the middle of the scale. Obviously, in all cases we are talking only about tendencies, about the predominance of a particular type of governance, but not about predetermined conformity.

Isolated communities of natural development are more likely to implement two extreme governance strategies: true local self-government and landlord municipalities. The first strategy is often inherent in small societies with few communities; generally, only some of them demonstrate this type of governance. The second strategy—landlord municipalities—is more common for societies with vast territories and abundant natural resources (forest, river, and marine resources). The social positions of individuals are largely determined by factors of influence and clan affiliation, whereas disposable income is virtually of no importance.

For isolated communities of coercive development, two other, polar, governance strategies are more common: "Soviet-type" and "politicized" municipalities. This is most often observed in young societies, where power is still in the hands of "appointees" from the economic sphere, former enterprise bosses, who grew up in the hierarchy of managerial relations and retained the style of "command management" and, accordingly, adherence to the state hierarchy. Besides, such societies are characterized by significant groups of industrial workers, existing trade unions, and competition between large enterprises and their management teams; all this drives the struggle for power and contributes to the emergence of "politicized" municipalities. In fact, this is typical for all communities of coercive development—i.e., "politicized" municipalities emerge in this specific type of community. They can also develop in any turbulent communities. Landlord municipalities are rare, but they also exist. A person's social status is primarily determined by clan affiliation and formal power position.

"Ordinary" communities of natural development, just as the first type (isolated natural development) more often implement two governance strategies: true local self-government and landlord municipalities. And similarly, personal influence and clan affiliation are the main factors that determine an individual's status. In this respect, this type of local society coincides with the type of isolated natural development communities in terms of the frequency of governance strategies and status determinations. All other types of isolated natural development communities implement these two municipal administration strategies extremely rarely or not at all.

"Ordinary" communities of coercive development more often implement the same governance strategies as isolated societies of coercive development, namely, the "Soviet-type" and "politicized" ones. Thus, in terms of governance strategy, the above four types of communities are split into pairs depending on the nature of their development: naturally developed communities tend to implement "true local self-government" and "landlord" strategies, whereas coercively developed communities lean toward "Soviet-type" and "politicized" ones. (This does not apply to turbulent communities at all; they are different from all the other types.) In "ordinary" communities of coercive development, clan affiliation, formal power position and, partly, capital largely determine personal statuses.

In turbulent communities of both types (natural and coercive), municipal authorities can implement a "politicized" governance strategy; all others are extremely rare. True local self-government was not found here at all (and it would be unrealistic to capture such a strategy). The socio-occupational factor (influence), formal power position, and capital determine a person's social status. Clan affiliation has little or no importance. The capital factor, by contrast, is more pronounced here than in any other type of society.

In summary, polar governance strategies, when manifested, correlate with the types of communities in three ways. In one case, only isolated and ordinary communities of natural development implement a pair of strategies—true local self-government and "landlord administration"; the other four types of communities hardly ever resort to them. In the second case, specifically communities of coercive development, both isolated and ordinary, apply another pair of strategies—"Soviet-type" and "politicized." In the third case, only turbulent communities have a "politicized" strategy, while the rest do not.

Formal power and capital are relatively more important in turbulent and coercively developed communities, whereas clan affiliation—in isolated and naturally developed ones. Above, I considered the likely reasons for the observed differences in governance strategies and status determination.

References

Artyomova, O. Y. (1999). Clan. In V.A. Tishkov (Ed.), *Peoples and religions of the World: Encyclopedia* (pp. 886–887). Great Russian Encyclopedia. Артёмова О.Ю. (1999). Клан. В кн.: В.А. Тишков (Ред.) *Народы и религии мира: Энциклопедия*, (pp. 886–887). М.: Большая российская энциклопедия.

Barsukova, S. Y. (2013). Thug Soviet Union, or the economy of mutual services. *Economic Sociology, 14*(1), 111–119. Барсукова С.Ю. (2013). Блатной Советский Союз, или Экономика взаимных услуг. *Экономическая социология*, 14(1), 111–119.

Blyakher, L. E. (2008). Archaic mechanisms of legitimization of power in Russia, or essays on the origins of nostalgic consciousness. *Politia, 3*(50), 7–29. Бляхер Л.Е. (2008). Архаические механизмы легитимации власти в России, или очерки об истоках ностальгического сознания. *Полития*, 3(50), 7–29.

Bondarenko, D. M. (2007). Difficulties with "complexity" (Heterarchy, homoarchy and categorical differences between social anthropology and synergetics). *Social Sciences and Modernity, 5*, 141–149. Бондаренко Д.М. (2007). Сложности со «сложностью» (Гетерархия, гомоархия и категориальные расхождения между социальной антропологией и синергетикой). *Общественные науки и современность*, 5, 141–149.

Bondarenko, D., Grinin, L., & Korotayev, A. (2002). Alternative pathways of social evolution. *Social Evolution and History. Studies in the Evolution of Human Societies, 1*(1), 54–80.

Brumfield, E. M. (1995). Heterarchy and the analysis of complex societies: Comments. In R. M. Ehrenreich, C. L. Crumley, & J. E. Levy (Eds.), *Heterarchy and the analysis of complex societies. Number 6* (pp. 125–131). Archeological papers of the American Anthropological Association.

Chirikova, A. E., & Ledyaev, V. G. (2017). *Power in a small Russian town*. HSE Publishing House. Чирикова А.Е., Ледяев В.Г. (2017). *Власть в малом российском городе*. М.: Издательский дом НИУ ВШЭ.

Collins, K. (2004). The logic of clan politics: Evidence from the central Asian trajectories. *World Politics, 56*(2), 224–261.

Crumley, C. L. (1979). Three locational models: An epistemological assessment for anthropology and archaeology. In M. Shiffer (Ed.), *Advances in archaeological method and theory* (Vol. 2, pp. 141–173). Academic Press.

Ehrenreich, R. M., Crumley, C. L., & Levy, J. E. (Eds.). (1995). *Heterarchy and the analysis of complex societies* (Vol. 6). Archeological Papers of the American Anthropological Association.

Grigoriev, L. M., & Salmina, A. A. (2013). The "structure" of social inequality in the modern world: measurement problems. *Sociological Journal, 3*, 5–21. Григорьев Л.М., Салмина А.А. (2013). «Структура» социального неравенства современного мира: проблемы измерения. *Социологический журнал*, 3, 5–21.

Kordonskiy, S. G., Plusnin, J. M., Krasheninnikova, Y. A., Tukaeva, A. R., Boykov, D. V., Morgunova, O. M., & Akhunov, D. E. (2011). Russian province and its inhabitants (observation experience and attempt at description). *World of Russia, 20*(1), 3–33. Кордонский С.Г., Плюснин Ю.М., Крашенинникова Ю.А., Тукаева А.Р., Бойков Д.В., Моргунова О.М., Ахунов Д.Э. (2011). Российская провинция и её обитатели (опыт наблюдения и попытка описания). *Мир России*, 20(1), 3–33.

Kordonsky, S. G. (2006). *Power markets: Administrative markets of the USSR and Russia*. OGI. Кордонский С.Г. (2006). Рынки власти: Административные рынки СССР и России. М.: ОГИ.

Kordonsky, S. G. (2010). *Russia. local federation*. Publishing House "Europe. Кордонский С.Г. (2010). *Россия. Поместная Федерация*. М.: Издательство «Европа.

Ledeneva, A. V. (1998). *Russia's economy of favours: "Blat", networking and informal exchange*. Cambridge University Press.

Ledyaev, V. G., & Chirikova, A. (2017). Power in local Russian communities: Patterns of interaction between legislative and executive branches of local government. *Urban Affairs Review, 53*(6), 990–1024.

Ledyaev, V. G., & Chirikova, A. E. (2019a). Governors and local elites in Russia: Patterns of interaction. *European Politics and Society, 20*(3), 315–332.

Ledyaev, V. G., & Chirikova, A. E. (2019b). Urban regimes in small Russian towns. *City & Community, 18*(3), 812–833.

Ledyaev, V., Chirickova, A., & Seltser, D. (2014). Who governs? Power in the local Russian community. *Journal of Political Power, 7*(2), 211–231.

McCulloch, W. S. (1945). A heterarchy of values determined by the topology of nervous nets. *The Bulletin of Mathematical Biophysics, 7*, 89–93.

Mote, V. L., & Trout, W. (2010). Political territoriality and the end of the USSR. *Space & Polity, 7*(1), 21–43.

Plusnin, J. M. (1999). The life far off the state. *ECO, 12*, 117–126.

Plusnin, J. (2000). A new Russia – Or the same old Russia? An alternative worldview in the making. In H. Isham (Ed.), *Russia's fate through Russian eyes. Voices of the new generation* (pp. 15–29). Westview Press.

Plusnin, J. M. (2002). Power and control in the eyes of the provincial society. In P. L. Kapitsa (Ed.), *Russia in a global context. Issue 3. Evolution of Russian statehood over 10 years* (pp. 52–55). Nikitsky Club. Плюснин Ю.М. (2002). Власть и управление в глазах провинциального общества. В кн.: П.Л. Капица (Ред.), *Россия в глобальном контексте. Вып. 3. Эволюция российской государственности за 10 лет* (pp. 52–55). М.: Никитский клуб.

Plusnin, J. M. (2008). Factors in the development of local self-government. Assessing the importance of isolation and isolationism. *Issues of Public Administration, 3*, 38–50. Плюснин Ю.М. (2008). Факторы развития местного самоуправления. Оценка значения изоляции и изоляционизма. *Вопросы государственного и муниципального управления*, 3, 38–50.

Plusnin, J. M. (2009). The structure of local government in municipalities of different types. *Region 86. Journal of State and Municipal Management of Yugra, Khanty-Mansiysk Autonomous Okrug, 2*(10), 63–68. Плюснин Ю.М. (2009). Структура местной власти в муниципалитетах разного вида. *Регион 86. Журнал государственного и муниципального управления г. Югры, Ханты-Мансийский автономный округ*, 2(10), 63–68.

Plusnin, J. M., & Mitroshina, E. N. (2017). On the other side of the concept of openness, transparency and ethics in public administration: informal relations between municipal leaders and their interaction strategies. In E. G. Yasin (Ed.), *XVII April International Scientific Conference on the Development of Economy and Society. Book 2* (pp. 297–309). HSE Publishing House. Плюснин Ю.М., & Митрошина Е.Н. (2017). По другую сторону концепции открытости, прозрачности и этичности публичного управления: неформальные отношения муниципальных руководителей и их стратегии взаимодействия. В кн.: Е.Г. Ясин (Ред.), *XVII Апрельская международная научная конференция по проблемам развития экономики и общества.* Книга 2 (pp. 297–309). М.: Издательский дом НИУ ВШЭ.

Schwab, K., & Malleret, T. (2020). *COVID-19: The great reset*. Forum Publishing.

Shkaratan, O. I. (Ed.) (2009). *Socio-economic inequality and its reproduction in modern Russia*. ZAO OLMA Media Group. Шкаратан О.И. (Ред.), (2009). *Социально-экономическое неравенство и его воспроизводство в современной России*. М.: ЗАО «ОЛМА Медиа Групп».

Shkaratan, O. I. (2012). *Sociology of inequality. Theory and reality*. NRU HSE Publishing House. Шкаратан О.И. (2012). *Социология неравенства. Теория и реальность*. М.: Издательский дом НИУ ВШЭ.

Small, D. B. (1995). Heterarchical paths to evolution: The role of external economies. In R. M. Ehrenreich, C. L. Crumley, & J. E. Levy (Eds.), *Heterarchy and the analysis of complex societies* (Vol. 6, pp. 71–85). Archeological papers of the American Anthropological Association.

Tikhonova, N. E., Lezhnina Yu, P., Mareeva, S. V., Anikin, V. A., Karavay, A. V., & Slobodenyuk, E. D. (2018). *Model of income stratification of Russian society: Dynamics, factors, cross-country comparisons*. Sankt-Peterburg: Nestor-History. Тихонова Н.Е., Лежнина Ю.П., Мареева С.В., Аникин В.А., Каравай А.В., & Слободенюк Е.Д. (2018). *Модель доходной стратификации российского общества: динамика, факторы, межстрановые сравнения*. М.; СПб.: Нестор-История.

Wodtke, G. T. (2016). Social class and income inequality in the United States: Ownership, authority, and personal income distribution from 1980 to 2010. *American Journal of Sociology, 121*(5), 1375–1415.

Young, J. F. (2009). Russia's elusive pursuit of balance in local government reform. In C. Ross & A. Campbell (Eds.), *Federalism and local politics in Russia* (pp. 248–262). Routledge.

Zhukov, D. S., & Seltzer, D. G. (2019). System dynamics of the Russian regional elite (1985-2019): Alternative scenarios. *Journal of Political Research, 3*(4), 40–74. Жуков Д.С., Сельтцер Д.Г. (2019). Системная динамика российской региональной элиты (1985-2019 гг.): альтернативные сценарии. *Журнал политических исследований*, 3(4), 40–74.

Chapter 11
Conclusion

To the best of my ability, I attempted to review numerous empirical observations and present a generalized picture of the real structure of Russia's modern provincial society. Data were collected over a period of almost four decades, and I believe all these years many of the described phenomena remained largely unchanged. Others are versatile or transient. Their correlation is different. Stable components refer to the deep, natural foundations of social life. Slightly versatile components pertain primarily to the socio-political sphere; they follow developments in the structure of state power. Therefore, over short stretches of time, such transformations are far from dynamic. However, there are also very rapid and significant shifts in provincial social life, which involve people's behavioral responses to the political and economic environment. Hence, they are widely represented in the population's daily subsistence practices. The specific feature of Russian provincial life transformation manifests itself in the different rate at which various components of the social structure change. In conclusion I would like to make a brief overview of the above and for the third time summarize the key research findings.

I am considering the provincial society in Russia exclusively at the local level, since I believe only here reality is observable. The local provincial society consisting of communities whose members do not define themselves as such because they do not realize it, is structured from below, with the structure developing from the very depths of social life. Its own, natural structure is subtle and barely noticeable. It is fragile and can be easily disrupted. Therefore, for the outside world the local society has a special protective armor, and a double one. It consists of a kind of "chain mail" and "cuirass" imposed on the body of every community from above by the state. The former is an estate structure determined and cherished by the state. The estate "chain mail" is coarse; it wounds and deforms the tender fabric of the community's grassroots structure. The "chain mail" is covered by the "cuirass" of the state administrative-territorial framework, which determines the spatial borders of social life. The state armor shapes the body of the community. It is not quite clear what image this metaphor corresponds to: a hermit crab in someone else's shell, or a chained prisoner. But it nevertheless figuratively captures the peculiar arrangement

J. Plusnin, *Russian Provincial Society*, Societies and Political Orders in Transition,
https://doi.org/10.1007/978-3-030-97829-7_11

of the provincial life in Russia: its dual structure—flexible communal and rigid estate-based—forms a phenomenon, the integrity of which has been constantly questioned by generations of observers-sociologists.

Since I am interested in the grassroot levels of social life, I focused on the flexible communal body extracted from state-imposed armor and undertook to describe it from two different angles. The first aspect is the physical projection of the community in space; an attempt was made to describe the territorial structure. The second aspect is the totality of direct sustainable relations between people on their territory; an attempt was made to describe the grassroots social structure. In doing so, I deliberately avoided presenting such a structure as linear, as stratification of households by income.

Since it is difficult to grasp "flexibility," I split my description into three components, assuming they form the three main axes of the skeleton palpable under the soft communal skin. The most important is the axis of kin and neighborly relations based on the kinship of many generations of people living together; on their territorial conservatism; on negligible migration activity; and on the stability of interpersonal ties. This structure forms the basis on which everyday life grows. Everyday life is the habitation, existence, and activity of relatives and neighbors within the boundaries of the controlled territory. Everyday life determines the second axis—interdependent cooperative relations between households based on both altruistic (gift and help) and mutually beneficial exchange behavior. These relations shape the system of local economic ties and differentiate people along the axis of economic activity, its poles represented by "rent-seeking" (passive) and self-employed (active) population. The third axis is the relationship of people's interdependent positions—their local personal statuses attributing them to the "upper" or "lower" strata. Status depends on several—four principal—factors (personal influence, clan affiliation, power position, and controlled capital). By basing my description on these three axes—us/them, passive/active, and upper/lower strata—I attempted to capture the grassroots social structure.

Empirical analysis unveiled the complexity of the provincial society's social structure, its multiple components and even hierarchy. On the upper level, the grassroots social and estate structures—with their disparities and interpenetration—are complementary. However, since their nature is different, they are hierarchical rather than congruent. On the lower (grassroots) level, a community's social structure is made up of three—this time congruent—components; moreover, all three components have a single source, and they are interdependent. This grassroots social structure resembles a *dicotyledon,* with one cotyledon being the territorial structure that organizes communities in space, and the other one—the economic structure and the social one itself. As shown above, their functional roles differ.

In addition, it was necessary to classify local communities on external grounds. I selected four principles, two of which proved to be most heuristic: (1) degree of spatial isolation and (2) the specifics of a community's emergence and development depending on the extent of government impact. The two other principles—age of the community and layout of its administrative center—proved to be useful, but secondary. Generalization produced typologies of local communities. Of the maximum

18 possible types of communities, only six were shown to be relevant, and even they could be eventually reduced to four. Two types are polar in their main features: (1) spatially isolated ancient and old communities that developed naturally, without significant intervention from the state; and (2) "turbulent" communities located on transport thoroughfares, with a well-developed infrastructure, generally quite recent, established and developing under significant coercive political or economic government impact. The other two types are intermediate; they are distinguished on different grounds: (3) turbulent and non-isolated ("ordinary-type") ancient and old communities of natural development; (4) isolated and non-isolated ("ordinary-type") old and young communities of coercive development. The developed typology enabled to classify the diverse empirical data relating to the territorial and social structures, and to explain the specific features of the local economy and informal economic practices of the population.

The typology has the utmost value for analyzing the territorial structure. Considerable differences in the territorial structure are observed between two polar types: isolated communities of natural development, on the one hand, and turbulent communities of coercive development, on the other. In the first case, the administrative center is secondary; it is formed from the rural district, emerging initially as either a religious or economic center. Subsequently, it is additionally vested with state military and administrative functions. The rural district is primary; it develops spontaneously and is not limited by its neighbors' compressive impact. The rural district develops in the form of "clusters" consisting of several settlements. The settlements—villages—are small in terms of population, but numerous and located all over the territory. The density gradient from the center to the outskirts is low. The territory is large; its size is determined by the need to control natural resources for daily existence. The population can live autonomously using the procured natural resources. Borders are determined by natural barriers and tradition; they are controlled by local inhabitants; they have been stable for long; and do not always coincide with administrative boundaries.

In the second type of territorial structure, which is polar to the first one, the administrative center is primary, and the rural district is secondary; it evolves in the form of suburbs spreading from the center to the periphery. Due to this, the rural district is drawn to the center, and the periphery remains unpopulated. Settlements in the rural district are large in terms of population, but few; usually, they are industrial townships rather than villages. The entire community concentrates around the administrative center. In certain periods of life, the center attracts the population of the rural district, and the district itself falls into neglect. The density gradient from the center to the outskirts is high. The central settlement itself does not emerge naturally but is established close to resources that have no immediate vital importance for the community. The residential structure of both the central and rural settlements did not develop in a slow and natural manner but was formed "as if in a flash." The inhabited and developed territory is almost always much smaller than the administrative borders and does not coincide with the area of vitally important natural resources. Generally, the population does not develop these resources.

Borders are neither protected, nor maintained; for their subsistence, the inhabitants depend on external sources, primarily on the state.

The territorial structure of the third, "mixed," type of community developing naturally but not isolated, is characterized by a well-developed transport, energy, and utilities infrastructure. The territory is small, and the population controls its boundaries. Numerous villages with relatively few inhabitants are spread evenly throughout the entire territory. The centers of the communities have emerged in a natural manner and consist of ancient and old towns.

The territorial structure of the fourth, "mixed," type of young coercively formed communities, is characterized by an inadequate or moderately developed transport infrastructure. The territory is large but not controlled by the population. Settlements in the rural district are few but populous. They concentrate around the administrative center; the density gradient from the center to the outskirts is high. A substantial part of the local population settles along major transport routes.

Throughout the text, I emphasize that the territorial structure of provincial communities is extremely conservative: it does not change for ages, and the community strives to maintain this stability by all means. This is probably the most stable component of the social structure. In a sense, it is the *backbone* that stays "intact" outliving the "*bodies of its masters*"—local communities—which succeed each other there over ages. The "territorial backbone" survives even the estate forms, which vary at different stages of the country's political life. Moreover, the very "cuirass" of the state administrative-territorial framework mentioned above has largely developed on this ancient *backbone,* which is in fact the spatial invariant of social life.

By contrast, the economic structure is the most versatile, labile component of the grassroots social structure because it is indeed the focus of the community's adaptive potential. I have come to this conclusion based on empirical evidence. The very first, urgent reaction of a community to any change in the external environment is to transform its economic practices as forms of adaptive behavior essential for the continuous existence of the population. It is indeed in the economic structure that we observe a variety of transitions from one strategy to another in response to any significant external developments. Changing household strategies on a mass scale means altering *economic patterns,* which characterizes the adaptive capacity of society, its potential. In this respect the versatile, labile economic structure is the opposite of the "territorial backbone," although it actually develops within the territorial structure.

The provincial economy exists in two forms, different by nature and origin but deeply interpenetrating. In terms of scale and significance, the first, or formal economy is not primary for the livelihood of the local inhabitants. This place is firmly occupied by the "second economy"—the domestic and economic practices of households beyond the reach of formal state regulation. This is the wild field of informal economy, locally legitimate in its scope but far from legal. It largely consists of shadow and criminal economic activity. Both forms of the provincial economy have distinctive features.

The most notable and most important feature of the formal economy in the Russian province is its uniformity. It is the same everywhere, primarily because its backbone is the public sector. Of all the working-age population engaged in the local economy, the share of public sector employees ranges from two to three-fifths and more. Against this "publicly funded" setting, the other components of the local economy—material production and services—appear substantially less developed. The formal economy of the province creates a homogeneous background with shades barely discernible from area to area and region to region.

Against this bleak background, a vibrant diversity of "gray" informal economic practices is flourishing. Latently, in the "shadow" rather than the light, the people's economic activity is bubbling. Every household and every person, young and old—the elderly, adults, and children—are engaged in it. Therefore, considering the provincial economy, we must first and foremost focus on informal economic activities of households. This is primarily the economy of archaic crafts. We define "crafts" as independent domestic and economic activities of households based on in-house means and technologies and aimed at supporting the life of the family and achieving other, usually social, goals. As a domestic practice, crafts imply neither entrepreneurship nor business in their primary meaning. As an economic practice, crafts are aimed at generating additional income. Crafts are largely part of informal economy, i.e. they are not regulated by the state, not taxed, and not recorded in official statistics. Their scope in the province is high: from a third to over half of the working-age population provides for itself through various crafts and trades rather than being engaged in the local economy. If we consider the entire adult population, including pensioners, this share will exceed two-thirds. In fact, almost everybody employed in the local (formal) economy is also involved in crafts and trades.

Earnings from crafts are at least on the level of official incomes ("second income"), but more often they exceed them manifold. In the case of criminal crafts, common in some territories, informal incomes are incomparably higher. By structure and dynamics, the budget of households engaged in crafts and trades differs significantly from that of an average urban family relying on official sources of income.

Crafts and trades are diverse. We have recorded over 130 kinds and groups of them. We have also made a phenomenological classification of crafts based on several criteria. The main criteria are: (1) location of activity, (2) type of resources, and (3) traditional character of the craft. The nature of the craft and its kind are associated with the residential structure of the province and determined by the local labor market. The kinds of crafts depend on two principal factors: (1) spatial isolation of the community and (2) availability of economic support from the state. Thus, the kinds of crafts are directly determined by the type of local community.

Each local community practices many kinds of crafts (from several dozens to a hundred). Each household usually practices several (up to a dozen) kinds of crafts. Due to the different availability of resources, and dissimilar labor intensity and profitability of the crafts, households seek to specialize in certain kinds of them. Specialization can involve many households and entire settlements (communities). This tendency toward specialization leads to the phenomenon of "homologous series" of crafts: if the main types of resources available to the population in different regions of the country are similar, local communities in different territories demonstrate the same "set" of crafts. However, such specialization threatens the economic stability of households and entire communities, and, as a result, aggravates latent social tension and social deprivation.

The adaptive potential of provincial communities, expressed in informal household activities, is enormous. It is in this sphere of life that local communities demonstrate a "transition" to new economic practices and subsequently to new social arrangements and possibly to rudimentary political ones. At the same time, they revert to "long-forgotten," archaic practices, thus displaying the existence of a deep "social memory." All these economic practices are essentially forms of self-organization paving the way for the development of self-government mechanisms. Locally, self-organization and self-government are based on self-sufficiency. That is why I am referring to the phenomenon of *"life apart from the state,"* inherent not only in our remote province but also in local societies adjacent to major urban agglomerations. Entire local societies can exist independently if the rely on self-sufficiency and the economic activity of the population, its widespread ability to "live beyond the reach of the state." The government machine painstakingly tries to eliminate any trace of the "virus of independence" from local soil. But as we already witnessed in the 1990s—the time when the state was prostrate—this "virus" immediately breaks out putting forth not only healthy shoots but also taking the ugliest forms. Such is the nature of the economic component of social structure.

Between the "backbone" and adaptive components—the territory and informal subsistence practices—the third component of the structure, which, for lack of a better name, I called "the social structure itself," is balancing. It includes all the institutional elements that evolve from "Tönnies' tetrad" of relationships—family, neighborly, and reciprocal ties united by the spirit of Kürwille. This is the component that is clearly visible even to its bearers, because in contrast to the other two components, it is explicated in the minds of ordinary people. And it is the one that is most closely associated with the *"state-imposed chain mail"* of the estate structure. Due to constant pressure from the estate structure, "the social structure itself" is resilient but amenable to change. Its transformations are not always targeted and can hardly be captured; anyway, "resilience" appears to prevail over "transformism."

Habitation (territory) and activity (crafts) are the basis of existence. Existence is everyday life in the system of kin and neighborly relations and behavior in accordance with the position acquired, mastered, and approved by a person in his community—according to his local social status. In the provincial society, almost everyone is an insider; there are no "them-like-us" here. All outsiders are visible; they "pass by," hardly affecting and not deforming the long-established structure of relations. But the "us/them" ratio depends on the type of community. Even the structure and composition of "us" demonstrate such dependence. Different types of communities have different ways of establishing and developing "affinity" relationships.

A social structure based on kin and neighborly relations develops in two ways. It can proceed either through agglomeration—heterogeneous composition of the inhabitants, or through layering—settling the territory at different times. In an agglomerated structure, the population is heterogeneous by origin, it comes from different territories and regions, from different clans and ethnic groups. Agglomerates indicate that diverse groups of people settled the area almost simultaneously, regardless of the reason—of their own accord or under government coercion. Agglomerations are typical of young communities formed coercively, and of "turbulent" ones, where the share of migrants and their diasporas is significant. A "layered" structure is composed of groups of people diverse by origin, which settled the territory at different times. "Layering" is formed by various ethnic, religious, social, or occupational groups. "Layering" is identified in naturally developing old and ancient communities. Very few modern communities were established and exist as an expanded single community, without the participation of migrants and without the introduction of compact groups of outsiders, who in two-three generations become insiders.

In isolated communities, "affinity" is based on family and ethnic ties. The ancient ethnic substrate has also been preserved here, albeit implicitly. On the contrary, in non-isolated communities, the composition and structure of "us" is predominantly "layered" rather than agglomerated. The individual agglomerate components have long merged, leveled out, and dissolved in each other. Due to the destruction of family ties, the structure of "us" is fragmented and homogeneous: there are no large kin groups in the community, just as there are few isolated ethnic groups, and if they do exist, they merge with each other. This is especially evident in "turbulent" communities, where migratory pressure is high, thus over time promoting the adaptation and assimilation of migrants of other ethnicities. In such communities, the rural area is underpopulated, and the administrative center is excessively overpopulated. As a result, kin and neighborly relations are destroyed and degraded not only in the administrative center, but also in the rural district.

The composition and structure of "outsiders" in "turbulent" and "ordinary-type" communities differs from those in isolated ones. Here, the number of migrants is much higher and, accordingly, the share of "flow-through," random people is substantial. It is important that "outsiders" are widely present not only in the administrative center, but also in the rural settlements. There is not much ethnic or religious filtering, so both the town and the rural district attract many migrants of various ethnicities and people who are alien to the locals in their mentality. At the same time, the composition of "outsiders" in all types of communities is the same. It is represented by individual families and groups that differ from the locals in social, occupational, ethnic, and religious or ideological terms.

An individual's social status in the local community is determined by social, ethnogenetic, political, and economic factors. Status, therefore, depends primarily on the person's influence—the public respect he or she has, which is determined by moral qualities, moral behavior, and professional competencies (only indirectly related to education). The second most important determinant of the status is clan affiliation (belonging to a family and/or ethnic group). The other major but less significant factors are the position in the formal power hierarchy and money income (disposable capital). This hierarchy of factors determining status positions stems from the fact that the determinants of status in a provincial society, in contrast to urban ones, are not anonymous. The social structure is heterarchical rather than hierarchical.

To a certain extent, the factors determining status positions depend on the type of community. In different types of communities, the significance of these factors varies. In ancient and old isolated communities of natural development, the social positions of individuals are largely determined by influence and clan affiliation, whereas disposable income is virtually of no importance. The same is true for ancient and old "ordinary-type" communities of natural development. In this respect, they coincide with the above type. By contrast, in isolated communities of coercive development, a person's social status is primarily determined by clan affiliation and formal power. In "ordinary-type" communities of coercive development, personal statuses are largely determined by clan affiliation, formal power and, partly, capital. In all "turbulent" communities, the social status of a person is determined by the socio-occupational factor (influence), by the formal power position, and by capital. Clan affiliation is of little importance here. The capital factor, by contrast, is more pronounced here than in any other type of community. In general, formal power and capital are relatively important in "turbulent" and coercively developed communities, whereas clan affiliation—in ancient and old isolated naturally developed ones. The differences in status determination are probably due to several reasons: first, ability to be self-sufficient; second, dependence on public resources; and third, the extent of routine state control over the local authorities.

Factors determining individual statuses also affect the political organization of the community's life. We identified four styles of local government in the power system, and they prove to be related with the type of community and the status determination factors dominant there. The established style of administration correlates with the type of community in order to draw on the prevailing stratification factors giving access to leadership positions in local government.

In ancient and old isolated naturally developed communities, two governance strategies prevail: real local self-government and municipalities in the form of estates. The first strategy is inherent in small communities with few communes; generally, only some of them demonstrate this type of governance. The second strategy—"estates"—is more ordinary for communities with vast territories and abundant natural resources. Coercively developed isolated and "ordinary-type" communities tend to demonstrate two other governance strategies: "Soviet-type" municipalities and "politicized" governance. This is typical for young communities with strong positions of "appointees" from the economic sphere, who have retained the "command management" style and are committed to government hierarchy. Thus, in terms of governance strategy, these types of communities are split into pairs depending on the nature of their development: naturally developed communities tend to implement "real local self-government" and "estate" strategies, whereas coercively developed communities lean toward "Soviet" and "politicized" ones. By contrast, it is difficult to distinguish a particular style of governance in "turbulent" communities—"politicized" governance is more likely, whereas the other strategies are rarely implemented. We detected no signs of real local self-government here.

As can be seen from the foregoing, all three components of the social structure—the "us/them," "active/passive," and "upper/lower strata" relationships—are interrelated among themselves. They are associated with both the economic and territorial structure of the community. Together they form an integrity, which at the grassroots level we call "community" or "commune" ("Gemeinshcaft") as defined by Ferdinand Tönnis, and at a higher level—local society, which in fact is a conglomerate of communities. Communes retain their archaic nature and that is why they are invisible at the level of a large city or a large society. And it is precisely because of the invisible presence of archaic elements in its social structure that the provincial society remains sustainable under any conditions.

This high sustainability and the desire to preserve what is already in place are determined by the specific combination of various structural components I have depicted. These components are organically complementary and congruent. Some of them (the territorial structure) are conservative and invariant in a sense, remaining unchanged for centuries and longer. Others (the social structure itself) are complex in composition, flexible, and capable of change, but only to a limited extent. The composition depends on the multiple social positions (statuses) of each community member. Versatility is triggered primarily by changes in the state-imposed estate structure (the aforementioned *"chain mail,"* which is also a factor in determining status positions), and not by some remoter external factors. Hence, over the life of one or several human generations, the social structure itself appears unchanged. Still others (the economic structure) are variative and adaptive and serve as a "rapid reaction force." Each time establishing new *"economic patterns,"* mastering new crafts and trades, "forgetting" some and "recollecting" others, the economic structure of provincial communities acts as a trigger for evolutionary transition. It is these mechanisms that allow us to talk about ongoing social transformation, perhaps also about social progress, even if it backtracks. This is, therefore, a structuralist deconstruction of the "social organism," which is how we generally perceive the provincial local society in Russia.